Small Business

AN ENTREPRENEUR'S PLAN

Small Business

AN ENTREPRENEUR'S PLAN

THIRD CANADIAN EDITION

RONALD A. KNOWLES

CLIFF G. BILYEA

Based on *Small Business: An Entrepreneur's Plan,* Fourth Edition, by J.D. Ryan, Lee A. Eckert, and Robert J. Ray

Harcourt Canada

Toronto Montreal Fort Worth New York Orlando
Philadelphia San Diego London Sydney Tokyo

Canadian Cataloguing in Publication Data

Knowles, Ronald A.
Small business: an entrepreneur's plan

3rd Canadian ed.
Includes bibliographical references and index.
ISBN 0-03-922727-8

1. New business enterprises–Management. 2. Small business–Planning.
3. Business planning. I. Bilyea, Cliff G. II. Title.

HD62.5.K568 1999 658.1′141 C98-931751-X

Acquisitions Editor: Ken Nauss
Developmental Editor: Su Mei Ku
Production Editor: Stacey Roderick
Senior Production Coordinator: Sue-Ann Becker

Copy Editor: Georgina Montgomery
Cover and Interior Design: Sonya V. Thursby, Opus House Incorporated
Typesetting and Assembly: Bookman Typesetting Co.
Printing and Binding: Kromar Printing
Cover Art: © Elle Schuster/Image Bank

Harcourt Canada
55 Horner Avenue, Toronto, ON, Canada M8Z 4X6
Customer Service
Toll-Free Tel.: 1-800-387-7278
Toll-Free Fax: 1-800-665-7307

This book was printed in Canada.
2 3 4 5 6 04 03 02 01 00

preface

We were excited when Harcourt asked us to prepare a third edition of *Small Business: An Entrepreneur's Plan*. It validated the quality of the book and meant we were on the right track in entrepreneurial education. It also meant we'd found a significant niche in the marketplace.

From the first — pulling together case studies and matching them with Action Steps, Business Plan Building Blocks, explanatory boxes, figures, tables, and marginal notes — we wanted *Small Business: An Entrepreneur's Plan* to be helpful, informative, easy to read, accessible, interesting, and fun. Luckily, we found a publisher with the same goals, and the book was born.

Entrepreneurs are an adventurous lot. They chafe under authority, and they love controlling their own destinies. They know that 60-hour work weeks are normal, and that working the 100-hour week is often reality, especially at start-up. So, if you're an entrepreneur at heart and you want to make your vision a reality, then this book is for you.

Your Personal Road Map

This book, with its 87 Action Steps, is your personal road map to success in small business. Beginning with Action Step 1, the book will guide you through the competitive marketplace — through trends, target customers, pricing, and promotion; through shopping malls, spreadsheets, and hushed, grey bank buildings; through independent businesses that are up for sale and through franchise opportunities — all the way to your own small business. Along the way you'll meet other entrepreneurs and hear their stories of success and failure. You'll have some fun building your business plan. Furthermore, by completing the Action Steps, Business Plan Building Blocks and Checklist Questions and Actions to Develop Your Business Plan, you will be drawing a customized road map for small business success: a complete business plan that clearly evaluates and illuminates your opportunity for entrepreneurial success.

BUSINESS PLAN BUILDING BLOCK

Each chapter will have a Business Plan Building Block component. As you work through the text, you'll automatically assemble the components that allow the seamless construction of a well-wrought and well-thought-out business plan.

ON THE WAY

You will start your journey by taking a careful look at yourself and your skills. What is your personal and business vision? What gives you satisfaction? What internal drives make you an entrepreneur?

Next, you'll step back and look at the marketplace. What's hot? What's cooling down? Where are the long lines forming? What are people buying at the supermarket or on the Internet? How is it packaged? What distinguishes the up-and-comers from the down-and-outers?

Then you will brainstorm a business that will fit into an industry niche or fill a gap. You toss numbers around to get a feel for how they turn into money, and you keep having fun.

Then it will be time to profile your target customer, assess the competition, develop some clever promotional strategies, and select a location. By that time you will be almost halfway through this book, you'll know where you're going, and you'll feel that you're in control of your own destiny.

That's when you can get serious. Chapter Eight will help you look ahead to the day you open the doors of your own business. It will help you manage the unexpected and anticipate trouble spots and problems that could slow you down or even cripple your effort. Chapter Nine continues this line of probing by helping you pull some numbers together. Here, we'll introduce you to some of the basic financial statements a business needs to survive and grow. If you have a well-considered plan, somewhere there will be a backer for your business. Chapter Ten will help you "shake the money tree" and guide you in finding the money you need. Next, in Chapter Eleven, you will start to consider the best legal form for your business, and Chapter Twelve will help you put together a winning team and a management strategy.

OTHER DOORWAYS AND OPTIONS

At this point, you will have completed more than 55 Action Steps. These steps help you start your own business from scratch, and to build a business that will help you achieve your vision and dreams. Starting out on your own is one option to owning your own small business — and it is clearly our favourite, though it is not the only small business doorway. In Chapters Thirteen and Fourteen, we look at two other doorways or options: buying an existing business and franchising.

What does buying an ongoing business involve? Why is it important to know why a seller is selling? What is a reasonable price? How much is good will really worth? We'll answer all these questions and help you learn how to negotiate a price. We'll also remind you to take along a notebook but leave your emotions — and your chequebook — at home until the time is right to go further.

If you're a neophyte entrepreneur, just testing the waters of small business for the first time, you will certainly want to examine another doorway — franchises — to see what they offer. Chapter Fourteen will help you do this. For the first-time entrepreneur who is accustomed to the power, image, and family feeling of a large corporation, franchising can provide a helpful security blanket. But we warn you: get lots of advice before you sign a franchise agreement.

In Chapter Fifteen, we open your eyes to another small business option: exporting. We want to convince you that no matter how small your business is, exporting is a real possibility if you have the vision, knowledge, and plan. We'll help you draft an export strategy so you're ready to enter and profit from international opportunities from day one.

YOUR COMPLETE BUSINESS PLAN

By the time you reach Chapter Sixteen you will have gathered enough material to write a complete business plan for showcasing your business to the world — that is, to bankers, vendors and lenders, venture capitalists, credit managers, key employees, your family, and your friends. Your finished plan will be a blueprint for your business. It will provide a walk-through of your industry, generate excitement in potential lenders, demonstrate your competence as a thoughtful planner, and underline the reasons customers are going to clamour for your product or service. Your plan will also serve you as a means of channelling your creative energies.

Let's think about that for a moment.

One reason you're reading this book is that you're creative. You like to build, to pull things together, to plant seeds and watch things grow, to develop projects, to produce. When your mind is creative, you probably come up with more ideas than you can handle. *That* is why you need a plan that helps give structure to your entrepreneurial aspirations. Perhaps you've always dreamed of working for yourself, being your own boss. Well, you can have that dream if you're *prepared*.

Features That Will Help

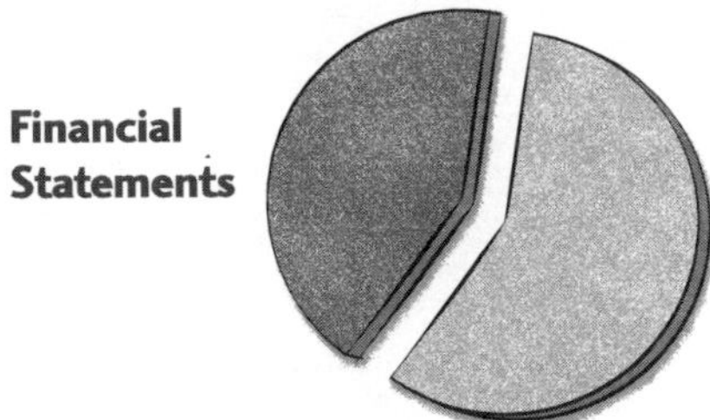

The Action Steps, Business Plan Building Blocks, and Checklist Questions and Actions to Develop Your Business Plan demonstrate exactly what belongs in your business plan.

KEEPING TRACK OF YOUR SLICE OF THE PIE

The three figures in the right margin portray a complete business plan as a pie chart, with each slice of the pie representing a part of the plan. Each chapter of the book is designed to help you complete one or more of the parts of your business plan. You will notice that a pie illustration appears at the beginning of each chapter. Those pies show which part (or parts) of the plan is addressed by the Action Steps in each chapter. The pies will also help you track your progress as an entrepreneur. When all the pieces of the pie are in place, your business plan will be completed and you'll be ready to open your doors.

A. The product or service
B. The market and the target customer
C. The competition
D. Marketing strategy
E. Location
F. Management
G. Personnel

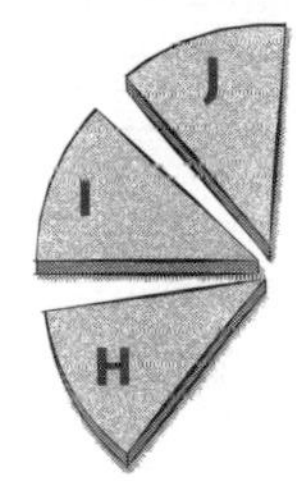

H. Projected income statement (Profit and loss)
I. Cash flow projection
J. Projected balance sheet

ACTION STEPS

Our road map to success in small business is composed of 87 Action Steps. Completing these steps should significantly help your chances of reaching your business vision and goals. You see, the world of business is like a maze — a series of challenges and obstacles — and the Action Steps are designed to lead you through the maze. Each Action Step is an exercise that accompanies our explanation of a particular portion of the maze.

OPENING WINDOWS

In each chapter, figures and tables provide useful information and concepts to illustrate the text. Examples include Internet databases (throughout the book), tips for developing successful, strategic alliances (Chapter Four), the best places to set up your booth at a trade show (Chapter Six), and a strategy for selecting your mentor (Chapter Twelve). All of these offer the new entrepreneur windows onto the world of small business.

STAYING ON TRACK

Other features help you stay on track and focus on the task at hand. Learning Opportunities at the beginning of each chapter identify the educational goals of the chapter. Business Plan Building Blocks help you identify future trends. Margin definitions help you build your business vocabulary. Think Points for Success push you to think further, deeper, and more successfully about what you have learned. If you need more information about any of the topics, the Notes and Other References section at the end of every chapter will help you.

NEW TO THE THIRD EDITION

Writing a business plan often seems to be a daunting and cumbersome task to students and experienced business people alike. In this third edition, we have demystified the process with Business Plan Building Blocks, a step-by-step guide to writing a fully developed plan for any type of business, and Checklist Questions and Actions to Develop Your Business Plan to make sure you've put together all the details. The 87 Action Steps help set the stage, the building blocks help pull the plan together in an orderly and logical fashion, and the checklists ensure that you have considered all the details.

We have also included in this new edition a number of improvements designed to make *Small Business* the most exciting, current, comprehensive, and useful small business and entrepreneurship textbook available. You'll find in this edition:

- integrated Web sites throughout the text that address the implications of the Internet and the World Wide Web on small business;
- updated Canadian sources for information concerning small business and entrepreneurship, including relevant World Wide Web addresses;
- an updated list of relevant references for further information;
- increased focus on youth entrepreneurship;
- updated stories, profiles, and examples, many of which are based on the research of *Profit: The Magazine for Canadian Entrepreneurs* editor Richard Spence;
- a more streamlined presentation; and
- updated graphical and statistical information.

VIDEO SUPPORT

Thanks to TVOntario, Harcourt Brace Canada, and Lockwood Films, this edition continues to be supported by a thirteen-part video series entitled, *Writing a Small Business Plan*. We encourage you to take advantage of this video support. TVO has also created a course guide, available at Harcourt Brace, that will help you through each part of the business plan.

Additionally, this edition is supported by another set of eight videos entitled *Micro Business Video Series*. Prepared for the Business Development Bank (BDC) by Barbara Frank and Gordon McLeod of Corporate Catalysts, these videos offer supplemental information and exercises on small business marketing and finance.

This Book Is for You

TO DREAMERS AND BEGINNING ENTREPRENEURS

This book can be used on at least two levels. One is a fast-track approach for the action-oriented entrepreneur who wants to get on with the start-up. The other is a step-by-step process for the creative dreamer who can afford to take the time to savour the atmosphere of the business arena.

As you're reading the book, keep your computer or pencil and paper close by so that you can note or jot down ideas. Get used to brainstorming. Also, it's not a bad idea to carry a cassette recorder in your car so that you can record ideas that occur to you while you're driving. The inspiration that you get from a freeway billboard 400 kilometres from home might be the seed from which your winning business will grow.

Our point is that this is *your* book. Use it in whatever way suits your needs. Make notes in the margins, mark it up with a highlighting pen. Use the book as a handbook, as a textbook, or as both. It's designed for a wide range of creative, energetic people who want to own their own business, and someplace in that range of people is *you*. Good luck!

TO THEIR INSTRUCTORS AND MENTORS

As for previous editions, a useful Instructor's Manual is available, with lecture outlines, sample business plans, test items, and more. Like this book, the Instructor's Manual is improved thanks to comments from you and your colleagues. Thanks again for selecting *Small Business: An Entrepreneur's Plan* for your students. And please keep writing. Hearing from you keeps us in touch with our customers.

Acknowledgments

We couldn't have written this book without significant contributions from a number of people. The book is built on a foundation of case studies, and the Action Steps are taken from real-life tactics in the marketplace. Many entrepreneurs have succeeded in the real world, and we've just tried to tell you how they've done it.

Our special thanks go to:

Richard Spence, editor of *Profit: The Magazine for Canadian Entrepreneurs*
Larry Mah, Manager, Intervision, The Canadian Youth Business Foundation
Orville Lahey (Lahey Consultants Inc.)

We are truly indebted to our colleagues who graciously devoted their time to review and improve this third edition. Especially Arthur Coren (Kwantlen University College); Laurence Hewick (Wilfrid Laurier University); Norman Hotchkiss (Department of Foreign Affairs and International Trade); Ed Leach (Dalhousie University); Lois Stevenson (Industry Canada); and Peter Young (George Brown College).

Thanks also to Lori Kapshey for her efficient secretarial support.

Of course, this third edition could not have been completed without the endless help, guidance, and advice of the Harcourt Brace staff, notably Ken Nauss (Senior Acquisitions Editor) and Stacey Roderick (Production Editor).

A special thanks goes to Su Mei Ku of SMK Editorial Services. It was her excellent work that helped shape the manuscript into a book we were all proud to publish. Thanks also to Georgina Montgomery of West Coast Editorial Associates whose thorough copy editing of the book made us look good.

Last, this book would not have been possible had it not been for all those who contributed to the U.S. edition. We truly appreciate the help and guidance of J.D. Ryan, Lee A. Eckert, and Robert J. Ray.

Thank you, and we hope you enjoy your small business adventure.

RONALD A. KNOWLES, Algonquin College, Ottawa
CLIFF G. BILYEA, Wilfrid Laurier University, Waterloo, and Senior Consultant at KPMG

Statistics Canada information is used with the permission of the Minister of Industry, as Minister responsible for Statistics Canada. Information on the availability of the wide range of data from Statistics Canada can be obtained from Statistics Canada's Regional Offices, its World Wide Web site at http://www.statcan.ca, and its toll-free access number 1-800-263-1136.

A NOTE FROM THE PUBLISHER

Thank you for selecting *Small Business: An Entrepreneur's Plan,* Third Canadian Edition, by Ronald A. Knowles and Cliff G. Bilyea. The authors and publisher have devoted considerable time and care to the development of this book. We appreciate your recognition of this effort and accomplishment.

We want to hear what you think about the book. Please take a few minutes to fill in the stamped reader reply card at the back of the book. Your comments and suggestions will be valuable to us as we prepare new editions and other books.

brief contents

contents

twelve

thirteen

fourteen

one

Doorways to Small Business — Your Great Adventure

BUSINESS PLAN BUILDING BLOCK

At the end of each chapter, you will begin a preliminary draft of what will become a complete and free-flowing business plan.

LEARNING OPPORTUNITIES

After reading this chapter, you should be able to:

- Learn how you can fit in, grow, develop, and prosper in the new economy and the third millenium.
- Identify the role, skills, and characteristics of successful Canadian entrepreneurs.
- Describe the rationale for a business plan and list the main components.
- Improve your research and information-gathering skills.
- Expand your knowledge of small business by interviewing small business owners.
- Discover your personal strengths and what success means to you.
- Identify your personal visions, values, and goals.

He sucks up the air in a room as he enters it.

Brash and cocky, 24-year-old Carmine Coletti already runs his own business, employing four other people full-time.

His company, TireNet, sells tires to consumers and small businesses through the Internet. Coletti is determined to grow the high-tech company to a point where he can hire someone to run it, and then he'll start up something new.

"My edge is in the application of technology. I'm not just selling tires." Asked what motivates him, Coletti steps from behind his desk, unbuttons his expensive suit jacket and pulls up his turtleneck sweater to reveal the "swoosh" symbol tattooed on his navel.[1]

George Cohen, the "burgermeister," is senior chairman of McDonald's Restaurants of Canada Ltd. and vice-chairman of Moscow McDonald's. The man with chutzpah and "ketchup in his blood" opened his first McDonald's franchise in Moscow in 1990. Today, there are thirteen outlets in what was the former Soviet Union. In just one outlet at Pushkin Square, as many as 50 000 people line up each day for a taste of Western capitalism. Why has George Cohen been so successful? *Pravda*, a major newspaper in Moscow, described him this way: "George Cohen stands out with his unequalled spirit of entrepreneurship."[2]

Figure 1.1 Before you begin to write your business plan, investigate the doorways to small business.

ACTION STEP PREVIEW

1. Assess your job security.
2. Look into your business future by drawing a "future wheel."
3. Brainstorm three new businesses capitalizing on the "cocooning" trend.
4. Use "new-eyes" to investigate the marketplace for fresh opportunities.
5. Assess your interests and abilities.
6. Assess your accomplishments.
7. Organize your information.
8. Mind map and list your core values.
9. Define your personal visions and goals.

Life is short, and you only go around once. So you want to make sure you're achieving what you desire, having fun, making money, and being the best person you can be.

How do you do that?

Some people do it by going into business for themselves. If *you* are thinking about owning your own business, this book is written for you.

Try this line of thought: What do you want to be doing in the third millennium? What is your personal vision? What's the best course of action for you right now? What might be the best business for you? What are your strengths? This chapter will address these questions and many others.

This is the Age of the Entrepreneur. According to Industry Canada, there are 2.5 million small businesses in Canada. Each year, about 140 000 new corporations are started. Over 60 percent of the new jobs in the private sector are being created by firms with fewer than 20 employees. Yes, it's a great time for the entrepreneur. You could be fulfilling your dream. If you're thinking about owning your own business, come along with us!

What's Happened to the Forty-Hour Week, the Golden Parachute, and the Gold Watch?

Good question. Just how serious are you about entering the bustling arena of small business? Can't get a job — executive recruiters call it a "position" — in "big business"? How much pressure is there on you to travel the entrepreneurial road into small business?

Let's say you read this book — enough of it, anyway, to begin to get the picture about entrepreneuring. You try some Action Steps and find them stimulating and even fun (though they take time away from your weekend, the beach, the movies). You also discover in the process that you don't thrive on competition, that you think a 60-hour work week is madness, that you'd be edgy if you ever had to mortgage your house for start-up money. You take refuge in the dream of wearing a suit to work, driving a snappy sports car, and always having your weekends free.

So you close the book on small business planning with a snap and snatch up the classifieds, telling yourself you're going to work for a big company, something visible, something with clout and prestige and a logo and great perks. You're going to find a *real job*.

The fact is, however, that may not be as easy — or as realistic a proposition — as you believe.

If you're thinking about entering the corporate ranks, here are some labour market facts you might want to consider:

- As of 1997, the jobless rate for youth was about 17 percent — nearly double that for those over the age of 25.[3]
- The proportion of those 15- to 24-year-olds who have never worked doubled over the last 15 years.[4]
- Those 18- to 30-year-olds — the so-called "baby busters" — represent about one-fifth of the labour market, but accounted for three-fifths of the job losses over the recession of the early 1990s.[5]
- Canadian productivity barely increased over the latter part of the 1990s.[6]
- Large firms have not been hiring. The number of large firms (500^+ employees) has not increased since the early 1980s. By the latter half of the 1990s, only about 40 percent of Canadian workers were employed in large corporations — down from 45 percent in the early part of the 1980s.[7] (See also Figure 1.2.)

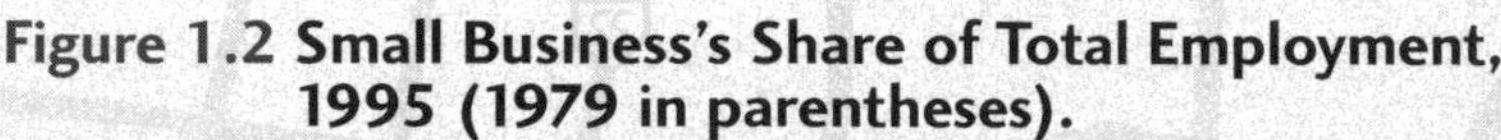

Figure 1.2 Small Business's Share of Total Employment, 1995 (1979 in parentheses).

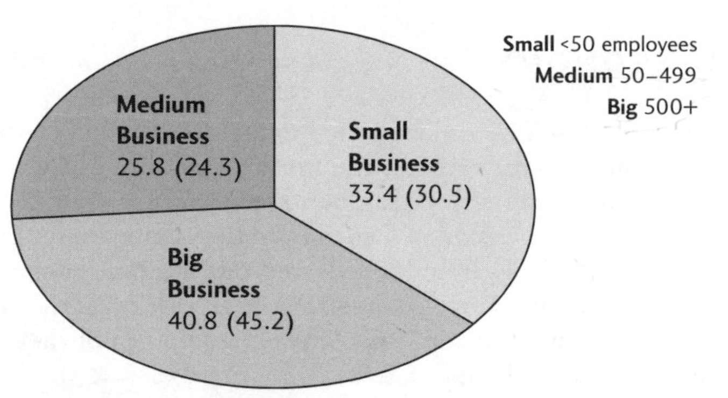

Source: Statistics Canada, "Small Business's Share of Total Employment," adapted from "Small Business Profiles — Ad-hoc Requests," Cat. No. 61C0002. Reprinted with permission.

ACTION STEP 1

Assess your job security.

On a sheet of paper, write down your present job title, the firm or organization you work for, how long you've worked there, how many hours a week you work, and the three tasks that take up most of your time.

Are you on the phone a lot? Do you shuffle paper? Do you spend time in meetings? Does your job put you on the road more than once a week? How do the three tasks you listed square with your job title?

Now, rank your job security on a 1–10 scale. How easily could you be replaced? If you currently are not working, rank the job security of your mother or father, brother or sister, friend or relative.

The world has changed, and in many cases it's hard to understand the logic of big business in responding to these changes. One thing is for certain: a job in the large corporate sector is no longer, and will no longer be, a ticket to security. How sure are you that you will find that "job of a lifetime"? To stress this point, we want you to complete Action Step 1.

You want to do more than survive. You want to have fun. You want your life to have value and meaning. You likely value substance, honesty, security, and success. So, in order to decide which road to take, you are going to have to do some research and keep your eyes and ears open. To get you thinking about opportunities, let's take a moment and look at the two major growth engines of the Canadian economy.

The Engines of the Canadian Economy

Over the last few years, our economy has undergone the most significant shift since the pivotal unfolding of the Industrial Revolution. The reality is that our traditional resource-based industries (mining and forestry, for example) and our smokestack industries (such as autos and steel) are no longer the engines

Box 1.1 They Said It

"Then came the upheavals of the 1980s and 1990s, as an epidemic of large corporate mergers and downsizings left many supposed lifetime employees at loose ends and contemplating self-employment. Even the public sector was forced to face the grim reality of retrenchment during this period, releasing yet another pool of potential small business owners or employees."

CATHERINE SWIFT, president and chief executive,
Canadian Federation of Independent Business (CFIB)

Source: Catherine Swift, "It's a Small World After All," *Post 2000*, Issue 8, November 15, 1997, p. 5.

of economic growth. Today, and into the third millennium, the global marketplace and knowledge- and technology-based industries are the engines of our economy.

GLOBAL ECONOMY

About 43 percent of our Gross Domestic Product (GDP) can be attributed to Canada's economic success around the world. One-third of Canadians owe their livelihood to the strength of the country's global economy. Foreign markets are fuelling the expansion of Canada's hottest companies. "Eighty percent of our revenue comes from the U.S., but our international market also includes Japan, Germany, Portugal, Australia, and New Zealand. We couldn't exist if we stayed within Canada," says Jane Somerville, publisher and president of Somerville House Books Ltd.[8]

KNOWLEDGE- AND TECHNOLOGY-BASED ECONOMY

Brenda, the owner of Tomorrow Travel Inc., has convened a "virtual" meeting from her home office with her colleagues from around the world. From her "electronic cottage," she pushes a button on her computer, and one by one, the televised images of meeting participants pop up on her screen. Everyone exchanges greetings before getting down to business.[9]

Welcome to the age of technology and the electronic cottage. As we enter the next millennium, many Canadians like Brenda will work and play out of their homes, connecting with their friends and business associates at the speed of electronic mail (e-mail). Don Tapscott, author and Canadian cyberguru, tells us that the new economy is a:

- knowledge economy made up of knowledge workers and knowledge consumers,
- digital economy in which physical things can become virtual, and
- networked economy in which producers and consumers operate directly through digital networks.[10]

Nuala Beck, another influential Canadian thinker, estimates that about 60 percent of our economic activity and 70 percent of our jobs are now tied up in new industries such as telecommunications, computer hardware and

Box 1.2 Small Business Tips

Says Nuala Beck, "It's not what you study, it's where you apply what you've learned — that is the key. And you'll be further ahead if you apply your special talents in an industry that has a future, rather than in one than doesn't." For example:

- If you study English, think about starting a business in the fast-growing software industry, editing manuals or new product literature.
- If your interest is photography, think about starting a business taking photographs for media journals and pharmacology journals.

Source: Adapted from Nuala Beck, *Excelerate: Growing in the New Economy* (Toronto: Harper Perennial, an imprint of Harper Collins Publishers Ltd., 1995), pp. 16, 18.

software, and pharmaceuticals.[11] Smart entrepreneurs will have to take advantage of this new knowledge-based, technology-driven economy.

The Internet is the latest indicator of the complete shift in the nature of our economy. Today, the Internet is a ubiquitous part of Canadian business and culture. Successful businesses have already embraced this new technology, and the trend to get on the Net will continue. According to the 1997 Profit 100 (*Profit* magazine's survey of Canada's 100 fastest-growing companies), 55 percent of the companies have Web sites and 77 percent use the Net for e-mail and 66 percent for research.[12] As well, according to Statistics Canada, almost one in three Canadian households owned a computer in 1996 — a number that has tripled in growth within a decade — and about 8 percent of these were connected to the Internet (see Figure 1.3). If you haven't already done so, we strongly suggest that you find access to the Net. When you do, you will be joining millions of others in the new digital economy.

The global market and technology are the two major engines driving our economy. Other trends affecting the direction of the Canadian economy will be discussed in the next chapter. The key, at this point, is to understand that technology and the global economy are creating opportunities for the enterprising entrepreneur. For example, in the opening vignette, Carmine Coletti took advantage of the cocooning and information trends by establishing TireNet — a business selling tires over the Net. Figure 1.4 shows a mind map of some of the opportunities resulting from this cocooning trend — the tendency for people to retreat to the safety, security, and convenience of their homes. Action Step 2 gives you an opportunity to stretch your imagination and fantasize about your own "enchanted fortress." After you have designed your dream home, go to Action Step 3 and explore the small business implications of cocooning.

ACTION STEP 2

Look into your business future by drawing a "future wheel."

Get a pencil and paper and spend ten minutes modifying our future wheel (Figure 1.4) into your own enchanted fortress. There is no such thing as a wrong idea or a wrong direction. Just close your eyes for a moment and allow your imagination to take over. See how many additional lines and balloons you can add. This will also introduce you to brainstorming. You can predict the future as well as anyone else; all you need to do is mesh information with your imagination and see what happens.

Figure 1.3 Computers in Canada

HOUSEHOLD COMPUTER MARKET

- The percentage of Canadian households in 1996 with computers totalled 31.6.
- Of those households, 49.2 percent had a modem and 7.4 percent had access to the Internet.

GROWTH TRIPLES IN A DECADE

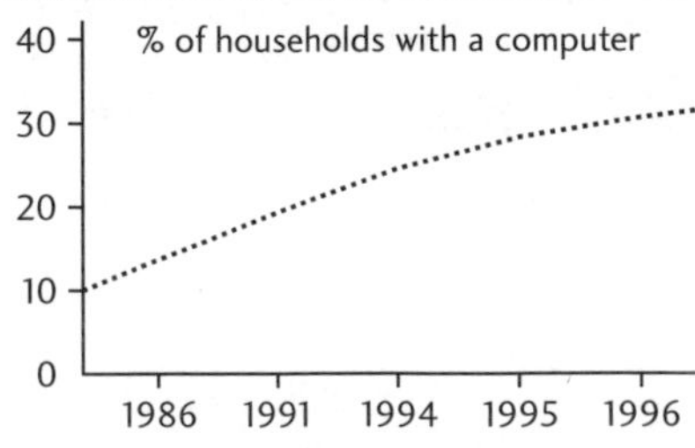

- Income levels and children determine the likelihood of there being a computer in the home.

- Forty-five percent of single-family households with children under 18 years of age (or about 1.7 million) had a computer compared to 18 percent a decade ago.
- Sixty-five percent of households with an income of over $70 000 reported having a computer.

INTERNET PENETRATION

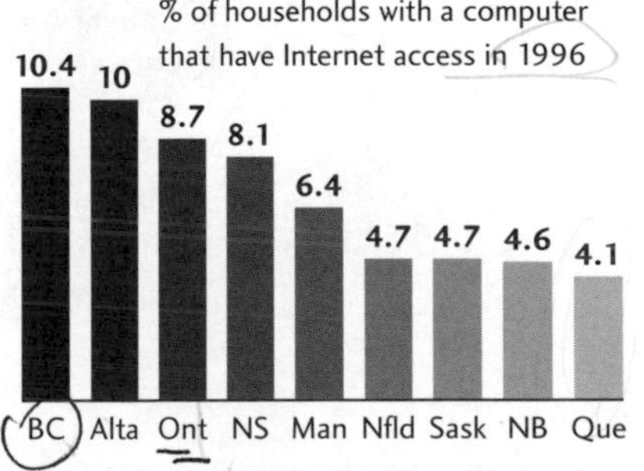

Source: Statistics Canada, "Computers in Canada," adapted from "Household Facilities by Income and Other Characteristics," Catalogue No. 13-218. Reprinted with permission.

ACTION STEP 3

Brainstorm three new businesses capitalizing on the "cocooning" trend. Open your eyes.

Get a pencil and paper. Write the word "cocoon" in the centre of the page and draw a mind map, using the trends that radiate out from it. Repeat the same process you used in Action Step 2. Allow yourself to let your creativity run. Refer to Figure 1.4 for inspiration.

This is a mind-mapping process (see Box 1.3). Mind mapping allows you to plot a chain of ideas graphically without losing your train of thought. If you are mind mapping with a group, use a large writing board or poster board to encourage participation.

In the next few chapters, you'll get more chances to practice with this technique.

Figure 1.4

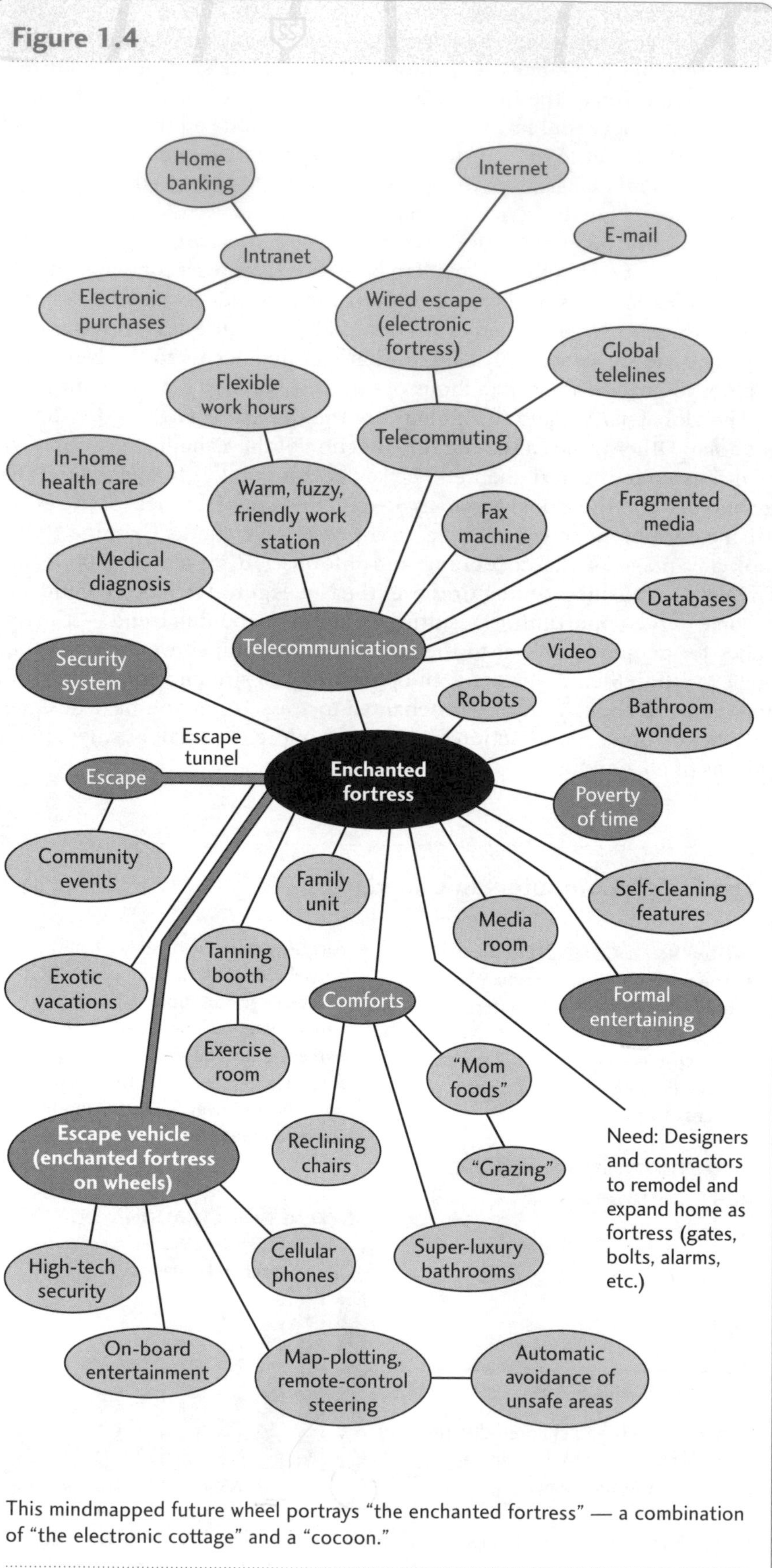

This mindmapped future wheel portrays "the enchanted fortress" — a combination of "the electronic cottage" and a "cocoon."

Box 1.3 Doodling with a Purpose

A mind map — sometimes called a spoke diagram, thought-web, or clustering diagram — is a sketch using circled words connected by lines to form units. It is a form of doodling, only it has a purpose — to generate ideas. It works like this:

1. In the centre of a page, you write your vision or goals and draw a circle around the words.
2. Every time you get an idea related to this vision or goals, you write it down, circle it, and connect it with a line to the theme.
3. Ideas are connected to one another with more lines, which are, in turn, connected to the vision or goals. Before you know it, you have a gigantic spider web or idea tree full of opportunities.

Mind mapping is meant for individual "brain dumps," but it can be easily adapted for group or team brainstorms.

The Age of the Entrepreneur

As much as 50 percent of all the jobs that will exist ten years from now do not exist today.[13] The business world is changing faster and faster, so what do you do? Life may not be what you thought it would be, so what do you do? The big firm you wanted to work for may not be hiring or is now closed. The job you trained for is obsolete. What do you do?

Establish your vision, plan ahead — you live in a great country. Canada enjoys the highest level of human development in the world. In 1997, the United Nations ranked us number one for the fourth consecutive year.[14] Canadian entrepreneurs have played a central role in this success. According to Industry Canada, independent businesses accounted for over 80 percent of the 600 000 jobs created between 1996 and 1997, and almost half of those jobs came from new businesses.[15] Small businesses are the main source of energy in our private enterprise system. This sector is the major contributor to job creation, productivity, and economic growth and wealth.

Here are a few more facts (also see Table 1.1):[16]

- Canada has over 2.3 million small businesses (including the self-employed) with fewer than 100 employees.
- The number of self-employed continues to rise. As of 1998, about 16 percent of the labour force were self-employed, compared with 12 percent in 1981.
- Including the self-employed, more than 95 percent of all businesses in this country are small.
- Small business is Canada's largest employer, accounting for over 50 percent of private sector employment and 43 percent of economic output.
- Small businesses account for more than a quarter of all business sales in Canada, one-third of all profits, and one-fifth of all assets.
- Twenty-five percent of all small businesses in Canada are owned by people aged 18 to 29.
- According to surveys conducted by the Canadian Federation of Independent Business (CFIB), Canadian small and medium-sized businesses pay higher wages and spend more on training, research, and development as a percentage of sales than do large businesses.
- Over 15 percent of Canadian households (about 1.5 million families) have a family member who operates a business from the home.
- About 50 percent of all new businesses start up in the home.

Table 1.1 Number of Businesses in Canada, Total and as a Percentage of the Total Business*

	1981		1991		1994	
	Number	%	Number	%	Number	%
Self-employed	678 000	49.3	1 146 000	55.4	1 393 000	59.9
Employer business						
< 5 (employees)	522 358	38.0	678 447	32.8	707 886	30.5
5–19	125 928	9.2	174 966	8.5	163 155	7.0
20–49	30 024	2.2	43 588	2.1	38 300	1.6
50–99	10 049	0.7	13 897	0.7	11 638	0.5
100–499	7 753	0.6	9 334	0.4	8 486	0.4
500+	2 030	0.1	2 020	0.1	2 023	0.1
Subtotal	698 142	50.7	922 252	44.6	931 518	40.1
All businesses	1 376 142	100.0	2 068 253	100.0	2 324 518	100.0

*Numbers may not add up to 100 percent because of rounding.

Source: Adapted from Industry Canada, *Your Guide to Government of Canada Services and Support for Small Business: Trends and Statistics, 1996–1997,* Catalogue No. C1-10/1997E; and John Manley and Paul Martin for Industry Canada, *Growing Small Business*, February 1994, p. 4. Reproduced with the permission of the Minister of Public Works and Government Services Canada, 1998.

- Over 60 percent of Canadians think small business owners are happier at their jobs.
- One in three Canadian jobs depends on trade.

Entrepreneurs are the fuel of our private enterprise system. They provide the competitive zeal; create jobs, new ventures, and opportunities for others; and improve our economic growth and social fibre. Entrepreneurs are visionary self-starters who love the adventure of a new enterprise. They have swoosh and chutzpah, providing a spirit of energy, initiative, and potential for progress.

The hours for entrepreneurs are often long and lonely. But just in case you think entrepreneurs are not a happy bunch, here is what Peter Sagar, director-general of the entrepreneurship office of Industry Canada has to say: "Surveys show that people with the highest life satisfaction levels are people who own their own businesses." Supporting this, a survey of Canadian entrepreneurs by Padgett Business Services found that 75 percent said they would take the route all over again.[17]

Hundreds of research studies have attempted to determine the common skills, personality, and behavioural traits of successful entrepreneurs. The simple deduction from all this research is that most entrepreneurs cannot be cloned. They tend to defy stereotyping and broad-brush labelling. "I have seen people of the most diverse personalities and temperaments perform well in entrepreneurial challenges," concludes business guru Peter Drucker.[18]

Nevertheless, if generalizations must be made, we can say that most of our entrepreneurs are:[19]

Goal-oriented individuals. Entrepreneurs tend to be task or goal driven rather than activity oriented or socially motivated.

Opportunists. Entrepreneurs are driven by opportunity. They are motivated by the belief that they can satisfy a need through an innovative activity.

Agents of change. Entrepreneurs invariably identify their primary motivations as "seeing a need and acting on it."

- *Moderate risk takers.* Entrepreneurs are innately curious and take calculated risks.
- *High energy performers.* Entrepreneurs wake up "excited" in the morning because they believe they can control and change their lives and the lives of others. They crave the excitement of the unknown and lose interest quickly when situations become repetitive.
- *Independent thinkers.* Entrepreneurs have a need for freedom — a need to control their own destiny and "be their own boss."

In a ground-breaking Profit 100 study of successful Canadian business entrepreneurs in the 1990s, Rick Spence, editor of *Profit* magazine, isolated ten key characteristics of successful entrepreneurs (see Box 1.4). Here's what Spence has to say about these factors: "What's important in perusing this list is noting how few of these characteristics are personality-driven. Most of them represent behavioural characteristics that can be learned, as opposed to inherited abilities (an affinity for math, say, or an outgoing personality) that confer ongoing advantages on just a lucky few."

According to this research of successful growth firms, most entrepreneurs are *made*, not born. This is good news for the thousands of Canadians who don't think they have the innate abilities to start up on their own.

To find out whether you have what it takes to be a small business owner, ask yourself some of the questions in Action Step 10. We also suggest you visit the Web site of the Canadian Youth Business Foundation" (Box 1.5) and meet others like yourself who have decided to investigate the entrepreneurial option.

Knocking at the Entrepreneurial Doors

There are three doorways to small business ownership. Doorway One is buying an ongoing business: you look around, find a business you like, and buy

Box 1.4 The Ten Characteristics of Successful Canadian Business Entrepreneurs

According to Profit 100's study, successful Canadian entrepreneurs of the 1990s possess the following characteristics:

1. **Experience.** They have an in-depth knowledge of their field and its products.
2. **Strategic vision.** They are driven by a compelling vision.
3. **Impatience.** They react quickly to change and seize the opportunity of the moment.
4. **Willingness to share.** Old fashioned as it sounds, they believe in sharing.
5. **People oriented.** They are not loners. They have to like people — after all, people are what drives business.
6. **Enthusiasm.** They are professional optimists. A problem is always an opportunity in disguise.
7. **Ability to deal with stress.** They are able to channel stress into positive energy.
8. **Persistence.** They don't give up easily when things look bleak. In their eyes, the glass is always half full.
9. **Lifelong learning.** They make lots of mistakes. Successful entrepreneurs consider mistakes a learning experience.
10. **Ability to communicate.** They are deliberate, strategic, and eager communicators.

Source: Adapted from Rick Spence, *Secrets of Success from Canada's Fastest-Growing Companies* (Toronto: John Wiley & Sons Canada, Ltd., 1997), p. 228. Reprinted with permission of the author.

Box 1.5 Bookmark This

Canadian Youth Business Foundation: http://www.cybf.ca

Interested in becoming more involved with the entrepreneurial community? Even if you are not so young — chronologically, that is — we suggest you visit the Web site of the Canadian Youth Business Foundation (CYBF). You'll find some great information and sources of help. It is the only comprehensive Canadian Web site dedicated to developing, supporting, and promoting entrepreneurs in Canada.

Here is some of the help you can access:

- the support of other entrepreneurs and other like-minded individuals;
- advice from experienced entrepreneurs, business executives, and professionals; and
- a wide range of small business information, such as how to register your business, how to market yourself and your business, and how to prepare a business plan.

According to Larry Mah, Manager, Intervision, CYBF: "The best quality of this site is that it is all genuinely provided with no ulterior motives. It is a community. We have no plans to hit our users with 'in their face corporate advertising' or other stuff."

it. Sounds pretty easy, doesn't it? A business broker will make it sound even easier, so beware.

Doorway Two is buying a franchise: you find a concept you like, one with national visibility, and you buy it. In exchange for your money, the franchisor supplies you with inventory, advice, and a product or service that is well known in the marketplace. Sounds pretty easy, doesn't it? A slick franchisor will make it sound even easier.

Doorway Three, our favourite, is starting a new business from scratch — a business that is compatible with your interests and skills, one that is backed up by careful research that shows strong customer need.

BUSINESS PLAN
a blueprint for your business start-up or expansion

Entering the world of small business by *any* of these doorways demands a carefully designed **business plan** — words and numbers on paper that will guide you through the gaps, the competition, the bureaucracies, the products, the services. The 87 Action Steps presented in this book will help you write a business plan; the Building Blocks and the Checklist Questions will help you keep on track. As additional sources of information, you will also find World Wide Web references in each chapter. Now enjoy the journey as an entrepreneur!

WHAT ABOUT THESE THREE DOORWAYS?

About two-thirds of all entrepreneurs enter the world of small business by buying an existing business or a franchise operation. When these people have gained some experience and confidence, many of them, like Carmine Coletti, decide to start a totally new business from scratch. Others, like George Cohen, however, are not happy with just one business. They start up. They sell. They start up again. And they become experts at writing and implementing business plans.

No matter which doorway you choose, you're going to need a business plan. If you buy an ongoing business, you may inherit the seller's business plan. It's still wise to write one of your own, however. Ask the seller (again and again, if necessary) for the data you need for writing your own plan. That way, before you commit to purchase, you can check out those claims of huge potential profit and endless good will for yourself. The business plan is written by you for your direction.

If you buy a franchise, you'll be buying a business plan from the franchisor. But until you see it, you won't know for certain if you'll need to prepare one of your own as well. If you don't understand the franchisor's plan, by all means ask questions and write your own. Writing a business plan is a lot cheaper than spending money on a franchise that may not work.

If you start your own business, a business plan is a must, an *absolute must.* That plan stands between you and success.

Creating a Business Plan — Why Bother?

By the time you reach Chapter Seventeen, you will have gathered enough material to write a personal business plan to showcase your business to the real world — that is, to bankers, vendors and lenders, suppliers, venture capitalists, credit managers, key employees, your family and your friends. Your completed plan will be a blueprint for your business, whether it's a start-up or expansion. Here are a few other reasons why a business plan is important:

- *Lays out goals.* A written business plan provides an orderly statement of goals for ready reference at all times. It clarifies what you want to achieve and helps you work toward these goals.
- *Provides an organizing tool.* A plan, when completed, will provide you with the guidance to manage your business and keep it on track.
- *Acts as a financial guide.* You will know before you start your business how much money you'll need and how much you are going to earn.
- *Helps obtain advice.* A plan will provide you with a structure and format to get advice.
- *Helps secure investment.* A well-written plan will help you get the much needed start-up capital.

SO WHAT DOES A PLAN LOOK LIKE?

The particular format and content of a plan all depend on a number of factors, such as the kind of business you want to start, how much time and patience you have, and who is going to be involved with your business — that is, your target reader. If you are planning to go into business alone, or if you're in a hurry or can afford to loose a small investment, you may want to consider the fast-start plan provided in Chapter Seventeen. If, on the other hand, you have some time to think about it and other people (such as bankers, investors, and advisors) are involved with your business, you will very likely have to write a comprehensive plan like the one shown in Chapter Sixteen. Our template for this kind of detailed plan is provided in Box 1.6.

Although we have provided you with one particular format — one that has worked for us over the last ten years — there are all kinds of business plan variations. For example, all major chartered banks and accounting firms provide their version of a business plan to their customers. Scotiabank's *Scotiabusiness® Plan Writer* is one such plan (Box 1.7).

Box 1.6 Business Plan Outline

When you start a business, you must create a business plan. Your plan should contain the following broad components (a detailed outline is provided in Appendix I):

Cover Sheet
Table of Contents
Executive Summary
Description of the Business
- A. The Product or Service
- B. The Market and the Target Customer
- C. The Competition
- D. Promotion Strategy
- E. Location
- F. Management and Form of Ownership
- G. Personnel

Financial Section
- I. Projected Cash Flow (monthly, first year)
- J. Projected Income Statement
- K. Projected Balance Sheet

What Is a Small Business?

Honestly, nobody really knows for sure.

Strange as it may seem, there is no standard Canadian definition of small business. Here are three different interpretations.

- According to the Entrepreneurship and Small Business Office of Industry Canada, a small business is any firm with fewer than 100 paid employees in the manufacturing sector and fewer than 50 paid employees in all other sectors.
- Our major banks generally agree that small businesses are those which have loan authorizations of less than $500 000.
- The Small Business Loan Act, one federal government small business program, defines an eligible small business as one that has an annual revenue of less than $5 million.

Box 1.7 Small Business Tips

Scotiabank will provide you with its *Scotiabusiness® Plan Writer* free of charge. This software will assist you in creating a professional business plan, one that will really help you sell your ideas. The step-by-step format guides you through the entire process required to:

- Organize your thoughts and objectives.
- Develop strategies to achieve business goals.
- Produce financial projections.
- Identify problem areas through "what if" scenarios.

The *Scotiabusiness® Plan Writer* is a smart way to begin putting your ideas to paper.

We tend to like the rather open definition provided by the Canadian Federation of Independent Business, that a small business is "a firm that is independently owned and operated and is not dominant in its field of endeavour." A typical small business owner, according to this description, would employ anywhere from 1 to 20 employees. This represents over 80 percent of all businesses in Canada today.

The small business we are talking about is any venture with spirit, any business you want to start, or any idea you want to bring into the marketplace. It may be part-time, something you do at home, something you try alone, or something you need a team for. The ideas for a small business are almost limitless.

Your Chances of Success

Do some small businesses fail? Of course they do. Failure is a part of life. Just like some students fail a course. Over the latter part of the 1990s, about 3,500 bankruptcies occurred in Canada every year. Many of these involved small companies. Studies have shown that 65 percent of new businesses survive their first year; 30 percent their first five years; and only 15 percent make it for ten years. The cold, hard fact is that there is a chance that your idea may flop. That's why we want you to work through the chapters of this book. If you prove your business idea on paper first — in your business plan — there's a good chance you'll be successful. This is where conducting a lot of primary and secondary research comes in.

Conducting Research

Research opens doors to knowledge. There are three approaches to research. You'll need a combination of all three to make it big in small business.

PRIMARY RESEARCH

Primary research is carried out by interacting with the world directly or by talking to people, perhaps interviewing them. This includes talking to people "virtually" over the Net. You might ask small business owners questions like: Where were you when the entrepreneurial bug bit? Whom do you bank with? How did you choose your lawyer? Your accountant? What would you do if you started up tomorrow, knowing what you know today? Customers can be asked questions like: Is there something we don't carry that you need? How else can we be of help to you? How did you learn about our business? Vendors and suppliers may be asked questions like: What advertising works best in a business like ours? What products are hot? What services are being offered? In Chapter Two, we ask you to conduct your own primary research on your small business idea.

PRIMARY RESEARCH
interacting with the world directly by talking to people

SECONDARY RESEARCH

When you read second-hand what someone else has discovered, you're carrying out **secondary research.** You switch on your computer and surf the

SECONDARY RESEARCH
reading about someone else's primary research

Net. You go to the library and look up "small business" in the Business Index. You locate and read magazine and newspaper articles that contain information you think will be helpful. Databases and information from trade associations are also secondary sources of information. Or you write to trade associations in your industry. You find data on sales that will help you project how much money you can make in small business. Good techniques here will save you lots of footwork.

NEW-EYES RESEARCH

NEW-EYES RESEARCH
the use of intuition and observation to learn about the marketplace

New-eyes research provides a variety of fresh ways to look at a business. Many successful entrepreneurs have conducted new-eyes research. Claire Davenport, president of Blue Dog Bagels in Waterloo, Ontario, for example, visited about 150 different bagel shops to observe customers and the way the business is run before she opened her shop. In new-eyes research, you play detective. You might become a "mystery shopper" to check out your competition. When **target customers** appear, you observe them so that you can profile them later. You may stand in a supermarket and, trying not to look nosy, watch what people put in their shopping carts. For example:

TARGET CUSTOMERS
customers with the highest probability of buying your product or service

Steak + Beer + Veggie tray + Twelve-pack of cola = Party time
Cereal + Dog food + Diapers + Baby food = Family with young children

Doing this type of work allows you to develop a **psychographic profile** of your target customer.

PSYCHOGRAPHIC PROFILE
a description of a group (or groups) based on an analysis of people's lifestyles

New-eyes research is fun. Doing it along with using the Internet, studying books, magazines, trade journals, and publications like *Profit* magazine, and talking to people, you will be able to develop a credible and valuable business plan. Remember that the business plan may become your guide to success — or it may show you that your idea isn't worth any more of your time.

It's time to investigate the market for new opportunities. Action Step 4 will get you going.

Plotting Your Future

You have looked at your job situation and at the potential job market; and you've tried a mind map and begun investigating the marketplace with new eyes for opportunities. Now it's time to see if you have what it takes. To begin, step back for a moment and assess your interests and abilities. We want you to complete Action Step 5, a sort of self-assessment guide to the world of entrepreneuring. It'll help you learn some things about yourself.

Next, we'd like you to meet Judd O'Herlihy.

At 40, Judd O'Herlihy was unhappy with his dead-end job as branch manager of a major electrical manufacturer. He needed a change and a new direction. So he registered for a career guidance class at a local community college. At the second session, the instructor-counsellor gave the class some aptitude tests. She asked all the participants to list every accomplishment in their entire lives that gave them a good feeling.

Judd hated writing and he resisted the process, but his list soon took shape.

1. ball monitor, third grade
2. second prize, paper drive, fourth grade

3. pole vault, new high school record, age 16
4. organized Lions Club pancake breakfast for 5 000 high school seniors

He was playing with the idea, making fun of it, when he remembered something else from his high school years. He'd bought old cars and fixed them up. The first car was an Alfa Romeo 916. He'd bought it for $800 and resold it, after fixing it up, for $1 500. Remembering the cars made him think of other accomplishments. He'd been a Queen Scout, a decorated war hero, a carpenter and cabinetmaker, and a fair trumpet player. After he and his wife bought a house, he'd designed and contracted to build their swimming pool. After catching the spirit of the exercise, he filled up three pages. But only one thing on his list held his attention: building that swimming pool.

The instructor asked Judd to explain why this was so high on his list.

"Well," Judd said, thinking back, "we wanted a pool for the kids, so I asked several pool contractors for bids. I have five kids. I wanted a bigger-than-average pool so that they wouldn't be fighting over territory. My specs were simple: 12-metres long, 9 metres wide, 3 metres under the diving board. My pool didn't fit the specs of any of the contractors. They had standard plans, with only 2.75 metres under the diving board. One contractor even told me that to go deeper would violate the city code. So, since their plans didn't fit my yard, and since they had knocked each other pretty hard trying to get my business, I lost confidence in the whole crowd. Only one contractor offered to do the pool. It would cost double, he said, and he was certain I wouldn't like it."

The instructor asked Judd what he did then.

"I was discouraged, but summer was coming and my kids kept pressing me. I began to think, 'What's the big deal with a swimming pool? It's just a concrete hole in the ground attached to some plumbing.' So I looked in the Yellow Pages and located a civil engineer who considered himself a pool specialist. For less than $300, the engineer got me all the permits and showed me how to find the best subcontractors.

"My friends and neighbours tried to dissuade me," Judd went on, "but I collected bids anyway. I got them from diggers, steel riggers, electricians, tile people, gunnite and concrete contractors. When I tallied the bids up, I discovered I could get my pool — with the 3-metre depth I wanted — at about half the cost of the lowest bid from the big-time pool firms.

"So I built the pool myself. Along the way, every subcontractor showed me how to save money. I photographed the process and kept detailed notes. In less than a month, the pool was finished. It was perfect. The neighbours came around asking questions, and I helped them subcontract their pools. I even wrote a 16-page booklet, 'How to Contract Your Own Concrete Pool and Save 50%.' I advertised the booklet in the pool sections of some newspapers and sold 2 000 copies for $9.95 each. My cost, including mailing, was about $1.50. We got the pool we wanted, and the profit from the booklet paid for it twice."

"A great story, Mr. O'Herlihy!" said the instructor. "But tell me. If this was so rewarding, why didn't you go on building?"

"Too busy," Judd said.

"That's too bad," said the instructor. "With talent like *that*, you should *make* time."

ACTION STEP 4

Use "new-eyes" to investigate the marketplace for fresh opportunities. Interview at least three people who are self-employed. One of them should be in your area of interest. (If you're a potential competitor, you may need to travel 80 kilometres or more to get real help.)

Successful entrepreneurs love to tell the story of how they made it. Be up front about what kind of information you want from these people and why you want it; make appointments with them at times and places convenient to *them*. You may be amazed at how much help you get.

Open-ended questions are best because they leave room for embellishment. Here are some suggestions to start you off:

- When did you decide to start your own business?
- What was your first step?
- Do you remember how you felt?
- If you had it to do all over again, what would you do differently?
- How large a part does creativity play in your particular business?
- Are your rewards tangible or intangible?
- What was your best advertisement or promotion?
- What makes your business unique?
- How important is price in your business? Would a price war increase your customer base?

Depending on how you hit it off, you might be able to think of these first interviewees as sources of marketplace experience. They may be able to help a lot when you start to assemble your "squad" — your lawyer, accountant, banker, and so on.

It's helpful to take some notes during the interviews. If you want to use a cassette recorder, however, be sure to ask permission first.

Don't worry about evaluation at this stage. The information will fall into patterns sooner than you think.

ACTION STEP 5

Assess your interests and abilities.
Do you have what it takes to make it in small business? To find out, profile yourself as an entrepreneur. You won't be a perfect fit, because there is no such thing. Nonetheless, you will get much more out of this book if you fantasize yourself in the role of a successful entrepreneur. Keep your mind open and your pencil sharp. Opportunities are unlimited. This Action Step will help you assess your abilities and interests and get your creative juices flowing. You will probably come back to this step several times.

- How would your best friend describe you?
- How would your worst enemy describe you?
- How would you describe yourself?
- How much money do you need to survive for six months? For twelve months?
- How much money can you earn in your present position in three years? Five years? What is the maximum potential of your earning power?
- Are you comfortable taking moderate risks?
- Are you constantly looking for newer and better ways to do things?
- What can you do better than most people?
- Where do you live now? (Describe your home, residential area, geographical area, amenities, etc.)
- In what way would you like to change any of the above?
- Do you enjoy being in control?
- How do you spend your leisure time?
- Do you look forward more often than backward?
- How important is winning to you?
- Whom do you know whose strengths might complement some of your weaknesses?

Later that night when Judd was about to fall asleep, he was still glowing with the memory of his pool building. He woke up his wife. "Honey!" he said. "Wake up. I'm going to build us a *house*!"

The memory of a single past accomplishment changed Judd's life. With new confidence, he quit his job and started building rental units. Today, Judd O'Herlihy has his own company and is financially independent. He'll never work for someone else again.

Action Step 6 focusses on some of your past accomplishments and shortcomings. The purpose of the exercise is to give you confidence. After all, you've come *this* far, right? It should also trigger your imagination and get you rolling. Small business is your dream, your venture. When you get going on it, you'll learn more about yourself than you likely thought possible. But first you are going to learn to get organized.

Some people have the feeling that getting organized will stifle their creativity. Marci Reid was like that until she saw the value of her adventure notebook.

Marci Reid loved to travel, so when she graduated from high school, she got herself a job with a travel agency. For fourteen months she worked as a secretary, learning the business. From her first week, Marci kept a notebook diary, listing elements of the travel business that seemed to be important.

Over the next dozen years, Marci worked for three different travel agencies and her diary notebook grew. She spent four years in Europe and when she returned home, she knew it was time to strike out on her own. By then her diary notebook filled four volumes.

"I know the travel business," Marci said to a friend. "All I need are a few more business skills. Then I can have my own agency."

Marci read and reread her notebooks. She spent time boiling down the information. Then she consulted with her family and with a friend she'd been considering for a partner. Everyone she talked to was excited. Marci's friend was also tired of working for other people and enthusiastically agreed to be her partner. So, for three months, the two friends hunted for a location for their new business. When they'd found three they thought would work, Marci enrolled in a course in entrepreneurship. She knew she needed help refining her voluminous notes into a workable business plan.

"In the first class, it was made really clear that you've got to plan every move," said Marci. "I admit I fought the idea at first, mostly because I was so eager to get started, but also because I thought that too much planning would throttle my creativity. But then as I examined each step of building the business plan, the patterns began to appear, and I saw how things would work out in the long run. Then I didn't feel cramped at all. My travel industry diary became my adventure notebook.

"It was high anxiety when we opened up for business. Our contractor was four months behind, so we had to rent temporary space almost 15 kilometres away from our target customers. And since we couldn't get our location right away, our banker chopped our line of credit in half. Luckily, we had followed the advice of our instructors and had a back-up bank. Then an airline strike forced us to stay up three nights rerouting customers. Without a plan, we'd have gone under.

"Adventures in Travel is 3 years old now, and my partner and I are thinking about another start-up. The other evening, I brought out my adventure notebook — the one I'd used to plan our travel agency — and read through it. I was amazed at its accuracy. I think that shows that you can do a lot in life if you get organized.

"On this next start-up, believe me, we'll do even more planning. You can dream yourself silly, but when you go into business for yourself, you need to put those dreams behind you and get down to the nitty-gritty: customers, sales, profit, winning."

Most people begin a new business with less planning than they give a family vacation. Marci's adventure notebook was the incubator for ideas that helped her prepare her business plan, which proved, on paper, that she could be successful. Marci and her partner had a vision and they continue to update their plan.

How do you learn to operate like Marci? First, you need to get organized. Action Step 7 will help you do that.

Now we want you to think about what success means to you.

Thinking about success can be stimulating and enlightening. What makes a business successful? Unsuccessful? How do *you* measure success? How do your friends measure it?

You and your friends can speculate about what businesses are doing well. But only a detailed examination of their business operations and their books would give the whole picture. Still we still urge you to exercise your marketplace intuition. Personal observation is a good way to become more aware of what is happening to small firms in your community. For example, the next time you eat out, try this:

- Estimate the number of customers in the restaurant.
- Estimate the total number of customers the restaurant serves each day.
- Estimate the average price per meal.
- Multiply that average by the total number of daily customers.

Do this for other businesses and soon you'll get the feel for which businesses are losing, which are winning. Observe with new-eyes and success factors will emerge.

Success is a personal, subjective thing, whereas income and return-on-investment are measurable. You need to think about these different faces of success as you start your adventure. The success checklist below will help you. At the end of it, add other items that might signify success to you.

Do you measure success in dollars? How many?

- ❑ $50 000 a year?
- ❑ $100 000?
- ❑ $250 000?
- ❑ $1 000 000?
- ❑ As a return-on-investment? How much? ______________

Or do you measure success in other ways?

- ❑ Being able to enjoy a certain lifestyle
- ❑ Having friendly customers who appreciate the service

ACTION STEP 6

Assess your accomplishments and shortcomings.

Begin by listing all the things in your life that have made you proud. What, for example, has given you the most satisfaction? What is your sweetest memory? How old were you when that event occurred? What were you doing at the time? Were you alone or with someone? How did it feel to be victorious? How did it feel to be in control?

Then move to the present. Where are you now with your accomplishments? What have you done lately that you're proud of? What about the future? Where do you want to be in three years? In five years? In ten? In 20?

Now, list the things that you *don't* like to do or that you don't do well. All entrepreneurs have their weaknesses. What you want is a business that takes advantage of your strengths. If you can identify your likes and dislikes, then you can direct yourself toward the things that you enjoy and avoid the things you hate. You may find some surprises when you review your lists.

ACTION STEP 7

Organize your information.

If you're the typical aspiring entrepreneur, you probably write 90 percent of your important data on the back of an envelope. That's fine, but now that you're doing this for real, get yourself some kind of container (a shoebox, a briefcase, a folder) to put those envelopes in. Even better, compile an adventure notebook, ideally using something with pockets so that you can keep track of small items like brochures.

Your adventure notebook should have:

- a twelve-month calendar
- an appointment calendar
- a priority list of things you need to do
- your name, company address, and phone number (at the front, in case you leave it somewhere)
- an idea list
- a "new-eyes" list for keeping track of successful and not-so-successful businesses you come across, plus notes about the reasons for their success or failure
- a list of possible team members (Who impresses you and why? What are their key attributes?)
- a list of possible experts to serve as resource people when you need them, such as a lawyer, an accountant, some bankers, successful businesspeople, and so on

ACTION STEP 8

Mind map and list your core values.
Take a quick look at your own unique talents that can catch an emerging opportunity.

Start with a clean sheet of paper. Draw a circle with your name in it on the middle of the page. Begin to mindmap the values in your life that are important to you. This could include achieving financial security, producing things, helping others, having fun, making things grow, developing trust, and so on.

When you are finished, and after you have thought about it for a while, make a list of your ten core values. The best business for you is the one that includes what best fits your core values and matches emerging market opportunities — the topic of the next chapter.

ACTION STEP 9

Define your personal vision and goals.

1. Define your personal vision.

Personal and business success starts with a vision of who we are, what we know drives us, and what we want. This personal vision is the pillar of foundation that will give us guidance and direction in the conduct of our lives and our business. It is a clear mental picture of what we want to be known for over the next five to ten years. Here are a few examples to help you get started:

- To be loved and respected by my family and friends.
- To be known as a caring and helpful human being.
- To have others remember me with respect.

Now it's your turn. Write a short statement (say 15 to 25 words) of your personal vision in life.

2. List your personal goals.

Guided by your personal vision, it is now time to write down the things you would like to achieve over the long run — your personal goals. Here are some examples of what we mean by personal goals:

- To be financially independent.
- To control my own time.
- To be able to choose whom I work with.

Now it's your turn. Take as much time as you need and make a list of your personal goals. You don't have to be too specific. You can refine your goals later on.

- ❑ Having power (you know how things should be done; when they're done your way, you feel terrific)
- ❑ Being able to live where you want
- ❑ Providing employment for others
- ❑ Being the best business in your area
- ❑ Seeing long lines waiting for your service
- ❑ Hanging loose, doing what makes you happy
- ❑ Having time to do what you enjoy doing
- ❑ Achieving teamwork (a smooth operation, employees reporting to you)
- ❑ Having fame (your face on TV, your name a household word)
- ❑ Being in control (you want things done *your* way.)

Do you measure success by the type or location of your dream house?

- ❑ In the heart of a lavish, up-scale residential area
- ❑ A penthouse atop a tall building in a stylish area
- ❑ Anywhere that's safe
- ❑ A place where your kids can play
- ❑ A cosy cabin on a quiet lake
- ❑ A fancy, beautifully decorated city apartment
- ❑ A tropical island, isolated, quiet
- ❑ A building with your name on it

Now we want you to step back for a moment. What did success really mean to you? Was it spending quality time with your family; having the trust and love of others; obtaining material wealth or security? We have really asked you to think about your **personal values**: those things that guide your day-to-day

Box 1.8 It's a Head-Heart Issue

Creating a vision demands both the "head" and the "heart."

According to John Kotter, author of *Leading Change*, there are at least six characteristics to an effective vision.

1. **It conveys an imaginable picture of what the future — the far future — will be like.**
2. **It appeals to the long-term interests of employees, customers, stockholders, or anyone else with a stake in the firm.** Poor visions that ignore the legitimate interests of some groups are going to be counter-attacked — by customers who stop buying, for example, or employees who kill change through passive resistance.
3. **It consists of realistic, attainable goals.** Visions must be ambitious enough to force people out of comfortable routines. But setting such "stretch" goals is not the same as setting impossible goals. Impossible goals lack credibility and don't motivate action. Pipe dreams aren't visionary.
4. **It is clear enough to guide decision making.** Effective visions are focussed enough to help employees decide which actions are important and which are out of bounds.
5. **It is flexible enough to allow individual initiative as well as adjustments to changing circumstances.** Visions shouldn't be vague, but neither should they be so specific that they kill initiative.
6. **It is easy to explain.** If you can't explain the vision to someone in less than five minutes without hooking their interest, then the vision is unfocussed or uncompelling. Go back to the drawing board.

Source: Adapted from John P. Kotter, *Leading Change* (Boston: Harvard Business School Press, 1996) in *Soundview Executive Book Summaries*, Vol. 18, No. 10, (2 parts) Part 2, October 1996. Reprinted with permission of Soundview Executive Book Summaries.

activities, behaviour, and decision making. The things that matter to you most. It is now time to hone in on your values. Close your eyes, think about what things in life are really important to you. You may not die for them, but they are principles that mean a great deal to you. Complete Action Step 8, which will help you come to grips with your values — those qualities that you care about most in life.

In your own small business, you will not be able to work the long hours with any enthusiasm unless you have a compelling vision and a corresponding set of goals. As we have already learned, a vision and goals are dominant characteristics among successful entrepreneurs. A **personal vision** is a deeply held aspiration or mental picture of who you are and where you want to be in your life at some point in the future. **Personal goals** are statements of things you would like to achieve at some point in the future. Take a stab at Action Step 9. Define your personal vision (Box 1.8 will help) and list your goals. Note that as you develop your business plan, you will come to realize that your personal vision and business vision have a great deal in common.

Now you are ready to move on to Chapter Two and begin honing in on market opportunities that match or are confluent with your personal values, vision, and goals.

PERSONAL VALUES
those intrinsic activities, behaviours, and processes of decision making that guide a person's day-to-day activity

PERSONAL VISION
a deeply held aspiration or mental picture of who you are and where you want to be at some point in the future

PERSONAL GOALS
statements of what you would like to achieve over the short term (up to five years)

In a Nutshell

The Canadian workplace is and will continue to be bombarded by change. Perhaps the most important areas of change are the explosion in information technology and the expansion in the global marketplace, both of which are upsetting the nature of work and dramatically altering our industrial structure. Foreign markets are fuelling the expansion of Canada's hottest companies. About 70 percent of all jobs are tied up in knowledge-based industries that are primarily concerned with the creation and use of data and knowledge — welcome to the knowledge-based economy. We have entered the Age of the Entrepreneur where knowledge, not physical capital, is the driving force.

Entrepreneurs, as agents of change, need to sharpen their skills — mindmapping, networking, developing teamwork, conducting research and so on — to deal with the realities of this new economy. As if this isn't enough, they must then apply many of the traditional business skills — accounting, finance, management — by means of a business plan, to translate their entrepreneurial skills into dollars. This book will provide you with a business plan road map and the ideas and tools to succeed . . . but the challenge is yours!

Think Points for Success

- ✓ Change is accelerating everywhere, and that includes the world of business. Change creates problems. Entrepreneurs are problem solvers.
- ✓ The knowledge-based society is no longer big news. It's here. To see what's next, scan the environment with new-eyes. What does 2010 hold for you?
- ✓ To find your doorway into your own business, gather data and keep asking questions.
- ✓ Be creative on paper, test your assumptions, and develop your business plan for the marketplace. Mindmap. Draw a future wheel. Confirm your venture with numbers and words before you enter the arena.
- ✓ Even though you may not be in business yet, you can intensify your focus by writing down your thoughts about the business you think you want to try. Stay flexible.

ACTION STEP REVIEW

The keys to success in small business are planning and momentum. In this chapter, nine Action Steps help you focus on both.

1. Assess your job security. Do you have any? By looking at your current work situation, you can assess your motivation for wanting to take the entrepreneurial plunge.
2. Look into your business future by using a "future wheel."
3. Mindmap the "cocooning" concept to generate ideas for new businesses.
4. Interview small business owners who are doing something similar to what you'd like to do with your own business.
5. Find out if you have what it takes to make it in small business.
6. Assess your past achievements.
7. Organize your information. Compile an adventure notebook.
8. List the values that are important to you.
9. Formulate your personal vision and list your personal goals.

✓ Be clear on your personal vision and goals before you develop your business vision.
✓ Remember: We are entrepreneurs. Work is our fun. And personal satisfaction can be very rewarding.

Business Plan Building Block

WHERE AM I NOW?

From the point of view of the potential readers of your business plan (bankers, loan officers, rich relatives, close friends with money, venture capital professionals), the most important part of the plan is information on you, the entrepreneur who wrote the plan.

Your goal, from the very first sentence on the very first page, is to inspire confidence.

Before you write your business plan, study how you look from some of your old résumés. What picture do the résumés present? Who are you? Where have you been?

Since the résumé work is for your eyes only, jot notes to yourself about strengths and weaknesses. To trigger your brain to perform this task, review the nine action steps in this chapter as you search for ways to transfer your skills and aptitudes to an entrepreneurial situation.

If you already have a business up and running, use this same start-up energy to improve it.

No one is perfect. Recognize your own shortcomings and make a list of people who have talents that you might lack. It's never too early to think about team building. With hard work and an honest look at your own skills picture, you'll be able to fine-tune this information when you showcase your founding team in your final business plan.

WHERE AM I GOING?

Now that you have looked at the past and present, think about where you are going. Return to Action Step 9. Refine your personal vision. How do you want to be known? Take a closer look at your personal goals. Will these help you reach your personal vision?

Checklist Questions and Actions to Develop Your Business Plan

DOORWAYS TO SMALL BUSINESS — YOUR GREAT ADVENTURE

❑ What is your small business venture?
❑ Assess your interests, abilities, and weaknesses as they relate to your business venture.
❑ Assess your past accomplishments and shortcomings as they relate to your business venture.
❑ Which of the three ways to small business ownership do you prefer? Why?
❑ Develop a questionnaire and survey at least 20 individuals who you view as your target customer.
❑ What is your personal and business vision?

NOTES

1. Excerpted from Tanya Talaga, Jonathan Ferguson, and Vinay Menon, "Lives on Hold," *Toronto Star*, December 7, 1997, p. BE2. Reprinted with permission of the *Toronto Star* Syndicate.
2. Adapted from Donna Jean Mackinnon (SouthamStar Network), "Delivering on Capitalism — on a Bun," *Ottawa Citizen*, April 29, 1997, p. E3; and Kara Kuryllowicz, "The Best Businesses to Get into Now," *Profit*, December/January 1997, p. 62. See also Louis E. Boone, David L. Kurtz, and Ronald A. Knowles, *Business*, 1st Canadian edition (Toronto: Dryden, an imprint of Harcourt Brace & Company, Canada, 1998), pp. 57–58.
3. Entrepreneurship and Small Business Office of Industry Canada, *Small Business Quarterly*, Winter 1997. Available at <http://strategis.ic.gc.ca/cgi-bin/basic>.
4. Talaga, Ferguson, and Menon, "Lives on Hold," p. BE1.
5. *Ibid.*
6. 1997 Statistics Canada data, as reported in Barrie McKenna, "Canadian Productivity Posts Weak Growth in 1996," *Globe and Mail*, June 6, 1997, p. B9. See also Boone, Kurtz, and Knowles, *Business*, pp. 12–13.
7. Catherine Swift, "It's a Small World After All," *Post 2000*, Issue 8, November 15, 1997, p. 5.
8. Kuryllowicz, "The Best Businesses to Get into Now," p. 60. See also Boone, Kurtz, and Knowles, *Business*, p. 57.
9. Adapted from Swift, "It's a Small World After All," p. 4.
10. From an interview with Don Tapscott, "Cyberwhiz Don Tapscott Is Mapping the Digital Frontier," *Royal Bank Business Report*, November 1996, p. 21. See also Boone, Kurtz and Knowles, *Business*, p. 245.
11. Nuala Beck, quoted in Colin Campbell with Carole Hood, *Where the Jobs Are* (Toronto: Macfarlane Walter & Ross, 1997), p. 9.
12. 1997 Profit 100 data is cited in Rick Spence, *Secrets of Success from Canada's Fastest-Growing Companies* (Toronto: John Wiley & Sons Canada, Ltd., 1997), p. 135.
13. Campbell with Hood, *Where the Jobs Are*, p. 5.
14. 1996 United Nations data, as reported in Paul Knox, "Canada Still Place to Live, UN Says," *Globe and Mail*, June 12, 1997, pp. B1, B9. See also Boone, Kurtz, and Knowles, *Business*, pp. 5–6.
15. Industry Canada, Advertising Supplement, "Small Business Tomorrow's Giants," *Profit*, December/January 1998, p. 49.
16. Industry Canada, *Your Guide to Government of Canada Services and Support for Small Business: Trends and Statistics, 1996-1997*, Catalogue No. C1-10/1997E; John Manley and Paul Martin for Industry Canada, *Growing Small Business*, February 1997, p. 4. See also Boone, Kurtz, and Knowles, *Business*, pp. 115–17; and Industry Canada, Advertising Supplement, "Small Business Tomorrow's Giants," p. 49.
17. Industry Canada, Advertising Supplement, "Small Business Tomorrow's Giants," p. 49.
18. Peter Drucker is quoted in Boone, Kurtz, and Knowles, *Business*, p. 113.
19. Ron Knowles and Debbie White, *Issues in Canadian Business* (Toronto: Dryden, 1995), pp. 26–39.

OTHER REFERENCES

Beck, Nuala. *Excelerate — Growing in the New Economy*. Toronto: Collins Publishers Ltd., 1996.

Bridges, William. *Creating You & Co.* Reading, MA: Addison Wesley Longman, 1997.

Carey, Elaine. "Many More Working for Themselves. Stats Can." *Toronto Star*, October 25, 1997, p. C7.

Gray, Douglas A. and Deanna L. Gray. *The Complete Canadian Small Business Guide*, 2nd edition. Whitby, ON: McGraw-Hill Ryerson Ltd., 1997.

Lewin, Marsha D. *The Overnight Consultant.* New York: John Wiley & Sons, Inc., 1995.

Spence, Rick. *Secrets of Success from Canada's Fastest-Growing Companies.* Toronto: John Wiley & Sons Canada, Ltd., 1997.

Spence, Rick and Richard Wright. "Canada's Hottest Startup." *Profit*, September 1997, pp. 34–37.

Tapscott, Don. *Growing Up Digital: The Rise of the Net Generation.* Toronto: McGraw-Hill, 1998.

Tarkenton, Fran. *What Losing Taught Me About Winning.* New York: Simon & Schuster, Inc., 1997.

Worzel, Richard. *The Next Twenty Years of Your Life.* Toronto: Stoddart Publishing Ltd., 1997.

Journals and Magazines

Bootstrapping' Entrepreneur; e-mail: ibootstrap@aol.com

Canadian Business, 21 issues/year, Canadian Business Subscriber Service, 777 Bay Street, 8th Floor, Toronto, ON M5W 2B8.

The Canadian Invention and Innovation Newsletter; free by calling 1-800-265-4559.

Entrepreneurships and Small Business Management, 5 issues, Abaco Communications Ltd., 145 Royal Crest Court, Univ 2, Markham, ON L3R 9Z4.

Home Business Report, 4 issues, 2949 Ash Street, Abbotsford, BC V2S 4G5.

Inc. — The Magazine for Growing Companies, 12 issues, P.O. Box 51534, Boulder, CO, 80323-1534

Journal of Small Business and Entrepreneurship, 12 issues, Centre of Entrepreneurship, Centennial College, P.O. Box 631, Station A, Scarborough, ON M1K 5G9.

Profit — The Magazine for Canadian Entrepreneurs, 6 issues, P.O. Box 80027, Station B, Room B, Toronto, ON M7Y 5C7.

two

The Big Picture — Charting Trends for Your Small Business

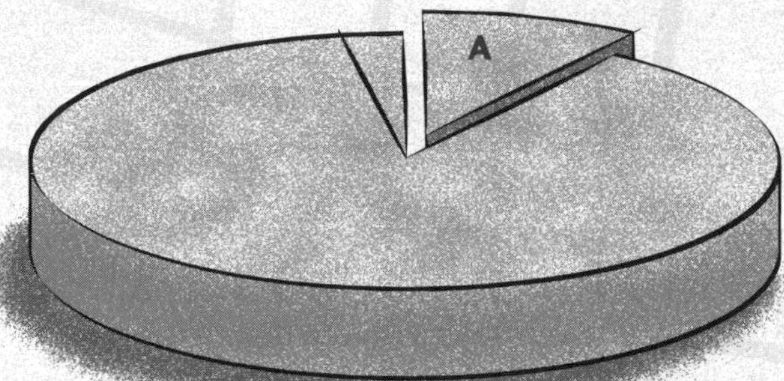

BUSINESS PLAN BUILDING BLOCK

This chapter will help you describe the industry and market trends — the big picture — for your business. It will show you how to expand your knowledge of customer needs and your market niche, and how to begin writing the description of your business.

LEARNING OPPORTUNITIES

After studying this chapter, you should be able to:

- Understand how to analyze the potential for small business success by applying the life-cycle yardstick to industries, products, services, and locations.
- Determine what business you're really in.
- Become acquainted with the technique of brainstorming.
- Use diagrams and mind maps to explore market segmentation.
- Discover market signals that indicate trends and opportunities.
- Discover market forces that underlie the trends.
- Deduce a person's lifestyle from the contents of his or her shopping cart.
- Identify trends that will affect your business.
- Select helpful information sources.
- Begin your search for the business that best fits your aptitudes and skills.
- Increase your ability to read market signals that forecast needs.

Back in 1991, the Pacific Western Brewing Co. closed its doors. This small brewing company, located in Prince George, B.C., could not compete with the likes of Labatt and Molson. That's when Kazuko Komatsu, a seasoned businessperson with 20 years of successful marketing, brewing, and exporting experience, came to the rescue. Kazuko bought the company. She retrained the staff, improved the quality of the beer, and targeted the lucrative Japanese market. What a tribute to Canadian entrepreneurship! Today, Pacific Western is healthy again. Its beer is the third most popular imported beer in Japan, behind the giant Budweiser and Heineken brands.[1]

In the 1980s, Allan Millman took the plunge, risked his financial future, and bought Iona Appliances Inc. (located in Welland, Ont.) from a U.S. multinational. It wasn't long before reality set in and Millman found himself "knee deep in alligators." The Canadian market was just too small to support Iona's broad product line. No wonder the American company sold at such a good price. But Millman was no stranger to innovation. He had an MBA in chemical engineering and a few years of experience in product development at Warner-Lambert Canada. He also knew an industry starved for new products when he saw it, and zeroed in on the household vacuum cleaner.

Figure 2.1 Chapter Two will help you prepare part A of your business plan, "The Product or Service."

ACTION STEP PREVIEW

10 Travel back in time and observe a marketplace of the past.

11 Define your business and test your definition.

12 What's new? What's hot? What's cooling down?

13 Assess the lifestyle of your potential target customer by walking his or her neighbourhood.

14 Have some fun with segmentation and gap analysis.

15 Decode the secrets of the shopping cart, using your new eyes.

Millman stepped back and realized that vacuum cleaners had not changed in almost 100 years. He made his plan and moved quickly: he reduced the number of product lines, focussed on this single product, and invested heavily in research and development. Success did not come overnight. But by 1997, the company made its first appearance on the Profit 100 with a five-year growth rate of 650 percent. Its key product was the Fantom, a dual cyclonic vacuum cleaner with a gleaming sci-fi look. This single product became so successful that the company decided to change its name to Fantom Technologies Inc. — a tribute to Canadian ingenuity and the power of technology to turn a company around.[2]

Industry or market trends reflect our economy's response to change. And change creates entrepreneurial opportunities. In the first chapter, we introduced you to the two dominant trends affecting the Canadian economy: the export market (see Chapter Fifteen) and technology. These trends were a major factor contributing to the success of Pacific Western Brewing Co. and Fantom Technologies Inc. Kazuko Komatsu of Pacific Western jumped on the export trend. She realized there was a niche for quality Canadian beer in the lucrative Japanese market. Allan Millman of Fantom seized the opportunity to use technology to improve on the old vacuum cleaner. Other major trends affecting Canadians into the next millennium are shown in Box 2.1. Figure 2.2 takes a look at employment trends in Canada over the past 20 years.

A business plan begins with the "big picture" — the industry or market overview. Industries go through life cycles. Products and services within industries also progress through a life cycle: birth, growth, maturity, and

Box 2.1 Market Trends

Ten major trends will affect Canadians into the next century.

1. **The ecological movement toward sustainable development.**
2. **Downsizing, delayering, and outsourcing.** Large corporations will continue to shed their corporate fat. A "free agent" movement toward just-in-time employment will grow as large corporations subcontract and contract out everything they can.
3. **Knowledge-based industries.** The shift to knowledge-rich employees and the digital economy will continue.
4. **Media change.** The digital shift from broadcast (television, for example) to interactive media (the Internet, for example) will continue.
5. **Demographic changes.** There will be a growing importance in the over-50 age group who, while preparing for retirement, will do everything in their power to push back the aging process.
6. **Democratization of information.** The Internet and the World Wide Web will gradually give small businesses and individuals the same power to access information as large firms have.
7. **Telecommuting and home-based business.** The number of people working out of their homes will continue to grow, increasing the presence of so-called "electronic cottages."
8. **Cocooning.** Outside stresses will be reduced as people spend more leisure and work time at home.
9. **Social equality.** A gradual movement to a more permissive "egalitarian" society will occur.
10. **Globalization.** The shift toward an export-based economy will continue.

Figure 2.2 Canadian Employment Trends, by Sector, 1977–1997

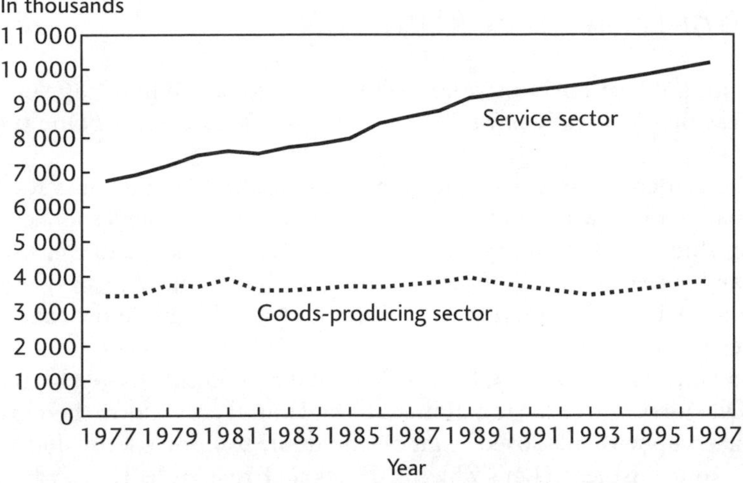

Over the last few decades, the service sector has dominated our economy. For example, the total service sector employment grew about 20 percent from 1980 to 1990. In contrast, employment in the goods-producing sector remained relatively constant over this same period. However, over the latter part of the 1990s, a new trend seemed to emerge. The goods-producing sector, fuelled by telecommunications and manufacturing, began to pick up steam. Over the period of 1993 to 1997, employment in the goods-producing sector increased by about 9 percent, whereas employment in the service sector increased by only 6 percent. "Good old manufacturing is alive and well and driving a lot of growth in the Canadian economy," said Michael Fradette, national director of Deloitte Touche Tomatsu International, in a 1996 report.

Source: Statistics Canada, "Canadian Employment, by Sector, 1977–1997," adapted from "Labour Force Information," Cat. No. 71-001; and "Historical Labour Force Statistics," Cat. No. 71-201. Reprinted with permission. Also available on <http://www.statcan.ca/english/Pgdb/economy/Economic/econ40.htm>.

decline. The industry overview helps you gain a perspective on your "niche" and helps the reader of your business plan (a lender or investor) understand why you have chosen to pursue a particular segment of the market.

Why Look at the Big Picture?

To be successful in small business, you need to know two things: what business you are really in, and where your business is positioned on the industry life cycle. Entrepreneurs tend to be in a hurry. They want to push on, to throw open the doors to customers, and to read the bottom line. That's not all bad, but before *you* charge into the arena, step back and examine your industry **segment**. Where are the lines? What are people buying? Where do you see "Going Out of Business" signs? Where are the start-ups? What's hot? What's cooling down? What business segments will still be thriving five years from now? If you opened the doors of your new business today, how long would it be before your product or service was no longer valuable?

SEGMENT
an identifiable slice of an industry

So look before you leap. Brainstorm with your family and friends and interview your potential customers. Study the marketplace. Read industry journals.

Use your new eyes. And use this chapter to help you define the trends and gaps in your industry — in other words, to see the big picture.

RECOGNIZING OPPORTUNITIES

What are the best business ventures to pursue today? Where can you find a business that will really pay off? One that will make you rich? One that you will enjoy?

Only you can answer the question, because the best business for you is one that you enjoy. The best business for you uses those experiences, skills, and aptitudes that are unique to *you*. The early action steps in this book are designed to help you discover what is unique about you. Who are you? What are your skills? What excites you? What do you already know that distinguishes you from others?

As a consumer, you know, for example, that restaurants have a high failure rate. One week you're having dinner at The Hound and Glove; the next week it's locked up with a "Closed" sign on the door. You don't want that to happen to your business That's why *you* do **market research**. That's why you're going to make sure your business serves a *need*. This means that you will enter the marketplace from a position of strength.

MARKET RESEARCH
collection and analysis of data pertinent to an existing or potential market

Let's back up and get the big picture. Before the Industrial Revolution, most people were self-employed. In this so-called agricultural or first wave, farmers and sheepherders were risk takers because they had to be. There were few other options. The second wave, or the Industrial Age, began with the Industrial Revolution and was characterized by machine power and mass production.

We are now firmly entrenched in the so-called information wave. Some have termed these times the knowledge-based era. We like to think about it as the entrepreneurial age. These times, to a large extent, are marked by the growth of a new craft economy distinguished by quality, small customized quantities, technology, and service. As in the first wave, working from home has again become both popular and common.

The existence of the megacorporation in the new millennium should not be considered a threat to the small entrepreneur, but an opportunity. First, most large corporations depend on small business to produce support products and services. This outsourcing is going to continue in the years ahead. They know that this is the most efficient and effective way to do business. Second, bigger isn't better, and many small businesses — even those whose markets are expanding rapidly — are barely noticed by the large corporation.

The exploding need for specialized products and services from beer and vacuum cleaners to coffee brewing and personal fitness training is mind-boggling. You may see as much change in the next ten years as your parents have seen in their lifetime. Such change creates opportunities for fast, flexible, and focussed firms. If you stay in touch with change and the exploding market niches that change creates, you will always see more opportunities than you can pursue. Action Step 10 will give you some perspective on change.

ACTION STEP 10

Travel back in time and observe a marketplace of the past.
Place yourself in a time warp and take a look at a marketplace of the past. What was selling 25 years ago? 50 years ago? 100 years ago?

To get this picture, look at old magazines, old catalogues, old movies, old TV shows, old high school yearbooks, and old family photographs. What do you see? Are all of the people dressed alike? Does everyone have the same smile, the same frown, the same serious look? How small is their world? How small is their horizon?

Study the advertisements in old magazines and newspapers and then:

1. List the products that are still around today.
2. List the products that are no longer on the market.

Which list is longer? What does this tell you about the changing marketplace?

Brainstorm Your Way into Small Business

Sharon and Amelia liked to travel. For seven years, they worked for other people while looking for a business that would pay them to see the world. Sharon taught English at the local high school. Amelia was a manager for a computer products firm.

At school, Sharon discovered the technique of mind mapping, a method of note-taking using clusters and bubbles, letting the information flow along its own course. Amelia thought they could mindmap their way into business.

In the centre of a large sheet of paper, they wrote "segments." In a bubble next to "segments" they wrote "travel." Momentum built up. They wrote "world," "people," "profit," "tickets," "theatre lovers," "affluent shoppers," "English wool," "archaeology," "art," "Picasso," "Paris," "caves," "rocks," "rock climbing," "veterans," and "health nuts."

They drew a double circle around "affluent shoppers," surrounding that with "Hong Kong," "London," "Paris," "Morocco," and "Rome."

"This is fun," Amelia said. "This smells like money," Sharon added.

The two friends kept on mapping until they had developed an idea for their business: taking affluent shoppers on guided tours of world-famous shopping districts.

Yes, their idea requires a lot of work to develop a business plan, but Amelia and Sharon now have a vision of what they want to do.

BRAINSTORMING TECHNIQUES

The point of this example is to show what can result from a simple exchange of ideas. If you gather people around you with wit, spark, creativity, positive attitudes, and good business sense, the synergy will almost always surprise you, and could lead to new ideas, company growth, expanded profits, or perhaps the information for a new industry. The possibilities are limitless, but the trick is to structure brainstorming sessions in a way that maximizes creativity. A few suggestions follow.

1. Pick a Saturday, Sunday, or a day when everyone has some free time.
2. Find a site where you'll have few interruptions.
3. Invite 10–15 people (some will drop out and you want to allow for the no-shows).
4. Schedule the starting time at 9:00 A.M., serve coffee and doughnuts, and really begin at 9:30.
5. Allow time for self-introduction. Tell participants not to be modest. They're getting together with winners. Have them talk in terms of accomplishments.

Tips:

- Have everyone arrive with a potential business idea.
- Before the close of the first meeting, select one or two hot ideas (cast a vote) and ask participants to prepare a one-page checklist summary and analysis of the ideas.
- Get together again within two to four weeks and brainstorm the hot ideas. Make it clear that the basic purpose is to spin ideas off one another, not to form a huge partnership.
- The best brainstorming sessions occur when you come brain-to-brain with other creative, positive people. Brain energy is real and you need to keep tapping it.

When gathering participants and planning your meeting:

- Try to find imaginative people who can stretch their minds, and who can set their competitive instincts aside for a while.

- Remember that in brainstorming sessions, there's a no-no on no's. You're not implementing yet, so don't let skepticism kill an idea.
- Find a neutral location.
- Try to focus on one problem or opportunity.
- Encourage the members of a group to reinforce and believe in each other.
- Use helpful equipment, such as a cassette recorder and flipchart. And don't forget to bring a supply of paper and pencils.

Know Your Real Business

THE IMPORTANCE OF STEPPING BACK

Watch a carpenter framing a new house, working close to the wood, nailing with quick hammer strokes. But to get a view of the total house — the structure that will become someone's home — the carpenter must step back from the detailed work, cross the street, and examine the shape of the whole.

What business is the carpenter in? The nail-driving business? The framing business? The home-building business? Or the business of satisfying the age-old "nesting" need?

Only by stepping back can you answer the question of what business you are in. This is a very important question.

Let's see how the process of stepping back transformed Canada's postal services from a national disaster in the early part of the 1980s to a major success story throughout the 1990s.

That Was Then and This Now: The Canada Post Story

From the 1950s onward, the government-run Post Office Department in Canada found itself amassing larger and larger deficits. By the end of the seventies, the yearly deficit was well over $500 million, and reaching the $1 billion mark was almost a foregone conclusion.

Thank goodness, the government of the day had the presence of mind to step back and take a hard look at this aging dinosaur. Here's what it saw: inefficient plants, outdated equipment, fragmented operations, and a dismal labour relations record. The result? The old department was told to operate like a real business, and Canada Post Corporation was born in 1981.

Since the early 1980s, Canada Post has shown itself to be a remarkable commercial and financial Canadian success story, recording several profitable years. Why? First and foremost, Canada Post management, like Kazuko Komatsu and Allan Millman in the opening vignettes, stepped back and redefined what business it was really in. Through brainstorming and honest discussions, management discovered that the company was no longer in the "mail business." That was the business of the old Post Office. Canada Post was really in the communications, advertising, and distribution business. The management team then built the business plan around this new vision.

The lesson here is to know what business you are in — to know who your customers are and what satisfies their needs. Mary Clark's experience illustrates the importance of understanding what business you are really in.

Mary Clark was a 40-year-old teacher who had always been more interested in riding her prize-winning saddle horses than in teaching school. When her grandmother died and left her $200 000, Mary made a down payment on a boarding stable and left teaching forever, or so she thought.

The boarding stable was run down. It had stalls for 100 horses, but only 40 were occupied. Mary did everything she could think of to make the place better for horses. The $57 000 she spent on rebuilding, painting, and grading made Clark's stables a very attractive place. She bought the highest quality of feed and gave the horses the best care money could buy.

When owners began to move their horses to other stables, Mary couldn't understand. She had not increased her fees, and she treated the horses like friends. In six months, only three customers remained. In nine months, she was behind on her mortgage payments. In her tenth month, Mary had to sell the stables.

Mary had made the simple mistake of thinking horses were her target customers. Her real target customers were girls between the ages of 7 and 14. Mary thought she was in the business of stabling horses. The business she was in was providing service for girls who rode horses. The girls wanted recreation, training, and social activities. Mary's customers left because other stables were providing lessons, trail rides, barbeques, and a fun experience. Today, Mary is back in the classroom, wondering why people don't care more about their horses — and why they didn't care about the quality of her stables.

DEFINE YOUR REAL BUSINESS

What business are *you* really in? What business do you want to be in? Naming anything is a game of words, and a small business is no exception. The examples in Table 2.1 can help you define your business. If you're hesitant about defining it at this early stage, remember what happened to Canada Post — and to Mary Clark's stable.

Now complete this sentence:

I'm in the business of ______________________________

Table 2.1 Defining Your Business

If you're in:	Try saying:
Software sales	"I'm in the problem-solving business."
Pie baking	"I'm in the reward and satisfaction business."
College teaching	"I'm in the information business."
Medicine	"I'm in the healing business."
Auto manufacturing	"I'm in the ego-gratification business."
Mattresses	"I'm in the sound sleep business."
Cameras/camcorders	"I'm in the happy memory business."
Gourmet cookware	"I bring fun back into the kitchen."
Locksmithing	"I'm in the security business."
Badge manufacturing	"I'm in the recognition business."
Operating a coffee bar	"I provide a gathering spot."

ACTION STEP 11

Define your business and test your definition.

Follow these steps:

1. Brainstorm what business you're really in. Let your mind play at this. Try to keep negative statements to a minimum.
2. Once you've decided what business you're in, visit your printer and order some one-colour business letterhead stationery. (One colour is cheaper, so you save money right from the start.)
3. Next, go to the library and look for a thick publication called the *Directory of Associations in Canada.* Locate the name of a trade association your business would be a part of. Write down the address, phone number, and name of a contact person.
4. Before you leave the library, check the *Gale Directory of Publications* for a trade journal that covers your industry. Try to find one that's not connected to the association you found listed in the *Directory of Associations in Canada.* Write down the name of the publication; the publisher's name, address, and phone number; and the cost (if any) of a subscription.
5. Look in the *Dun & Bradstreet Key Business Directory* or the *Robert Morris Annual Financial Statements* of similar companies to see how they have performed.
6. Finally, write or telephone the publications and trade associations that are in your area of interest. Ask them for a rate card and for demographic studies. It's free because you are a prospective advertiser. The trade association will tell you about itself and provide membership details.

You will soon have a wealth of information for your research.

BABY BOOM
the increase in the national birth rate from 1947 to 1966

Explain why you chose this definition and how it relates to your target customer (include benefits).

Keep honing your definition of your business. Once a month is not too often to redefine it, especially before the start-up. Check your definition against the signals you get from your potential target customers, since they may perceive your business differently. You may have new letterhead stationery printed after you talk to them, but as business expenses go, that's a small price to pay to prevent customer confusion. By developing a questionnaire about your business idea and getting feedback from a number of potential customers, you will be able to redefine the business you are in.

Now you're ready to do Action Step 11.

How to Minimize Marketplace Heartache — Watch Trends

Let's say you've tried a small business and failed. Let's say you followed in the footsteps of Mary Clark, the teacher who loved horses; you opened a business out of love, and it fell apart. Your customers left you, and your creditors scared you to death. Okay, you failed once. Worse, you're still unhappy in your job. So, after licking your wounds, you've decided you'd like to try it again. After all, this is the Age of the Entrepreneur, right? So what's the next step?

Well, you look around with those new eyes. Study that list you made of products from 5, 10, and 25 years ago (Action Step 10) and try to make some generalizations about how things have changed. Here's a quick overview.

THE SPLINTERING OF THE MASS MARKET

Today's consumers are informed, individualistic, and demanding. Their buying habits are often difficult to isolate because they tend to buy at several levels of the market. For instance, a materials management person may buy the office copier from Xerox but the paper from a discount office supply warehouse. Some high-fashion, high-income consumers patronize the up-scale boutiques and yet buy their household appliances at discount outlets.

For the consumer, three key factors have splintered the mass market: (a) a shrinking middle class — there are both more high-end, affluent consumers and more consumers who live at or near the poverty level; (2) shifting sizes of age groups; (3) new living arrangements, including smaller houses, smaller furniture, enclosed patios, and twin master suites for working roommates. If you look around with new eyes, you can see major market segments emerging that were not here a decade ago: **baby boomers**; vigorous, healthy over-50-year-olds; teens; single parents; and affluent over-80-year-olds.

To get a better view of today's trends, contrast consumer values of the two decades between 1970 and 1990 with those we can project into the next millennium (see Table 2.2). Action Step 12 will take you out into your community to conduct some trend research.

A LIST OF TRENDS TO START YOU OFF

Let's say you like taking care of people and you have worked for ten years in an infant day-care centre. However, the neighbourhood is aging, affluent families have moved away, and the day care is closed. You decide to go into business for yourself. What business do you choose? How about a care centre for elderly people?

Box 2.2 Small Business Tips

What's hot? What's booming? What looks like fun?

If you're in a small business, or thinking about getting into one, you can make it easy on yourself by identifying industries in the growth phase of their life cycle. How do you do that? You play marketplace detective.

Where are the lines? The crowds? What's on the bestseller list? What are people into? Health? Diet? Exercise? Do-it-yourself? What are people talking about at parties? Personal computers? Videocassette recorders? Travel? Rock climbing? A little selective listening tells you where consumers are spending their money.

Now look around you. When you focus on a particular business, can you sense growth over the long term? Or is the operation involved with a fad that won't last? For your business, you want a growth industry that will generate new customers at a fast clip, allowing you to build a customer base quickly.

Customers are your survival mechanism in any business. If you enter a mature industry (railroads, buggy whips, automobiles, microcomputer hardware), you'll have to seduce customers away from established competitors.

Let's think about where other opportunities exist.

There is a continuing increase in dual-income families and single parents. That means very few people are at home during the day, unless they are working from the home. Obvious business opportunities are child care and home security systems.

With both adults working to pay the bills, no one has enough time (the "poverty of time" trend). Obvious business opportunities are easy-to-fix meals, fast food, teleconferences.

Canadian society is more ethnically diverse than ever before.
Opportunity: helping schools and business integrate.
People are exercising for fitness and health, and they want to look good while sweating.
Opportunity: attractive sports clothes.

Table 2.2 Changing Consumer Values

1970–1990	1990–2000
Quantity	Quality
Things	Experiences
Initial cost	Total use cost
High expectations	Modified expectations
Liberal credit	Tightened credit
Conformity	Individuality
Impulse shopping	Planned expenditures
Experimental lifestyles	Return to old values
Video games	Home entertainment
Car status	Home status
Stable middle class	Shrinking middle class
Child-oriented homes	Adult orientation
Throw away	Reuse
Broadcast TV	Interactive media

ACTION STEP 12

What's new? What's hot? What's cooling down?

1. Take your new eyes out into the marketplace and observe what's happening at the local (or regional) level. Your community is a marketing lab. To discover what this means for you and your business, prowl around a supermarket and analyze what's going on. A locally owned store will give you a clearer picture than a chain will, because it serves the needs of your area. Chains normally show you what the country is buying, and that's not much help for an entrepreneur.

   What's on sale? What's dusty? What's wilted? What is the store promoting? What conclusions can you draw about the store's marketing strategy? Which department has the most space? The longest customer lines? The most workers? The highest prices? What products must move fast? Can you guesstimate how quickly or slowly a product moves from shelf to customer in the various departments? Move on to the other locally owned stores — hardware stores, drugstores, restaurants, gift shops, and others.
2. Give your new-eyes research a database by going to the local newspaper. Visit the display advertising department and ask to see research they've completed on the area.
3. Go to the public library and study Statistics Canada's *Market Research Handbook* (Catalogue No. 63-224) or *Canadian Markets* by *The Financial Post* for your area. Note:
   - The total dollars spent on clothing and housing
   - The percentage of households with incomes above the national average
   - The total city/province population

How do your new-eyes research findings correlate with what you found in the secondary sources?

Box 2.3 Small Business Tips

What is the future of consignment clothing? Computer repair? Women's classic ready-to-wear? Videocassette rentals, cyberspace, direct response retailing, coffee bars?

Use your marketplace radar to choose a growth segment of a growth industry. Ride the crest of the wave. Get off before the trend turns down. Choosing the hot growth sector is usually the right way. Occasionally, however, it sours.

How times change. What do you see here that you didn't see much of ten years ago? What marketplace items can you add to this list?

- Personal computer repair
- Downsizing consultant
- Communication systems consultant
- Theme tours
- Adventure travel
- $200 sweatsuits
- Personal digital assistance
- Electric cars
- Online databases for home users
- Home banking
- Genetic engineering
- Chemical detoxification
- Internet
- Chip cameras
- Ceramic engines
- CD-ROM entertainment
- Digital tapes
- Virtual reality
- Direct satellite TV
- Cellular communication
- Post-It notes
- Video marketing
- Modems
- Desktop publishing
- Wristwatches that receive messages
- Intranet

People must change jobs, and they need retraining.
Opportunity: education.

Continue the list here.

TREND	OPPORTUNITY

The Life-Cycle Stages

LIFE CYCLE
four stages, from birth to death, of a product, business, service, industry, or location

When you have produced a long list of trends, divide them into four groups according to the stage of their **life cycle**. See Figure 2.3. If a trend is just beginning, label it *embryo*. If it's exploding, label it *growth*. If it's no longer growing and it's starting to cool, label it *mature*. If it's beyond maturity and is feeling chilly, label it *decline*. Think about these life-cycle stages often. Everything changes: products, needs, technology, neighbourhoods.

Looking at the life-cycle diagram, you can see that the auto industry as a whole is very mature. Nonetheless, some of its segments are promising — for example, minivans, sports models, and up-scale imports. Convertibles are back, and in the suburbs you see young mothers driving around in Jeep 4 × 4s. Despite traffic jams, people are still driving. But the cars they drive reflect changing lifestyles. What you have with this example is a growth segment in a mature industry.

Figure 2.3

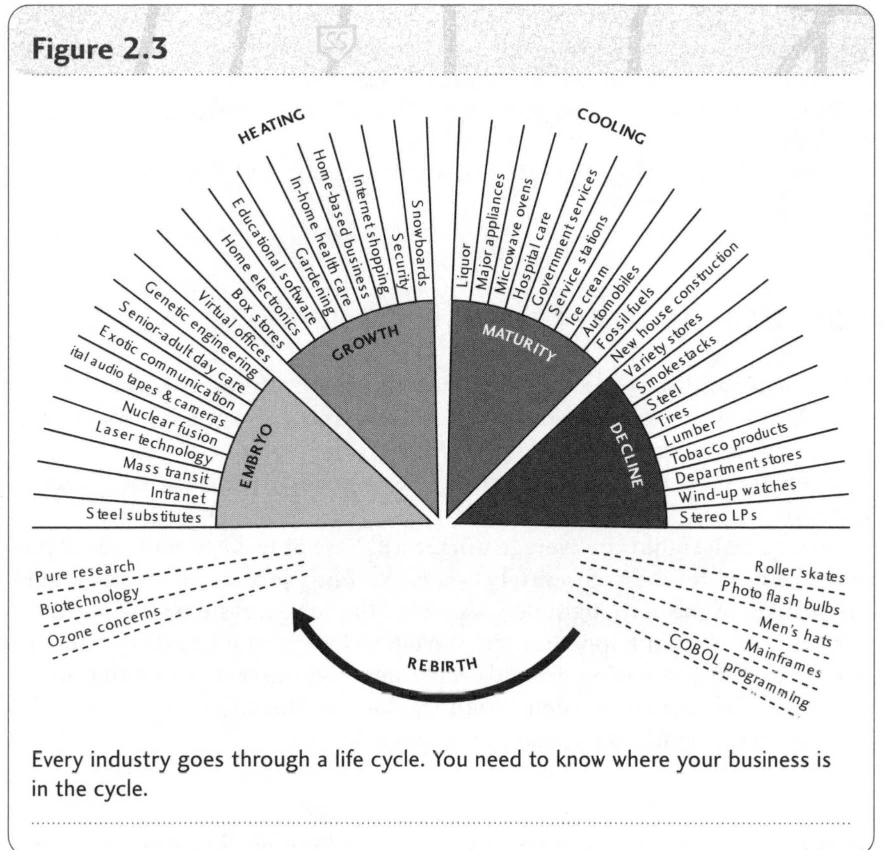

Every industry goes through a life cycle. You need to know where your business is in the cycle.

How do consumer habits determine trends? Well, people are keeping their cars longer, so one growth segment in the auto industry would be the **aftermarket**. Examples of business in that segment would be paint, detailing, electronic accessories, and engine rebuilding. If you're interested in the auto industry, consider the aftermarket.

AFTERMARKET
the marketplace where replacement items can be purchased, such as auto tires and sewing machine belts

In the computer business, competition and the microchip have brought down the price of computer hardware. A personal computer system that sold for $5 000 three years ago can be purchased for one-third of that today. And that same $5 000 buys a system with more speed, more power, more features. With the gain in power comes more sophisticated software. Some of the software, despite claims of being "user-friendly," has a long learning curve. So one opportunity in the computer field is computer instruction. What about the Internet? Can you sell your product or service over the Net?

Where can you find gaps in the life-cycle diagram? Where is your business in its four-stage cycle?

WATCH FOR MARKET SIGNALS

Market signals are everywhere — on the Internet, in electronic display bulletin boards, in the newspaper (classified ads, bankruptcy notices, display ads), in the lines at the theatre, in the price-slashing after Christmas, in discount coupons, rebates, store closings, grand openings. With practice, you can follow a product in the market right through its life cycle.

For example, consider designer jeans. In the early 1980s, massive ad campaigns convinced otherwise-sane Canadians they should pay $40 and up for jeans carrying designer labels. The jeans were available only in the posh stores. A year later, designer jeans had reached the discount stores. Jeans that had sold for $55 were now selling at deep discount, like $9.99. A bargain? Yes, and also a trend. But what has now replaced that trend? Custom-fit jeans with over 440 combinations to ensure the exact fit.

What items have you seen go through their life cycle, from up-scale to deep discount?

Now go back to the life cycle and see if you can add some products and industries to it.

HOW DEEP IS DEEP?

When merchandise slides into deep discount, the profit party is over. The air is cool. The market is flooded; sinking is likely, and drowning is possible. The product is at the end of the life cycle. If that's happened to your job — or to your business — it's time for you to find a **growth segment** of a **growth industry**.

GROWTH SEGMENT
an identifiable slice of an industry that is expanding more rapidly than the industry as a whole

GROWTH INDUSTRY
an industry whose annual sales increase is well above average

Experts tell us that the average worker will have at least seven kinds of jobs in his or her lifetime and several careers. No one's job is completely secure. Rhonda Van Warden thought hers was, until the school system eliminated her position. When that happened, she started to look at the trends in her community and in the nation. Rhonda has some great assets, including intelligence and being a good listener, and she has the flexibility to see herself in a totally new role when opportunity knocks.

After being downsized from her job as a school counsellor, Rhonda started to attend seminars, read books about job hunting, surf the Internet, and network with her friends for leads. One day she was talking to two friends, and their conversation turned to lingerie.

"What I wish," said Kary, "is that I could buy some of that semi-sexy stuff without having to go into Le Sex Shoppe to buy it."

"There're always the catalogues," Marsha pointed out, "and there are ads in the back of every magazine I subscribe to."

"I don't trust those catalogues," Kary replied. "When I pay that much money for something that small, I want to see what I'm getting!"

Marsha turned to Rhonda. "You're sitting there not saying a word, Rhonda. What're you thinking about?"

"I think," Rhonda said, "I've just discovered the business I want to be in."

Rhonda's idea was to tap her women friends for potential target customers who would like to come to her home for a private showing of women's intimate undergarments. Rhonda named her business Private Screenings, and had letterhead stationery printed. Then she began to contact suppliers and manufacturer's reps. They were interested in her idea.

Her first "private screening" was well attended. Only women were present, and Rhonda sold almost a thousand dollars' worth of merchandise. The women loved what they saw, and they had fun. Ten years earlier they probably wouldn't have considered buying the things they bought that night, but times and people change.

Rhonda went on from her success in selling to develop a line of products that she sells through her own catalogue and on her Web page. Her husband has joined her in the business, and she has hired a woman to present her intimate merchandise through seminars. (The seminars also are held in private homes.) Rhonda spends most of her time recruiting personnel and developing new products.

"When I started in this business," Rhonda admits, "I thought it might help to supplement my husband's income. But it's expanded so much that we have to scramble to keep up with orders. We travel a lot, talking to manufacturers about trends, picking up ideas. This business is full-time job for *both* of us."

Rhonda was a sharp reader of market signals — the trends that reflect changes in how people think. What trends have helped to make Rhonda's business successful?

1. Specialized consumer tastes. Rhonda's target customers are discreet middle-class women in their forties and fifties, many of whom would be uncomfortable walking into a specialty shop to see intimate lingerie. When Rhonda brings the merchandise to them, they feel comfortable, special, and adventurous.
2. High-tech/high-touch. We can't stop the entry into our lives of computers and the Information Age. But we all try to balance the electronic effects of whirring machinery with human responses — just look at EST, dance, the arts, feeding our fantasies. Private Screenings capitalizes on the desire for softness in these high-tech times.
3. Relaxing attitudes about sex. Private Screenings was founded in the 1990s, a time when attitudes toward sex were becoming much more relaxed.

What other trends do you see contributing to the success of Private Screenings?

THE RIGHT PLACE AT THE RIGHT TIME

There are two other kinds of opportunities for growth that you should be aware of. The first lies in the fact that various age groups will grow faster than the average population. Canada's changing population profile is shown in Table 2.3. For example, the 50+ age group represented about 19 percent of the population in 1961. By the year 2011, it will represent over 33 percent of our total population. We know that about 55 percent of disposable income and about 80 percent of the savings account dollars are controlled by the 50+ group. Therefore, knowing the needs of this growing demographic force can reap huge benefits for the imaginative entrepreneur.

The second is the growth and potential buying power in your geographic area. For example, Table 2.4 shows the growth of the Canadian population by province. Also shown are "buying power indices," which help clarify the relative strength of the consumer markets for each of these areas. This information is also available for smaller metropolitan areas. In which area do you intend to start your business? Is the local population growing? Are consumers buying in your area, or are they travelling to other municipalities?

Conduct Your Own Research

This is a good time to walk the neighbourhood to observe clues to lifestyle first-hand. Action Step 13 will get you out into the neighbourhood of your target customers. Take along your new eyes and conduct **eyeball (informal) research.**

EYEBALL (INFORMAL) RESEARCH research that involves playing detective and observing the habits and buying preferences of potential customers

ACTION STEP 13

Assess the lifestyle of your potential target customer by walking his or her neighbourhood.

The best time to walk a target neighbourhood is on the weekend, when people are home and the garage doors are open. What you're looking for are clues to lifestyle.

How many cars do you see? What makes and models? How old are they? What's their condition? Sports cars and low-slung two-door hatchbacks indicate owners who are young, or trying to be. Station wagons suggest families. Trucks, four-wheel drive vehicles, and luxury cars tell you other things.

Do you see any sports or recreation equipment? Any tools? Any pets, doghouses, stables?

What's the maintenance level of the homes? Are they patio homes, condos, townhouses, or single-family dwellings? Estimate the average number of bedrooms, bathrooms, square feet, and so on.

Visit a real estate office and get a ballpark figure on housing costs in the neighbourhood. Use these costs to estimate household income. (If the average price for a home in your target neighbourhood is $300 000 and buyers can finance $150 000, the household income is probably $60 000–$90 000.)

If you don't have time to walk the neighbourhood, bike it or drive it.

Commonly available secondary information can help you confirm your observations. See what data your community newspaper or cable station has already gathered. Also, review information from the latest census track. It's all free!

Study your target customer from all angles. You can't afford to make any blind guesses.

Table 2.3 Canada's Changing Population Profile (Millions)

Age	1996	2001	2011
0–4	1 991.5	1 924.3	1 980.1
5–9	2 036.9	2 082.2	2 016.6
10–14	2 035.2	2 124.8	2 104.8
15–19	1 996.3	2 124.5	2 259.2
20–24	2 027.0	2 115.2	2 332.3
25–29	2 217.5	2 177.7	2 392.8
30–34	2 615.4	2 366.4	2 416.1
35–39	2 657.3	2 723.4	2 443.0
40–44	2 377.8	2 716.3	2 544.5
45–49	2 146.6	2 399.6	2 801.9
50–54	1 667.4	2 140.1	2 722.0
55–59	1 327.3	1 651.4	2 362.2
60–64	1 209.4	1 300.9	2 063.6
65–69	1 129.7	1 154.0	1 544.5
70–74	980.4	1 027.1	1 142.5
75–79	704.9	831.9	906.1
80+	842.9	1 017.7	1 398.1
Total	29 963.7	31 877.3	35 420.3

Source: Statistics Canada, "Canada's Changing Population Profile," adapted from "Population Projections for Canada, Provinces, and Territories, 1996–2011," Cat. No. 91–520. Reprinted with permission.

PRIMARY RESEARCH SOURCES

It is also time to conduct some primary research. Develop a questionnaire for potential customers on your product or service. Box 2.4 is an example of a product analysis questionnaire on a device called a "Water Waiter," which monitors the water level in hanging flower baskets. Other ways you can conduct primary research include talking to successful and not-so-successful entrepreneurs who are operating businesses similar to yours. Talk to potential suppliers and a banker to get their perspectives on your endeavour.

Rich Cameron is a very precise and careful person, and he understands research and trends. If you're considering a venture you know very little about, you should work in that kind of business for a while to get experience. Recall from Chapter One that experience is a key characteristic of successful Canadian entrepreneurs (Box 1.3). If you can't get direct experience, then perhaps you can do what Rich did.

When Rich Cameron celebrated his 35th birthday, he was a supervisor in an auto plant. In this smokestack business, he knew that it was only a matter of time before he would lose his job. It was a declining business.

"I was your typical workaholic," Rich said. "I'd do overtime at the office, put out a lot of energy for the company, and then wonder why I didn't feel terrific. If someone had told me I was experiencing corporate burnout, I'd have laughed in his face."

Rich had been in the habit of changing jobs when he got frustrated. He started working as a grocery bagger when he was twelve, and since then he'd

Table 2.4 The Provincial Markets (Comparative Market Data), 1997

	CAN.	NFLD.	P.E.I.	N.S.	N.B.	QUE.	ONT.	MAN.	SASK.	ALTA.	B.C.	YUKON	N.W.T.
Population, June 1, 1997													
Total (000s)	29 181.7	545.8	133.5	907.6	749.1	7150.6	10 969.8	1 127.0	996.8	2 705.0	3 7978	31.6	67.1
Total (%)	100.00	1.87	0.46	3.11	2.57	24.50	37.59	3.86	3.42	9.27	13.01	0.11	0.23
Change 1991–97 (%)	6.90	1.94	2.97	0.72	5.06	3.49	8.60	3.10	1.02	6.33	15.84	14.49	20.37
Avg. annual rate of growth (%)	1.12	−0.33	0.49	0.12	0.83	0.57	1.38	0.51	0.17	1.03	2.48	2.28	3.14
Households, June 1, 1997													
Total (000s)	10 697.2	169.7	45.7	327.9	262.4	2 749.4	3 952.9	417.1	364.2	949.2	1 428.1	11.6	19.0
Personal Income, 1997													
Total (millions $)	563 339.5	7338.6	1 934.6	14 759.0	1 119.3	125 599.6	238 833.7	19 565.3	14 304.5	52 007.9	75 805.9	601.3	1 069.8
Total (%)	100.00	1.30	0.34	2.62	2.04	22.30	42.40	3.47	2.54	9.23	13.46	0.11	0.19
Per capita ($)	19 300	13 400	14 500	16 300	15 400	17600	21 800	17400	14 400	19 200	20 000	19 100	16 000
Income rating index*	100.00	70	75	84	80	91	113	90	74	100	1-3	99	83
Retail Sales, 1997													
Total (millions $)	230 928.1	3 683.5	896.3	6 946.1	5 409.9	56 059.2	84 253.9	8 243.6	7022.5	24 492.7	33 294.0	250.3	376.3
Total (%)	100.00	1.60	0.39	3.01	2.34	24.28	36.48	3.57	3.04	10.61	14.42	0.11	0.16
Per capita ($)	7900	6 700	6 700	7700	7200	7800	7700	7300	7000	9 100	8 800	7900	5 600
Market rating index**	100	85	85	97	91	99	97	92	89	114	111	100	71

*Income rating index: Average personal income of residents in each area as measured against the national average personal income. This index gives an indication of the purchasing power of each market.

**Market rating index: Average retail sales per capita in each area as measured against the national average retail sales per capita. This index gives an indication of the relative retail sales power of each market.

Source: The Financial Post Datagroup, *Canadian Markets 1997/98*, 71st ed., pp. 14–16, and 611.

Box 2.4 Water Waiter Questionnaire

Have you ever had a plant die because it just didn't get watered at the right time? It's an all too common occurrence. The Water Waiter (patent pending) is designed to help people maintain healthy plants. The device attaches to hanging plants and indicates when they need water. Your comments on this watering-level indicator would be appreciated.

1. What is your reaction to the idea of a device that measures a hanging plant's need for water?
   ❑ Very interested? ❑ Not interested?
2. Have you ever lost plants due to dryness in the past?
   ❑ Yes ❑ No
3. Would you expect to find the Water Waiter included as part of a hanging basket or available only as an extra?
   ❑ Included ❑ An extra purchase ❑ Doesn't matter
4. How many hanging baskets do you buy each year?
   ❑ 0 ❑ 1 ❑ 2–4 ❑ 5 or more
5. What price would you expect to pay for the Water Waiter? (Note: The Water Waiter can be reused in following years.)
   ❑ If sold as part of the basket ❑ If sold as a separate feature
6. In order of preference of location, where would you expect to buy the Water Waiter? (1 - most likely, 5 - least likely)
   ❑ Canadian Tire/Home Depot
   ❑ Nursery
   ❑ White Rose
   ❑ Grocery store garden centre
   ❑ Other: ____________________
7. Who do you feel is the most likely person to buy the Water Waiter?

   ____

Please provide any other comments on your impression of the Water Waiter.

____

____

____

____

If you wish further information, please write your name and phone number below.

Name: ____________________

Phone Number: ____________________

Thank you.

Source: Questionnaire courtesy of Water Waiter Inc., Philip M. Rajotte Sr., President and William Rozak, C.M.A. Reprinted with permission.

worked in sales, management, real estate, and insurance. Now he started to look around for something else to do. He arranged to work a four-day work week — ten hours a day — and spent the three other days exploring.

"When I was a kid in high school, my dad took me aside and gave me some valuable advice. 'Son,' he said, 'remember this. You are your greatest resource.' So one of the first things I did, before I checked out the marketplace, was take some aptitude tests. They told me three things: I'm good with spatial problems, I like being creative, and I like to play. The last one — play

— is the one that threw me. I grew up in a family where we learned to work hard, and *play* is a word we didn't use much. It took me more than a year to accept the fact that I like to play."

While Rich was digesting this news about himself, he attended some seminars, mostly in small business, and kept to his work schedule of four days for his boss and three days for himself. He walked more than a hundred neighbourhoods and interviewed more than a hundred small business owners. He studied traffic patterns, shopping habits, and trends. After a year, he knew that he wanted to combine work and play by opening a toy store. He was about to settle on a location in a major shopping centre when he happened to interview the owner of an antique store.

Rich asked the antique store owner why he'd chosen this location.

"We did research," the man said. "My wife is the mathematician of the family. She worked the whole thing out on paper."

"Great," Rich said. "I've been at it for more than a year, myself. What kind of things did she do?"

"We counted the cars in the parking lot," the owner said. "We counted them every day for two weeks. This lot was packed solid from dawn to dark."

Rich looked out. Today, the parking lot was packed. "What about weekends?" he asked.

The antique store owner looked at the floor. "Now there," he admitted, "we've been having problems, ever since we lost our anchor tenant."

"How long ago was that?" Rich asked.

"Six months ago tomorrow," the man said.

Rich thanked the owner and kept on exploring. He had liked this centre. It was close to a perfect target neighbourhood. Yet, something was wrong. He could feel it.

Rich was still talking to store owners when evening rolled around and the parking lot began to empty, fast. He stopped interviewing to do some new-eyes observing. Cars full of people kept pulling into the lot and stopping. Everyone except the drivers got out and walked to parked cars. None went into the stores. Rich quickly saw the light: a parking lot used by car-pooling commuters!

"I'd been interviewing the store owners all afternoon," Rich said, "and not one told me about this 'park and ride' situation. Maybe they didn't know it. Maybe they were hiding something. Either way, it was a signal for me to keep on looking."

It took Rich Cameron two years to find what he was looking for — a location near a target neighbourhood packed with kids, young parents, station wagons, and toys. He named his store Toys from Middle Earth.

"The main thing you've got to watch in the toy business," Rich says, "is how fast a trend can end. One week you're selling war crafts like crazy. The next week, war crafts won't even move at deep discount and the kids are coming in the store asking for software they've seen on a new TV show or on the Net. To make it in toys these days, you need to keep one eye on the kids, the other on the future." He grins. "If you'd told me this a couple years back, I wouldn't have believed you. But you learn to read the customers in this business, or you go under."

Rich Cameron won't go under. He likes to win too much.

Rich took a hard look "inside" and then spent two years researching the toy industry. His business is located near a high-tech park and today it is growing steadily because he planned well and because he matched his skills with his business. Rich is a researcher to model yourself after. He integrated new-eyes research with hard data from secondary sources.

SECONDARY RESEARCH SOURCES

Now we're going to introduce you to some valuable secondary research sources that you can use for gathering hard data.

Hard Data

Newspapers Study the local newspaper, starting with the classified and display ads. For a bigger picture, read *The Globe and Mail, The Financial Post,* or the business section of your local paper.

Magazines There is almost an endless list of great magazine reads — *Profit, Maclean's, Canadian Business, The Financial Times, Inc., Success, Omni,* and so on. Remember to study the ads. They tell you what's hot and where the money is flowing. In Chapter Four you'll read a case study about Mina Cohen who found a niche in the travel business. Her idea germinated from a great deal of soul-searching and reading *Equinox*. The point is, keep reading with your new eyes. Look for articles on new trends, new ideas, and new opportunities.

Trade Journals These are a valuable source once you know what industry and business you're in. Use your new business letterhead to write trade associations. You can find these listed at your local library. You might also want to try, for example, the *Directory of Associations in Canada,* the *Encyclopedia of Associations,* or the *Gale Directory of Publications.*

Banks Banks are in the business of lending money. Banks have economists, marketing experts, and individuals who evaluate trends and research and write forecasts and reports of economic trends. Ask to see those reports. Most major banks also have a number of publications and brochures on starting and operating a small business.

Planning Offices Cities and regional municipalities employ planners to chart the future and plan for growth. Check the city and regional offices listings in the phone book to find out where these offices are. For the best service, however, you'll need to visit the office, make friends with the staff, and be pleasant and patient. Ask for a copy of the profile on your city.

Box 2.5 Small Business Tips

You can get lots of free advice. All you have to do is ask. The National Bank of Canada, for example, will provide you with its booklet, *Your Key to Success,* a guide to preparing a business plan for independent business. It includes a diskette with information and advice that will help you prepare your business plan. It's a useful source of "how to" information. We suggest you add it to your collection.

Reports from Colleges, Universities, and Investment Firms Many colleges and universities publish annual and semi-annual reports on economic conditions in the province. You can probably get copies of these by writing to the university public relations office. Reports are also published by private institutions of higher learning with special interests in business.

Real Estate Firms Large commercial and industrial real estate firms have access to developers' site research. The more specific you can be on your requirement, the easier it will be for them to help you. Familiarize yourself with the dynamics of the area. What firms are going into business? What firms are leaving business? (For more details on this, see Chapter Seven.) They can supply you with a listing of rental space in your community.

The Business Development Bank of Canada The BDC publishes all kinds of materials of interest to small business. The BDC also provides a wide range of financial alternatives (see Chapter Ten) and sponsors numerous seminars on small business. For information, call or visit your nearest BDC office. You can also write to Business Development Bank, 5, Place Ville-Marie, Suite 400, Montreal, QC, H3B 5E7; visit its Web site at <http://www.bdc.ca>; or call 1-888-INFO-BDC (1-888-463-6232).

Industry Canada <http://info.ic.gc.ca> Industry Canada has been given specific federal responsibilities in the area of small business. The Canada Business Service Centres of Industry Canada should be one of your first stops for small business information. There are eleven CBSCs — one located in each province and the Northwest Territories (for locations, see Appendix 2.1 of this chapter). Key activities of each centre include toll-free telephone help; CBSC Web sites (see discussion below); CBSC resource and information with in-person service, directories, publications, and access to external databases; a toll-free, fax on-demand service; and "Pathfinders" — brochures, organized by topic, with overviews of services and programs.

Statistics Canada <http://www.statcan.ca> Statistics Canada produces a large volume and variety of statistics that are available to all Canadians. For most subjects, Statistics Canada will probably be one of your major sources of secondary information. How reliable is this information? *The Economist* asked a panel of experts from various countries to rank statistical agencies. All agreed that Canada has the best statistics in the world. Yes, our number crunchers were ranked number one. If you haven't used Statistics Canada before, you may find it a little overwhelming. Persist, for it's well worth the effort. You might want to start with its Catalogue No. 11-204, which provides a guide listing over 1 000 reports and documents, as well as numerous electronic databases. It's even available on diskette or CD-ROM. Their annual publication, *Market Research Handbook* (Catalogue No. 63-224), is also a useful starting place. In Chapter Seven, we will introduce you to Census Canada data. The point is, Statistics Canada has all kinds of invaluable business information.

Computer Databases

As you know by now, we are bound up in the knowledge-based economy. Unique databases are cropping up daily. A discussion of this new generation of information would be a book in itself; however, there are five Industry Canada data sources and one Statistics Canada source that warrant special mention.

Industry Canada

- *Canadian Company Capabilities.* This database of over 25 000 Canadian company profiles allows you to search for a firm by product, geography, or activity. You can also register your company and promote your products or services worldwide in cyberspace.
- *Trade Data Online.* This source provides reports and graphs on 6 000 exports and imports to and from over 600 countries, as well as five-year trends. You can also use the information to help forecast domestic and foreign market opportunities.
- *International Business Information Network.* Contacts, country information, and trade fair venues from the world are provided here.
- *dISTCovery.* Here you will find a list of over 35 000 worldwide technologies that can be licensed and are ready for use. You can use the technologies to solve a problem in your manufacturing process or increase your sales through innovation by acquiring the rights to license a technology in Canada.
- *Contact! The Canadian Management Network.* This is a source of Canadian contacts for business management advice, skills development, software tools, services, and useful management publications. *Contact!* also hosts on-line forums where business people and experts can get together electronically to discuss topics of mutual interest. What a great way to do your primary research!

Statistics Canada

CANSIM (Canadian Socioeconomic Information Management System) is a massive data retrieval system maintained and operated by Statistics Canada. This source provides access to historical and current statistics on all kinds of economic and demographic information. Tailored data analysis packages, graphics, and a bibliographic search service are also available. For more information on CANSIM or other data retrieval systems, call or write your nearest Statistics Canada Regional Reference Centre.

In today's knowledge-based world, the list of secondary data sources just keeps growing. The point is, there's massive information out there. All you have to do is start looking, and we suggest that you start at your local public, college, or university library.

Internet Databases

In the last few years, the Internet has become a predominant sources of secondary business information. There are literally hundreds of Web sites that can help you start and run your business. Some major sites include:

- Strategis: <http://strategis.ic.gc.ca> Industry Canada, in partnership with the business community and universities, has created the largest, most comprehensive business information Web site in Canada. It contains over 75 000 reports, 600 000 pages of text, and 2 gigabytes of statistical data. You can also get updated information ranging from business diagnostic and benchmarking data to all the government forms you need to incorporate.
- Online Small Business Workshop: <http://www.sb.gov.bc.ca/smallbus/workshop/workshop.html> This on-line site covers all the basics in "how-to," from fashioning the initial product idea to marketing, research, sales forecasting, financing, planning, and everything in-between.
- Contact! The Canadian Management Network: <http://strategis.ic.gc.ca/sc_mangb/contact/engdoc/search.html> This is the primary Canadian source on the Internet for business management information and advice. It gives access to a full range of small business support organizations in

Canada, and provides a wide range of educational materials and tools to help entrepreneurs start a business.

- Canadian Technology Network: <http://ctn.nrc.ca> Here is a site that helps Canadian businesses look for technological assistance. Advisors work with individual entrepreneurs to identify needs and to find the right source of assistance for almost every technology imaginable.
- Business Development Bank of Canada (BDC): <http://www.bdc.ca> According to the BDC, this is a cyber destination that small- and medium-sized Canadian businesses can call their own. The Web site includes more than 300 hyperlinks to small business resources, coast to coast.

Other secondary research sources include:

- Canadian Industrial Innovation Centre
  Waterloo, Ontario
  <http://www.innovationcentre.ca>
- Human Resources Development Canada
  <http://www.hrdc-drhc.gc.ca>
- Chamber of Commerce
- Local Business Development Centre
- Local Entrepreneurs Network

ACTION STEP 14

Have some fun with segmentation and gap analysis.

Form some of your friends into a focus group and poll them about gaps in the marketplace. Ask them to respond to such questions as:

What products do you need that you can't get?

How could you increase your productivity without working more hours?

What products or services would enhance your quality of life?

Make a list of the gaps that the group identifies. Then project the list out as far as you can, and follow the wants and frustrations of your friends into the marketplace. Are any of the needs they mentioned national in scope?

Segmentation and Gap Analysis

The idea of **market segmentation** is to keep breaking down potential markets into as many similar subsegments as possible. The more you learn about an industry, the better informed you will be to write your business plan. This procedure will help you identify opportunity gaps and see combinations of gaps that may constitute markets. Segmenting the consumer market can be done geographically (e.g., by province), demographically (e.g., by age under 20, 20–30), psychographically (e.g., concern for safety), by benefits sought (e.g., sports utility in cars), and by the rate of product/service usage (e.g., one-time purchase for a number of years of a vacuum cleaner or weekly purchase of dry cleaning service). Figure 2.4 illustrates a mind map that dissects one segment of the health-care industry into subsegments. This is the kind of thinking we want you to do in Action Step 14. It's another brainstorming activity, so have fun with it.

MARKET SEGMENTATION breaking down potential markets into homogeneous groups with similar characteristics and qualities

Entrepreneur Fred Hayes searched for gaps and opportunities by taking a long look at a major, far-reaching trend — the baby boom. Fred explains:

"I got into baby bedding by studying the home. What did it need? What would it be like in five years? Then I targeted the last wave of baby boomers; they were in their late twenties when I founded Sweet Dreams Bedding. My market research showed me that these people were having fewer kids, but were spending more money on the ones they did have. That info told me to position my products in what we called "the New Nursery." My first year, sales were spotty. My second year, I grossed over a million dollars. I listen to my customers, and they tell me what they want me to produce. That nursery is my marketplace."

Fred Hayes is a big man, 188 centimetres tall, 95 kilograms. He served in the military, later learned to sew on industrial machines and do construction work, and after that made good money in commercial construction. An on-the-job accident put an end to that career, however.

Figure 2.4

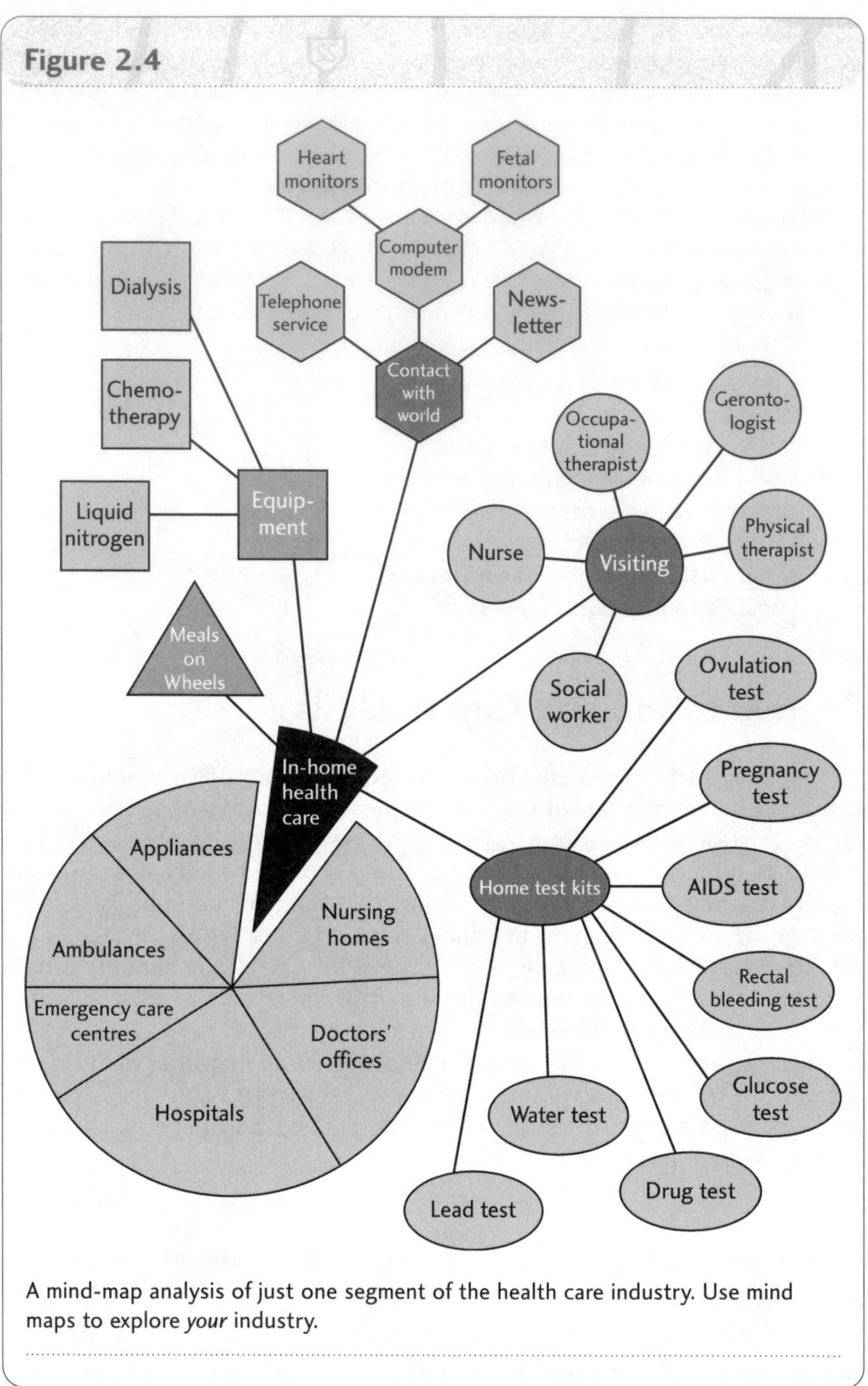

A mind-map analysis of just one segment of the health care industry. Use mind maps to explore *your* industry.

Fred was hospitalized for three weeks, and when he got out, his back pain told him he would no longer work in construction. Fred was bitter, but willing and able to shift careers.

"Okay, I was 41 years old. I had great kids and a good marriage. I started collecting workman's compensation and looking around for a job, but it soon became clear that no one wanted to hire me.

"That meant I was going to have to work for *myself*.

"I signed up for a seminar in small business. I was a stand-up student, because it hurt to sit for more than 20 minutes at a stretch. But I got the message of small business loud and clear.

"'Know what business you're in,' the prof said. 'Scrounge up some customers who agree with you. Ask them what products they need and want. Find out what they can pay. Make the product. Ship it. Always pay your bills. And make sure you're pals with your banker before you run short of cash.'"

It was good advice, and Fred took it. Market research told him there was room in the baby bedding business, and he found a job sewing for a mattress manufacturer — to learn the business from the inside. In his spare time, he designed a nursery set for some neighbours who had a new baby, and they were impressed. That's how Sweet Dreams Bedding began.

Fred worked out of his home the first year. When orders came in, he hired some help and moved into a small warehouse. As someone else took over the sewing, Fred went into sales. He kept an accurate customer file and was always careful to ask the customers what they liked about his product.

The second year, Fred discovered that although young couples were having fewer children, they were spending a lot more money outfitting the children they did have. This gave Fred the clue that he should expand into coordinated nursery items: pillowcases, dust ruffles, and coverlets that go together.

"'Trends are like customers,' my small business prof used to say. 'You can spot some of them by standing outside and staring through the window. But others don't show up until you're in business, working and sweating away, wondering whether or not you'll make it.'"

Action Step 15 can help you make some informal judgements about the marketplace. Shopping cart analysis is another window through which you can view the market.

ACTION STEP 15

Decode the secrets of the shopping cart, using your new eyes.

Use your new eyes to uncover the lifestyle of your target customer by analyzing the contents of a supermarket shopping cart. Play detective the next time you're in a supermarket and make some deductions about lifestyles as you observe the behaviours of shoppers.

Give each subject a fantasy name, perhaps associated with a product (Susan Cereal, Steve Steak, Eloise Sugar) so that you can remember your insight. What can you deduce about each shopper's lifestyle? What do their shoes say? Their clothes? What does their jewellery tell you? Or their hairstyles? Put these deductions together with a demographic checklist (sex, age, income, occupation, socioeconomic level), and then decide how many of these shoppers are potential target customers for your business.

Trained marketeers look for a category of buyer known as a "heavy user." A heavy user of apples would eat ten to fifteen a week. A heavy user of cigarettes would smoke two packs a day. A heavy user of airlines — called a frequent flyer — flies 10–30 times a year. Who are the heavy users in your business?

In a Nutshell

A trend is a direction of movement. For example, the trend of our present civilization is away from the smokestacks of the Industrial Age and toward the computers and the Internet of the Entrepreneurial Age. An easy way to start studying trends it to step back in time and observe a marketplace of the past. Then move one to your own arena — the neighbourhood, nearby shopping malls, Main Street, your trade association, your supermarket.

Two tools will help you chart trends: looking around with new eyes (that is, eyeball research, playing marketplace detective) and applying the life-cycle yardstick to products, industries, and so on. As you learned earlier in this chapter, a life cycle has four phases: embryo, growth, maturity, and decline. Before you open the doors of your small business, you need to be aware of what phase your product is in. For example, if you think there's easy money in selling microcomputers, you need to know that this industry is now maturing. If you want to install security products, you need to know that this industry is in the growth stage. If you're thinking about opening a toy store, you need to know that the toy industry is mature and may be on the decline, and that you may be forced to steal customers from other people.

Just for fun, select three to six businesses at random — for example, a foreign auto repair business, a restaurant-bar, a flower shop, a bedding manufacturer, a

ACTION STEP REVIEW

10 Travel back in time and observe a marketplace of the past. How has it changed?
11 Define your business and test your definition by reaching out beyond the classroom.
12 What's new? What's not? What's cooling down?
13 Assess the lifestyles of your potential target customer by walking in his or her neighbourhood.
14 Have some fun with segmentation and gap analysis.
15 Decode the secrets of the shopping cart, using your new eyes.

travel agent, and a computer school — and determine their life-cycle stages. While you're doing that, remember how the old post office had to adjust. Is the same thing happening to some of the smaller firms you know because they're failing to see what business they're really in?

Information on trends is all around you: on the highways, in the stores in mid-December and after Christmas, in the headlines and classifieds, at government agencies, in the many trade associations. This information can give you the big picture if you know how to seek it out.

Think Points for Success

- ✓ A valuable tool you can use for charting trends is the four-stage life-cycle yardstick.
- ✓ The life-cycle yardstick helps you find a growth industry, decide what business you're really in, and discover gaps and segments that are promising.
- ✓ Once you know what segment you're in, you can focus on market research with new eyes.
- ✓ Try to latch onto a trend that will help you survive (in style) for the next ten to fifteen years.
- ✓ Trends don't develop overnight. The signs are out for all to read, months — even years — in advance.
- ✓ Develop and circulate your primary research customer questionnaire to your target customer.

Business Plan Building Block

INDUSTRY OVERVIEW

You need to demonstrate your knowledge and understanding of the business opportunity you want to pursue. How big is the total industry? How old is it? Is it growing, and if so, in what direction?

What segment have you chosen? It is vital that you present a comprehensive understanding of who your customers are and why they will buy from you. Get on the Internet. Use some of the secondary sources provided in this chapter and definitely do some primary research.

TANNING BUSINESS
THE TEENAGER IN THE INDUSTRY LIFE CYCLE
STILL GROWING REGARDING TECHNOLOGY AND INDUSTRIAL MARKET
20-40 AGE RANGE
DON'T WANT TO GET SUNBURN WHEN GO ON VACATION, TAN CONSUMERS (TIME, RELAXATION, LESS DANGEROUS THAN SUN)

CURRENT POSITION AND FUTURE OUTLOOK

Example:

This is what you learn about Big Wheels, a growing bike shop in town: The two owners are well-known trail bike riders who, for the past two years, have been repairing and servicing all kinds of bicycles out of the oversized garage of one of their partners. In the past twelve months, this part-time venture grossed $161 000 without the benefit of advertising or a retail location.

The market for high-quality and custom-made bicycles has grown over 10 percent per year for the past ten years, and industry observers expect the trend to continue into the next century. The new retail store will have 5 000 square feet in showroom space and another 3 000 square feet for doing repairs and stocking goods.

The bicycle industry in North America sells two dollars' worth of accessories and clothing for every one dollar spent on bicycles. The store conservatively expects sales to at least double the first year (they previously had not sold clothing) and to reach $1 million in three years.

It's your turn again. Develop your section on the current situation and future outlook. It's important to demonstrate an understanding of growth problems (such as choosing the right location and attracting customers), as well as cash management, gross margins, inventory control, and vendor sources. Ready or not, start writing down what you already know and what you need to know. You will have many opportunities to upgrade this section as you gather data. Your primary research, when complete, will help.

MANAGEMENT AND OWNERSHIP

Needed now is a mini-résumé of the key player (or players) you'd like to have on your founding team. Lenders, capital firms, and vendors consider the founding team to be the most important factor in a business plan.

At this point, keep the résumés brief, focussing on the past experience that will give this start-up a competitive edge. (Save the full-blown résumés of the management team for the appendix at the back of the plan.) Explain your business form (that is, corporation, partnership, or sole proprietorship) and, if you have more than two people on the team, include an organizational chart.

Your turn again: Who are the players?

DESCRIPTION OF YOUR BUSINESS

Think of yourself riding up 50 floors in an express elevator. You have 30 seconds to explain to a stranger what your business is about.

Example:

My partner and I retail high-end bicycles from our store in Halifax. We repair, service, and modify off-road bikes for the serious trail rider. Ninety percent of our customers are from Halifax and they see us as a valuable resource in helping them to achieve a healthy and enjoyable exercise lifestyle.

Note that this description is not only short and to the point, but it also includes important customer benefits.

Now it's your turn: My business is:

____

____

____

____

____

Checklist Questions and Actions to Develop Your Business Plan

THE BIG PICTURE: CHARTING TRENDS FOR YOUR SMALL BUSINESS

- ❑ What trends will influence your small business?
- ❑ What business are you really in?
- ❑ What segment of the market will be your niche?
- ❑ What gaps will you fill within that segment?
- ❑ Is it a growth segment in a growth market?
- ❑ Initially define your target market, and determine how large that customer base is.
- ❑ Identify the secondary sources you will use as part of your market research.
- ❑ Does this business fit your vision and values?
- ❑ Other than making money, what are the goals of your proposed venture? (You should be able to establish four to six over the next three years.)
- ❑ For your business, what objectives do you wish to achieve this next year?

NOTES

1. Adapted from Daphne Bramham, "Japan Taps into Pacific Western Beer: The Various Brands Are Brewed to Suit Japanese Tastes, Entrepreneur says," *The Vancouver Sun*, March 7, 1997. Reprinted by permission.
2. Adapted from Rick Spence, *Secrets of Success from Canada's Fastest-Growing Companies* (Toronto: John Wiley & Sons Canada, Ltd., 1997), pp. 35–37. Reprinted with permission of the author.

OTHER REFERENCES

Celente, Gerald. *Trends 2000*. New York: Wagner Books Inc., 1997.

Cork, David (with Susan Lightstone). *The Pig and the Python: How to Prosper from the Aging Baby Boom*. Toronto: Stoddart Books, 1996.

Gates, Bill. *The Road Ahead*. New York: Viking Press, 1996.

Harris, Lesley Ellen. *Digital Property, Currency of the 21st Century*. Whitby, ON: McGraw-Hill Ryerson Ltd., 1997.

Hise, Phaedra. *Growing Your Business Online: Small Business Strategies for Working the World Wide Web*. New York: Henry Holt, 1996.

Peters, Tom. *The Circle of Innovation*. New York: Knopf, 1998.

Thurow, Lester C. *The Future of Capitalism*. New York: William Morrow & Co., Inc., 1996.

Appendix 2.1 Key Contacts

CANADA BUSINESS SERVICE CENTRES

Nova Scotia
Canada/Nova Scotia Business Service Centre
1575 Brunswick Street
Halifax, NS B3J 2G1
Tel.: (902) 426-8604
Toll free: 1-800-668-1010
Fax: (902) 426-6530
Info-Fax: (902) 426-3201
Toll free: 1-800-401-3201
Teletype: 1-800-797-4188

New Brunswick
Canada/New Brunswick Business Service Centre
570 Queen Street, P.O. Box 578
Fredericton, NB E3B 6Z6
Tel.: (506) 444-6140
Toll free: 1-800-668-1010
Fax: (506) 444-6172
Info-Fax: (506) 444-6169
Teletype: 1-800-887-6550

Prince Edward Island
Canada/Prince Edward Island Business Service Centre
75 Fitzroy Street, P.O. Box 40
Charlottetown, PE C1A 7K2
Tel.: (902) 368-0771
Toll free: 1-800-668-1010
Fax: (902) 566-7377
Info-Fax: (902) 368-0776
Toll free: 1-800-401-3201
Teletype: (902) 368-0724

Newfoundland
Canada Business Service Centre
90 O'Leary Avenue, P.O. Box 8687
St. John's, NF A1B 3T1
Tel.: (709) 772-6022
Toll free: 1-800-668-1010
Fax: (709) 772-6090
Info-Fax: (709) 772-6030

Quebec
Info Entrepreneurs
5, Place Ville-Marie, Plaza Level
Montreal, QC H3B 4Y2
Tel.: (514) 496-INFO (4636)
Toll free: 1-800-322-INFO (4636)
Fax: (514) 496-5934
Info-Fax: (514) 496-4010
Toll free: 1-800-322-4010

Ontario
Canada/Ontario Business Call Centre
151 Yonge Street
Toronto, ON M5C 2W7
Tel.: (416) 954-INFO (4636)
Toll free: 1-800-567-2345
Fax: (416) 954-8597
Info-Fax: (416) 954-8555
Toll free: 1-800-240-4192

Manitoba
Canada Business Service Centre
330 Portage Avenue, 8th Floor
P.O. Box 2609
Winnipeg, MB R3C 4B3
Tel.: (204) 984-2272
Toll free: 1-800-665-2019
Fax: (204) 983-3852
Info-Fax: (204) 984-5527
Toll free: 1-800-665-9386

Saskatchewan
Canada/Saskatchewan Business Service Centre
122 3rd Avenue North
Saskatoon, SK S7K 2H6
Tel.: (306) 956-2323
Toll free: 1-800-667-4374
Fax: (306) 956-2328
Info-Fax: (306) 956-2310
Toll free: 1-800-667-9433

Alberta
The Business Link Business Service Centre
10237 104 Street, Suite 100
Edmonton, AB T5J 1B1
Tel.: (403) 422-7722
Toll free: 1-800-272-9675
Fax: (403) 422-0055
Info-Fax: (403) 427-7971
Toll free: 1-800-563-9926

British Columbia
Canada/British Columbia Business Service Centre
601 West Cordova Street
Vancouver, BC V6B 1G1
Tel.: (604) 775-5525
Toll free: 1-800-667-2272
Fax: (604) 775-5520
Info-Fax: (604) 775-5515

Northwest Territories
Canada/NWT Business Service Centre
Northern United Place
5004 54th Street, 3rd Floor
Yellowknife, NT X1A 2L9
Tel.: (403) 873-7958
Toll free: 1-800-661-0786
Fax: (403) 873-0101
Info-Fax: (403) 873-0575
Toll free: 1-800-661-0825

BUSINESS DEVELOPMENT BANK OF CANADA (BDC)

For the BDC office nearest you, please contact:
Tel: 1-888-INFO-BDC
(1-888-463-6232)

INTERNATIONAL TRADE CENTRES

Nova Scotia
International Trade Centre
1801 Hollis Street, 5th Floor
P.O. Box 940, Station M
Halifax, NS B3J 2V9
Tel.: (902) 426-7540
Fax: (902) 426-2624

New Brunswick
International Trade Centre
1045 Main Street, Unit 103
Moncton, NB E1C 1H1
Tel.: (506) 851-6452
Toll free: 1-800-332-3801
Fax: (506) 851-6429

Prince Edward Island
International Trade Centre
75 Fitzroy Street, P.O. Box 1115
Charlottetown, PE C1A 7M8
Tel.: (902) 566-7426
Fax: (902) 566-7450

Newfoundland
International Trade Centre

Atlantic Place
215 Water Street, Suite 504
P.O. Box 8950
St. John's, NF A1B 3R9
Tel.: (709) 772-5511
Fax: (709) 772-2373

Quebec
International Trade Centre
5, Place Ville-Marie, Suite 700
Montreal, QC H3B 2G2
Tel.: (514) 283-6796
Fax: (514) 283-8794

Ontario
International Trade Centre
Dominion Public Building
1 Front Street West, 4th Floor
Toronto, ON M5J 1A4
Tel.: (416) 973-5053
Fax: (416) 973-8161

Manitoba
International Trade Centre
400 St. Mary Avenue, 4th Floor
Winnipeg, MB R3G 4K5
Tel.: (204) 983-5851
Fax: (204) 983-3182

Saskatchewan
International Trade Centre
123 2nd Avenue South, 7th Floor
Saskatoon, SK S7K 7E6
Tel.: (306) 975-5315
Fax: (306) 975-5334

Alberta — Edmonton
(also responsible for the Northwest Territories)
International Trade Centre
Canada Place
9700 Jasper Avenue, Suite 540
Edmonton, AB T5J 4C3
Tel.: (403) 495-2944
Fax: (403) 495-4507

Alberta — Calgary
International Trade Centre
639 5th Avenue SW, Suite 300
Calgary, AB T2P 0M9
Tel.: (403) 292-4575
Fax: (403) 292-4578

British Columbia
(also responsible for the Yukon)
International Trade Centre
300 West Georgia Street, Suite 2000
Vancouver, BC V6B 6E1
Tel.: (604) 666-0434
Fax: (604) 666-8330

EXPORT DEVELOPMENT CORPORATION (EDC)

General Inquiries:
Tel.: 1-800-850-9626

REGIONAL ECONOMIC DEVELOPMENT AGENCIES

Atlantic Canada Opportunities Agency (ACOA)

ACOA — Head Office
Blue Cross Centre
644 Main Street, P.O. Box 6051
Moncton, NB E1C 9J8
Tel.: (506) 851-2271
Toll free: 1-800-561-7862
Fax: (506) 851-7403

ACOA — Newfoundland
Atlantic Place
215 Water Street, Suite 504
P.O. Box 8950
St. John's, NF A1B 3R9
Tel.: (709) 772-2751
Toll free: 1-800-668-1010
Fax: (709) 772-2712

ACOA — Prince Edward Island
100 Sydney Street, 3rd Floor
P.O. Box 40
Charlottetown, PE C1A 7K2
Tel.: (902) 566-7492
Toll free: 1-800-871-2596
Fax: (902) 566-7098

ACOA — Nova Scotia
1801 Hollis Street, Suite 600
P.O. Box 2284, Station M
Halifax, NS B3J 3C8
Tel.: (902) 426-6743
Toll free: 1-800-565-1228
Fax: (902) 426-2054

ACOA — New Brunswick
570 Queen Street, 3rd Floor
P.O. Box 578
Fredericton, NB E3B 5A6
Tel.: (506) 452-3184
Toll free: 1-800-561-4030
Fax: (506) 452-3285

Enterprise Cape Breton Corporation
Commerce Tower
15 Dorchester Street, 4th Floor
P.O. Box 1750
Sydney, NS B1P 6T7
Tel.: (902) 564-3600
Toll free: 1-800-705-3926
Fax: (902) 564-3825

FEDERAL ECONOMIC DEVELOPMENT INITIATIVE FOR NORTHERN ONTARIO (FEDNOR)

FedNor — Sault Ste. Marie
302 Queen Street East
Sault Ste. Marie, ON P6A 1Z1
Tel.: (705) 942-1327
Toll free: 1-800-461-6021
Fax: (705) 942-5434

FedNor — Sudbury
30 Cedar Street, Suite 407
Sudbury, ON P3E 1A4
Tel.: (705) 671-0711
Toll free: 1-800-461-4079
Fax: (705) 671-0717

FedNor — Thunder Bay
201 North May Street, Suite 201
Thunder Bay, ON P7C 3P4
Tel.: (807) 626-1800
Toll free: 1-800-465-6870
Fax: (807) 623-5392

FedNor — North Bay
107 Shirreff Avenue, Suite 203
North Bay, ON P1B 7K8
Tel.: (705) 494-7050
Fax: (705) 494-7588

FEDERAL OFFICE OF REGIONAL DEVELOPMENT — QUEBEC (FORD-Q)

Head Office
800, Place Victoria Tower, Suite 3800
P.O. Box 247
Montreal, QC H4Z 1E8
Tel.: (514) 283-6412
Fax: (514) 283-3302

Liaison Office
Place du Portage, Phase II
165, Hôtel de Ville
P.O. Box 1110, Branch B
Hull, QC J8X 3X5
Tel.: (819) 997-8299
Fax: (819) 997-3340

Abitibi-Témiscamingue
906 5th Avenue
Val-d'Or, QC J9P 1B9
Tel.: (819) 825-5260
Toll free: 1-800-567-6451
Fax: (819) 825-3245

Bas Saint-Laurent, Gaspésie, Îles de la Madeleine
2, St-Germain Street East, Suite 310
Rimouski, QC G5L 8T7
Tel.: (418) 722-3282
Toll free: 1-800-463-9073
Fax: (418) 722-3285

Côte-Nord
701 Laure Boulevard, 2nd Floor
Suite 202B, P.O. Box 698
Sept-Îles, QC G4R 4K9
Tel.: (418) 968-3426
Toll free: 1-800-463-1707
Fax: (418) 368-0806

Estrie
Place Andrew Paton
65 Belvedere Street North, Suite 240
Sherbrooke, QC J1H 4A7
Tel.: (819) 564-5904
Toll free: 1-800-567-6084
Fax: (819) 564-5912

Laval, Laurentides, Lanaudière
Tour du Triomphe II, Suite 204
2540 Daniel-Johnson Boulevard
Laval, QC H7T 2S3
Tel.: (514) 973-6844
Toll free: 1-800-430-6844
Fax: (514) 973-6851

Mauricie, Bois-Francs, Drummondville
Place du Centre
150 Marchand Street, Suite 502
Drummondville, QC J2C 4N1
Tel.: (819) 478-4664
Toll free: 1-800-567-1418
Fax: (819) 478-4666

Trois-Rivières
Immeuble Bourg du Fleuve
25 des Forges Street, Suite 413
Trois-Rivières, QC G9A 2G4
Tel.: (819) 371-5182
Toll free: 1-800-567-8637
Fax: (819) 371-5186

Montérégie
Complexe Saint-Charles
1111 Saint-Charles Street West, Suite 411
Longueuil, QC J4K 5G4
Tel.: (514) 928-4088
Toll free: 1-800-284-0335
Fax: (514) 928-4097

Nord du Québec
800 Place Victoria Tower, Suite 3800
P.O. Box 347
Montreal, QC H4Z 1E8
Tel.: (514) 283-5174

Outaouais
259 Saint-Joseph Boulevard, Suite 202
Hull, QC J8Y 6T1
Tel.: (819) 994-7442
Toll free: 1-800-561-4353
Fax: (819) 994-7846

Québec-Chaudière-Appalaches
905 Dufferin Street, 2nd Floor
Québec, QC G1R 5M6
Tel.: (418) 648-4826
Toll free: 1-800-463-5204
Fax: (418) 648-7291

Saguenay — Lac-Saint-Jean
170 Saint-Joseph Street South, Suite 203
Alma, QC G8B 3E8
Tel.: (418) 668-3084
Toll free: 1-800-463-9808
Fax: (418) 668-7584

WESTERN ECONOMIC DIVERSIFICATION CANADA (WD)

Manitoba
The Cargill Building
240 Graham Avenue, Suite 712
P.O. Box 777
Winnipeg, MB R3C 2L4
Tel.: (204) 983-4472
Toll free: 1-800-561-5394
Fax: (204) 983-4694

Saskatchewan
S.J. Cohen Building
119 4th Avenue South, Suite 601
P.O. Box 2025
Saskatoon, SK S7K 3S7
Tel.: (306) 975-4373
Toll free: 1-800-203-9041
Fax: (306) 975-5484

Alberta
Canada Place
9700 Jasper Avenue, Suite 1500
Edmonton, AB T5J 4H7
Tel.: (403) 495-4164
Toll free: 1-800-550-9558
Fax: (403) 495-4557

British Columbia
Bentall Tower 4
1055 Dunsmuir Street, Suite 1200
P.O. Box 49276
Vancouver, BC V7X 1L3
Tel.: (604) 666-6256
Toll free: 1-800-663-2008
Fax: (604) 666-2353

Ottawa
Centennial Towers
200 Kent Street, 8th Floor
P.O. Box 2128, Station D
Ottawa, ON K1P 5W3
Tel.: (613) 952-9378
Fax: (613) 952-9384

STRATEGIS: INDUSTRY CANADA ON-LINE

On-line: <http://strategis.ic.gc.ca>

Help Desk
Tel.: (613) 954-5031
Toll free: 1-800-328-6189
Fax: (613) 954-1894

three

Positioning Yourself as an Entrepreneur for Market Opportunities

BUSINESS PLAN BUILDING BLOCK

This chapter will help you align your personal vision and values with your business mission, goals, and objectives, and guide you as you start to develop your strategy. It will also help you collect data that will allow you to focus on the most promising unmet needs, and identify the industry or market trends — the big picture — for you and your business.

Figure 3.1 Chapter Three will help you prepare part B of your business plan, "Positioning Yourself as an Entrepreneur for Market Opportunities."

LEARNING OPPORTUNITIES

After reading this chapter, you should be able to:

- Mesh your personal business objectives with one of the many opportunities in the marketplace.
- Understand that your business objectives provide a positive and unique thrust to your business.
- Narrow your industry research until viable gaps appear.
- Gain insight into hidden pockets of the life cycle by using an industry chronology.
- Understand how problems can be turned into opportunities.
- Combine demographic (population) data with psychographic (picture of a lifestyle) data to produce a customer profile.
- Identify heavy users of your product or service.
- Brainstorm creatively.
- Use a matrix grid for blending your objectives with your research findings to produce a portrait of a business.
- Create a mission statement for your business.

The voice at the other end of the telephone was gritty and determined. Its owner, Beverly MacIntyre, is talking from Dieppe, which is just outside Moncton, New Brunswick. "I have always wanted to make a difference, whatever I do," she says. "That's my vision and it's very important to me."

Six years ago, she and an associate, Terry Miller, started BKM Research & Development Inc. The company talks to employers, figures out what skills they're looking for, then creates a training program to teach clients. Often this involves bringing in industry experts to help out. Recently, BKM launched another teaching option in the virtual-solutions division. It now provides educational support to business via the Internet. The company currently offers its services in Atlantic Canada and the Caribbean. "Our mission is to find meaningful employment for our graduates. Around 83 percent of our full-time graduates find work," says MacIntyre, so "we must be doing something right."[1]

ACTION STEP PREVIEW

16 List your business goals for the next three years.
17 Research your favourite industry.
18 Identify three or four market gaps that look promising.
19 List problems that need solutions.
20 Brainstorm for solutions.
21 Mesh possible solutions with your goals and objectives, using a matrix grid.
22 Narrow the gaps and see your target customer emerge.
23 Draft your mission statement.

"My personal vision is to live my life sharing the true beauty of the North with others," says David Loeks, successful owner of Arctic Edge, an adventure and outfitting company based in Whitehorse, Yukon.

It wasn't a Cinderella beginning for Loeks, however. After a slow start, he decided to put everything on hold and went back to university for a graduate degree in business administration. He returned to Whitehorse with a renewed focus, new skills, and a broader perspective — a bigger picture — of the tourism industry and its changing markets.

Today Arctic Edge provides a well-to-do international clientele with adventures that combine wilderness and outdoor activity with information about the natural history of the Arctic. "We run high quality trips that appeal to the up-scale North American and European traveller," says Loeks. "My mission was to carve out a market niche that would enable us to attract the type of people that could afford Club Med, but who want an education as well."

There is a market need for increased awareness and appreciation of the Arctic community. Loeks saw this need and turned his vision and deep love for the beauty and history of the Arctic into a competitive advantage. His personal vision and the market's needs were in sync. Loeks says that the key to competing successfully is having a strong personal vision and good sense of what you think people would like.[2]

In Chapter One, we asked you to step back, take a good hard look at your strengths and weaknesses, and think about your personal vision, values, and goals. In Chapter Two, we introduced you to the big picture: market and industry trends that signal entrepreneurial opportunities. Now we want to help you align your personal vision and values with the market opportunities. Think for a minute: this "alignment" was a major factor contributing to the success of Beverly MacIntyre of BKM and David Loeks of Arctic Edge. MacIntyre had a personal vision, "to make a difference, whatever I do." She positioned her business in the growth markets of education and technology. Her business mission "to help people find meaningful employment" guided her along the life-long path to make a difference. In the same fashion, Loeks's personal vision, "to live my life sharing the true beauty of the North with others," was in keeping with the eco-tourism trend and his resulting business mission.

As you work your way through this self-assessment chapter, you will better understand what type of business best suits you. The sky is the limit on ideas for your small business. On the other hand, you may already have very firm ideas on what type of business you plan to start. If you are not sure, keep your options open at this stage. As you assess your vision and values, establish your mission, goals, and objectives and let your ideas percolate. In the final analysis, you want to match your business idea with your interests. Box 3.1 diagrams the flow of the thought process from your vision to your strategy. Your best business opportunity will be where your personal vision and values meet your business mission.

Your Values

I believe that the owner and/or president of a company determines its culture. His or her personal qualities of doing business and treatment of others are disseminated through the rest of the organization: the company ends up

Box 3.1 It Is All Connected

YOUR VISION
is
Based on YOUR VALUES and beliefs.
It is spelled out in
YOUR MISSION statement
fleshed out in
YOUR GOALS and OBJECTIVES
and accomplished through
YOUR STRATEGY.

with the reputation of its leader." So says Alex Tilley, owner and chairman of Tilley Endurables Inc.[3]

Art Coren, instructor at Kwantlen University College, agrees with Tilley. "A business reflects the values and personality of the people that own and operate it. If, for example, your core values are respect for others and upholding the traditional family structure, could you start an escort service? As a small business owner, your business must embody your values. Starting a business that violates one or more of your core values could lead to chaos and misery."[4]

So you need to ask yourself what intrinsic values guide your day-to-day activities, behaviour, and decision making. Think about what things in life are really important to you. You may not die for them, but they are principles that mean a great deal to you. Now make a list. The following is a cross-section of both personal and business values one may have. Use this as a guide, but don't just incorporate them as yours unless you firmly believe that they are important to you.

- Customer service
- Quality
- Family
- Friends
- Money
- Material items
- Trust of others
- Security
- Benefits of a socially aware community
- Confidence in others
- Work ethics
- Desire for ownership
- Desire for power
- Desire for affiliation
- Desire for achievement
- Desire for recognition

What does your list look like? Which are business values and which personal values? You may find, as you develop your list, that it will consist of values and priorities. If one of your values is security, then think what this means to you. Does it mean being able to take care of others and provide opportunities? If to your spouse it means having a small business that allows flexible time, is close to home, enables weekends off, and does not involve travel, then you'll find your business choices are limited. Don't ignore your spouse's values and personal priorities or choices.

Values serve as guideposts for your actions. They help you deal with problems you have never seen before. As Alex Tilley points out, a business reflects the values and personality of the people that own and operate it. If you believe in treating people fairly, chances are your business will too. If you are socially aware, you may want your business to embody the same values. For example, you may budget an annual financial contribution to a charity in your business plan. Values, once crystallized, become the basis of your mission statement and goals (Figure 3.2). Now that you've had a chance to think about your values, it's time to focus on market opportunities that support these values.

Figure 3.2

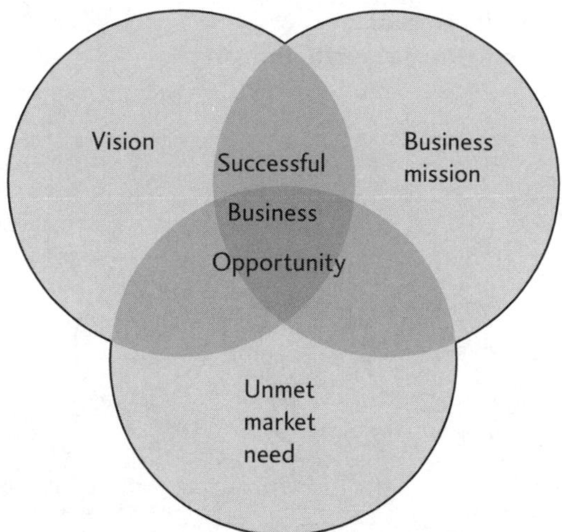

Success is where your personal vision, based on your values, connects with your busines mission and matches with an unmet need in the marketplace.

Welcome to Opportunity Selection

Think of the process for selecting the right opportunity for you as a huge funnel equipped with a series of idea filters. You pour everything into this funnel — your visions, values, long-term goals, short-term objectives, personality, problems, hopes, fears, and primary, secondary, and new-eyes research — and a valuable business idea drains out at the bottom. This opportunity selection process contains seven steps. It is a method to help you find market segments that match with your personal vision and goals (see Boxes 3.1 and 3.2). It connects your skills to your research, and shows you

Box 3.2 The Power of Vision

Five percent of the workforce — some 670,000 Canadians — is affected by depression every day. Depressive disorders cost Canadians more than $3 billion annually. Over the 1990s, downsizing — "laying off employees across the board without changing the basic corporate structure," — was a major source of stress for thousands of Canadians.

If your personal vision is to help people understand and deal with depression, then the downsizing trend and the resulting stress factor are problems that can translate into a real business opportunity. CHC-Working Well, a Financial Post "50 Best Managed Private Companies," is one of Canada's leading firms that has taken advantage of the downsizing trend. "We help people understand the early signs and symptoms, so they can be aware of depression before it becomes a serious problem. We're part of the solution," says Jack Santa-Barbara, head of CHC-Working Well. This Mississauga, Ont., firm started out small in the 1980s and has since grown to a $20 million medium-sized company with over 700 employees.

Source: Rod McQueen, "Canada's 50 Best Managed Private Companies: CHC-Working Well," *The Financial Post*, December 13, 1997, p. 17.

the skills you need to develop. It aims the power of your mind at the particular segment of small business that suits you (see Figure 3.3).

Here is a quick preview of the seven steps to opportunity selection:

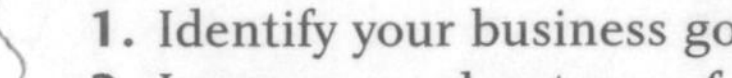

1. Identify your business goals.
2. Learn more about your favourite industry.

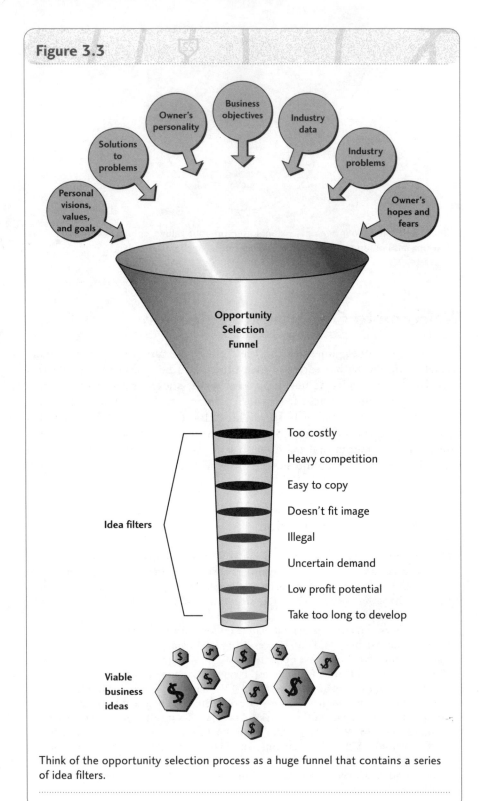

Figure 3.3

Personal visions, values, and goals

Solutions to problems

Owner's personality

Business objectives

Industry data

Industry problems

Owner's hopes and fears

Opportunity Selection Funnel

Idea filters

Too costly

Heavy competition

Easy to copy

Doesn't fit image

Illegal

Uncertain demand

Low profit potential

Take too long to develop

Viable business ideas

Think of the opportunity selection process as a huge funnel that contains a series of idea filters.

3. Identify promising industry segments.
4. Identify problems that need solutions.
5. Brainstorm for solutions.
6. Mesh possible solutions with opportunities in the marketplace.
7. Take stock of, and focus on, the most promising opportunities.

To understand how this process works, let's see how Steve and Anne found their business opportunity. Steve, a graduate from a technical school, had been bounced from job to job over the last few years. Anne graduated with a major in marketing and still hadn't found a real job — but then she'd not been looking that hard. They weren't too sure whether they wanted to start a business together, so they took a night course in small business to help sort things out. Both had a good handle on their personal visions and goals, and now it was time to see if they could come up with a good business idea.

We'll show you how they worked through their idea using the seven steps of opportunity selection. This case study also introduces another important concept: teamwork. Let's start with Steve and Anne's business goals.

STEP 1: IDENTIFY YOUR BUSINESS GOALS

Anne and Steve's first step was to develop a list of business goals. Their small business professor had asked, "If you were to start a business, what would your goals — in relation to your values — be? Security, money, independence, control?" She added that eventually these general goals would have to be refined as short-term objectives and made much more specific and measurable (as noted in Box 3.3).

It took a few days — more time than they thought — but Steve and Anne finally came up with a list of broad goals that sounded like heaven:

1. *Psychological rewards.* They wanted to plant a seed and watch it grow into a business that they and their future family would be proud of.
2. *Teamwork.* All their lives they had planned to work together to build a strong family unit. Now they wanted to practise these teamwork skills in business. They wanted their business to be something bigger than they could accomplish as individuals — the value of synergy. As a team, both Anne and Steve had listed their strengths and weaknesses. They wanted to build on their strength.
3. *Money.* They wanted to earn a respectable family income — a minimum of $50 000 per year.
4. *Safety.* There was no way they wanted to lose money now. They had a family to think about.
5. *Growth industry.* They wanted to find a booming segment of a growth industry (an industry whose annual sales growth is considerably above average).

Box 3.3 Small Business Tips

In the final analysis, each of your broad goals will boil down to a set of specific business objectives. These objectives should be S M A R T:

Specific
Measurable
Achievable
Realistic
Time-framed

ACTION STEP 16

List your business goals for the next three years.

What do you want from small business? Money? Fame? Job security? To be your own boss? Freedom to explore the marketplace? Control of your own destiny? Just want to be a president?

Think back to the forces that made you interested in small business in the first place. What were those forces? Where were you when you first thought about owning the store? How have circumstances changed your goals?

You probably won't have trouble writing down goals, but if you do, flip back to the notes you made for Action Step 4 and to your skills analysis (Action Step 8).

List everything you want, even if it seems unreasonable or embarrassing to you. This is your personal list, after all, and you will sift through the ideas later.

6. *Time.* They knew that getting a business up and running could take a year at the very least. They wanted to define and develop their business so that they could make a little money the first year, get their feet wet, and then go bigger in the next two to four years, once they knew what they were doing and what the market really wanted.
7. *Key people.* They wanted to operate the business themselves for the first year. But as the business grew over the next four years, they wanted to be able to attract the best people to work with them.
8. *Fun, adventure, excitement.* They knew that starting a small business, even in a growth or glamour industry, would involve hassles, problems, and surprises. So they decided to make sure their business would be one with which they would have some fun.

Now it's your turn. Why would you want to start your own business? What are your goals? Action Step 16 will help you work through this.

STEP 2: LEARN MORE ABOUT YOUR FAVOURITE INDUSTRY

As you searched for trends in Chapter Two, you probably found a dozen industries that seemed interesting. Now it's time to explore one of them in more depth. The industry should be the one that interests you most and about which you have at least some knowledge, whether it's genetics, robotics, entertainment, food service, travel, education, publishing, retailing, construction, manufacturing, information, or whatever.

As you move into your selected industry, collect information from previous Action Steps. For secondary data, visit a resource centre or library, study periodicals like *The Globe and Mail, Canadian Business, Profit,* and other general business or news sources. Most libraries have computer databases to help you search. The Internet is also a great source of secondary research, but you need to sift through a lot of information. Check out Strategis. As discussed in Chapter Two, it's a useful source of industry research (see Box 3.4). In addition, the Canadian Business Index and other such sources will point you to

Box 3.4 Bookmark This

Strategis: http://Strategis.ic.gc.ca

As we noted in the last chapter, Strategis — Industry Canada's Web page — is a great source of secondary research. It is devoted to providing information, resources, contacts, and hard-to-get information in a pre-arranged, easy-to-use format.

Main Menu

- Company Information
- International Business Opportunities, Trade and Investments
- Business Information by Sector
- Micro-Economic Research and Statistical Analysis
- Technology, Innovation and Licensing
- Business Support Services
- The Marketplace: Services, Laws and Regulations
- Human Resources Training
- Consumer Information

dozens of articles in your field. Is there a trade show you can attend? What you're looking for is an accurate picture of trends in the industry that interest you. You need to learn what's breaking, what's cresting, and what's cooling down.

In focussing on your industry, break down your search into categories such as life cycles, speed of change, history, competition, recent industry breakthroughs, costs of positioning yourself, target customers, and so on. Later, after you have gathered the data, you can use these categories as idea filters for sifting information through the power marketing funnel.

For example, using the life-cycle concept discussed in Chapter Two will sharpen a first look at any industry. When you're reading a newspaper and you see a headline that says "CBC tries to shed stodgy image in prime time — but can it be hip?", you make three fast-reflex judgements. First, the industry is entertainment. Second, the segment is network television. Third, the shows are in the mature phase, on their way to decline.

And when you're driving down the street and you see a shopping mall being renovated, you know that the face lift is an attempt to move the mall back from a mature or decline phase into a growth phase. The point of all this is to find an industry segment where there is room for growth.

A second helpful category is competition, which we'll be analyzing in detail in Chapter Five. Competition, which varies with each stage of the life cycle, is an idea filter that can save you years of grief.

A third helpful category is the concept of industry breakthrough or hot button. What really hums in your industry or segment? Remember, the first computers filled large rooms and ran on punch cards. The first industry breakthrough was the printed circuit. The second was the microchip. And the third was computer networks. Could the fourth be the network computer — a personal computer with no hard drive?

Let's return to Anne and Steve. They had a firm idea of their favourite industry. They had done a lot of primary and secondary research and had decided to focus on the information industry. All the numbers told them the information industry was still a growth market. On a personal level, Steve loved the technical world and Anne knew there was a real need for marketers in the technology sector, and she liked working with techies. They had chosen a growth industry, which meshed with their personal visions and goals.

Now it is your turn. Research your favourite industry. Is it in a growth phase? What breakthroughs are occurring? Does your business capitalize on the latest advances in technology and imagination? Put this kind of thinking into Action Step 17.

ACTION STEP 17

Research your favourite industry.
What industry really attracts you? What's out there that has a magnetic pull you cannot resist? To help you get started, recall what you discovered in Action Steps 12 (What's new? What's hot?) and 14 (segmentation, gap analysis) and dive in. Also, think about what you discovered when you interviewed small business owners in Action Step 11.

A good idea at this stage is to remember the Canada Post Corporation and stay wide-angle in your views. Look at genetics, robotics, entertainment, food service, travel, education, publishing, the auto industry, retailing, construction, small manufacturing, information — anything that looks interesting.

After you've decided on "your" industry, research it like crazy. It might help to organize your research into categories such as life cycle, speed of change, history, competition, recent industry breakthroughs, costs of positioning yourself, customer base, and so on.

If you're working alone, it will help to write your industry overview. If you're working with a team, you'll save yourself some confusion if everyone writes an overview, sharing his or her perspective with the others.

STEPS 3 AND 4: IDENTIFY PROMISING INDUSTRY SEGMENTS AND PROBLEMS THAT NEED SOLUTIONS

When you write your business plan, you'll need to explain why you have chosen a particular **market gap** and what you believe the resulting business opportunity is. If you have selected a promising opportunity and have communicated your excitement about it, you'll have developed a "hook" for the banker or investor who will read your plan. One example of a market gap is shown in Box 3.5.

MARKET GAP
an area of the market where needs are not being met

Anne and Steve had done a lot of primary and secondary research. They knew that computers and the Internet were explosive market segments (see Figure 3.4). They also learned that there was a growth market for computer networks — especially for the small businesses (Table 3.1). From their research they had isolated four breakthrough segments: the home computer

ACTION STEP 18

Identify three or four market gaps that look promising.
Now that you're hip-deep in your industry, scrutinize segments where you think you could survive and prosper. It's time to begin to profile your target customer.

Prepare a combination demographic-psychographic checklist to help you explore target markets. Include items for evaluating:

- Demographic data — age, sex, income, family size, education, socioeconomic status, place of residence, religion, political affiliation, and so on.
- Psychographic data — occupation, lifestyle, buying habits, dreams, interest and leisure activities, ambitions, and so on.

Or, if you're going after a commercial/industrial market, use company size, type of industry, number of employees, location, departments of large companies, and so on.

Tailor your checklist so that it provides a thorough profile of your target customer.

ACTION STEP 19

List problems that need solutions.
When you surveyed your friends in Action Step 14, you were approaching the list of problems you need to develop now. The difference is that the problems you are seeking now are those that are unique to the industry you've been exploring.

Follow your success with Action Step 14 and get together with people who know something about your industry. Ask them for input and write down everything. Use this input to develop your list.

Each problem you identify multiplies your opportunities to prosper in your segment.

Box 3.5 Internet Commerce

Highlights from the 1998 Canadian Internet Marketplace indicate that through the first half of this year:

- Approximately 5.2 million Canadians will use the Internet on a daily or weekly basis.
- Approximately two million Canadians will be connected to the Internet.
- British Columbia will maintain its position as Canada's most "wired" province.
- Canadians will use the Internet primarily for e-mail and access to subject-specific content.
- Canadian business will be most interested in electronic commerce solutions.
- Sympatico will establish itself as one of the fastest growing Internet service providers in North America.
- Netscape will maintain its leadership position as browser-of-choice.

Source: 11 CORINFO Research and Information Services, *Canadian Internet Marketplace*, 1998. Reprinted by permission.

market, the Internet, Intranet, and computer networks. It would be hard to argue that any of these are not growth segments. The numbers are quite clear — at least for the next couple of years. Wisely, Anne and Steve also listed some of the major problems in the industry: product and service distrust, speed change, information overload, security, cost, and so on.

The secret to focussing on market gaps is to find a target customer — a person or business that needs a particular product or service that you could provide. You then profile your target customer (we do this in detail in the next chapter), and that profile becomes one of your idea filters. Now it's your turn to focus on the segments within your industry and spot some that look promising. Complete Action Step 18. Action Step 19 will help you spot opportunities in your industry segment. If this exercise draws a blank, go back and do some more brainstorming. Remember, the process of idea generating is not linear. You may have to bounce around for a while.

STEP 5: BRAINSTORM FOR SOLUTIONS

Brainstorming is a process used by many groups to generate fresh ideas: think tanks, middle managers, major corporations, and especially small businesses.

What follows is a short recap of the brainstorm held by Anne and Steve — with their best friends, Carol and Rick — as they started to transform problems into business opportunities.

"Anne and I have invited you guys over for a pizza and to get some ideas on business opportunities," Steve began.

"As you guys know," said Anne, "we are thinking about starting our own business. We have done all kinds of research and have decided to focus on the information industry. We have even identified a few hot segments. We want to brainstorm for more ideas and some solutions to industry problems."

The four spent the first hour throwing out ideas. Some of these did not appear at first to be going anywhere. Rick, for example, thought the company should design computer games and go head-to-head with Sega and Sony. Ideas kept coming out — virtual training, leveraged buyouts, virtual games,

Figure 3.4

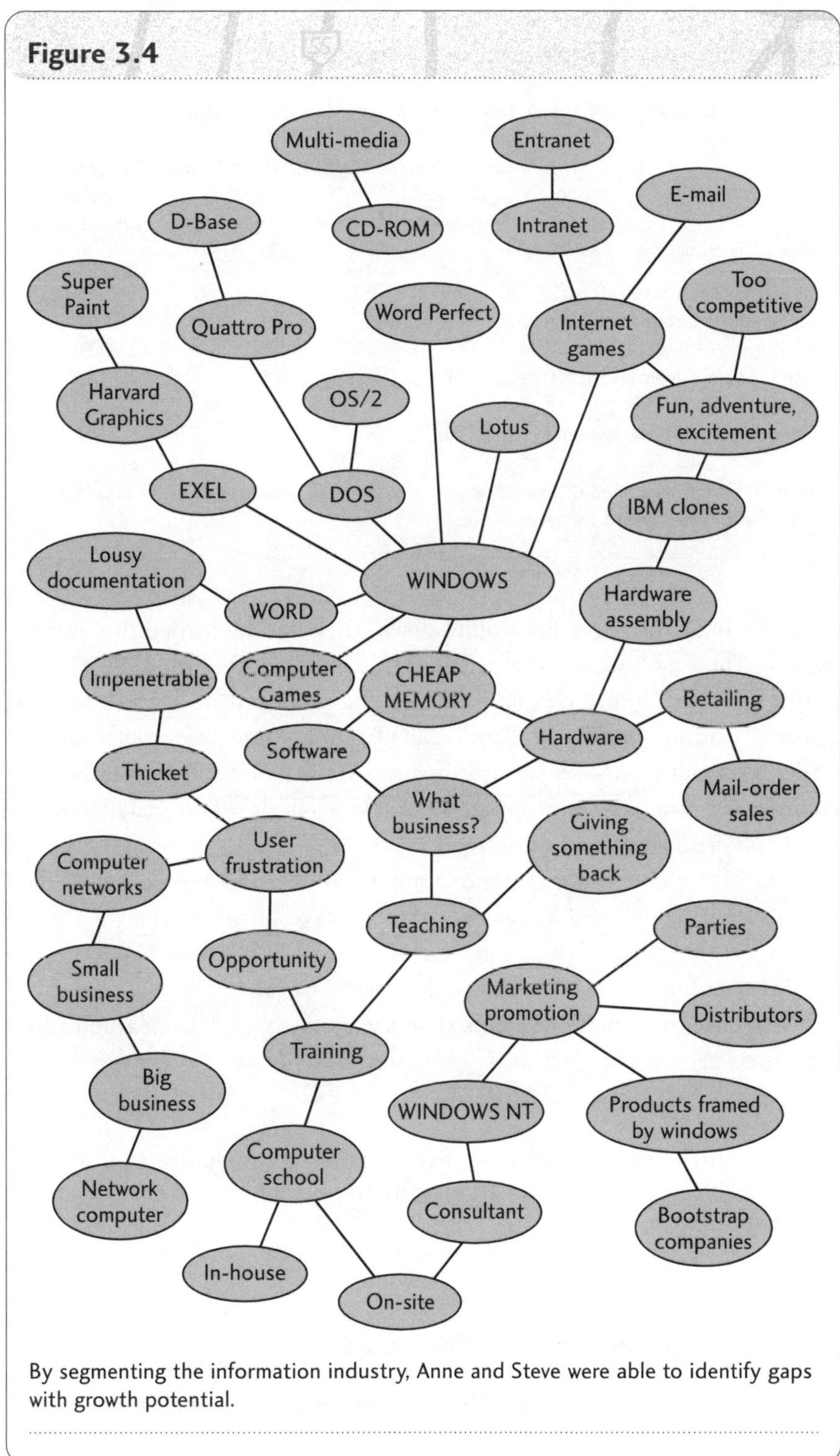

By segmenting the information industry, Anne and Steve were able to identify gaps with growth potential.

software manufacture, hardware assembly, retailing, Web design, and on and on. Anne kept writing them down on a flip chart. Finally she said, "I'm exhausted. Time for a break."

When they came back, it was Steve's turn to keep track of the ideas. He flipped to a clean sheet on the chart. Over the next hour, the four friends created a mind map loaded with ideas for a business (see, for example Figure 3.4).

Table 3.1 Small Business Gets Wired

According to Statistics Canada, the larger you get, the more technology you use.

Use of Technology	Small Firms (6–50 employees) %	Medium-sized Firms (51–250 employees) %	Large Firms (<250 employees) %
Network computer systems	44	75	95
Stand-alone computers	78	84	92
Packaged software	72	94	100
Use custom-developed software daily	41	73	89
Embedded computer systems	10	12	42

Source: Statistics Canada, "Small Business Gets Wired," adapted from *The Daily*, Cat. No. 11-001. Reprinted by permission.

As the brainstorm session wound down, they had identified two areas to explore. The first area was the installation of and training for network computing systems. Their target market would be small business. Steve had just finished reading about a Statistics Canada survey that said computer networks (especially LANs) were now being installed in small businesses at a record pace. Their second option was Intranet design and installation for small and medium-sized businesses.

"Well, this about wraps it up for tonight. Anne and I have a lot of ideas to mull over," concluded Steve. "We're going have to think about these two options."

"Wait a minute. How will you decide?" asked Carol.

"We'll have to do more research, then use a matrix grid. We learned about the matrix grid in class last week," Anne responded.

It's helpful — and in most cases necessary — to summarize after a brainstorming session so that you can identify the useful ideas. Let's summarize what happened in this session:

Box 3.6 Brainstorming — The Rules

Brainstorming is not a way of thinking but rather an environment in which innovative thinking can occur. In a brainstorming session, everyone is encouraged to contribute ideas. Stimulation is provided by the ideas of others. The goal is to come up with lots of ideas, some of which may seem far-fetched or even erroneous, and then, as momentum grows, to see where concepts develop. A key to brainstorming is to reserve judgement initially so that creativity is not stifled. Lastly, brainstorming must be conducted in an environment in which "anything goes." People must not be made to think that their ideas are silly or stupid. Negative statements or actions, reservations, or criticisms are not allowed.

1. Using brainstorming, the team identified problems and possible solutions.
2. Most ideas were good ideas.
3. The two ideas that looked best involved computer networks and Intranet systems.
4. It did not seem that Anne and Steve could pursue both ideas at once. They had two different target customers. So, one might have to go on the back burner. (This is not a bad thing. It is always helpful to have budding ideas in your pocket, since every product or service has a life cycle.)

Now that you understand what brainstorming is and what it can accomplish for a business, give it a try with your own business. Assemble your partners or friends and go for it. Action Step 20 gives you some directions.

ACTION STEP 20

Brainstorm for solutions.
Now you need to get really creative. Dig out the list of problems in your industry that you made in Action Step 19. Every problem can be turned into an opportunity.

You'll generate better ideas in the long run if you just let your imagination roll. Don't be concerned with a lot of logic and reason — not at this stage. You might begin with a quick overview of what you know so far and then slide into possible (and impossible?) solutions. A cassette recorder can be useful.

Have fun.

STEP 6: MESH POSSIBLE SOLUTIONS WITH OPPORTUNITIES IN THE MARKETPLACE

While some people like to use lists or mind maps for arriving at opportunities, others prefer a more systematic method. A **matrix grid** can provide the desired structure for decision making. After you have brainstormed some possible solutions, you need to improve your focus on them and evaluate them. The matrix grid in Figure 3.5 helped Steve and Anne do this. The next day, after their brainstorm with Carol and Rick, they reviewed the various criteria on the list. Then they ranked the top three in order of greatest importance and the bottom three in order of least importance. The top three were then assigned a value of three, while the bottom three were given a value of one. This way, each criterion did not receive the same value.

MATRIX GRID
a screen through which ideas are passed in order to find solutions

Figure 3.5

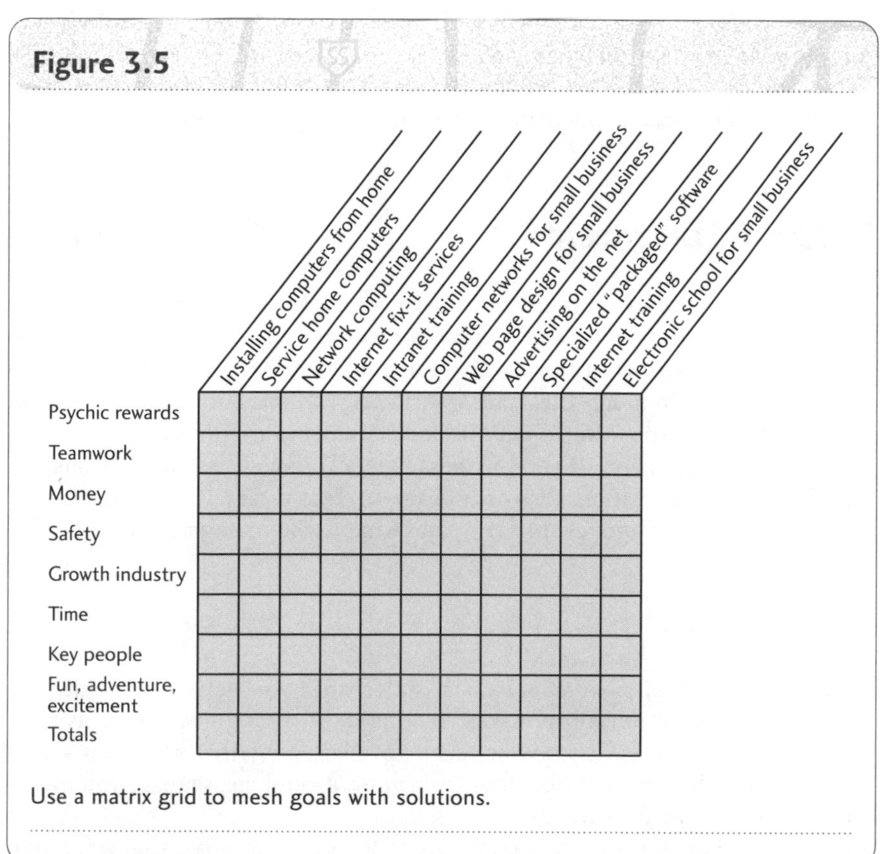

Installing computers from home
Service home computers
Network computing
Internet fix-it services
Intranet training
Computer networks for small business
Web page design for small business
Advertising on the net
Specialized "packaged" software
Internet training
Electronic school for small business
Psychic rewards
Teamwork
Money
Safety
Growth industry
Time
Key people
Fun, adventure, excitement
Totals

Use a matrix grid to mesh goals with solutions.

ACTION STEP 21

Mesh possible solutions with your goals and objectives, using a matrix grid.
A matrix analysis will help you focus, especially if you're working with a group and you have diverse objectives to satisfy. If you prepare a large grid and put it on the wall, all members of the team can participate.

Down the left side, list the goals you brainstormed in Action Step 16. Along the top, list the possible solutions you came up with in Action Step 20. Select a rating system to use for evaluating the match of each possible solution with each of your goals. It could be a ten-point scale or a plus-zero-minus system:

Plus (+) = 3
Zero (0) = 2
Minus (–) = 1

When you've rated all of the combinations, find the total for each column. The totals will indicate your best prospects. The rest is up to you.

ACTION STEP 22

Narrow the gaps and see your target customer emerge.
All right: you've found your segment and you've tested parts of it. Now you need to stay with this segment until you know whether or not it will work for you.

One way to keep concentrating is to make a simple sketch or list that sums up what you've learned so far. Figure 3.4 may help guide you. Use a large sheet of paper, because you need to consider all the important things you've learned here. Begin with your personal vision, values, and business goals and move on through a review of what has happened. After you've done your sketch, identify the gap in your industry that looks most promising for you.

The group voted on several of the possible solutions they brainstormed. When the numbers were tallied, they decided the network computer business was the preferred option. They liked the idea of working with small businesses. This segment was really starting to heat up. They would provide advice and consulting in computer networks. Their target market would be smaller, independent business that wanted growth. If they succeeded, the Intranet would be the next focus.

Now prepare a matrix grid and weigh your criteria to help you focus on the best course of action. Action Step 21 tells you how to do it.

STEP 7: TAKE STOCK AND FOCUS

What have you learned about the opportunity selection process? Before you answer this, take some time to rethink what you want to achieve in your small business. If you feel a little uneasy about how fast you've run the last couple of laps, perhaps it's because you haven't yet identified your industry. It's time to take stock.

What is your industry?

____

What is your market gap?

____

What are some opportunities for you?

____

____

Now, before you lose the feel for the process, try sketching a rough picture of your journey through your favourite industry. If it doesn't feel like home, you should sense it now. Action Step 22 will help you to do this. Now it's time to get started on writing a mission statement for your business.

Mission Statement

Now that you have identified your market opportunity — one that reflects your values — you need to think about a business mission.

Your personal vision and values give you guidance and direction in the conduct of your life. In much the same way, a business mission is a statement of your company's purpose and aims. Mission statements are normally connected to the values and vision of the business owner. In small business, a mission statement is concise (about 25 words or fewer), briefly describing the product or service, who the target customer is, and what niche or segment is the focus.

YOUR MISSION

Your mission is your road map. First, it states what you believe in — the difference that the organization makes. Second, it becomes a way of measuring your success as you evaluate your results over time against what you stated you wanted to do. Third, it becomes your promotional message, as you incorporate it as part of your printed material.

Peter Drucker, in his book, *The Practice of Management*, notes that we should think about a number of factors in developing a mission statement:[5]

1. *Customers.* Who is your target customer?
2. *Product or service.* What is your business all about — in a sentence or two?
3. *Geographic market.* Are you serving your local city, the province, Canada, or — if you are exporting — maybe even world markets?
4. *Concern for financial contribution and growth.* What returns do you expect on your investment and what growth pattern do you expect to achieve (e.g., growth of 5 percent per year)?
5. *Core values and beliefs.* Look back at your values in Box 3.1. Are these values consistent with what you want to do?
6. *Self-concept.* Because of knowledge and expertise, you may bring to the business a special skill that will give you a unique niche.
7. *Concern for public image and stakeholders.* Are you an environmentally friendly business, or will you be contributing a percentage of all sales to charity, or are you actively involved in your community?
8. *Concern for employees.* Are you planning to run your business on a team basis? Or will you alone be it?
9. *Technology and systems.* Does your business offer a value-added benefit by using technology or a particular system?

Your mission statement is unique. Some people capture their thoughts in a few words, some take pages. Some people express them in poems, some in music, and some in art. But in all cases, an empowering mission statement:[6]

- represents the deepest and best within you,
- fulfils the contribution your business will make, and
- deals with your vision and principle-based values.

For example, Anne and Steve's mission statement for their business might read like this:

To help growing small businesses improve their profitability, effectiveness, and long-term growth through the implementation of, and training in, computer networks.

Here are a few other examples of mission statements:

To own a flower and gift shop that specializes in highly stylized floral arrangements for "special occasions," and that services the local community.

To be a proud and profitable home-based business providing responsive and efficient word-processing services and laser-quality correspondence to local small businesses.

To sell environmentally friendly cleaning products to convenience stores in our city, to reduce the growing need for our dependence on chemicals

In some cases, the guiding principles of the company or owner are embedded in the mission statement. For example, the following six guiding principles are embedded in the Starbucks mission statement:

Starbucks Mission Statement[7]
Establish Starbucks as the premier purveyor of the finest coffee in the world while maintaining our uncompromising principles as we grow. The following six guiding principles will help us measure the appropriateness of our decisions:

1. *Provide a great work environment and treat each other with respect and dignity.*
2. *Embrace diversity as an essential component in the way we do business.*
3. *Apply the highest standards of excellence to the purchasing, roasting, and fresh delivery of our coffee.*
4. *Develop enthusiastically satisfied customers all of the time.*
5. *Contribute positively to our communities and our environment.*
6. *Recognize that profitability is essential to our future success.*

If you have been able to isolate an opportunity gap in your industry, it is now time to draft your mission statement. Complete Action Step 23.

ACTION STEP 23

Draft your mission statement.
In a short paragraph, describe the purpose or main goal of your business.

What is your product or service?
Who is your target customer?
What is the niche or market segment you aim to exploit?

You may also want to expand your statement by including your core set of values and beliefs, concern for stakeholders and the environment, or your concern for employee well-being.

Now go back and revisit your personal vision. Does your personal vision connect with your business mission? It should. If you are having trouble, here is one example:

Beatrice had a personal vision: "To live a life in which others would remember her with dignity and respect." Her business mission was "to be a respected flower and gift shop owner specializing in highly stylized floral arrangements for 'special occasions' and catering to her local community needs."

As her business mission, Beatrice wanted to be remembered with respect and dignity through her gift of flowers.

Your Strategy

STRATEGY
the broad program for achieving an organization's objectives and implementing its vision

A **strategy** is a broad program for achieving an organization's objectives and thus implementing its vision. It creates a unified direction for the organization in terms of its many objectives. It also guides those choices that determine the nature and direction of an organization.

Before you start developing the strategy for your business, it is helpful to have a context in which competitive strategy is formulated. Figure 3.6 presents a model developed by Professor Michael E. Porter of Harvard Business School. As you review the model, you'll see that the left side refers to "Factors Internal to the Company." You are required, as an entrepreneur, to look at your own strengths and weaknesses — after all, you are the company! Figure 3.6 helps you do that.

Your "Personal Values" will be contained in your value analysis and also in your mission statement. Don't take this section lightly, as it will be your internal guide to your overall business plan.

The right side of the competitive strategic model outlines the two major components to the "Factors External to the Company." "The Industry Opportunities and Threats" are critical to success and survival as a small business. As well, it is important to understand the "Broader Societal Expectations" — the trends discussed in Chapter Two that your business will face.

Figure 3.6 Context in Which Competitive Strategy Is Formulated

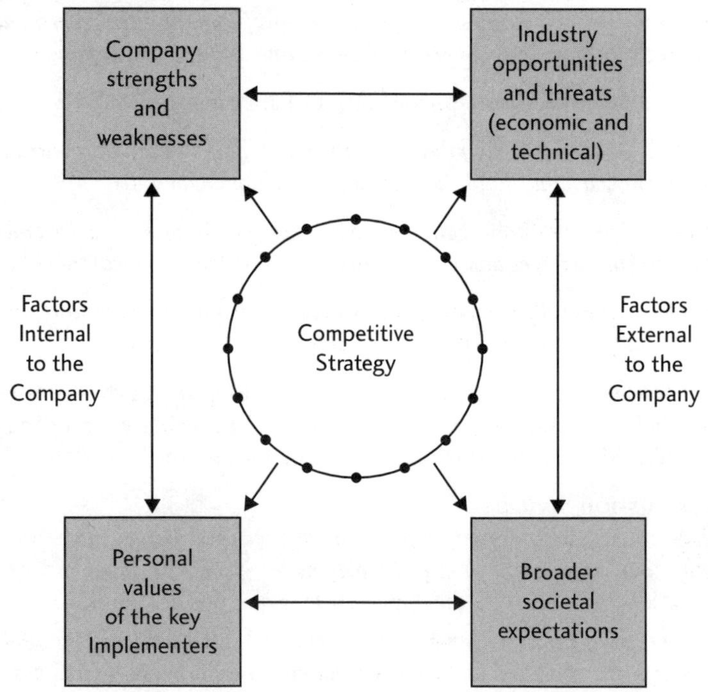

Use this model, developed by Michael E. Porter, to understand the context from which your business strategy will be formulated.

Source: Adapted with the permission of the Free Press, a Division of Simon & Schuster from *Competitive Advantage: Creating and Sustaining Superior Performance* by Michael E. Porter. Copyright © 1985 by Michael E. Porter.

To help you understand strategy, the following case study outlines how it actually works.

Med-Eng Systems Inc.[8]

Before land mines became a global cause, a Canadian engineering company was developing high-tech body suits to protect people who were dismantling the explosive devices.

Now, Med-Eng Systems Inc. hopes to capitalize on its early entry into the mine-removal market, after delegates of 120 countries met in December 1997 in Ottawa to sign a historic anti-land mines treaty.

"With the mine clearance [equipment], it's a new market, a bigger market," says Vince Crupi, executive vice-president of Med-Eng, which first built its reputation on high-tech bomb protection helmets.

"People are buying equipment to donate, so we're participating in trade shows and United Nations shows."

This potential breakthrough comes four years after Ottawa-based Med-Eng developed a full body suit and helmet to protect Canadian soldiers from land mine explosions in Bosnia. Two Canadian soldiers had already been killed by mines in Bosnia and the army wanted to end the casualties.

Today, about 90 percent of Med-Eng's revenue — projected at $7-million for fiscal 1997 — still comes from standard bomb disposal gear, but Mr. Crupi expects the mine suits to fuel future growth. More than 60 million mines are buried in former war zones around the world.

"Canada was the leading nation saying we wanted zero tolerance of death or injury [in mine clearance]," says Danny Gunn, a retired major who, in the early nineties, was responsible for finding a mine suit for the Canadian Armed Forces. "We're not at war. We don't want our people killed cleaning up somebody else's mess."

While armies are Med-Eng's most obvious clients, they only clear mines from land necessary for their operations, says Mr. Gunn, now an explosives and mine specialist with Med-Eng. The bigger jobs, including clearing fields and forests in Cambodia, Bosnia, and Lebanon, are being contracted out by the United Nations to private firms.

It's these customers that Med-Eng needs to meet its sales projections. While the suits — at a minimum price of $10 000 — are not cheap, Med-Eng is betting consumers will recognize quality and specialized design.

The strategy of Med-Eng Systems Inc. builds on the worldwide attention focussed on land mine disposal. What are the critical components of their strategy?

In a Nutshell

In the first few chapters, we encouraged you to come to grips with your personal vision and goals and to look at the industry trends with new eyes. In this third chapter, we want you to begin to match your personal vision, values, and goals with market needs. Here we provide you with a seven-step opportunity selection process, and encourage you to brainstorm and complete a matrix grid to help you get your personal vision in sync with your business mission. To illustrate how this process works, we followed the progress of Steve and Anne, who ended up deciding to start their business in the field of network computers. Next, we wanted you to begin thinking about your mission statement. In the final analysis, we hope that we have helped you connect your personal vision to a mission statement for a new business opportunity, and that you are on the way to establishing your strategy for achieving your vision.

ACTION STEP REVIEW

16 List your business goals for the next three years.
17 Research your favourite industry.
18 Identify three or four market gaps that look promising.
19 List problems that need solutions.
20 Brainstorm for solutions.
21 Mesh possible solutions with your goals and objectives, using a matrix grid.
22 Narrow the gaps and see your target customer emerge.
23 Draft your mission statement.

Think Points for Success

- ✓ Your business must reflect your personal values. They provide you with guidance and direction in the conduct of your business and life.
- ✓ Select an opportunity by using the seven-step opportunity selection process as a guide.
- ✓ Align your mission statement with your personal values. The statement must state the purpose and aim of your firm.
- ✓ Establish a strategy that attains your vision.

Business Plan Building Block

CURRENT POSITION AND FUTURE OUTLOOK (REFER TO EARLIER WORK IN CHAPTER TWO.)

You will need to explain your current position and future outlook for this business projected out three to five years. If you are planning for an existing business, you must perform a critical analysis of your current situation and how you will grow the business over the next few years.

Focus on how you are unique and how to build on your strengths. If this is a start-up venture, base your forecast on research and your plans to exploit your market niche.

You began this process in Chapter One. Now it's time to build, correct, and polish your first attempt.

My business is:

____

____

____

____

____

UNIQUENESS AND DIFFERENTIATION

It is important that you demonstrate that you are addressing an unfilled need. You are different and unique, and you understand the meaning of pricing and value from your potential customers' perspective.

YOUR BUSINESS IS UNIQUE BECAUSE ...

Your product is smaller, faster, neater, more flexible, lighter, more attractive, stronger, and so on. Or your service is quicker, more reliable, mobile. Your people are better trained, your location more convenient. Your prices are competitive and your business has many advantages over existing competition.

Nobody wants to hear about a "me too" business. Stress your differentiation, your position — and translate features into market-hungry benefits. It is important to show how you have an edge over the competition. Try to think in terms of a "personal niche monopoly."

____

____

____

____

____

MARKET OPPORTUNITIES

Based on your research, arrange the most promising opportunities in the marketplace according to the following categories:

1. New or emerging markets — gaps and niches.
2. Neglected customer needs.
3. Failing competitors
4. Complementary product mix.
5. Expanded use of existing facilities.
6. New geographical and international opportunities

Rank by priority order those that are most attractive now and up to five years forward.

Checklist Questions and Actions to Develop Your Business Plan

POSITIONING YOURSELF AS AN ENTREPRENEUR FOR MARKET OPPORTUNITIES

- ❑ How is your product or service addressing the needs of the target market and offering benefits?
- ❑ What are your business and personal values?
- ❑ Define your market niche.
- ❑ Define the idea filters you used to establish the business viability for your product or service.
- ❑ Complete your mission statement.
- ❑ Revisit and update your business goals and objectives under Checklist Questions and Actions on p. 48.
- ❑ Identify market segments that have market potential.
- ❑ List industry problems that your business may face, and how you would address them.

NOTES

1. Excerpted from "Clear Visions: The Top 40 Under 40," *The Financial Post Magazine*, April 3, 1997, p. 22. Reprinted by permission of *The Financial Post Magazine*.
2. Adapted from Industry Canada, *Connection and Strategies for Success: Participants Workbook*, 1990, p. 36. Reproduced with the permission of the Minister of Public Works and Government Services Canada, 1998.
3. Alex Tilley, March 27, 1995.

4. Personal contact with Art Coren, Kwantlen University College, June 1998.
5. Adapted from Peter F. Drucker, *The Practice of Management* (New York: Harper and Row, 1954).
6. Stephen R. Covey et al., *First Things First* (New York: Simon & Schuster Inc., 1994).
7. *Starbucks Mission Statement*, copyright 1996. Reprinted by kind permission of Starbucks Coffee Company.
8. Ijeoma Ross, "Body Suit Maker Finds Perfect Fit in Mines Treaty," *The Globe and Mail*, December 4, 1997, p. B11. Reprinted with permission from The Globe and Mail.

OTHER REFERENCES

Brennar, Charles D. Jr. *Proactive Customer Service*. New York: AMACOM Publishing, 1997.

Covey, Stephen R. et al. *First Things First*. New York: Simon & Schuster, Inc., 1994.

Compuserve, Dialog, Dow Jones News/Retrieval, and The Source are a few of the major database distributors you can access with a PC and a modem. All these services can provide you with an excellent way to do initial and ongoing research for both general and specific data. Costs are relatively low.

Crawford, Michael G. "The Seven Deadly Marketing Sins." *Profit*, January/March 1997, pp. 32–35.

Farber, Barry G. *State of the Art Selling*. Franklin Lakes, NJ: Career Press, 1995.

Gershman, Michael. *Getting It Right the Second Time*. Reading, MA: Addison-Wesley, 1991.

Hutchinson, Brian. "Merchants of Boom." *Canadian Business*, May 1997, pp. 39–48.

Johansson, Johny K. and Ikujiro Nonaka. *Relentless: The Japanese Way of Marketing*. New York: Harper Business, 1997.

Newell, Frederick. *Learn More About Customers and Use What You Learn*. New York: McGraw-Hill, 1997.

Sterne, Jim. *Customer Service on the Internet*. New York: Wiley Computer Publications, 1996.

four

Profiling Your Target Customer

Figure 4.1 Chapter Four will help you complete part B of your business plan, "The Market and the Target Customer."

BUSINESS PLAN BUILDING BLOCK

This chapter will help you begin collecting information to understand, develop a profile of, and connect with your target customer.

LEARNING OPPORTUNITIES

After reading this chapter, you should be able to:

- Understand that your key to survival in small business is the target customer.
- Use your intuition to forecast what will happen in your industry.
- Use primary and secondary research to profile your target customer.
- Simplify the messages you communicate through your business.
- Discover how popular magazines aim at the target customer.
- Match your target customer with what he or she reads, watches, and listens to.
- Become more aware of, and start being on the look-out for, potential partnerships, alliances, and associations.
- Recognize the market and the target customers who are about to surface.
- Gather critical market input from target customers through surveying field interviews.

During the late 1990s, small business retailers in Canada had a rough ride. Retailing was not a growth market (see Figure 4.2) — just as Canadian giants Consumers Distributing and K-Mart found out. Growth, if any, was mostly in the "big box" format imported from the United States with the likes of Home Depot, Price Club/Costco, and Wal-Mart.

One small Canadian retailer who bucked the retail trend and seemed to thrive over the 1990s was Just Kid'n Children's Wear Ltd. of Langley, B.C. Owned by the brother-sister team of Kelly Cahill and Colleen Hazelwood, Just Kid'n was a Profit 100 success that racked up sales of over $1.5 million in 1997 — up from just over $200 000 six years earlier.

According to the owners, the major reasons for their success were threefold. First, they latched on to a growth niche in the mature retail market. Their target was the so-called **echo boom**, the junior baby boom of the mid-1980s during which baby boomers finally decided to have kids of their own.

Second, they knew who their target customer (TC) was and what the TC wanted. Of their customers, 90 percent were women: 70 percent parents and 30 percent grandparents, relatives, and friends. They ranged in age from 25 to 45, and they tended to have mid to high incomes. According to Hazelwood, their customers were well-off boomers who were prepared to spend more for high quality, hard-wearing, designer clothes for their kids.

ECHO BOOM
period in the mid-1980s during which baby boomers finally decided to have kids of their own

ACTION STEP PREVIEW

24 Use your new eyes on some mass-market magazines to develop your profiling reflexes.

25 Research specific magazines to profile your TC.

26 Profile three firms using the "Canadian Company Capabilities" Internet site.

27 Back up your profile with primary data you collect by interviewing and surveying prospective target customers.

Third, everyone at Just Kid'n constantly kept in touch with the TC. Simply knowing who the customer is and what they want is not enough. The heart of the Just Kid'n strategy is a customer list with over 100,000 target customer names, addresses, and phone numbers. This database enables store managers to send a handwritten letter of thanks to the top 20 customers for their business and offer them discount coupons. Says Cahill: "With this database we can develop a relationship with the customer, who will have a good feeling about us and want to come back and shop again and again." The result has been pure gold — 80 percent of the company's business is repeat.[1]

The Thumper Mini-Pro is a $300 hand-held therapeutic massage device. Wellness Innovations Corp., founded by a Markham, Ont., chiropractor, conceived and sells the Thumper throughout North America. Interestingly enough, Wellness neither designs nor manufactures its product. Instead, it relies on **outsourcing** — a fast growing trend in which a company farms out one or more of its in-house operations to outside specialists. For example, the design and manufacturing of the Thumper was outsourced to Baranti Group Inc. Baranti, in turn, outsourced the manufacturing to another firm. "We're their virtual R&D and their virtual manufacturing company," says Barry Papoff, president of Baranti.

OUTSOURCING
farming out one or more company operations to specialists

This outsourcing trend has given birth to a wave of entrepreneurs and tiny companies — niche players like Baranti — whose sole purpose is to provide services or products on a contract basis to other businesses. Outsourcing has become a way of life for many companies, large and small, who have stripped away all their functions except their so-called "core competencies." The target customers of companies like Baranti are other businesses, not the end users, as was the case for Just Kid'n. Their success depends on their ability to profile and ultimately to satisfy the needs of other business.[2]

The major focus of the last chapter was the product or service. Your prime concerns there were the following: "Do I have a product or service that is in a growth segment or a growth market?" and "Are my business goals consistent with my own personal values, goals, and long-term vision?" By now, we hope you have some pretty solid ideas as to what products or services are right for you. In the old way of thinking, entrepreneurs would have next focussed their attention on the basic features of the product, such as size, colour, or price. We call this old view a "product-push" mentality, and it goes like this: "I think that there's a market there somewhere, and all I have to do is to produce what I think to be a quality product at a competitive price, and the market will respond with a sale."

Most marketers tell us that a product push strategy does not work well in today's marketplace. If you want to increase your chances of being both happy and rich, we suggest a new approach, one that emphasizes the "pull factors" of the market. The key to getting your product or service to the marketplace is to determine what the customer wants through a customer profile and then adapt or create a product or service to satisfy this want or need. You design your business around what the customer wants rather than try to make the customer purchase what you want to produce.

The market pull approach explained, to a large degree, the success of Just Kid'n and Baranti Group in the opening vignettes. These thriving companies

Figure 4.2 Retail Sales, Canada and the United States

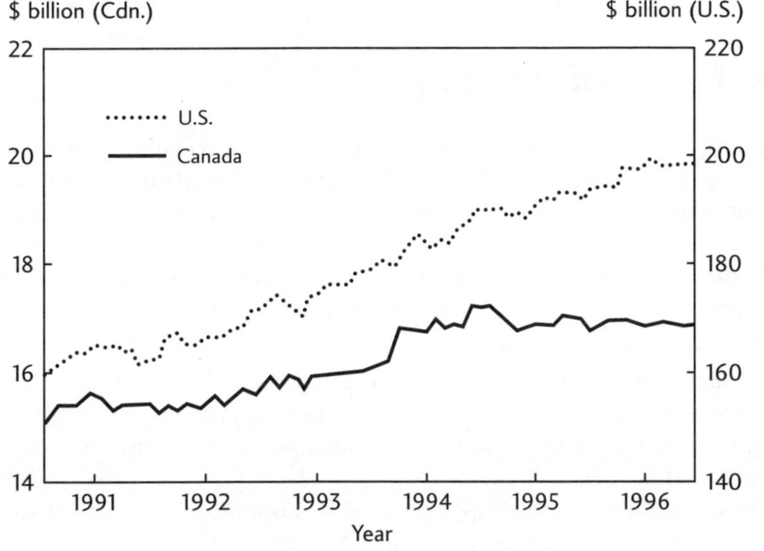

In 1992 dollars, seasonally adjusted

Unlike the U.S., the Canadian retail industry did not see much growth during the late 1990s.

Source: © Datastream International Limited, 1996. ALL RIGHTS RESERVED. Reprinted by permission.

knew who their target customers were and what they wanted. In this chapter, we want you to start thinking about how you can develop a market pull strategy. This means you will have to begin with a customer profile. But don't make it too narrow. For example, one approach to defining a market is to determine a customer's needs or applications: "We are in the market of cleaning dishes."

Box 4.1 They Said It

"As long as you keep collecting and updating names, a database can continue to perform for you, year-round. The only limit is your ability to come up with relevant and imaginative uses for your list, and that depends mainly on your ability to think up legitimate excuses for contacting your customers, and new, value-laden reasons why they should come back to your business."

RICK SPENCE, editor, *Profit* magazine

Source: Rick Spence, *Secrets of Success from Canada's Fastest-Growing Companies* (Toronto: John Wiley & Sons Canada, Ltd., 1997), p. 90.

Box 4.2 Bookmark This

An excellent example of what the Web is good for at a niche retailer level: Brigittine Monks Fudge at <http://greatbend.com/brentw/fudge.htm>.

Another is to define it by product: "We make dishwashers." Still another focus is on a customer group: "We sell to restaurants." View your market from multiple perspectives.[3]

The Power of Profiling

TARGET CUSTOMER (TC)
a person, type of person, or business that has the highest probability of buying your product or service

PROFILING
describing the needs and behaviour of your target customer

Your **target customer** (TC) is your key to survival in small business. For that reason, you need to do a profile of your customer. **Profiling** is about describing the needs and behaviour of your TC. In this chapter, we'll focus on specific profiling techniques and sources to help you understand that elusive customer. But first, let's take a look at the different kinds of target customers. Entrepreneurs that we have known tell us you should be watching for at least three target customer groups:

1. *Primary.* This TC is perfect for your business and could be a heavy user.
2. *Secondary.* This one almost slips away before you can focus the camera. Sometimes your secondary TC will lead you to the third customer, who is invisible at first.
3. *Invisible.* This customer appears after you open the doors, after you have the courage to go ahead and start your business.

Your primary and secondary target customers are the only customers that you can see right now. However, once you open your business, a new customer may arrive on the scene, and you must always be ready to change so that you can take advantage of new market opportunities. In this chapter, we focus on your primary and secondary customers, but we encourage you to always remember that there are elusive "invisible" customers — the ones that seem to come out of the woodwork once you start your business.

There are two basic types of customer profiles:

1. Consumer (or end-user)
2. Business-to-business (or supply chain)

We will begin with a consumer profile.

CONSUMER OR END-USER PROFILE

DEMOGRAPHICS
key characteristics of a group of people, such as age, sex, income, and where they live

PSYCHOGRAPHICS
segmenting of the population by lifestyle behaviour

In some cases, your TC may be the end-user or consumer. This was the situation for Just Kid'n in the opening vignette. Just Kid'n sold its products directly to the customer through its retail outlets. If your "heavy" TC is the consumer or end-user, your customer profile will require **demographics** — the segmenting and statistical analysis of your TC by age, sex, income, education, location, and the like. Recall, for example, that in the case of Just Kid'n, the primary TCs were parents, mainly women between the ages of 25 and 45. To profile your heavy customer, you'll have to use demographics. But you'll also need a new tool called **psychographics** — the first-hand intuitive insight into lifestyle, buying habits, patterns of consumption, and attitudes. Just Kid'n's psychographic target was the high-income boomers who were prepared to pay more for quality, hard-wearing, designer clothes. Although demographics is an important profiling tool, marketers today are beginning to place more emphasis on the reasons for people's buying behaviour. Let's step back for a moment and understand the reasons for this recent marketing trend.

We've talked about the importance of demographics and how the boomers, in particular, have and will continue to affect market trends. In a strange way, this "bulging" phenomenon (social change), combined with our knowledge-based/change economy (economic change), has forced marketers to ask why people purchase products or services, not simply who is buying. Although the demographics of the population are still predictable, the lifestyle and buying habits are no longer tied to demographics. Today, we have to know *why* people are buying. For example, two adults with a combined income of $75 000, but with no children (**D**ouble-**I**ncome-**N**o-**K**ids) have different spending patterns than two adults earning $75 000 to $125 000, but with four children. Why? Because these two groups have completely different wants and values. People now buy products and services that reflect the needs of their lifestyles, not necessarily their sex, age, or income. The whys and wants of consumer purchases are what psychographics is all about. It is a process of segmenting the population by lifestyles and values, recognizing that people in each segment or slice have different reasons for making a purchase.

There are a number of "propriety" psychographic models in use in North America. Two of the most prominent are the VALS (value and lifestyle model) from SRI International in the United States and the Goldfarb model, which is Canadian but has also been adapted in the United States. We'll focus here on the Goldfarb model, which classifies the Canadian population into six psychographic segments. Some key characteristcs are shown in Table 4.1 and Box 4.3. Note that almost 50 percent of Canadians are either "Day-to-Day Watchers" (22 percent) or "Joiner-Activists" (27 percent). Between 1988 and

Table 4.1 Key Characteristics for Each of the Six Goldfarb Psychographic Segments

	% of Canadian Population 1988	1996
Day-to-Day Watchers — Traditional values Research purchases. Need to be comfortable with products before purchasing. Early followers as opposed to leaders.	22	22
Old-Fashioned Puritans — Very conservative and traditional Home and family oriented. Heavily insured. Tend to resist change.	11	13
Disinterested Self-Indulgents — Hedonistic Risk takers. Like to be on the leading edge of product innovation. Heavy impulse buyers. Travel.	10	15
Joiner-Activists — Leading edge thinkers Willing to spend especially on clothes. Day-to-Day Watchers follow this segment. Heavy pleasure trip takers. Like new technology.	24	27
Responsible Survivors — Cautious, not risk-takers Enjoy self-rewards. Accept direction well. Brand loyal. Heavy TV viewers.	14	11
Aggressive Achievers — Confident, success oriented Want to be leaders. Love status-signalling goods. Bargain hunters. Flaunt material possessions.	12	12

Source: *Goldfarb Psychographics: A New Dimension in Data Analysis*, July 1988; and *The Goldfarb Report*, 1996. Reprinted by permission of Goldfarb Consultants.

Box 4.3 Goldfarb Psychographic Profile of the Adult Canadian

Day-to-Day Watcher:
Percent of Adult Population: 22%
Characteristics:

1. Followers, not leaders.
2. Family-oriented, particularly when related to their purchasing decisions.
3. Socializing is limited to close friends and relatives.
4. Most entertainment done at home.
5. Patronize well-known brands, are often the market leaders, and are rarely moved to something new.
6. Extremely brand loyal because they doubt their own capabilities and react positively to authority.
7. Shop at established stores.
8. Not buyers of generic products.

Joiner-Activist
Percent of Adult Population: 27%
Characteristics:

1. Quest for on-going self-improvement.
2. They want change, not the status quo.
3. They identify with the underdog brand.
4. Willing to experiment.
5. Actively join organizations.
6. Busy and happy people.
7. The most rational decision makers and most liberal.
8. Prime purchase motivator is information.
9. Not strong impulse buyers.
10. They are into nature, nutrition, exercise.
11. Like home entertainment because they enjoy things like cooking.
12. Away from home a lot, pursuing various activities.
13. Success is measured on a personal basis, not in a social context.
14. Not competitive from a business perspective, but excel in recreational and personal endeavours.
15. Product quality is more important than price, but only for high-interest items.
16. New products will be accepted if accompanied by strong selling arguments. Heavy into magazines, newspapers, but not TV.

Source: *The Goldfarb Report*, 1996. Reprinted by permission of Goldfarb Consultants.

1996, the percentage of "Disinterested Self-Indulgent" risk-takers increased dramatically from 10 percent to 15 percent.

Let's return to Just Kid'n for a moment. To a large degree, psychographics explained the reasons for the success of this small niche player. Its target market is Goldfarb's largest, and growing, psychographic group — the Joiner-Activists. Note the characteristics of this group as shown in Table 4.1 and Box 4.3. With their extensive customer list, Just Kid'n was able to target its products to the "Activists" lifestyle needs.

Several Canadian companies can provide you with a psychographic or lifestyle profile for a specific area. For example, Compusearch can provide lifestyles data by postal code. These kinds of data can be obtained in published form for large areas, but when it comes to a specific neighbourhood, you have to pay for the data on that. The cost can range from hundreds of dollars to hundreds of thousands of dollars, depending on the detail you might need. When it's all said and done, you will probably have to do a lot of your own research to get a psychographic handle on your target customer — mainly because of cost factors. This is your opportunity to practise your new-eyes research and learn why people buy things. At worst, you will have fun playing marketing detective.

Now, if you just can't afford the cost of contracting out a psychographic analysis, don't fret. This may be your opportunity to piggyback all of the information gathered for use by media sources. Let's see what information can be gleaned from the media.

Box 4.4 Target Market — The Nexus Generation

Businesses, governments, or other organizations trying to reach Generation X soon come up against a major roadblock: no one knows *exactly* who or what Generation X is!

According to some, Generation X is all about the year you were born: 1963, 1969, or (depending on who's talking), 1976. On the one hand, Generation Xers have been described as wanderers, slackers, and couch-potatoes interested only in watching *Simpsons* reruns. On the other hand, they have been portrayed as the most conservative, hard-working generation since those born during the Great Depression. Similarly, some experts say Xers are serious about marriage, while others see the X-generation as a group reluctant to make commitments.

Robert Barnard feels the term Generation X, as a label, is widely over-used, ambiguous, and a cliché. "It means too many things to too many different people," says Barnard, a 29-year-old Xer from Toronto. Barnard founded d~Code Inc., a small consulting firm that helps companies and govnerment departments better understand what makes 18- to 34-year-olds tick. In place of the term "Generation-X," d~Code uses the phrase "Nexus generation" to characterize this target group. Nexus means a bridge or connection; in this case, the connection is between the industrial age and the birth of the information age.

d~Code helps its private- and public-sector clients decipher the aspirations, preferences, and unique features of the age group born at this critical nexus. It works with them to design marketing, human resource, or public policy strategies that connect with the Nexus generation, consumers, employees, and citizens. In the process, d~Code strives to build bridges across generations.

According to d~Code, there are a few psychographic likes and dislikes of the Nexus generation:

- For Nexus, financial compensation is not as important as it is to the preceding generations. Nexus ranks quality of life (e.g., longer vacations) and opportunities for on-the-job training ahead of a whopping paycheque.
- Nexus is more sceptical and has less confidence in traditional institutions such as the Church, the University, the nuclear family, the State, and the Corporation.
- Nexus is more media-savvy, techno-literate, educated, and worldly than any previous generation.
- Nexus is composed of "experience seekers" who put off marriage, kids, and house payments longer than those in previous generations.
- Nexus is more comfortable — and less anxious — about change.
- Nexus makes up about 32 percent of the voting population.

Sources: Based on personal correspondence with d~Code Inc.; and adapted from Gayle MacDonald, "The Eyes and Ears of a Generation," *The Globe and Mail*, February 4, 1997, B11. Reprinted with permission from The Globe and Mail. Visit d~Code's Web site at <http://www.d~code.com>.

WHAT WE CAN LEARN FROM MEDIA SOURCES

Mina Cohen was an archaeologist and teacher by training. She had worked on numerous excavations and had been a pedagogic adviser of External Affairs and a teacher at a local high school. Despite her talents and extensive training, it seemed that she was always worried about her next job. The market just wasn't there for her talents. She even had to take a few secretarial jobs to supplement her income.

One day in late summer, she decided to take control of her life and entered a small business program at a local college. At first the course seemed incomprehensible. Techniques such as brainstorming and mind mapping were foreign to her; up to this point, she had been taught, in a "right-brained" manner, to be logical. In the end, however, she decided to persist and stay in the course. Finally, after a few group brainstorming sessions and extensive primary and secondary research, she had an idea: Why not offer archaeological excursions? She would be in the "holidays-with-a-purpose" business. But who were her target customers?

One fall evening, she was curled up, browsing her favourite magazine, *Equinox*. It suddenly occurred to her that these readers might just be her target market. After all, this was *her* favourite magazine. That's when it hit her. Why not send away for the publisher's secondary data on its target readership? In less than a week, the information arrived.

After a quick study of the *Equinox* secondary data, she began to realize that her idea had a real chance to make it. Her primary target market would be well-off couples who wanted to travel and learn. The publisher's data confirmed her intuition and ideas based on her ad-count analysis. Now she was sure that she had a growing market for her services. Her target customers were affluent (they could pay for her services), influential (they would tell and influence others about them), active (they liked travelling and learning), and increasing in number (a large segment would be boomers aged 25 to 49). It didn't take her long to summarize the demographic and psychographic information from the publisher, which would become an important part of the marketing section of her business plan.

As we learned from Mina Cohen, an easy way to understand the power of profiling is to analyze media sources that are aimed at different target markets.

Most, if not all, of the major media sources have conducted extensive research on the demographic and psychographic profiles of their target customer. In many cases, these profiles are available through media kits from the advertising departments of the media sources. For example, if your target customer were travel oriented, you could ask a travel-related magazine for its readership profile. The key here is, if you know which media sources your target customer reads, listens to, or watches, you can get in-depth profiles from these media companies because they need to know this information for their advertising.

In this section, we focus on magazines (while still recognizing the Internet as an important media source). However, you can take advantage of almost any of the media — especially commercial ones — because of the useful information contained in ads. We could just as easily expand our discussion to include TV programs and radio stations and, to a lesser extent, books and movies.

Often, we walk past magazines without giving them a sideways glance. That's unfortunate, because magazines hold the key to many questions about marketing. One way to regard a magazine is as a glossy cover wrapped around pages of ads and editorial copy. With new eyes, however, you can see that a mass-market magazine exists because it is a channel to the subconscious of a certain type of reader.

That knowledge is power.

What can you learn about target markets, consumption patterns, and buying power from the advertisements in a magazine? Put yourself in an analytical frame of mind. Begin by counting the ads. Then notice the types of products that dominate the ads; these ads are probably aimed at the heavy users of those products. Next, study the models; they are fantasy images with which the target customer is expected to identify, connect, remember. The activities pictured in the ads enlarge the fantasy, and the words link it to real life. A good ad becomes a slice of life, a picture that beckons the customer inside, toward the product.

We took an issue of *Equinox* (it has a carefully profiled reader) and did a new-eyes analysis. After we looked at the data, we drew a few conclusions. We developed categories as we went along (one of the nice things about new-eyes research is that you can expand the model as you collect data). Here is what we looked for:

- total number of ads one-third page or larger
- ads aimed at heavy users (type of products that are advertised the most)
- large ads (two pages or more)
- demographics models (estimated age, occupation, sex)
- main activities depicted
- objective depicted (including mail order ads, if any)
- message the media is trying to convey

New-eyes research helped us develop a demographic and psychographic profile of the average *Equinox* reader. The target reader seemed to be our classic Joiner-Activist (see Box 4.3). The ads implied that the target audience was affluent, influential, and active. The TCs were socially active and loved to travel, especially out of the country. Into health and recreation, they were well educated and relied heavily on new technology and electronic toys for information and leisure pursuits. They lived in suburbia and took pride in their homes as a place to entertain and relax with friends. There seemed to be an equal split between male and female readership. Most readers appeared to be age 25 to 50, married (or family oriented), with a family income exceeding $40 000. We checked our research with the display ad department people at *Equinox*, who sent a detailed demographic and psychographic profile of their typical customer — and yes, that person turned out to be the Joiner-Activist (see for example, Table 4.2).

In addition to magazines, customer profiles are also available from newspapers and radio and TV stations. The point is, media advertisers spend lots of money on trying to get the attention of their prospective target customers. We can benefit from this big business advertising. Action Step 24 will help you get a feel for media advertising through your new-eyes research. After practising new-eyes research in your particular area of interest, it's time to focus your attention on some specific media sources. Use Action Step 25 to conduct research on your target customer at little or no cost to you.

ACTION STEP 24

Use your new eyes on magazines that would better help you understand your business idea.

Study some magazines and their target readers. Then do a comparative analysis, following the example of our analysis of *Equinox*. Glance quickly at each magazine's cover. What qualities does it project? Flip through the magazine. What strikes your eye? Are the ads aimed at men? At women? At teens? At seniors? At everyone? What appears to be the age range of the target customer? The income range? Is the marketing effort national or regional?

You're just beginning to look at magazines as marketing tools, so you can start anywhere. Begin with magazines in your home, or buy a couple at a newsstand or drugstore. Ask the above questions about each one.

The next time you're in a store where magazines are sold, observe shoppers at the magazine rack. Note which magazines they buy. How many of these purchases could you have predicted? Record your observations in your adventure notebook. If you have a chance, interview a couple of these magazine buyers. Ask them why they bought what they did. Use what they say to build reader profiles in your mind. Without being too obvious, collect as much demographic data as you can on these shoppers. Could any of them be your target customers?

BUSINESS-TO-BUSINESS PROFILE

The outsourcing trend of the 1990s has given birth to thousands of companies or individuals whose sole purpose is providing services or products, on

ACTION STEP 25

Research specific magazines in your business area.
Choose at least two magazines that you think your target customer would read. Begin by conducting some new-eyes research, following the example of our analysis of *Equinox*. What strikes your eye? Are the ads aimed at men? At women? At teens or seniors? What appears to be the age range of the target customer? What's the income range? What Goldfarb psychographic group are they targeting? What message are they trying to convey?

Next, turn your attention to primary research. Interview magazine buyers. Ask them why they buy the magazine. Use what they say to add to your reader profile. Without being too obvious, collect as much demographic and psychographic data as you can on these shoppers. Could any of them be your target customer?

Now we want you to do some secondary research. Using your business letterhead, write to the magazines' display advertising departments. Ask for media kits and reader profiles. (If you don't have stationery yet, or if you are in a hurry, see if you can contact them over the Internet or give them a call.)

When the profiles arrive, check them out. How close were your new eyes and primary research profiles? Are you starting to get a clearer picture of who your target customer is and what she or he wants?

Table 4.2 Summary of *Equinox* Readership Profile

Demographic Profile	National Average %	*Equinox* %
Household income: $50,000+	42	56
Occupation		
White collar	25	48
Education		
College graduate or more	43	58
Age		
25-49	47	49
Marital Status		
Married/living together	57	51
Sex		
Male/female	49/51	53/47
Psychographic Profile		
Joiner-Activists who: entertain for business travel on business spend money on high-tech equipment travel for pleasure are socially and physically active	24	35

Source: PMB Print Measurement Bureau PMB 98. Reprinted by permission.

a contract basis, to other businesses. As a result, many small businesses do not deal directly with the final consumer. Instead, they are a sub-contractor and part of the so-called supply chain. Suppose, for a moment, that you decide to start your own editing business. Your target customer may be a publisher, whose customers may be university and college faculty and teaching staff, whose customers are the consumer — the student. As an editor, you have become part of the supply chain in the production of a book. Your target customer will not be the consumer or end-user (the student); it will be another business or supplier (in this case, a publisher). As a sub-contractor, you will need to profile other businesses — target customers — that could use your services.

As a member of the supply chain, your ultimate goal is to create partnerships, joint ventures, alliances, or associations with your target customer. Rick Spence, in his analysis of Canada's fastest-growing Profit 100 companies, concluded that these types of associations were a key offense weapon of fast-growth companies in the nineties, helping them to:[4]

- develop better products
- stretch their marketing dollars
- reach more customers
- obtain more feedback on their products or services
- provide better customer service
- extend their operations around the block or around the world

Ten tips for developing and nurturing a successful alliance are shown in Box 4.5. You'll want to keep these in mind, but first you should start a list of possible TCs. You'll need to conduct business profiles of potential partners or business associates. There are all kinds of secondary information you can draw on. In the next few chapters, you'll learn about a number of "hard copy"

Box 4.5 Ten Tips for Joint Ventures and Strategic Alliances

Successful business alliances are like standing on one foot: easier to start than to maintain. Here are ten tips from Canada's fastest-growing companies on developing and nurturing the most productive joint ventures and strategic alliances possible.

1. **Do your homework.** Assess your organization's strengths and weaknesses. Know where you want to go, and then identify the areas where you need help. Research the market to learn who can help you reach your goals.
2. **Think win-win.** Before you propose an alliance or joint project to another organization, ask yourself, "What's in it for them?"
3. **Feel out potential partners.** Make sure your potential associates share your values and level of commitment. As a number of Profit 100 entrepreneurs commented, you should also like your associates. Today potential alliance associates have to go through an intensive two-way, two-day interview to determine if there is a good fit both strategically and operationally.
4. **Put the best available person on the project.** Your associates and allies deserve quick access to the relevant decision makers.
5. **Put it in writing.** Spell out your mutual expectations and responsibilities in a contract. Determine allocation of costs. Both sides should obtain legal advice.
6. **Set measurable objectives and realistic deadlines.** Nothing spoils a partnership faster than a perception that one side is letting the other down. Both sides need ways of determining that the other associate is doing its share of the work.
7. **Stay in touch**. Keep open lines of communication with your partners. They can be formal (regular reports) or informal ("let's meet for coffee").
8. **Keep tabs.** Use regular feedback sessions to review the project's progress. Is it meeting the goals of both parties? If not, how can you fix things?
9. **Do it right.** Your associates expect you to give a joint project your best shot. If you can't, let them know. Internally, your goal should be to make your associate the real winner; that will help you snare more joint projects in future.
10. **Exit stage left.** Before forming an alliance, determine how either side can get out.

Source: Rick Spence, *Secrets of Success from Canada's Fastest-Growing Companies* (Toronto: John Wiley & Sons Canada, Ltd., 1997), pp. 117–18. Reprinted with permission of the author.

sources, such as Fraser's Canadian Trade Directory. For now, to get you started, we want to introduce you to what we think is the key source of business information, "Canadian Company Capabilities," which can be found on Industry Canada's Web site, Strategis at <http://strategis.ic.gc.ca>. Connecting to Canadian Company Capabilities will help you:

- Locate a list of your potential target customers
- Promote your new business venture
- Provide market research
- Locate Canadian suppliers
- Discover potential partnerships and associations
- Research your competition
- Uncover export opportunities

The database contains over 35 000 company profiles and over 200 000 products, services, and technologies. As of 1998, this free Industry Canada on-line service allows you to search for and profile your potential TC by

ACTION STEP 26

Profile three firms using the "Canadian Company Capabilities" Internet site.
The Strategis "Canadian Company Capabilities" Web site at <http://strategis.ic.gc.ca> allows you three ways to profile a company — complete, short, or custom.

As of 1998, a complete profile of a company contains the following information:

- Legal name
- Operating name
- Source (where the information originated)
- Company ownership (Canadian or foreign)
- Mailing address, telephone number, e-mail address
- URL (Web address)
- Language
- Company profile
- Primary and alternative industry
- Year established and number of employees
- Export sales
- Exporting (yes or no)
- Date updated
- List of contacts
- Products/services/technologies
- Interest in alliances (foreign and domestic)
- Countries exporting to or interested in exporting to

Go to the site and click on "Canadian Company Capabilities." Select three companies that could be your target customer and carry out a "complete profile" of each of these firms. Just follow the instructions on the site.

If your target customer is not another business, or you're still not sure exactly who your TC is, we suggest you use this Action Step to practise your profiling skills. It is a great source to learn about your competition. Select any three companies to profile and begin learning about the power of the Internet. You may also want to try a "custom" profile and see what happens.

product, geography, or activity. When you are ready to start your business, you will want to register your company in the Canadian Company Capabilities database and promote your products or services worldwide. For now, we want you to learn about this amazing Web site, get some practice in profiling potential target companies, and begin learning about the power of the Internet. You will even need this source when it comes time to research your competition. Complete Action Step 26.

Primary Research Can Help Too

Secondary sources of demographic, psychographic, or business profiling information may be enough to allow you to get a fairly accurate profile of your target customer. Chances are, though, that you'll need to test your profile against reality. Field interviewing and surveying are two important primary research tools that can help you get a more accurate profile of your target customer.

FIELD INTERVIEWING TARGET CUSTOMERS

A lot of people go into small business because they don't have much choice. Many of them have to learn new skills and learn them fast. Fortunately, entrepreneurs tend to be bright, creative, and hard-working. Julia Gonzales is a good example.

"It's no secret that I was distressed when my husband was transferred. I didn't blame him wanting the transfer; I would have wanted it, too. But I had a terrific job as manager of a full-line baby furniture and bedding store, and to keep both job and husband I'd have had to commute over 160 kilometres daily, five days a week. So, I quit my job.

"But I missed the store, and it was hard living on one salary when we'd gotten used to two. When I started to look for work, I found that my reputation had preceded me. Store owners knew of the place where I'd worked, and they were pretty sure that all I wanted was to work for them to get a feel for the area so that I could open a store of my own and compete with them.

"This gave me an idea. I hadn't *considered* doing that. So when I couldn't find work, I decided to go for it, to go ahead and compete with them. Their fear gave me confidence!

"One thing I learned on my way up from stock clerk to store manager was that it pays to know your customer. So, in the mornings I'd get the kids off to school, do a few chores, and drive to a baby store. I'd park my car a block away and when customers came out of the store, I'd strike up conversations with them.

"'Hi!' I'd say. 'My name's Julia Gonzales, and I'm doing market research for a major manufacturer who's interested in this area. I'm wondering if you might have a minute to answer a few questions about babies.'

"My enthusiasm must have helped. I like people and babies, and I guess it shows. Being a mother helps me understand other mothers, too. I always dressed up a little bit and carried a clipboard. I'd ask the obvious questions like:

- What do you like about this store?
- What things did you buy?
- Were the people helpful and courteous?

"Sometimes I parked in the alley to research the delivery trucks. At the beach and the shopping malls, I would stop every pregnant woman I saw. I developed a separate list of questions for pregnant women:

- Have you had a baby shower?
- Which gifts did you like best?
- Which gifts seemed most useful?
- What things are you buying before your baby comes?
- What things are you waiting to buy?
- How are you going to decorate the baby's room?
- What do you really need the most?

"The research was time-consuming, but after 30 interviews I had enough information to make some very sound decisions. I also knew the weaknesses of my competition.

One way to get primary data is to interview or conduct focus group discussions among potential target customers, and in some cases this may be the way to go. You could also interview other businesses if your target customer is the consumer or end-user.

We saw how Julia Gonzales used interviewing to help her locate her new store. In the next chapter we'll come back to interviewing again when we're researching our competition. In the meantime, we'll move on and use another skill: surveying to get a more refined picture of our target customer.

SURVEYING TARGET CUSTOMERS

Let's see how Elizabeth Wood used the survey technique to get her started on her own business.

Elizabeth was a supervisor at a local textile plant. Over the last few years, things had been tough. It seemed that she was always hearing about someone being laid off. She wondered when it would be her turn. But as time rolled on, she was becoming less and less concerned. She loved to be creative with food, and she had set her goal: opening a small neighbourhood restaurant.

For some time now, she had been developing her skills in business. She had taken several courses in restaurant and bar management. Next, she entered a small business course at a local university. In an attempt to get a handle on her target customer, she read many studies on the eating-out habits of Canadians. She knew that there was a trend to eating outside the home, but what did this mean for her local market? This secondary research was very revealing, but she just couldn't risk her future on someone else's research. She decided to do her own survey. She studied survey design and got plenty of advice from her professor, who had lots of experience in surveying. Crazy's Roadhouse was one of the most popular eating spots in town. Often, Elizabeth would have a bite to eat there, and she got to know Crazy's owner, Max, quite well. She told Max about her dream to open a small restaurant some day, and about how much she was learning in her small business course. They got to talking, and at last Max agreed to let Elizabeth do her survey of his customers. After all, the price was right. She would do the survey free of charge and would give Max her results — a classic win-win proposition.

Elizabeth spent the next few weeks designing her survey. How many customers should she survey? When should she survey? How should she conduct herself? There was so much to do. Fortunately, with the help of her small business teacher, Max, and the team she had been working with in school, she launched a week-long survey of Max's customers. To Max's surprise, customers wanted to fill out the questionnaire. To Elizabeth's surprise, she heard Max explaining to someone that he thought it was about time he learned a little bit more about what the customer wanted.

Stay tuned. We'll hear more about the results of Elizabeth's survey later on. But for now here are three of the major findings related to Max's target customer:

1. The lunch trade (Monday to Friday) customers were older than expected: almost 40 percent were 35–44. In contrast, the weekend customers were younger: 52 percent were 25–44. As for the "after five" crowd, the average customer was even younger — almost 33 percent were under 25.
2. Regarding income, Elizabeth found that the major customer base was the affluent (those with $48 900+ in total family income). As a matter of fact, almost 50 percent of the customers had a professional as the head of the family, and 87 percent had two or more wage earners in the family unit.
3. From a psychographic perspective, Elizabeth found that, at lunch, Max was getting the Joiner-Activists who were there on business and who were eating salads and sipping Perrier. Over 60 percent ate at a restaurant at least once a week. In the evening, Max was getting mostly Aggressive Achievers and Disinterested Self-Indulgents. He called them his bar crowd.

Elizabeth tried to answer a number of questions regarding the customer base: Why did the customer come to Max's? Where did his customer live and work? Who did the customer think the competition was? When her work was completed and she handed Max her results, Elizabeth got a pleasant surprise. She received a cheque from Max. "Small token of my appreciation," Max said. "It's not a lot, but I really did learn something. I thought I knew my customer before you came along."

Elizabeth didn't earn enough to quit her real job, but it was nice to get paid for developing a customer profile, one she could use to help her start her own restaurant. In the next chapter, we'll come back to Elizabeth and find out what her survey said about Max's competition.

When Julia Gonzales and Elizabeth Wood discovered that they would have to work for themselves, they quickly began to research their target customers. The method they chose was interviewing and surveying. You can do the same thing for your business. Action Step 27 tells you how to do it.

ACTION STEP 27

Interview or survey prospective target customers.

Now that you've profiled several target customers, it's time for you to take a big step. It's time to move from the tidy world inside your head to the arena of the marketplace. It's time to rub elbows with the people who'll be buying your product or service.

You know your TC's habits, income, sex, personality, and buying patterns, and can guess at his or her dreams and aspirations. You've identified the heavy users of your product or service. Now you're going to check out these things by interviewing these potential customers.

Make up some questions in advance. Some of them should be open-ended — that is, calling for more than just a simple yes or no. Here are some questions to help get you started:

Do you like to shop at this store?
What products did you buy today?
Are the salespeople helpful and courteous?
How did you learn about this store?
Is this your first visit? Or, How often do you shop here?
What are you looking for that you didn't find in the store today?
Where do you live?
What do you read?

Make Customer Profiling a Reflex

We've tried to help you make customer profiling a reflex. If you keep at it, it will help you adjust your focus continually on the all-important marketplace.

Predicting the needs of every customer is almost impossible to accomplish with 100 percent accuracy. The invisible customer will emerge with needs that have not been anticipated. These customers were previously invisible. An alert entrepreneur will listen carefully to unexpected requests and be quick to respond to these opportunities. The following case provides a typical example.

INVISIBLE CUSTOMERS

Some people go into business for themselves because they can't work for someone else. Some are mavericks who don't like to take orders. Others are dreamers who love their own ideas. Still others, like Fred Bowers, have some handicap that keeps them from getting a job with a large firm.

Fred's experience illustrates that customers sometimes "come out of the woodwork."

Fred Bowers had planned to have a career in the military until he was injured in a fall from a training helicopter. He could still walk, painfully, but his military career was over. With a medical discharge in his pocket, Fred looked around for work.

"I'd always loved soccer," Fred said, "I'd been a pretty fair player, and my coaching experience had given me a good understanding of kids. I thought there might be a place for a soccer specialty shop in our community, but before I went for financing I spent a year checking it out."

Fred found eighteen sporting good shops in the area he was interested in. None of them carried a full line of soccer products. When he began profiling his target customers, Fred came up with two identifiable targets:

Primary target: boys, ages 6–17
Secondary target: girls, ages 6–12
Household income (both target): $28 000–$32 000
Socioeconomic level: middle, upper middle
Interest: sports

Then Fred segmented the youngsters into two groups: members of school teams and members of Canadian Soccer Association teams.

His description of his target customers was so good that when he showed his 52-page business plan to a couple of investors, they put up all the money he needed to start up Soccer City. Because of Fred's knowledge of the game, his store prospered. Schools counted on him for an honest deal, and parents of players counted on him for advice on equipment.

"I had thought I'd just be selling," Fred said. "What I was really doing was providing a service."

After he'd been in business a year, a third market began to emerge. The customers in this third group were adults, mostly foreign-born, from places such as Great Britain, Germany, Mexico, and South America. They had grown up playing soccer and they loved the game. To them, it was a fiercely fought national sport, and they still liked to play. These previously invisible customers would drive 80–120 kilometrres to Fred's shop for equipment they couldn't find anywhere else.

"They didn't show up in my research," Fred said. "If I hadn't opened up, I wouldn't have known about them. Now they make up at least 30 percent of my business. One day they weren't there; the next day, they were. I like that. I like it a *lot*. It makes this whole adventure more interesting."

In a Nutshell

Your target customer is the key to your survival in small business. Constructing a customer profile is like drawing a circle around that customer in order to turn the circle into a target at which you can aim your product or service. Before you open your doors, you should profile your target customer at least five times. After your doors are open, it's a good idea to gather data through surveys, interviews, and so on, and to refine the profile monthly.

An "end-user" profile combines demographic data (age, sex, income, education, residence, cultural roots) with psychographic insight (observation of lifestyle, buying habits, consumption patterns, attitudes). The magazines read by your target customer will reveal a well-drawn profile, because the chasers of this very expensive advertising have already researched the customer thoroughly. The Internet is also a useful secondary profiling tool, especially if your target customers are other businesses. Surveying and field interviewing are primary research tools that will also help you find your target customers.

Profiling your target customer is important because it shows you:

1. how to communicate your message with a minimum of confusion,
2. what additional service your target customer wants, such as delivery, credit, gift wrapping, installation, post-sale service, and so on,
3. how much the target customer can pay,
4. what quality the target customer wants,
5. where large groups of target customers are located, and
6. who else is after your target customer.

Think Points for Success

✓ *Psychographics* is derived from *psyche* and *graphos*, Greek words for "life" or "soul" and for "written," respectively. Thus, psychographics is the charting of your customer's life, mind, soul, or spirit.

✓ Profiling draws a "magic" circle around your target customer. Placing the customer in the centre of that circle transforms the whole arena into a bullseye.

✓ Segmenting is like slicing pie; it allows you to help yourself to a piece of the pie.

✓ You can save a lot of steps by using market research that has been done by others.

✓ Contact magazines and newspapers. They employ market researchers.
✓ Be sure to use the Internet.

Business Plan Building Block

CUSTOMER PROFILE

Describe your potential customers and why they will want to do business with you. If your TCs are end-users or consumers, segment them by demographics (age, sex, income, etc.) or psychographics (lifestyles and buying behaviour). If your TCs are business, profile them using the "complete profile" categories provided in Action Step 26.

You are demonstrating that you know your market and your research shows that there are enough customers to support your business idea.

Go back and review the material you have developed in the first three chapters of this textbook. You are now ready to explain your customer profile.

It's your turn:

Explain your customer profile: you will need 1–3 pages to elaborate.

BUILDING ASSOCIATIONS/PARTNERSHIPS

Creating associations or partnerships is a key marketing strategy. Try to list some businesses or associations you can create an alliance with. For example, if you want to retail second-hand books, can you associate with a business that is in the coffee business? You could complement each other. While your customers are browsing, for example, they could have a cup of coffee. Make a list of some of the businesses or firms with whom you could strike up an association. Don't forget the non-profit sector. What associations could you create with the Boy Scouts or Cancer Society?

It's your turn:

List potential associations or partnerships, then rank them by priority: this will take at least a page.

Checklist Questions and Actions to Develop Your Business Plan

PROFILING YOUR TARGET CUSTOMER

❑ Profile your target market in terms of primary, secondary and invisible customers.
❑ What do the results of your primary research questionnaire tell you about your target market?
❑ What information have you developed about your target customer from your secondary research?
❑ What characteristics are unique or clearly definable about your target customer?
❑ What is the best way to reach your target market?

NOTES

1. Rick Spence, *Secrets of Success from Canada's Fastest-Growing Companies* (Toronto: John Wiley & Sons Canada, Ltd., 1997), pp. 88–89. Reprinted with permission of the author.

ACTION STEP REVIEW

24 Use your new eyes on magazines that would better help you understand your business idea.
25 Research specific magazines in your business area.
26 Profile three firms using the "Canadian Company Capabilities" Internet site.
27 Interview or survey prospective target customers.

2. Based on Greg Ip, "Outsourcing Becoming a Way of Life for Firms," *Globe and Mail*, October 2, 1996, p. B8. Reprinted with permission from The Globe and Mail.
3. Simon Hermanne, *Hidden Champions* (Boston, MA: Harvard Business Press, 1996).
4. Spence, *Secrets of Success from Canada's Fastest-Growing Companies*, p. 103.

OTHER REFERENCES

Foot, David. "Boomers Dance to a New Beat." *Globe and Mail*, January 9, 1998, p. B21.

Retail Council of Canada. *Consumer Pulse Check Survey*, 1997.

Reynolds, Cynthia and Sean Silcoff. "In the Lap of Luxury." *Canadian Business*, January 30, 1998, pp. 40–54.

Ries, Al. *Focus: The Future of Your Company Depends on It*. New York: Harper Collins, 1996.

Sherlock, Paul. *Rethinking Business-to-Business Marketing*. New York: Free Press, 1991.

Walker Smith, J. and Ann Clurman. *Rocking the Ages*. New York: Harper Business, 1996.

Whiteley, Richard C. and Diane Hesson. *Customer-Centred Growth*. Reading, MA: Addison-Wesley, 1996.

five

Learning from the Competition

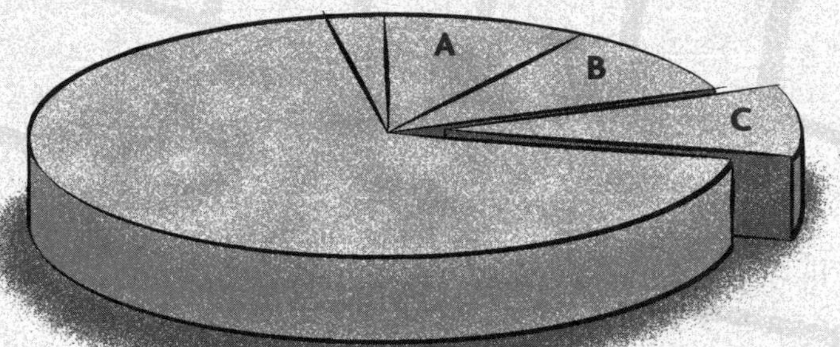

BUSINESS PLAN BUILDING BLOCK

This chapter will help you learn from and define the competition. It will help you build distinctive value for your product or service and further define your specific niche. It will also help you establish what drives your strategy. At the completion of this chapter, you will be able to write a brief competitive overview.

Figure 5.1 Chapter Five will help you prepare part C of your business plan, "The Competition."

LEARNING OPPORTUNITIES

After reading this chapter, you should be able to:

- Discover how to create and grow your market with the help of your customer and competition.
- Define your real competitor through a benefits analysis and customer research.
- Find your position on the competitive ladder through primary and secondary research.
- Evaluate your potential competitors using a competitive test matrix.
- Use the four-phase life cycle to change the arena and establish your competitive positioning strategy.
- Discover ways to create uniqueness through service and product change.
- Benefit from partnerships and associations with your potential competitors.
- Develop a perceptual map positioning your business and competition.

MPact Immedia Corp. is a Profit 100 company in Montreal. It helps firms convert paper-based transactional documents such as invoices, cheques, and bills into a much more efficient electronic system. Competition in the world of electronic commerce is fierce. The lack of industry standardization means that the market is always ripe for new players with new ideas. Among MPact's most feared competitors are the chartered banks. The banks could potentially dominate the market through their financial infrastructure, sheer size, expertise, and massive customer base.

Brian Edwards was president of MPact from 1995 to 1997. When he got wind that the Royal Bank of Canada was eyeing his market, he moved swiftly with a pre-emptive strike. He managed to convince the Royal Bank to join forces with MPact. Together they formed a joint venture that established Can-Act, a system that allows the bank's customers to make recurring business payments to governments, utilities, or trading associates electronically. It was a win-win association. The Royal Bank was able to quickly provide its customers with a distinctive, value-added service. In turn, MPact gained a new customer base along with the marketing clout of a new partner.[1]

ACTION STEP PREVIEW

28 Do a benefits analysis.
29 Find your position on the competitive ladder.
30 Construct a competitive matrix.
31 Practise your new competitive strategy.

Ron Taylor's family had been in the business of building new homes until the early 1990s when there was a recession in the housing market. When the market fell out of new-home construction, the family business closed up and Ron was left with the opportunity to find another career. It wasn't easy. It took healing time and a lot of soul-searching.

In time, his new-eyes research led him into the business of renovating basements. People could not afford high-priced new homes or high interest rates, so they renovated. Secondary research from Statistics Canada and CMHC (Canada Mortgage and Housing Corporation) told him that this was a growth segment. His psychographic research led him to the conclusion that his primary target customers would be those who could not afford to build new homes but who wanted to build a sanctuary for their teenage offspring. He would be in the business of cocooning for teens.

It then came time for him to research his potential competitors. At first, he thought this was obvious. His major competitors were other contractors and builders — after all, if you could build a house, certainly doing a basement renovation would be no problem. But he soon realized that this was the same type of logic that got his family into trouble in the early nineties. His new business couldn't survive with a market sharing/price-cutting mentality. He could no longer afford to share a market. So, using primary research — interviewing, focus group discussions, and just plain listening — he began to build a list of the benefits that his TCs were looking for, and a list of who, in the eyes of the customer, were the best companies or individuals to satisfy their wants. His first list included benefits such as:

- electrical outlets — lots of them for teen toys;
- soundproofing;
- an area equipped for dancing; and
- a bathroom with a full-length mirror.

One night, after a long session with his mentor and some close friends, Ron realized that his competition wasn't other contractors at all. His competition was anyone who could provide the customer with the same benefits. In a strange way, he began to realize that even his customer could be a major competitor.

Only a few years ago, the subject of competition conjured up warlike terms such as "beat the competition," "disarm your competitor," "take a piece of their market," and so on. This market-sharing mentality assumed that when you went into business you would take a piece of the action away from someone else. In a steady-state environment in which industries changed at a slow and predictable pace, the focus was on attacking the competition. Since there was little change going on, this strategy seemed to be the only way to drum up new business.

The knowledge-based economy and the new informed customer have changed the way business has to view competition. As we learned from MPact's partnering strategy, the new economy is about learning from and forming alliances and strategic arrangements with the competition. It's about creating your own market niche and continually changing and improving your product or service as the customer dictates. Today, competition is healthy, and it's there to help you change and respond to the market.

In the last few chapters, we learned about the power of marketing and profiling the customer. We've tried to get you to focus your business toward the growth industry segments and customer needs. This chapter explains how your perceived competition can help you further define your specific niche and the ways you may in fact work with your competition. But remember, it all starts with the customer.

Who Is Your Competition?

Think back. Recall in Chapter Two that we talked about defining your business, not in terms of a product or service, but in terms of the benefits your product or service provides to the potential customer. Well, in the same vein, your competition is not necessarily other businesses that provide a similar product. For example, in the opening vignette, MPact's real competitors were almost invisible. Its most dangerous competitors were the major banks, not other firms that had developed comparable technology. MPact was really in the business of providing efficient electronic transfer of business documents. Major banks were MPact's competitors because they could potentially provide this same service and benefits.

In today's economy, your real competition is anyone who provides similar products, services, or benefits to your customer. But you must also be aware of what's called the **invisible competition** — that is, any business that has the capacity and desire to provide similar products, services, or benefits to your customer. For example, imagine you are in the fast-food business in a small town that doesn't have a McDonald's. Then Wal-Mart comes to town. Your invisible competition has just arrived with a McDonald's within its store.

INVISIBLE COMPETITION
people or businesses that have the capacity or desire to provide the same products, services, or benefits that you do

As we learned from Ron Taylor, your competition is not necessarily who you think it is (although your views are important). Your customers define the competition in terms of who can best satisfy their needs. Ron used the primary research techniques of interviewing his customers to learn about his competition. Strangely enough, he learned that his real competition might even be his customers. Let's return to Elizabeth Wood (from Chapter Four) and see how she uncovered the real competitor for Max, the owner of Crazy's Roadhouse, by using another primary research technique: the survey questionnaire.

Max, the owner of Crazy's Roadhouse, didn't think he needed to know what the customer thought. He knew who the competition was. It was that other roadhouse down the street. Fortunately, Elizabeth knew better. In her restaurant questionnaire, she asked the customers themselves who the competition was: "If you did not eat here today, what restaurant would you have chosen?"

The results gave Max a new perspective on his business. He learned that his competition depended on the dining-out time. At noon, his competition was any restaurant within a 2-kilometre radius that could serve the customer fast. The noon hour trade was more concerned with "getting in and out" than with the quality of the food.

Weekdays from 6 to 9 P.M. and weekends his competition was any restaurant within an 18-kilometre radius of his roadhouse that provided great food and a fun atmosphere. During this period, Crazy's was perceived as a "destination" restaurant. In contrast to the noon hour trade, these customers did not value quick service as much as quality food and dining atmosphere.

The crowd after 9 P.M. on both weekdays and weekends had a different need: fun time. Max's competition was not the great eateries, but establishments that catered to the entertainment side of the business. Customers were prepared to drive as much as 50 kilometres to enjoy a good evening out.

Max was taken aback by the survey results. He didn't have a specific competitor at all. He had a number of potential competitors, depending on the dining-out period. With Elizabeth's help, not only did Max get a much clearer picture of his somewhat elusive competitors, but he also began to get some new ideas about how he could promote and grow his business.

In developing your market strategy, you need to anticipate your competitor's strategy and accordingly be proactive. After you have identified your competitors, including the invisible ones, the first step is to identify their strengths. This puts you in a position to anticipate their actions. Therefore, study their decisions about products, geographic markets, and customers.

One common mistake is to believe that all competitors within an industry behave the same way. This is just not true. Think of the different ways restaurants try to position themselves to attract their target customers. Once you understand a competitor's strategy, the next step is to understand the driving force behind it.

What is the driving force? Most companies, small and large, have one key component that gives them a competitive edge. This key component is what Michael Robert calls the company's driving force.[2] All decisions, including those about which products to develop, customers to target, and markets to enter, are based on the driving force. Taking the Porter model of competitive strategy (Figure 3.6 in Chapter Three) a step further, you can select a driving force for your business. You may have more than one of the following components, but only one can drive your strategy. The full list appears in Box 5.1.

Product-driven strategy. A product-driven company ties its business to a single product. Future products will resemble current and past products in look and function.

User/customer class-driven strategy. A user/customer class-driven company builds its business around specific customers or users. Johnson &

Box 5.1 What Drives Your Strategy?

Most companies have one key component that gives them a competitive edge. Identify your small business strategy from the following:

a) product-driven strategy (e.g., Cow Brand Baking Soda)
b) user/customer class-driven strategy (e.g., Johnson & Johnson)
c) market type/category-driven strategy (e.g., John Deere)
d) product capacity/capability-driven strategy
e) technology/know-how-driven strategy (e.g., Nortel)
f) sales/marketing method-driven strategy (i.e., Avon)
g) distribution method-driven strategy (e.g., Rogers Cable)
h) natural resources-driven strategy (e.g., oil companies)
i) size growth-driven strategy (e.g., Coke, Pepsi)
j) return/profit-driven strategy (e.g., banks)

Source: Michael Robert, *Strategy Pure and Simple II* (New York: The McGraw-Hill Companies Inc., 1998). Reprinted by permission of The McGraw-Hill Companies.

Johnson, for example, makes health-related products for doctors, nurses, and patients.

Production/capacity/capability-driven strategy. A production capacity/capability-driven company focusses its strategy on its production facilities. Specialty printers, for example, exploit the special capabilities of their production facilities.

Technology/know-how-driven strategy. Technology/know-how-driven companies get their edge from a distinctive technology.

PERCEPTUAL MAPPING

Perceptual mapping is another way to begin learning about your competitors. It is based on segmenting your market into more homogeneous markets. You can segment the restaurant business by a range of factors, such as type of menu (e.g., Chinese, Canadian), clientele (e.g., business people, children), type of service (e.g., self-serve, personalized service), or price (e.g., low, medium, high). You can think of further segmentation — for example, by meals served (breakfast, lunch, and/or dinner) and services (such as music or entertainment) provided.

Once the market analysis is complete, then your competition can be placed on a number of different perceptual maps depending on your descriptive axes. Using the restaurant example, Figure 5.2 helps clarify who your closest competition is by identifying the various competing products that are similar to yours.

For your product, you should be able to identify three or four different axes, and for each set of axes, place competing products in the appropriate segment. If you are a fancy restaurant, you don't monitor what McDonald's has on its menu; instead, you are concerned about what your competition has to offer and how it is marketing its services.

Now it is your turn. Who is your real competition? Try a benefits analysis by completing Action Step 28. Then look at Box 5.2 to help you identify your competitors.

ACTION STEP 28

Do a benefits analysis.

Start with a brainstorm and then try a perceptual map. Get some paper and collar a few of those primary target customers you have been collecting in your adventure notebook — yes, get your potential customer to help. Begin by defining what business you're in. Write down all the potential benefits. Try to stay away from the features of the product. Remember Ron Taylor. His benefits were for adults living with teenagers — soundproofing, for example. Add to your list of benefits by conducting other kinds of primary research. Recall how Elizabeth used the questionnaire approach and Ron Taylor used interviewing.

Figure 5.2

McDonald's

Wendy's

Burger King

Catering to children

Economic Price — **High Price**

Harvey's

Mr. Sub

Swiss Chalet

(Fine dining in your area)

Winston's

Old School House

Mature TC

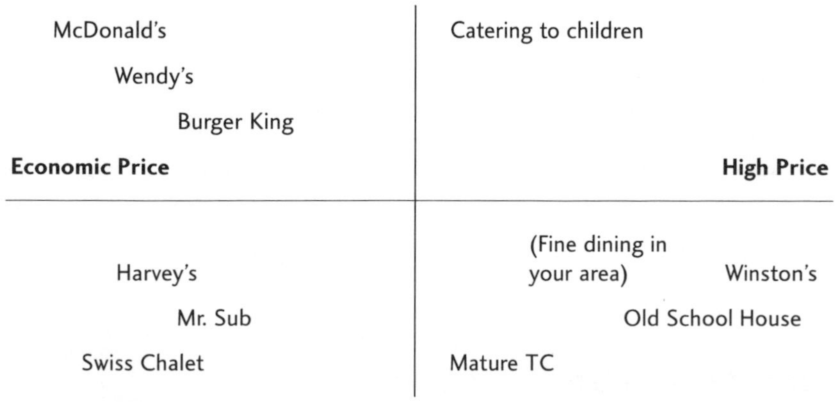

Perceptual mapping helps you learn about your competition.

Box 5.2 A Quick Guide to Identifying Your Competitors

To identify your competitors, you need the following:

1. an understanding of your current competition,
2. an understanding of your future competition, and
3. an understanding of your customer

Current Competition

Some ways to better understand your competition may involve:

a. **Trade shows.** Visit industry trade shows and conferences to examine competitors' products, meet their sales representatives, and learn their product line. Look for product substitutes (domestic and foreign) that can add value to your product and customers.
b. **Reverse engineering.** Purchase a competitor's product and dissect it to determine costs of production, methods of manufacture, and possible suppliers.
c. **Competitors' literature.** Request, as a potential customer, product brochures and price lists from existing competitors. They will give insight into the product concepts, promotion, and corporate image.
d. **Industry association journals.** Read industry journals and learn about the publicity competitors are receiving on new products and services.
e. **Site visits.** Walk through competitors' place of business and observe their corporate image, product displays, level of service, and corporate ambiance.

Future Competition

Some likely sources of future competition include:

a. **Product expansion.** A competitor may decide to take advantage of its technology, marketing, or brand name by expanding an existing line.
b. **Market expansion.** A firm outside your geographic area may expand into your territory.
c. **Backward integration.** One of your suppliers who provides many of your components may decide to put them all together, resulting in a competing product.
d. **Forward integration.** One of your customers might decide that he or she can do what you do, but better or cheaper.

Your Customer

Here are some things you should ask your customers in order to determine their product selection process and why they may likely choose a competitor's product over yours:

a. What product names came to mind when you first decided to shop for the product?
b. Why did you think of these names?
c. For what applications or on what occasions are you likely to use the product?
d. What other kinds of products would be just as satisfying in the same situation?
e. Was it price, quality or something else that determined the purchase of the product?

Source: Contributed by Laurence Hewick, Wilfrid Laurier University, 1998.

Competition and Positioning

Basically, competition is a mind game played out in the customers' minds, since that is where buying decisions are made. Inside customers' minds are

Box 5.3 Bookmark This

The Internet is a great source of competitive information.

Strategis (at <http://strategis.ic.gc.ca>) should be your starting point. In the last chapter, we encouraged you to use the Canadian Company Capabilities link, containing information on over 26 000 businesses. Now we want you to investigate other Strategis links. To get started, we suggest you click on the Strategis' Company Directories. Here you will find all sorts of detailed Internet sites that provide competitive information. For example, we found a link to the Canada Yellow Pages (at <http://www.canadayellowpages.com>), in which you can search for businesses by type, name, and location across the nation. The Canadian Trade Index (at <http://www.palantir.ca/the-alliance/public/cti.html>) is another link we found. It offers a comprehensive directory of over 25 000 manufacturers. The Company Directories site will also give you information on foreign competitors.

many "ladders" — for products, for services, for sports figures, for TV programs, for banks, wines, rental cars, and so forth. To compete for a position at the top of the ladder, a business must first get a foothold and then wrestle with other businesses to improve its position. Looking at competition from this perspective helps you focus on the mind of the target customer.

Competition is always changing. You are therefore faced with a constant process of positioning your product or service to meet the changing needs of the customer. Action Step 29 will help you define your position on the competitive ladder, using your primary, secondary, and new-eyes research skills.

SCOUTING THE COMPETITION

The better you understand your competition, the more clearly you will see how you can position yourself for success. Figure 5.3 is a sample **competitive matrix** that will help you evaluate your potential competitors. Action Step 30 will assist you in developing your competitive matrix. Work from your strengths, and remember that strengths are built on knowledge. Knowing your competitors will increase your confidence. Then everyone can win.

Up until now, we've talked about positioning your business idea in the mind of the customer. Now we're going to turn our attention to your product or service.

The Competition Life Cycle

Like everything else in life and business, competition has a life cycle that can be grouped into four broad stages: embryo, growth, maturity, and decline. These stages are, for the most part, determined by the product life cycle (see Figure 5.4). Briefly, we can describe the four stages of the competition life cycle as follows:

1. In the *embryonic* stage, the arena is empty. There's just you and your idea for a product or service and a tiny core market.
2. As your industry *grows*, competitors smell money and attempt to penetrate the arena to take up positions they hope will turn to profit. Curious

ACTION STEP 29

Find your position on the competitive ladder.

Using your primary research techniques, make a list of your competitors as perceived by your customers. Try not to forget the possibility of the invisible competitor. From Action Step 28, you now have a list of customer benefits. So remember, you're looking for those people or organizations that can provide the same benefits as you. Add more potential competitors to this list, using your secondary sources of information. Here, the telephone book is a great place to begin. You might also want to consult the *Canadian Business Guide* or *Fraser's Canadian Directory*; and to search the Internet and look in the magazines that would appeal to your target market. Don't worry if your list of potential competitors gets too long. The more competitors you detect, the more you can learn.

Now you're ready to find your position on the competitive ladder by answering the questions in each step below:

1. Which firm is at the top? Why is it up there? What's unique about the firm? Who are its target customers? What are the company's strengths? What are its weaknesses? Where is it vulnerable?
2. Who holds the number two spot? The number three spot? Ask the same questions about them.
3. Now look at your own business. What image are you trying to project? What is unique about your business? Where are you strong? Where are you weak? What are your major groups of target customers?
4. Ask yourself if you really want to compete on this ladder (in this arena). Might a different ladder be better suited — and thus more fun — for you?

A couple of tips: First, if you want to compete on this ladder, you must capitalize on your unique strengths. Second, evaluate your prospects on a different ladder by going through Steps 1–4 with a different product or service in mind.

COMPETITIVE MATRIX
a grid used to get a clear picture of the strengths, weaknesses, and sales volume of your competitors

ACTION STEP 30

Construct a competitive matrix.
Now that you have a good idea of who your major competitors are, it is time to construct a competitor test matrix as shown in Figure 5.3. List all those competitors or potential competitors and the benefits and features resulting from Action Step 29. Remember, your competitor may not be providing the same products. If you want to sell healthy water, for example, your potential competitors are those who are in the health business. The purpose of this Action Step is to learn from their strengths so you can borrow from their experience and create a better, more unique product or service.

Next, rank each competitor on a scale of 1 to 10 for each benefit category. By the time you're finished, you will have an instant overview of your competition and your opportunities.

What are the strengths of your competitors, and how can you learn from them to improve your idea?

Figure 5.3

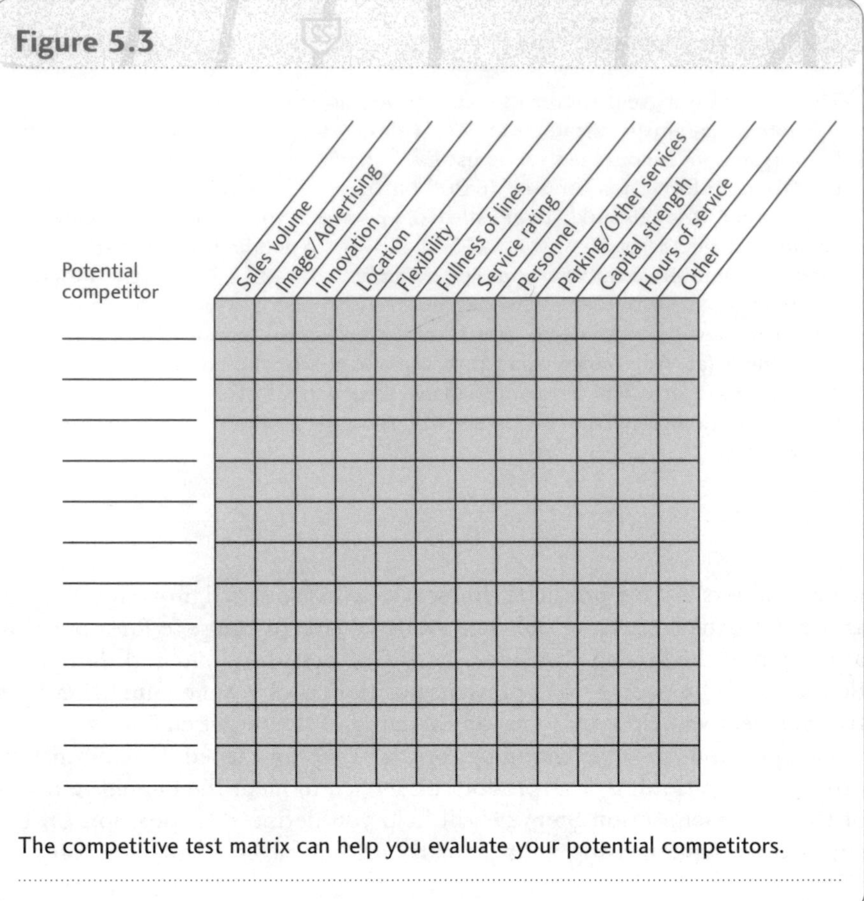

The competitive test matrix can help you evaluate your potential competitors.

target customers come from all directions. You have visions of great success.

3. As the industry *matures*, competition gets fierce and you are forced to steal customers to survive. Shelf velocity slows. Production runs get longer. Prices begin to slide.

Figure 5.4

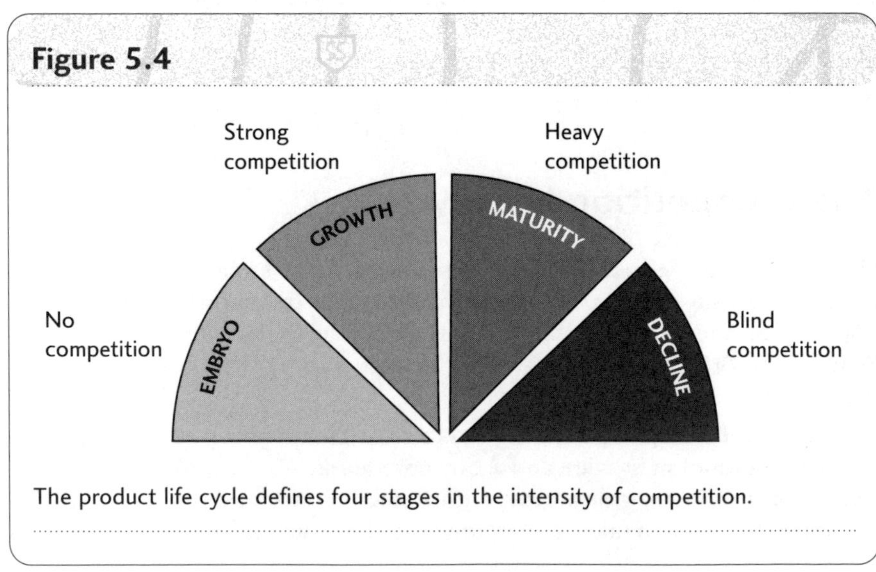

The product life cycle defines four stages in the intensity of competition.

4. As the industry goes into *decline*, competition becomes desperate. Many businesses fail, and weary competitors leave the arena, which is now silent except for the echoes of battle.

Remember Hugh Hefner and his *Playboy* empire? Well, *Playboy* readers got older (the moving target concept) and the kingdom became a dukedom. It took Hefner and *Playboy* some 30 years to move through the competition cycle, and that arc was rather smooth and even. Hefner's experience was typical of the way competition used to evolve. Changes occurred slowly. Products, services, and even markets would get stuck in a particular stage. A few years ago, for example, the embryonic stage for a computer software package might have lasted up to two or three years.

No more. The new economy has changed all that. Today, movement from one phase to another can be at lightning speed. It's not unheard of for a product to go through the four cycles in a matter of months. In the high-tech business, for example, a common rule of thumb is six months — that is, you've got six months from the birth of an idea to **product penetration**. After six months, competitors have already entered the market, and the product begins to enter the declining phase. What this means is that, to survive, you

PRODUCT PENETRATION
a calculated thrust into the market

Box 5.4 The Competition Life Cycle

The Embryonic Stage
The embryonic stage is marked by excitement, naïve euphoric thrust, clumsiness, a high failure rate, and much brainstorming. Pricing is experimental. Sales volume is low because the market is very small and production and marketing costs are high. It's difficult to find distributors, and resellers demand huge gross margins. Profit is chancy and speculative. Shrewd entrepreneurs, however, can close their eyes and divine the presence of a core market. Competition has not yet appeared.

The Growth Stage
The growth stage is marked by product innovation, strong product acceptance, the beginnings of brand loyalty, promotion by media sizzle, and ballpark pricing. Product innovation occurs. Distribution becomes all-important. Resellers who laughed during the embryonic stage now clamour to distribute the product. Strong competitors, excited by the smell of money, enter the arena of the marketplace, as do new target customer groups. Profit shows signs of peaking.

The Mature Stage
The mature stage is marked by peak customer numbers and zero product modifications. Design concentrates on product differentiation instead of product improvement. Competitors are going at it blindly now, running on momentum even as shelf velocity slows. Production runs get longer, so firms can take full advantage of capital equipment and experienced management. Resellers, sensing doom, are cool on the product. Advertising investments increase, in step with competition. Some firms go out of business. Prices are on a swift slide down. Any competitor who enters the market now is either dumb, overconfident or both. In the once-hot marketplace, there's a pervasive air of depression.

The Decline Stage
The decline stage is marked by extreme depression in the marketplace. Competition becomes desperate. A few firms still hang on. Research and development ceases. Promotion vanishes. Price wars continue. Opportunities emerge for entrepreneurs in service and repair. Diehards fight what remains of the core market. Resellers cannot be found — they've moved on.

must be constantly in touch with the market and compete with the right strategies accordingly. Figure 5.5 and Box 5.4 will help you understand the life-cycle stages more clearly.

Your Competitive Positioning Strategy

In the last few chapters, we've learned that a major objective when starting or owning a business is to position your product or service in a growth segment. If your market is growing at 25 percent a year, you may be able to make a lot of mistakes and still succeed. If, however, you're competing in the mature or declining stage, one mistake can spell disaster. In these stages you'll be forced to lower prices, take business away from others, or invest lots of advertising money. These are market-sharing conditions, and you don't want to — or shouldn't plan to — share a market.

You really don't want to position yourself in an embryonic competitive stage either. In this initial stage you will be all alone with virtually no proven market. We know that if you expect to make it, you'll need customers — a receptive market. But this means that you will need some competition, something that is virtually nonexistent in the embryonic stage.

In today's changing economy, there is no choice. Your strategy must be a constant "war of movement" (for those of you who still think that your competitive strategy should be warlike) or a constant process of positioning and moving your product or service toward a growth market. The name of the game is change and creating uniqueness as dictated first and foremost by

Figure 5.5

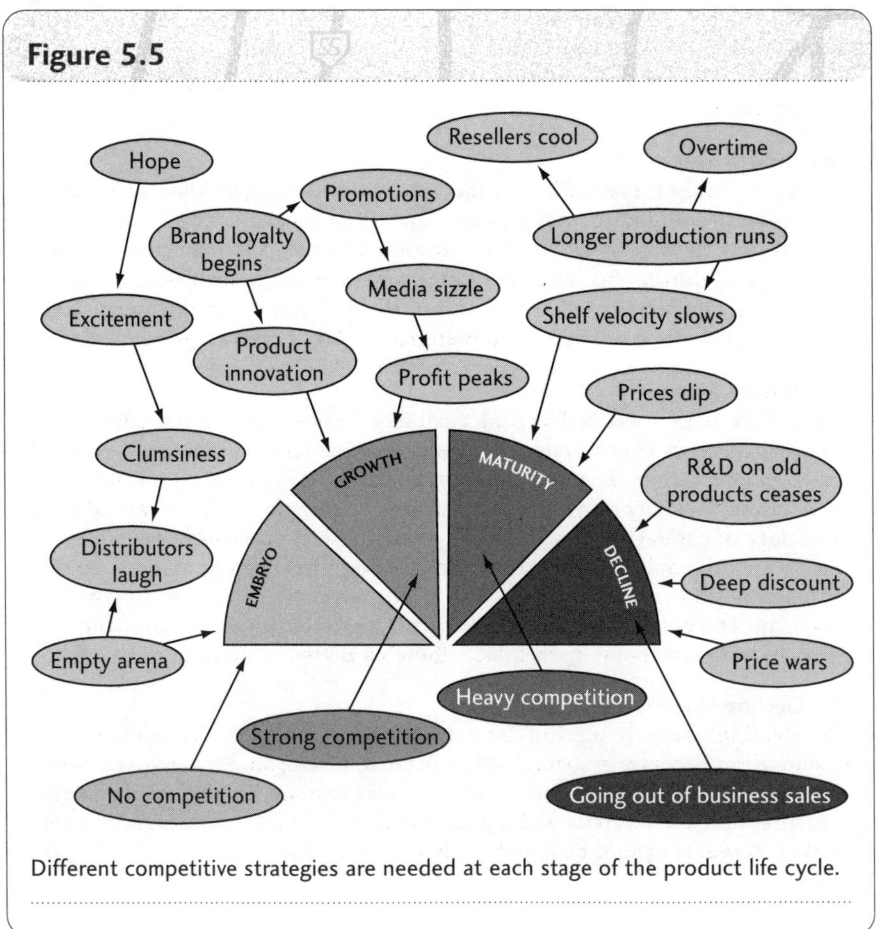

Different competitive strategies are needed at each stage of the product life cycle.

your customers and secondly by your potential competitors. Figure 5.6 depicts this new competitive positioning strategy. Yes, you will always have competition, because you need their advice. The secret is to continually learn from your competitors and customers so that you can adjust your product or service to meet the needs and wants of the market. Your competitive strategy is all about changing the arena. By constantly adding benefits to your product or service, you will guide your business into growth segments.

At the beginning of this chapter, we learned how Brian Edwards of MPact changed the arena by initiating competitive partnering. Let's see how this technique also worked for Mina Cohen, owner of Archaeological Encounters.

You'll recall Mina from Chapter Four. She decided she wanted to be in the "travel-with-a-purpose" business. Her product was archaeological excursions. The bad news was that she had created an embryonic product. No one else was offering this kind of service, so she was faced with such questions as: What price do I charge? How can I attract customers without massive advertising? To complicate things even more, her competitive analysis told her that her target customers valued their time and would likely get travel agencies to help them plan their vacation experience. Her competition would be travel agencies that could easily enter her market if they wanted to, and they would have a strong customer base to draw from. Here she was with an embryonic product, trying to position herself and do business in the fiercely competitive travel industry. What a challenge!

She tackled perceptual mind mapping. Eventually, as she was sifting through her ideas, a creative solution gradually took shape. Why not partner with a travel agency interested in the eco-tourism market? She would locate the best travel agency in town and offer her excursions as an add-on service. The agents would handle the advertising, pricing, and booking since this was their strength — organizing and planning. Mina could then focus on her strengths — teaching and archaeology — and get paid from the travel package for her knowledge and expertise.

Figure 5.6

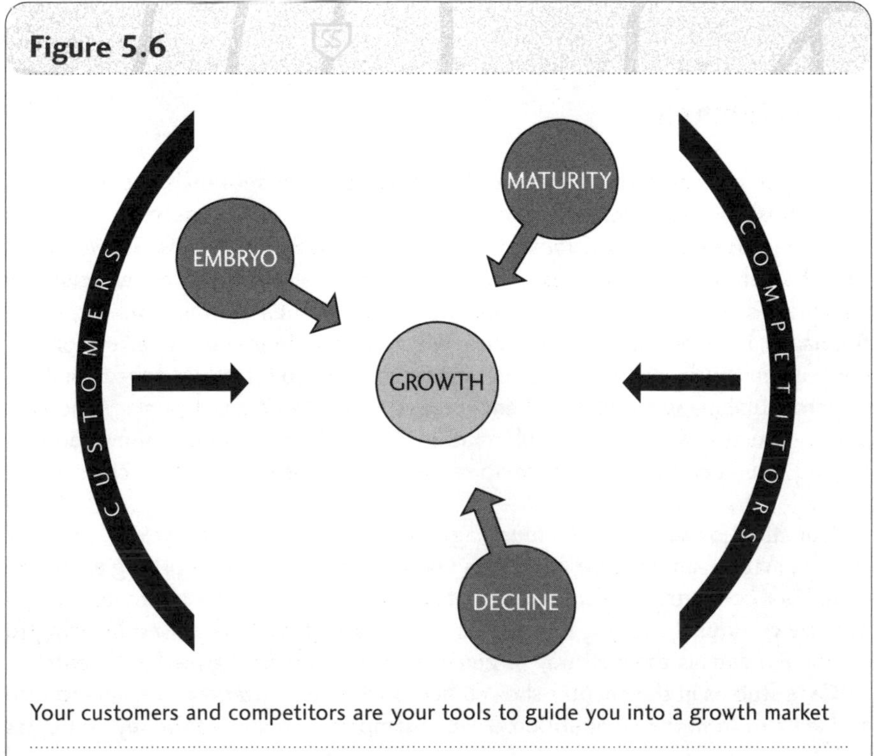

Your customers and competitors are your tools to guide you into a growth market

ACTION STEP 31

Practise your new competitive strategies.

Make this a perceptual mapping or a brainstorming session with family or friends. Start with a novel idea (such as packing expensive gear in popcorn) and let go with the wild ideas.

Keep your mind on the industry ladder as you brainstorm. What's unique about your product or service? Are you supplying something your target customer wants or needs? How can you create a new arena? What might you do to establish presence? What image would be good for your business? Is there some way that you could become so unique that you would build your own pie? Are there potential competitors you might be able to partner with?

Consider what you might do if you start out in an embryonic industry and the arena soon fills with competitors. Come up with a Plan B.

Think. Imagine. Create. Surprise. And have fun.

Box 5.5 Small Business Tip

"There are more competitors coming in, and we're trying to partner with them," says Brian Edwards, President of MPact Immedia Corp.

Likewise, Rick Spence, editor of *Profit* magazine, points out that teaming with competitors is a growing trend. Respected competitors are beginning to turn to each other more often for the mutual benefit of both organizations. The key driver is the customers' ever increasing expectations of quality and service.

Source: Adapted from Rick Spence, *Secrets of Success from Canada's Fastest-Growing Companies* (Toronto: John Wiley & Sons Canada, Ltd., 1997), pp. 114. Reprinted by permission of the author.

The lesson from Mina's experience is clear. She moved her embryonic product and service into a competitive market by creating an association with her potential competitor. By understanding the needs and strengths of her competitors, Mina was able to create a win-win situation.

YOU CAN DO IT

We have provided you with a number of cases about innovators who worked with and learned from competitors and brought about big changes in the marketplace. It's altogether possible that we may someday be telling such a story about *you*. Yes, you too can do it. You just need to:

- know what business you're in,
- know your target customer,
- know your competition,
- know the benefits of your product or service, and
- give rein to your creativity and your entrepreneurial spirit.

Get going! Surprise us! Action Step 31 will help.

In a Nutshell

Your key source for learning about and defining your competition is your customer. Customers help us determine who our competitors are. Competition is a mind game, because buying decisions are made in the customers' minds. So, we began this chapter by asking you to conduct a benefits analysis. In this exercise, we encouraged you to use primary research techniques such as brainstorming, questionnaires, interviewing, and surveying. We asked you to identify one key component of your business that is your driving force. We also introduced the technique of perceptual mapping. Next, we encouraged you to search out primary and secondary sources of competitive information. Our goals here were to show you how to find your position on the competitive ladder and construct a competitive matrix.

Our attention turned to the four stages of the competitive life cycle — embryo, growth, mature, and decline — and its implications for the enterprising entrepreneur. Your competitive positioning strategy, we said, should be to create uniqueness by continually adding benefits to your product or service. And listening to customer needs is the best way to guide your business into growth segments.

Case studies in the chapter showed how successful entrepreneurs worked with and learned from the competition. These examples emphasized the key strategies

ACTION STEP REVIEW

28 Do a benefits analysis.
29 Find your position on the competitive ladder.
30 Build your own competitive matrix.
31 Practice your new competitive strategies.

of creating uniqueness through continuous change and establishing special partnerships or associations — even with your competitors.

Think Points for Success

✓ Customers help you determine who your competitors are.
✓ A benefits analysis can be conducted by using primary research techniques such as brainstorming, questionnaires, interviewing, surveying, and perceptual mindmapping.
✓ Learning from the competition will help you position your business.
✓ Knowing your driving force will help you make better decisions.
✓ Your competitive positioning creates uniqueness by continually adding benefits to your product or service, and it guides your business into growth segments.
✓ Establishing partnerships or associations with your competitors also gives you a competitive edge.

Business Plan Building Block

MARKET OPPORTUNITIES

Based on your research, identify the most promising opportunities in the marketplace according to the following categories:

New or emerging markets — gaps and opportunities
Neglected customer needs
Failing competitors
Complementary product mix
Expanded use of existing facilities
New geographical and international opportunities

Now rank those that are most attractive now and up to five years forward.

____

____

____

____

____

____

COMPETITION

Even though you believe you have little or few competitors, you must make an assessment of whom you are competing with. You should list your major competitors, their dollar volume, market share, marketing methods, financial conditions, prices, service levels, geographic areas served, and weaknesses. Start with a rough draft here and fine-tune it again as you keep developing your plan. Stress unmet needs and niches. Your first draft of this section should use one to three pages.

List major and minor competitors. Estimate their dollar volume by product type and consider their strengths, weaknesses, markets served, and unmet needs. A map of the area is useful — show distances from your site and proximity to market and competition. Back this up with industry data, market surveys, and primary research.

Your turn: this should take 1–2 pages.

MARKET SHARE

Review the total market and estimate your anticipated share penetration from the first through the fifth year.

Your turn:

COMPETITIVE ANALYSIS

Summarize the material you have developed in this chapter to demonstrate that you have not underestimated your competitors. A brief competitive overview could be sufficient for a small firm serving a local geographic area, a specialty distributor, a short-run manufacturer, or a professional service (1–2 pages).

A detailed competitive analysis is needed for larger firms ($2 million to $200 million in projected sales). Write a comprehensive analysis of market share, marketing strategies, pricing, positioning, promotion, distribution, finances, and customers' perceptions (3–10 pages).

Note that the competitive marketplace is imperfect. Sometimes a few miles or a few hundred miles can make a significant difference in how competitive a business must be. If a mature marketplace is oversaturated, keep exploring other areas. You may find an underserved market that will welcome you instantly with warmth and healthy profit margins.

Checklist Questions and Actions to Develop Your Business Plan

LEARNING FROM THE COMPETITION

- ❑ Define and analyze your primary and secondary competition.
- ❑ Identify your position on the competitive ladder.
- ❑ Construct a competitor test matrix.
- ❑ What is your major competitive positioning strategy?
- ❑ What is unique about your product or service?
- ❑ What do customers think of the competition's product or service?
- ❑ What is the size of the total market, and what share do you expect to achieve in the first, second and third years, and why?

NOTES

1. Adapted from Rick Spence, *Secrets of Success from Canada's Fastest-Growing Companies* (Toronto: John Wiley & Sons Canada, Ltd., 1997), p. 114. Reprinted by permission of the author.
2. Michael Robert, *Strategy Pure and Simple*, 2nd edition. (New York: McGraw-Hill Companies, Inc., 1998).

OTHER REFERENCES

Bishop, Bill. *Strategic Marketing for a Digital Age*. Toronto: Harper Collins, 1996.

Hope, Jeremy and Tony Hope. *Competing in the Third Wave*. Boston, MA: Harvard Business School Press, 1997.

Lewis, Herschell Gorden, and Robert D. Lewis. *Selling on the Net*. Lincolnwood, IL: NTC Business Books, 1997.

Tyson, Kirk W.M. *Competition in the 21st Century*. St. Lucie Press, 1997.

Wecker, David. *The Maverick Mindset: Finding the Courage to Journey from Fear to Freedom*. New York: Simon & Schuster, 1997.

six

Marketing Strategies and Promotion: Connecting with the Customer

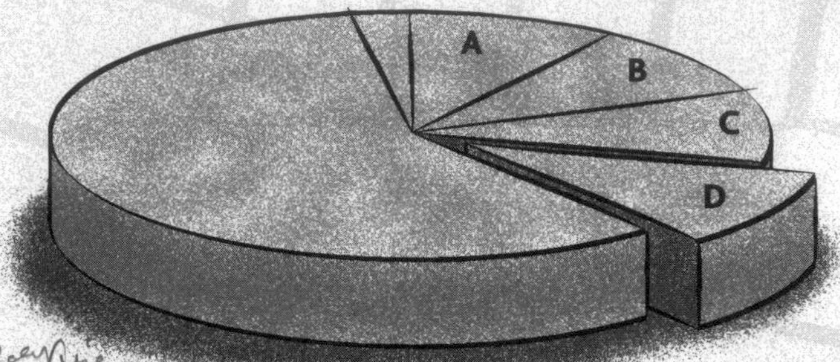

LEARNING OPPORTUNITIES

After reading this chapter, you should be able to:

- Develop a marketing strategy for your product or service.
- Learn to communicate with target customers, using both conventional and creative promotional methods.
- Use research to determine a marketing strategy.
- Get free publicity.
- Maximize economy in advertising and promotion.
- Understand the value of personal selling.
- Use creative techniques to arrive at the right promotional mix.
- Develop a customer list.
- Promote through networking.
- Build your own network.

BUSINESS PLAN BUILDING BLOCK

This chapter will aid you in developing the first draft of your marketing strategy, and in shaping your plan to communicate with, service, and provide value-added services or products to your customers.

In Antigonish, Nova Scotia, John Dobson built a five-store giftware retail chain across Atlantic Canada that grew 1 264 percent in five years. At South of the Border, he says, "our game plan has been to have the best customer service." That means cash refunds, free gift-wrapping year round, and employees who are trained to know their products and empowered to make decisions that favour the consumer. The result is loyal customers who return again and again, and spend $500 to $700 in the stores every year.[1]

IKOR Integrated Facilities Inc., a Toronto office-furniture dealership, is another Profit 100 company that has prospered over the nineties. IKOR's major promotional strategy is "Wow." Throughout the company's showroom are signs that say "Wow service by IKOR." It's a concept that Igor Korenzvit, founder and president, constantly drums into his staff. According to Korenzvit, "There are three kinds of service you can give to people: less than they expected, which we call 'Yuck'; what they expected, which we call 'Blah'; and more than they expected, which we call 'Wow.' We only deliver Wow." [2]

ACTION STEP PREVIEW

32 Brainstorm a winning promotional campaign for your business.
33 Attach a price tag to each item of your promotion package.
34 Develop resource files on your computer.
35 Build your network.

Figure 6.1 **Chapter Six will help you prepare part D of your business plan, "Marketing Strategy."**

Chapter Three discussed the importance of market research, while Chapter Four focussed on your target customers. In Chapter Five, you learned how to analyze your competition. Understanding your market, your target customer, and competition are all part of developing your market strategy. Your strategy may be one of differentiating your product from that of the competitor's, segmenting your total market, positioning it in relation to other products, or carving out and defending a certain niche. The marketing strategy in your plan is a "what-to-do" section. In all cases, it is implementing a plan that considers the product or service benefits and values, the primary objectives you want to accomplish, where you are going to locate your business, and finally how you plan to promote your business. Before you reach the point of promotion, you need to be very clear about the focus of your product or service, location, and pricing strategy. Product and price have been discussed in earlier chapters; location is discussed in Chapter Seven.

Now that you have profiled your target customer and gained a sense of competition and market niche, it's time to plan a promotional strategy. But each business is unique, and you don't want to throw away money on promotional schemes that don't work.

For example, if your target customer is a college-educated suburban female aged 45–55, who makes over $100 000, owns three cars, rides horseback ten hours a week, and reads *Practical Horseman* and *Performance Horseman*, your best chance of reaching her is with direct mail.

On the other hand, if your target customers are males and females aged 24–57, with a high school education and income of $17 000, you'll have to resort to some form of mass-market advertising or, better still, rethink your target market.

Promotion is the art or science of moving the image of your business into the prospective customer's mind. *Promotion* comes from the Latin verb *imovere*, which means "to advance," "to move forward." It's an aggressive word, so learn to say it with a $mile!

PROMOTION
the art or science of moving the image of your business into the prospective customer's mind

As we have learned from the opening vignettes, customer service and quality are the cornerstones of any marketing or promotional strategy. This is where we begin our promotion discussion.

Your Promotional Cornerstones: Service and Quality

According to Jim Clemmer, author of *Firing on All Cylinders*, "Customer service and quality are back in vogue." Numerous surveys during the 1990s have consistently shown that improved customer service and quality are key factors contributing to business profit and growth. A Statistics Canada study — *Strategies for Success* — of almost 1 500 companies, found that customer service and product quality were the most important success factors among growth firms.[3] A 1998 study by Deloitte & Touche Consulting came to the conclusion that customer service was the currency of the digital age: "The most profitable companies ... are adapting to a new customer value paradigm and proactively changing the basis of competition."[4] (Translation: Be more useful to your customer than your competition and you will make a whack of cash.)

Why is delighting the customer with service and quality so important? Here are a few additional market facts:

- You can charge up to 10 percent more if the customer perceives quality service.

Box 6.1 Small Business Tips

There are seven service secrets that you should keep in mind:

1. Set a new standard for your industry.
2. Don't make clients pay for your mistakes.
3. Measure the service you provide.
4. Provide speedy service.
5. Relieve your customers' stress.
6. Use feedback to stay in touch with the customer needs.
7. Surround your product with customer benefits.

Source: Rick Spence, *Secrets of Success from Canada's Fastest-Growing Companies* (Toronto: John Wiley & Sons Canada, Ltd., 1997), pp. 143–44. Reprinted by permission of the author.

- Firms with high service records are 12 percent more profitable than firms without, and their yearly sales growth is 12 percent higher.
- About 68 percent of customers stop doing business with a particular establishment because the employees appear indifferent toward the customer.
- It costs five times more to get a new customer than to keep your present customer satisfied.
- A happy customer will tell five new people, but an unhappy customer will complain to ten people.
- What's worse is that only one customer out of 26 will bother to tell the owner. This means that if only one customer complains, 25 others also have complaints, and each one is telling ten people.
- Remember, the 80-20 rule: Eighty percent of the world is influenced by the other 20 percent. Word of mouth by the customer is a major way to get your message out once you are established. A customer who is happy because of quality service is the way to make word-of-mouth work for you.

Where to begin? If you want to start your own customer service strategy, we suggest the following:

- Recognize that all of us are captive in the midst of a customer service epidemic.
- Think of a customer as "the next person to whom you give your work," at home and in your business.
- Think of service as treating people with genuine care, dignity, and respect.
- Start to practise customer service at home. Serve your family and friends as you would a customer.
- Don't tolerate bad service any more. Make quality service part of your personal and business culture. If we don't do anything about this service disease that has infected Canada, many of us will end up shopping across the border where someone else takes service a little more seriously.

Promotional Strategies

THE PROMOTIONAL MIX

Once you have your service and quality in line, the key to connecting with customers is to consider a variety of promotional strategies and then pick the right one. There are four main elements to a promotional strategy:

Paid advertising
Personal selling
Sales promotion
Publicity or unpaid promotion

Within the four elements is a wide range of other elements, the **promotional mix**, which include:

PROMOTIONAL MIX
all the elements that you blend to maximize communication with your target customer

Paid media advertising
Point-of-purchase displays
Catalogue sales
Direct mail
Money-back guarantees
Free ink and free air
Personal selling
Trade shows
Industry literature
Work visibility
Discount coupons
Brand yourself
Promotion in cyberspace

All these elements together make for an overall promotional strategy. You may use some at one time or with one product, and others at another time or with a different product.

POTENTIAL STRATEGIES

Paid Media Advertising A sure-fire way to reach out is through advertisements on radio, television, display boards (written or electronic), newspapers, magazines, and trade journals. Advertising tickles the target customer's mind. With a good ad, you can reach right into your TC and create the desire to buy from you.

Advertising has some obvious drawbacks: 1) it can be expensive to create; 2) if you don't spend even more money, your ad won't get exposure; and 3) major advertisers get preferred placements (i.e., the best locations within a publication, store or business area; or the best time slots on TV or radio).

Advice:

- Make sure that a large percentage of the listeners, viewers, or readers are in one of your TC groups. Otherwise your message is wasted.
- Your best ad is often yourself. Stay visible and remember the importance of personal selling.
- Check with vendors. Ask for tear sheets, copy, and co-operative advertising money, and help on advertising design and layout.
- Check with marketing departments of newspapers. Ask for help, advice, information.
- Newspapers sometimes offer advertising in special supplements, such as a small business section, at reduced cost. The offer includes free editorial copy.
- Explore creative co-op advertising, in which suppliers share a portion of the cost.
- Don't be afraid to piggyback. Let Madison Avenue build the market. Then use your promotional mix to tell the TC to buy at your place.
- Start small, and test and analyze the results of each promotional campaign.

Point-of-Purchase Displays These displays, situated usually at or near the check-out counter or front desk, encourage impulse purchases of last-minute items like paperbacks, pantyhose, candy, magazines, and gum. A sharp P-O-P (point-of-purchase) display can improve your image, and it serves as a tireless, silent salesperson, always on duty. A good P-O-P can be used for customer education. If it is hard to understand how to use your product or the benefits aren't clear to the TC, your silent salespeople can deliver the message.

There are, at the same time, a few problems with these displays: 1) you can't sell large items because they crowd customers at the cash register; and 2) the display must sell itself as well as the product. (A tacky P-O-P will turn prospective customers *off* instead of *on*.)

Advice:

- Do weekly evaluations of all P-O-Ps. Make certain your silent salespeople are doing their work.

Catalogues This sales tool is just right for isolated shoppers and shoppers in a hurry. Because we are becoming so "time poor," even general items are now being purchased via catalogues. Customers can shop at their convenience and not have to worry about store hours, parking, or traffic. Catalogue houses such as Lillian Vernon or Lands End don't usually manufacture anything, so they are always looking for good products. Use catalogues as another kind of silent salesperson to reach customers if your TC tends to be a catalogue shopper.

If you try printing your own catalogues, you'll run into at least three problems: 1) cost (they are expensive to print and to mail); 2) size limitations (it's tough to sell anything by catalogue that's big, bulky, or inconvenient to ship); and 3) the challenge of establishing and maintaining a reliable mailing list.

Advice:

- Be prepared to take advantage of on-line catalogues. They are growing in number, especially in business-to-business transactions (see Box 6.2).
- Let major catalogue houses do your promotion, but make sure you can deliver if your product takes off.
- Before you get in too deep, approach a few major houses with a product description plus photographs. If they don't like your product, they may help you locate a catalogue house that will. The feedback will be invaluable.

DIRECT MAIL
advertisement or sales pitch that is mailed directly to target customers

Direct Mail This promotional tool lets you aim your brochures and flyers where they will do the most good. **Direct mail** is very important for small business because it can go to the heart of your target market.

The success of direct mail depends on your ability to define the target market. Recall from Chapter Four, for example, that a key to the success of Just Kid'n was its customer list of over 100 000 target customer names, addresses, and phone numbers. This list allowed the company to direct mail and develop a special relationship with its target customers. If the market is too fragmented for you to do this, direct mail is not for you.

Advice:

- Develop customer lists. (Action Step 34 will help you get started later on in the chapter.)

Money-back Guarantees You may not have thought of a guarantee as a form of promotion, but it is. You can reach security-minded customers by emphasizing the no-risk features of your product.

The problem is that you must back up your guarantee with time and money. Therefore, if you have a guarantee, don't overlook the cost implications in your income and expense statements.

Advice:

- Figure 5 percent into your pricing to cover returned goods. If the product is fragile or easily misused — and people have been known to misuse just about everything — build in a higher figure.

Box 6.2 Bookmark This

More and more, retailers are going on-line to sell their products. Here are a few examples:

The Internet Mall: http://www.internet-mall.com (a list of on-line retailers supported by advertising)

The Internet Plaza: http://www.internet-plaza.net (a collection of Web links to retailers who have their own Web site)

Downtown Anywhere: http://www.awa.com (a list of on-line retailers)

Cybersuperstore: http://www.cybersuperstore.com (lower end of the on-line shopping experience)

The Internet Shopping Network: http://www.internet.net (largest and most established of on-line shopping retailers)

Similarly, catalogue shopping is going on-line, especially in business-to-business transactions. Dealer-to-dealer network programs, for example, are quickly replacing the infrastructure of store departments and workers who verify, invoice, label, and ship goods. These new programs have the capability of doing everything but picking up and packing your purchase and getting it to the door — and yet even this is possible at a click of the mouse through such companies as Purolator.

At the leading edge of this branch of the electronic revolution is the network-based program called "Smart Catalog," developed by Calgary's Vicom Multimedia Inc. Smart Catalog is used by large companies such as Gulf Canada Resources Ltd. in Calgary. Here is what Bob Henderson, purchasing manager at Gulf Canada, has to say: "It gives a three-dimensional, pictorial view of a product, eliminates errors in selection, and helps prevent getting the wrong product. We can order on-line. At the end of the month, we have one invoice for all transactions that are summarized. It's slick." Although these types of multimedia network catalogues may never completely replace touch-and-feel shopping, they are certainly a welcome efficiency.

Visit Smart Catalog at <http://www.vicom.ca/irf.html>.

Source: Adapted from Andrew Allentuck, "Network Selling: Catalogues Are Going Multimedia," *Globe and Mail*, November 12, 1996, p. C5. Reprinted by permission of the author.

Free Ink and Free Air Free publicity through reviews, features, interview shows, press releases, and newspaper columns cost you nothing and can be effective. Free ink and free air are excellent ways to promote because they establish your company in a believable way. The target customer is likely to attach more credence to words that are not paid advertising. The obstacle here is getting media people to think your business is unique and noteworthy.

Advice:

- *Every* business is newsworthy in some way. Dig until you find a different twist. Know the media people. Aim your release at *their* target readers, viewers, or listeners.
- Make your press kit visually appealing, include your story, and send accompanying photos of your principals, your facility, and your product being used or your service being performed.

Personal Selling It doesn't matter if you've never sold before; no one is a better salesperson than you are if you believe in your product or service. You are the business. If you listen carefully, your TCs will *tell* you how to sell them your product or service. That's why a good salesperson is a creative listener, not a fast talker. Most customers like to talk with the owner of the business. Use that to your advantage. (See Box 6.3.)

PERSONAL SELLING
the selling and taking of orders by an individual salesperson

Unfortunately **personal selling** is expensive, especially if you have to pay others to do it, and it will boost your overhead unless you pay your salesperson only by earned commission. And if you try to do it all yourself, you won't have the time and energy for other things that only you can do. But for small businesses, the best form of promotion is personal selling.

Advice:

- Make everyone in your business a salesperson: delivery people, warehouse people, computer programmers, bookkeepers, clerical people, switchboard operators. If nothing sells, they're out of a job. Remind everyone who works for you that your TC needs a lot of TLC (tender loving care).
- Consider developing a network of sales reps who will work on a percentage of sales. Keep cheerleading. Reps need encouragement, too.
- Increase your personal visibility. Join a business or service club and trade associations. Write a newspaper column. Be bold (see Box 6.4).
- Stay in touch with your customers and listen to them. If you don't, you may lose your business.

Trade Shows These shows display your product or service in a high-intensity way. Trade shows focus on customers who have a keen interest in your business area. Your appearance at a trade show asserts your position in your

Box 6.3 Direct Sales Is Alive and Thriving

"People are being downsized and let go. Direct selling (personal selling) is an industry that is offering income-earning opportunities to people who want to be independent," says Ross Creber, president of Direct Sellers Association. In the nineties, direct sales was still alive and thriving, but few firms made house calls like the Fuller Brush salesman or Avon lady of the fifties and sixties. Direct selling mainstays like Avon Canada Inc. and Amway of Canada Ltd., or Canadian upstarts like Weekenders, adjusted to the "ding dong" tactics of the past. House parties, offices, and technology were their new stomping grounds — and in many cases, their roads were electronic and their doors were on computer screens. Here are some facts:

- Over the first half of the 1990s, sales of the Direct Sellers Association's members — who represent roughly half of all direct sellers in Canada — jumped 116 percent to $1.1 billion.
- The number of independent sales representatives in the association rose 67 percent to 600 000 people (over the first half of the nineties). Of these, about 81 percent were women, of whom 78 percent worked part-time and the remainder more than 30 hours per week.
- Roughly 53 percent of all sales come from personal care products (cosmetic, skin care, jewellery), 32 percent from home and family-care products, 8 percent from leisure and entertainment products, and the remainder from a cross-section of categories.
- About 70 percent of direct sales take place in the home (almost three quarters by appointment or through group parties), 20 percent in the workplace, and 8 percent at public events such as fairs.
- The World Federation of Direct Selling Associations, with members in 43 countries, reports that direct selling soared 102 per cent between 1988 and 1994 to $67.6 billion (U.S.). The total number of direct-sales people jumped 108 percent to 18 million.

Source: Adapted from Gayle MacDonald, "Who's Still Knocking at the Door?" *Globe and Mail*, May 6, 1996, p. B6. Reprinted with permission from The Globe and Mail.

Box 6.4 Bite a Lion on the Tail

For whatever reason, many people are afraid of personal selling. You can make that fear your challenge. Have you ever heard of the surefire cure for fear of lions? You just bite a lion on the tail.

It's the same way with fear of elevators. The best cure is to ride in lots of elevators.

If you're afraid of selling, go out and become your own best salesperson. *You can do it,* not only because you know the business better than anyone else, but because your very hesitancy indicates that you will be sensitive to your customers' needs.

But don't just go out there and be sensitive. Go out and bite a lion on the tail.

industry. The local library should have a copy of the publication *Canadian Industry Shows and Exhibitions*. This will help you learn where to display your products. You may also want to check the CARD (Canadian Advertising Rates and Data), which lists many publications under various occupational and industrial classifications.

However, if the show is not in your area, you'll have transportation costs, as well as booths and rental space. Furthermore, unless you're careful and make a study of the layout, you may rent a space that is thin on traffic. See Figure 6.2.

Advice:

- Share a booth with another small business owner.
- Combine functions by doing some market research while you're promoting.
- Try to obtain space in a high-traffic area.

Industry Literature Become a source of information in your industry by producing brochures, newsletters, handbooks, product documentation, annual reports, newspaper columns for the layman, or even the "bible" for your industry (how would you like to be recognized as an expert in your field?). We think this is one of the best promotional devices around if your business lends itself to trade literature promotion.

Becoming a source of info

Remember that expertise is admired and sought out by others. As you grow in expertise, you'll also grow in confidence.

Advice:

- If you're not a good writer, encourage a friend to help.
- Talk is cheap. If you get your thoughts down on paper, you're two steps ahead of the talkers.
- Sometimes joint advertising with a manufacturer in a trade magazine is possible.

Box 6.5 They Said It

Only a few facts are known for sure about the Internet. Here they are:

- The Internet will change the way business is done.
- No one knows how, when, why or how much.

Source: Rick Spence, *Secrets of Success from Canada's Fastest-Growing Companies* (Toronto: John Wiley & Sons Canada, Ltd., 1997), p. 134.

Figure 6.2

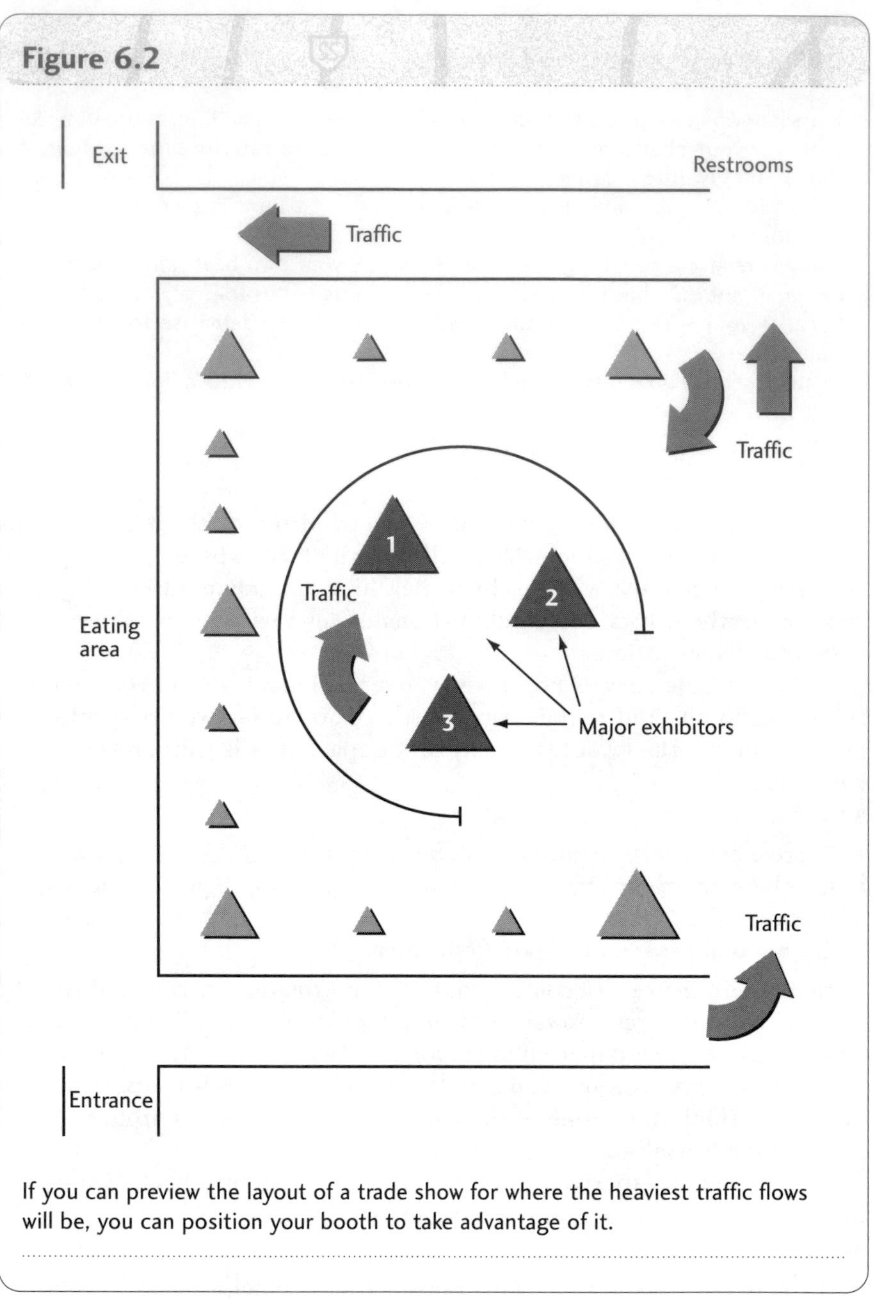

If you can preview the layout of a trade show for where the heaviest traffic flows will be, you can position your booth to take advantage of it.

Working Visibility Most service firms display their presence as they work. In other words, they put signs on everything: their business, their trucks, and their work sites. Wherever they're busy, they let people know it. They make themselves visible.

The drawback here is similar to one of the drawbacks with point-of-purchase display. If the presence you maintain doesn't sell itself — if it is unattractive or if it calls attention to an unappealing part of your business — you will lose potential customers rather than gain them.

Advice:

- Exploit your public activities with signs that tell people who you are.
- Be unique and professional in your image and message.
- Make sure the message is working.

Discount Coupons Discount coupons are a special form of freebie because they give you positive feedback on your promotion. They should have an expiration date and multiple-use disclaimers (as, for example, a disclaimer that the coupon cannot be used in conjunction with other promotions or discounts). They should also be coded to identify the source so that you can find out where your advertising is paying off, and tested in small quantities before major use.

Everyone seems to like coupons. Even if your product or service is "upscale," consider trying coupons as an introduction or at your slow times of the year.

Another twist on the coupon is the entitlement card: "Buy five cups of coffee and get the sixth cup free." There are numerous variations on this theme.

Advice:

- Consider giving away freebies that will catch your customer's attention. Box 6.6 shows some examples of effective freebies.

Brand Yourself The coffee mug you carry often has its own identity— maybe telling everyone, for example, that you are a Tim Hortons customer. And maybe it's the same with the baseball cap you wear: the "swoosh" on it tells everyone who's got you branded. A **brand** is a name, sign, symbol, design, or combination of these used to identify the products of one firm and to differentiate them from competitive offerings. A brand is the promise of the value your customer will receive from you. Smart entrepreneurs figure out

BRAND
a name, sign, symbol, design, or combination of these used to identify the products of a firm

Box 6.6 How Street Smart Are Your Freebies?

Every business has a "freebie" that will help grab the mind of its target customer. This book is full of examples: the toy store retailer who gave away a large jar of pennies in exchange for a start on a customer mailing list; the inventor who gave away one computer lock box in exchange for a mailing list of 1400 names. Here are some more examples of effective, street-smart freebies.

Orange juice. A manufacturer of a new juice squeezer served freshly squeezed orange juice at a trade show.

Hot dogs. A retailer obtained hot dogs and buns from a local hot dog maker, then advertised with promotions that read "Bring your buns to our August Sale at noon." At noon, the line of hot dog lovers stretched around the block. Curious customers, lured by free food and the carnival atmosphere, walked into the store to check out the sale. The cost of this promotion was $66.

Health drink. The distributor of an expensive food blender gave away cups of a health drink and a booklet of recipes at a trade show. Salespeople were on hand to take orders for the blender.

Advice. A men's clothing store employed a woman fashion consultant during the month of December to give advice to women who came in to shop for presents for men.

A flower shop passed out "Green Thumb" information leaflets on plant care.

A hardware store expanded into the parking lot for a "home improvement weekend." Professionals were on hand to give tips and instruction on laying tile, repairing garden hoses, fixing leaky faucets, and installing dead-bolt locks.

Often, suppliers will have promotional give-aways.

Source: Adapted in part from Toni Delacorte, Judy Kimsey, and Susan Halas, *How to Get Free Press* (San Francisco: Harbor Publishing, 1981), pp. 120–21, 125, 131–32.

ways to make themselves — and thus their business — distinctive. They brand themselves. Tom Peters, a management icon, offers the following advice to help you brand yourself and your business:[5]

Advice:

Start with answering the following questions:

- What is it that I add to my product or service that makes it different?
- What will I do to make myself and my business stand out?
- What would your customer say is your greatest strength?
- What is your most noteworthy personal trait? How is this trait tied to your business?
- How do you provide distinctive value to your business and the customer?
- What will you and your business be famous for?

Promote in Cyberspace In 1997, Jean J. Robillard, owner of Profit 100 company Avant-Garde Engineering Inc. in L'Assomption, Quebec, had a gut feeling that his potential customers were looking for new product information. So, he ordered up a 25-page Web site with lots of pictures and product descriptions. His site caught the attention of a Texas contractor who eventually placed an order worth $217 000.

According to Profit 100, now is the time to be on the Web — even if you don't think your target customer is a potential Web-surfer. Every business should have a Web site. It's your electronic telephone number and a valuable key to success.[6]

Today, anyone can have a Web site. And almost anyone does. But a site with no visitors is of little benefit to you. How do you make your site worth bookmarking? Three sites (as of 1998) can help you stay current with the technology:

Search Engine Watch: http://searchenginewatch.com/
Advertising Age: http://adage.com/
Web Sites That Work: http://www.yes.net/

Advice:[7]

- Promote your Web site off-line. Off-line promotion of a Web site can account for a major portion of first-time buyers. Include, for example, your Web site address in your letterhead and business cards. Be innovative; use every opportunity you have to promote your Web site with your company name.
- Get your Web site listed with search engines and directories. This will help your customer find you.
- The title of your Web page should clearly indicate the contents or purpose of the site.
- Design your message so that it is simple and easy to update.
- The Web is good for selective reading. Help your customers quickly select what they want.
- Remember that your customers may not have the most recent Internet technology. If you design a site that requires the latest technology, you are going to lose some customers — how many will depend on your target market.
- Make your Web page "action oriented." Provide your customer with the benefits of purchasing from you.
- In the interactive world, the ad is only there if the person finds it. Therefore, promoting on the Internet must give the customer a compelling reason to search out the site. According to Don Tapscott, one of Canada's premiere cyber gurus, your Web site must be rich in content, entertaining, and integrated with content.

How to Make the Right Decision

Any promotion or promotional mix that advances the image of your business is worth considering. However, before you select any promotional strategy, be clear on the promotional objectives you want to accomplish. They could be:

- to establish a presence in the marketplace,
- to obtain a certain level of sales,
- to position your product in a certain niche relative to your competition, and
- to expand the size of your market.

Therefore, be clear on your objectives before you decide on your promotional strategy. That's why we ask you to keep an open mind throughout this chapter, as you brainstorm for strategies, examine promotion campaigns, and come to understand the importance of an overall marketing plan. Then you will be able to spend your marketing dollars wisely to connect with your target customer.

Sales Reps as Connectors

Suppose you have a new product that has immediate sales potential across the country. How can you connect with the whole country? Should you hire your younger brother to take care of it for you, or should you seek out a professional sales representative, who will act like a commissioned sales agent for you?

An army of sales reps awaits your call. Make your selection carefully. Exercise caution, because the reputation of your sales reps will become your reputation.

The best way to find good reps is to interview potential buyers of your goods. Ask them to recommend some reps who have impressed them. When the same name surfaces several times, you will know where to start your contacts. Also, look carefully at who calls most frequently on your TC.

Aggressive reps may contact you. Prepare yourself to ask them the right kinds of questions:

- Who are your customers?
- How many salespeople do you have?
- What geographic areas do you cover?
- What lines have you carried?
- What help can you offer in collecting overdue accounts?
- What ideas do you have for trade show presentations?
- Do you have a showroom?
- Could you work with us on a regional analysis while we get ready for national coverage?
- Do you promote over the Internet?
- What percentage commission do you expect?
- Can I participate in your sales meetings?
- Do you handle competitive lines?
- What kind of reports on your sales calls can I expect?
- What kind of performance guarantees do you offer?
- How can the agreement be terminated?
- Can I pay out after I have collected from customers?

Provide all the encouragement and support to your reps that you can, and never stop being a cheerleader. At the same time, insist on sales call reports

Box 6.7 Partnerships Can Help: 101 Big Ideas

Barbara Lambesis, founder of Marketing Methods, a company based in Phoenix, Arizona, and Margaret Swaine, founder of Pierce Communications, a company based in Toronto, formed a cross-border partnership to help small business with affordable promotion strategies. To get your creative juices moving, listed below are a few of their street-smart ideas. By the way, Barbara and Margaret are constantly looking for "big ideas," so they encourage you to send them your promotional ideas. They will pay $10 if they print your idea, and you'll get your name and company in their book. (This is one of their promotional techniques, referral incentives, put into practice to help small businesses and sell more books.)

Walking signs. Hire a student to model or walk near your store with a sandwich board sign advertising your business.

Yellow Pages. The Yellow Pages are popular because they have a reputation for producing results.

Guarantees. Tom Stoyan, author of *Sell More . . . 101 Ideas to Increase Sales Now!*, has a guarantee: "The exercises in this book are guaranteed to work for you. If they do not, I will gladly refund your full purchase price if you provide me with evidence you have worked the ideas for 30 days, along with your sales receipt." As Tom Stoyan will attest, guarantees work.

Special sales. Don't just have a sale, have a happening. Try to be unique. In their book *101 Big Ideas*, Lambesis and Swaine talk about one store that had a "crack of dawn" sale. At this event, the owners gave a free breakfast, in the parking lot, for everyone who purchased at least $25 worth of goods.

Referral incentives. Remember that Lambesis and Swaine will offer you $10 for a good idea they use in print.

Special events. A restaurant called Marble Club holds an annual marble shooting contest, with the proceeds going to a local charity.

Greeting cards. Often, cards at holiday time get "lost" in the shuffle. Pick a different time to remember your customer — maybe an "unbirthday" card.

Free talks and presentations. In Chapter Seven you will meet Sheila Mather, who gives free talks to groups of small business students as a part of her strategy.

Home parties. Even if you deal mainly with the business community, invite them to your home on a Friday at noon for a light lunch and a swim. If you don't have a pool, try a picnic.

Statement stuffers. It doesn't cost much to include a coupon, flyer, or announcement with your invoice.

The list goes on. *101 Big Ideas* is recommended reading.

Source: Adapted from Barbara Lambesis and Margaret Swaine, *101 Big Ideas for Promoting a Business on a Small Budget* (Toronto: Pierce Communications Press, 1990). Reprinted by permission.

that will keep you informed on what is going on in the field, and pack your bags and make some calls with your reps. Write monthly sales letters and encourage feedback from both your reps and their customers. You *could* learn the worst — that a new line has taken your place or that the reps have been sleeping. This feedback will help you to evaluate your product line and your reps.

Courtesy as Promotion

A dealer in luxury imported autos mailed 5 000 postcards to high-income prospects. The postcard message read something like "Come in and test-drive this road warrior and receive a nice gift."

One potential customer travelled 65 kilometres for his test drive. The gift was a good incentive, but he'd been looking at cars for a year and was about to make a decision, so he wanted the test drive. That morning he had transferred funds to his chequing account. "Honey," he said to his wife as he left the house, "I'll be home with a car." His pink slip on his trade-in smouldered in the glove compartment.

Mr. Serious Prospect entered the dealer's showroom wearing old clothes and clutching his postcard. Four dapper salesmen in three-piece suits had seen him coming and had left the showroom quickly.

Without a salesperson in sight, the prospect spent ten minutes waiting, reading the literature. The demos were locked, so he couldn't even sit behind the wheel for a fantasy drive. At last, a secretary entered the showroom, asked him for his postcard, and gave him the premium gift. About this time, one salesman returned, hands in his pockets and looking bored. The prospect took the opportunity to ask some questions about the car, to which the salesman responded without enthusiasm in monosyllables — and with a yawn.

Mr. Prospect took his business elsewhere that morning. He found the car he wanted and wrote a cheque for $45 000.

The promotion objective was to bring in customers for a test drive, not to give away premiums. Everything worked except the last person in the chain. How many other deals did that dealer lose during the promotion?

Be dramatic. Impress your employees with the fact that you mean business about customer courtesy. Close down your business for a day and have all employees attend a sales retreat that stresses the importance of potential customers to your remaining in business. Follow up the retreat with incentive programs that reward employees for acts of exceptional courtesy to customers.

Planning Ahead

You need to make a lot of intelligent noise before you open your doors for business. When you open, open with a bang. Start-ups are ironic: you often need to spend a large sum of money to overcome buyer inertia, yet you don't have those dollars to spend. What are you to do? Use your head instead of your chequebook.

Plan for your opening now. Few businesses are profitable at first, so yours probably won't be either. Many of the promotional tools we've just discussed cost very little. You will need to use them to lure customers and build confidence that you are in this game to win. Use your head instead of your chequebook. And keep your target customers clearly in mind so that you'll be able to tell them how your product or service will benefit them.

DON'T KEEP YOUR BUSINESS A SECRET

When it comes to promotion, if you fail to plan, you're planning to keep your business a secret.

One way to avoid keeping your business a secret is to brainstorm an ideal **promotional campaign** with no holds barred and no worries about costs. Action Step 32 makes sure you consider all of your creative ideas before you discard them because you think they are unrealistic. Save the ideas you come

ACTION STEP 32

Brainstorm a winning promotional campaign for your business.

Disregard all budgetary restraint. Pretend that money is no object. Close your eyes, sit back, and develop the ideal campaign for connecting with your target customers. It's okay to "get crazy" with this, because excellent workable solutions often develop out of such unleashed mental activity!

- If your product or service needs a multimillion-dollar advertising promotion with endorsements by your favourite movie star, fantasize that it's happening now.
- If you need a customer list created in marketing heaven, specify exactly what you need and it is yours.
- If you are looking for the services of a first-class catalogue house, just whisper the name three times and you are in business.
- If your business at its peak could use a thousand delivery trucks with smiling drivers who make your TC feel terrific, write down "1 000 smiling delivery people."
- If your product is small, brainstorm the perfect point-of-purchase device, perhaps one with slot machines whose money-tubes are connected to your private bank vault.
- How would you promote your product or service over the Internet? Design the perfect Web site. Watch the money roll in.

This chance to ignore cost won't come around again (reality is right around the corner). But for now, have fun.

PROMOTIONAL CAMPAIGN
a sales program designed to sell a specific product or service or to establish an image, benefit, or point

Box 6.8 Creative Promotional Ideas From *Streetfighter*

Don't be afraid of being different. What's hot? What's cool? What's melting in your arms?
Problem: Salespeople at Wisman's Trusted Appliance & TV, Inc., feared they were losing business when customers left the store to comparison-shop. The solution? The owner packed a freezer with ice cream. Every customer who looked at a freezer got a half-gallon carton, *free*. Instead of comparison shopping, the customers raced home to their refrigerators. That gimmick kept Wisman's in the mind of the prospect and helped increase sales by 11 percent.

Contest? Fat prize? Insure yourself at Lloyd's
The owner of a small print shop was tapped for $750 by the organizers of a charity golf tournament. Wanting as much mileage as possible for his promotional dollar, he offered a hole-in-one contest prize of $10 000, to be split between the first golfer to ace the ninth hole, and the charity. The owner's picture was taken with an oversize cheque, and the media kept cameras trained on the ninth hole. And if the golfer had sunk one? No problem. The shop owner was insured with Lloyd's of London against business loss, with a premium of $450 — $300 less than his name on the donors' board would have cost.

Source: Adapted with permission from *Street Fighter Marketing*, a book published by Street Fighter Marketing, Inc. 467 Waterbury Court, Cohanna, OH 43230, USA. Written by Jeff Slutsky. Web site: <http://streetfighter.com>

up with in this Action Step because we'll use them later. Box 6.8 shows how two entrepreneurs applied ingenious — and cost-effective — solutions to their promotional needs. Later in the chapter, we share four case studies from our own file on creative promotions.

As you'll see throughout this chapter, the entrepreneurs who succeeded are the entrepreneurs who have the best fix on their target customers. They are also the entrepreneurs who understand the importance of market research.

Promotion and Market Research

CORE BENEFIT PROPOSITION
a statement about the benefits of your product or service to your target market

As you gain experience in promoting your small business, you'll see for yourself just how much your promotional strategy and the target customer are interlocked. That's why you can't plan your promotional strategy without building on your market research. This helps you develop your **core benefit proposition**. Your TC is interested in what your product or service will do for them. You are selling benefits, not features. Your research will help you clarify the benefits of your product or service. That's why you can't plan your promotional mix without dipping back into market research. The pros do both at the same time. But don't take our word for it — ask entrepreneur Frank Williams. He combined his research with promotion, and he used a freebie for a come-on.

Frank Williams was really happy with his microcomputer until the switch went out two days after the 90-day warranty was up. Frank put the micro into his car and drove to the repair shop.

"You turn it on and off a lot?" the repairman asked.

"Of course," Frank said. "Several times a day. Why?"

"That's what wore it out," the repairman said. "The switch is the only moving part. The rest of this baby will last ten years, at least."

The repair bill was $150, and when Frank got back home he gave the situation some thought. The reason he had to keep turning the machine off was to stop his youngest child from messing up his files. What alternative had he to turning the machine off?

The lock box idea came to Frank as he was dropping off to sleep that night. The following weekend, he designed a prototype of wood. His model had a hinged lid, a brass lock, and a space-age look. Frank took it to a friend of his who was a manufacturer. The friend thought it would fly. They consulted their wives on colours, and the group came up with eight colours: red, orange, yellow, black, beige, blue, white, and avocado.

"That's a lot of paint," the manufacturer said. "How can we narrow it down?"

"Market research," Frank said.

Frank took a prototype lock box to a computer trade show. He put up a large sign that said: "Register for a Free Micro Lock Box." People crowded into Frank's booth to sign up for his drawing. The card had a place for their name, address, phone number, type of computer, and the colour they would like.

It worked. Frank's market research was cheap and fast. In a day and a half, he got 1 400 people to tell him what colour of lock box they wanted. The overwhelming favourite was beige. Furthermore, he had a good start on a customer mailing list.

By being curious and thorough, Frank Williams had discovered one of the secrets of the marketplace. You can promote and do market research at the same time. He also learned that if you don't know what your target customers want, all you have to do is ask them.

ASK THE CUSTOMERS QUESTIONS TO DEVELOP YOUR MARKETING STRATEGY

When you're trying to brainstorm your marketing strategy, ask your customers how they perceive your business. Then ask them questions such as:

- Is there anything you couldn't find?
- Is this your first visit to this store? (or some other greeting instead of "Can I help you?")
- What do you want and do we have it?
- How does our product or service fit your needs?
- How do we compare in price to the competition?
- Is there more value to you in shopping here than elsewhere?
- Where are you from?
- How did you find us?
- How else might our company be of service?

Listen to the answers your customers give you, and value the information for what it is: primary market research data. Write down each customer's exact words in your adventure notebook.

ACTION STEP 33

Attach a price tag to each item of your promotion package.

What will your customer connection cost? To get some idea, go back to Action Step 32 and list the top four or five connections you want with your customers. Then find their cost.

Let's imagine that you have chosen this promotional mix:

1. *Magazine ads.* This choice assumes you know what your TC reads. Good. Contact the display ad department of the magazines. Ask for its media kit and a reader profile. At the same time, ask for the rates for its mailing lists for the geographic areas you want to reach. Many magazines will sell lists by a code.
2. *Direct mail.* Look up mailing list brokers in the Yellow Pages under Direct Mail. Tell them what business you are in and ask for information, strategy tips, and sample names to check for mailing list accuracy against your TC profiles. Compare the costs of buying the lists from brokers and from magazines.
3. *Press releases.* Visit the marketing department of your local newspaper for information on targetting its readers. Use this information to angle your release. Type the release double-spaced. Catch the reader's attention, but keep the message simple. Be sure to wield the five *Ws* (who, what, where, when, why) and the noble *H* (how) of journalism.
4. *Personal selling.* If you cannot reach customers this way yourself, you will need to budget for someone who can. If you are planning on selling yourself, locate lead clubs in your area and start building a network of contacts. Figure your salary and expenses as a promotional cost. (For tips on how to profile your personality and how it can be balanced by others, see Chapter Twelve.)

Once you know what each item of your promotional package will cost, you can decide which ones you can afford. Your final plan should look something like Table 6.1.

FREEBIES IN GENERAL

Freebies are a tremendously effective promotional gimmick. You can use them to get your customers' attention, to create interest in a new product, or (like Frank Williams) to gather market research. Give-aways don't have to be expensive to help you connect with customers. Box 6.6 describes some inexpensive freebies that entrepreneurs have used to grab the mind of the target customer. (Note that many of the freebies are purely informational. Could you boost sales by offering free advice?)

Making Decisions

By now you should be ready to make a few decisions about your marketing strategy and promotional mix. Let's begin with price.

ATTACH PRICE TAGS TO YOUR PROMOTION STRATEGIES

A give-away, like any other promotional strategy, costs money. Look at the ideal promotional strategies you identified in Action Step 32 and pick the top four or five elements. Then determine the price of each. Action Step 33 walks you through the process. The promotional plan for Flower Warehouse will help you put a price tag on your strategy (see Table 6.1). Box 6.9 gives you some sample media rates. This is only a guide, so check with your local media for exact rates.

Don't be discouraged if price knocks out part of your ideal promotional mix. Always evaluate if there is a way to achieve the same result, but with less cost. That's why we've filled this chapter with so many inexpensive promotional ideas. Use the powers of your imagination to brainstorm the best possible promotional effort for your business.

Even as you make a decision, keep thinking of the best possible effort — and of your target customer — and you can't go wrong.

Table 6.1 Sample Promotional Plan — Flower Warehouse

Promotional Method	Frequency	Annual Cost	Comments
Yellow Pages	Daily	$2 400	Monitor results
Window signs	12/year	$ 360	Support promotions
Point of purchase signs	12/year	$ 240	Support promotions
Newspaper ads	2/month	$3 000	Support promotions
Fliers	12/year	$ 800	With sales promotions
Sales promotions	1/month	$4 500	Holidays and specials
Publicity	12/year	$ 200	Publicize promotions
Personal sales calls	1/week	$ 0	Corporate accounts
Sampling and gifts	As needed	$1 000	Door prizes and referrals
Networking	1/week	$ 600	Sales leads
Thank-you letters	As needed	$ 0	Customer referrals

Source: Adapted from Barbara Lambesis and Margaret Swaine, *101 Big Ideas for Promoting a Business on a Small Budget* (Toronto: Pierce Communications Press, 1990), p. 90. Reprinted by permission.

Box 6.9 Sample of Media Rates

Local Newspaper:	Between $0.75 and $1.25 per line; 1/6 of a page is $200 to $335.
Radio:	A 30-second ad costs $97, including preparation of the ad to reach 250 000. A four-hour remote on site costs $3 500 which includes three 60-second ads every hour plus twelve 30-second pre-ads. A 30-second ad to reach 80 000 is approximately $24.
ValPak: (Direct Mail)	Ten thousand addresses in a predetermined zone is 3.5¢ per unit or $350 if art work — about 5¢ per unit. Note: Direct mail is number one in N.A. in advertising spent $198 billion.

Source: American Direct Mail Association

CONCENTRATE YOUR EFFORTS

One promotional strategy may prove to be a big winner for your business. The examples that follow show how several entrepreneurs discovered their winning strategies. While reading what these entrepreneurs have to say, you may discover your own winning strategy. Look for inspiration.

Earth-to-Air Travel, Inc. — Newsletter

Two years ago we missed the ironclad deadline for getting out an ad in the Yellow Pages, so we tried to make up for that by placing fun-type ads in community newsletters within a 2-kilometre radius of our agency. The ads didn't cost much, and we hoped they would help to keep our visibility high. Our best response came from a mobile home park less than a kilometre away. It's a gold mine of retirees with steady incomes and who dearly love to travel.

By studying the community newsletters, we came up with our own format, and now we send out our own agency newsletter every couple of months. On the front page we feature a catchy travel theme, along with a picture of our employees. The picture helps us connect, especially with first-time customers. They see our smiling faces, and most of them feel they know us when they walk through our door. We're already on the way to being friends.

Computer Master — Direct Mail

When we started Computer Master, we quickly discovered that the major newspaper covered the city, while the market we'd targetted — 50⁺ age group and small business microcomputer owners — lived in the valley community. The one sure way to reach the centre of the market was with a direct mail piece. Our promotional strategy was to develop a list of local library customers and to offer them free seminars.

The response was terrific. We generated enough business for a healthy start-up, and satisfied customers sold for us after that by taking us up on our training seminars.

Direct mail allowed us to go right to the heart of our market. When you're just starting out in a new venture, that kind of accuracy is worth every penny it costs.

Argosy Auto Parts — A Sign on Your Car

The main reason we chose Argosy was because we thought it was a good name. In Toronto my husband had 32 years of experience in the auto parts trade — in retailing and also in distribution — and when we opened our store in Victoria, we felt it was a guaranteed money-maker.

We opened in mid-summer, but by September we were ready to call it quits. Sales had averaged only $2 000 a month, and that wasn't even enough to pay the rent.

Fortunately, we got help from a small business seminar. It was made clear to us that although everyone was familiar with the name Argosy in Toronto, few in Victoria knew who we were.

Our first step was simple: we parked our car on the main street near our store. On the back we placed a large sign, with an arrow pointing to our store. The sign read "Argosy Auto Parts." Business picked up right away, and that gave us the confidence to make contact with service stations in the area. Gradually, we built up our own network. I joined some local service clubs, and that led me to a sales lead club.

Things are all right now, but when I look back, I know that without that sign on the car we'd have been out of business in no time.

Garment Guide — Free Ink

When my partner and I got the idea for guiding shoppers through the Montreal garment district, we thought it would be so exciting we wouldn't have to do much except stop off once a week to make bank deposits.

Were we ever wrong.

We ran a good-sized ad in the local paper. It filled a couple of tour buses, but then our market ran out because those customers didn't need a return visit. We had some flyers printed up, and we covered every car in every parking lot in our community. Two thousand flyers netted us half a bus.

Then I just happened to read a feature story in the "View" section of the *Montreal Gazette* about a tour to Quebec City. On an impulse, I called up the reporter and told her about Garment Guide. It worked.

On the next tour, the reporter came along and brought a staff photographer. Two weeks later, our story was on the *front page* of the "View" section — a beautiful third of a page — and customers began calling us! Our local papers followed a month or so later with features about the service, and after we got bigger, a TV reporter profiled us for one of the evening news magazines on television.

Now business is great. We haven't had to advertise for eighteen months. When people ask me what kind of promotion I believe in, I tell them, "Free ink!"

We hope you found inspiration by reading about these entrepreneurs who, through planning or perseverance, found successful promotional strategies. Now let's go on to two of the most useful promotional tools for *every* small business: mailing lists and networking.

Mailing Lists

Sometimes the winning component of a promotional mix is a mailing list that goes to the heart of your target market. An accurate and up-to-date mailing list can mean money in the bank. Entrepreneur Mel Cartwright developed a database on his target customers in a fun and painless manner — and in the midst of his Christmas promotion.

Mel had worked for three large corporations before he decided to start a business of his own in Calgary, Mel's Toys.

For the first six months, business was fair and Mel broke even. Then sales picked up dramatically the last Saturday of November. The parking lot in the shopping centre was crammed with cars, and Christmas-conscious people came in, hunting for gifts for their children. That Saturday, Mel made more money than he had in all of September.

"The toy business is seasonal," Mel said. "And with all those people coming through the door, I wanted to make sure I developed a solid customer base."

So, for three weeks, Mel hired a Rent-a-Santa and a professional photographer. Every child that came into Mel's Toys was photographed, free, on Santa's knee. While the children were being photographed, the parents filled out information cards with their child's name, age, toy preferences, and date of birth.

At the end of the three weeks, Mel had developed a fine customer list. He also had one valuable piece of information: the birthday of every child who had been photographed.

Every time a birthday rolled around, Mel mailed a small, inexpensive toy along with some copies of the Santa photograph. As an added bonus, he made the negatives available to parents, many of whom ordered Christmas cards picturing their child talking to Santa.

As his mailing list grew, Mel came up with another idea.

"I was at the cash register one day when one of my employees was sick with the flu, and I noticed five customers in a row who spent more than $50. I kept those cheques and credit card slips separate, and at the end of the day I photocopied them and started a Big Spender list. Today, my Big Spender list has grown to several hundred customers and I've developed a special mailer aimed just at them.

"I wish someone had told me how important a mailing list would be in this business before I got into it. With what I know now, I think I could branch off into at least a dozen industries and do very well."

You may not need a Rent-a-Santa to get started, but you do need well-organized information. Action Step 34 asks you to organize the information you

ACTION STEP 34

Develop resource files on your computer.

Begin with a study of what your target customer reads. Move from there to a reader profile and a mailing list to find out where your TCs are concentrated.

For every customer you contact, make up a computer file. Use your handy demographic set-up (sex, age, income, education, and residence — or size of company, type of industry, what department does the buying, and so forth) and launch yourself early into analyses of lifestyle or business style. If you have a computer, this is a great time to use it.

Try to segment the big spenders and develop a special strategy for them. (Every industry has its heavy users. Who are the heavies in your industry?)

Start a media file on your computer by contacting all potential advertising media in your area. Ask for rate cards and demographics.

If you have not done it yet, start a file on your competitors and how they promote. Try to learn what is working. What ideas can you borrow?

Start a "How Can They Help Me?" file on your vendors and suppliers. Most vendors have been in the industry awhile. Get to know them, ask for advice, and listen carefully. You may not buy from them, but the information you obtain could save your neck.

already have. See how the concept of a mailing list may begin with a customer file and then expand to include your other contacts as well. You can't help but gather information as you operate your small business. With good files, that information becomes useful. Organized information is power — and Action Step 34 shows you how to get that power.

Networking

Another source of promotional power is the technique of **networking**. Networking carries the image of your business to a support group of non-competitive helpers. It is the wave of the future in small business. Gena D'Angelo speaks for many when she gives this testimonial for networking.

When Rob and I decided to go into business for ourselves, we looked around for more than a year. I had some training in graphics and Rob is good with numbers, so what we finally decided on was a franchised mail-box operation. We paid the franchiser a flat fee and agreed to pay a percentage of our gross as well. In turn, we received assistance and a well-developed business plan.

What they didn't tell us about was networking.

When you're in the mail-box business, giving good service is how you forge ahead. We knew we had to promote our image, and we tried everything — brochures, leaflets, flyers, and full-page display ads in the local newspapers. But the business didn't start rolling in until I joined my first network.

It's a sales lead club, and the membership is varied. We have a real estate broker, an insurance agent, the president of a small bank, the owner of a coffee service, a printer, a sign manufacturer, the owner of a chain of service stations, a sporting goods store owner, a travel agent, two small manufacturers, and a contractor. We meet once a week for breakfast. If you don't bring at least one sales lead for another club member, you have to put a dollar in the kitty. I've gotten more business from that club than from all my other promotional efforts combined.

I then decided to join another club, and I used the contacts I made to build my own network. Business has been good ever since. We opened our second shop last April, put in a computer to keep track of our customers, and added an answering service. That first year, we networked our way to even more business, and we're planning to open a third shop 10 kilometres south of here by this time next year.

Networking gives you confidence, and it allows you to pass on helpful information to people who aren't competing with you — and to receive that kind of information too.

As a small business entrepreneur, you can network your way to a surprising number of new customer connections, which can spell success in big letters. If you don't have a network, use Action Step 35 to build one. Develop your network and build core groups of people within it. Because a network grows naturally from the loose association of people you already know, and because you are at the *centre* of the net, it has to help you.

ACTION STEP 35

Build your network.

Visualize yourself as being in the centre of a web of interpersonal contacts and associations. This web connects you with your family, friends, neighbours, acquaintances, business associates — everyone you know — and it is your potential network.

To develop a functioning network for yourself, write down what you know about each person in your web: business, hobbies, residence, children, interests, and whom they might know. Recall where you met the person. Does the meeting place tell you anything helpful? Are you members of the same group or club? What interests do you share? What is the connection between you and the person?

Now, from all these people, build a couple of core groups. Start with two or three people. Are they interested in networking? Are they diverse enough? (You'll need doers, stars, leaders, technicians, an organizer or two — people who will tend to "balance out" your own talents. See Chapter Twelve on team building.) Make sure the people you contact are not competing for the same target customers. The members of a core group must *not* be competitors; if they are, the group won't function as it should.

Set up a meeting. If you are working, breakfast usually works best. If the core group catches on, you can share phone duties and arrange further meetings.

Before you know it, you will be networking your way through the channels of your community, business to business.

NETWORKING
communicating through person-to-person channels in an attempt to sell or gain information; talking to people with the purpose of doing business

Box 6.10 Your Entrepreneurial Know-Who

Rein Peterson is one of Canada's entrepreneurial gurus. Here is what he has to say about networking.

"Networking is a basic and critical resource for Canadian entrepreneurs. Nurturing and building personal 'know-who' entrepreneurial skills is often a prerequisite for success in pursuing opportunities beyond resources currently in place. People make use of other persons to pass on recommendations, solicit jobs, obtain funds, and so on, but this is often denied in public, for it is regarded as wrong to do so. But research continues to show that:

1. Successful entrepreneurs spend more than 50 percent of their time maintaining their personal networks.
2. Personal entrepreneurial networks outlast individual business ventures.
3. Managing a personal entrepreneurial network requires initiative.

"As a result, entrepreneurial students (at the Schulich School of Business, York University) are taught the Nine Rules for Developing Your Entrepreneurial Know-Who:

1. First, you must admit that entrepreneurial know *who* is as important as entrepreneurial know *how*. Be diplomatic, but don't be inhibited about developing contacts that will assist you in starting your new venture. Reciprocity is a universal value. If you help someone else, they are likely to respond in kind. If they do you a favour, consider it an invitation to reciprocate.
2. Be systematic, explicit and forthright in creating and managing your network. Successful entrepreneurs use annotated name card files. There is also software available for your computer to record your contacts' addresses, telephone numbers, birthdays and other relevant information.
3. Assess your network in terms of the specific types of ventures that you peruse. For growing ventures, does your network provide access to financial resources you will continually need — bankers, private investors, angels, other entrepreneurs, etc.? What are your links to knowledgeable professionals — lawyers, accountants, venture capitalists, industry experts, etc.? Are you a member of important industry associations, clubs or civic organizations where you will meet others with similar goals? A typical entrepreneurial network includes about 800 members, only 12 percent of whom are professionals. The vast majority are doers and risk-taking peers like yourself.
4. It helps to place your business venture close to your natural contacts and where others in a similar business are located. For example, the importance of networking among like-minded businesses is evident in the following areas: Kitchener-Waterloo, Kanata, North Toronto, parts of Montreal, Calgary and Vancouver.
5. Use your network regularly. Just like physical fitness requires exercise, networks become stronger and more effective through use. The strengths and weaknesses of your network become apparent only when used.
6. Identify and communicate continuously with the "gatekeepers" in your network. The gatekeepers are the select few special people who are truly committed to you. Not only do they provide you with a sounding board, but they also keep in touch with other potentially useful people of whom you may not be aware or unable to keep in touch with. They know whom you can contact to get help. They form a part of your "virtual" business organization.
7. Assess your network in terms of the entrepreneurial functions you are required to perform: opportunity recognition and risk management. Do you have contacts who can help you spot a potential window of opportunity before the rest of the pack? How many of your contacts are strong enough to tell you when you are wrong?

(Continued)

Box 6.10 Your Entrepreneurial Know-Who *(Continued)*

8. Contribute regularly to your personal network. You need to put something into the well to keep drawing. Social banking, whereby people keep informal track of those who contribute and those who don't, is a fact of life.
9. Don't become a slave to developing your network. Effective entrepreneurship requires a balance between know-how and know-who. You can become ineffective by spending too much time managing your network. It is not a social club, but a business resource.

Source: Rein Peterson, "How Is Entrepreneurship Different in Canada?" in *Mastering Enterprise*, Part One (sponsored by Doane Raymond, Compaq, and Bank of Montreal), *Financial Post* and *Financial Times*. Reprinted by permission of Rein Peterson, Professor and Director of Entrepreneurial Studies, Schulich School of Business, York University, Toronto.

Box 6.11 Bookmark This

So, you find it hard to go out and talk to people. Or you can't get the answers you want. Why not chat in cyberspace? Visit the Web site of the Canadian Youth Business Foundation (CYBF) at <www.cybf.ca>.

Click on the "Ask an Expert" button. Here you will have the opportunity to access and ask questions of small business experts who donate their time to help. The CYBF also has a "Just Ask" button for those times when you have a specific question and need experienced small business advice. The CYBF even has a "Live Chat" service that allows you to speak to other entrepreneurs directly.

In a Nutshell

The marketing strategy describes what you have to do to reach your goals and objectives. Within that strategy is promotion. Promotion is the art or science of moving the image of your business into the prospect's mind. Anything that will advance that image is a good tactic to consider. The foundation of any promotional strategy is customer service and quality.

In this chapter, we recommended that you survey the whole range of promotional strategies available to you and then choose the promotional mix that will work best for your unique business. Potential strategies include paid media advertising, point-of-purchase displays, catalogue sales, direct mail, money-back guarantees, free ink and free air, personal selling, trade shows, industry literature, work visibility, branding, and promoting in cyberspace.

We also recommended that you seek creative solutions to the problem of promoting within a small budget, and we gave examples of how other entrepreneurs have responded to that challenge. Other topics covered included the proper place of freebies, the reasons why an accurate and up-to-date mailing list is a must for survival, and the importance of networking for sales leads and other information.

Throughout the chapter, we stressed the relationship between market research (your strategy for locating target customers and learning their needs) and promotion (letting your customers know your business can serve their needs and make them happy in the process). The overall message of the chapter is to use your head as well as your chequebook in connecting with the customer.

Think Points for Success

- ✓ Be unique with your promotions. Instead of Christmas cards, send Thanksgiving cards or April Fool's Day cards.
- ✓ Stand in your target customer's shoes. Think like your TC. Find the need. Find the "ladder" in the TC's mind.
- ✓ Maintain a visual presence.
- ✓ A world in transition means opportunities for entrepreneurship. Fast footwork can keep you in the game.
- ✓ To start your own mailing list, give away something for free. In return, potential customers will give you their names.
- ✓ Rent a Santa. Rent a robot. Rent a hot-air balloon. Rent a talking dolphin. Brand yourself. Create some excitement, because excitement sells.
- ✓ When you think you have it made, keep connecting with that customer anyway. You will never be so big that you can afford to disconnect. Remember this and it will make you rich.
- ✓ Remember to promote the benefits and value of your product or service.
- ✓ Use the Internet to promote.

ACTION STEP REVIEW

32 Brainstorm a winning promotional campaign for your business.
33 Attach a price tag to each component of your promotional package.
34 Develop your resource files on your computer.
35 Build your network.

Business Plan Building Block

ADVERTISING AND PROMOTION

Describe your advertising and public relations plan. What are the most cost-effective ways to reach your customers? Use the data you have developed from the text.

Public Relations — Unpaid Advertising

- Sample news releases (attach).
- Research articles or contributions to trade or technical journals.
- Participation in, or sponsorship of, events.
- Contributions to local media (air, press, and others).
- Community charities and/or networking activities.

Media Advertising and Direct Mail

- Mail list applications
- Advertising-space buys
- Yellow Pages
- Computer bulletin boards and Web sites
- TV and radio commercials
- Point-of-purchase displays, signs, billboards
- Brochures and selling sheets
- Business cards and ad specials
- Trade shows and informational seminars

Don't be afraid to be different and unique. Your message has to penetrate a lot of clutter.

Your turn: this will take a page or more.

SERVICE AND SUPPLY

Once the sale is consummated, explain delivery of the product. Take out? Will call? UPS? Purolator? FedEx? and so on. Follow with sales support. What will your customer need from you once the product or service has been delivered? Look for techniques to turn your service into additional sales opportunities.

Your turn:

SALES FORECAST

It's time to start firming up your numbers. Forecast the first year by month and the second through fifth years by the quarter. Expect a slow start and adjust for seasonal months that are consistent with your industry. It is helpful to develop a minimum, maximum, or realistic sales forecast.

Support your numbers with data on total market available, your anticipated share, orders already booked, letters of commitment, and anything else that will support your assumptions.

MARKET STRATEGIES

You have already made sales projections. This section will demonstrate how you plan to achieve your sales goals.

In this section, outline your activities to identify your target customers' unmet or undeserved needs. How will you communicate with customers to explain how your firm would benefit them?

This is a general statement that demonstrates that your business is customer driven. Use information in Chapter Four to develop a one-page marketing strategy philosophy.

SERVICES AFTER THE SALE

Once you have a customer, what will you do to keep him or her? Phone call follow-up? Correcting shipping or product mistakes? and so forth.

Checklist Questions and Actions to Develop Your Business Plan

MARKETING STRATEGIES AND PROMOTION: CONNECTING WITH THE CUSTOMER

- ❑ What is your marketing strategy?
- ❑ What are the promotion mix goals and objectives?
- ❑ What stimulates your target market to buy or use your product or service?
- ❑ What has the primary and secondary market research told you about promoting your business?
- ❑ Develop a promotional strategy for your business.
- ❑ What percentage and what amount of your promotional budget will be spent on each of the components of a promotional mix, and why?
- ❑ Does your business have a unique twist for a possible publicity story?
- ❑ Why did you select the business name you are using?

NOTES

1. Rick Spence, *Secrets of Success from Canada's Fastest-Growing Companies* (Toronto: John Wiley & Sons Canada, Ltd., 1997), p. 140.
2. *Ibid.*, p. 140.
3. *Ibid.*, p. 142.
4. Geoffrey Rowan, "Customer Service Forms the Currency of the Digital Age," *The Globe and Mail*, March 18, 1998, p. B25.
5. Adapted from Tom Peters, "The Brand Called You," as first published in *Fast Company*, August/September 1997, pp. 83–94. Copyright © 1998.
6. Spence, *Secrets of Success from Canada's Fastest-Growing Companies*, pp. 134–35.
7. Thea Partridge, "Building a Site Profile: Print Invitations, Search Opportunities," *The Financial Post*, March 8, 1998, p. N4; and Don Tapscott, *Growing Up Digital: The Rise of the Net Generation* (Toronto: McGraw-Hill, 1998), p. 197.

OTHER REFERENCES

Anderson, Kare. *Pocket Cross-Promotional Marketing*. Master Media Ltd., 1996.

Bodean, Nat. *Direct Marketing Rules of Thumb*. Whitby, ON: McGraw-Hill Ryerson Ltd., 1997.

Brethour, Patrick. "Guru's Guide to Online Marketing." *Globe and Mail*, May 14, 1997, p. 13.

Church, Elizabeth. "How Firms Should Handle Bad Publicity." *Globe and Mail*, November 8, 1996, p. B9.

Dru, Jean-Marie. *Creative Advertising: Breaking with the Past*. New York: John Wiley & Sons, Inc., 1996.

Heinzl, John. "In-Your-Face Service Leaves Customers Cold." *Globe and Mail*, January 16, 1998, p. B23.

Qubein, Nido R. *How to Be a Great Communicator*. New York: John Wiley & Sons, 1997.

Siskind, Barry. "100 Reasons to Exhibit at a Trade Show." *Globe and Mail*, September 17, 1997, Ad Feature.

Stone, Kayle. "Promotion Commotion." *Report on Business*, December 1997, pp. 102–106.

Tulenko, Paul. "The Key to a Successful Presentation." *Globe and Mail*, December 29, 1997, p. B6.

seven

Location

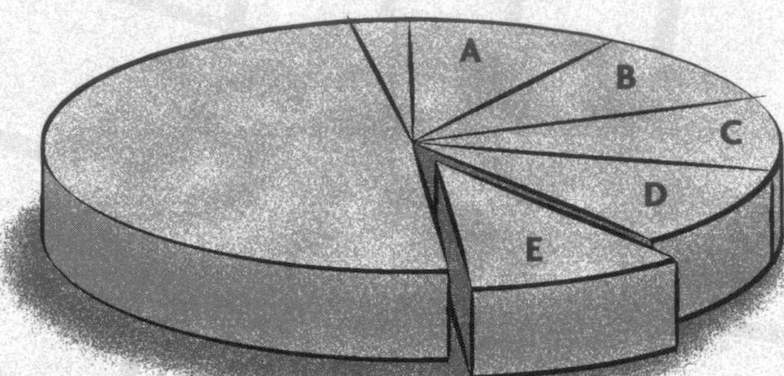

BUSINESS PLAN BUILDING BLOCK

This chapter will help you select the location that is best for your type of business and the options that may be available.

Figure 7.1 Chapter Seven will help you prepare part E of your business plan, "Location."

LEARNING OPPORTUNITIES

After reading this chapter, you should be able to:

- Understand the contribution of location to small business success.
- Understand the uniqueness of your business-location needs.
- Focus on customer needs when evaluating a location.
- Develop a checklist for evaluating potential sites for your business.
- Think about if and when you should locate your business out of the home.
- Use both secondary and primary sources of information in locating your business.
- Understand and negotiate a lease contract.

"In Halifax, there's nothing really like us," Moira Lloyd, co-owner of Ceilidh Connections, says of the Barrington Street bar. "We're a restaurant on one side, with computers on the other. People can sit here and have a beer and plate of fries while they surf [the Net]." The target customer is between the ages of 20 and 35. The on-line lounge is particularly appealing to tourists and business travellers who can "return home" in cyberspace.

Choosing the right location was a critical decision for Moira and her partner, Fiona Merry. They wanted to be close to the tourist trade and the downtown core, and within walking distance of the two universities, St. Mary's and Dalhousie. It looks like all their research has paid off. The restaurant is busy and the cyber lounge is booming. "Once the computers caught on, the lounge became our main income here," says Moira.[1]

Exercise + people + fun + work + stress = start a physical fitness program in the workplace. Psychographic thinking and the guidance of visionaries such as Faith Popcorn have been put into practice successfully by Sheila Mather. There she was, on an early Saturday morning, sharing her experience with an audience of soon-to-be business people. She operates her business out of her home, but today this seminar was her location, and she was marketing herself at a local small business seminar called "Look Before You Leap."

ACTION STEP PREVIEW

36 Fantasize your perfect location.
37 Use your new eyes to evaluate business locations.
38 Seek professional help in finding a location.

Her talk began with a few minutes of low impact aerobics. When everyone was energized, she said, "You don't have to be a rocket scientist. I'm not in the high-tech business per se. But my job is to increase productivity in our growth high-tech sector. I'm in the 'feel good, energy, and people business.' These are the benefits that my customers want. You're also my potential customer, and after exercising, I hope you feel a little better now."

She explained that her home-based location strategy was not about finding a physical site. It was about finding ways to locate herself and her business in front of the customer. "Yesterday, for example, my location was an empty office where I conducted my exercise program for one of my company clients. Today, my location is here at this seminar. In home-based business, your location is fluid, and one thing is for sure: you should plan to be out meeting people, because it is people who will drive your business." The trend in the third millenium is definitely towards the mobile entrepreneur — the one that goes to the target market.

One of the most important decisions the small business entrepreneur makes is where to locate the business. "Location, location, location" have been touted as the three most important reasons for business success. To some extent, and especially in "store-front" operations, this philosophy has a great deal of merit. For example, if you're a business like Ceilidh Connections and renting a location for a number of years, a good site selection is critical — and most retail leases reflect this importance in their length and complexity, with 30 to 50 pages not being unusual.

This chapter will lead you through the steps involved in finding a good physical location for your business, and the process, should you need it, of negotiating a lease that will serve you well.

And what if you want to operate your business out of your home? First, congratulations! This is a growth market and you may just be on the right track. We have now entered the age of the "gold-collar," or home-based, worker. More and more of us are working at home like Sheila Mather. The gold-collar worker now represents about one-quarter of the Canadian workforce. In the next few years, as many as 30 percent of us could be working out of the home. All kinds of services and products are now provided by home-based businesses. With the growth in services and the knowledge-based industries, chances are you will, one day, be operating some sort of business out of your home.

That said, in planning to set up your business at home, your location analysis is still just as important as if you were to lease. There are a number of critical location questions that you're going to have to think about: Do the municipality by-laws allow me to operate a business at home? How do I balance my family and work life? How do I deal with my target customers from my home? and so on. In this chapter, we'll also encourage you to consider all the pros and cons of locating your business out of the home, and to establish your location strategy as part of your overall marketing strategy.

The Importance of Location

WHAT IS THE PERFECT LOCATION?

The perfect location is different for every enterprise. If you're in the housecleaning business, you can work out of a van equipped with a cellular

ACTION STEP 36

Fantasize your perfect location.
Sit down where you won't be disturbed and brainstorm the ideal location for your small business. Get a pencil and paper and let yourself dream. Draw a mind map, or use a list format; the idea is to get your thinking on paper.

For example, if you were going to open a candy-cigarette-cigar stand, you might want to locate in the West Edmonton Mall, where people pass by every hour. Or, if you were goining to open an extremely up-scale boutique, you might visualize a location in Toronto's Yorkville.

Once you have the general idea of the type of neighbourhood you have in mind, write down what else is terrific about this location. Writing everything down will give you a starting point as you move out to explore the world.

telephone. If you're in the mail-order business, you can work out of a "cocoon" or a post office box. Action Step 36 asks you to brainstorm the perfect location for *your* business.

A good location can make everything easier for a new business. A highly visible building that's easy for your customers to reach will save you advertising dollars. Once you've been discovered and your customer base is well established, however, location is less important. Nonetheless, for a retailing firm, a good location is absolutely essential. As well, if you are a retailer, your location will depend on the kind of goods you sell — convenience, shopping or specialty goods.

Work through Action Step 37. It will help you analyze the effect of location on your shopping habits. Use new eyes to examine your own consumer behaviour.

A Location Analysis Checklist

Before you charge out to scout possible locations for your business, you need to decide what you really need. The checklist below will help you zero in on the criteria that are important to your business. Use a scale of 1 to 10 to rate the relative importance of each item in terms of your target customers. When you finish scoring, go back and note the high numbers, say, anything above 5. Then, after you've read the rest of the chapter, come back to this list to see if your priorities have changed.

RATING IMPORTANCE (1–10)

✓ *Neighbour mix.* Who's next door? Who's down the street? Who's going to help pull your target customers to the area? Which nearby business pulls the most customers? If you're considering a shopping centre, who's the anchor tenant (the big department store or supermarket that acts as a magnet for the centre)?

✓ *Competition.* Do you want competitors kilometres away or right next door? Think about this one. If you're in the restaurant business (a service that customers shop for, at least in their minds), it can help you to be on "restaurant row."

✓ *Security, safety.* How safe is the neighbourhood? Is it as safe as a nursery at noon but an urban jungle at midnight? Is there anything you can do to increase the security?

✓ *Labour pool.* Who's working for you, and how far will they have to commute? Does your business require more help at certain peak periods of the year? How easy will it be to find that kind of skilled or technical help you need? How far will they travel? Don't overlook the potential of part-timers, teens, seniors, and homemakers. Are there any zoning restrictions?

✓ *Services.* Police and fire protection, security, trash pick-up, sewage, maintenance: What is included in the rent, and who pays for those services that are not? Is your location near a bus or subway stop?

✓ *Costs.* What is the purchase price if you're buying; or what are the rent or lease costs (and what is the type of lease)? Insurance, improvements, association dues, routine maintenance: who pays for what? Can you negotiate a few months' free rent?

✓ *Ownership.* If you're still planning to buy the property, who will you get to advise you on real estate? Consider a lease with an option to buy, but have the contract reviewed by a real estate lawyer.

- ✓ *Past tenants.* What happened to the past tenants? What mistakes did they make, and how can you avoid those mistakes?
- ✓ *Space.* If you need to expand, can you do it there, or will you have to move to a new site?
- ✓ *Accessibility.* Is your business where your target customer might expect to find you?
- ✓ *Parking.* Most people like to park free and close to your door. Is that possible?
- ✓ *History of the property.* How long has the landlord owned this property? Is it likely to be sold while you're a tenant? If the property is sold, what will happen to your business? What will happen to your tax obligations? If the property goes on the market, do you want the first right to make an offer?
- ✓ *Physical visibility.* Does your business need to be seen? If so, is this location easily visible? Can you make alterations to increase its visibility? Can you install the type of sign you want?
- ✓ *Life-cycle stage of the area.* Is the site in an area that's embryonic (vacant lots, open space, emptiness), growing (high-rises, new schools, lots of construction), mature (building conversions, cracked street, sluggish traffic), or declining (vacant building, emptiness)? What will the area be like in five years? What effect would that have on your business? What do the municipal planners have in mind for the area? When will the highway department tear up the street? (See Figure 7.2.)
- ✓ *Image.* Is the location consistent with your firm's image? How will nearby business affect your image? Is this an area where your customers would expect to find a business like yours? (Look for a place that reinforces your customers' perception of your business.)
- ✓ *Local/municipal licensing.* A wide variety of trades and establishments require a licence fee that can range anywhere from $5 to thousands of dollars. In many Canadian municipalities, for example, licences are required if you operate a limousine service, refreshment vehicles, auctioneer service, billiard and pool hall, and skateboarding facilities. You'll also want to find out about local regulations on the installation, alteration, and maintenance of exterior signs and parking.
- ✓ *Hours of operation.* Most municipalities have by-laws regarding the hours of operation. These hours may be different for various areas within a region. If you're planning a retail operation, be sure to look into this detail.
- ✓ *Utilities.* The high cost for water, sewage, gas, or other utilities may bring some unpleasant surprises. You should list all your utility requirements. Are they adequate? What would it require to upgrade them?
- ✓ *Local zoning by-laws.* Check out the present and future zoning. What restrictions may apply to your business?
- ✓ *Taxes.* Property and business taxes can change from street to street. Try to find out if there are any plans for reassessment.
- ✓ *Approval.* Have you considered necessary approvals, such as those required from health officials, the fire marshal, the city planning office, and the liquor licensing board?
- ✓ *Transportation.* How much will your business depend on trucks, rail, buses, airports, or shipping by water? If you're in manufacturing or distribution, you'll need to determine your major transportation channel. It's also a good idea to have a back-up system. A good technique here is to make a diagram of the location and all the lines of transportation your business will use in both receiving goods and customers and shipping goods.
- ✓ *Your target customers.* This is the last but most important criterion. Will your customers — lured by your terrific promotions — find you easily but have no place to park? Consider highway access and potential obstacles that

ACTION STEP 37

Use your new eyes to evaluate business locations.

Think about how location affects your spending habits. For example, where do you buy gas for your car? Do you buy it on your way to work or school, or on your way home? Why?

Now, with your adventure notebook in hand, look through your home. How important was the location of the retailer when you bought the items you see? For example,

- candy, sodas
- washing machine
- paintings, wallhangings
- carpeting, paint
- mail-order items such as books, magazines, clothing, CDs
- custom-made golf clubs
- eyeglasses
- prescription drugs
- designer clothes
- wristwatch, jewellery
- power lawn, and garden tools
- TV set, VCR
- car, motorcycle
- collectibles
- your home itself

A random look through your chequebook might trigger your memory. Feel free to add to this list.

How far did you travel, for example, for your last dinner out with a friend? For a carton of milk? A magazine? A lounge chair? A video cassette rental? How far would you travel to consult a brain surgeon?

What conclusion can you draw about the importance of location in making a purchase or providing a service?

Remember also that the cheapest location may not always be the best location.

You can expand on this Action Step by interviewing purchasing agents and buyers of commercial and industrial goods. Ask them what impact location has on their choice of vendors or on their recruitment of employees.

Figure 7.2

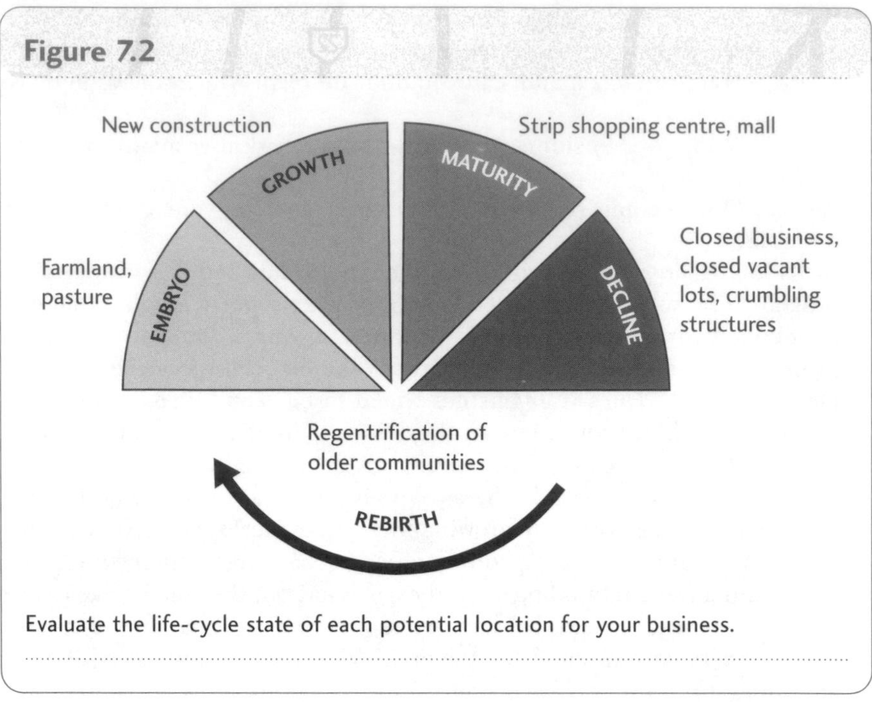

Evaluate the life-cycle state of each potential location for your business.

could make coming to your place of business inconvenient or unpleasant. What do your customers really want? Ease of parking? Convenience? Atmosphere? Proximity to work? Even the side of the street is important. (For example, a dry cleaner would want to be on the inbound side of the street so customers can easily drop off their cleaning on their way into the city to work.) Your location must satisfy the needs of the customer, not your own personal needs. This is a particularly important consideration if you're planning to operate out of your home. Are you setting up a home-based business because it is convenient to you or your customer? Remember: you work from home, not at home!

The Rise of the Gold-Collar Worker

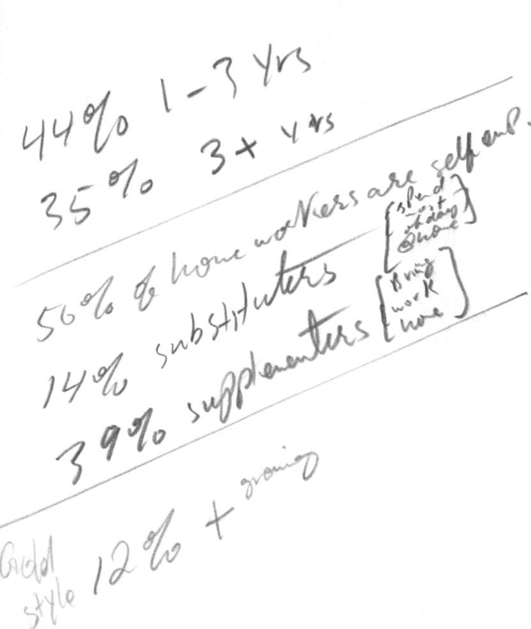

Working at home has become a major trend in the way Canadians do business. About two million Canadian households create jobs, stimulate local economies, and provide a growing commercial market. Most of these home businesses have been in operation for more than one year (44 percent, one to three years; 35 percent, more than three years). Almost half of the home workers are self-employed; 14 percent are substituters (employees who spend part of their day at home); and 39 percent are supplementers (employees who bring work home). According to these statistics, chances are that you will be working out of your home in the future — even if you have another job. In their report on home business, Barbara Orser and Ted James dispel a number of myths about the nature of home-based business (see Box 7.1).

Home business is one of the "golden" industries of the next decade, with the annual growth rate expected to be in the 12 percent range. Major reasons for this trend include:[2]

Cocooning. Many of us are attempting to reduce outside stresses by spending more leisure and work time at home.

Box 7.1 Dispelling the Myths About Home-Based Businesses (HBBs)

Myth: HBBs are fairly small in number.
Fact: One in four of all Canadian households operates some form of home business.

Myth: HBBs spend all their time at home.
Fact: Less than 40 percent of the work day is spent at the home base; 30 percent is spent on the road and 32 percent at the customer or client's premises.

Myth: HBBs are mostly service providers.
Fact: About 50 percent of HBBs provide service and the remainder are manufacturers and wholesalers.

Myth: HBBs typically occur only in urban areas.
Fact: Nearly half (48 percent) of people primarily running an HBB live in a non-urban area.

Myth: HBBs are motivated by financial reward.
Fact: Intrinsic factors like independence and flexibility are more important motivators for being home-based than financial rewards.

Myth: HBBs create problems for the neighbourhood.
Fact: The number of registered public complaints about HBBs is so small as to be insignificant.

Myth: HBBs deliberately ignore municipal by-laws.
Fact: Forty percent of home-business owners surveyed were not even aware of existing by-laws regulating their business activities.

Source: Barbara Orser and Ted James, *Home Business: A Report Prepared for the Home-Based Project Committee*, Industry, Science and Technology Canada and Employment and Immigration Canada, p. 8. Reproduced with the permission of the Minister of Public Works and Government Services Canada, 1998.

Computerization. New high-tech equipment such as fax machines, personal computers, and modems for e-mail and the Internet have made it a lot easier and more convenient to operate out of the home.

Two-income families. It makes it a lot easier to work out of the home when both parents are trying to raise a family and make a living.

Growth of the service industry. A service business generally has lower start-up costs, operational expenses, and equipment costs, making it much more sensible to run your operation out of the home.

Higher productivity. Studies show that productivity increases by 20–60 percent when employees can work during peak times at their own pace. In fact, such statistics have influenced the new knowledge-based companies to encourage telecommuting.

Increased efficiency. The home worker saves on transportation, rental, furniture and equipment costs.

"Egonomics." The new consumer demands more individual attention. Home-based businesses are well positioned to adapt to changing and individualistic consumer needs.

Vigilante consumer. The new customer is fragile and fickle and craves superior service. This consumer does not tolerate the mediocrity of mass production and sameness.

Downsizing. Today, companies are encouraged to go small and to contract out whenever possible.

Mobility. With the growth in personal care and home care, more and more businesses are going to their customers, which means that a store front is not always necessary.

Starting your business out of the home does not mean that your plan is written on the back of an envelope. It takes just as much care to open and operate a home business as it does to establish a traditional retail business. Before you decide on a location, consider the advantages and disadvantages of operating out of your home. Box 7.2 will help you get started. Weigh the pros and cons carefully. See also Box 7.3 for tips that could help you run a successful home business.

Box 7.2 Is Home the Best Place? A Location Checklist

The following checklist may help you determine if you should operate your business out of the home.

- **Target market.** How far will your customers be willing to travel to get to you? Can your business travel or deliver to the customer? How efficient is it for you to serve customer from your home?
- **Neighbourhood mix.** Do you need other businesses to pull your customer to you?
- **Physical visibility.** Does your business need to be seen?
- **Competitors.** Why would your target customer deal with you out of your home-based business rather than with your competition? What advantages does your home business offer over that of your competitors?
- **Life-cycle stage.** Is your area in an embryonic (e.g., vacant land), growing (e.g., plenty of construction, new schools), mature (e.g., cracked streets, sluggish traffic), or decline (e.g., vacant buildings) stage? Do you want to be doing business in the same location five years from now?
- **Image.** How would your target customers react if they learned that you were operating out of your home? For example, right or wrong, some customers might not take you seriously.
- **Local/municipal.** Do you require a licence, and can you get a licence to operate out of your home?
- **Local zoning by-laws.** Do local by-laws allow you to operate your business out of your home?
- **Space/physical requirements.** Do you have enough space to serve the customer and your business needs effectively? What are your physical requirements? For example, do you need to add a washroom? Do you have a designated area to work? How will the customer enter your location? Do you need a separate entrance?
- **Approvals.** Have you considered the necessary approvals related to health, fire, transportation, environment, and labour?
- **Insurance.** Will your insurance company allow you to operate a business out of your home? How will this affect your insurance premiums?
- **Utilities.** Are there any extra utilities requirements (e.g., extra telephone line)?
- **Work habits/behaviour.** Do you need to "get away in the morning?" Many business people like to completely separate their business and personal lives. Do you have the discipline to work in your home?
- **Lifestyle.** Will your business disrupt your family and personal lifestyles? How will your neighbours feel about you running your business out of your home?

Source: Ron Knowles, *Writing a Small Business Plan: Course Guide* (Toronto: Dryden, an imprint of Harcourt Brace & Company, Canada, 1995), p. 44.

Box 7.3 Tips for a Successful Home-Based Business

- Make sure that all your printed materials communicate that you are a serious business professional.
- Have a separate business telephone line.
- Have a separate space for your office.
- Establish a work schedule.
- Minimize household distractions and treat them as if you were at the office.

Getting the Information You Need to Find the Right Location

Business people tend to stay in a location for a while because it is expensive to renovate and move. Thus, selection of your location will be one of your most important start-up decisions. You will want to make sure that you are right in the heart of your target market. So, where do you go for information? We'll begin with secondary sources of location information — that is, published data that has been gathered and compiled by others.

STATISTICS CANADA

Data collected by Statistics Canada could be one of your major sources of secondary information, especially if you are planning to rent, lease, or buy a retail or manufacturing business. But even if you plan to operate your business out of your home, Statistics Canada data can still be useful. For example, you are going to want to know where your target customer lives and works.

Census

The Census is one of the major Statistics Canada sources of information. Census data is gathered every five years (e.g., 1991, 1996, 2001, and so on) through a massive survey of the Canadian population (for more details on the Census, see Box 7.4). The data is organized into a number of categories (age, sex, household income, etc.) that are then described and published by Statistics Canada. Census data is produced for a number of standard geographic areas. Some of the most common ones are shown in Box 7.5. Finding the right Census information can be time-consuming and sometimes frustrating. To get started, we suggest that you go to the Statistics Canada Web site <http://www.statcan.ca>. Once you have become familiar with Census terms and information, we then suggest you visit a main library that carries Statistics Canada information. You should find the information clearly indexed, but don't be afraid to ask the librarian for help.

The major advantages of the Census are twofold:

1. It is comprehensive. Data can be tabulated by age, sex, employment status, sex, income, and so on.
2. It is detailed. Data can be tabulated for small geographic areas, the smallest of which is the enumeration area (about 300 dwellings).

The major disadvantage of the Census is timeliness. A census is conducted once every five years. By the time the data is published, it could be as many

Box 7.4 The Canada Census

What it's about. Provides demographic, social, economic, and cultural information on the Canadian population.
Who is surveyed. All Canadian citizens and landed immigrants aged 15 and over, excluding institutional residents and refugee claimants.
How we collect the data. Household survey; labour market data are collected from a 20 percent sample of the population through self-enumeration, or by canvasser enumeration in remote and northern areas and on Indian reserves.
Frequency. Labour market and income data are collected every ten years (decennial census), as in the 1991 Census, and occasionally collected in the five-year (quinquennial) census, as in 1996.
Response rate. Approximately 95 percent (varies according to questions).
Reference period. The previous calendar year for income and weeks worked; the week worked; the week before Census Day for labour force activity and for class of workers, occupation, and industry of employed persons; the previous seventeen months for class of worker, occupation, and industry of persons not employed the week before Census Day.
Geographic detail. Canada, provinces and territories, counties, federal electoral districts, census metropolitan areas, census agglomerations, municipalities, census consolidated subdivisions, enumeration areas, provincial census tracts and block faces (geocoding allows data users to obtain estimates for very specific geographic areas).
Demographic detail. Includes age, sex, education and major field of study, marital status, household relationship, ethnic and cultural origin, mother tongue, language spoken at home, knowledge of official languages, place of birth, citizenship, period or year of immigration, and disability.
Information collected.

- occupational (approximately 500 codes)
- industry (approximately 400 codes)
- class of worker (paid worker, self-employed, unpaid family worker)
- weeks worked in calendar year preceding Census
- labour market activities in week preceding Census
- wages and salaries
- farm and non-farm self-employment income (net)

Time frame. Wage and salary data since 1901, labour force data since 1951, employment income and total income since 1961.
What makes the data valuable.

- very extensive geographic detail
- extensive number of characteristics available for cross-tabulation
- population coverage includes the Yukon and Northwest Territories
- consistent historical database
- very accurate data

Source: Statistics Canada, "Census of Population," adapted from *Labour Market and Income Data Guide.* April 1992 Cat. No. 75F0010XPB. Reproduced by authority of the Ministry of Industry, 1994.

as seven years out of date. However, in many cases, Census data can provide much-needed historical trend information. (See for example, Figure 7.3.)

Other Sources of Statistics Canada Information

The Census can be a powerful tool for locating your customer or your business. But it's not the only source, and you should not stop here. A good source

Box 7.5 Sample Census Data by Geographic Areas: Census Geography, 1996

Census data are produced for a number of standard geographic areas. These are some of the common ones.

Administrative Areas

- **provinces and territories census divisions**
  counties, regional districts, regional municipalities
- **census subdivisions**
  municipalities
- **federal electoral districts (1987 and 1996 Representation Orders)**
  The 1987 Representation Order refers to electoral boundaries set as a result of population counts from the 1981 Census. The 1996 Representation Order refers to those set after the 1991 Census.
  forward sortation areas
  the first three characters of the postal code

Statistical Areas

- **census metropolitan areas**
  very large urban areas, together with adjacent urban and rural fringes. The urban core has a population of over 100 000.
- **census tracts**
  neighbourhoods
- **enumeration areas**
  smallest unit, usually about 300 dwellings

Source: Statistics Canada, 1996 Census, http://www.statcan.ca/english/census96/

of other Statistics Canada information is the Statistics Canada *Market Research Handbook* (Catalogue No. 63-224). Here you will find all kinds of consumer and location information. For example, profiles are provided of key industries in all provinces and 45 major cities. A second important "hard copy" resource document available in most reference centres or libraries is the *Statistics Canada Catalogue* (Catalogue No. 11-204E). This publication has an excellent subject index at the back. Lastly, we encourage you to visit the Statistics Canada Web site (see Figure 7.4).

OTHER SOURCES OF SECONDARY INFORMATION

As we know by now, Statistics Canada is not our only source of secondary information. Local municipality and regional governments have all kinds of information, such as traffic counts, so a visit to your local planning office is a must. While you're there, check the zoning by-laws and future plans. For example, you might be awfully disappointed if you decide to locate your home-based business in a municipality that forbids home-operated enterprises. Or locating your business on a road scheduled for sewer work might be your quick ticket to bankruptcy. If you are going into a mall, the mall owners should have a detailed location study. Get their analyses, or don't locate there. Consider potential suppliers. They should know which outlets are doing the greatest business. If you approach them in the right way, they may be pleased to help you. After all, this could mean more future business for them.

ACTION STEP 38

Seek professional help in finding a location.
Visit a commercial real estate office to gain information. Commercial real estate firms have access to planning reports and demographic information that will tell you a lot about growth in the community. Have your plan well in mind and make an appointment beforehand. Dress conservatively.

And leave your chequebook at home!

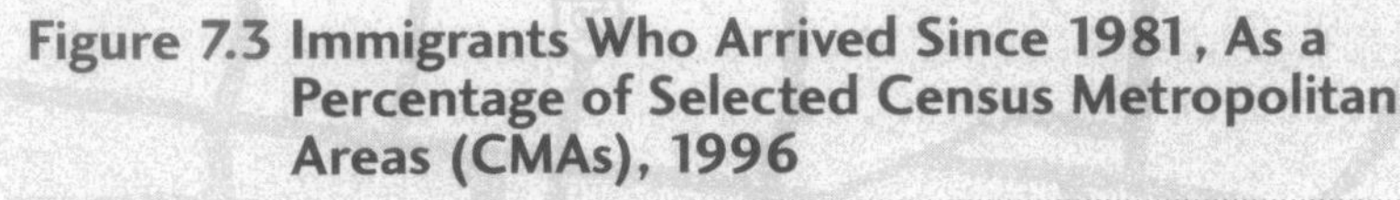

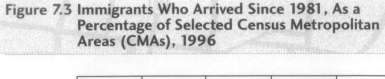

Figure 7.3 Immigrants Who Arrived Since 1981, As a Percentage of Selected Census Metropolitan Areas (CMAs), 1996

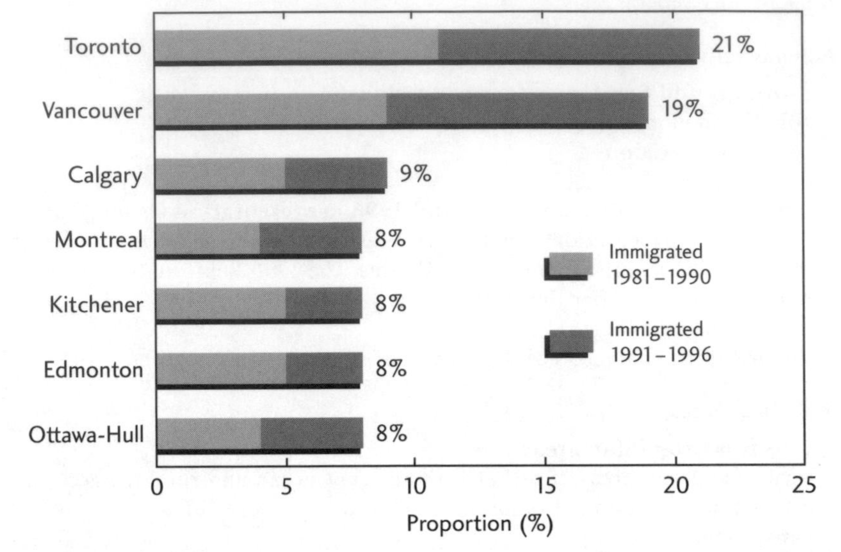

Census data provides useful information such as historical trends.

Source: Statistics Canada, "Immigrants Who Arrived Since 1981 as a Percentage of Selected CMAs, 1996," adapted from "The Daily," Catalogue No. 11-001, November 4, 1997. On <http://www.statcan.ca/Daily/English/971104/c971104d.gif>. Reprinted with permission.

Private companies also will, for a price, get you some pretty detailed information. One such firm is Compusearch, which maintains location databases that are highly targetted and include names of facilities and offices within a specific area.

Commercial real estate agents can be very helpful, particularly if you're thinking about a retail or manufacturing operation.

Finally, we encourage you to get on the Net. Strategis, at <http://strategis.ic.gc.ca>, is probably your best place to start. In Chapter Five, we encouraged you to use Strategis to seek out competitor information. Now we want you to go back to this research and see if you can discover some valuable information for locating your business. Action Step 38 will help you further.

Primary Sources of Location Information

In the last six chapters we have talked about your primary research techniques such as brainstorming, interviewing, mind mapping, and so on. As you know by now, we cannot rely strictly on secondary research because it is just that — secondary. For your location analysis, you are also going to have to do some of your own primary research. But the hitch is that there is no formula or set framework to follow. Nevertheless, this is a real opportunity to practise your new-eyes research. To help, we will provide examples of how some enterprising entrepreneurs did theirs. We then encourage you to find your own creative way.

Figure 7.4

STATISTICS CANADA SEARCH

Welcome to Statistics Canada!

▸ Daily news
Highlights of newly released data, schedules for major releases and announcements of new products and services.

▸ 1996 Census
Free tabular data from the latest Census results.

▸ Education Resources
Programs and products to integrate Canadian statistical information into teaching and learning.

▸ Service centres
Information on our regional offices, libraries and other distributors of Statistics Canada data.

▸ Site Map

▸ Links to other sites

▸ Français

▸ Canadian statistics
Free tabular data on aspects of Canada's economy, land, people and government.

▸ Products and services
Catalogue; research papers; online statistics ($); downloadable publications ($); information on seminars, conferences and other services.

▸ Concepts, definitions and methods
Program documentation; standard classifications; discussion papers; questionnaires; information on new surveys.

▸ About Statistics Canada

▸ Canada Quiz
Explore our site and learn about Canada and Canadians.

Are you getting your information on the Canadian economy first hand?

Subscribe to Canadian Economic Observer

Visit the Statistics Canada Web site to make use of some of the products and services.

Source: Statistics Canada, "Welcome to Statistics Canada," from the Statistics Canada website <http://www.statcan.ca/start.html>. Reprinted with permission.

Henry wanted to start a dry cleaning business. He knew that the success of his business would depend on the number of cars that passed by a specific point during peak hours. Through experience in the business, he had found a direct relationship between the number of cars and the volume of dry cleaning. What did he do? He did not rely on the traffic counts from his local municipality, although this secondary information was useful in narrowing down possible sites. His answer was to sit in his car for several days and count the number of vehicles that went by his potential sites. After doing this a few times for various locations, he finally found the "perfect" spot.

Today, Henry has fifteen outlets and we find him out counting cars, getting ready for his sixteenth store. He tells us that he is in the business of counting cars because, if he can get that right and competition is not a serious factor, then everything else should unfold nicely.

Now let's see how Martha did her primary research by counting people.

Martha wanted to start a gift store that her favourite grandmother would be proud of. The name of her new business would be Gramma's, so the location had to be right, for she wanted to keep this name for a long time. She also knew from working in gift stores that most of the business would come from the impulse buyer.

A new mall was opening down the street, and the manager, fresh from business school, had loaded her down with site plans, traffic studies, and potential store locations. "You had better hurry," he said. "The good spots are being snapped up awfully fast." Fortunately, her small business teacher was close by and added a little sanity to her life. "It's easy," she said. "Just replicate, and you will know for sure. Find a mall that is under construction and tell me how much business the gift store is doing."

"That's crazy," exclaimed Martha. "You can't possibly know how much a business is doing before the mall is built."

"That's true," said her professor. "Why don't you wait until you know what is going on."

"I'm going to miss this one," protested Martha.

"Yes, you may, but when you find the right location, you will know it, because you will be able to back up the mall research with some of your own primary research."

About six months later, Martha finished doing her pedestrian counts in front of an empty store at a more established mall on the other side of the city. Her own traffic counts and the mall studies convinced her that this was the location for her. Today, Martha's gift store at the more established mall is doing well. She is not making a million, but she is making a good living, and her grandmother is very proud of her.

Here is the lesson she learned: If your business relies on impulse buying, you had better know exactly how many people will go by your door and how many will enter and make a purchase — *before you open your doors.*

By the way, it took over two years to fully lease the new mall that Martha first looked at.

Specific primary research techniques worked for Henry and Martha. The key to their success was knowing who their customers were and what they wanted. Their businesses were driven by the amount of traffic passing by their doors — in one case it was cars and in the other, people. Now let's return to Elizabeth Wood (remember Crazy's in Chapters Four and Five) and see how she helped Max, the owner, determine whether he had a good location.

"That's a stupid question," quipped Max. "Of course I have a great location — just look at my sales."

"Just a minute," cautioned Elizabeth. "Because you are fortunate enough to have customers, this does not mean you have the perfect location." Elizabeth knew what she was talking about because she was standing in front of Max, a little smugly, with the results of her customer survey. "Let me ask you: where do your customers live?"

"That's easy," said Max. "They live in the neighbourhood. That's why I chose this location." Not wanting to burst Max's balloon, Elizabeth agreed he was partly right. "The fact is, your lunch trade lives at the workplace. That is, 'place of work' is the most important location criterion at lunch. As a matter of fact, the perfect luncheon location would be within walking distance of 'white-collar' industry — one of those new industries that Nuala Beck talks about."

Then Elizabeth explained to Max that most of his lunch customers were forced to drive to his restaurant, and that's why there were always a few empty seats at lunch during the first part of the week. "Now, as for your night and weekend trade," she continued, "most live at least 15 km from your restaurant. Your TCs are 'grazers' who say that their household income is $50 000 plus per year and who come from all over the city. The most important thing to them is that they can get here within 20 minutes and there is adequate parking. Yes, parking is very important to them. You should begin thinking about the potholes in your parking lot before you start losing business."

Now that Elizabeth knew where Max's customers lived and worked, there was a lot more they could talk about. For the next few hours, they brainstormed new ideas and approaches to making the location more accessible to the customer. For example, how could Max speed up the food service at lunch?

Now let's consider the importance of primary research for the home-based business. Remember Mina Cohen from Chapter Four? She was in the travel and learning business. She worked out of her home, but her location was at the dig site. There is no doubt the archaeologists at the site demand that she and her customers "dig" with care. Her location analysis concerns itself with finding prime dig sites for her customers to visit.

For Ron Taylor (Chapter Five) and the business of cocooning (basement recreation rooms) for teens, what is his location? His customer's house, of course. His location strategy is all about finding homes where teens live.

We can't stress it enough. If you operate a service business from home, your location analysis is just as important as if you are renting. After all, your location is at your *customer's* home or place of work. All of these cases point to the need for primary research before you decide your location. If you can support primary analysis with secondary data, so much the better.

Many of you will choose not to operate your business out of the home, although we encourage you to give serious thought to this strategy. For those who plan to rent a location, we'll go now to the complex world of leases.

Some Things You Must Know About Leases

A lease document is drawn up by the property owner's lawyer. Although its language is very specific, the terms spelled out are provisional — that is, the terms are proposed as a starting point for negotiation. Nothing you see in the contract is cast in stone . . . unless you agree to it. Obviously, the terms proposed will probably favour the property owner. Consider the proposed lease seriously. Discuss it with your own lawyer and with others who have experience with leases, and determine how best to begin the negotiation. The following pages will guide you through this process.

ENTREPRENEUR, READ YOUR LEASE

Entrepreneur Mick Beatty failed to read the terms of his lease. He thought he had a "gentlemen's agreement" with his landlady, but he was wrong. His story points up the importance of *assuming nothing* when it comes to leases.

I was on vacation from the East when I discovered the perfect location. It was in the sleepy tourist town of White Rock, on the edge of the world in a fabulous part of British Columbia.

It was late summer, I remember, and I'd just spent a week driving through the mountains from Calgary. When I reached White Rock, I thought I was home.

I discovered Eddie's Pub my first evening in town. It faced the beach, and sitting there sipping a cool one, I could watch the sun reflect off the water. From time to time, people would drift in for a casual drink, and while sitting there, feeling like a million, I must have talked to 20 different folks.

They loved the place, too. And most of them looked up-scale.

Vacations don't last forever, and when I got back home, I kept thinking about Eddie's in White Rock. I was working then for one of the giant mega-corporations, making good money in a pressure cooker of a job, and even though I was enough of a culture freak to appreciate Toronto, I wanted more out of life. After one particularly hectic day at the office, I sat and stared out the window, thinking about those three days I'd spent in White Rock, on the beach.

A business trip took me to Vancouver that next spring, and I managed to haggle for an extra day so that I could stay overnight in White Rock and stop in for a drink at Eddie's.

Double surprise.

The sun was shining — and Eddie's Pub was for sale.

I called my banker back East. He said I was crazy. I phoned two buddies, one from college, one from the squash club. They thought it would be fun to be part of a new venture and were ready to invest. I talked to Eddie, the owner, made a deal to pay him so much down and the rest out of profits, and suddenly I owned a small business.

When I phoned my boss in Toronto, he said I was crazy, too. "Living somewhere on a beach is just a dream," he said. But what he said next saved my life. "Tell you what, Mick. Don't pull the plug until you're absolutely sure. We'll give you six months. If you're still out there dreaming, send in your resignation. Meanwhile, have fun. Every man needs a fling before he settles down."

I said okay, and thanks. And that was that.

The location at Eddie's is only 200 square metres. The layout is long and narrow, and we used mirrors from the Gay Nineties to give the place atmosphere. The traffic is mostly walk-in — beach people, stray tourists — and the only promotion I had to do was to put up a sign that said "Happy Hour

4–6:30." I shook hands with my customers, passed out complimentary drinks, served the best espresso in the Vancouver area, and started making money my first day.

Then trouble showed up.

I hadn't been open a week when I got a call from my landlady. She was a crusty-voiced lady I'd barely talked to, and she said over the phone that there had been some complaints about the music.

"Hey," I said. "I'm sorry. Who's complaining?"

"Your neighbours," she said. "They have rights, too, you know."

"Is it too loud?"

"No," she said. "It's not the volume. It's that rock stuff that's causing the trouble. It irritates the other customers."

"Rock?" I said. "It's not rock, it's more like —"

"I don't know what you call it," my landlady said. "But it's got to stop. And right now."

"My customers like it," I argued. "The music is part of my atmosphere."

"Young man," she said, "what your customers like is neither here nor there. I own that property, and I have other tenants to think about. And if you have any questions, I'd advise you to read your lease." She hung up.

Well, I read the lease, carefully. And then I saw a lawyer. He confirmed what I'd read — according to the terms of the lease, my landlady had the power to tell me what kind of music I could play in my own small business.

Incredible, but true.

I tried turning off the music. Right away, my customers missed it. Drink orders fell off. I surveyed my neighbours and made a list of songs they didn't find offensive, but when I played that junk in the bar, my steady customers (who were becoming less steady) asked me to turn it off. As a last resort, I even visited my landlady and tried to **renegotiate the lease**. But she wouldn't budge.

RENEGOTIATE A LEASE
obtaining a new or modified contract for occupancy

There was only one thing to do. I sold the business. I went back to my job in Toronto. I still owe some money to my partners, and when the tension builds at work, I always think of the sun on the water at White Rock. I'll go back sometime. But right now I'm a little soured on the place. It's too bad. They've got a great beach. And a great little bar where you can sit and watch the sun go down.

My advice? Have a plan, get some experience before you start, and last of all, read the small print in your lease.

ANTICIPATE THE UNEXPECTED

Bette Lindsay has always had a soft spot for books, and when she finally chose a business, it was a book store in a shopping centre. She had researched everything — trends, census data, newspapers, reports from real estate firms, suppliers — but she failed to anticipate an important potential pitfall: dependency on an anchor tenant (a business in a commercial area that attracts customers).

Few small businesses are themselves "destination locations." They must count on anchor tenants to draw traffic. Bette made an assumption that the anchor tenant in her centre would be there forever. This case study shows the importance of having Plan B ready.

My husband and I researched the small business field for almost two years, and my heart kept bringing me back to books. I've read voraciously since I was 7 years old, and I love a well-written story. So when a new shopping centre was opening ten kilometres from our home, I told my husband, "This is it."

Everything looked perfect. They had a great anchor tenant coming in — a supermarket that would draw lots of traffic. The real estate agent we'd been working with during most of our search showed us the demographics of the area, which documented that we were smack in the middle of a well-educated market. According to statistics put out buy the federal government, a book store needs a population of 27 000 people to support it. Our area had 62 000 people, and the closest book store was more than eight kilometres away.

Everything else looked good, too. We had lots of parking. The neighbours (three hardy pioneers like ourselves) were serious about their business and pleasant to work with.

We wanted to be in for the Christmas season because December is the peak season for book stores. So we set a target date of mid-October. The contractor was still working when we opened a month later.

We started off with an autograph party and we ran some best-seller specials. And even though construction work from our anchor tenant blocked our access, we had a very good Christmas that year. We started the new year feeling very optimistic.

One day in mid-January, construction work stopped on our anchor tenant's new building. The next day we read in the paper that the company had gone bankrupt.

Well, the first thing I did was call the landlord. He was out of town, and his answering service referred me to a property management company. They said they knew nothing about what was happening and that all they did was collect the rent. January was slow. So was February, and March. In April, two of our neighbours closed up. The construction debris still blocked customer access. It was a mess.

In May, I finally succeeded in getting in touch with the owner and tried to renegotiate the lease, but his story was sadder than mine.

Fourteen months after we moved in, we finally got our anchor tenant. If I'd suspected it would take anything like that long, I could have built some provision for it into our lease.

Bette and her husband learned the hard way.

HOW TO REWRITE A LEASE

LOCATION ESCAPE HATCH
a way to cancel or modify your lease if the landlord fails to meet the specified terms

You live with a lease (and a landlord) for a long time. If you're successful in a retail business, your landlord may want a percentage of your gross sales receipts. If you're not successful or if problems develop, you're going to want several Plan Bs and a **location escape hatch** — a way to cancel or modify your lease if your landlord fails to meet the specified terms. For example, your lease should protect your interest:

- if the furnace or air conditioning system breaks down
- if the parking lot needs sweeping or resurfacing
- if the anchor tenant goes under
- if the building is sold
- if half of the other tenants move out

The possibility of such grief-producing eventualities needs to be dealt with — with precise words and precise numbers in the lease.

Read the lease slowly and carefully (Box 7.6 will help you). When you see something you don't understand or don't like, draw a line through it. Feel free to rewrite the lease if you need to. It's *your* lease, too, you see. If you need help from a lawyer, get it. And make sure that the owner (or the leasing agent) indicates his or her agreement with your changes by initialling each one.

Here's a checklist to start you on your rewrite.

1. *Escape clause.* If the building doesn't shape up or the area goes into eclipse, you will want to get out fast. Be specific. Write something like this into your lease: "If three or more vacancies occur in the centre, tenant may terminate lease."
2. *Option to renew.* Most businesses need at least six months to a year to get going. If your business does well, you will want to stay put. If it does not, you don't want to be saddled with a heavy lease payment every month. Get a lease for one year, with an option to renew for the next two or three.
3. *Right to transfer.* Circumstances might force you to sublet. In the trade, this is called "assigning." Make sure the lease allows you to transfer your lease without a heap of hassle if such circumstances arise.

Box 7.6 The Language of Leases

Before signing on the dotted line, be certain you understand the language of the lease. These terms will get you started:

Building gross area. The total square-foot area of the building when the enclosing walls are measured from outside wall to outside wall.

Usable building area. The square-foot area within the building actually occupied by tenants, measured from centre partition to centre partition.

Common area. The square-foot area of the building servicing all tenants in common, such as lobby, corridors, lavatories, elevators, stairs, and mechanical equipment rooms. The building common area is usually between 10 and 12 percent of the gross building area.

Rentable area. A combination of the tenants' usable building area plus each tenant's pro rata share of the common area.

Gross rent. A rental per square foot, multiplied by the rentable area, to determine the annual rent due on a lease, where the landlord provides all services and utilities, including tenant janitorial services.

Net rent. A rent per square metre (or foot) multiplied by the rentable area to determine the annual rent due under a lease, whereby the tenant also pays, in addition to the rent, its pro rata of all utilities and services and real estate taxes.

Loss factor. The proportion of usable building area to total rentable area. The usable area is that in which you may put furniture and equipment for actual office use. The rentable area often includes a proportionate share of ancillary building services. The lower the loss factor, the more usable space there is. Loss factors can vary from floor to floor in the same building. Rentable area may be calculated in a different manner for one building than it is for another, and this will affect your comparison of rental proposals.

4. *Cost-of-living cap.* Most leases allow the owner to increase rents along with inflation according to the consumer price index (CPI). To protect yourself, insist on a cost-of-living cap so that your base rate won't increase faster than your landlord's costs. Try for half of the amount of the CPI increase, a standard measure. Thus, if the CPI rises 10 percent, your rate will go up only 5 percent. It's fair, because the owner's costs won't change much. Major tenants in your centre will insist on a cap, so you should be able to negotiate one also. Proceed with confidence.
5. *Percentage lease.* Percentage leases are common in larger retail centres. They specify that the tenant pays a base rate plus a percentage of the gross sales. An example: $.00 per square foot per month plus 5 percent of gross sales over $500,000 per year.
6. *Floating rent scale.* If you're a pioneer tenant of a shopping centre, negotiate a payment scale based on occupancy. For example, you may specify that you'll pay 50 percent of your lease payment when the centre is 50 percent occupied, 70 percent when it's 70 percent occupied, and 100 percent when it's full. You can't build traffic to the centre all by yourself, and motivation is healthy for everyone, including landlords.
7. *Start-up buffer.* There's a good chance you'll be on location fixing up, remodelling, and so on, long before you open your doors and make your first sale. Make your landlord aware of this problem and negotiate a long period of free rent. The argument: if your business is successful, the landlord — who's taking a percentage — will make more money. If your business doesn't do well or if it fails, the landlord will have to find a new tenant. You need breathing space. You've signed on for the long haul. By not squeezing you to death for cash, the landlord allows you to put more money into inventory, equipment, service, atmosphere — the things that make a business go.
8. *Improvement.* Unless you're a super fixer-upper, you don't want to lease a place equipped with nothing but a dirt floor and a capped-off cold water pipe. You need a proper atmosphere for your business, but you don't want to use all your cash to pay for it before you open. Negotiate with the landlord to make the needed improvements and spread the cost of them over the total time of the lease. Otherwise, find a space that doesn't require heavy remodelling.
9. *Restrictive covenants.* If you're running a camera store and part of your income derives from developing film, you don't want a Fotomat booth to move into your centre. If you're selling hearing aids, you don't want a

Box 7.7 Before You Sign . . .

Before you sign a lease, ask these questions:

- Does the lease contain an escape clause?
- Does it have an option to renew?
- Can you "assign" the lease if you need to sublet?
- Do you have a ceiling on rent increases?
- Do you have a floating lease scale, according to how much of the centre is occupied?
- Have you tried to negotiate a period of free rent while you are preparing to open the doors?
- Have you negotiated to have the landlord make the needed improvements and charge you for them over the total time of the lease?

stereo store next door. Build restrictive covenants (things that your landlord cannot do) into your lease to protect yourself.

10. *Maintenance.* When the parking lot needs sweeping, who pays for it? If the air conditioner goes out, who pays? If the sewer stops up, who is responsible for the repairs? Get all of this written down in simple language. Your diligence with words and numbers will pay off.

In a Nutshell

The main purpose of this chapter was to help guide you through the process of finding a location that is right for you, your business, and your customer. We encouraged you to use your new-eyes research as well as secondary sources, and to keep asking the question "What is the best location according to my target customer?"

If you are planning to retail or manufacture your product or service, your choice of location is probably the most important decision you will make. You'll have to live with your selection for a long time. We encouraged you to complete the location filter checklist and begin to understand the language and consequences of leases. Many of you will plan to start your business from your home. This is fine, but don't think that your location analysis is not important. A location checklist for your home-based business was also presented. We wanted you to make sure that your home office will satisfy the needs of your customer and won't destroy your personal life. Lastly, we discussed the need to understand the language and consequences of leases.

Think Points for Success

✓ The irony of the search for a start-up location is that you need the best site when you can least afford it.

✓ Take your time selecting a location. If you lose out on a hot site, don't worry; another one will eventually turn up.

✓ Even if you start up your business at home, you will need a location analysis.

✓ A site analysis for a street-side location should include everything that is unique to a specific building or space. Many successful centres have some dead traffic areas.

✓ Who are your business neighbours? Are they attracting *your* type of customers or clients? What will happen if they move or go out of business?

✓ Know the terms and buzzwords — *net, gross, triple net, industrial gross,* and so on — and be aware that they may mean slightly different things in each contract or lease agreement.

✓ Everything is negotiable: free rent, signage, improvement allowances, rates, maintenance. Don't be afraid to ask; a dollar saved in rental expenses can be worth more than $10 in sales.

✓ Talk to former tenants; you may be amazed at what you learn.

Business Plan Building Block

This section of your business plan explains why you have selected your location and how it satisfies the needs of your target customers and your business.

Your description should include the following key considerations:

- How close or accessible your location is to the target market.
- The distribution channels you intend to use to reach the target customer if you do not have a store-front location.

ACTION STEP REVIEW

36 Fantasize your perfect location.
37 Use your new eyes to evaluate business locations.
38 Seek professional help in finding a location.

- How the location satisfies the exterior and interior requirements for the business (if possible, include a floor plan or photos in an appendix).
- How close the competition is to your location.
- The possibility of expansion.
- Whether the building is leased or owned. Indicate whether the lease has been reviewed by a lawyer (include proof of ownership or a copy of the lease in an appendix)
- Whether the location is in conformity with municipal by-laws and environmental regulations.

Your turn: Using materials from this chapter, describe why you have chosen this site.

____

____

____

____

____

____

Checklist Questions and Actions to Develop Your Business Plan

LOCATION

- ❑ What criteria are important to your location?
- ❑ What secondary research do you need to make a decision about location?
- ❑ If you plan to operate a home-based business, be sure to answer all the questions in Box 7.2
- ❑ Define the importance of location for your target customer.
- ❑ If you are a home-based business, how have you separated work from home?
- ❑ Why have you chosen the site that you have selected?
- ❑ If you have a home-based business, identify any zoning issues you face.

NOTES

1. Based on Jeffrey Simpson, "Quite the Little Spot," *The Halifax Herald,* January 24, 1998. Republished with permission from the Halifax Herald Limited.
2. Gray, Douglas A. and Diana Lynn. *Home Inc.* (Toronto: McGraw-Hill Ryerson, 1989).

OTHER REFERENCES

Bredin, Alice. *Set Up a Home Office That Works.* New York: John Wiley & Sons, 1996.

Deschamps, Michelle, Jack Dart, and Graham Links. "Home-based Entrepreneurship in the Information Age." *Journal of Small Business & Entrepreneurship,* Vol. 14, No. 1, September 1997, pp. 74–97.

Eggerston, Laura. "Canada Is Cheap Location for Business Start Ups: Study." *Globe and Mail,* October 10, 1997, p. B4.

Entrepreneur Magazine. *Starting a Home-based Business.* New York: John Wiley & Sons, 1997.

eight

Surprises You Can't Afford

LEARNING OPPORTUNITIES

After reading this chapter, you should be able to:

- Anticipate potential troublesome events that could occur in your business.
- Develop Plan B (C, D, . . .) in order to minimize the ill effects of unfortunate surprises.
- Learn the cost of each item you will need to do business, so that you know your total start-up expenses.
- Develop a personal financial statement in order to know how much you will have to borrow to go into business.
- Weigh the opportunity costs of going into business.

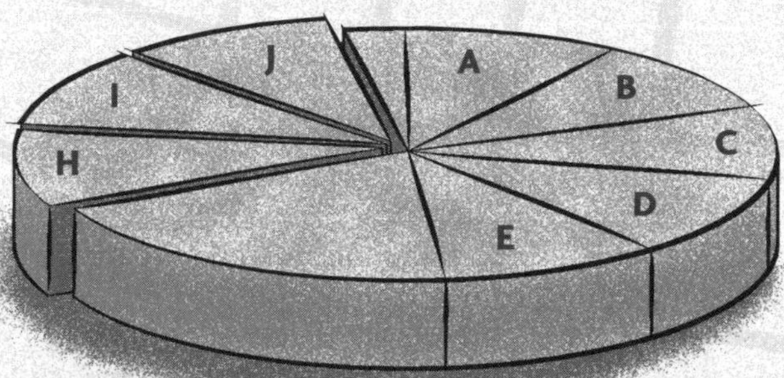

BUSINESS PLAN BUILDING BLOCK

You can't include surprises in your business plan, but you can demonstrate to the reader that you have thought of almost everything. This chapter will help you anticipate potential problems and show you how to minimize their effects.

Calvin Johnson started out as just another young man with a pick-up truck, doing odd delivery and moving jobs. With his eyes for marketing, he noticed that PriceCostco, the American retail giant, was losing sales to other furniture dealers like The Brick simply because it offered delivery and PriceCostco didn't. He had Plan B: "I went to Costco (now PriceCostco) and said 'Hey, I can do that for you,'" says Johnson. "And they said fine." He launched his own company, Cost-Less Express Ltd., to serve PriceCostco customers — with the warehouse giant's unofficial sanction. He became a gypsy company, depending on the crumbs left behind by a much larger, more established business.

By 1996, Johnson had some 3 000 regular clients and distributed between them some 80 000 catalogues promoting about 2 500 different items. Sales had grown to over $3 million — good for twelfth place on the Profit 100 list of fastest-growing companies. He has now moved his business out of his home into a real office and has signed his first formal contract with PriceCostco to become its official catalogue and delivery partner.[1]

Figure 8.1 Chapter Eight will help you prepare parts H, I, and J of your business plan, the financial section.

ACTION STEP PREVIEW

39 Prepare your Plan B checklist.
40 Attach price tags to your business.
41 Develop a personal financial statement.
42 Determine how much you can make if you do not go into business.

Although a business plan is designed to demonstrate how the business will prosper, there is a need to demonstrate flexibility when things do not go exactly as planned. What can go wrong and what can be done to eliminate downside risk? When you interview successful entrepreneurs and ask them what surprises they had not anticipated when they started, they usually have quite a few. Almost always, you hear that it cost more and took longer than they had planned.

Having at least one Plan B — an alternative strategy for bailing the business out of a tight spot created by some unforeseen or unfortunate situation — is a must for every entrepreneur. Developing one can start with new-eyes research and a list of potential problems and their solutions. That's how Calvin Johnson started his business on the road to success. He saw a gap in PriceCostco's distribution chain that he could fill better than the multinational corporation that created it. We will help you create your plan B in this chapter. This kind of thinking can help you cut down your surprises by half.

There are countless ways to test the market without making major financial commitments. The worst surprise is finding that there is no market for your product, service, or concept. For example, before you lease a building or buy inventory or machinery, see what you can do by "outsourcing" everything. There are others who can fabricate, assemble, purchase, sell, ship, demonstrate, sample, or give you some space at a trade show. In the opening vignette, we learned how Calvin Johnson started out with an informal partnership to test his market. Nobody can know exactly what to expect until she or he starts. We encourage you to try to start at the lowest level with the least investment so your missteps will be small and correctable.

Avoiding a Play from Left Field

There's always something coming that you can't see, perhaps something like what this case study illustrates.

Tommy Mankiewicz was playing poker with a couple of his university buddies when the idea of starting a small business came up.

"Dry cleaning," Rick said. "You can work out of the garage. All you need is a panel truck and a customer list. It's like coining money, right from the start."

"Sandwiches," George said. "And I know just the place. Traffic 24 hours a day — beach traffic, commercial, commuters, blue-collar workers, school kids. Gimme two cards." George had been in sandwiches on the East Coast. Rick and Tommy often called him George, the King of Sandwich. They assumed he knew a lot about business.

"How much would it cost?" Tommy said.

George whipped out a pencil and pushed some numbers around. "Figure 20 grand apiece, tops," he said. "Plan to double your 20 in eighteen months, easy."

"Those are nice numbers at the end," Tommy said. "But which one of you big spenders can loan me the 20 at the beginning?"

"Hey," George said. "No problem! They don't call me the Sandwich King for nothing. Give me a handshake now and your name on a paper later, and we're in business."

So Tommy and Rick shook hands with George.

George was between jobs, so he handled lots of the details. He found the location, negotiated with the owner of the building, talked to equipment vendors, bought a great-looking sign. Tommy and Rick prepared financial statements to give to the banker George knew, and Tommy contacted relatives and friends to ask for start-up money.

Tommy and Rick and their wives spent some weekends fixing up the place. Tommy worked hard. He was handy with tools, and he built cabinets and shelves. He was building one of his creations the day the city inspector dropped in at the shop to make his inspection. He was a heavy-set man with beady eyes and was carrying a clipboard. He walked around the place, frowning and making notes. After a while he asked Tommy, "Where's the restroom for the disabled?"

"What?" Tommy said, feeling a chill on the back of his neck.

"The disabled restroom. You know, wide enough for a wheelchair, regulation railing along the wall, special raised toilet facility. You gotta have one."

"Can you wait for my partner to come back?" Tommy asked. "He just stepped out. If you'll talk to him, I'm sure he —."

But the inspector just stood there, shaking his head. And Tommy knew that George hadn't taken care of it, and even when George did get there, all the inspector did was read them chapter and verse of the city code. Every public place must have a restroom for the disabled. They had to tear out a wall, put in a drain, move some machinery around in the kitchen, and replumb everything. It would cost $12,000.

The inspector came back to check the work when they'd finished. He sat down at the counter, and Tommy brought him a sandwich. He told Tommy that they were lucky not to have been fined. The inspector paused and then said, "Your sandwiches are great. Once you guys get going, they'll make you famous."

The work on the new restroom delayed the opening of Tommy's shop more than a month.

ACTION STEP 39

Prepare your Plan B checklist.

Now that you've got your business well in mind, take a few minutes to brainstorm a list of surprises that could cost you money or time, and, if possible, how you can turn these problems into opportunities. Use our checklist to help you get started. Talk to businesspeople in your industry. If you don't know anyone, get on the Contact! chat line (see Box 8.2) and ask questions. If you are intending a street-side location, ask the neighbours what has happened to them and how they're doing in this location. Talk to vendors, suppliers, customers, and insurance brokers. If you are going to operate out of the home, ask the opinion of other home entrepreneurs. Ask. Probe.

When you finish your list, put a checkmark beside each item that will cost money.

Reading about these fellows' experience, it's all too easy to say "I told you so." It's easy to second-guess in such a situation and to say to yourself, "They should have known about that requirement. They just didn't do their homework."

But Tommy and his partners were experiencing the heady excitement of entrepreneurship. They were having fun and were caught up in the busy work of opening a business.

The same thing could happen to you. That's why you've got to plan for everything, even surprises. Box 8.1 provides you with a Plan B checklist that could help eliminate surprises, while Box 8.2 gives you some Web sites that you can check out to find useful information like registering your business.

If you get into the habit of making lists, doing mind maps, and writing everything down, you'll improve your chances of surviving in small business. Action Step 39 will help you anticipate potential surprises.

PAYING THE PIPER WHEN THE PURSE IS THIN

Small businesses are especially vulnerable at start-up time because that's when they're least able to afford surprises. If Ginny Henshaw had anticipated possible surprises, she'd have been better prepared for what happened to her.

Box 8.1 Plan B Checklist

Here's a checklist of some obvious start-up concerns. Add to this list as you think of things.

I. Advisors

- A. Lawyer
- B. Banker
- C. Accountant/bookkeeper
- D. Insurance agent
- E. Commercial real estate agent
- F. Mentor (advisory board)
- G. Consultants
- H. Suppliers
- I. Chamber of commerce
- J. Professional association
- K. Other organizations

II. Organization

- A. GST registration (if necessary)
- B. PST registration
- C. DBA ("Doing business as" = fictitious business name)
- D. Partnership agreement
- E. Corporation
- F. Other

III. Licences, Permits

- A. Business licence
- B. Resale permit
- C. Department of Health
- D. Liquor licence
- E. Fire inspection permit
- F. Local building inspection
- G. Other

IV. Location

- A. Lease review (lawyer)
- B. First and last months' rent (Rent may have to be paid while making improvements. Estimate time needed to do improvements.)
- C. Security deposit
- D. Leasehold improvements
- E. Insurance
- F. Security system
- G. Utilities, deposits, estimated monthly costs
  1. Electric
  2. Gas
  3. Water
  4. Phone installation
- H. Other

V. Auto (Consider new, used, leased)

- A. Autos
  1. New/used
  2. Lease/purchase
- B. Trucks
  1. New/used
  2. Lease/purchase
- C. Insurance
- D. Maintenance, repairs

VI. Equipment

- A. Office
- B. Retail space
- C. Warehouse
- D. Manufacturing area
- E. Kitchen
- F. Dining area
- G. Communication
- H. Computer
- I. Other

VII. Fixtures

- A. Tables
- B. Chairs
- C. Desks
- D. File cabinets
- E. Work benches
- F. Storage cabinets
- G. Display cases
- H. Lighting
- I. Shelving/storage

VIII. Supplies

- Pencils, pens, notepaper, tape, letterheads, dictionary, calendar, appointment book, coffee, tea, soft drinks, bottled water, and so on

IX. Inventory

- What are the minimum and maximum average inventory requirements you need on hand to do business on your first day?

X. Advertising/Promotion

- A. Signs
- B. Business cards
- C. Flyers/brochures
- D. Displays
- E. Ad layouts and graphics
- F. Media (newspaper, radio, other) costs
- G. Trade show booths
- H. Other

(Continued)

Box 8.1 Plan B Checklist *(Continued)*

XI. Banking

- A. Chequing account
  1. Cheque charges
  2. Interest on account
- B. Chequing/bookkeeping system
- C. Deposit box
- D. Savings/chequing account
- E. Credit
  1. Credit cards
  2. Personal lines of credit or letter of credit
  3. Loans and interests
  4. Credit from suppliers/vendors

XIII. Employees

- A. Application/employment forms completed (e.g., employer registration number from Revenue Canada)
- B. Training program

Box 8.2 Bookmark This

Registering Your Business.
http://www.fin.gov.bc.ca/corpg.default.htm
The *One Stop Business Registration System* is a quick and unique way of completing the most common business registration forms.

Business Name Registration. The Ministry of Consumer and Commercial Relations.
http://www.ccr.gov.on.ca/mccr/welcome.htm

Business Number (BN).
http://www.revcan.ca/menu/EmenuNBA.html
The Business Number replaces many of the old numbers that businesses use to deal with government.

Goods and Services Tax.
http://www.revcan.ca/menu/EmenuNBA.html
Every individual or business engaged in a commercial activity with annual sales and revenues of GST-taxable goods or services totalling more than $30,000 must register and charge the GST.

The Canadian Management Network.
http://strategis.ic.gc.ca/sc_mangb/contact/engdoc/homepage.html
Canada has a nation-wide network of small business support organizations.

The reason I decided to start a day-care centre was because I really like kids. I talked it over with my husband, who said he'd help out if I got in over my head.

I think we planned things pretty well. We found a good location — smack in the middle of a neighbourhood of young families with an average of 2.3 children — and then we spent weekends painting and fixing up. We worked hard, but it was fun, and it made us feel a part of something warm and cozy.

Well, about three weeks before our opening, we called the light and power people to ask them to turn on the lights. "Sure thing," they said. "Just send us a cheque for $700, and the lights will be on in a jiffy."

"What?" I asked. "Did you say $700?" We had around $800 in the kitty, but that was earmarked for emergencies.

"That's right. You're a new commercial customer with a good credit rating. That's the reason the figure's so low."

"You think $700 is low?" I asked. I was shocked.

"For your tonnage," they said, "it's right on the money."

"Tonnage? What tonnage?"

"Your air conditioner," they said. "You have a five-ton unit on your roof.

"But we're not planning to run it!" I said. "The breeze here is terrific. We don't need the air conditioner."

"Sorry, ma'am. Our policy is pretty clear. Sometimes we get three months' deposit, but for your business, we'll only require the two. Is there anything else I can help you with today?"

"No," I said. "Nothing."

SHAREHOLDERS AGREEMENTS WITH BUY-SELL OPTION

If you have business partners or associates, it is very important that you draw up a shareholders agreement to spell out the rules and regulations of the partners. The agreement should include a buy-sell option that clearly states what happens if one partner should die, become disabled, or want to sell his or her interest in the business. When partners split up, and most eventually do for one reason or another, a shareholders or partnership agreement with a buy-sell formula will very likely save the business and keep you out of court. Think of it as a prenuptial agreement.

Often, these agreements are funded by joint life insurance on the owners, so that if you die, the business or the other owners will collect the life insurance proceeds and use those funds to buy out your interest in the business. Otherwise, your surviving family members may find it very difficult to sell the interest in the business they inherit from you, except at a give-away price.

Many small business owners ignore the need for shareholders agreements, or dislike having a will drawn up. They keep putting it off. The few hundred dollars you may spend in legal fees to draw up a partnership agreement is probably one of the best investments you and your associates will ever make.

Managing the Unexpected

Most business surprises will cost you money, and your ability to cope with them will depend on your ability to pay for them. The estimated cash reserve form in Figure 8.2 and Action Step 40 will help you prepare your cash flow and thus reduce the risks of doing business.

RISK MANAGEMENT

You, the entrepreneur, may be the best judge as to how much risk you can manage and how much should be transferred. But most likely, you will need some sort of business insurance. You'll likely need a business insurance professional who will probably not be the same person who brokered your homeowner's or auto policies. We suggest you network your way to a good business insurance agent — the same way you select a lawyer. You will want someone who understands your business, worker's compensation, product liability, errors and omissions, bonding, burglary coverage, and key employee insurance — health, fire, life, and so on.

Figure 8.2 Estimating Total Funds Required (Application of Funds) to Start a Business

PART A Estimate cash reserve you need to cover unexpected surprises over the first few months.
PART B Estimate starting costs you have to pay only once.
PART C Add A and B. This equals the total funds required to start your business.

PART A Estimated Cash Reserve to Cover Unexpected Surprises

Item	Your estimate of monthly expenses based on sales of $ ________ per year.	Your estimate of how much cash you need to start your business (see column 3).	What to put in column 2. (These figures are typical for one kind of business. You will have to decide how many months to allow for in your business.)
	Column 1	Column 2	Column 3
1. Salary of owner-manager	$	$	2 times column 1
2. All other salaries and wages			3 times column 1
3. Rent			3 times column 1
4. Advertising			3 times column 1
5. Delivery expense			3 times column 1
6. Supplies			3 times column 1
7. Telephone and Internet			3 times column 1
8. Other utilities			3 times column 1
9. Insurance			2 times column 1
10. Taxes, including Employment Insurance			4 times column 1
11. Interest			3 times column 1
12. Maintenance			3 times column 1
13. Legal and other professional fees			3 times column 1
14. Miscellaneous/ unexpected			3 times column 1
15. Total cash required to cover start-up operations		$ ________	Add rows 1-14. This amount will be recorded as cash in the current assets of your opening balance sheet.

(Continued)

ACTION STEP 40

Attach price tags to your business.
Sit down at your desk and look around with new eyes.

1. List the items on your desk: pencils, paper, telephone, computer, cell phone, business cards, calendar, and so on. List the desk itself, the lamp, chair, bookcase, filing cabinet, coffee machine. Now go through the drawers, writing down every item you use to make your work run easier and smoother.

   When you finish the list of things you can see and feel, make another list, this time of your expenditures for things you cannot see, some of which you might take for granted. These include insurance, protection, rent, utilities, taxes, legal services, accounting services, and so on.
2. Beside each tangible item and each intangible expense, write down how much it cost or still costs you. If you don't know precisely, jot down a ballpark figure and move on. You can learn the exact amount later. Add up these figures.
3. Move all your items to the work sheet (Figure 8.2). Note that we differentiate costs as either start-up expenses or operating expenses. This is an easy way to think about costs.

   As you gather more information, you'll be able to refine the numbers of this sheet.

Figure 8.2 Estimating Total Funds Required (Application of Funds) to Start a Business *Continued)*

PART B Starting Costs You Only Have to Pay Once		
16. Prepaid expenses - Grand opening advertising - Deposit with public utilities - Prepaid insurance - First and last months' rent - Licences/permits - Other	Total prepaid $________	Expenses paid before opening, part of which will be "used up" during the first year of operation. (These expenses will be recorded under current assets of your opening balance sheet.)
17. Opening inventory/office supplies	Total inventory $________	Your suppliers can help you on this. (These estimates will be recorded under current assets of your balance sheet.)
18. Equipment and fixtures (including installation)	Total equipment $________	You will probably have to fill out a separate sheet showing all the details. (These estimates will be shown as fixed assets on your opening balance sheet.)
19. Leasehold improvement (decorating/remodelling, etc.)	Total leasehold $________	Talk it over with a contractor. (These costs are recorded as fixed costs in your opening balance sheet.)
20. Organizational costs - legal and other professional fees - franchise fees	Total organization $________	These organizational expenses are paid before you open your business and are recorded as other assets on your opening balance sheet.
21. Other start-up costs	$________	
22. Contingency - equal to at least 10 percent of your start-up total	$________	
23. Total costs you have to pay only once		Add rows 16–22
PART C Total Start-Up Funds Required		
24. Total funds required to start your own business (Part A + Part B)	$________	Add lines 15 + 23. This will be the total assets in your opening balance sheet.

Insurance companies frequently put together packages for particular types of businesses, such as retail, wholesale, and service. Also explore group rates through your trade association or your local chamber of commerce. Most chambers of commerce offer a small business insurance package. Joining a group insurance program can save you a lot of money.

Remember that insurance is only one of the options to reduce risk — and in some cases, it should be considered the last resort. Insurance can reimburse you only for unintentional, unforeseen, and uncontrollable losses, not for everyday business risks. Other options include eliminating the risk with a Plan B or C, reducing it, assuming it, or transferring it to someone else.

GETTING ADVICE

Yes, you must be prepared because there's a boatload of surprises awaiting every entrepreneur who enters the marketplace. We've talked about Plan B, formulating your strategy, thoroughly researching your market, and peering into the future to see what lies ahead. But there's another angle to planning: it's called seeking advice.

Think for a moment about where you are right now on your road to the marketplace. You're halfway through this book. You've analyzed your skills and needs. You've probed your past and surveyed your friends. You've discovered what success means to you, and you've plotted trends and found your industry segment. You've profiled your target customer, studied the demographics, and developed a marketing strategy, including your promotion campaign. You've examined the prime and indirect competition. You've used your new eyes to find a dynamite location. Now you need to find a small business guru or establish an advisory board and get some advice.

Where might you find a business guru or someone who should be on your advisory board? Well, what about your banker? Many people come to him or her for money — some of them carrying business plans, others not knowing a spreadsheet from a bed sheet. What about your accountant? What about the real estate broker who helped you with your search for a location? What about your business insurance specialist or a retired person who is very knowledgeable about your industry? An advisory board should be no more than three to five people. Have you contacted your local Canada Business Service Centre? You can even get advice over the net. Strategis is a key resource (see Box 8.3).

You can use your network to find other people who may help you. Show them your goals, objectives, and list of potential surprises and ask for their advice. Ask them for their ideas about what other surprises might be in store for you. If one of those persons gives you wonderful advice, consider putting him or her on your advisory board or, if you're incorporated, on your board of directors. Remember, you can make anyone part of your team — your lawyer, accountant, small business professor, even your customer.

THE RISK OF DISHONEST EMPLOYEES

One of the nastiest surprises for a budding entrepreneur is employee dishonesty. You might think that because you're small, employees won't steal from you, but that is wrong. Small firms get hit more often than big ones. Here's a list of precautions that will help minimize the opportunities for employee theft and fraud.

- Sign all the cheques yourself.
- Don't let any one employee handle all the aspects of bookkeeping.
- Insist that all bookkeeping be up-to-date and clear.
- Insist that your bookkeeper take scheduled vacations.
- Do regular physical inventories.
- Open all mail containing payments yourself.
- Track all cash transactions and maintain a rolling annual cash flow on a monthly basis.

Box 8.3 Bookmark This

Online Help: http://strategis.ic.gc.ca/contact

Contact!, the Canadian Management Network, part of industry Canada's "Strategis" Internet site is a great source of information for small business and small business support organizations, 24 hours a day. The vision of Contact! is to provide a forum for Canadian small businesses and their support organizations to meet, learn from each other, develop business opportunities, and connect with people who are otherwise outside their network. The vision includes input from the very users of Contact! who have, over the years, provided advice and ideas through focus groups and meetings across the country. The people at Contact! work with over 40 partners in the private sector and several federal and provincial government bodies who share the vision. Contact! is:

Informative

- Canada's most comprehensive information on small business support organizations, providing detailed descriptions of their programs and services, and relevant names, addresses and phone numbers.
- Accurate and up-to-date information through regular on-line updating.
- Contains a search tool that makes finding help easy; an index permits you to browse.
- "How-to guides" and interesting articles on management for small business.
- A federal government handbook helps you find what government offers business.
- A catalogue of educational, diagnostic, and management software tools for your convenience.
- A database of people and organizations that can help you understand foreign cultures and business practices.
- Descriptions of business awards and profiles of successful business.

Interactive

On-line forums help you network with other entrepreneurs and small business counsellors nation-wide. Share your expertise and learn from others. Small business counsellors from across Canada will be able to share expertise, retired experts can give advice, students of business can learn, and small business can network for business solutions.

A Source of Business Opportunities

With the support of over 65 trade associations behind the Canadian Business Networks Coalition, you can gain additional networking opportunities, and benefit from the educational resources created by all involved to help you form business partnerships.

Source: Adapted from Industry Canada, Strategis Web site, <http://strategis.ic.gc.ca/contact>, November 11, 1997. Reproduced with the permission of the Minister of Public Works and Government Services Canada, 1998.

- Use numbered order forms, and don't tolerate missing slips.
- Insist on fidelity bonds for every employee who handles cash.
- Triple-check references on résumés and employment applications.
- If your business is a cash business, be there. Absentee owners, beware!
- Try to eliminate cash by accepting debit, credit, and "smart cards."

THE BOTTOM LINE

Financial return may not be your number-one reason for starting a business, but it is a strong motivator. Just thinking about it can help you keep on the business success track. Here are some things to think about:

Income stream. What can you count on from your business? How much salary? profit? What benefits? Company car? Retirement fund?
Profit from sale. What is the potential profit if the business is sold? If and when that point comes, what could you make if you took the company public via a stock offering?
Life cycle. How long will it take to move from start-up to a profit position? Most businesses take two years, even three. What happens to your investment projected two or three years hence?
The rule. Every business should provide the owner with an income stream *and* growing equity. Income without equity means trouble; equity without income means starvation.

The Personal Financial Statement

HOW MUCH MONEY DO YOU HAVE NOW?

The next question to ask yourself is: Do you have enough start-up money? You can find out by getting a total for your assets (what you own), getting a total for your **liabilities** (what you owe), and then doing the easy arithmetic to determine your net worth — in other words, you need to prepare a personal **financial statement** to see what you are worth right now.

An easy way to do this is to visit the Web site of a major financial institution (see Box 8.4). It will look something like the one in Figure 8.3. Pulling together a personal financial statement is important because it tells you where you are with money now, and it will indicate your borrowing capability.

Get some practice by doing Action Step 41.

LIABILITIES
the sum total of what you owe

FINANCIAL STATEMENT
a list of assets and liabilities that will show your net worth or equity

ARE YOU PREPARED TO WAIT?

We've said before that it's going to be a while before your business starts making money. In small business, you don't just rent a location, throw open the doors, and begin to show a profit. You need to be aware of time lags.

What does this awareness mean? It means you've planned everything down to the doorknobs. It means you don't quit your job until you've finished your business plan and checked with your banker about a line of credit or, as we

Box 8.4 Bookmark This

The Web sites of major financial institutions can be a great help to you in preparing your personal financial plan. For example, we found the following information on the Toronto Dominion Web site at <http://www.tdbank.ca>:

- Goal Planner
- Cash Flow Calculator
- Net Worth Calculator
- Retirement Planner
- Education Planner
- Savings Calculator
- Advice and Strategies
- RRSP Loans

ACTION STEP 41

Develop a personal financial statement. Sit down with a pencil and paper and do some figuring.

1. List everything you own that has cash value and estimate its worth. Include: cash, securities, life insurance, accounts receivable, notes receivable, rebates/refunds, autos and other vehicles, real estate, pension, and so on.

   Don't stop now. Go on to list the market values of your home furnishings, household goods, major appliances, sports equipment, collectibles, jewellry, tools, computer, livestock, trusts, patents, memberships, interests, investment clubs, an so on.

   Add up the amounts you've written down. The total represents your *assets.*
2. List every dime you owe to someone or something: accounts payable, contracts payable, notes payable (such as car loans), taxes, insurance (life, health, car, liability, etc.), mortgage or real estate loans, and anything else you owe. These are your *liabilities.*
3. Subtract your liabilities from your assets to find your net worth. It's that simple.

Now you know how much you have and therefore how much you need to raise so that you can start your business.

Figure 8.3

Assets (what you own)	**Current Value ($)**	**Current Value ($)**
1. Liquid Assets		
Cash (chequing, savings, etc.)	$________	
Stocks, bonds, etc.	$________	
Cash surrender value of life insurance	$________	
Other liquid assets	$________	
Total Liquid Assets		$________
2. Investment Assets		
Mutual funds, real estate, investments, etc.	$________	
RRSPs/pension fund	$________	
Other investments	$________	
Total Investment Assets		$________
3. Personal (Fixed) Assets		
Furniture	$________	
Residence	$________	
Auto/boat	$________	
Jewellry/art	$________	
Other	$________	
Total Personal (Fixed) Assets		$________
4. Total Assets (1 + 2 + 3)		$________
Liabilities (what you owe)	**Current Value ($)**	**Current Value ($)**
5. Short-Term Debt (Liabilities)		
Credit cards owing	$________	
Personal loans (amount outstanding)	$________	
Income tax owed	$________	
Other loans outstanding	$________	
Total Short-Term Debt		$________
6. Long-Term Debt (Liabilities)		
Mortgages (amount owing)	$________	
Loans to purchase investment and other personal assets	$________	
Other long-term debt	$________	
Total Long-Term Debt		$________
7. Total Debt (5 + 6)		$________
8. Personal Equity (4 – 7) (Total Assets - Total Liabilities)		$________

A personal financial statement form will tell you how much you are worth

will discuss in Chapter Ten, an angel. The angel is a special person (often a relative) who is prepared to finance you until you get started. It means you're not surprised when your business does not support you (right away) in the manner to which you've become accustomed.

A business is a living, breathing entity, and it takes time for the golden egg to hatch. Be financially prepared to wait awhile.

Opportunity Costs

BEFORE YOU TAKE THE PLUNGE

Before you jump into your own venture, make sure that you are being honest with yourself. What are the **opportunity costs**? What would your financial situation be if you kept working for someone else and did not go into business?

OPPORTUNITY COST
the cost of making an investment

Any business will take time — 50 to 100 hours per week — so you will have to love what you're doing in order to succeed. Box 8.5 will help you measure the value of the time if you had spent it elsewhere. Doing this will also force you to consider the value of the benefits you are probably earning while you work for someone else.

Complete Action Step 42. The dollar projection you come up with should let you know precisely what you're getting into. If it hurts you to think about what you'll be giving up if you go into business, maybe you're not ready for the plunge.

In weighing the opportunity costs of going into business, ask yourself questions such as these:

- Can you afford to leave your job or, as a student, do you need to work for someone right away to pay off your debts?
- What are your gut feelings as you approach the point of no return?
- How comfortable are those "golden handcuffs"?

Box 8.5 How to Project Opportunity Cost

Project your salary for the next twelve months
Add in benefits from your employer:

- Life insurance
- Disability insurance
- Health insurance
- Pension plan
- Dental plan
- Extended health care
- Vacations
- Sick days
- Company car
- Employment Insurance (EI) contribution
- Expense account
- Bonuses
- Other
- Total

Calculate the interest you could earn in the twelve months on the capital you're planning to invest in your business.
Example: $25 000 × 6% = $1 500
Add in your time.
Hours per week you plan to work in your new business:
Subtract the number of hours you now work.
Hours available for moonlighting:
Multiply moonlighting hours by hourly rate and then by 50 weeks
Total opportunities cost (your potential income for the next year)

ACTION STEP 42

Determine how much you can make if you do not go into business.
Calculate what will happen to you financially if you keep on with what you are doing. Attach a value to the extra time you're going to have to spend in your new business. Box 8.5 can help you.

1. Project your salary for the next twelve months.
2. Add in the value of the benefits you receive from your employer: insurance, pension plan, company car, expense account, bonuses, unemployment insurance and Canadian Pension (employer's contribution), parking, free photocopying, complimentary paper clips, and so on.
3. Now figure in the capital you're planning to invest in the business. What would you make on this money if you invested in a no-load family of money-market funds that allows you to switch from stocks to money markets and back to stocks when interest rates change?
4. Add in the value of your time. If you're planning to work 60 hours a week in your new business (many entrepreneurs work 100 during peak seasons), subtract 40 (your normal work week) from 60. That would leave you 20 hours a week available for moonlighting. Say you could make $20 per hour moonlighting. Then, 20 hours a week times 50 weeks a year times $20.
5. Find the total.

THINK AGAIN ABOUT WHAT SUCCESS MEANS TO YOU

As we've pointed out before, money isn't the only measure of success. You need to keep your focus on what you really want. Make a list. Do a mind map. Dig deep into yourself and learn what makes you tick.

Risks and Off-Setting Actions

When survivors from any field or profession get together, they like to share horror stories. We have collected a few of these in the small business "surprise" area and come up with some preventive actions for them. They're listed in Table 8.1. You can probably think of more for your business.

TURN A LEMON INTO LEMONADE

At some time in your business life, you're going to need to find a way to capitalize on one of those unfortunate surprises. When that time comes, we hope you will be as resourceful as Terry Adkins.

Terry and Susan Adkins' Donut Place got off to a slow start. They grossed only $275 a day the first month, when what they needed was closer to $700. But then things started picking up. They had weeks with daily averages of $310, $380, and then $475, and they could see that they were going to make it after all.

By Easter of the second year, they were pulling in $850 on weekdays and $600 on weekends, when trade naturally slowed down. They were beginning to look forward to taking their first vacation in a long time, when the city decided to put in new sewers right in front of the store. Almost overnight business dried up. They were in despair.

After a week of no business, they had an idea. They borrowed a shopping cart from the supermarket and put in it a 50-cup coffee urn — full of steaming coffee — and boxes of doughnuts, disposable cups, cream and sugar packets, and napkins. Then Terry wheeled the cart down to the next corner.

While he sold doughnuts, he got to know people. The second day he went out, he took along a paper and pencil. He wrote down the people's names and what kind of doughnuts they liked. He didn't know that this is called "market research"; it just seemed like the smart thing to do.

Terry and Susan didn't make as much money as they had before the crisis, but they made enough to keep going until things got back to normal. And when it was all over, they had more than a hundred new customers. And because of Terry's market research, they knew what kinds of doughnuts the new customers liked.

Terry and Susan transformed their problem into an opportunity. Terry likes to think they turned lemons into lemonade.

Table 8.1 Preventive Actions to Counter Surprises

SURPRISE	OPPORTUNITIES
Your landlord decides to evict you and your business.	Always have a lease reviewed by a lawyer so you know the grounds under which you could be evicted. Get legal help to rewrite the lease so that it favours your business. Keep in contact with the landlord if there are any potential troublesome areas. Make sure you have a renewal clause.
The newspaper does not run the ad for your grand opening.	Make connections with all media. Develop a **tickler file**. Make sure you see proof sheets. Withhold payment until they do it right.
An hour after you sign your name to guarantee the lease, your best friend and partner gets cold feet and pulls out. You do not have a thing in writing to protect you against partner's remorse.	Have a written shareholders (partnership) agreement up front. Open a special **escrow account**. Everybody deposits. Everybody signs.
For eight weeks, during your peak season, the city has the sidewalk in front of your store torn up. The noise is deafening.	Network your way into city hall. Make sure you know your council member. Try to rally media sympathy. Use the underdog angle.
Your general contractor goes bankrupt.	Get a **completion bond**. Ask the bonding agency to expedite.
Your bookkeeper disappears with $100 000, your books, two trade secrets from the company safe, and your spouse.	A fidelity bond would have protected you. Join a singles club.
Your best salesperson is hired away by the competition.	Woo key employees. Keep them involved and informed. Don't take them for granted. Think about giving them a piece of the business. Check the horizon for pirates.
Due to an administrative error, the bank calls in your loan. It is payable in 30 days. If you would like to cash out, they will give you 25 cents on the dollar.	Take a banker to lunch. Take a back-up banker to lunch. Try to get a cash flow going in your operation without a line of credit, except for seasonal circumstances. Also be prepared to put extra personal funds into the business.
A new customer pays you by cheque, takes delivery of the goods, and then stops payment on the cheque before you get it to the bank. You were too busy to get a cheque verification/authorization.	No matter how busy you are, take time for important survival tasks. Retain all your invoices and the initial letter of agreement of all goods until they are paid for in full.
Your largest customer declares bankruptcy. The money owed you in receivables is 77 percent of your gross annual sales.	Don't keep all your eggs in one basket.
The bank where you have your chequing account refuses to extend you a $20 000 line of credit to buy a piece of equipment that will double your business.	Keep your banker in your information loop. Make sure you give your banker updates on your business plan, including your planned capital purchases. Get a back-up bank. Discuss money long before you need it.

TICKLER FILE
a calendar-based reminder system

ESCROW ACCOUNT
funds held by a neutral third party until the stated conditions are met

COMPLETION BOND
an insurance policy that will pay for finishing a project

ACTION STEP REVIEW

39 Prepare your Plan B checklist.
40 Attach price tags to your business.
41 Develop a personal financial statement.
42 Determine how much you can make if you do not go into business.

AFTER PLAN B

The reason for many small business successes is fast footwork. A small business can move more quickly than a big business. The idea is to keep informed, alert, and flexible. After you develop Plan B, work on Plans C and D. Planning is a process that doesn't stop.

TWELVE-MONTH START-UP CHECKLIST

Think about the things you need to start action on twelve months before you open your door for business. For example, if you want to place an advertisement in the Yellow Pages, you may need to plan for it ten months before the business opens or wait until the next edition comes out. Refer to Box 8.6 for an example of a twelve-month checklist.

Box 8.6 Complete Your Own Start-up Appendix for Your Business Plan

1 year before launch

- Research the demand for your product or service from both primary and secondary sources.
- Read an environmental scan that addresses your project.
- Prepare a test market analysis including an analysis of competition, price, market share.
- Register your product or service
- Write out your mission and goals and start your business plan.
- Establish your form of ownership.

10 months

- Establish the strength of your equity base and need for venture capital.
- Identify your potential fixed and variable costs.
- Investigate all channels of distribution.
- Identify potential suppliers and establish prices.
- Investigate packaging, design, and potential promotion approach.
- Start search for site location to be established three months before opening.
- Establish a good relationship with a banker and a lawyer.

8 months

- Evaluate the results of the field test and establish prices and promotion strategy.
- Confirm suppliers and prices.
- Start getting confirmed prices on promotion material.
- Prepare an overall capital and operating budget.
- Prepare position descriptions for staff.
- Complete competitive analysis.
- Establish an advisory board.
- Investigate all external funding sources.
- Complete your business name search.

6 months

- Start listing potential locations.
- Meet board of advisors to assess progress and problems.
- Clearly identify target market for your promotion strategy.
- Order any fixed assets that require long delivery time.

(Continued)

Box 8.6 Complete Your Own Start-up Appendix for Your Business Plan *(Continued)*

- Establish leases where appropriate.
- Gain approval from the appropriate government bodies if producing a product that requires it.
- Place advertisement if necessary in the Yellow Pages (may need to be sooner depending on your start date and the new phone book release).
- Establish bank line of credit.
- If a home business, verify the city/township by-laws.

5 months

- Finalize location.
- Prepare a design and schedule for leasehold improvements.
- Order signs.
- Order inventory and supplies.
- Contact telephone company for information about home office service options 1-800-387-5185.

4 months

- Contact the leasehold improvements.
- Finalize packaging including design.
- Finalize your promotional approach.
- Complete details for GST with Revenue Canada.

3 months

- Sign for all utilities and hook-ups.
- Develop job descriptions and place ads for staff.
- Take possession of location.
- Start renovations and install fixed assets.
- Meet with board of advisors.

2 months

- Select staff to start.
- Start marketing approach depending on nature of business, and finalize renovations.
- Start receiving fixed assets.

1 month

- Shelve and price inventory.
- Start staff as required.
- Train new staff.
- Get marketing campaign under way.
- etc. etc. etc. — all you forgot about!!

Launch

- Hold grand opening.
- Offer opening specials.

Note that *almost all* the work takes place before the official opening.

In a Nutshell

Start-up needs to go smoothly. What you don't need are expensive surprises that knock you and your business for a loop. Before you open your doors, you need to have anticipated as many potential unpleasant surprises as possible and have a plan of action for each one of them. For example, how would you turn the following unwanted surprises into opportunities?

- Your landlord decides to evict your business.
- Your Yellow Pages ad is terrible.
- The customer that accounts for 75 percent of your business declares bankruptcy.

Expecting and *planning for* the unexpected can make the different between life and death in business. Looking closely at your present assets and liabilities — by developing a personal financial statement — and calculating the opportunity costs of going into business for yourself will help you eliminate some surprises, and they may cause you to question whether you're truly ready to take the plunge. Just remember two things: no one can anticipate everything, and setting up will probably cost more and take longer than your planning indicates.

Think Points for Success

✓ Listen to your competition so that you can change and improve.
✓ Create partnerships and outsource what you can.
✓ Be aware of closing dates for Yellow Pages advertising and other key media.
✓ Keep a time log that tells everyone (you, your founders, your key employees) how you are progressing on the plan.
✓ Make sure your partners are as committed to the business as you are, and have a shareholders or partnership agreement.
✓ Keep an ongoing list of unfortunate surprises that could hurt your business. Write down how you can turn these surprises into opportunities.
✓ Always have a Plan B. And a Plan C. And a Plan D.
✓ Let some key customers in on your planning; let them see it with their own eyes. Go one step further — create a customer board of directors.

Business Plan Building Block

Develop a list of issues that are unpredictable and difficult to control. List the actions that might be taken to mitigate their impact on this business venture.

Problem	**Opportunity**

Complete Figure 8.2. Estimate the total funds required to start your business.

Total cash required to cover start-up operations (line 15, Figure 8.2) $__________

Total costs you have to pay only once (line 23, Figure 8.2) $__________

Total funds required to start your own business (line 24, Figure 8.2) $__________

List the total equity you can invest in the business

Total personal equity (Line 8, Figure 8.3) $__________

Total personal equity available to invest in your business

Cash $__________

Other (specify) ____________________ $__________

Total (other) $__________

Total Equity $__________

Checklist Questions and Actions to Develop Your Business Plan

SURPRISES YOU CAN'T AFFORD

- ❑ What operational goals and objectives do you want to achieve?
- ❑ What risks and challenges does your business face, and how will you address each one?
- ❑ Develop a start-up schedule beginning twelve months from the launch, indicating all the activities you must undertake (e.g., place Yellow Pages phone advertisement), along with related costs up to start-up. Note, this could be a two- or three-page schedule.
- ❑ What are the major cash drains in your business?
- ❑ What types of insurance and employee bonding will you have for your business?

NOTES

1. Adapted from Rick Spence, *Secrets of Success from Canada's Fastest-Growing Companies* (Toronto: John Wiley & Sons Canada, Ltd., 1997), pp. 59–61. Reprinted by permission of the author.

OTHER REFERENCES

Baxter, Sarah Jane. "10 Smart Start-up Moves." *Profit*, September 1997, p. 37.

Carroll, Jim and Rick Broodhead. *Canadian Internet Advantage.* Toronto: Prentice Hall, 1997.

Holloran, Ed. *Credit and Collection: Letters Ready to Go!* New York: NTC Business Books, 1998.

Jacks, Evelyn. *The Complete Canadian Home Business Guide to Taxes.* Whitby, ON: McGraw-Hill Ryerson Ltd., 1997.

Kaplan, Robert S. and David P. Norton. *The Balanced Scorecard.* Whitby, ON: McGraw-Hill Ryerson Ltd., 1997.

Scott, Gini Graham and John J. Harrison. *Collection Techniques for a Small Business.* New York: Oasis Press, 1994.

nine

The Power of Numbers

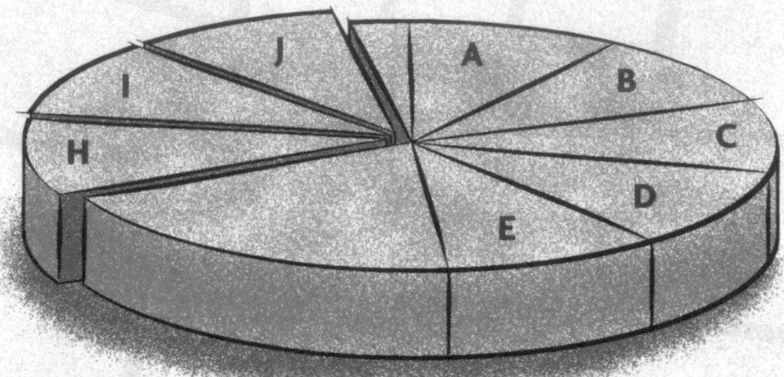

Figure 9.1 **Chapter Nine will help you prepare parts H, I, and J of your business plan, the financial section.**

LEARNING OPPORTUNITIES

After reading this chapter, you should be able to:

- Use numbers to project your business future.
- Develop cash management strategies.
- Project monthly sales and propose a sales forecast.
- Search your personal financial situation for creative ways to deal with shortfalls.
- Understand that bills are paid with cash, not profit.
- Use ratios as a management tool.
- Create a cash flow projection.
- Create an income statement and balance sheet.
- Create a financial plan to start your business.

BUSINESS PLAN BUILDING BLOCK

Cash management need not be complicated. But you need to pay attention. Cash is the lifeblood of your business. Here is how to build a financial plan and stay in control of the flow.

Brent Trepel graduated at age 22 from the University of Western Ontario in London, Ontario, with an honours degree in business. Then he jumped in his car and drove west to one of the jewellery stores owned by his family. For the next two years, he worked in both the Calgary and Edmonton outlets of Ben Moss Jewellers.

And what he found was a near-crisis situation. The family had expanded the stores too quickly. In the early 1990s, unplanned growth had substantially driven up debt-to-equity ratios and reduced working capital to anorexic levels. "I understood the importance of financial ratios," said Trepel. "We didn't have many options. If we didn't put a plan together, we would not be around. There was some resistance; some people wanted to stick with the old ways, but my father was fantastic. He said: 'Go with it.'"

Over the next five years, Brent introduced tight financial controls and slashed expenses. Each store was required to maintain a strict level of inventory and set specific inventory turnover objectives. "If a product category was not achieving its turn, we took it out of the assortment," Trepel said. His belt-tightening and tight inventory controls worked. By the late 1990s, inventory turnover was 50 percent better than the North American average. Working capital improved by 30 percent and, with the increased cash flow, Trepel was able to cut the debt-equity ratio in half. Ben Moss Jewellers became one of Financial Post's "50 best privately managed companies."[1]

ACTION STEP PREVIEW

43 Recall hard times to plan for the future.
44 Spread out the year in an income scenario.
45 Project your cash flow — spreading out the green.
46 Project an income statement — a moving picture of your business.

In this chapter, we urge you to move beyond your start-up plans and venture out into the uncertain future. It's time to set some numerical goals for your first year of operation and beyond. Brent Trepel depended on financial planning to chart a course away from the financial ruin of his family-owned business. This chapter will show you how to begin charting your financial future. Our main purpose here is to help you avoid running out of money. We'll also introduce you to some of the basic financial statements a business needs to survive and grow. When you are ready to write your financial plan, we suggest you follow the step-by-step format provided in the Building Blocks section of this chapter.

Chart Your Business Future with Numbers

Which months will be strong in your particular business? Where are the seasonal weaknesses? What is your sales forecast for the first year? For the second? For the third? How much profit will you make? Or how much will you loose? How can you project cash flows, bank loans, lines of credit, vendor credit? When do you add people to the team? Will they bring in cash and at what cost? What will your cash picture look like when your start-up costs are spread over a whole year? What would rapid growth do to your cash picture? Have any of your life experiences prepared you for handling money in business?

START WITH THE PAST

One easy way to chart your business future is to face your past. Everyone has financial ups and downs. What were some of your good and bad times? Let Action Step 43 help you face your financial past so you can chart your financial future.

Now prepare a realistic Personal Financial Cash Budget. Follow the model shown in Table 9.1.

COLLECT SURVIVAL INFORMATION

In the previous chapter, you worked out a personal financial statement. Then, in Action Step 43, you recalled personal survival tactics — how you dealt with money problems in the past. Your next step is to begin building a sales and cash forecast, and a profit and loss statement. We'll discuss them briefly before moving on.

1. *Sales forecast.* Before you jump into a business, you need to figure out how many sales dollars you can produce in a given period of time. You can develop a first-year forecast by combining information on sales from business owners, trade associations, your prime research questionnaire, and your own marketing plans.
2. *Seasonality scenario.* Almost every business will have its peaks and valleys during the year. You may need to write a brief seasonality scenario for the first year of your particular business.
3. *Cash management.* Because of time lags (cheques clearing, dating, credit sales, credit cards, bad risks, human factors, paperwork, weekends, and so on), you may not get paid the same day you make a sale. Meanwhile, you have to pay cash out for labour, taxes, rent, utilities, and inventory. If your business is going to stay afloat in this turbulent trough between

ACTION STEP 43

Recall hard times to plan for the future. List the times in your life when you ran out of money. Now look ahead.

Part A. Your Personal Money Past. Look back over your life to the days when you were not so street smart, and try to remember hard times.

Where were you, and what were you doing? What was your age at the time? How much training did you have? Who was there with you? How many people did you have depending on you? How did you feel about running out of money? Angry? Sick? Depressed? Victimized?

How did you solve the problem? Did you moonlight? Did you get a loan? Did you take out another mortgage? Did you try to tighten your belt and run leaner?

Part B. Your Personal Money Future. Look ahead into the next year. List your expenses, such as those for shelter, food, medical bills, transportation, insurance, phone, school, clothes, and utilities — and then add in 10 percent for a contingency fund. If you need a form with blanks, Table 9.1 will help. You can also ask your banker, or check out the Web sites of major financial institutions.

Next, list the tactics you have developed to handle these expenses. If it looks as though you are not going to have enough money, what is your Plan B?

Table 9.1 Personal Financial Cash Budget — Monthly Expenses

Category	Item	Estimated Expenses (Add 10% for contingencies)	Actual Expenses
Housing	Rent/mortgage Heating Electricity Telephone Maintenance Other		
	******Subtotal***		
Food	Weekly groceries and staples extras during weeks Restaurant meals/week		
	******Subtotal***		
Transportation	Car, operating, repair Public transit Other (taxis)		
	******Subtotal***		
Personal	Leisure activities Personal care items Hair styling Laundry/dry cleaning Other		
	Subtotal		
Clothing	Work clothes Family/personal		
	******Subtotal***		
Care-Dependents	Children Adults		
	******Subtotal***		
Debts	Charge accounts/credit cards Loans Other		
	******Subtotal***		
Sundry	Entertainment Newspapers Business search costs/supplies		
	******Subtotal***		

(Continued)

Table 9.1 Personal Financial Cash Budget — Monthly Expenses *(Continued)*

Category	Item	Estimated Expenses (Add 10% for contingencies)	Actual Expenses
Insurance	Dental/medical Personal/life Car Household Other		
	Subtotal* (Subtotal*)		
Medical	Doctor/dentist/optician Prescription drugs Other		
	**Subtotal*		
Taxes	Property Income tax Other		
	**Subtotal*		
Miscellaneous	Education (course fees, books, etc.) Licences (e.g., driver's licence) Church and charity Other		
	**Subtotal*		
Savings	Target your monthly savings		
	**Subtotal*		
Total Monthly Expenses:			

Source: Adapted from Human Resources Development Canada, "Working Solutions: Preparing a Realistic Budget," *Take Charge Self-Help Series*, No. 6. Reprinted with the permission of the Minister of Public Works and Government Services, 1998.

credit and creditors, you have to know where every dollar is. Long before the dollars stop trickling in, you have to make arrangements for help. Cash management means knowing where every dollar is coming from every month and where every dollar is going so you can maximize the benefits of the money you are holding. The idea is to speed up the inflow of cash and slow down the outflow.

4. *Profit and loss.* Unless you are the exception to the rule, you are not going to make lots of money your first year in business, and if you get rich, it will probably happen slowly. A projected (pro forma) profit and loss statement will tell you when you are going to start making a profit, which has to come before you start to get rich. And if you're not going to make a profit for a while, you might want to structure your business so that your losses can be deducted from personal taxable income.

FORECAST SALES

The following case study illustrates the value of planning and the art of sales forecasting. The case is about a bookstore operation, and it is valuable because the owners went through four important steps:

1. They developed a seasonal scenario so that they were not surprised by the Christmas crunch and February blues.
2. They gathered data from their trade association and private companies such as Dun & Bradstreet, which gave them a benchmark for comparisons.
3. They developed their own method of projecting sales by using ratios.
4. They tracked sales monthly, compared them to the forecast, and adjusted expenses according to changes in actual sales.

In any operation, you want to separate your product mix according to how fast it moves. The term for this is "shelf velocity." In the bookstore case, industry data told the owners to separate paperbacks from hardbacks because the shelf velocity of each category is different.

Patricia French — DISCovery Bookstore

We planned every phase of our bookstore operation. My husband, Don, has always been a great reader, and my friends at university used to accuse me of being a bibliophile, but we quickly discovered when we did our research that a bookstore is a business. In business, you either grow fast or you don't survive, so we found ourselves mastering a lot of new skills, fast.

Running a bookstore is not the same as being a happy-go-lucky English major in university.

We worked and saved for several years — employed in bookstores, teaching advertising — so that when we started our business, we had over $30 000. In addition, we got our friends interested, and they contributed over $50 000 more. With that in hand, we wrote up a comprehensive business plan and went to our banker, who loaned us $35 000 against our inventory as collateral.

The location we found has about 700 square metres of floor space, and data from a major trade association indicated that sales for that size of store in this demographic area would be around $150 000 annually.

The first question was how much to spend on inventory. To answer that, Don used a ratio method of inventory projection.

TURN RATIO
a measurement obtained by dividing the average inventory into annual sales or cost of goods sold

First, we found the annual **turn ratio** for hardcover, which was 3. This is a measurement obtained by dividing the average inventory into annual sales or the cost of goods sold. Then we found the annual turn ratio for paperbacks, which sell faster. That was 5.

To find the amount we needed for initial inventory, we first multiplied the percentage for gross sales times the annual sales figure.

Industry figures told us hardcovers would account for 60 percent of sales (that meant paperbacks would equal 40 percent of sales):

$$60\% \times \$150\ 000 = \$90\ 000 \text{ annual hardcover sales}$$

Next, we figured cost of sales, which was 60 percent. We got this number from our suppliers, and we checked it out with Dun & Bradstreet's key business ratios, and Statistics Canada's "Small Business Profiles." We multiplied

60 percent times \$90 000. That came to \$54 000, which was the annual cost of (hardcover) goods sold.

In order to develop the start-up hardcover inventory, we divided the cost of goods sold by the annual ratio, which for hardcover was 3:

$$\frac{\$54\ 000}{3} = \$18\ 000$$

So we knew our estimated cost for the initial hardcover inventory would be \$18 000.

We went through the same procedure for paperbacks, multiplying annual sales by percentage of sales and by cost of sales, and then dividing by the turn ratio:

$$\frac{\$150\ 000}{5} \times 40\% \times 60\%$$

$$\frac{\$60\ 000}{5} \times 60\% = \frac{\$36\ 000}{5} = \$7\ 200$$

Finally, when we added the two figures, we came up with \$25 200. Don checked this out with our suppliers, and, to be on the safe side, we calculated we would need \$30 000 for initial inventory.

It was a lot of money. It was also a relief to know where we were going.

Next, we plotted out a sales forecast for a year, and we assigned percentages of sales for each month.

A scenario gives you a feel for the future. We knew that Christmas would be our peak time. That holiday season accounts for at least a third of our business. When you realize that, you can be better prepared. Here's our scenario:

January (6.5 percent). January is an anticlimax to Christmas, but it's still busy because of gift certificates and exchanges. Don and I will run some good specials at the end of January, before taking our yearly inventory. Even though sales are slowing down, we have to order new titles, because publishers (our suppliers) will be giving us advance notice on their list for spring.

February (4.5 percent). Very quiet. We take inventory, weed out stuff that doesn't sell, send it back. We meet a lot of publisher's reps, who are out on the road pushing new titles.

March (5 percent). On March 15, we have an Ides of March Sale. Next year, we're planning a St. Patrick's Day tie-in.

April (5 percent). Still slow. We estimate a slight jump in sales after the fifteenth, mostly because spring vacation gives some people time to read.

May (8 percent) and June (8 percent). Two holidays — Mother's Day and Father's Day — plus weddings and graduation, give us our second busiest season. Art books and gift editions will do well. Also encyclopedias and how-tos.

July (6 percent) and August (7 percent). We're not in a tourist area, and summers for us will be slow. We sell mostly easy-to-read paperbacks, and our minds will be on ordering books for Christmas.

September (9 percent). Saved by back-to-school purchases. We're interviewing people for Christmas jobs and making last-minute purchases on gift items.

October (10 percent) and November (12 percent). The start of the busy season. Customers sense it, and we can feel the momentum. The rush is just around the corner.

December (19 percent). The crunch. I work the front while Don stations himself in back, inputting our sales into the computer. We gather information daily so we can spot the direction holiday sales will take. It will be different every year, but this exercise by Don will help us chart sales and plan for future years.

Don and Patricia prepared Table 9.2 (Monthly Cash Flow) before they opened their business. This is a good example to follow. Be sure you can justify income and expense items. Also note that most income and expense items will vary month by month as sales fluctuate. You should prepare a monthly cash flow for the first year, then quarterly for the next two years.

After the first year of business, sales forecasting will become easier. Keep records monthly the first year so you'll know how your peaks and valleys correlate with the seasonality of your industry.

Most businesses are seasonal, and you'll need to develop strong control systems to manage your cash resources. Start now to identify alternate sources of credit and also ways to collect cash from customers before all of your products or services are delivered.

ACTION STEP 44

Spread out the year in an income scenario.

Write out a monthly revenue for your first year of operation.

You can do part of the scenario with new eyes — just look around at obvious forces such as weather, heat, cold, time, and expense, and mix these carefully with life cycle, location, and competition as they relate to your business.

You will have to do the rest of the scenario with information gleaned from other small business owners or secondary data from Dun & Bradstreet, Statistics Canada, or trade associations.

When does your industry collect money? Before the sale? During the sale? After the sale? Long after the sale?

When will you have to pay for your inventory?

What is the shortest time lag you could see between the time you pay for inventory and the time you receive money (payment, hard dollars) for the sale of that same inventory?

What is the longest time lag? When will you declare a lag a bad debt?

If you are in manufacturing, and you have to alter or reshape or rebuild the raw materials into a product, what kind of time lag will there be?

Now that you have seen your sales percentages for a year, what management strategies do you need to develop to get more control of your cash flow?

FORECAST COLLECTIONS

What businesses are seasonal? When can you collect ahead of time?

If you're in the ice cream business, sales will heat up in summer. The same is true of hardware (especially home improvement supplies) and auto parts, when everyone is getting the travel bug. If you run a ski shop, you might have to order your skis at a summer trade show, pay for them when they arrive in September, and wait until late March to make the final sale.

If, on the other hand, you're in the bed-and-breakfast business, you can collect your money ahead of time — when the customer books the accommodation — and have it spent or invested long before you have to deliver the bed and breakfast. The same is true for airlines, insurance companies, magazines, newspapers, advertising agencies, travel agents, printers, and caterers. If you're on the receiving end, it's nice to know there are businesses that collect the dollars up front.

Often, service trades will bill for their services and may not be paid for 30 or 60 days after the work is completed. What's it like for your business? As one example, Box 9.1 shows the typical payment and collection timelines for an electrical service company.

CHART YOUR PRO FORMA INCOME AND EXPENSE STATEMENT

Now it's time to prepare a pro forma income and expense statment. Action Step 44 takes you through the process. Note that more than just sales are involved: you will also need to project times of collection and other time lags so that you can get a feel for the way cash will flow through your business. The Action Step winds up by asking you a pointed question: Now that you have seen your sales percentages, what management strategies will you develop to get more control of your cash flow?

Box 9.1 Electric Works — Payment and Collection Timelines

Payments

- Wages: weekly
- CP Deductions: monthly
- Income Tax Payments: quarterly
- Raw Materials: 30 days
- Hydro Inspector: 10 days

Collections (even though the terms may be net 30 days)

- 3 or 5 contractors: 45 days
- 1 contractor: 60–90 days
- 1 contractor: 90–120 days

It's better to tackle that question before you open your doors. Think about that as you read the following case study. It tells the story of how Laserian, Ltd., a flashy company in a glamorous growth industry, got into money trouble because its CEO didn't bother with cash management.

He was a creative kind of guy.

Jerry Fiske's Laserian, Ltd., a manufacturer of laser optics, was just going into its second year of operation when it started to run out of money. The research and development people, who ran the company, came to Jerry to tell him the company needed a cash injection.

"We're out of money, Jerry. What's the story?"

Jerry didn't know. So he went to see Phil Brill, his banker.

First Visit

Jerry handed Phil a roughed-out profit and loss statement on the back of an envelope. Phil took the envelope, glanced at the figures, then looked at Jerry.

"How's the laser business, anyway?"

"Booming," Jerry said. "We've got orders pouring in for this new scanner. Every food chain in the country wants one the day before yesterday. We're starting up production of a new holographic camera — one that will take pictures of automobile tires to check for defects. The Canadian Forces have sent six guys around because they want us to sign a contract to work on a new cryptographic device. The numbers speak for themselves, Phil. We did $300 000 in sales this month and had a profit of $52 000 plus."

The banker looked at the numbers on the envelope:

Sales	$300 000
Cost of Goods Sold	$172 000
Gross Profit	$108 000
Expenses	$ 76 000
Profit	$ 52 000+

"How much do you need?"

"Thirty thousand should do it, Phil. Just for odds and ends until our receivables start pouring in."

Table 9.2 Monthly Cash Flow — DISCovery Bookstore

Step I	Opening Balance	6% July	7% Aug.	9% Sept.	10% Oct.	12% Nov.	19% Dec.	6.5% Jan.	4.5% Feb.	5% March	5% April	8% May	8% June	Total
Step II														
1. SALES		7 800	9 100	11 700	13 000	15 600	24 700	8 450	5 850	6 500	6 500	10 400	10 400	150 000
2. —														
3. TOTAL SALES		7 800	9 100	11 700	13 000	15 600	24 700	8 450	5 850	6 500	6 500	10 400	10 400	150 000
Step III														
Receipts														
4. Cash In														
5. — Cash Sales		7 800	9 100	11 700	13 000	15 600	24 700	8 450	5 850	6 500	6 500	10 400	10 400	150 000
6. — Receivables Collected														
7. — Loan Proceeds														
8. — Personal Investment														
9. — Sales of Assets														
10. — Equity	80 000													80 000
11. — Loans	35 000													35 000
12. —														
13. Total Cash In (lines 5 through 12)	115 000	9 000	10 500	13 500	15 000	18 000	28 500	9 750	6 750	7 500	7 500	12 000	12 000	265 000
Step IV														
Disbursements														
14. Cash Out														
15. — Purchases		5 255	9 880	9 305	8 030	8 720	6 575	5 080	3 760	3 045	6 545	7 440	8 420	82 055
16. — Advertising (2%)		200	200	200	200	400	400	100	100	200	100	100	200	2 400
17. — Auto and Truck														
18. — Bank Charges and Interest		300	300	300	300	300	300	300	300	300	300	300	300	3 600
19. — Insurance		450												450

(Continued)

Table 9.2 Monthly Cash Flow — DISCovery Bookstore *(Continued)*

	Opening Balance	6% July	7% Aug.	9% Sept.	10% Oct.	12% Nov.	19% Dec.	6.5% Jan.	4.5% Feb.	5% March	5% April	8% May	8% June	Total
20. — Professional Fees														
21. — Rent		1 200	1 200	1 200	1 200	1 200	1 200	1 200	1 200	1 200	1 200	1 200	1 200	14 400
22. — Business Taxes and Licences														
23. — Telephone		50	50	50	50	50	50	50	50	50	50	50	50	600
24. — Utilities (Heat, Light, Water)		150	150	150	150	150	150	150	150	150	150	150	150	1 800
25. — Wages — Employees														
26. — Principal Draw or Management Salaries		1 600	1 600	1 600	1 600	1 600	1 600	1 600	1 600	1 600	1 600	1 600	1 600	19 200
27. — Term Debt (Principal Portion Only)		250	250	250	250	250	250	250	250	250	250	250	250	3 000
28. — Purchase Fixed Assets	60 790													62 790
29. — Taxes														
30. — Materials and Supplies (1%)		100	100	100	100	100	100	100	100	100	100	100	100	1 200
31. — Miscellaneous (3%)		325	325	325	325	325	325	325	325	325	325	325	325	3 900
32. — Start-up (Application of funds excluding cash reserve)	44 210													44 210
33. —														
34. Total Cash Out (lines 15 through 33)	105 000	9 880	14 055	13 480	12 205	13 095	10 950	9 155	7 835	7 220	10 620	11 515	12 595	237 605
Step V														
Summary														
35. Total Cash In (line 13)	115 000	9 000	10 500	13 500	15 000	18 000	28 500	9 750	6 750	7 500	7 500	12 000	12 000	265 000
36. Plus: Cash Forward (Prev. Mon. — line 39)		10 000	9 120	5 565	5 585	8 380	13 285	30 835	31 430	30 345	30 625	27 505	27 990	
37. Equals: Total Cash Available	115 000	19 000	19 620	19 065	20 585	26 380	41 785	40 585	38 180	37 845	38 125	39 505	39 990	265 000
38. Less: Total Cash Out (line 34)	105 000	9 880	14 055	13 480	12 205	13 095	10 950	9 155	7 835	7 220	10 620	11 515	12 595	237 605
39. Equals: Closing Bank Balance	10 000	9 120	5 565	15 585	8 380	13 285	30 835	31 430	30 345	30 625	27 505	27 990	27 395	27 395

"From the look of these numbers," Phil said. "I'd say you'd be good for it."

Jerry smiled. This was easy street. "I never argue about money," he said.

Later that week, he had a cheque for $30 000. He turned it over to his manager and got back into the lab, where he was happy.

One month later, Laserian ran short of cash again.

Second Visit

"Sorry to bother you again, Phil," Jerry said, "but we need another short green transfusion." Jerry was smiling. He had received money before, and he knew this was a piece of cake.

"How much this time?" the banker said.

"What about ninety grand?" Jerry asked.

"Sounds steep," Phil said. "What's your cash picture?"

Jerry smiled. "We're in terrific shape, Phil." Jerry handed the banker a sheet of graph paper that contained a short column of numbers. "Take a look at this month."

February:	
Sales	$320 000
Cost of Goods Sold	$184 000
Gross Profit	$136 000
Expenses	$ 87 000
Profit	$ 49 000

The banker studied the figures without saying anything.

"Feast your eyes, Phil. Sales are up over last month. The total profit for the last two months is over a hundred grand. If things keep up at this rate, we'll have $5 million in sales by the end of the year. And that means a million in profits."

The banker looked up at Jerry. "What's the money for?" he asked.

"Plastic," Jerry said. "Everything we build is housed in plastic, and my purchasing guy found a real deal. That stuff's made with oil, you know, and if the world runs short of oil, we've got to have enough plastic to get us through."

"A sound point," Phil said. "Can you have your accountant get me a completed profit and loss statement?" Phil asked. "And do something on cash flow?"

"Can do," Jerry said. "I'll get my people right on it."

"Let us see the numbers," Phil said. "I'll get back to you."

Walking out of the bank, Jerry was disappointed in the banker's conservative attitude. He thought briefly of changing banks, then swung his mind back to the excitement of lasers.

Back at the plant, he told his manager to do a profit and loss statement and a cash flow projection, and then he got back to his inventing.

This time, it took the bank almost three weeks to approve the loan. And two loan officers came out to have a look at Laserian, Ltd.

Apparently, they liked what they saw, because the cheque came through just in time.

The $90 000 lasted only a couple of months, so Fiske went to see his banker for a third time.

Third Visit

"I'll bet you know why I'm here," Jerry said.

"You'd better tell me, just the same," Phil said.

This time Jerry was ready with some computerized **spreadsheets**. He unrolled them in front of the banker. "Look at those numbers, Phil. Feast your eyes. That's over a million in sales you're looking at. It's also over $220 000 in profits, counting next month. The sales are already on the books, and we're showing a backlog that will carry us for two more months."

SPREADSHEETS
displays of critical accounting data

The banker studied the spreadsheets (see Table 9.3). He'd seen thousands of spreadsheets come across his desk. He knew that fast growth could kill a company that wasn't ready for it.

"How much do you need this time, Jerry?"

Jerry smiled. He thought he'd found a money tree.

"Thirteen thousand looks like what we need, but I thought we could double that, just to be on the safe side." Jerry paused. "Let's say $30 000."

"You're already into us for $120 000," the banker said. "Before you get any more, I'd like to discuss how we're getting that back."

"Hey," Jerry said. "I'm good for it. Look at those numbers!"

The room was silent. For a long time, the banker didn't say anything. When he finally said something it was a two letter word — NO!

Table 9.3 The Laserian Ltd., Income and Expense Statement

	January	February	March	April	Totals (four months)
Sales	300 000	320 000	360 000	380 000	1 360 000
Cost of Goods Sold	172 500	184 000	208 000	218 500	782 000
Gross Profit	127 500	136 000	153 000	161 500	578 000
Expenses					
Sales — Commissions	27 000	28 800	32 400	34 100	
Advertising/Promotional	1 500	1 600	1 800	1 900	
Travel	500	5 000	2 000	5 000	
Equipment Rental	800	800	800	800	
Auto/Truck	1 300	1 300	1 300	1 300	
Repair/Maintenance	800	800	900	900	
Rent	12 000	12 000	12 000	12 000	
Supplies	1 500	1 600	1 800	1 900	
Telephone	4 000	4 400	4 900	5 300	
Utilities	1 200	1 200	1 200	1 200	
Insurance	1 700	1 700	1 700	1 700	
Legal/Accounting	2 500	2 500	2 500	2 500	
Dues/Subscription	250	400	400	400	
Salary — Management	14 000	15 000	16 000	17 000	
Salary — Staff	3 000	5 000	7 000	9 000	
Miscellaneous	1 000	1 100	1 100	1 200	
Interest on Bank Loan	1 900	1 900	1 900		
Payroll Taxes	1 300	1 500	1 700	1 900	
Depreciation	1 000	1 000	1 000	1 000	
Total Expenses	75 350	87 600	92 400	101 000	356 350
Net Before Taxes	52 150	48 400	60 600	60 500	221 650
Tax Reserve	23 450	21 800	27 300	27 300	99 850
Net Profit After Taxes	28 700	26 600	33 300	33 200	121 800

WHAT WENT WRONG?

Bankers don't like surprises. The banker's job is to protect bank depositors, and bankers all over the world worry about small firms that don't maintain an up-to-date business plan. Jerry Fiske's banker did not feel that the bank could afford to underwrite Laserian's prosperity, which was based on uncontrolled growth, regardless of Laserian's **gross profit**.

GROSS PROFIT
net sales minus cost of goods sold

Therefore, Jerry Fiske did not get the money he needed to sustain the rapid growth of his company. The company was out of control, and Jerry didn't see it even when the numbers were down on paper.

What could Jerry have done differently? If he had prepared a cash flow projection ahead of time, his shortfall would have been predicted and he could have applied for one big loan instead of a series of smaller, haphazard loans. Table 9.4 shows what that ideal cash flow would look like with an adequate loan of $200 000 in place. The bottom line in Table 9.4 is Cash Flow for Month.

What you aim for — over and above paper profits — is positive cash flow. You want enough money available so that you can achieve your business plan and stay in business. Now let's revise Table 9.4 by taking Jerry's one-time loan

Table 9.4 How Jerry Fiske Wishes the Laserian, Ltd., Statement of Cash Flow Looked

	January	February	March	April
Cash-on-Hand/Start of Month	10 000	170 800	74 900	52 100
Cash Received/Accounts Receivable	210 000	280 000	316 000	352 000
Three-Year Bank Loan	200 000			
Total Cash Available	420 000	450 800	390 900	404 100
Cash Disbursements				
Manufacturing Disbursements				
Packing, etc.	18 000	19 000	21 000	23 000
Material	123 000	224 000	172 000	198 000
Outside Labour	44 000	49 000	53 000	57 800
Other Disbursements				
Sales — Commissions	14 000	27 000	28 800	32 400
Salary — Management	12 000	12 800	13 600	14 400
Salary — Staff	2 700	4 500	6 000	7 600
Payroll Taxes	4 500	4 500	5 300	6 000
Advertising/Promotional	1 400	1 500	1 600	1 800
Travel	500	500	5 000	2 000
Auto/Truck	1 300	1 300	1 300	1 300
Equipment Rental	2 400		2 400	
Repair/Maintenance	800	800	900	900
Rent	12 000	12 000	12 000	12 000
Supplies	1 400	1 500	1 600	1 800
Telephone	2 500	4 000	4 400	4 900
Utilities	1 200	1 200	1 200	1 200
Insurance	4 000			
Legal/Accounting	2 500	2 500	2 500	2 500
Dues/Subscriptions		1 200		
Miscellaneous	1 000	1 100	1 100	1 200
Loan		7 500	7 500	7 500
Total Disbursements	249 200	375 900	338 800	378 700
Cash Flow for Month	170 800	74 900	52 100	25 400

of $200 000 and watch why Jerry had to run to the banker so often. January's cash flow becomes negative ($170 800 – $200 000 = –$29 200). No wonder Jerry needed to borrow $30 000 in a hurry! This negative cash flow carries on through. If we assume that Jerry wasn't able to borrow any money at all, our revised cash flows for each month would be:

	January	February	March	April
Cash-on-Hand/Start of Month	$10 000	$(29 200)	$(117 600)	$(132 900)
Cash Received/Accounts Receivable	210 000	280 000	316 000	352 000
Bank Loans	—	—	—	—
Total Cash Available	220 000	250 800	198 400	219 100
Total Disbursements	249 200	368 400	331 300	371 200
Cash Flow for Month	$(29 200)	$(117 600)	$(132 900)	$(152 100)

If you're figuring along, you'll notice that Total Disbursements now differ from the Total Disbursements in Table 9.4. That's because if there is no loan, there won't be any loan payments of $7 500 in February, March, and April. Note also that in spreadsheets, a negative amount like –$29 000 is often shown in parentheses, as $(29 000).

Fortunately, Jerry bagged a few loans, but another quick revision of the cash flow shows that $30 000 in January and $90 000 in February weren't enough:

	January	February	March	April
Cash-on-Hand/Start of Month	$10 000	$800	$2 400	$(12 900)
Cash Received/Accounts Receivable	210 000	280 000	316 000	352 000
Bank Loans	30 000	90 000	—	—
Total Cash Available	250 000	370 800	318 400	339 100
Total Disbursements	249 200	368 400	331 300	371 200
Cash Flow for Month	$800	$2 400	$(12 900)	$(32 100)

And remember, for these same four months, Laserian, Ltd., showed $121 800 of net profit after taxes.

WHAT'S THE MORAL?

Although Laserian was profitable on paper (see Table 9.3), every month that sales increased saw an increase as well in accounts receivable (money owed the company but not yet paid). Because the company was expanding, money had to flow into inventory. Past sales could not generate enough cash to support the growth. Without outside sources of cash, the company could not keep up.

This is very typical of a company going through a rapid change. Project your cash flow and prepare a pro forma income and expense statement before you open your doors — for at least two years in advance. If your numerical projections are sound, your banker may grant you a line of credit or a loan for start-up costs. If your projections are haphazard, you may get the same answer that Jerry Fiske got when asking for a lesser amount: *no*.

ACTION STEP 45

Project your cash flow — spreading out the green.

If you don't have access to a computer and an electronic spreadsheet program, get yourself a spreadsheet from your bank or adapt the worksheet from the Business Development Bank (see "Other References") and begin projecting your cash across the first year of your business.

1. Write down all the cash you'll start the year with. In the case of DISCovery Bookstore, this was $10 000.
2. For each month, enter the amount of cash you'll receive from sales or accounts receivable.
3. Enter any loans in the month you receive the cash from the lender.
4. Total the above, which will give you the cash available for each month.
5. Now list all disbursements (cash going out). Spread these out, too.
6. Then subtract disbursements from cash available, which gives you a monthly cash flow.
7. Examine your work. Have you explored the quirks of seasonality? Have you discovered the minimum and maximum time lags between when you make a sale and when the business gets paid in cash for the sale? Does the picture look accurate? Have you checked with an expert?
8. Try the "what-if" test:

   If your cash flow picture looks good, test your money management skills by dropping in a couple of "what ifs." What surprise expenses could throw a monkey wrench into your new business?

Cash Flow and Income Statement: Important Projections

A pro forma income statement tells you when you're going to make a profit on paper. A cash flow projection tells you whether or not you can pay the bills and when you'll have to visit the banker. Both the income statement and the cash flow projection are necessary for the survival of your business. First we want you to start with a cash flow.

CASH FLOW PROJECTION

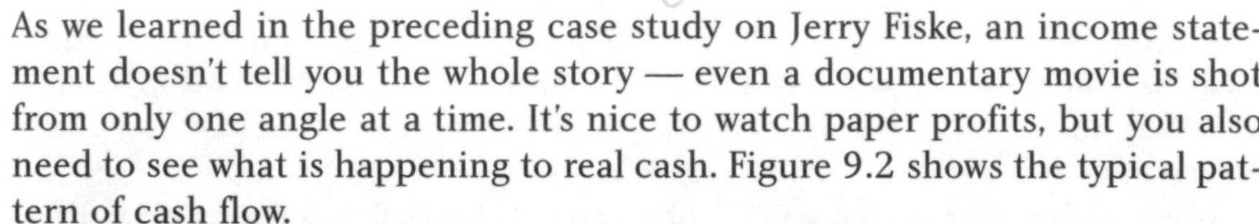

As we learned in the preceding case study on Jerry Fiske, an income statement doesn't tell you the whole story — even a documentary movie is shot from only one angle at a time. It's nice to watch paper profits, but you also need to see what is happening to real cash. Figure 9.2 shows the typical pattern of cash flow.

A monthly cash flow projection is a tool to help you control money. Now that you understand the need for not running out of cash, here's a tool to help you control its flow. Action Step 45 leads you through a monthly cash flow projection. We also supply you with a worksheet you can use to prepare your projected cash flow (Table A9.4, page 196). Also, all the banks and most major accounting firms can supply you with a disc for preparing your cash flow and income statement. Box 9.2 provides you with some points to consider while you're working out your cash flow. Take your time with your cash flow. It's not an easy job. There are lots of things to think about.

When you're through with Action Step 45, show the results to an expert. Does the picture look accurate? It's better to know the truth now, while you're working on paper. Paper truth is a lot easier on the pocketbook than real truth.

PRO FORMA INCOME STATEMENT

Once you have completed your cash flow, you are now ready to create your own pro forma income statement. You have a head start because your cash flow projection (Action Step 45) has a lot of the information you need. For

Box 9.2 Cash Flow — Points to Consider

The three most important ingredients in managing and operating a business? CA$H, CA$H, and more CA$H.

And yet more than 80 percent of small businesses do not use a Cash Flow Forecast.

- Two factors ensure that you have sufficient cash to operate comfortably:
  1. A twelve-month forecast of sales and expenses.
  2. A workable and realistic policy stating when you pay your bills and when you can turn sales into cash.
- Cash flow includes principal, bank payments, and interest — separately.
- Cash flow does not include accounts payable, accounts receivable, or depreciation, only cash in and cash out.
- Your year-end cash flow provides the basis for your projected income statement.
- Before offering credit, do a cash flow.

Box 9.3 Year-End Income Statement — Points to Consider

- All sales are included, even if you have not collected the money.
- All operating costs are included, even if you have not paid the bills.
- Principal payments are not included, but interest is.
- Depreciation is included.
- You can create your income statement from your cash flow. The end of the cash flow is the start of the year-end income statement.

Always remember:
Profit Is Not Cash!

those of you who are not familiar with an income statement, Box 9.3 provides some helpful hints. To show you how this works, we have constructed a projected year-end income statement for DISCovery Bookstore (see Table 9.5). A quick glance at the cash flow of DISCovery books (Table 9.2) makes it obvious that profit is not cash. DISCovery's profit was $8 450, but its cash increase was $17 395 ($27 395 – $10 000). In this case, Patricia and Don's

Table 9.5 Pro Forma Income Statement — DISCovery Bookstore

Sales (Revenue)	$150 000
Cost of Goods Sold	
Opening inventory	30 000
(plus) purchases	82 055
Subtotal	112 055
(minus) closing inventory	22 055
(equals) cost of materials	90 000
Total Cost of Goods Sold	90 000
Gross Profit	60 000
Operating Expenses	
Rent	14 400
Utilities	1 800
Salaries — Employees	
Salaries — Principal Draw (Man. Sal.)	19 200
Advertising	2 400
Office supplies	1 200
Insurance	450
Maintenance and cleaning	
Legal and accounting	
Delivery expense	
Licences	
Boxes, paper, etc.	
Telephone	600
Depreciation	4 000
Miscellaneous	3 900
Total Operating Expenses	47 950
Other Expenses	
Interest	3 600
Total: Other Expenses	3 600
Total All Expenses	51 550
Net Profit (Loss) (Pre-tax)	8 450

ACTION STEP 46

Project an income statement — a moving picture of your business.
You may want to adapt the format shown in Table 9.5 (a blank form is provided in Table A9.5 (page 197). Generate the numbers for the projected period as follows:

1. Using data from your cash flow, forecast your sales for the year.
2. Figure your cost of goods sold, subtract that from sales, and you have gross profit.
3. Add up all expenses and subtract those from gross profit. That gives you the net before taxes.
4. Subtract taxes. (Governments will tax you on paper profit, so you have to build this figure in.)

The figure at the bottom is net profit after taxes for the year.

Figure 9.2

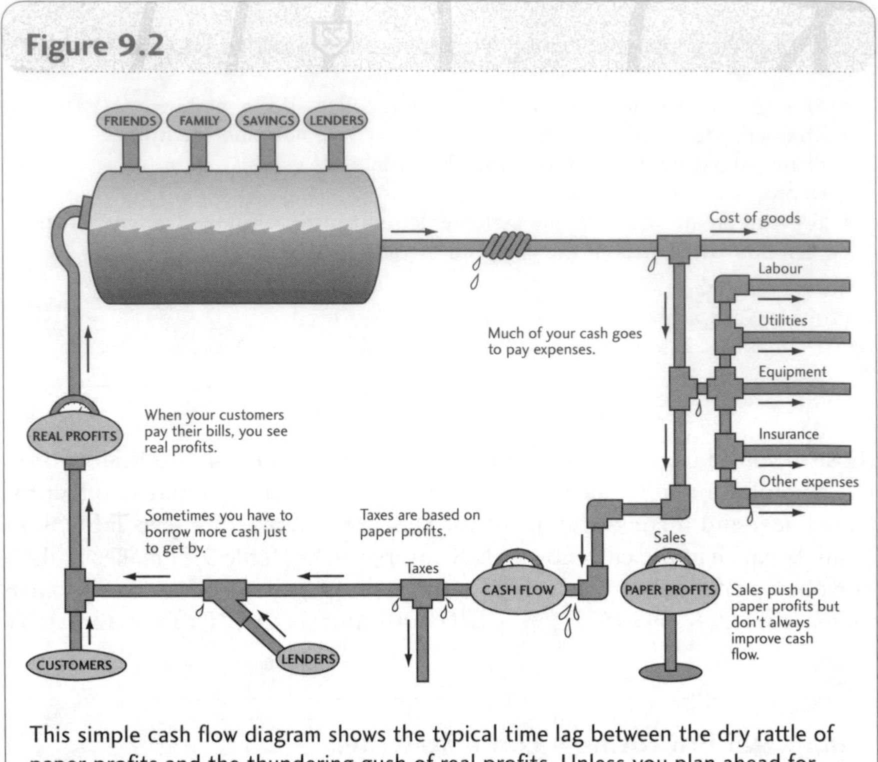

This simple cash flow diagram shows the typical time lag between the dry rattle of paper profits and the thundering gush of real profits. Unless you plan ahead for the lag, you could find yourself high and dry.

excess cash might have given them the illusion that they were doing better than they actually were.

The main point here is that you need both a cash flow statement and an income statement to know how you're doing. If you discover that you won't be making a profit or you will have a cash shortfall for the first few years, you're going to need a very good plan, a group of terrific investors, and an understanding banker who can give you a line of credit.

Action Step 46 will ask you to create your own income statement.

What Are the Key Numbers in Your Business?

Knowing a few key numbers can help you avoid painful surprises. If you know your cost (variable and fixed) and your gross sales, you can calculate your break-even to tell you when you will start making money. Break-even is handy at start-up time, after you have completed your cash flow projections, and also on an ongoing basis to establish your product or service price.

BREAK-EVEN ANALYSIS

A small manufacturing company was completing a plan for its second year of operation. Its first-year sales were $177 000. Its fiscal year ended in December. A sales breakdown for the last three months of the first year looked like this:

October	$24 000
November	$29 000
December	$15 000
Total	$68 000

The owners took a look at the numbers and called in a consultant to help. The consultant gathered information from sales reps, owners, and customers and projected sales for the second year at a whopping $562 000. The owners reacted with disbelief.

"You're crazy," they said. "That's over three times what we did last year."

The consultant smiled. "Didn't you tell me you were going to add three new products?"

"Yes."

"And new reps in March, June, and September?"

"Yes, but —"

"And what about those big promotions you've got planned?"

"Well, sure. We've planned some promotion. But that doesn't get us anywhere near three times last year."

"All right," the accountant said. "Can you do $275 000?"

The owners got into a huddle. Recalling the fourth quarter, they were sure they could stay even, and 4 × $68 000 (fourth-quarter sales) was $272 000. They knew they had to do better than last year.

"Sure. No problem. We can do $272 000."

"All right." said the consultant, rolling out his break-even chart.

"I've just projected $562 000 in sales for the year. To break even, you need only $275 000."

"Hey," the owners said. "We're projecting $90 000 in the first quarter."

"I'm glad you're thinking my way," the consultant said. "Because if you don't believe you can reach a goal, you'll never get there." He paused, then said "By the way, that "$90 000 is three times what you did in your first quarter last year!"

"Just tell us what to do," the owners said.

Following a careful cash flow analysis, the consultant determined that the company would need to borrow money. They knew their business — industry trends, product line, competitors, sales, and promotion plans — but there was no way the bankers would believe a tripling of growth. The key to getting the loan was to convince the bankers the company could do better than the break-even, at $275 000. The break-even chart (see Figure 9.3) was built on the $562 000 sales figure. Note on the chart that after $280 000 in sales, the firm has passed its break-even point and is making a profit.

Box 9.4 Bookmark This

Calculation of Financial Indicators: http://www.slu.edu/eweb/
Breakeven Analysis: An Essential Tool:
http://www.enterprise.org/enet/library/be.html
Revenue Canada Tax Service: http://www.rc.gc.ca
Robert Morris Annual Financial Statement: http://www.bmatters.com

Box 9.5 Bookmark This

We suggest you start with Contact! the Small Business Library link, at <http://strategis.ic.gc.ca/SSG/mi03933e.html>.

Here you will find over 650 educational articles and self-help guides written by leading business experts. Their finance section contains all kinds of how-to financial advice and sources of help.

The Library

Find over 650 educational articles and self-help guides by leading business experts.

Share your publication

Ideas for new articles

Contact!'s Key Links!

- **Business Chat/Coffee Break**
- **150+ Multi-cultural Advisors**
- **2500+ Support Organisations**
- **300+ Software Tools**
- **Search Contact!'s Database**
- **Contact! Us**
- **Contact!'s Homepage**

Accounting	**Business Plans**	**Competitive Intelligence**	**Electronic Commerce**
Finance	**Home Business**	**Human Resources**	**Innovation**
Internet	**Legal**	**Marketing**	**Media**
Networking	**Newsletters**	**Operations**	**Product Development**
Research	**SME Statistics**	**Sales**	**Starting a Business**
Taxation	**Trade**	**Year 2000**	**What's New !**
More Sections to Come...			

Industry Canada, Strategis Web site, <http://strategis.ic.gc.ca/contact>. Reproduced with the permission of the Minister of Public Works and Government Services Canada, 1998.

The banker granted the loan because he realized the company could pass the break-even point, and then some. The key, as usual in business, was a combination of numbers and human confidence.

In a Nutshell

Not surprisingly, many entrepreneurs find it difficult to project numbers for their business. There are several explanations for this:

- They're action people who are in a hurry; they don't think they have time to sit down and *think*.
- They're creative; their strengths are greater in the innovation area than in the justification area.
- They tend to think in visual terms, rather than in numbers or words.

Nonetheless, business is a numbers game and cash is king. In spite of the entrepreneur's feelings about numbers and projections, survival in the marketplace depends on having the right numbers in the right colour of ink. This chapter helps you establish your cash flow, propose your pro forma income statement, use ratios to plan your business, and understand the value of break-even analysis.

Figure 9.3

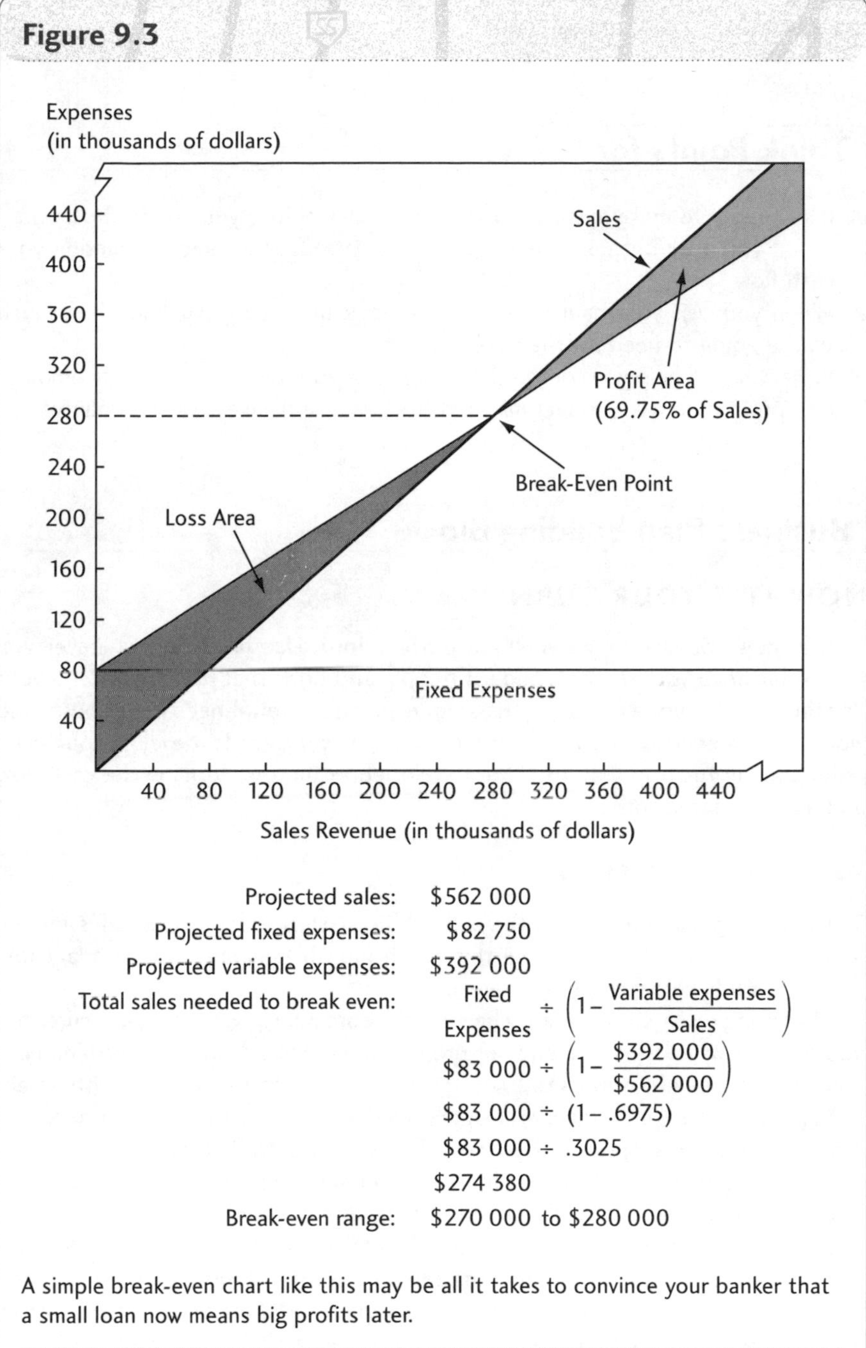

Projected sales: $562 000
Projected fixed expenses: $82 750
Projected variable expenses: $392 000

Total sales needed to break even:

$$\text{Fixed Expenses} \div \left(1 - \frac{\text{Variable expenses}}{\text{Sales}}\right)$$

$$\$83\,000 \div \left(1 - \frac{\$392\,000}{\$562\,000}\right)$$

$$\$83\,000 \div (1 - .6975)$$

$$\$83\,000 \div .3025$$

$$\$274\,380$$

Break-even range: $270 000 to $280 000

A simple break-even chart like this may be all it takes to convince your banker that a small loan now means big profits later.

ACTION STEP REVIEW

43 Recall hard times to plan for the future.
44 Spread out the year in an income scenario.
45 Project your cash flow — spreading out the green.
46 Project an income statement — a moving picture of your business.

The idea in projecting numbers is to make them as realistic as possible. That is the key. Your numbers may seem reasonable to you, but you must make them seem reasonable to others as well. You make them believable by keeping them realistic and documenting them properly. You need to relate each projection to your specific business and to industry standards, and then to *document* them (tell where they came from) in your business plan. The case studies and the examples in this chapter will help you make your projections believable to your banker as well as to yourself.

For those of you who are ready to complete your financial plan, Appendix 9.1 will guide you through this process.

Think Points for Success

- ✓ It's cheaper to make mistakes on a spreadsheet before you go into business.
- ✓ When you work out numbers for a business plan, spend time completing your cash flow.
- ✓ When you visit your banker to ask for money, make sure you know how much you're going to need for the long run.
- ✓ Projecting will help you control the variables of your business: numbers, employees, promotion mix, product mix, and the peaks and valleys of seasonality.

Business Plan Building Block

NOW IT'S YOUR TURN

Explain how you developed your sales projections. Use hard data wherever you can. Summarize your research and list people and firms that have influenced your conclusions. Include cost of goods sold, expenses, capital needs, and best- and worst-case scenarios. If you are using computer software to develop your plan, enter the information that you have developed in the text to fill in the cash flow and income statement.

SALES PROJECTION

The most important and often the most difficult step is estimating sales for the first year of a new business. The thirteenth month becomes more manageable because you have a year of experience.

Marketing research is the key. The financial community wants to make sure that you have spent a lot of time on your projection because it drives everything else. You want to minimize surprises. Even "good surprises" can raise havoc with a well-thought-out plan (for example, imagine you receive ten times the orders you expected and you simply don't yet have the resources to fill them).

You have already conducted an industry overview. You may have identified total sales internationally, nationally, province-wide, and in your service area. Your task after factoring in industry and local growth is to determine what part of the market you can reasonably expect to penetrate in the first, second, third, fourth, and fifth years. Trade magazines, census data, suppliers, and major newspapers often have already performed your secondary market research. Don't forget to do your research on the Internet and CD-ROM. Attach appropriate printed data to your market research section in the appendix of your plan to substantiate your numbers. Fine-tune these numbers by showing your own research and notes from industry experts that support your assumptions on projected sales. When you list your competitors, don't forget to estimate their market share and the part of their market that you have targetted.

Explain the segment or niche you have chosen, make growth projections, and detail the suitability of this opportunity for you. Projections are with documented estimates. A third party's estimate will have more value than yours, so quote as many sources as you can to support your financial forecast.

Write one to two pages on why you believe your sales forecast is reasonable. Avoid phrases like "I think" and "We feel." Say instead "research demonstrates." Be positive, but don't try to sell too hard.

Checklist Questions and Actions to Develop Your Business Plan

THE POWER OF NUMBERS

- ❏ Validate your sales forecast based on your primary and secondary market research. Update the last checklist item in Chapter Five, p. 102.
- ❏ Identify all your cost and pricing assumptions.
- ❏ Prepare a monthly cash flow the first year, and a quarterly cash flow for the next two years. Wherever there is a cash shortfall, it will require new equity, debt, or a bank line of credit. Maintain a minimum $5 000 cash balance.
- ❏ What percent of your initial cash will go into overhead and fixed costs versus operating costs?
- ❏ What is your fallback position if your sales forecast and cash flow do not reach expectations?
- ❏ Prepare a monthly income statement for the first year, and a quarterly statement for the next year.
- ❏ What concerns might the banker have about your pro forma cash flow, income and expense statement, and balance sheet, and what is your response?
- ❏ Is your break-even within range of your minimum sales forecast?
- ❏ How do your financial ratios compare to industry averages obtained from sources such as Robert Norris Annual Financial Statements or the Dun & Bradstreet rates?
- ❏ What will you use as collateral to ensure your line of credit?
- ❏ Prepare your own personal net worth statement.

NOTES

1. Adapted from Rod McQueen, "Proactive Approach Puts New Polish on the Family Business," *The Financial Post*, December 14, 1996, p. 13. Reprinted by permission of The Financial Post.

OTHER REFERENCES

Business Development Bank. Business Planning Package. [Consists of a series of do-it-yourself kits providing forms and financial information required by a new business owner. The BDB also publishes a newsletter, *PROFITS*, and many free booklets.]

Business Development Bank. *Minding Your Own Business.* [This pocketbook series deals with topics important for small business success: Volume 1, General Management; Volume 2, Retail Management; Volume 3, Service Business; Volume 4, Manufacturing.]

Canadian Bankers' Association. *Financing a Small Business — Working with Your Bank.* [Free. Write: The Canadian Bankers' Association, Box 1500, Station A, Toronto, ON M5W 2N6.]

Canadian Small Business Financing and Tax-Planning Guide. Toronto: CCH Canadian (updated monthly).

Coopers & Lybrand. *Profit Improvement Opportunities for Retailers 142.* [This clever set of checklists will help you plan and manage your retail business. Other major accounting firms also can be very helpful in providing you with financial information on starting a business. For example, Thorne, Ernst & Whinney distribute free brochures titled "Presenting Your Case for a Loan" and "Starting a Small Business."]

Costales, S.B. and Geza Szurovy. *The Guide to Understanding Financial Statements.* Whitby, ON: McGraw-Hill Ryerson Ltd., 1997.

Riding, Allan and Barbara Orser. *Beyond the Banks: Creative Financing for Canadian Entrepreneurs*. Toronto: John Wiley & Sons Canada Ltd., 1997.

Royal Bank of Canada. *Your Business Matters*. [This series of sixteen publications covers topics from market planning and finance to operations and exporting. Most Royal Bank branches will have booklets on hand. Other major Canadian banks also have free material that could help in starting and financing your business. Visit them and see what they have. For example, the Bank of Montreal provides a series of helpful booklets for small business called "Problem Solvers."]

Scott, Rankin, Gordon & Gardiner. *New Business Kit — A Guide to Financial, Tax and Accounting Considerations of Starting a New Business*. Ottawa. [Copies of this guide can be obtained by contacting Scott, Rankin, Gordon & Gardiner, 1130 Morrison Drive, Suite 120, Ottawa, ON K2H 9N6. Telephone (613) 596-2767; fax (613) 596-2775.]

Sidford, Colleen. "Designing an Effective Cash Flow Forecasting Program." *CMA Magazine*. September 1997, pp. 18–21.

Appendix 9.1

Step-by-Step Instructions for Completing Your Financial Plan

This section will help you complete a financial plan for your business.

STEP 1. CREATE AN APPLICATION AND SOURCES-OF-FUNDS TABLE

In this first financial table, you are required to state what you intend to spend your money on for start-up expenses (i.e., application of funds) and where you will get your money (i.e., sources of funds). Let's begin with your application of funds — those expenses that you will incur before starting your business. When you're completing this table, keep Figure 8.2 (Chapter Eight) handy because it will also help you organize your information.

First, we want you to divide your start-up expenses into four categories:

Application of Funds (Start-up)

1. General Start-up Costs
2. Leasehold Improvements
3. Equipment Costs
4. Cash Reserve Fund

Table A9.1 provides examples of the types of expenses in each category. In basic terms, leasehold improvements are expenses you pay to make your location ready for the customer: carpeting, lighting, plumbing, painting, and so on. Equipment costs relate to items you need to produce your product or service. These items normally last more than one year: desks, chairs, tables, cash register, and so on. Your general start-up costs will contain expenses not included in leasehold improvement and equipment costs — anything from prepaid insurance to paying for your opening inventory. Table A9.1 divides these expenses into three categories: (1) organizational costs, (2) prepaid expenses, and (3) opening inventory and office supplies.

Your cash reserve fund is your cash on hand before you start your business — a pool of uncommitted cash.

Next, create a list of sources of funds divided into two categories: equity and loans. Equity, or what the business owes the owner, includes what the owner puts into the business: cash, equipment, inventory, and supplies.

Table A9.1 Sources and Application of Funds

Sources of Funds

1. Equity (What the business owes the owner)
   — cash
   — equipment
   — material
   — inventory
2. Loans (What the business owes others)
   — short-term
   — long-term
   — line of credit
3. Near Equity
   — venture capital contribution
   — angel money

Application of Funds

1. General Start-up Costs
   Organizational Costs
   — legal, accounting, government registration, franchise fees, etc.
   Prepaid Expenses
   — insurance, licences and permits, first and last months' rent, security deposits, utility deposits, opening advertising and promotion, etc.
   Inventory and Office Supplies
   — total inventory and office supplies on hand in order to do business the first day
2. Leasehold Improvements
   — carpeting, mirrors, light fixtures, electrical, plumbing, signage, washrooms, air conditioning, wallpaper and painting, etc.
3. Equipment Costs
   — tables, chairs, desk, filing cabinets, work benches, storage cabinets, cell phone, computer, copier, fax machine, auto, etc.
4. Cash Reserve Fund
   — total cash on hand immediately before the business opens (a minimum of 10 percent contingency)

Note: Your applications of funds (i.e., what your business needs the money for) must equal your sources of funds (i.e., where you get your money).

Loans, or what the business owes others, is money that comes from outside investors who want to get in on a business but not own it. Your likely source will be the bank.

STEP 2. CREATE YOUR OPENING BALANCE SHEET

Your next step is to create an opening balance sheet based on your Application and Sources of Funds Table. Your opening balance sheet is a statement of your business financial health at a point in time (i.e., immediately before you start your business). Table A9.2 shows you how to map your estimates from your Applications and Sources of Funds Table into your opening balance sheet. At this point, you should check the financial health of your business by calculating, at the very least, your liquidity ratios (quick ratio and current ratio) and your solvency ratio (total liabilities to net worth or equity ratio). You should also check to see how these ratios compare with any other industry ratios related to your business. A complete list of ratios you should consider for your business appears in Table A9.7.

To help you get started, a typical opening balance sheet is shown in Table A9.3.

STEP 3. CREATE YOUR PROJECTED CASH FLOW

Your next step is to create a projected cash flow for the first year. Normally, this will be on a monthly basis. A blank cash flow has been provided for you in Table A9.4. We suggest you review the instructions contained in Box 9.2 before you start your cash flow.

After completing your cash flow estimates, be sure to check that your "bottom line" cash balance is positive, and to determine your cash break-even point. We suggest that you next project your cash flow for two more years. In some cases, depending on the nature of the business, this may not be required, but you should try and "crystal ball" your future — even if the numbers might be a little rough.

STEP 4. DETERMINE YOUR PROJECTED OR PRO FORMA INCOME STATEMENT

After you complete your cash flow, calculate your year-end (end of period) income statement (forecasted operating statement). To get you started, a

Table A9.2 Creating an Opening Balance Sheet

Sources of Funds	
Equity — Total	Equity
Cash	
Equipment/Material/Labour	
Loans — Total	Liabilities
Short-term	Current liabilities
Long-term	Long-term liabilities
Other	Other liabilities
Total Sources of Funds	*Total Equity and Liabilities*
Application of Funds	**Balance Sheet**
General Start-up Costs — Total	
Organizational Costs	Other assets
Prepaid Expenses	Current asset
Opening Inventory/Office Supplies	Current asset
Leasehold Improvements	Fixed asset
Equipment Costs	Fixed asset
Cash Reserve Fund	Current asset
Total Application of Funds	*Total Assets*

Notes:

1. Your total sources of funds will equal your total application of funds.
2. Your total application of funds will equal your total assets.
3. Your total sources of funds will equal your equity + liabilities.
4. Your total assets will equal your equity + liabilities.

Table A9.3 Opening Balance Sheet (period ending ____________)

Assets			
Current Assets			
Cash			
Accounts receivable	________		
Inventory/office supplies	________		
Prepaid expenses	________		
Other current assets	________		
Total Current Assets	________		
Fixed Assets		________	
Equipment, furniture, fixtures	________		
Leasehold improvements	________		
Land/buildings	________		
Auto/truck	________		
Other fixed assets	________		
Total Fixed Assets		________	
Other Assets			
Organizational costs	________		
Total Other Assets		________	
Total Assets			________
Liabilities and Equity			
Liabilities			
Current Debt (due within the next twelve months)			
Bank loans — current portion	________		
Loans — other	________		
Accounts payable	________		
Other current liabilities	________		
Total Current Liabilities		________	
Long-Term debt			
Long-term (minus current portion)	________		
Mortgage and liens payable	________		
Loans from shareholders	________		
Other long-term debts	________		
Total Long-term Liabilities		________	
Total Liabilities			________
Owner's Equity			
Shareholder's Equity	________		
Retained Earnings	________		
Total Equity			________
Total Liabilities and Owner's Equity			________

Note: The cash in your balance sheet must equal the closing cash at year-end in your cash flow statement.

blank statement for a new business is provided in Table A9.5. We suggest that you also review Box 9.3 before you get started. Again, you should try to project your income for the next two years. And last, evaluate the financial health of your business in terms of break-even and the relevant efficiency and profitability ratios shown in Table A9.7.

Table A9.4 Projected Cash Flow Statement — Worksheet

STEP I													
Opening	Month												Total
Balance	1	2	3	4	5	6	7	8	9	10	11	12	
STEP II													
1. Sales													
2.													
3. Total Sales													
STEP III Receipts													
4. Cash In													
5. Cash Sales													
6. Receivables Collected													
7. Loan Proceeds													
8. Personal Investment													
9. Sales of Assets													
10. Equity													
11. Loans													
12.													
13. Total Cash In (line 5 through 12)													
STEP IV Disbursements													
14. Cash Out													
15. Accounts Payable													
16. Advertising/Promotion													
17. Auto and Truck													
18. Bank Charges and Interest													
19. Insurance													
20. Professional Fees													
21. Rent													
22. Taxes and Licences													
23. Telephone													
24. Utilities (Heat/Light/Water)													
25. Wages: Employees													
26. Principal Draw or Management Salaries													
27. Term Debt (Principal Portion Only)													
28. Purchase Fixed Assets													
29. Taxes													
30. Materials and Supplies													
31. Miscellaneous													
32. Start-up Application of Funds (Excluding Cash Reserve)													
33.													
34. Total Cash Out (line 15 through 33)													
STEP V Summary													
35. Total Cash In (line 4)													
36. Plus: Cash Forward (previous month — line 39)													
37. Equals: Total Cash Available													
38. Less: Total Cash Out (line 34)													
39. Equals: Closing Bank Balance													

Table A9.5 Projected Income Statement (period ending ____________)

Sales (Revenue)			______
Cost of Goods Sold			
Opening inventory	______		
(plus) purchases	______		
Subtotal		______	
(minus) closing inventory	______		
(equals) cost of materials	______		______
Total Cost of Goods Sold			______
Gross Profit			______
Operating Expenses			
Rent	______		
Utilities	______		
Salaries — Employees	______		
Salaries — Principal Draw (Man. Sal.)	______		
Advertising	______		
Office supplies	______		
Insurance	______		
Maintenance and cleaning	______		
Legal and accounting	______		
Delivery expense	______		
Licences	______		
Boxes, paper, etc.	______		
Telephone	______		
Depreciation	______		
Miscellaneous	______		
Total Operating Expenses			______
Other Expenses	______		
Interest	______		
Total: Other Expenses			______
Total All Expenses			______
Net Profit (Loss) (Pre-tax)			______

STEP 5. CALCULATE END OF PERIOD OR YEAR-END BALANCE SHEET

This financial statement will give you a final indicator of the financial health of your business. A typical end-of-period (year-end) balance sheet is shown in Table A9.6.

Using the list of ratios provided in Table A9.7, test the financial health of your business in terms of liquidity, solvency, efficiency, and profitability ratios. Compare your ratios with related industry ratios, if they exist.

Table A9.6 Closing Balance Sheet (period ending ___________)

Assets			
Current Assets			
Cash	________		
Accounts receivable	________		
Inventory/office supplies	________		
Prepaid expenses	________		
Other current assets	________		
Total Current Assets		________	
Fixed Assets			
Equipment, furniture, fixtures	________		
Leasehold improvements	________		
— Depreciation/amortization	________		
Land/buildings	________		
Auto/truck	________		
Other fixed assets	________		
Total Fixed Assets		________	
Other Assets			
Organizational costs	________		
Total Other Assets		________	
Total Assets			________
Liabilities and Equity			
Liabilities			
Current Debt (due within the next twelve months)			
Bank loans — current portion	________		
Loans — other	________		
Accounts payable	________		
Other current liabilities	________		
Total Current Liabilities		________	
Long-Term Debt			
Long-term (minus current portion)	________		
Mortgage and liens payable	________		
Loans from shareholders	________		
Other long-term debts	________		
Total Long-term Liabilities		________	
Total Liabilities			________
Owner's Equity			
Equity at start of period	________		
+ Profit over period	________		
— Owner's draw	________		
Total Equity		________	
Total Liabilities and Owner's Equity			________

Table A9.7 Definitions of the Ratios

Area	Ratio	Formula	Purpose	Conclusion
Profitability	Profit Margin	$\frac{\text{Net Profit}}{\text{Total Sales}} \times 100$	To determine % profit on each sales dollar	High — Congratulations Low — Increase sales — Decrease costs — or both
	Gross Profit Margin	$\frac{\text{Gross Profit}}{\text{Total Sales}} \times 100$	To determine % of gross profit on each sales dollar.	
	Return on Investment	$\frac{\text{Net Profit}}{\text{Total Assets}} \times 100$	To determine effective use of all financial resources.	High — Congratulations Low — Might signal unwise investments — Analyze assets for possible disposal and conversion to cash
	Return on Owner Investment	$\frac{\text{Net Profit}}{\text{Owner's Equity}} \times 100$	To determine adequacy of owner's investment plus effectiveness of use.	High — Congratulations Low — The question must be asked, "Is this the most profitable use of my money?"
Cash Flow (Short-Term Position)	Working Capital	$\frac{\text{Current Assets}}{\text{Current Liabilities}}$	To measure the ability of a business to meet its current (next 12 months) obligations.	In many businesses 2:1 usually acceptable, but needs will vary with industry. In general: High — Possible excessive investment in inventory or ineffective use of cash. Low — If low or less than 1, the amount and term of money owed by business should be carefully analyzed. Possible debt restructuring or further investment may be necessary.
	Acid Test	$\frac{\text{Current Assets Less Inventory}}{\text{Current Liabilities}}$	To determine ability to pay current liabilities using only the highly liquid assets (cash and receivables).	1:1 viewed favourably, but if: High — analyze for ineffective use of cash and/or excessive accounts receivable, possibly indicating adjustments to credit and collection policy. Low — See above, Working Capital
Efficiency	Inventory Turnover	$\frac{\text{Cost of Goods Sold}}{\text{Average Inventory}}$ Average Inventory = $\frac{\text{Opening + Closing Inventory}}{2}$	To show number of times inventory is sold and replaced over a given period. Assesses quality of inventory.	Acceptable ratio varies with industry (i.e., perishable goods must turn quickly, while clothes may only turn over on a seasonal basis). Obvious deviations from industry standards may indicate excessive inventory resulting from improper purchases or poor marketing.
	Inventory Supply	$\frac{\text{365 Days}}{\text{Inventory Turnover Ratio (see above)}}$	To show average days' supply in inventory (actual number of days to sell and restock inventory)	See comments above. Use as a guide to improve purchases.
	Receivable Turnover	$\frac{\text{Net Sales}}{\text{Average Accounts Receivable}}$ Average Accounts Receivable = $\frac{\text{Opening Receivables + Closing Receivables}}{2}$	To measure effectiveness of firm's credit and collection policy.	High — Congratulations. Either an effective credit and collection policy or a basically cash business Low — More attention to control of receivables required

(Continued)

Table A9.7 Definitions of the Ratios *(Continued)*

Area	Ratio	Formula	Purpose	Conclusion
	Average Days Receivable	365 Days / Receivable Turnover Ratio (see above)	To show the average number of days your customers take to pay their accounts.	Low — Congratulations High — Amounts to interest-free loans to your customers. Inform your supplier terms of repayment and if necessary upgrade credit and collection policy to bring Average Days Receivable and Average Days Payable closer together.
	Average Days Payable	Average Payables × 365 / Purchases Average Payable = (Opening Accounts Payable + Closing Accounts Payable) / 2	To show the average number of days you are taking to reimburse your suppliers.	Relate to suppliers' terms of repayment. Over your stated terms, your reputation and future dealings may suffer.
Equity (Long-Term Growth Potential)	Debt Capital Ratio	(Current Liabilities + Long-Term Liabilities) / Total Liabilities	To measure level of creditors' support of your business.	High — Creditors have large claim. Possible warning of excessive debt. Low — Indicates continuing commitment by owner, but refer to profitability area - return on investment ratio for further analysis.
	Owners' Equity Ratio	(Current Liabilities + Long-Term Liabilities) / Owners' Equity	To measure level of owners' commitment to business.	— See above, Debt Capital Ratio — Horizontal analysis will indicate if your investment is increasing or decreasing in value.

ten

Shaking the Money Tree

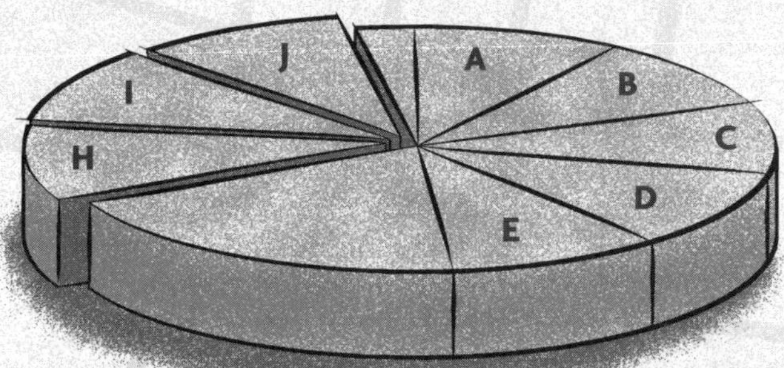

BUSINESS PLAN BUILDING BLOCK

This chapter will explain the sources of funds available to you and the usual conditions for repayment. Most businesses underestimate capital needs. Demonstrate in your business plan that you have planned for all contingencies.

LEARNING OPPORTUNITIES

After reading this chapter, you should be able to:

- Understand that you, the owner, will be the major source of start-up capital for your business.
- Create a framework to save and budget money to start your business.
- Understand that your personal equity and credit cards will be a primary source of capital.
- Practise personal money management skills before you start your business.
- Develop a strategy to get the most from your suppliers.
- Partner with, and gain the most support possible from, your banker.
- Investigate the lending arena, including venture capitalists, for money to fund your new business.
- Identify the pros and cons of debt versus equity financing.
- Determine the types of financing options best suited for your business.
- Take advantage of government and community-based sources of financial help.

Image Processing Systems Inc., in Scarborough, Ont., is one of Canada's leading Profit 100 companies. It develops and sells machine-vision manufacturing-inspection systems, and is a past master at balancing its financing sources. Where did it get its start-up money? In nine years, it has looked almost everywhere for sources of funds. It tapped owner's equity, bank funds, friends and relatives, export financing, "angels," venture capitalists, grants from the National Research Council and other government sources, and, finally, a public stock issue. But Terry Graham, the firm's president, does not see anything unusual about his firm's financial history. "Any start-up company in Canada finds it difficult to get money," he comments, and then adds a sobering note: "The bank was only supportive in the past year, when we didn't desperately need them anymore." In fact, the only resentment he seems to feel is towards the labour-sponsored venture capital funds, which were specifically set up in recent years by the federal government, and armed with generous federal and provincial tax incentives, to invest in promising small business. "The labour funds are incredibly conservative," he says. "They are set up as venture-capital funds, but they don't act like it."[1]

ACTION STEP PREVIEW

47 Make a list of money sources.
48 Design a vendor statement form.
49 Befriend a banker.
50 Prepare to meet your lenders.

Figure 10.1 Chapter Ten will help you prepare parts H, I, and J of your business plan, the financial section.

Every business, regardless of its size or stage of development, will need some sort of financing. Where do successful entrepreneurs find money to start their business? The answer seems to be "almost everywhere," as we learned from the experience of Image Processing. A snapshot of the financing histories of Canada's most successful firms is shown in Table 10.1. It should come as no surprise, however, that the major source of financing is personal capital from savings, credit cards, a new mortgage on the house, and so on, injected into the business by the owners themselves. You, the owner, will probably be the major source of financing. Aside from internal or owner financing through personal investment and profits, the banks are by far the most important source of financing. Nevertheless, the creative talents of entrepreneurs are displayed when it comes time to shake the money tree. Some enterprising companies, for example, receive their financing from suppliers, customers, and even employees.

But, as we have noted, the major source of start-up money for your new venture will have to come from you, the owner. Thus, before you begin to shake the money tree, we encourage you to get your personal finances in order and begin thinking about creative ways to save money. We'll help you prepare to meet your banker and introduce you to some of the major sources of external capital, including the government We also want you to be aware of the pros and cons of debt versus equity financing. Throughout this chapter, we encourage you to persist in your search for money. In Rick Spence's insightful analysis of Canada's Profit 100 companies, one of the important lessons he says he learned about successful independent companies was "If your story truly has merit, there is a backer for your business somewhere."[2]

Before You Shake the Money Tree

What action should you take when you need money to start a business? Do you ask the bank? Do you ask Aunt Alice or a co-worker? Do you write your Member of Parliament? Do you refinance your home?

Table 10.1 Sources of Financing

Sources of Financing	No. of Companies
Owner(s)	93
Chartered banks	86
Public stock issues	33
Friends and relatives	27
Government	18
Other financial institutions	17
Venture capital	12
Informal investors	11
Suppliers	8
Customers	3
Employees	3
Overseas lenders/investors	3
Barter	2
Commercial paper	1

Source: Adapted from Rick Spence, *Secrets of Success from Canada's Fastest-Growing Companies* (Toronto: John Wiley & Sons Canada, Ltd., 1997), p. 161. Reprinted by permission of the author.

As we have seen, most new ventures begin with the entrepreneur's own capital. Funds can usually be borrowed if you have other sources of income and collateral, such as sufficient equity in a home.

In this section we'll help you begin the search for start-up financing.

PREPARE FOR THE SEARCH

Before hunting the money tree, prepare, prepare, prepare.

Research the World of Money Money creates its own world, with its own customs, myths, and rules. Before you go around with your hand out asking for money, we suggest you spend at least three months studying the world of money.

If you are new at this, a good place to start is *The Wealthy Barber* by David Chilton. Then go on to books like those listed in the "Other References" section at the end of this chapter.

Sit at the Feet of a Money Guru Think of three people who know more about money than you do. Seek out one of those people. Begin to build a money network.

Buy Some Stock Invest in a few common stock shares of a business you want to know about. When you read its financial reports, monitor your emotions. Write down how you feel as you open up *The Globe and Mail* to check the rollercoaster of your ups and downs. When it comes time to ask people to invest in *your* business, read over what you wrote.

Watch Your Four Cs Why? Because that's exactly what lenders will do. Continually ask yourself these questions:

1. *Cash.* How much **liquid cash** (savings and chequing accounts) do I have?
2. *Character.* Do I pay my bills on time? How would an investor view me?
3. *Capacity.* Do I have the ability to repay the loan out of the planned business profits?
4. *Collateral.* Which of my tangible assets — such as my car, securities, condo, life insurance — can I use to secure a loan? Banks want collateral.

LIQUID CASH
funds that can be used immediately, usually held in chequing or other accounts

Check out Your Personal Credit Ask the credit bureau for a copy of your credit report. The cost is minimal, and they are required by law to make it available to you. You may find some surprises, such as black marks that may have been posted in error. Make sure your credit report is clean or explainable before you go to the bank.

Write out a Detailed Business Plan Now The business plan is your showcase for displaying all the ideas and information you've gathered for your venture. A suggested format for the plan appears in Chapter Sixteen. Start thinking about your plan now and test it on family, friends, and bankers.

Befriend a Banker, and a Back-up Banker Banks are conservative, and they probably will not want to lend you start-up money unless you pledge real property or security. However, bankers can lead you to money sources you hadn't considered. Seek your banker's advice on pulling your business plan together. If you get your banker's input, he or she will have a hard time refusing help later on. Your banker is one gateway to the world of money. But you should know more than one banker. We'll give you help with this later in this chapter.

PLAN TO SAVE AND BUDGET

The time to think about your personal financial status is right now. Down the road, you're going to need to show lenders that you manage your own finances and that you will have enough money to live on when you open the doors of your new cash-hungry business.

Most entrepreneurs will draw heavily on their own finances to start their own business. And if you are like most Canadians, you are already in debt as it is. This means that you are going to have to change your spending habits if you want to run your own business and still maintain your lifestyle. So we want you to take a moment and consider some street-smart ways for saving money. We suggest you begin with a brainstorm. That's what we did and the results are shown in Box 10.1.

Lenders will want to know as much as possible about your money management skills, so it's a good idea to concentrate next on your personal household budget. After all, personal money management and business money management involve the same skills. You'll need to determine how much money you need each month and what you have coming in each month. That is why we asked you to work out a budget in the last chapter (Box 9.2). Now we suggest that you go back to Box 9.2 and check out how much you can save from your monthly budget. Target for at least a 10 percent saving. But you can save even more. You just have to keep looking.

Box 10.1 Save Money, Brainstorm and Have Some Fun

"We threw a party to brainstorm with our friends on how to save money. We had a lot of fun, and now save hundreds of dollars every year. Our saving party is now an annual event, with a prize going to the most creative suggestions. By the way, everybody gets a prize because everyone is creative. Each participant is required to bring his or her own hand-made prize for distribution. Last year, our award went to the couple who suggested that we form a baby-sitting club which works on a barter system. Now, if we need a baby-sitter, we have ten parents ready to help."

Make saving money fun. Here are a few suggestions:

- Practise energy conservation. Turn off the lights when you don't need them and turn the heat down.
- Wash only dirty clothes and use cold water.
- Go on vacation when there's a sale for plane or train tickets or other travel discounts.
- Make your own liquid refreshment — especially for the festive season.
- Eliminate credit card expenses.
- Wrap your gifts in newspaper.
- Make your own treats.
- Quit smoking.
- Take your own lunch to work.
- Make your own coffee and bring it to your meetings.
- Own one car.
- Ride a bike.
- Buy second-hand and barter when you can.
- Use coupons and buy in bulk.
- Before shopping, make a list and buy only what is on your list.
- Go out for dinner and a movie in your own home.
- Look for a better deal on your personal life insurance and car insurance.

These are a few suggestions. But we are sure there are hundreds more. We want you to make a plan to save and keep track of how much you save (see Action Step 47). Most importantly, we want you to reward yourself when you have accomplished your saving goals.

It's time to look at your personal financial situation and lifestyle. Figure out how much money you need to live on if you go into business and still want to keep a roof over your head. Complete Action Step 47.

Now we want you to begin thinking about your business. Shrewd entrepreneurs leverage the dollars they have, so they won't have to shake the money tree so hard. Box 10.2 provides some tips that could save you money for your business. Read through the list. How many of these ideas have you thought of? How many are new to you?

ACTION STEP 47

Make a list of money sources.
Before you start looking for outside money, review the personal financial statement you developed in Action Step 41. Now go back to Box 9.2 in Chapter Nine. See how you can save money and reduce your personal expenses each month. (If there's more than one owner, each owner should do this.)

Once you have worked out your personal budget, determine where you will get money to live on for at least six months — in some cases, twelve or eighteen months. The longer you can go without drawing money out of your business for your living expenses, the higher the probability of your future success.

LEARN HOW MUCH CREDIT YOU HAVE

Rand A Technology Corp. is a very successful reseller of hardware and software for computer-aided design and manufacturing (CAD/CAM). It provides customized solutions to clients' information-age problems. This Profit 100 company started from zero in the mid-1980s and grew into a $175 million company by the late 1990s. It now claims to be the world's largest CAD/CAM value-added reseller — a computer industry term for distributor/consultant. Rand is now in the enviable position of having bankers knocking at its doors, asking what they can do for Rand. "They call me every week asking if we want more money," says Dennis Semkiw, one of the original owners. But, as he recalls, it wasn't always that way.

Box 10.2 Tips for Saving Money in Your Business

- Ask your customers for cash deposits when they place orders.
- Persuade your vendors to give you more **trade credit or dating** and more time to pay.
- Lease your equipment.
- Run a lean operation; do not waste anything.
- Work out of your home if you can.
- Get your landlord to make on-site improvements and finance the cost over the term of the lease.
- Stay on top of your receivables. Be aggressive.
- Keep track of everything. Try to resell whatever by-products you have in your business.
- Return goods that aren't selling.
- Take mark-downs quickly on dead goods.
- Use as little commercial space as you can.
- If your customers do not visit your business facility, it does not have to be higly visible or attractive.
- When you have to borrow money, shop around.
- Make sure your extra cash is used to earn interest.
- Shop non-bank lenders such as credit unions.
- Do not offer collateral on your loans unless you have no other alternative.
- Survey your friends and relatives for loans. They might lend you money at rates higher than they would get in the money markets, but lower than you would have to pay institutional lenders.
- Befriend a venture capitalist who funds your type of firm.
- Consider selling limited partnerships. You could become the general partner, with little or none of your own capital invested.
- Consider selling stock. (Consult a lawyer.)
- Always maintain an up-to-date cash flow on a monthly basis.

TRADE CREDIT OR DATING
a vendor's extension of the payment term into the near future

When Rand started, it had all the usual cash-flow problems. "Our first form of financing was credit-card debt," says Semkiw. In the early days, the owners' main goal was to make sure the employees got paid before themselves. "My brother, Brian, who runs the finances of the company, would hand us the cheques and tell us when we could cash them," recalls Semkiw. When times got tough, he admits, Rand used Visa to pay MasterCard, or vice versa.[3] According to an article in *Inc.* magazine, "credit cards are now among the most common small-bussiness financing tool. Used carefully, they can work for you."[4]

Now it is time to have a little fun. Let's find out how much unsecured credit you have. This will give you a very general picture of how the financial world rates you at this time. On the business side, once you've done this, you can determine whether there are any untapped sources of funds for your start-up, or fallbacks and emergency sources for your business or personal expenses. Use Table 10.2 or a sheet of blank paper. To learn your credit limits on your charge accounts, look at your most recent statements. You may need to call or write to some businesses for this information. When you've filled in the amounts for each account you have, add them up.

Surprised? Few people are aware of how much credit they have. Before you start your business, we want you to consider:

Table 10.2 Your Current Financial Sources

Source	Amount/Limit
Department Stores	
Sears Bay Others	
Oil Companies	
Esso Petro Can Shell Others	
Bank Credit Cards	
Visa MasterCard American Express Diner's Club Others	
Personal Lines of Credit	
Bank Trust company Credit union Others	
Any Other Unsecured Credit	
Total Credit Available	

1. Applying for two (additional) credit cards — one Visa and one MasterCard. Set them aside to use only for business expenses when you start. Pay the bills when they come due with a company cheque. The banks don't care who writes the cheque, as long as it clears. In addition, it will give you good documentation for your bookkeeper and Revenue Canada. Plus, you will have some additional credit for your business.
2. Applying for a personal line of credit with your bank. Usually, depending on the four *Cs* of credit (your cash, character, capacity, and collateral), you can obtain anywhere from $5 000 to $50 000 of secured or unsecured credit at very attractive rates. If you have a personal line of credit, you are in a much more flexible position with your new business. If you need additional short-term financing, it's available. If not, it can be your security blanket, to be there for you if unexpected expenses should pop up. Other than the cost to establish the line, you only pay when you need to borrow.

With regard to these considerations, bankers and credit companies are much more relaxed about extending credit to a "steady citizen": a person with steady employment income. Also, you would be making arrangements for the money when you don't need it. Bankers tend to like lending money to people who don't really need it.

One reason we suggest that you obtain two bank cards is that your business will have at least limited sources of credit for which payment can be delayed up to 45 or even 60 days without interest. As we learned from Dennis Semkiw of Rand A Technology, personal credit cards can sure help the cash flow. For example, take a look at Table 10.3. Notice that the two cards in the example complement each other in that they allow the holder to get 45 to 60 days of free credit on charge purchases made any day of the month, provided the proper card is used. As you can see, the technique provides the maximum credit when purchases are charged early in the billing cycle. (Warning: Payments must be in the bank's hand on or by the payment due dates.) This technique will also work with suppliers who offer credit terms.

THE VENDOR STATEMENT FORM

An often overlooked technique for reducing your capital requirement is to probe your vendors (major suppliers) for the best prices and terms available. Professional buyers and purchasing agents ask their vendors to fill out an information sheet, writing down the terms and conditions of their sales plans. This is a good idea for you as well.

Table 10.3 How to Get 45 to 69 Days Free with Two Credit Cards

		When to Use		
Card	Closing Date of Billing Cycle	Start	Stop	Time from Purchase to Payment (Example)
Visa	4th of the month	5th	19th	Charge July 5th, pay September 3rd (60 days)
MasterCard	19th of the month	20th	4th	Charge July 20th, pay September 18th (60 days)

VENDOR STATEMENT
a personally designed form that allows you to negotiate with each vendor from a position of informed strength

ACTION STEP 48

Design a vendor statement form.
One of the best ways to save money is to get help from your vendor/supplier. To do that, you need to create your own special form that specifies, in writing, the terms to be negotiated.

Be tough. Be firm. Be pleasant.

Personalize this form by putting the name of your business at the top. Prepare your list of needed information, using the list of eighteen suggestions we've given you.

The vendor form will give you points to speak to. Most vendors hold something back; design your form to help you learn what those things are and get the best deal for your business. When negotiating, use a lot of open-ended questions like "What else can you do for me?"

A small business must buy professionally, and a **vendor statement** will help you do just that. With this form, your vendors' verbal promises become written promises. How well you buy is as important as how well you sell, because every dollar you save by "buying right" drops directly to the bottom line. To compete in your arena, you need the best terms and prices you can get. The statement will help you get the best.

Personalize your form by putting your business name at the top. Then list the information you need, leaving blanks to be written in. Some of the basics include:

1. Vendor's name
2. Vendor's address, phone number, fax number, e-mail, and Web site, if applicable
3. Sales rep's name
4. Business phone (will vendor accept collect calls?)
5. Home phone (for emergencies)
6. Amount of minimum purchase
7. Quantity discounts? How much? What must you do to earn?
8. Are dating or extended payments terms available?
9. Advertising/promotion allowances
10. Policies on returns for defective goods (who pays the freight?)
11. Delivery times
12. Assistance (technical, sales, and so on)
13. Product literature available
14. Point-of-purchase material provided
15. Support for grand opening (will supplier donate prize or other support?)
16. Nearest other dealer handing this particular line
17. Special services the sales rep can provide
18. Vendor's signature, the date, and some kind of agreement that you will be notified of any changes

Remember, the information the vendor writes on this statement is the starting point for negotiations. You should be able to negotiate more favourable terms with some vendors, because these people want your business. Revise your application form as you learn from experience how vendors can help you. Now it is time to prepare your own vendor statement form. Action Step 48 will help you.

PREPARE TO MEET YOUR BANKER

Norbert Bolger of Nor-Built Construction, a homebuilder, recalls being initially impressed with his bank. But in five years he watched four bank mangers breeze through his local branch, to the point where he no longer even knew his account manager's name. When Bolger finally went to meet manager number three a year or so ago, he expressed some dissatisfaction with the high interest rate the bank was charging. "It doesn't sound like you want my business," said Bolger, looking for reassurance. Instead, the banker's reply was, "Not really." "Well," said Bolger, "maybe I should go look somewhere else." "Go ahead," said the banker. Bolger recently completed his switch.[5]

Although banks are in the business of lending money, they also have a responsibility to their depositors. As such, they have a major aversion to risk-taking and tend to choose the safest deals. Their main objective is to make profit for their stockholders, not to create opportunities for you to make money. They can help businesses to start up and expand, but they have to be picky. Their target for bad debt losses ranges from half to 1 percent. This means that they target to get their money back in 99 out of every 100 loans.

In a start-up case, the odds are that you, the owner, will be the banker and your money will come from personal loans or savings. In the case of an established small business, banks are much more co-operative because the venture is less risky — providing, of course, that the financing is backed up by loads of collateral security. The point is, in a start-up situation, you will most likely deal with a bank or major financial institution because you will need a personal loan, and you are also going to have to set up some sort of business-related account. Where possible, it is advisable to deal with the bank's small business advisor, but not all bank branches have such a position.

As your business grows, you will also have to deal with a bank for expansion funding. And as Norbert Bolger of Nor-Built Construction learned, sometimes it is difficult for small businesses to maintain a solid relationship because bank managers tend to move around a lot.

The banking attitude towards small business is changing. Historically, it has often been said that a banker is a person who lends his umbrella when the sun is shining and wants it back the minute it begins to rain. But like it or not, the small business community is going to have to learn how to keep a banker happy, rain or shine. Here are some strategies for dealing with bankers.

Make Your Banker (or any Lender) Part of Your Team Take the time to visit your local banker before you apply for the loan. Find out what he or she wants and be sure to deliver. Bring your banker into the information loop. Make sure your banker understands your product or service before you apply for the loan. In fact, many small business advisors would like to visit you at your location. Make sure your banker knows what you are up to. Try to get him or her excited about your idea. Yes, bankers are people and they can get excited.

Befriend a Banker Build a trusting relationship — even before you ask for the money. Under-promise and over-deliver. Be clear, honest, and thorough.

Don't Surprise a Banker Keep your banker informed. In many cases, keeping a banker informed may be a requirement of your loan. But even if it isn't, savvy entrepreneurs let their banks know about the good and the bad on a regular basis. Bankers are more willing to help if they understand your needs and know that you are trying to anticipate your expected financial needs. If you have a problem, don't procrastinate. Tell the banker right away what you are going to do about it. When you have a line of credit, banks will want to know the status of your accounts payable and receivable. We suggest you plan to send your banker regular updates, even if not requested.

Invite Your Banker to Your Business On your own turf, you won't feel so intimidated and the banker will better understand your business. Communications will flow more easily and your enthusiasm may just become contagious.

Have a Back-up Banker Shop around as you would for any major purpose. Make your banker aware — in a non-threatening way — that you do have other options, but don't bluff. Seek out other options even after you get the loan. Bankers respect healthy competition for good clients.

Respect the Banker's Rules Understand the banker's rules to have paperwork completed correctly and on time. Most account managers are overworked. Try to make their job easy.

Have an Up-to-Date Plan You must have a properly prepared financial plan, and you must be able to justify every number.

Get Professional Advice Make sure your banker is aware you are receiving professional advice. Have your loan agreement reviewed by an accountant, lawyer, and, most importantly, an experienced business person — your financial mentor.

Be in Sync Make sure you and your banker see eye to eye before you apply for the money. If you foresee a personality conflict, start looking for another banker.

Ask for Enough Show your banker you can forecast and understand your situation. It helps the banker sleep at night, too.

Get Ready for Personal Guarantees Many entrepreneurs say, "I incorporated so I won't have to sign my life away." From a banker's perspective, if you have a new corporation, few assets, and no track record, you'll probably have to personally guarantee your loan. If you do have to sign personally for a loan, make a decision right away to begin finding a way to get rid of personal guarantees. If your business is running smoothly for three to five years, be ready to switch your account to another bank if your bank doesn't want to lift the guarantees.

Negotiate the Best Deal You Can The bank will respect you for being a good negotiator. If you still have a job, negotiate for a line of credit or loan while you are still employed. Personal lines of credit are reviewed each year and chances are you can maintain this line if you keep up a good credit rating.

Understand the Banker's Discretionary Limits Different managers have different maximum amounts they can lend depending on their position and bank policy. Try to find out what the lending limit is for your prospective banker. If it is below the amount you are asking, he or she will need to get approval from a supervisor.

If you are planning to make a loan for your business, remember that banks and financial institutions are in the business to make money for their shareholders. Before you get a loan and "sign on the dotted line," *read the fine print* of your loan agreement. Remember the "buyer beware" rule and be prepared for the following:

Spousal Guarantee In certain provinces, laws governing matrimonial assets might mean that the guarantee of your spouse would be required. Needless to say, you should try to avoid spousal guarantees, but if you do get your spouse to sign on the dotted line, your relationship had better be rock solid.

Premium Rates Be prepared to pay a premium interest rate. Banks consider small business high risk and charge accordingly. For the privilege of controlling your destiny, you can expect to pay as much as the prime rate plus 3 percent on unsecured loans, and usually prime plus 1 percent on secured loans.

Demand Loans Most loans, both operating and term, to small businesses are demand loans. This means that there is a footnote on your financial agreement that says your financial institution can "demand" full payment at any time for virtually any reason. If, for example, your bank manager gets cold feet because of the faltering economy, he or she can call your loan and go after you personally if you have signed a guarantee. Try to avoid this type of demand loan arrangement and, at the very least, try to limit the demand portion of the loan. Always have your own back-up plan in place if the bank calls your loan.

Collateral If you have no assets or security, you will not get a loan — period. Banks are not in the business of risking their stockholders' money. All banks will ask for business and personal (if they can get it) security or collateral for your loan. It is common practice to request a collateral amount, which always far exceeds the value of the loan. One Canadian study, for example, estimated that the average bank collateral requested by banks for start-ups was four times the value of the loan. Collateral for established business was at least double the amount of the loan. In effect, banks will ask you to personally guarantee an amount, far in excess of what you are asking for — even if you are an existing business. The more collateral the banks have, the more secure they feel. We reiterate: You should negotiate to limit your collateral, especially if it is personal.

Insurance Most banks and financial intuitions will require you to have the standard personal and business insurance (fire, theft, etc.) to protect them should you have an unexpected problem. In many cases, a bank or financial institution may even require you to sign over your life insurance and disability policies to them. You should make absolutely sure that those close to you are also protected should you die or become incapacitated.

Covenants There are literally dozens of covenants or legal conditions that could be built into your loan agreement to protect the lender. Some of these are likely to include:

- An environmental assessment.
- Maintaining a minimum level of cash.
- Restrictions on certain financial activities, such as the payment of bonuses and dividends without the lenders approval.
- A mandated time period (for example, 90 days after year-end) for providing financial statements to the bank. (If this covenant is in your agreement try not to agree to providing an audited statement. It could cost you thousands of dollars.)
- A shareholders' or partnership agreement.
- A maximum on the size of capital purchases you can make without bank approval.

Fees Banks may require you to pay a range of user and service fees for setting up your line of credit, requesting your loan balance, writing cheques, and using credit card facilities. Some of these fees are negotiable and some are not. Here are the two major user fees that you should try to avoid or at least negotiate.

- Application fee. You may be asked to pay a loan application fee (usually ranging from $100 to $200), which is the bank's cost (including the cost associated with preparing a credit application form) for evaluating its opportunity to deal with you.
- Loan management fees. You may very well be subjected to additional fees if your bank is required to spend time on activities such as monitoring your accounts receivable or inventory, meeting with clients, and preparing statements.

The point here is that many small business owners don't become aware of these extra charges until after the fact. Find out what your obligations are before you sign anything.

We also encourage you to keep a running list of questions to ask prospective bankers. These will get you started:

- What are your lending limits?
- Who makes the decisions on loans?
- What are your views on my industry?
- What experience do you have in working with businesses like mine?
- Could you recommend a qualified lawyer? Bookkeeper? Accountant? Computer consultant?
- Are you interested in writing equipment leases?
- What kind of terms do you give on accounts receivable financing?
- What is the bank rate on Visa or MasterCard accounts? What credit limit could I expect for my business credit cards?
- What interest can I earn on my business chequing account?
- Do you have a merchants' or commercial window?
- Do you have a night depository?
- If you can't lend me money, can you direct me to people who might be interested in doing it?
- Do you make **Small Business Loans Act — guaranteed loans?**
- If I open up a business chequing account here, what else can you do for me?

SMALL BUSINESS LOANS ACT (SBLA)—GUARANTEED LOANS
loans where up to 90 percent of loaned funds are insured by the federal government

ACTION STEP 49

Befriend a banker.
Money creates its own world. There are several doorways into that world. Your banker sits at the threshold of one of those doors. (In a sense, your banker is the guardian of the gate.)

Start with a familiar place, the bank where you have your chequing account. Make an appointment to talk to the branch manager. Here are some questions to ask:

1. Do you lend money to new small business?
2. Do you make Small Business Loans Act-guaranteed loans?
3. What are your criteria for loans?
4. What is your loan approval process?
5. What do you think of my business plan?

If you are happy with your banker's answers, talk over the possibility of opening an account for your business. If you have money tucked away in life insurance or a mutual fund somewhere, ask about the bank's accounts offering premium interest rates.

Now read about how Steve McWhorter handled his cash-flow problems by helping a banker to understand the business he was in.

Things went really well our first year. My third invention — a battery-operated fuel monitor for the new diesel turbos being made in Germany — was selling like hotcakes, and I'd found a great production manager to keep things going down on the line.

Then cash flow troubles developed.

It happened in February of our second year, when a couple of the big car makers — customers that purchased at least half our product — slowed down on their payments. Some payments were more than 90 days past due.

I stay pretty much in the lab and the shop because that's the fun part of the business for me, so I didn't find out about the cash problems for almost three weeks. When I did find out, we invoiced the customers again. Still no money. The first week in March, I had trouble meeting the payroll. The second week I had to pay a couple of crucial supplier accounts. The third week, except for petty cash, the company was almost out of money.

I gave my banker a call. We were on good terms, and I had four accounts at her bank. When I told her my problem, she simply asked me how much I needed for how long. Instant line of credit. What a relief.

Well, we got that squared away, and when things were rolling smoothly again, my banker sat down with me and the company books, and we worked out a strategy for bridging the gap between billing and customer payment.

Those sessions really bothered me, so I started looking around for someone to help out on the numbers. My banker helped here, too, with advice and recommendations about what kind of person would be best at keeping track of money.

When I worked for someone else, I never thought of a banker at all. Since I've been in business, I've come to realize a banker can be a business person's best friend.

Action 49 will get you started in developing a relationship with a banker.

Show Me the Money

SOURCES OF START-UP CAPITAL

By now, you should have improved your money savvy and developed a firm grasp of your personal finances. And ideally, you've also prepared, if necessary, a vendor statement and befriended a banker. Now it's time to zero in on other sources of start-up capital. Provided below is list of all kinds of possible sources. We begin with you, the owner, the main source of start-up capital. But, like James Brown, you never know what can happen when scouting the forest.

James Brown knows the benefits of looking around. When his doctors told him he would never work again as a fisherman in Nova Scotia, he was able to secure a small loan of $500 from Calmeadow Nova Scotia. He found a loan that was based on his character, "not on collateral." As the business grew, he borrowed a total of $16 000, including supplier credit. He now has two employees and operates year round.[6]

Owner Investment Savings and personal loans are the most likely source of financing for small business start-ups. As we have noted previously, personal lines of credit and cash advances from credit cards have also become a major source of financing for small businesses. One government report, for example, estimated that small business debt financing through credit cards alone might actually be in the billions of dollars. At least one bank understands this niche and has introduced a commercial charge card targetted at the small business community. Use your credit card advances only when absolutely necessary, and not as a source of start-up capital. Don't overlook paid-up life insurance, and note that policies issued before 1973 carry an interest rate of no more than 6 percent.

Banks and other Financial Institutions The odds are that you are going to have to deal with a major bank. But don't forget about other financial institutions such as trust companies, co-operatives, credit unions, and caisses populaire.

Love Money Investment from friends, relatives, and business associates is a major source of equity financing for business start-ups. Some say that as much as 50 percent of all start-up money comes from family and friends. If you are considering this type of ownership investment, you will require a partnership or shareholders agreement, detailing the roles of all concerned.

LOVE MONEY
investment from friends, relatives, and business associates

Business Angels **Angels** refer to wealthy individuals from the informal venture capital market (e.g., retired small business people) that are willing to risk their own money in someone else's business. In Canada, angels have financed approximately twice as many firms as have institutional venture capitalists. They usually tend to finance the early stages of the business with investments in the order of $100 000.[7] Angels often require an active management or operations role. They are most active in smaller firms where they may even get involved in the "hands-on" day-to-day operations. In larger firms, the role of the angel is more distant and usually takes the form of management advice and counsel through the board of directors.

ANGELS
wealthy individuals from the informal venture capital market

Angel investors are normally hard to find, but you can start with professional advisors (accountant, lawyer, etc.), your local chamber of commerce and local office of the Business Development Bank of Canada; or visit the Strategis Web site <http://strategis.ic.gc.ca>.

Suppliers Trade credit from suppliers is one of the most often used — and overlooked — forms of short-term financing. That is why we encouraged you to design your own vendors or suppliers form (Action Step 48) before you start your business.

Most suppliers will offer a small business at least 30 days to pay for their product once you are established. Suppliers may also allow you to defer your payments over a longer period of time if you pay some sort of interest charges on the deferred payment. You may even want to negotiate a consignment arrangement with some hungry suppliers. In this case, the supplier owns the goods until you sell them.

Customers Customers, especially for home-based service businesses, are a source of credit. Don't be shy to ask for a deposit before you provide a service or go out and purchase supplies and materials. For example, if you are in the "fix it" business, get your customers to pay for your materials before you start the job by asking them for a deposit. That way you can be a little more confident you will get full payment and you don't have to tie up your own money.

Leasing About one-third of all small businesses use leasing as a source of debt financing, which amounts to about $3 billion in contracts annually. Commercial banks are now getting more involved in the leasing business.

A leasing company (lessor) will purchase an asset such as equipment, computers, automobiles, or land. The small business (lessee) will then sign a legal agreement to pay the lessor a fixed amount over a specific period of time. There are several types of leasing arrangement, including a "walk away lease or net lease," which entitles the lessee to simply return the asset at the end of the term. A "capital or open end" lease requires the lessee to buy back the asset at the end of the term. Most leases can be tailored to the lessee requirements and the lease type will depend on the situational needs.

The obvious advantage is that a small business does not have to tie up its start-up or operating funds. Unlike loans, leases normally cover the total asset costs, including installation and transportation charges. Lease charges are usually fixed and are likely higher than a bank loan rate. They provide small businesses with a reliable payment schedule. A lease may be one of the few options in hard economic times when loans from financial institutions may not be available. As well, lease payments are a business expense.

Leasing also has its disadvantages. For example, chances are that the lease will cost you more over the long run. Leasing companies are in the business to make money and they have to make their profit margins. Unless you have a specific kind of lease, the small business owner will have no assets to show for after the lease is over. In other words, leases do not improve the asset base of the business. A lease payment commits the owner over a specific period of time, and thus limits the flexibility the owner might otherwise have to sell the equipment for a more efficient factor of production. One other note of caution: lease rates normally carry a high interest.

Employees and Employers If you have a good idea, a current or past employer might well be a possible source of start-up capital. When you hire employees, don't be afraid to offer them a part of the action in return for a small investment.

Micro Lending Programs Several non-government and community-based agencies have initiated innovative start-up programs to aid very small or micro businesses. One innovative model of the Canadian Youth Business Foundation is provided in Box 10.3. Another example is the Calmeadow program, used by James Brown to start his business in Nova Scotia (in the case

Box 10.3 Canadian Youth Business Foundation: Community-Based Funding Program

Look into the Canadian Youth Business Foundations (CYBF) community-based funding program. This business loan program provides essential start-up credit to youth (ages 19–29) who have good business ideas but not the resources to get up and running.

Loans are available only in locations where Youth Business has set up a program in partnership with a local community organization. The pool of funds available in each community is limited. Therefore, loans (up to $15 000) are granted on a merit and need basis, similar to a scholarship, to young people most likely to succeed and where the money will make a critical difference to beginning the enterprise.

At the very least, you're going to need a business plan and a mentor to qualify. For more information, visit the Web site of the Canadian Youth Business Foundation at <http://www.cybf.ca>.

at the beginning of this section). Calmeadow also operates (as of 1998) in other centres across Canada. There are basically two types of community-based models: the lending circle (also known as peer lending), and very small loans with no group affiliation but which require some sort of security. Since there is no central clearinghouse for these types of micro lending opportunities, you are going to have to start by getting in touch with local economic development departments and chambers of commerce. The Internet is also a good resource. We suggest you begin with the Strategis Web site.

Government Programs We encourage you to be on the look-out for community-based "grass roots" programs supported by provincial and local governments. For example, "pools" of start-up capital have been established by the Saskatchewan and Manitoba governments. The federal government also has a number of programs providing financial support to small business. A few of the major programs, like the Micro-Business Program of the Business Development Bank are briefly outlined in the final section of this chapter.

Venture Capitalists With venture capital firms, we enter the world of high rollers and high fliers. Unlike banks, which lend money that is secured usually by real estate or other "hard" assets, venture capitalists don't lend money. They are equity investors who buy a piece of the business with private or publicly sponsored pools of capital. Venture capitalists gamble on the business's rapid growth, hoping to reap a 300 to 500 percent return on their investment. They often expect at least 35 percent annual return on their investment.

According to the Canadian Venture Capital Association, venture capital people prefer to enter the financial picture at the second stage of a firm's development when the business has proven its potential and needs a large infusion of cash to support growth. The hungriest consumers of venture capital are technology companies with high growth potential. For example, high-tech firms secured about 66 percent of the $2 billion invested from venture capital in 1998.[8]

Co-operative Partnerships More and more, small businesses are beginning to realize the financial benefits of combining resources in some kind of co-operative arrangements. These types of arrangements go under many names: joint venture, strategic partnering, strategic alliance, corporate partnering, and so on. No matter what business you are in or what business you want to start, you can benefit from establishing strong collaborative alliances. For example, if you are establishing a home office, why not consider entering into an agreement with major customers or clients who need your services? They will supply you with an office and, in return you provide them with the services they require for a set number of hours per week. If you have a product you want to sell and need the distribution channel, why not enter into a marketing agreement with a larger, more experienced firm? It will market and sell the product that you supply. If you have a new idea and have built a prototype, you don't have to manufacture the product yourself: strike up an arrangement with a manufacturing plant to build the product and you sell it. The number of options available is only limited by your imagination.

Action Step 50 asks you to list potential lenders and investors and to develop your persuasive arguments. Without persuasive inducements to lenders, they have no reason to invest in your business. If you need help in listing your reasons, you might begin by profiling your target customer. You might list industry trends, and dovetail them with a scenario of where your product or service fits. Move from there to marketing strategy, selling, the profit picture, and return on investment.

In the final part of Action Step 50, you test your tactics on friends. Ask your friends to respond as though they were potential investors. You want to

ACTION STEP 50

Prepare to meet your lenders.
Know who your potential lenders are and why they should want to help you.

Part A. List potential lenders and investors. Begin with your family and friends and move on to business acquaintances and colleagues. Don't forget institutional leaders.

Part B. Now quickly list some reasons why lenders should want to invest in your business. What inducements are you offering potential investors? If you're offering them a very small return on investment (ROI), what are you offering that will offset that?

Think about the legal form of your business. Would you attract more investors if you incorporated?

Part C. Test your tactics by talking to a few friends. Tell them: "This is just a test, and I'd like your reactions to my new business venture." Watch their reactions, and make a list of the objections they give you — the reasons why they cannot loan you money.

Using your list of your friends' objections, write down your answers to those objections. Are there any you cannot answer? What does this mean for your business?

Box 10.4 Bookmark This

Here are some Web sites that will help you find finance-related information, including sources of funds.

Capital Quest
http://www.usbusiness.com/capquest/home.html

Prepare Yourself for the Venture Capital Inquest
http://www.datamerge.com/news/archives/vcinquest.html

Bank of Montreal: Business Plan Format
http://www.bankofmontreal.com

Bank of Montreal
http://www.bmo.com

Royal Bank
http://www.royalbank.com

Scotiabank
http://www.scotiabank.com

Toronto-Dominion Bank
http://www.tdbank.ca

CIBC
http://www.cibc.com

Business Development Bank of Canada (BDC)
http://www.bdc.ca
The BDC has developed a wide range of financing alternatives to respond to the unique and financial needs of every type of business.

Industrial Research Assistance Program
http://www.nrc.ca
National Research Council's Industrial Research Assistance Program (IRAP) can provide you with professional advice, technical assistance, and, depending on the type of business, a one-time grant of up to $15 000.

hear objections so they can be addressed. When you have completed this Action Step, you will be truly prepared to meet your lenders.

WILL THAT BE DEBT OR EQUITY?

EQUITY
financial investment that results in an ownership position of a business

DEBT FINANCING
obligation of a business to repay a lender the full amount of a debt (loan) in addition to interest charges

If you or others invest money in a business and expect, in return, a portion of ownership, this is called an **equity** or ownership investment. Equity investors, as owners, usually expect a say in the day-to-day operations of the business and how the profit or net income is to be distributed to the owners. When you or others lend money to a business, this is called **debt financing.** If a business is financed through debt (a loan), it is obliged to repay the lender the full amount of the debt in addition to interest charges on the debt. A lender does not usually get any ownership rights or say in the operations of the business.

How should you finance your business: debt or equity or some combination of the two? The trick is to find the right balance between debt and equity — one that will satisfy the needs of you the owner, the business, and the market. However, in looking for money to finance your business, remember that any "external" source of capital will always consider the extent of your own financial commitment to the business.

If personal funds (equity) are not sufficient, you must decide on debt or selling a piece of the ownership (also equity) or some combination of the two.

Generally, Canadian independent businesses rely far more on debt than on equity, with the banks playing a predominant role as sources of financing.

Listed below are some of the pros and cons of debt versus equity financing.

Advantage of Debt Financing through debt mainly by line of credit is useful in meeting a short-term deficit in the cash flow or in financing lower-risk projects. For example, it would be appropriate where money is needed to fund inventory before it's sold. Some of the advantages of debt are:

- the entrepreneur does not have to give up or share control of the company;
- the term of the debt (loan) is generally limited;
- debt may be acquired from a variety of lenders; and
- the kind of information needed to obtain the loan is generally straightforward and would normally be incorporated into the business plan.

Disadvantages of Debt Taking on debt can become problematic when a project is risky and the return is uncertain. For example, financing new product development makes no guarantee of success in the marketplace. It would be more appropriate to find an investor to share the risk rather than going into debt. Debt can also become a problem if it is not properly managed. The most frequent errors include:

- taking on more debt than the company needs to fund expansion;
- adopting too restrictive a policy toward debt and thus not accessing funds that might be readily available;
- misapplying funds in ways that yield inadequate returns and make it difficult for the company to repay its loans; and
- making mistakes in servicing the debt (accepting inappropriate repayment terms, encountering cash flow difficulties, taking on too large a debt-service burden).

Advantages of Equity Many entrepreneurs associate finding an investor with giving up control in their company. An appropriate investor, however, can contribute expertise, contacts, and new business as well as money. If the result is substantial growth in profitability, the original owner's overall wealth will increase, even if his or her share of the company is somewhat smaller. Equity investment is especially appropriate for:

- larger projects with longer time frames or additional skill requirements;
- high-risk ventures where the costs of debt would be prohibitive;
- rapidly growing ventures that may quickly exhaust available bank financing as they expand; and
- situations in which debt financing is not available.

Disadvantages of Equity Finding an investor brings another viewpoint to a company, and there is always the danger of incompatibility and disagreement. Because an equity owner is an integral part of the company, however, it becomes much more difficult to terminate the relationship if disagreements occur. With a partner, it is important to have a shareholders agreement.

There is another point to consider between debt and equity. Canada is a country with significant regional differences, and these may become apparent to entrepreneurs attempting to secure equity financing. In some parts of the country, business may not have the same access to equity capital as do their counterparts established closer to larger financial centres. Access will also be influenced by the availability of government funding through provincial programs and federal regional economic development agencies such as the Atlantic Canada Opportunities Agency and Western Diversification. Regionalism plays less of a role in securing business loans. For example, each of Canada's major chartered banks operates a nation-wide system of branches, all of which offer the same access to loans on the same terms in any member branch.

Lastly, equity investment should not normally be used for short-term obligations. For example, it would not make much sense to get a new partner to finance inventory fluctuations. Equity is usually thought of as a long-term financial instrument.

Primary Types of Debt Financing

The major types of debt financing for start-up business are spelled out below. Other, "secondary" types of financing are shown in Table 10.4.

SHAREHOLDERS LOAN
owner investment in the form of a loan

Shareholders Loans Should you decide to incorporate your business — and there are a number of good reasons for doing so, as we will learn in the next chapter — you have the option to invest as a shareholders loan. Although many banks will not lend money to a business per se, they will provide a personal loan to the owner who in turn lends the money to the business. There are a number of advantages for an owner to invest in the form of a loan as opposed to equity (through purchasing shares). First, you can deduct the interest payments as a company expense. If you buy shares (equity investment), however, you will receive payment in the form of dividends and these dividend payments are not tax deductible by the company. Second, in most cases it is easier to withdraw your money when it is in the form of a loan. And third, if your loan is properly secured, your investment will be safer in the event of a business failure. The main point here is that there are advantages to lending the company money, but you really should make sure you get sound professional advice.

Small Business Loans (SBLs) Under the Small Business Loans Act (SBLA), the federal government guarantees small business loans through Canadian chartered banks and a few other Canadian financial institutions such as caisses populaire, Alberta Treasury branches, and credit unions. The SBLA has become a major funding source for start-up business. Historically, of the total SBLAs granted, about one-third have gone to firms less than a year old.

These loans can be used to finance up to 90 percent of the cost of the purchase and improvement of three categories of fixed assets:

- the purchase of land required to operate the business;
- the renovation, improvement, modernization, extension, and/or purchase of premises; and
- the purchase, installation, renovation, improvement, and/or modernization of new or used equipment.

Loans cannot be used to acquire shares or provide working capital.

Small business loans are available to all businesses operating for profit in Canada — excluding farming, charitable, and religious enterprises — that have annual gross revenues of less than $5 million. The maximum loan may not exceed $250 000. Borrowers must pay the federal government a one-time, up-front loan registration fee of 2 percent of the amount of each loan. This amount may be added to the loan. The maximum rate of interest charged by the lending institution cannot exceed the prime rate plus 3 percent for floating-rate loans and the residential mortgage rate plus 3 percent for fixed-rate loans. This interest rate includes an administration fee of 1.25 percent, which is paid back annually to the government. Personal guarantees may not exceed 25 percent of the amount of the original loan. The maximum period over which a loan may be repaid is 10 years.

It is important to note that some of the terms and conditions and interest rates are negotiable. In the past, at least one major bank has eliminated the requirement for any personal guarantees under the SBLA program. Other banks have reduced the interest rate to prime and added automatic overdraft protection of up to 10 percent of the SBLA loan. Our advice: SBLAs are a great opportunity, but shop around for the best deal.

Table 10.4 Secondary Types of Loans and Credit Arrangements

Type of Loan	Explanation
Floor Plan Loan	These loans are mainly provided by manufacturers to stock up goods in the retailers' or distributors' premises. The retailer reimburses the manufacturer for the loan amount when the product is sold.
Bridge Financing	This type of interim financing provides short-term funding to cover the cost of a start-up project until long-term funds become available.
Mezzanine Financing	Mezzanine financing combines long-term lending with an equity position.
Factoring	This form of financing is available from specialized firms (and banks to a limited extent). A business sells its accounts receivable to a factoring company at a discounted rate (as much as 85 percent of a "high" quality account). This will reduce the risk of not receiving a payment and frees up needed cash.
Letter of Credit	Letters of credit are widely used in exporting and importing businesses. One of the most common exporting problems, for example, is collecting the accounts receivable. A popular method — and the most secure one — is a letter of credit issued by the bank of the purchaser. This is the purchaser's guarantee that the money has been set aside and will be paid to the supplier upon satisfactory delivery. Most banks and major financial institutions can provide this letter, given proper security, of course.
Inventory Financing	In some cases, banks and financial institutions will allow small businesses to borrow against a percentage value of their inventory. The business must have inventory that can be readily sold. Depending on the salability of the inventory, the owner could receive financing as high as 70 percent or as little as 30 percent of the market value.
Accounts Receivable Financing	In this type of financing, the money owed by customers of a business (accounts receivable) becomes the collateral for a loan. Banks and financial institutions have been known to provide as much as 75 percent of the value of the accounts receivable which are not more than 60 days old. Again, adequate security is an important consideration in determining the percentage value of the receivables.
Conditional Sale of Goods	Some manufacturers will provide financing to small businesses for a particular product on a conditional basis. They will require a substantial down payment and then allow the business to pay for the remaining portion on an installment basis over a period of time. This is termed a conditional sale because the business will own the product only on the condition that all the payments are made.

OPERATING LOAN
sometimes called a revolving loan, money used to help finance short-term business needs like inventory and accounts receivables

Operating Loans (Line of Credit) An operating loan (sometimes called a revolving loan) is used by more than 75 percent of small business borrowers to finance their short-term business needs. Normally, these loans help finance inventory and accounts receivable — that is, customers to whom a product has been sold but the money has yet to be received. Generally, the line of credit is the largest part of the loans outstanding of a small business' debt obligations.

How much can you borrow? In the normal course of business, the amount you can borrow will be determined by whichever is less of the following:

1. Your authorized borrowing limit, which is established by determining your projected maximum (peak) cash needs in any one month of the year. This is one of the main reasons why accurate projected cash flows are so important.
2. Your margin requirements, which means you can borrow only up to a specific percentage of accounts receivable outstanding and inventory on your books in any one month. Although you may have a pre-determined operating line of say $50 000, this does not mean that you can go out and use all of it when the need arises. These margins or limits will vary depending on the policies of the bank or financial institution. For example, in the past, banks have been known to finance up to 66 percent (sometimes as high as 75 percent) of accounts receivable that are less than 60 days old. But this margin or percentage will vary depending on the quality of the receivable and the type of industry. As for inventory, the margin or percentage may be as high as 50 percent of market value. This margin is often lower, depending on how easy it is to sell your inventory. The bottom line here is that if you need an extra $50 000 in a given period to finance inventory and receivables, you will only get a portion of this, and the rest will come from your resources.

PRIME RATE
the lowest rate of interest charged by banks on commercial loans to their most preferred customers

What interest rate will you pay? Depending on the financial institution and the business circumstances, you can normally expect to pay 1 to 3 percent above the **prime rate** for an operating loan. The so-called prime rate, set by each financial institution, is the interest rate the institution charges to its most credit-worthy clients. Expect to pay higher interest rates for smaller operating loans. For example, you might pay as much as 3 percent above prime for a $25 000 loan and only 1 percent above prime for a $2 million operating loan. The main point is that interest rates for operating loans can differ from financial institution to financial institution, so we encourage you to shop around. You can negotiate a rate closer to prime if you have good security.

What security is required? An operating line of credit will be secured by the accounts receivable or inventory as well as a personal guarantee. Personal guarantees are required because financial institutions will never recover the full value of an asset should your business fail. The amount of your personal guarantee is negotiable. At the very least you should try to limit your personal guarantee to the amount of the unsecured portion of the loan. So, if you have an operating loan of say $25 000 which is secured by inventory for $12 000, then you should try to keep your personal guarantee below $13 000.

TERM LOAN
loan used for medium- to long-term financing of fixed assets like equipment, furniture, expansion, or renovation

Term Loans Term loans are used by close to one-half of small businesses and are the major source of medium-term (two to five years) and long-term (greater than five years) financing. In most cases, term loans are used to finance the purchase of fixed assets such as equipment, a truck, or furniture. They may also be used to finance expansion or renovation.

How much can you borrow? Under normal circumstances you will be able to borrow up to 75 percent of the value of buildings or property. In the case of equipment, you should expect to get about 50 percent of the asset value. Normally, you will repay the loan through a fixed schedule of payments, which corresponds to the life of the asset. If you expect a piece of equipment to last five years, then the payments would be spread over five years.

What interest rate will you pay? Term loans can be repaid by either a fixed or floating interest rate. A **fixed rate** is one that remains the same over the period of a loan. A **floating rate** changes in accordance with the fluctuations in the prime rate. Many small businesses prefer a fixed interest rate because they know how much they have to pay and can budget accordingly. However, fixed rates are generally not available for loans of less than $25,000 and banks will normally charge higher interest for a fixed term. The reason is that a term loan usually commits the bank for several years, increasing the risk that a business might deteriorate. It should be noted that when short-term rates are low, financial institutions will be even more inclined to ask for a higher interest premium for a fixed term loan. Why? Because of the increased risk of rising interest rates. As with operating loans, the terms and conditions for term loans differ from bank to bank.

FIXED RATE
interest rate that remains the same over the period of a loan

FLOATING RATE
interest rate that changes with changes in the prime rate

What security is required? Financial institutions will require you to secure a term loan with the asset being purchased and, in most cases, a guarantee backed by personal assets. If you default on the term loan, the institution will be able to liquidate the asset and hold you personally responsible for any out standing balance. Again, you should always try to limit your personal guarantees to a specific amount.

Primary Types of Equity Financing

At some point, you are going to have to decide whether or not to incorporate your business. We'll cover the pros and cons of incorporating in Chapter Eleven. At this point, we want you just to understand that the type or form of equity that your business will require will depend, to some degree, on the legal structure of your business.

If you plan to run your business as a sole proprietorship or partnership, your investment into the business will simply be recorded as an owner's personal investment. You are the owner and your equity is what you personally put into the business. The main point here is that if other partners are involved in your business, a handshake is not enough. You must have some sort of agreement outlining the terms and conditions of each equity investor's contribution. You will need a partnership shareholders agreement that details such issues as: Who is investing what? How will the investment be paid back and under what conditions? What happens if someone dies? What is the procedure for selling out? What happens if the business fails? In the end, a formalized legal agreement should be drawn up and each equity investor must consult his or her own legal and financial advisor. The legal cost of a shareholders agreement is approximately $300 to $500 for a straightforward agreement.

Should you decide to incorporate, we strongly recommend you have a lawyer draw up a shareholders agreement to detail the rights and responsibilities of each equity investor. In the case of incorporation, there are a number of ways that you can structure an equity investment to benefit and protect both you and potential shareholders. For small businesses, the three principal forms of equity financing are common shares, preferred shares, and convertible debentures. Since any formalized equity arrangement can become quite complex, we strongly suggest that you do get some expert advice before you sign on the dotted line.

COMMON SHARES
equity investments that confer part ownership of the company, but are not as safe as preferred shares should the company fail

Common Shares Common shares confer part ownership of the company and are frequently issued in exchange for a company's initial capital. As the company grows, the shares increase in value and provide dividend income. If the company fails, however, common shareholders risk losing their investment. As an incentive to investors to place capital in small businesses, some provinces have set up development corporations that will repay as much as 25 to 30 percent of a shareholder's investment in such enterprises.

PREFERRED SHARES
equity investments that confer part ownership of the company, earn investors dividends at a fixed rate, and are safer than common shares

Preferred Shares Preferred shares may also be offered to investors. Such shares also represent partial ownership of the company. Preferred shares, however, usually earn a dividend at a fixed rate and, in the event of business failure, they are better protected than common shares, although their claim is still junior to that of debt holders. A company derives several advantages from issuing preferred shares. Unlike debts, preferred shares have no maturity date. And dividend payments are not as binding as interest payments on debt.

CONVERTIBLE DEBENTURES
loans that can be exchanged for common shares at a stated price, and are better protected than common and preferred shares

Convertible Debentures Convertible debentures are loans that can be exchanged for common shares in a company at a predetermined price. Like other debentures and bonds, they carry a fixed interest rate and a specified date by which they must be paid. As do shareholders, the holders of convertible debentures have the opportunity to benefit if the company grows. They are also better protected than are holders of common or preferred shares in the event of a failure. And because the debenture is a type of loan, interest is tax deductible. As a result, larger companies may find it easier to sell convertible debentures than other types of equity. Issuing convertible debentures is therefore a way to raise equity more cheaply than by selling common shares.

Government Sources of Financial Help

There are a number of local, provincial, and federal programs designed to assist small businesses. These plans also change from time to time, so it is important to maintain the most recent information from the respective government. Governments know a growth market when they see one, and they do make an effort to help. In recent years they have been moving away from helping finance small business to providing information and advice. However, there still remains a number of financial support programs for small business — the sources of which are far too numerous to detail here. We encourage you to visit a government information office, even before you begin putting the final touches to your plan. A good starting point would be a visit or call to the Canada Business Service Centre nearest you. You can also find a lot of information on government support programs via the Internet. We suggest you begin with Strategis. Here are a few helpful agencies that we found on the Strategis Web site in our 1998 search:

Business Development Bank of Canada A wide range of business financing programs are available including:

- *Term Loans.* Flexible loans are provided for projects such as the acquisition of fixed assets, expansion, plant overhauls, and the purchase of existing businesses.
- *Micro-Business Program.* Support is available to meet the early growth needs of the smallest businesses. This program provides counselling as well as financing of up to $25 000 to new businesses and up to $50 000 to existing companies whose business proposals demonstrate potential for growth and strong prospects for success.
- *Young Entrepreneur Financing Program.* This program is targeted to start-up entrepreneurs between the ages of 18 and 34. Up to $25 000 in term

financing and 50 hours of tailor-made business management support help are provided.

- *Venture Loans.* Venture Loans provide "quasi-equity" financing of between $100 000 and $1 million to businesses with a high-quality management team, a clear market niche, and a good potential for growth.

Atlantic Canada Opportunities Agency (ACOA) Key business support programs include:

- Business Development Program
- ACF Equity Atlantic Inc.
- Western Economic Diversification (WD) Program
- Commercial Loan Funds
- Capital Services

Other federal support programs and initiatives include:

- Community Futures Development Corporations
- Aboriginal Business Canada
- Community Economic Development Program
- Commercial Development Program
- Resource Access Negotiations Program
- Agriculture Financing: Farm Credit Corporation
- Canada Community Investment Plan
- Financing Assistance for Canadian Cultural Organizations

In a Nutshell

Money creates its own world. It has its own customs, rituals, and rules. Before you start asking people for money for your business, spend about three to four months researching the world of money. Here are some things you can do to streamline your research:

1. Get your personal finances in order.
2. Take some time, prepare, study the world of finance.
3. Find someone who knows more about money than you do, and keep asking questions.
4. Know that loans are made on the basis of the four Cs: cash, character, capacity (to repay), and collateral.
5. Start to develop your financial business plan. You need to show your plan to bankers, vendors, and lenders. For now, an outline is good enough. (See Chapter Sixteen for a model plan.)
6. Begin thinking of a banker as your gateway to the world of money.
7. Search out potential lenders.
8. Establish your balance between equity and debt.
9. Investigate sources of government assistance and community.

Think Points for Success

- ✓ Your banker can be a wealth of information. Maintain a good relationship with him or her.
- ✓ How well you buy is as important as how well you sell.
- ✓ Partner with your vendors. It's often the best way to get the best deals.
- ✓ In dealing with bankers, vendors, and lenders, use lots of open-ended questions like "What else can you do for me?"

ACTION STEP REVIEW

47 Make a list of money sources.
48 Design a vendor statement form.
49 Befriend a banker.
50 Prepare to meet your lenders.

Business Plan Building Block

POTENTIAL SOURCES AND EQUITY AMOUNT

List your potential sources and amount of equity for your start-up business. Complete the table below.

Potential Sources Equity

Sources of Equity	**Potential Amount ($) (Market Value*)**
Personal Equity	________
Savings	________
Borrow on your life insurance.	________
Mortgage your property.	________
Obtain a line of unsecured personal credit from your bank, credit union, or other financial institution.	________
Sell old stock you have been holding onto, even if it means taking a loss. Or get a loan using the securities as collateral.	________
Get a part-time job, moonlight your way to more money.	________
Invest your own equipment (computer, furniture, tools).	________
Automobile (Will the business own your vehicle?)	________
Inventory (paper, books, software)	________
Leaseholds (fixtures, plugs, paint)	________
Organizational costs (Have you paid for training or have you consulted a lawyer or accountant and paid for this out of your own money?)	________
Sweat Equity (the value of the time or labour that you can invest into the start-up of your business)	________
____________________	________
____________________	________
____________________	________
____________________	________
Total Personal Equity	________
Other Equity Sources	________
Friends and family	________
Angels	________
Venture capitalists	________
Government programs	________
Employer and employees	________
____________________	________
____________________	________
____________________	________
____________________	________
Total Other Sources	________
Total Equity	________

*Note: Market value is the price someone else ("the market") is prepared to pay for this asset.

Potential Lending Sources and Amount

List your potential lending sources and amount. Complete the table below.

Potential Lending (Debt) Sources of Capital

Potential Lending Sources	**Potential Amount ($) (Market Value*)**
Banks	
1. ____________________	________
2. ____________________	________
3. ____________________	________
Other financial institutions (trust companies/credit unions, etc.)	
1. ____________________	________
2. ____________________	________
3. ____________________	________
Friends and relatives	________
Co-operative partnerships	________
Suppliers and customers	________
Leasing	________
Employers and employees	________
Government programs	________
Total	________

*Note: Market value is the price someone else ("the market") is prepared to pay for this asset.

Checklist Questions and Actions to Develop Your Business Plan

SHAKING THE MONEY TREE

- ❑ What is the total amount of equity you need to establish and operate your business for the first year? Identify all the sources of funds.
- ❑ Identify your funding shortfall each month from the cash flow, and the funding sources and expected rate of interest.
- ❑ Are there any government, agency, or foundation funding (if you are a non-profit organization) sources for your venture?
- ❑ How much, if anything, do you expect from a venture capitalist, and what ownership are you prepared to forego? Note: If working with a venture capitalist or other partners, what do you expect in a shareholders agreement?
- ❑ Who are your prime vendors? What type of purchase agreement do you have with them?
- ❑ What is your debt to equity ratio, and how does that compare to industry ratios?

NOTES

1. Adapted from Rick Spence, *Secrets of Success from Canada's Fastest-Growing Companies* (Toronto: John Wiley & Sons Canada, Ltd., 1997), p. 162. Reprinted by permission of the author.
2. *Ibid.*, p. 160.

3. *Ibid.*, p. 156.
4. Pahedra Hise, "Don't Start a Business Without One," *Inc.* February 1998, pp. 50–53.
5. Spence, *Secrets of Success from Canada's Fastest-Growing Companies*, p. 166.
6. Adapted from "Growth in the Grassroots," *Profit*, October/November 1996, as appearing in Allan Riding and Barbara Orser, *Beyond the Banks: Creative Financing for Canadian Entrepreneurs* (Toronto: John Wiley & Sons Canada, Ltd., 1997), p. 93.
7. Riding and Orser, *Beyond the Banks*, p. 15.
8. Research by Macdonald & Associates Ltd. for Canadian Venture Capital Association, cited in John Heinzl, "Venture Capital Windfall Masks Danger," *Globe and Mail*, April 3, 1998, p. B23.

OTHER REFERENCES

Chilton, David. *The Wealthy Barber.* Toronto: Stoddart Publishing Co., 1989.

Dawson, George. *Borrowing to Build Your Business: Getting Your Banker to Say Yes*. Dearborn, MI: Dearborn Upstart Publishing, 1997.

Fiet, James O. "Fragmentation in the Market for Venture Capital." *Entrepreneurship Theory and Practice*, Vol. 21, No. 2, Winter 1996, pp. 5–20.

Ginsberg, Larry and Bruce McDougall. *Small Business, Big Money*. Scarborough, ON: Prentice Hall Canada Ltd., 1997.

Industry Canada. *Your Guide to Government of Canada Services and Support for Small Business*. 1996.

NRC/IRAP Industrial Technology Advisors.

Riding, Allan and Barbara Orser. *Beyond the Banks: Creative Financing for Canadian Entrepreneurs*. Toronto: John Wiley & Sons Canada, Ltd., 1997.

"The First Annual Definitive Guide to Small Business Financing in Canada." *Profit*, June 1997.

eleven

Legal Concerns

LEARNING OPPORTUNITIES

After reading this chapter, you should be able to:

- Decide which legal form (sole proprietorship, partnership, or corporation) is best for your business.
- Anticipate potential surprises if you are going into business with someone else.
- Understand legal escape routes.
- Develop tactics for finding the right lawyer.
- Develop questions for probing the mind of a lawyer.
- Explore the reasons for incorporating.
- Recognize signals that you should incorporate.
- Conduct secondary research into corporations and incorporating.
- Explore the various municipal, provincial, and federal legal regulations that may affect your business.
- Understand the importance of having your agreement in writing.

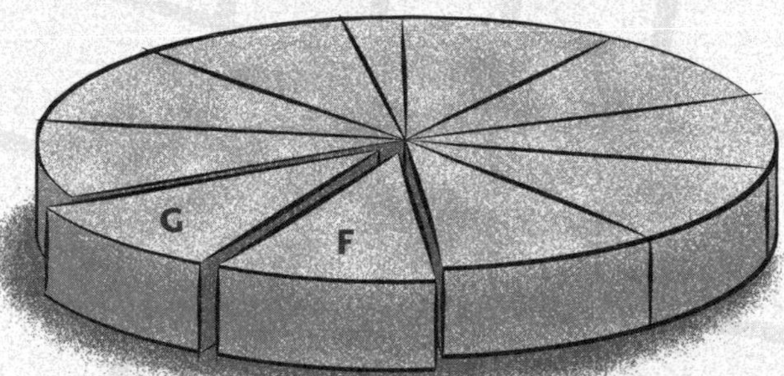

BUSINESS PLAN BUILDING BLOCK

In this chapter you will learn about different business forms and how to plan for the one which is right for you.

Henry Bemis was doing really well with his coffee service until one of his on-site coffee dispensers spewed boiling water all over the hands of Jody Dawn, a professional model.

Jody's hands earned her just over $200 000 a year. The day her hands were burned, she was at a branch of a major bank, doing a DeBeers-sponsored commercial for diamond rings and safety-deposit boxes.

Her model's hands were her living and her future. On the advice of her lawyer, Jody sued Henry and his Easy-Cup Coffee Service.

Henry had insurance, and the courts ended up awarding Jody $1 million.

Here's the way the court figured it:

- She made $200 000 a year.
- She could expect an active career of at least five years.
- Five years × $200 000 = $1 000 000

Luckily, Henry had the good sense to incorporate and had a lot of liability insurance. His personal assets were protected and his business insurance paid the bill.

Figure 11.1 Chapter Eleven will help you complete parts F and G of your business plan, "Management" and "Personnel."

ACTION STEP PREVIEW

51 Do some secondary research on corporations.

52 Take a lawyer to lunch.

Although Henry Bemis's story is fictitious, the situation is possible and could happen to you. You may run your small business as a sole proprietorship or in partnership with another entrepreneur, and be confident that it is in the best possible legal form. But are you sure? Or maybe you're in the planning stages of your new business and you don't know what legal form (sole proprietorship, partnership, or corporation) is best. In this chapter, we will look at clear financial signals and hidden business liabilities that should help you look ahead and decide which legal form will work for you. We'll also prepare you for some of the government red tape, and help direct you towards legal advice.

Legal Forms for Small Business

Generally, your small business can exist in one of three basic legal forms: a sole proprietorship, a partnership, or a corporation. For each of these standard forms of ownership (summarized in Table 11.1), we describe here some of the important business realities — and paperwork — you should be aware of.

The co-operative is a fourth type of legal form to consider. Technically, it's a particular type or variant of the corporate structure. Highlights of this lesser-known form of ownership are presented in the final part of this section.[1] It is also important to note that other business agreements, such as joint ventures, also exist.

Table 11.1 Characteristics of the Four Main Legal Forms

	Control	Need for Written Agreements	Raising Money	Taxes	Liability	Continuity
Sole Proprietorship	absolute	may be need for registration if own name not used	one-person show save, save, save	profit or loss go with personal income	personally liable for everything	restricted—business ceases to exist when owner gets tired of business or dies
Partnership (Limited)	total control by general partner	overwhelming	lots of laws	profit or loss passed on to ltd. partners	ltd. partners are liable only for $ invested	can be provided for in partnership agreement
Partnership (General)	divided	locate super lawyer	easier if more parties sign	profit or loss passed on to partners	personal liability for debts or misdeeds of partners	depends on buy-sell agreement
Corporation	shared (could be absolute)	locate super lawyer	market your "professional" appeal	some tax advantages to Canadian-controlled private corporations	limited to assets of incorporated entity; shareholders are usually not liable	perpetual existence

SOLE PROPRIETORSHIP

Most small businesses start out as a **sole proprietorship**. If you start a business on your own — without partners — you are a sole proprietor. A sole proprietorship, in the eyes of the law, is not a separate entity from the person: the business and the individual are the same. For example, the assets of the business are owned by the individual, and therefore the revenue and expenses are included in his or her personal income tax return.

SOLE PROPRIETORSHIP
a business that is owned by one person

The primary advantages of the sole proprietorship are:

- It is relatively easy and inexpensive to set up.
- It is directly controlled by the owner/operator.
- It is flexible and little regulated.
- Business losses can be deducted from other income.
- Wages paid for work performed by a spouse are deductible from the income of the business.
- Other investors may be added by written agreement.
- It offers some tax advantages in certain situations. For example, if the business suffers a loss and the owner has income from other sources, that loss can be used to offset the other income. If the business loss exceeds the other income, the unused portion of that loss can be carried forward to offset income in subsequent years. In this way, the business offers its owner a "tax shelter." Losses sustained by a corporation can only be used to offset income earned by the corporation.

The major disadvantages of a sole proprietorship are:

- The owner can be held personally liable for all debts of the business. Personal assets, such as the house and automobile, can be seized for nonpayment of bills, provided the necessary legal steps have been taken to do so. To avoid such an unfortunate occurrence, some entrepreneurs register certain personal assets in the name of their spouse. This is allowed as long as it is done at least one year before financial problems are encountered; otherwise, the court may construe the action as a deliberate attempt to out-manoeuvre creditors and will not allow it.
- Opportunity for continuity is restricted. The sole proprietorship ceases to exist when the sole proprietor goes out of business or dies.
- To some extent, the owner's ability to raise capital is limited. Many small businesses encounter financial problems, as their owners are reluctant to share ownership with others who are able to contribute the needed funds.
- The sole proprietor may be required to pay taxes at a higher tax rate in certain situations. Depending on the income level of the owners tax rates for a sole proprietorship can be higher than a corporation. The sole proprietor includes the revenues and expenses from the business on his or her personal tax return, and the income is taxed at whatever his or her personal rate happens to be either in the three previous years and for the following seven years.

PARTNERSHIP

Many small businesses start as a partnership and it works out well. A **partnership** is an association of two or more individuals carrying on a business to earn income. Legal requirements for forming a partnership vary from province to province, but generally a partnership can come into existence either through a written or oral agreement or, in some cases, even by implication.

PARTNERSHIP
an association of two or more individuals carrying on a business to earn income

GENERAL PARTNERSHIP
a partnership in which each partner has a hand in managing the business and assuming unlimited personal liability for any debts

LIMITED PARTNERSHIP
a partnership composed of at least one or more limited partners and at least one general partner

There are two types of partnerships: general and limited. In a **general partnership**, each partner has a hand in managing the business and assumes unlimited personal liability for any debts.

In a **limited partnership** — composed of one or more limited partners and at least one general partner — the general partner assumes both management duties and the downside risk. A limited partner's liability is limited to the amount of his or her original investment as long as he or she has had no role in management decisions.

Note that all partnerships must have at least one general partner.

The advantages to a partnership are:

- It is easy to set up.
- New partners can be added (some claim that this structure is more flexible and has a greater chance of continuity than a sole proprietorship).
- It involves few legal requirements. You can form a partnership with a handshake and dissolve it without one (though this is not a wise endeavour).
- Risk is generally shared equally among partners — except in the case of a limited partnership.
- Partners can provide mutual support and different skills. One of the best things about a partnership is psychological: it offers the moral support and contribution of teammates.
- It offers more potential sources of capital.
- Partners are taxed as individuals, and in some cases (as is with proprietorships) this can be advantageous.

Some of the major disadvantages are:

- Tax and estate-planning options are more limited than for a corporate structure (as discussed below).
- Partners and all their assets — personal and business — are, to some extent, at risk for any losses suffered.
- The reality is that sometimes business and personal liabilities of a particular partner aren't kept entirely separate. This can have potentially disastrous consequences to other partners whose shared business liability could result in unexpected personal losses.
- Decision-making may be difficult because each partner may want to have equal rights.
- One partner can make decisions that bind all others.
- Dissolution can be ugly, sometimes resulting in the closing of the business or damaged feelings.

On the surface, partnerships can make a lot of sense. Two or more entrepreneurs face the unknown together and pool their skills. They may be able to raise more capital than one person could alone. But forming a good partnership can be as challenging as forming a good marriage. We strongly suggest that you get everything in writing before you start the business. Write out a partnership agreement with legal advice. Each partner should get his or her own lawyer.

At the very least, your written partnership agreement should include the following:

- rights and responsibilities of the partners,
- capital contributions of each partner,
- role and time that each partner will devote to the business,
- provisions for retirement, death, termination and/or re-organization,
- how net income from business will be divided,
- means for settling disputes, and
- mechanism for dissolving the partnership or winding up the business.

So, while a partnership agreement is not legally required, it is highly recommended. If you don't think a written agreement is all that important, take a moment and see what happened to Phil Johnson when he did not have a partnership agreement.

Your Pal, Steve

I have to admit, the motor-sailor was my idea. I convinced my partner, Steve Savitch, to buy a boat — actually it was a fancy 14-metre rig called *The Ninja* — for the partnership. We could write off some of the payments as an expense, and it would do our company image a world of good.

Steve and I had been friends for a dozen years and partners in Savitch and Johnson, Business Consultants, for the past three. We'd done quite well and each of us was going to clear over $50 000 this year. I convinced him we could afford this perk. Besides, my marketing instinct told me it could really help close a few deals.

About two months after we bought the boat — and had a lot of fun — a fellow who sells radar equipment called me. Seems Steve had bought $2 000 worth of radar, and this chap was wondering when he'd get paid. After I hung up the phone, my secretary buzzed me with Mary, Steve's wife, on the line wanting to know where Steve was.

I thought he was on a business trip with a few of our best clients. As it turned out, Steve had disappeared with *The Ninja* and no one knew where. In the end, I got stung for all his business debts, including the payments on *The Ninja*.

The problem was that Steve and I never saw the need for having anything in writing. We were both men of good faith (or so I had thought). We had each pulled our weight in business and we had balanced each other's skills. For the first time in twelve years, I made an appointment to talk to a lawyer. He just shook his head. "You should have come to me a lot sooner, Phil," he said. "A *lot* sooner."

Last week, when I was closing the place down and getting ready to go back to work for my old boss, I got a postcard from Tahiti. "Sorry partner," Steve wrote. "Didn't mean to run out on you, but it was the only way I could handle the home front. These things happen.... Your pal, Steve."

CORPORATION

A **corporation** is a legal entity that exists under authority granted by provincial or federal law. It stands legally separate from the owners, and it does business in the name of the corporation. It can sue and be sued.

CORPORATION
a legal entity with the authority to act and have liability separate and apart from its owners

Because a corporation is an artificial entity, a creation on paper, it needs more paperwork to justify its existence. There are fees required, and meetings of the board of directors. The secretary of the corporation must keep accurate, complete records of what transpires at meetings.

Nonetheless, for many businesses, it's worth forming a corporation because it creates a shield between the creditors and the owner's personal wealth. To keep the shield in place, active owners can become *employees* of the corporation; their business cards have the corporate name and logo and specify their job title. At the same time, owners sign contracts as *officers* of the corporations.

Following are some of the reasons why you should think about incorporating or not incorporating your business. In the end, your decision to do so will depend on two key factors: your tax situation and your desire to limit your liability. However, we do want to emphasize that becoming a corporation won't solve all your problems. In most cases, it won't immunize you against your creditors. The banks, for example, will still want a personal guarantee, which could mean your house. Taxes won't be eliminated either. In fact, in the early years, the bank will treat a newly incorporated business as if it were a sole proprietorship. If you have losses, you are better off as a sole proprietor. Let's start with the major reasons for thinking about incorporating.

Liability A corporation acts like a shield between you and the world. If your business fails, your creditors may not come after your house, your beach condo, your Porsche, your first-born, or your hard-won collections — provided you've done it right.

To keep your corporate shield up, make sure you: 1) hold scheduled meetings; 2) keep up the minute book; and 3) act as if you are an employee of the corporation. Here's an everyday example of the corporate shield at work: One of your employees gets into a fender-bender while driving on company business. If you're a corporation, the injured parties will come after your corporation and not you. (If your employees use *their own* cars on company business, make sure they're insured for a minimum of $1 million.)

See how limited liability helped Henry Bemis in the opening vignette. Again, remember that banks and other creditors will want personal guarantees as well as business guarantees, thus the advantages of the corporation is lost.

You Might Enjoy Some Tax Advantages Taxation laws are complex, and a good accountant can dream up several ways to minimize taxes, regardless of what legal form you choose. However, a concept called "integration" attempts to ensure that income is taxed to the same degree whether it is held by an individual or channelled through a corporation. You won't get rich on your tax savings. Tax laws and rates vary slightly from province to province in Canada. We therefore strongly recommend that you see an accountant to help you determine the best organization form from a tax standpoint. In general, a special small business tax rate applies to income under $200 000 to a cumulative amount of $1 million. Once the $1 million limit is reached, the firm will be taxed at the full corporate rate. Small business tax rates vary from about 15 percent to 23 percent, depending on the province.

However, there are some tax advantages to being incorporated, and the obvious ones are listed below.

1. Only incorporated companies are eligible for manufacturing and processing tax credits.
2. Certain tax-free benefits, such as some insurance premiums, are available only to employees of incorporated companies.
3. In regard to pensions, there are still greater options for tax deferral under the corporate form.
4. Owners of corporations can enjoy potential personal tax savings. For example, once the income of a business reaches a certain level, the total tax paid by the corporation and the owner will be less than that which the owner of a sole proprietorship would pay. The exact level depends on the individual situation. As a ballpark figure, once you start earning $25 000–$30 000 (income after expenses), it would be time to consider incorporating to save you some personal tax.
5. Benefits can be paid to employees in different forms by a corporation, which could yield a tax saving. These forms include salaries, dividends,

and profit-sharing plans. In the case of a deferred profit-sharing plan, for example, a corporation can make contributions on behalf of employees. The contributions are allowed as a current business tax deduction, but the employee pays no tax until withdrawals are made. This type of plan is not available to the sole proprietorship. Careful analysis needs to be made in each situation to determine the optimal structuring of an owner/manager's earnings. You should be aware of the different forms of compensation and, if necessary, consult an accountant for advice on those your business should use.

If you want to learn more about the tax benefits of incorporating, a good starting point is the Revenue Canada Internet site at <http://www.rc.gc.ca>. Obviously, the whole issue of corporate tax benefits is complicated. You should always seek the advice of a corporate tax accountant in these matters.

You Upgrade Your Image What does the word "corporation" imply to you? IBM? Bell? GM? Heavy hitters, right? Let's look at the word with new eyes.

Corporation comes from the Latin, *corpus*, which means "body." To incorporate means to make or form a shape into a body. Looked at from that angle, incorporating starts to sound creative.

It will sound that way to lots of your TCs, too. As a corporation, you might be perceived to:

- have more longevity and solidity in the world.
- attract better employees.
- enjoy more prestige.

You Have the Opportunity of Channelling Some Heavy Expenses For example, with some legal help, you can write a medical assistance clause into your by-laws. Here's the way it works:

1. Your corporation pays the insurance premium on your health insurance.
2. Your corporation reimburses you for the deductible.
3. Your corporation writes off the money paid to you as a business expense.
4. You aren't liable to pay taxes on the reimbursement.

You Simplify the Division of Multiple Ownership For example, say you're going into the printing and graphic business with two very good friends.

- The business needs $110 000 to get started.
- You can contribute $60 000.
- Friend A delivers $25 000.
- Friend B delivers $15 000.
- You borrow the other $10 000 from your friendly banker.
- The way to handle the ownership is with stock. You get 60 percent. Friend A gets 25 percent. Friend B gets 15 percent.

You Guarantee Continuity If one of your stockholders or founders dies (or departs by motor-sailer or other means), the corporation will likely keep chugging along. That's because you've gone through a lot of red tape and planning to set it up that way.

It's one of the few justifications for red tape we know. However, if you are an individual incorporated and you die, the business will likely die with you.

You Can Offer Internal Incentives When you want to reward a special employee, you can offer stock options or a promotion (for example, a vice-presidential title) in addition to (and sometimes in place of) pay raises. Becoming a corporation officer may carry its own special excitement, which gives you flexibility. An ownership position (shares) can also motivate an employee to keep the company's best interest in mind.

You Are in a Good Position for Estate Planning As your company grows, you may want to set up other companies and include members of your family in your organization. At this point, you can engage in complicated share exchange and asset transfers. If you find yourself in this situation, you should consult a knowledgeable corporate estate lawyer.

There are also some potential disadvantages of incorporating. These include:

Potentially Fewer Tax Write-offs at the Beginning Business losses incurred by a corporation can be used for taxation purposes only to offset income of the preceding three years and the seven successive years. If your business suffers losses in its first few years of operation, the losses of the early years could conceivably never be used to reduce tax liability. As a sole proprietorship, losses from the business can be used to offset income from other sources in the year in which they are incurred. Thus, if losses are projected in the beginning years of the business and you have income from other sources, it may well be advantageous not to incorporate your business.

Higher Start-up Costs Start-up costs are higher if you choose to incorporate rather than carry on business as a sole proprietorship or partnership. For example, if you choose to incorporate federally, you will have to pay the government $500. Provincial incorporation is usually less expensive. As well, you will be required to do at least one name search, each at a cost of $75. You'll also have to pay additional legal and accounting services which could easily be $2 000–$3 000. While it is not necessary to obtain legal advice to incorporate, we strongly advise you to do so, particularly, if you are considering setting up with a complex share structure. Of course, legal advice means legal fees. These can easily add $200–$1 000 to the cost of incorporation.

Increased Paperwork Carrying on business as a corporation may increase the number of tax filings you are required to make. For instance, the Canada Business Corporations Act requires that you file an annual return (Form 22) each year and inform the Corporations Directorate of any changes in your board of directors or the location of your registered head office. You have to file separate income tax returns for yourself, which may lead to an increase in your ongoing professional costs. Your company is also required to maintain certain corporate records. Furthermore, you will likely be asked to register your company in any province or territory where you carry on business. Registration is different from incorporation. While a company may be incorporated only once, it may be registered in any number of jurisdictions to carry on business. You should contact the local corporate law administration office in each province or territory in which you plan to carry on business to determine what filing requirements you will have to fulfil.

Obviously, the issue of incorporation is somewhat complicated. For a good source of information, see Box 11.1. Some of the most frequently asked questions, and their answers, are summarized below.

Who Can Form a Corporation? Under most circumstances, one or more individuals who are 18 years of age or older can form a corporation. Similarly, one or more companies or "bodies corporate" may incorporate an additional company. These persons or companies are called incorporators. An incorporator may form a corporation whose shareholders, officers, and directors are other persons, or may serve as the sole director, officer, and shareholder of the company. An incorporator is also responsible for organizational procedures, such as filing the articles of incorporation and designating the first directors.

Do I Incorporate Federally or Provincially? A company can incorporate either federally (under the Canada Business Corporations Act), or provincially under the laws of a province or territory. Whether you incorporate federally or provincially, you will be required to register your business in the province or territory where you carry on business.

A major advantage of incorporating federally is that the head office can be located in any Canadian province, and it can be relocated if circumstances dictate. If you have the intention (either now or sometime in the future) of

Box 11.1 Thinking About Incorporating?

If you're thinking about incorporating, you should start with Industry Canada's *Small Business Guide to Federal Incorporation*. Here are some of the topics you'll read about:

- Why Should I Incorporate?
- Submitting Articles of Incorporation
- Organizing Your Company
- Complying with the Canada Business Corporations Act
- Shareholders
- Frequently Asked Questions

It will also provide you with:

- Sample Articles of Incorporation: One Class of Shares
- Sample Articles of Incorporation: Two Classes of Shares
- Sample Form 3 — Notice of Registered Office
- Sample Form 6 — Notice of Directors
- Sample Organizational Resolutions
- Sample By-laws
- Sample Notice of Annual General Meeting and Minutes of an Annual General Meeting
- Key Contacts

operating in more than one jurisdiction, you should probably choose to incorporate federally in order to simplify your business relations later. Still, the federal corporation must register in each province in which it is doing business.

Another reason given for choosing federal incorporation is the heightened name protection provided to federal corporations. While every incorporating jurisdiction in Canada screens potential corporations, the level of scrutiny varies. At the federal level, stringent tests are applied before the right to use a particular name is granted.

A final major advantage of federal incorporation is limited liability. A federally incorporated company is considered a legal entity anywhere in Canada. Therefore, its shareholders are protected by limited liability anywhere in the country. In contrast, a provincially incorporated company is a legal entity only in the province or territory in which it is incorporated. Thus, its shareholders are not protected by limited liability if it does business outside of its own jurisdiction.

Despite these advantages, many small businesses still decide against incorporating federally. We can only surmise that this is due mainly to the higher cost of federal incorporation.

What Kinds of Businesses Can Incorporate? Almost any type of business may incorporate. However, banking, insurance, loan and trust companies, and non-profit corporations are incorporated under different statutes. There are no restrictions such as minimum company size on the businesses.

Do I Need to Hire a Lawyer to Incorporate? No, though we recommend you do. A lawyer may provide valuable advice, but that is not required for incorporation. If you want to incorporate without a lawyer, get ready for a lot of paperwork.

Do I Need a Board of Directors? Yes. Your company must have at least one director. In your articles of incorporation, you are required to specify the number of directors. At each annual general meeting, shareholders elect directors (depending on the length or term of office the shareholders choose).

Shareholders may decide that, for various reasons, they want to remove a director they had previously elected. This is a simple procedure. It generally needs the approval of a majority of the votes represented at a meeting of shareholders called for the purpose of removing the director.

Who Can Be a Director? A director must:

- be at least 18 years old,
- be of sound mind (mentally competent), and
- be an individual (a corporation cannot be a director).

He or she must not be an undischarged bankrupt.

In addition, a majority of the directors of a corporation must be individuals who are ordinarily resident in Canada. You should keep this in mind when electing directors and filling vacancies. There is no requirement for directors to hold shares in the corporation, nor is there any restriction against their holding shares.

What Are the Responsibilities of the Board of Directors? The company's directors are responsible for the overall supervision of the affairs of the corporation. They approve the company's financial statements; make, amend, and repeal by-laws; authorize the issuance of shares; and call and conduct directors' and shareholders' meetings. The directors, in turn, usually appoint officers, who are responsible for day-to-day operations. In a small, private corporation, one individual may act as sole shareholder, director, and officer.[2]

Must a Company Have Shareholders? Yes. An active company must have at least one class of shares (ownership) and at least one shareholder (owner). A person or company who owns shares in a corporation is called a shareholder. Generally speaking and unless the articles of incorporation provide otherwise, each share in the corporation entitles the holder to one vote. A person becomes a shareholder by acquiring shares from the company (buying shares from the treasury) or from an existing shareholder. The larger the number of shares held, the larger the number of votes (and in most cases, control) a shareholder can generally exercise.

Shareholders have limited liability in the corporation, and usually are not liable for the company's debts unless, as noted earlier, the bank requires the owner/shareholders to pledge personal and company assets. On the other hand, shareholders generally do not actively run the corporation. Shareholders also have legal access to certain information about the corporation. For example, shareholders are entitled to inspect (and copy) the corporate records, and are entitled to receive the company's financial statements. Shareholders also elect directors, approve by-laws and by-law changes, appoint the auditor of the corporation (or waive the audit requirement), and approve certain major or fundamental changes to the corporation. These changes could include matters such as a sale of assets of the business, a change of name, and articles of amendment altering share rights or creating new classes of shares.

Do I Need a Shareholders Agreement? A shareholders agreement is not necessary, but we strongly advise that you have one, except, of course, if you are a one-person corporation. It is an agreement entered into usually by all shareholders. The written agreement must be signed by the shareholders who are party to it. While shareholders agreements are specific to each company and its shareholders, most of these documents deal with the same basic issues. A typical shareholders agreement includes the following clauses.

Article 1: Definitions
Article 2: Conduct of Affairs of the Corporation
Article 3: Transfers of Shares
Article 4: Real Property
Article 5: Death of a Shareholder
Article 6: Bankruptcy, etc.
Article 7: Powers of Attorney
Article 8: General Sale Provisions

Article 9: Arbitration
Article 10: General Provisions

The relationship among shareholders in a small company tends to be very much like a partnership agreement, with each person having a say in the significant business decisions the company will be making.

Here are some of the major provisions of a shareholders agreement:

- *Who sits on the board of directors.* A very common shareholders agreement provision for a small company gives all the shareholders the right to sit on the board of directors or to nominate a representative for that purpose.
- *How the future obligations of the company will be shared or divided.* The shareholders may agree, for example, that when other means of raising funds are not available, each shareholder will contribute more funds to the company on a pro rata basis.
- *How future shares are purchased.* For example, three equal partners could agree that no shares in the corporation will be issued without the consent of all shareholders/directors. In the absence of such a provision, two shareholders/directors could issue shares by an ordinary or special resolution (because they control two-thirds of the votes) to themselves without including or requiring the permission of the third shareholder/director.
- *The right of first refusal.* This provision states that any shareholder who wants to sell his or her shares must first offer them to the other shareholders of the company before selling them to an outside party.
- *Rules for the transfer of shares.* This provision details how the shares will be transferred in such an event as the death, resignation, dismissal, personal bankruptcy or divorce of a shareholder. Restrictions can be detailed in plans governing, for instance, when a shareholder can or must sell his or her shares, or what happens to those shares after the individual shareholder has left.
- *Other shareholders agreement provisions.* These may include non-competition clauses, confidentiality agreements, dispute resolution mechanisms, and details about how the shareholders agreement itself is to be amended or terminated.

Shareholder agreements are voluntary. If you choose to have one — and, as you now know, we recommend you do — the shareholder agreement should reflect the particular needs of your company and its shareholders. While undoubtedly the best advice is to keep your agreement as simple as possible, we strongly suggest that you consult your professional advisors before signing any shareholders agreement.

Do I Have to Get a Corporate Seal? Not necessarily. A corporation under the federal Canada Business Corporations Act, for example, is not required to have a seal. If you wish to have a corporate seal for your corporation, you may purchase one from a legal stationery store or commercial supplier.

If I Decide to Incorporate, What Next? Our advice: See a lawyer. However, if you want to do it yourself, contact your provincial authority if you want to incorporate locally or the Corporations Directorate of Industry Canada should you decide to incorporate federally. And, if you are going to do it on your own, get ready for lots of paperwork. You may also wish to check out the two Web sites listed in Box 11.2.

CO-OPERATIVE

Although relatively little has been written about co-operatives, you should give some consideration to this form, particularly if you are considering a home-based business that can benefit from a group pooling of talents.

Box 11.2 Bookmark This

Incorporate Online
http://strategis.ic.gc.ca

Federal Incorporation
http://strategis.ic.gc.ca/sc_mrksv/corpdir/engdoc/homepage.html

CO-OPERATIVE
an organization that is operated collectively by its owners

A **co-operative** is a special form of corporate structure, often formed by a number of small producers who want to be more competitive in the marketplace. As such, it can be somewhat complicated. Here are a few distinct features:

Incorporation Generally, at least three people are needed to incorporate a co-operative. You can incorporate provincially (each province has its own legislation) or federally under the Canada Co-operative Associations Act. Each government has its own legal wrinkles, so you are going to need some legal advice or do a lot of research.

Organization A co-operative is organized and operated for the purpose of providing its members with goods or services. There are various types and structures. Traditional co-ops, such as co-op retail stores, farming co-ops, or housing co-ops, supply service to their members. In worker co-ops, everyone is expected to work in the corporation, and all members are employed in this one business. Worker co-ops can be a useful format for home-based "craft" or "consulting" businesses, where members can pool their talents and benefit from each other's skills. Another format is the marketing co-op where members have their own business (product or service). The purpose of this co-operative organization is to market and sell the different products or services.

Capital Start-up funds for a co-operative are raised by member shares. The return on capital investment to the members is limited by federal or provincial/territorial legislation. For example, the co-operative surplus is normally returned to the members in the form of patronage refunds — sometimes called patronage dividends — and each member receives a share of that surplus proportionate to the business done or work carried out by the member with or through the co-operative.

Voting Each member can have only one vote, regardless of the number of shares he or she possesses.

Liability The co-operative is an entity distinct from its members, who thus benefit from the standard limited liability protection of a standard corporate structure.

Shares Shares cannot be transferred. They must be sold to members of the co-operative.

Priorities Employment security is usually more important than capital, especially in worker co-ops.

Here are a few of the major advantages of a co-operative:

- Given the number of members, there are potentially more sources of capital than in other business forms. In addition, government regulations for raising start-up capital generally favour co-ops.
- Members are owners and are therefore more motivated to produce and be successful.
- Co-operatives offer members plenty of opportunity to network and share ideas and expertise.

- Generally, co-operatives are entitled to receive the standard corporate protection such as limited liability.
- In most cases, it is relatively easy for members to sell their shares to other members.

A few disadvantages of co-operatives are:

- With large member groups it is sometimes difficult to get agreement. Conflict resolution becomes an issue.
- Management is supposed to be a co-operative (shared) responsibility. In some cases, management becomes unwieldy because of differing goals and objectives and, in other cases, a lack of experience.
- Some members find it difficult to work co-operatively or in teams.
- Some major institutions are not familiar or comfortable with how co-operatives work, making financing relatively more difficult to obtain.

Establishing a co-operative is tricky. We strongly advise you to consult with provincial or federal authorities and a lawyer. We also encourage you to network with co-ops in your area to understand how they are managed, and to learn first-hand the advantages and disadvantages of the co-op form of business.

Now it's time to do a little research on your own. Complete Action Step 51.

Your Business Name

So you now have a business idea you think will fly. You've spent a lot of time on your business plan and are beginning to think that it just might work. You've come up with a name for your business that you are proud of. Where do you go from here?

We suggest you next think about some legal protection for your name. After all, you don't want someone else to go out and start a business using your name. The process of protecting your business name will depend, in part, on the province where you want to conduct business and your legal form (which is one of the reasons we wanted you to consider your legal framework in the first part of this chapter). What follows is this whole procedure, simplified, but again we advise you to get some professional help.

According to provincial authority, a sole proprietorship or partnership does not necessarily have to register its name. Normally, if your business name is exactly the same as your own name, registration is not needed. For example, Mary Smith could operate a business as Mary Smith without registration. However, she would have to register the name of her business if the business name differed — even slightly — from her name. If she called her business Mary Smith *Consulting*, then she must register that name with the province where she is conducting her business.

Provincial registration does not require the business name to be unique. Thus, in some cases, you can register your business name without a search, but we advise that you do one since you may later find out that there are other businesses with similar names. If your registered name causes confusion with another business, you may be subject to penalties and may even have to change the name of your business. In other words, provincial registration does not necessarily protect your business name.

In searching a name you have two choices: doing a provincial search or doing a federal search. All incorporated businesses must register their corporate name with any province in which they do business. Although provinces will do a name search for you, your best bet is to ask for a federal name search report. If you incorporate federally, and we suggest you do, you will need a

ACTION STEP 51

Do some secondary research on corporations.

Before you take any action with legal forms, you need a lot of information.

We suggest you begin by logging on to the Internet. A good place to start is Industry Canada's Strategis Web site at <http://strategis.ic.gc.ca>. Enter the words "sole proprietorship" into the search box and you will find some 100 sources on corporate structures.

If you prefer hard copy, go to the library or the resource centre of your college or university. You can also check out the bookstores; handbooks on incorporation through various self-counsel series are helpful.

Once you get familiar with the broad concepts, you may want to do some specific research of companies in your industry. Write to the companies or get on the Net and visit their sites if they have one. You may also want to talk to a few small businesses you know. Get their opinion. What kind of structure would they suggest and why?

While you are doing this research, remember to keep looking around with new eyes.

NUANS (Newly Upgraded Automated Name Search) report. A NUANS report is a five-page document that includes a list of business names and trademarks that sound similar to the name you are proposing. The list is drawn from the national data bank of existing and reserved business names, as well as trademarks applied for and registered in Canada.

A NUANS will make you aware of any existing businesses that could prevent you from using your business name. It also lets you know whether your proposed trademark is already in use by another business. This saves you from having to change the name of your business later when you find out that you have been infringing on a trademark.

A NUANS report is obtained from private businesses known as Search Houses, which are listed under Incorporating Companies, Incorporation: Name Search, Searchers of Records, or Trademark Agents in the Yellow Pages.

Generally, when you register a name in federal incorporation, you must submit the NUANS report along with your proposed business name. The request for a numbered company is the same with one exception. You may request the federal government to grant your corporation a designating number, followed by the word "Canada" and a legal element, to serve as your corporate name. For this specific case, a NUANS report is not required. Any other kind of proposed name must be supported by a NUANS report. If there is another name that is similar to your name, you will be asked to make a new choice for your incorporated company.[3]

More Red Tape

When you start your business, you will be subjected to all kinds of federal, provincial, and municipal red tape. Box 11.3 provides a checklist of some of the requirements your business may be confronted with. One thing is for certain: you will have to deal with Revenue Canada. Thus, we focus here on the major Revenue Canada start-up requirements because these will be common for everyone.

THE BUSINESS NUMBER (BN)

Your first step in doing business with Revenue Canada is your business number (BN). The BN is the federal government's numbering system that helps to streamline the way it deals with businesses. It is based on the idea of "one business, one number."

You will need a BN (as of 1998) if you require one of the four Revenue Canada business accounts: corporate income tax, import/export, payroll deductions, or the Goods and Services Tax (GST) or Harmonized Sales Tax (HST). According to government, businesses will eventually be able to use their BN for other Revenue Canada accounts and other government programs. For instance, you will be asked to state the name of the business, its location, and its legal structure. You will also be required to outline what your business's sales will be. Without this type of information, you won't be able to complete the BN registration form.

If you decide you need a BN, you will have to complete Form RC1, Request for a Business Number. For more information, contact your local office of Revenue Canada. A good source of information is the Revenue Canada Publication, *RC2: The Business Number and Your Revenue Canada Accounts*. You can find this publication on the Revenue Canada site at <http://www.rc.gc.ca>.

GST/HST

The GST is a tax that applies at a rate of 7 percent to the supply of most goods and services in Canada. The HST is a sales tax that applies at a single rate of 15 percent to taxable supplies made in the three participating provinces of Newfoundland, Nova Scotia, and New Brunswick (as of 1997). The HST has the same basic operating rules as the GST. The federal component of HST is 7 percent and the provincial component is 8 percent.

If your taxable revenues do not exceed $30 000, you do not have to register for the GST or HST. However, you can register voluntarily and, in general, we suggest you do.

Although the consumer ultimately pays the the GST/HST, businesses are normally responsible for collecting and remitting it to the government. Businesses that must register or that register voluntarily for the GST/HST are called registrants. Registrants can claim a credit, called an input tax credit, to recover the GST/HST they paid or owe on their business purchases. If they pay more than they collect, they can claim a refund. Since there are goods and services that are tax-exempt (most medical and dental services and daycare services provided for less than 24 hours per day, for example), it is important that you check with Revenue Canada before you start your business.

To register for the GST or HST, contact your nearest tax services office. You will be asked to fill out an RC1, Request for a BN form, as we discussed earlier. You can get more information from the Revenue Canada publication, *General Information for GST/HST Registrants* or from Revenue Canada's Web site at <http://www.rc.ca>.

PAYROLL DEDUCTIONS

According to Revenue Canada, you are an employer if you: pay salaries, wages, bonuses, vacation pay, or tips to people working for you; or if you provide benefits such as lodging or room and board to the people working for you. If you are an employer, you will be responsible for deducting the following from your employees' pay cheques:

- income tax,
- Canada Pension Plan (CPP) contributions, and
- Employment Insurance (EI) premiums.

You may also be required to make payments and be subject to certain regulations under the workers' compensation legislation.

Payroll deductions can be complicated. So before you start your business, we strongly advise you to visit or call your local Revenue Canada office. An advisor may even come to your business and help you get started with all the forms you need. If you have a computer (and you should), Revenue Canada will give you a disk, *Tables on Diskette* (TOD) (T4143). It contains all the information you need to calculate deductions from your employees' pay for all pay periods. This disk is even available on the Internet on Revenue Canada's Electronic Distribution System. Another good source of information on payroll deductions is the Revenue Canada publication, *Employers' Guide to Payroll Deductions.*

FEDERAL INCOME TAXES

Generally, business income includes any money you earn with the reasonable expectation of making a profit.

ACTION STEP 52

Take a lawyer to lunch.

Canvass your business contacts for the names of three to five lawyers with experience in forming small business corporations and partnerships. Concentrate on those who have worked in your industry.

Talk to them by phone first and then take the most promising candidate to lunch. (Lunch is optional, but your inquiries are vital.)

The first thing you're looking for is someone you can get along with. Then look for experience in the world of small business. A hot trial lawyer may have a lot of charisma, but you want a nuts-and-bolts small business specialist who can save you time, pain, and money.

During lunch, find out about fees and costs. Compare the cost, for example, of having your lawyer write up a complex partnership buy-out agreement with the cost of setting up a corporation. Use some questions presented in this chapter to start you off in your discussion.

A good lawyer will offer you perspectives that will be helpful in the formation of your business. You may have to look awhile, and it may cost you some dollars up front, but there's no substitute for good legal help.

If you are a new business entity, your year end will be December 31 and your tax return will be due at the end of April each year. This business income (or loss) forms part of your overall income for the year. As a sole proprietor, your income tax return must include financial statements. It is most likely (if you are not in farming and fishing) that you will be required to submit one of the following two forms along with your T1:

- Form T2124, *Statement of Business Activities*
- Form T2032, *Statement of Professional Activities*

A partnership by itself does not file an annual income tax return. Each partner must include a share of the partnership income or loss on a personal, corporate, or trust income tax return. As such, partners must file either financial statements or one of the two proprietorship forms referred to above. Partnership taxes can get a little complicated, so you should get some accounting advice or, at the very least, consult with Revenue Canada.

A corporation must file a corporation income tax return (T2) within six months of the end of every taxation year, even if it doesn't owe taxes. Corporations report on an annual basis and are normally free to choose their year-end date. Corporations are also required to attach complete financial statements and the necessary schedules to the T2 return.

Corporate tax is complicated and you definitely should get professional help. But, if you really do want to try it yourself, the best place to start is the "Small Business Page" of Revenue Canada at <http://www.rc.gc.ca/menu/EmenuNBA.html>. It's a useful source of information, containing a list of all the Revenue Canada business publications.

Get a Lawyer

Businesses are built on people, of course, and this is why you need a business structure that will give you flexibility when the people in your business want to make a change. Don't underestimate the power of the psychological forces of a corporate structure.

A good small business lawyer can help you create the right business structure for a partnership or a corporation — a structure that gives you the flexibility you'll need. Network your contacts for a lawyer with experience in your industry. You need a lawyer on your team of advisors.

Once you've found one you think might be right for you, make an appointment with him or her.

Be sure to prepare your own agenda for each conversation with the lawyer. If you're organized, you will save money on your fee. Remember, only stay the time alloted or you'll pay extra.

Now you're ready to do Action Step 52.

If you don't use a good lawyer to help you structure your business, you probably won't have a plan to handle contingencies, and unforeseen events can take you by surprise. If Paul Webber had used his imagination to look ahead, his story might have turned out differently.

Paul was a computer programmer when he met Jerry Dominic. Jerry was a likable guy and a dynamic salesman, who knew there was money to be made in the information business, so he got together with Paul and formed a partnership in a software consulting business. They specialized in microcomputers. Their first year was okay — they netted over $40 000 apiece — but their second year was looking even better.

Box 11.3 Checklist of Requirements That May Impact Your Business

Have you considered the following?

Municipal

- regulations regarding home-based or home-occupation business
- zoning, rezoning, and obtaining a minor variance
- subdivision approval and consent to severance
- demolition control and permits
- site plan control approval
- construction permit
- licensing of business and trades
- signage regulations
- hours of operation
- food premises inspection
- municipal tax (e.g., realty tax, business tax)
- any more?

Provincial

- health and safety regulations
- workers' compensation
- provincial/territorial employment standards (e.g., hours of work, minimum wage, vacation pay, overtime pay, equal pay for equal work)
- health insurance
- environmental control regulations
- provincial tax (e.g., corporate, retail sales, tobacco, gasoline, land transfer tax)
- any more?

Federal

- Business Number (BN)
- GST/HST
- payroll deductions (e.g., Canada pension plan, insurance, income tax)
- food and drug regulations and inspection
- patents, trademarks, copyrights, and industrial designs
- federal corporation tax

By May of the second year, their projections told them they could make a $100 000 each before the end of summer. To celebrate, they went to a neighbourhood bar for a couple of drinks. Jerry got into an argument with a guy. There was a fistfight, and Jerry ended up on the floor. When Paul stooped down to help Jerry up, he noticed his partner felt heavy, like dead weight.

At 49 years old, Jerry Dominic was dead of a heart attack.

Two days after the funeral, Jerry's widow walked in to the office. Mildred had just inherited Jerry's half of the business.

Paul didn't like Mildred being his partner, but there was nothing he could do. He knew he would have to break his back to teach her the business. Computer software was fast-track and competitive — it changed before you could take a breath — and Mildred would have to learn an awful lot in a short time.

The first week, Paul was extra tired because he was handling his own customers while he spent long hours trying to teach Mildred the business. The second week, two of Paul's customers defected to a competitor. The third week, the company almost ran out of cash, and Paul had to dump in $5 000 from his personal account to keep suppliers happy.

The other problem was that Mildred wasn't learning the business. She was spending a lot of money and not holding up her end. There was no improvement in sight.

Paul hung on for a couple more weeks. Then he did the only thing he could do for his own survival: he took what customers he had left, rented another office, and tried to keep going. He figured he had paid his dues to Jerry.

Sometimes, Paul wishes he and Jerry had had something in writing to cover contingencies. In business, you always need a Plan B.

PARTNERSHIP AGREEMENT
a written agreement between two or more partners that specifies the role of the partners, including income sharing, capital gains distribution, and tactics for dissolution

If you still want to form a partnership, get a lawyer to draw up a **partnership agreement** and consult your insurance agent about getting some protective insurance. If you're able to look ahead, you'll avoid problems, regardless of the legal form of your business.

Get a Will

The importance of an up-to-date will cannot be overstated. Contrary to what most people believe, if you die without a will, things will not automatically work out as you would have wished. Disaster can result.[4]

DAVID CHILTON, author of *The Wealthy Barber*

If you die without a will, all your assets will be frozen. The courts will then pay off all debts and divide up your business assets according to a set of rigid rules. If you want your property, business, or shares transferred a certain way after your death, you must say so in a will. If you have partners or other owners, make sure they have a will and that you all understand what is going to happen if someone dies. Here are a few rules, drawn from *The Wealthy Barber*:[5]

1. Get a lawyer. Don't do it yourself. There are many issues to consider, both from a business and personal perspective.
2. Make your lawyer aware of your business arrangements.
3. Before you see a lawyer, decide exactly what you want to happen with your business should you die. Make sure that you discuss this with your business partners or other owners. Remember also that you have the right to know what is going to happen to the business if one of your key shareholders or partners dies.
4. Choose an executor. This is a person who will handle your affairs and carry out the will's instruction.
5. Don't procrastinate. Do it now!

In a Nutshell

There are three basic legal forms for your small business: sole proprietorship, partnership, and corporation (limited company). You can run a business as a sole proprietorship with a minimum of difficulty. You might only need a city licence, a resale licence, and a business name. If you use a business name other than your own, you will probably need to register the name with your provincial government. Be careful, however — this may not give you exclusive rights to use the name. The legal paperwork for a partnership is a little more involved. It may be possible to form a partnership with a handshake — but we wouldn't advise it. Get a lawyer and have a partnership agreement drawn up before you start. There are good skill-related reasons for forming a partnership. Let's say you're an inventor; you need a partner who can manage and sell. Let's say you're good at marketing; you need a partner who can run the office and keep the books. You may also form a partnership because you need the financial capital. Remember, however, these are the only two good reasons for forming a partnership — to provide skills and money. At least one of these needs must be met or you're asking for trouble. For example, friendship is not a good enough reason for a partnership arrangement. Forming a limited company or corporation takes the most paperwork and costs the most money. However, it gives you the most flexibility, as well as a shield in case your business hurts someone.

ACTION STEP REVIEW

51 Do some secondary research on corporations.
52 Take a lawyer to lunch.

Think Points for Success

✓ Know the advantages and disadvantages of the basic legal forms when you establish your business.
✓ Get a lawyer and a partnership agreement drawn up before you form a partnership.
✓ Incorporation can help limit your liability.
✓ Protect your business name and do a NUANS search to make sure you have not infringed on another business's name or trademark.

Business Plan Building Block

LEGAL STRUCTURE

State the type of legal structure — proprietorship, partnership, or a corporation — you intend to institute for your business. List the reasons why you chose this structure.

RED TAPE FILE

Set up a red tape file. Make a list of all the municipal, provincial, and federal regulations you are going to have to comply with. Beside each regulation, write the contact telephone number, address, and other pertinent information.

Checklist Questions and Actions to Develop Your Business Plan

LEGAL CONCERNS

- ❑ Explain why you selected your legal form of ownership.
- ❑ What professionals have you referenced in your business plan, and did you allow for the appropriate cost?
- ❑ What are the major legal risks for your industry, and how will you address them?

NOTES

1. Much of the research for this section was conducted on Industry Canada, Strategis Web site at <http://strategis.ic.gc>.
2. Industry Canada: Corporations Directorate, *Small Business Guide to Federal Incorporation,* Strategis Web site at <http://strategis.ic.gc.ca/SSG/cs01146e>.
3. *Ibid.*
4. David Chilton, *The Wealthy Barber* (Toronto: Stoddart Publishing Company, 1989), p. 67.
5. *Ibid.*

OTHER REFERENCES

Brandt, Steven C. *Stay Out of Court and in Business.* Archipelago Publishing, 1997.

Industry Canada: Canadian Intellectual Property Office. *A Guide to Copyright.* May 1997.

Industry Canada: Canadian Intellectual Property Office. *A Guide to Patents.* May 1997.

Industry Canada: Corporations Directorate. *Name Granting Guidelines.*

Industry Canada: Corporations Directorate. *Small Business Guide to Federal Incorporation.*

Rurka, Bean P. "Commercial Leases for the Small Business." *Law Now,* October/November 1995, pp. 10–11.

Tillson, Tamsen. "Common Sense Resolution." *Canadian Business,* March 1997, pp. 83–89. [Alternatives to litigation for settling business disputes.]

Revenue Canada. *RC2: The Business Number and Your Revenue Canada Accounts.*

Revenue Canada. *Employer's Guide to Payroll Deductions.*

Revenue Canada. *General Information for GST/HST Registrants.*

twelve

Building and Managing a Winning Team

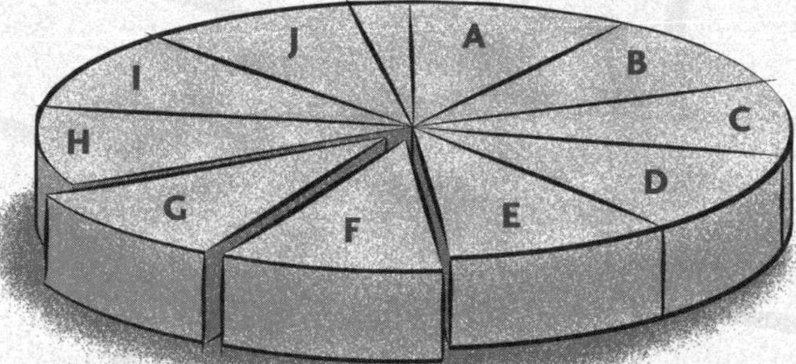

BUSINESS PLAN BUILDING BLOCK

This chapter will help you manage your business and develop a team that shares your vision and enthusiasm.

LEARNING OPPORTUNITIES

After reading this chapter, you should be able to:

- Know the basic management functions of planning, leading, organizing, and controlling.
- Chart your organizational structure.
- Consider the benefits of a virtual or network organization.
- Take another look at yourself and identify your strengths, weaknesses, and business needs.
- Use the idea of balance to brainstorm your ideal team and scout potential team members.
- Consider the merits of the just-in-time team, joint ventures, and strategic alliances.
- Take advantage of your board of directors and external advisors.
- Understand the value of an advisory board.
- Realize the need for a mentor.
- Find a winning team of employees and associates.
- Develop an action plan with your new team before you open the doors.
- Take a proactive approach to human resources.

MSM Transportation Inc. is a successful Profit 100 company, but when Robert Murray and Mike McCarron started out in the late 1980s, they knew they were combining two different types of management expertise, plus two very different personalities. Mike, the company's managing partner and primary marketer, is boisterous and outgoing, passionate and — as he admits — impulsive. Robert, MSM's president, trained originally as a credit manager, comes across as quiet, thoughtful, and more of a long-term thinker. Oil and water? Of course.

But Robert says the duo's strength lies in the fact that they can disagree, argue feverishly, work it out, and move on. With two partners who share a similar vision for the company, if not the same temperament, debate becomes a positive force that generates new ideas and better decisions. In an industry notorious for its lack of marketing and financial skills, MSM benefits from both personalities because they question each other's assumptions and strategies. Notes Robert, "My partner makes me much more effective and, I believe, much better at what I do."[1]

Figure 12.1 Chapter Twelve will help you prepare parts F and G of your business plan, "Management" and "Personnel."

ACTION STEP PREVIEW

53 Understand your personal strengths and weaknesses.
54 Consider a virtual team.
55 Find a mentor.
56 Tap your people resources by brainstorming with your team.

Your chances of success? Sixty-five percent of new businesses survive their first year; 30 percent survive their first five years; only 15 percent make it for ten years. The key to your small business survival is how you build and manage your team.

Business success is all about working with people you trust and respect to accomplish your personal and business goals and objectives. Way back in Chapter One, we explained that success meant different things to different people. Some say, for example, that success is the process of realizing goals that are driven by a compelling vision. We like this definition; however, it makes no mention of the importance of achieving results through people, and today we can no longer make it happen without others. To be successful in today's changing economy, we must start with a compelling vision and work at what we love. We must be able to satisfy the needs of a growth market, to focus on a particular niche or opportunity within that market, and to manage ourselves and others. This new changing economy has created the management need for people to work together to constantly generate new ideas. Today more than ever, business success will depend on how well we manage and work with people, and that is what this chapter is all about: working with people! We will start with the basics of management.

The Basics of Management

TO PLOC OR NOT TO PLOC

MANAGEMENT
process of planning, leading, organizing, and controlling

Management is the process of *P*lanning, *L*eading, *O*rganizing, and *C*ontrolling (or some may call it evaluating) — PLOCing. It's about effectively and efficiently getting things done with and through people (see Figure 12.2).

Figure 12.2

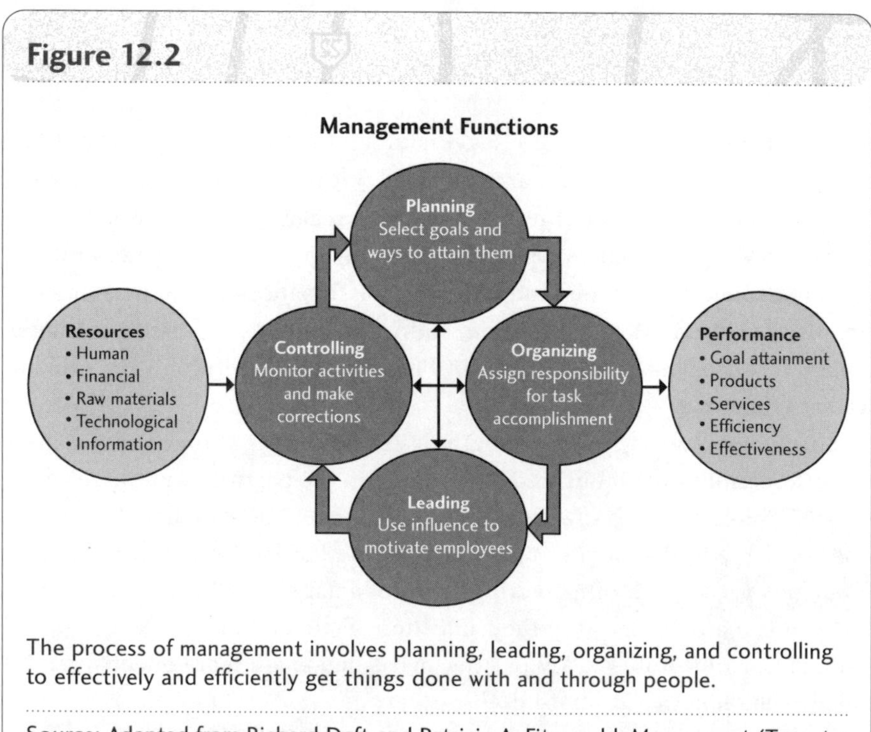

The process of management involves planning, leading, organizing, and controlling to effectively and efficiently get things done with and through people.

Source: Adapted from Richard Daft and Patricia A. Fitzgerald, *Management* (Toronto: Holt, Rinehart and Winston, 1992), p. 5. Reprinted by permission of Harcourt Brace & Company Canada, Ltd.

PLANNING

Step back for a moment and remember Chapter Three in which you first established a vision and then goals, followed by annual objectives that led to your strategic plan. In the old economy, planning was the sole responsibility of the owner/manager. Today, everyone does planning on an ongoing basis, and good business owners try to make it exciting and useful.

Planning is a process of outlining a business's objectives and goals and the ways in which everyone will accomplish the plan.

PLANNING
outlining goals and objectives and the ways in which everyone will accomplish them

Many entrepreneurs, though full of ideas, somehow cannot focus or target their energies. The reality is, good ideas are a dime a dozen, but people who can translate them into a profit are one in a thousand. The key to success is to focus through goal setting and meeting annual objectives. Only about 3 percent of the population become financially independent, and only about 3 percent set goals. Goal setting helps you translate your idea into a financial profit. Thus, the management section of your business plan should include the major goals and objectives of your business, which must be consistent with your personal vision and mission.

LEADING

In the old economy, you were the leader because you were the owner of the business. In the new economy, leadership has to be earned. **Leadership** is about creating the work climate that motivates people to do what is expected of them because they believe in what you are doing and share your vision.

LEADERSHIP
act of motivating others to do activities designed to achieve specific objectives

Researchers have identified the key ingredients of successful leadership. Studies consistently show that the so-called "transformational style" of leadership brings tremendous payoffs in company performance and innovation. This style has five types of behaviour that inspire exceptional performance:[2]

1. *Visioning*. The leader communicates a compelling vision of the future that is widely shared by the organization's members. The vision describes the ultimate outcome employees need to achieve. Transformational leaders lead by example and act in ways consistent with the vision.
2. *Inspiring*. The leader communicates the vision with passion, energy, and conviction, expresses optimism about the future, and shows enthusiasm about future possibilities. The leader generates excitement in the workplace and heightens others' expectations through symbols and images, which in turn build commitment to the vision.
3. *Stimulating*. The leader arouses interest in new ideas and approaches, and enables employees to think through problems in new ways. The leader who practises intellectual stimulation encourages the rethinking of ideas and the questioning of traditionally accepted ways of doing things. The leader considers "wild" ideas and supports divergent thinking. He or she uses reasoning and analytic thinking to problem-solve and select from the creative ideas generated.
4. *Coaching*. The leader coaches, advises and provides hands-on help for employees to develop their capabilities and improve their performance. He or she listens attentively, understands individual needs, motivations, and aspirations, and expresses encouragement, support, and confidence in individuals' abilities to meet the expectations inherent in the vision. The leader gives constructive feedback, encourages people to take on greater responsibilities, and provides opportunities for development by delegating challenging and interesting tasks.
5. *Team-building*. The leader builds effective teams by selecting team members with complementary skills and encouraging them to work together

toward common goals. He or she increases team confidence and commitment by giving positive feedback, sharing information, utilizing individuals' skills, and removing obstacles to team performance.

Peter Urs Bender tells us in his book, *Leadership from Within*, that this new style of leadership has five key steps:[3]

1. Know yourself: Identify your values, motivations, and personality type.
2. Have vision and passion: See what you love and love what you do.
3. Take risks: Be consistently courageous.
4. Communicate: Bring your vision to others, effectively and with confidence.
5. Check progress and results: Know where you are, so you can get where you want to go.

To learn more about what leadership is all about, see Box 12.1.

What is your leadership strategy? How will you empower — or give power to — your business? Be prepared to include a statement about how you are going to motivate your team to achieve the goals and objectives that will make you and them successful. Don't be afraid to show emotion. Emotion is a driving force and, in fact, some experts say that leadership is the emotional part of the management function.

ORGANIZING

Chapter Eleven discussed ways in which you might want to organize your business — sole proprietorship, partnership, corporation, or co-operative.

Box 12.1 Leadership from Within

Leadership is no longer about being in front of the pack, scoring the most goals, being first in sales, or having the highest position. Peter Urs Bender, "Canada's presentation guru," in his book, *Leadership from Within*, helps us understand a new kind of leadership that must "come from within."

According to Bender, leadership is about:

1. **People.** The other things — sales, profit, equipment, numbers, and systems — are important, but they are just tools and measures to help us make progress.
2. **Being the leader of you.** Find a vision, put it into action, and you will automatically become the leader of others.
3. **Internal motivation.** The command-and-control "shape up or get out" behaviour is quickly being replaced with an approach that involves coaching, empowering, and inspiring.
4. **Striving for perfection, while accepting our imperfections.** Being a leader means accepting that we are human.
5. **Change.** It's about making conscious choices to bring about positive change.
6. **Confidence.** You must truly believe that things can be better
7. **Growth.** Going beyond what we have done before.
8. **Energy.** Energy comes from your belief that something good is about to happen — a belief in a positive future. Energy is contagious.
9. **Creating a positive experience.** Leaders can motivate and make people feel excited and positive about work and life.
10. **Creating results.** True leadership is the ability to turn vision into results.
11. **Reducing fear and increasing hope.** Leaders are able to make changes and increase people's confidence and sense of hope.

Source: Peter Urs Bender, *Leadership from Within* (Toronto: Stoddart Publishing, 1997), pp. 7–11. Reprinted by permission of Stoddart Publishing Co. Limited, Toronto, Ontario.

The management section of your plan will explain what form of business ownership you plan to institute and why. But you are also going to have to come to grips with such questions as: What tasks are there to be done? Who does them? How are the tasks to be grouped? Who reports to whom? Where are decisions made? **Organizing** is the management function concerned with co-ordinating activities so that objectives can be met.

ORGANIZING
a management function concerned with co-ordinating activities so that objectives can be met

The key to developing an organizational structure or framework for your business is to remember that we are deeply entrenched in a business environment that demands innovation, proactivity, and risk taking. We can no longer form bureaucratic structures that inhibit the transfer of information. Table 12.1 shows the basic differences between the new "organic" structures and the old mechanistic structures. Bureaucracies inhibit the flow of information. In the management section of your plan, you will have to explain how you will organize your activities and structure your business to focus on your target customer and respond to a changing environment.

Traditionally, most small business structures have been organized on the basis of function, geography, or type of customer. Examples of these traditional types of structures are shown in Figure 12.3.

Today, small businesses have to work as a team. So, in your business plan, explain who is in your team and why. The process of developing an effective team is discussed later on in the chapter. At this point, we want you to consider the benefits of the new "virtual" type of organizational structure to your

Table 12.1 Organic Versus Mechanistic Organizational Structure

Organic	Mechanistic
1. Channels of communication open, with free flow of information throughout the organization	1. Channels of communication highly structured, with restricted information flow
2. Operating styles allowed to vary freely	2. Operating styles must be uniform and restricted
3. Authority for decisions based on expertise of the individual	3. Authority for decisions based on formal line management position
4. Free adaptation by the organization to changing circumstances	4. Reluctant adaptation, with insistence on holding fast to tried and true management principles despite changes in business conditions
5. Emphasis on getting things done unconstrained by formally laid-out procedures	5. Emphasis on formally laid-down procedures, with reliance on tried and true management principles
6. Loose, informal control with emphasis on norm of co-operation	6. Tight control through sophisticated control systems
7. Flexible on-job behaviour permitted to be shaped by the requirements of the situation and personality of the individual doing the job	7. Constrained on-job behaviour required to conform to job descriptions
8. Participation and group consensus used frequently	8. Superiors make decisions, with minimum consultation and involvement of subordinates

Source: Adapted from Dr. Pradip N. Khandwalla, *The Design of Organization* (New York: Harcourt Brace Jovanovich, 1977), p. 411. Reprinted by permission of the author.

Figure 12.3 Charting Your Organizational Structure: Three Traditional Approaches

FUNCTIONAL

The functional approach to an organizational structure is one of the most widely used forms in small business. Teams are formed in accordance with the duties or functions they perform, such as accounting, service, or sales. Shown below is a simple functional organizational chart for a restaurant.

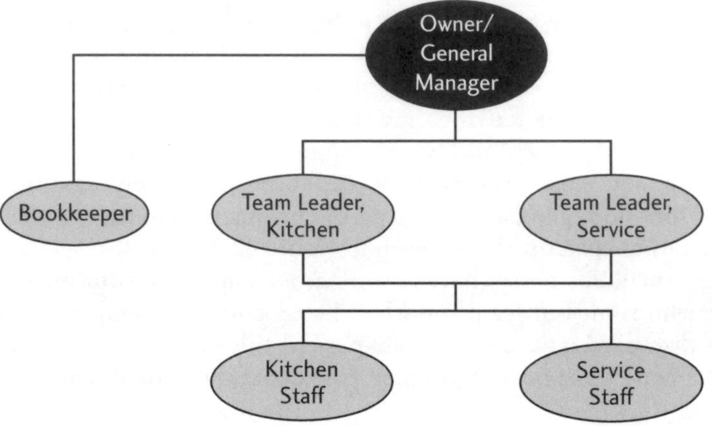

GEOGRAPHIC

Some types of independent businesses may decide to organize on the basis of geography. Provided below is an example of a "flat" service type of organization chart that has a structure based on territory or geography.

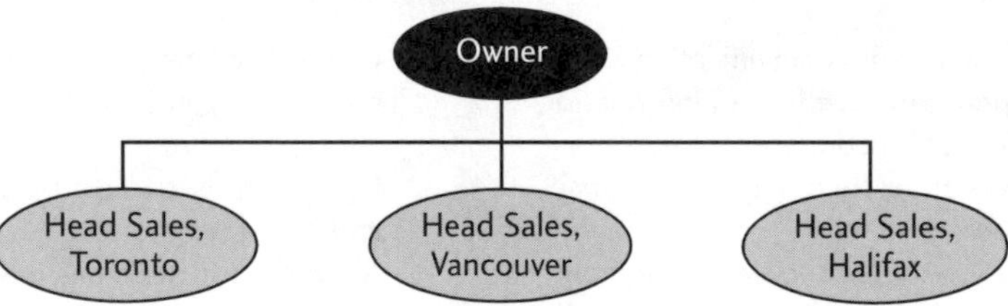

CUSTOMER-DRIVEN

Some independent businesses are starting to organize their company on the basis of type of customer. After all, it is the customer who drives the business. Here is one simple example of a small research and development organization that has a "customer-driven" organizational structure.

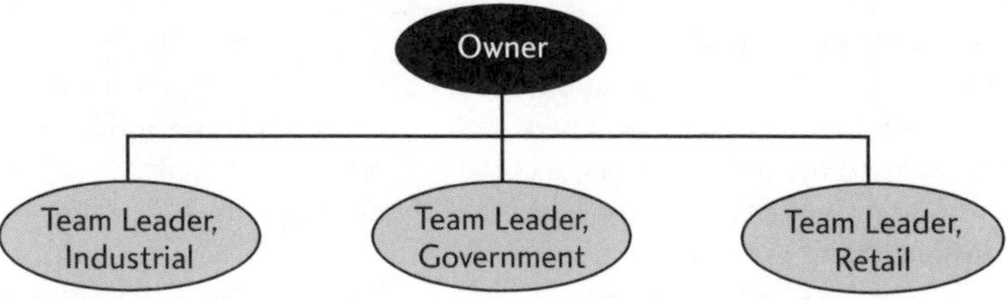

Source: Ron Knowles, *Writing a Small Business Plan: TVO Course Guide* (Toronto: Dryden, an imprint of Harcourt Brace & Company, Canada, 1995), pp. 49, 50. Reprinted by permission.

business. This network-type structure emerged because of its suitability in fostering and promoting a team approach to business.

The **virtual organization** became a buzzword in the late 1990s. Also called a **network organization**, it is one in which the core business functions (such as sales, accounting, retail, and manufacturing) are separated from the main business by small businesses or independent teams, often called **strategic business units**. What this means is that a business no longer has to compete under one roof. Jobs like human resources, advertising, maintenance, and sales can be contracted out to small businesses on an as-needed basis or handled by remote employees.

VIRTUAL ORGANIZATION (OR NETWORK ORGANIZATION)
organizational structure in which the major functions are broken up into strategic business units

STRATEGIC BUSINESS UNITS
independent teams or small businesses that support the functional needs of the main organization

Here's how the concept might work for an advertising agency. The entire agency may consist of only one person who presents the client with an idea. Once the idea is approved, the single person assembles "associates": graphic designers, copywriters, photographers, models, performers, and media experts to produce the package. The team is virtual — it is not housed in one central location, and might even have a "shamrock" structure as shown in Figure 12.4. This virtual ad agency has little staffing overhead, but can bring together the best talent to provide the client with a high-quality campaign at reasonable cost. Once the project is completed, the team of associates disbands, each member moving on to other projects.

For independent business, the virtual organization can allow the little guy to compete with the larger firm without sacrificing scale, speed, or agility. It is much like forming an all-star team to exploit a market opportunity. Here are some key characteristics of the virtual organization structure:[4]

- *It is customer-driven.* It is created to take advantage of a specific, customer-driven, time-based opportunity.
- *It is flexible.* It is disbanded when the opportunity ceases to exist.

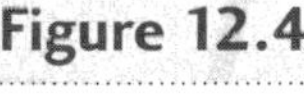

Figure 12.4

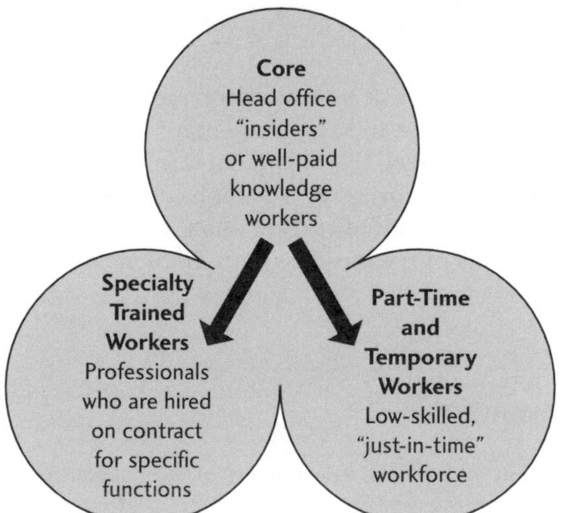

The Shamrock Model is a type of virtual organization with strategic business units.

Source: Adapted from Charles Handy, *Age of Unreason,* 2nd ed. (London: Century Business Books, Ltd., 1991). Reprinted by permission of the author.

- *It relies on mutual trust and teamwork.*
- *It is based on outsourcing.* Requirements are met with outside resources, not those from inside the organization.
- *It promotes supplier competition.*
- *It delegates selling duties to selling agents, not staff.*
- *It offers a web of associates or partners.* The corporate structure is linked by a web of alliances such as partnerships, joint ventures, and associates. This web replaces the traditional core functions such as manufacturing, warehousing, and supply.
- *It relies on outside expertise.* Emphasis is shifted from in-house knowledge to outside expertise.

CONTROLLING

Yesterday's management texts tell you that control is the final link in the functional chain of management — a process of monitoring to ensure that the activities of a business are being completed as planned. The manager/owner is expected to spend time checking up on the employee, making sure everything runs smoothly. In a static world, this might have been acceptable.

CONTROL
a system or procedure that allows people and the business to attain, together, mutually agreed upon goals in a directed or focussed manner

Today, **control** is a system or procedure that allows people and business to attain, together, mutually agreed upon goals in a directed or focussed manner. The controlling or evaluating process is everyone's responsibility, and it is a continuous process. It does not start after the job is completed. The key is to get everyone in your organization committed to your goals and concerned with evaluating their actions right from the start. As an owner, you need to help your staff reach their goals by removing obstacles and offering support. This is the essence of teamwork, the subject of the rest of this chapter (see Box 12.2).

Teamwork

THE FOUNDING TEAM

Your business plan reader will be most impressed by a founding team with industry-related experience and complementary skills as well as a record of achievement. When you finish this chapter, return to this section and develop two or three paragraphs proving your team has the experience, ability, and pedigree to ensure success. Information about the founding team is one of the most-read sections of the business plan. Here are a few examples.

Box 12.2 Teamwork

Today management is about the development of people, not the development of things, and the key is the

T ogether
E veryone
A chieves
M aximum

Manufacturing Example

Partners Bill and Lee Jones have spent over eleven years in the fitness business, Bill as a product designer and Lee as a sales representative. Bill developed and patented the Velopedical, an exercise bicycle that burns energy faster than a Stair Climber, and has sold over 10 000 units. Lee has been in the top 10 percent of the sales force of Acme Exercise Equipment for the past four years and has been personally responsible for over $8 million in sales.

They have hired Ed Riggs, a recently retired manufacturing manager of Sports Tech. Ed has a degree in industrial management from State Tech and has managed a light assembly operation for more than 20 years. Ed Riggs also teaches quality management classes at the community college on a part-time basis.

Edna Bloom is a retired CPA and has agreed to serve as CFO on a part-time basis.

Service Example

Teri Thorpe has served as Executive Chef of the Carlton Hotel and has won many awards and is well-known in the community.

Teri trained in Paris at the Culinary Institute and is certified as a Master Chef. She will supervise the kitchen. She owns a majority interest in the limited liability company.

Sally Chow was, until December, a training manager for the French Connection restaurant chain. Sally will act as general manager under the direction of Teri.

Patsy Emert is the minority investor. Patsy intends to retain her position as food and beverage manager of the Pelican Hill Country Club, but will be available as needed to monitor inventory and accounting activities.

Retail Example

Fast Stop Flower Shop is owned and managed by Bob and Susan Carter.

Bob opened the first shop five years ago in an abandoned gasoline station, and its high-profile Coast Highway location has made it a very busy and profitable business.

Susan Carter, Bob's sister, who has worked with Bob for two years, is going to run the second location four miles down the beach road in a high-traffice, tourist resort community. The second shop should allow volume purchase discounts that will have a significant effect on profit margins.

The Carters' mother has served as bookkeeper under the direction of J.T. Cook, CA.

The preceding management team examples are not full-blown résumés, but brief bios that demonstrate that the founders understand what they are doing. Vendors, bankers, investors, and teammates want to know about the founders. It is helpful to include a brief résumé, outlining your work experience, in your business plan. If you are light on experience, build on any success story you have to demonstrate that you know how to win. This is no time to be shy. Most people have a success story — use yours and it will give you confidence.

ACTION STEP 53

Understand your personal strengths and weaknesses.

What do you need to be successful? Money, of course, and tremendous energy and leadership. You need a vision, a terrific idea, the ability to focus, a sense of industry and thrift, and the curiosity of Sherlock Holmes. Do you have all these qualities or personality traits? Of course not. That is why you need a team — people to support your effort and to take over tasks that you're weak in or you don't understand.

So we want you to analyze yourself. Then you will know the kind of team you need. Take a few minutes and complete the personality analysis created by Peter Urs Bender in Appendix 12.1 of this chapter. Follow this up by asking yourself: What do I like? What am I good at? What do I hate? What does my business need that I cannot provide myself? Who can fill this need for me?

This simple exercise will help you start building a winning team.

BUILDING BALANCE INTO YOUR TEAM

As we learned in the opening vignette, balance, not sameness, is essential in a winning team. For many entrepreneurs, who have taken personal ownership of their ideas, finding this new freedom to let go and share their vision can be excruciatingly difficult. Entrepreneurs most in need of help are the stereotypical visionaries who founded a company and set out to do everything themselves. The day of the lone wolf operator is quickly coming to an end. Business today is just too complex. You need to realize that you cannot do everything yourself. You will need a team with different skills and personalities, depending on your strengths and the needs of the business. The key here is not to clone yourself. You need to surround yourself with people who can complement your skills.

The successful partnership at Tescor Energy Services Inc. provides a good example of this principle. It is a Profit 100 company that helps schools, hospitals, and governments reduce energy costs. Gary Johnston, chief administrative officer and minority partner, uses the analogy of the *Starship Enterprise* in *Star Trek: The Next Generation* to describe the ownership team. Tom Tamblyn, the founder and majority shareholder of Tescor, is like Jean-Luc Picard. His strengths are personal integrity and insightful strategic thinking, with a good intuitive sense of what is happening in the market. Tamblyn brought Mario Iusi, chief operating officer, and Johnston on board as minority shareholders to accomplish his business mission. Iusi is described as being like the *Enterprise's* Ricker. A make-it-happen type of person, he combines an understanding of systems with a focussed operational bent. Jonhston likens himself to the ship's counsellor, Deanna Troi, who always tries to go to the heart of the organization and wants to know how people are feeling. Together, says Jonhston, the three partners make a team worthy of the *Starship Enterprise*.[5]

This is a good time for a thorough self-assessment. Begin thinking about your strengths and weaknesses, and the kinds of people you are going to need to create your team. Complete Action Step 53.

CONSIDER THE VIRTUAL "JUST-IN-TIME" TEAM

You should be on the look out for people who complement your personality/skills characteristics and compensate for your weaknesses. Because you need to work with people who take ownership of your vision, the "9 to 5" employee mentality may no longer be in the equation. In the traditional team, business owners thought of their members as employees, but your new dream does not have to take the form of an employee/employer relationship. Think beyond the box. Think about such relationships as joint ventures or strategic alliances with other companies or formal associations/partnerships with individuals. How about subcontracting, or creating informal partnerships or associations?

Here are a few examples of how the virtual just-in-time teams can help you:

A general contractor pulls together a team of subcontractors who can be trusted to build a high-quality building. If the job goes well, there will be other opportunities for this team of specialists, but they only get paid while they are on contract.

A local printer discovers that her sales ability exceeds her ability to produce. She redefines herself as a "printer's broker" and uses her knowledge to select the most appropriate product from a wide variety of printers. She then sells her own small shop to an employee and increases her income several times over by providing assistance to customers who know little about printing. Her virtual organization now has just-in-time access to hundreds of experienced printers.

ACTION STEP 54

Consider a virtual team.
Make a list. Better still, create a mind map of the people or firms that might assist your efforts on an "as needed" basis — a virtual team. Think about a joint venture or strategic alliance with vendors, suppliers, co-workers, and even competitors. Look for those who share your vision. Keep on the look-out and be prepared to expand the list or mind map as new ideas emerge.

With continued corporate downsizing come mushrooming opportunities to alert "virtual team" entrepreneurs. The benefits include:

- Having access to the skills and experience of proven experts in their field.
- Paying only for services rendered.
- Reducing administrative and overhead costs.
- Gaining higher reliability.
- Achieving better quality and consistency.
- Having lower internal development costs.
- Getting a customer who is pre-sold.
- Maintaining flexibility to address new market opportunities instantly.

The virtual team needs to be customer-driven and opportunity focussed. There must also be agreement and a shared vision among all participants. Partners and opportunities must be selected with care. Performance standards are critical. The virtual organization might exist for a few weeks or a year or more. Then, when the opportunity has been fully exploited, the team must be prepared to disband quickly and move on to the next opportunity.

Now we want you to take a moment and consider a virtual organization. Complete Action Step 54.

JOINT VENTURES AND STRATEGIC ALLIANCES CAN HELP

At another level, consider as partners those firms with special capabilities that will share your risk in bringing a product or service to market. For example, if you have a new product, a team that includes retailers or end users could solve a lot of your marketing problems. Businesses usually form partnerships or associations in two fundamental ways: joint venture and strategic alliance.

JOINT VENTURE
partnership formed for a specific undertaking; it results in the formation of a new legal entity

Joint Venture A joint venture is usually a goal-oriented co-operation among two or more businesses. It involves the creation of a separate organization owned and controlled jointly by the parties. The joint venture usually has its own management, employees, production systems, and so on. Co-operation is limited to defined areas and, often, a predetermined time frame.

STRATEGIC ALLIANCE
goal-oriented partnership formed between companies to create a competitive advantage

Strategic Alliance A strategic alliance, sometimes called a business network, is a goal-oriented co-operation among two or more businesses, based on formal agreements and a business plan. In contrast to a joint venture, it usually does not involve the establishment of a separate new organization. The objective is to improve the competitiveness and capabilities of the individual members by using the strengths of the team. Depending on the need, the network may be organized in a variety of forms with regard to function, structure, and organization. If you don't know a lot about strategic alliances, the Canadian Business Networks Coalition (CBNC) is a great place to start. Spearheaded by the Canadian Chamber of Commerce and Industry Canada, the CBNC is made up of more than 60 business organizations and educational institutions across Canada. They can work with you to help you form a strategic alliance. Networks can grow and flourish. Check out their "Network Book." It is a practical guide for establishing a successful strategic alliance or business partnership.[6]

YOUR BOARD OF DIRECTORS OR ADVISORY BOARD

If you have decided to incorporate, now is the time to give some serious thought to your board of directors. In Chapter Eleven, you found out that, by law, you must have a board of directors. Many small companies take the easy route and simply elect key shareholders to the board. We want you now to think about forming a board that will provide true guidance and advice to your company. It is your chance to make a lawyer or accountant part of your team. If you need marketing help, elect a marketer. As we learned, your company's board of directors can make some very important decisions in the guidance and direction of your company. You do not want to lose this important opportunity to get outside expertise and advice.

But what happens if you have decided not to incorporate? You can also draw on the power of teamwork and advisors. Forward-looking entrepreneurs have created what is termed an "advisory board." You can include professionals such as bankers, lawyers, and accountants — even your small business professor. Again, you are looking for that skill set to complement areas where you have weaknesses. Colleagues, associates, and friends can also take on a semi-official responsibility for the company's welfare, and meet with you four or five times a year to review your updated business plan or new objectives, or to discuss difficult problems. Some enterprising entrepreneurs we know have even created a customer board of advisors. Sound a little unusual? Not at all. Since customers drive a business, it only makes sense to set up a formal mechanism like a focus group to listen to their concerns. Even if you are incorporated, an advisory board can be a big advantage. You will need as much help as you can get.

For example, Systems Integrator Les Systèmes Zenon Inc., another Profit 100 company, has an advisory board called "Friends of Zenon." It is a group of advisors who consult on strategy and help head off any problems they see looming. The voluntary, unpaid board includes experts in related technology fields, the company's lawyer, an accountant, and a venture capitalist. "We're very cautious and don't want to lose our focus," Eric Bourbeau explains. "Before we take any potentially risky decisions, we go to those guys and we check everything out. That way we have enough qualified people around us to make sure we rarely do anything stupid."[7]

GET A MENTOR

James and Brenda found their business mentor when they took a two-day "Look Before You Leap" small business seminar. In time, they were able to bounce ideas back and forth and get valuable feed back from a guest speaker at the seminar who had 25 years of experience in the school of hard knocks. "We couldn't have done it without her," says Brenda. "She gave us strength, direction, and confidence. She agreed to be our mentor on the condition that we become a mentor for a new business owner once we became successful. That made us feel good. For her, it was not a question of *if* we were going to be successful, it was a question of *when*. She believed in us — unconditionally."

For independent business, mentoring is a mutually beneficial partnership between a more experienced entrepreneur or business person, and an entrepreneur who is in the infant or start-up phase of a venture. The experienced partner is one who is reflective about his or her venture and is able to communicate and share his or her understanding and knowledge about what has made the venture grow. The inexperienced entrepreneur or protégé is receptive to the suggestions of the mentor and is also willing to try to implement some of them in the new business.

Mentoring is an ongoing partnership that may last for a number of months before any benefits are realized by either partner. The partners need to commit themselves to regular meetings with a focussed agenda. Usually, the mentor has more frequent and in-depth involvement than the advisory board.

Much of what is learned in small business comes from experience, since business, to a large extent, is an art. To be successful, we need to know how successful entrepreneurs think. We need help and direction, and in many cases we will not be able to get what we need from a book. That is why we need a mentor, someone who can give us start-up advice and encouragement.

Essential qualities of an effective small business mentor you should look for include:

- *A desire to help.* Individuals who are interested in, and willing to help, others.
- *Past positive experiences as entrepreneur.* Individuals who have had positive formal or informal experiences with a mentor.
- *A good reputation for developing others.* Individuals who have a good reputation for helping others develop their skill.
- *Time and energy.* Individuals who have the time and mental energy to devote to the relationship.
- *Up-to-date knowledge in the related field.* Individuals who have maintained current, up-to-date technological knowledge or skills.
- *A learning attitude.* Individuals who are still willing and able to learn and who see the potential benefits of a mentoring relationship.
- *Demonstrated effective managerial and mentoring skills.* Individuals who have demonstrated effective coaching, counselling, facilitating, and networking skills.

Although we strongly suggest you get a mentor, mentoring relationships do not always succeed the first time. Four of the most frequent problems with mentoring relationships include:[8]

- *Personality mismatch.* One or both members of the relationship may feel uneasy with the other or they may not be able to achieve the level of friendship necessary for rich communication.
- *Unrealistic expectations.* It is important that expectations are clearly defined from the beginning.
- *Breaches of confidentiality.* In order to develop the type of relationship in which the mentor can be effective, he or she must first be perceived as trustworthy and able to keep confidences, and visa versa.
- *Lack of commitment.* Both parties must do what they say and say what they do.

Table 12.2 provides some guidelines for choosing your mentor. Now it's your turn. Start looking for your mentor. Complete Action Step 55.

ACTION STEP 55

Find a mentor.

First develop a list of attributes you are looking for in a mentor, and areas where you need help. Network with your friends, co-workers, and business associates. Tell them what you're looking for — that is, a successful business owner with a good track record. The perfect mentor would be one with experience in your particular segment. You can also contact your local chamber of commerce or one or more of your local business clubs. See if your local small business centre can help. You can even look for a virtual mentor on the Internet (see Box 12.3).

Once you have located some candidates, develop a set of questions and set up a meeting to pick their brains. Here are some things to consider in selecting a mentor:

- Do you feel comfortable with this person?
- Can you trust him or her?
- Is he or she easy to communicate with?
- Does he or she have experience and contacts that can help your new business?
- Is he or she willing to devote the time to help you?

Once you have made your choice and the person has agreed to help you, keep in close contact. See the person at least once a month. Set up regular meetings with an agenda, and use the phone or e-mail to smooth out rough spots.

Table 12.2 Characteristics of Mentors

Mentors Are	Your Mentor Must
winners	have extensive business experience
humble	have at least one admitted failure
caring	truly care about you as a person
believers	truly believe you can move mountains
guides	be able to guide and direct without preaching
encouragers	be able to encourage the answer from within you
honest	have the strength and knowledge to be honest with you
empathizers	be able to empathize, not sympathize
listeners	want to spend time listening to you
excited	be excited about your ideas

Source: Ronald A. Knowles and Debbie White, *Issues in Canadian Small Business* (Toronto: Dryden, an imprint of Harcourt Brace & Company, Canada, 1995), p. 78. Reprinted by permission.

Staffing

THE INDEPENDENT CONTRACTOR OR ASSOCIATE

Although it is wise to build a web of complementary business associates — a virtual team — to assure success of your start-up, the reality is that you may need an employee, or several. Should this be the case, you should first consider the benefits of the "near employee" or the independent contractor.

Many people misunderstand government rules on independent contractors. If you tell the worker when to start and stop work, and if you supply the tools or office equipment, you have an employee. On the other hand, if the work assignment is task- or project-driven, if the worker sets his or her own hours, if you pay by the job and not by the hour, and if most of the work takes place away from your office using the worker's resources, then you may have an independent contractor or associate relationship. Many real estate agents, for example, that work on straight commission would qualify as independent contractors.

Think about using independent contractors or associates. If you pay by the job, on contract, you can save a lot of administrative costs. To start with, you only pay for work performed. You don't pay for coffee breaks. If the job is not done, you don't pay. Additional employee benefits that you, as an employer, pay take up a big chunk of your payroll. According to a KPMG survey, the wages and salaries that employers pay represent only about 58 percent of payroll costs. The remaining 42 percent are in benefits such as sick leave, employer's contribution to CPP, employment insurance, health insurance, and workers' compensation. What this means is that if you are expecting to pay $100 in wages, the real cost will be $172 — $100 for wages and $72 for benefits.[9]

A strong word of caution is in order. You need to be careful about the legal ins and outs of hiring on contract. We strongly recommend you check with both provincial/territorial and federal employment bodies, especially Revenue Canada, before you contract work out. Make sure, in writing if you can, that they will accept the conditions you set out for your associates or independent contractors.

Box 12.3 Virtual Mentoring

The Internet is quickly becoming a prime starting point for finding a mentor. It is a great source of help, particularly if you live in a remote community. As a matter of fact, with the power of the Internet, your mentor can now live a half way across the world. We suggest two prime sources to begin your virtual search: the Strategis and the Canadian Youth Business Foundation Web sites.

Strategis. Click on to Strategis and link to Contact's Coffee Break Listserv at <http://strategis.ic.gc.ca/conference/CONTACT/SSG/ec01032e.htm>. Here you will find a forum where you can ask business questions, share your thoughts and ideas, and build networks — a virtual meeting place for business advice and questions! Discussions are like an electronic meeting room, where any number of people can post messages to contribute to a discussion.

Coffee Break has become a major electronic discussion centre for as many small business-related questions as you can imagine. And it is a great place to find a mentor.

Canadian Youth Business Foundation (CYBF). Visit the CYBF's Mentoring program at <http://www.cybf.ca/frames/index.htm>. There is a physical and a virtual component to the mentoring program. It's designed to assist young entrepreneurs in the start-up phase right through to the first three years of business operation. Mentors are available as start-up advisors, personal mentors, counsellors, and electronic experts.

The CYBF has also created a mentoring discussion group — an open forum where mentors, protégés, practitioners, and interested individuals and organizations can discuss issues related to mentoring. Whatever your interest, you are welcome to contribute to the CYBF community of mentor network builders.

THE FIRST EMPLOYEES

When to hire your first employee is a question often asked. You may require people immediately, but many small firms do well using part-time or temporary workers until the owners have a strong feel for what needs to be done and who is best suited to do the job.

If the first worker needs to provide a high level of technical skill or is a person who can take your organization to the next level, you may need to provide an extra carrot, such as a profit-sharing option. A lot of talented workers prefer the entrepreneurial adventure to big business bureaucracy and will work for less if they share your vision and passion for entrepreneuring.

As you continue to add people, competence is not enough. You are assembling a venture team that wants to see growth and prosperity as much as you do. It is impossible to grow and expand until you have people who are equally capable and motivated to ensure success.

The quest for new employees begins with a written job description. You may not find a perfect fit so don't fence yourself in with too many specifications, yet don't overlook your future needs. Define the duties to be performed and the skills needed to perform them. A small business cannot afford a misfit or an unproductive person. If one person in a four-person organization doesn't work, you have lost 25 percent of your efficiency. Hiring and keeping good people is a critical factor in a firm's success.

If experience is not critical, consider vocational, trade, and professional schools. Local colleges and high schools have placement offices. Often programs are offered through social agencies where the government subsidizes worker training. Always check to see what's being offered. Government often creates programs to encourage employment and help small businesses. The best place to begin your search is the government Web sites on the Internet.

Stay out of trouble. In general, you can stay out of trouble if you avoid asking the following questions of a job applicant.

1. Age or birth date
2. Place of birth
3. A woman's maiden name
4. Racial or ethnic background
5. Religious affiliation
6. Marital status and sexual orientation
7. Number of children and ages
8. Medical condition or non-job-related physical data
9. Disabilities

Issues related to human rights, employment standards, and hiring are complicated, so the government has created brochures to help explain various regulations. About 90 percent of employee rights legislation comes under provincial jurisdiction, and provincial laws can vary extensively. Failure to follow any legal requirements can result in stiff penalties or even law suits from a disgruntled employee. So the best advice we can give you is to be very careful about what you say and check with your provincial labour departments if you have any doubts. You may find it beneficial to use an employment agency to hire your first few employees. Visit the sites shown in Box 12.4.

Ask the right questions. The trick is to prepare a list of questions that solicit responses to applicants' skills, experiences, or knowledge needed in the job. Similar questions should be asked of each applicant so that you can evaluate their responses and suitability. You may want to look over a few books that employees use to prepare for job interviews. These could give you ideas on questions to ask. To start, here are some questions that you could use:

1. How did you prepare for this meeting?
2. Why do you want to work for us?
3. How do your skills match the job description?
4. What would you do in the following situation? (Explain a problem they may face on the job.)
5. What type of training will you need to perform this job?
6. What are some of the obstacles you have overcome?

Box 12.4 Bookmark This

Federal Deductions: http://www.revcan.ca/menu/EmenuNBA.html
Under federal law, all employers are required to collect Employment Insurance Premiums, Canada Pension Plan contributions, and personal income tax on behalf of the federal government.

Provincial Deductions: http://www.wcb.on.ca
Employers must pay the accident fund of the Workers' Compensation Board through assessments on their payrolls.

Employment Standards: gopher://govonca.gov.on.ca:70/11/lab/epb/factsheets
This act provides for minimum terms and conditions of employment. It also establishes the minimum standards for working conditions, including paid public holidays.

7. What do you expect from a boss?
8. What gives you satisfaction in a job?
9. What do you think you will like most and least about this particular job?
10. What kinds of things disturb you on the job?
11. What have been your most pleasant work experiences?
12. What do you want to be doing in five years?
13. What would your references say about you?
14. What did you like or dislike about your last job?

The growth in part-time — sometimes referred to as the just-in-time — employment is exploding. Today, more than one in five workers are part-timers (working less than 30 hours per week). There are a number of advantages for firms in hiring part-time employees. First, since part-time wage rates are typically 60 percent of regular full-time wages, you can reduce your labour costs significantly. Part-time workers usually receive fewer benefits, which reduces yet another company expense. Part-time employment can also be an effective strategy for companies to benefit from the experience of the "retired" workforce, which, as we know, is a growth segment. You need to weigh these benefits against some of the negative long-term implications. For example, over-reliance on part-timers may leave your company without any experience or continuity. This could stifle your growth potential, since part-time workers normally have less commitment to you. In addition, the lack of continuity and loyalty becomes an issue if your company contracts out or outsources work. Contractors tend to go where there is money and where long-term contracts are available.

Now, let's see how Charlene Webb built her business using a team of high-energy part-time employees.

After Charlene Webb sold her gourmet cookware shop, she opened a women's specialty store. The shop is small — about 3 000 square feet — and is located in a neigbourhood centre in an up-scale community of about 10 000 people.

Charlene discovered that her ideal employees were local women who are active in community life and who prefer to work only one day a week. Monday's help is a golfer whose country-club friends come in to visit and buy from her on her day of work. Tuesday the tennis player is on, and her friends have followed her to the store. Wednesday is the yacht club member; Thursday, is a leader of hospital volunteers; Friday is a well-known club woman; Saturday is an attorney's wife. All of them are friendly women who know a lot about fashion and have a lot of energy, because they never have a chance to tire from the routine.

Charlene, who writes a society column (as free PR) in the community newspaper, has positioned herself as a social force, and many women have come to view her shop as *the one* to buy from for formal events at the country club and the nearby Ritz Carleton Hotel.

Her part-time helpers are not only an effective marketing tool; they also serve as local fashion consultants. They help Charlene make wise purchasing decisions. They are valuable members of her team, and they are friends as well.

Now it's your turn again. Action Step 56 is to be completed once you have built your team. It's your chance to brainstorm for ways to win. Make the most of all the creative human resources you have just brought on board! Action

ACTION STEP 56

Tap your people resources by brainstorming with your team.

Before you sign a lease, go into the hole for $50 000 worth of equipment, hire a lot of people, or spend $2 000 for a six-line telephone service, get your new team together and brainstorm the organization and objectives of your new business.

A flip chart is a handy tool for keeping track of ideas. One way to begin is to ask all members of your team to write down what they believe would be good objectives to achieve business goals.

You've found some good people, and it's taken some hard work. Make that work pay off by tapping your human resources. Participation leads to commitment. You'll be surprised at how this process can be a good team builder.

If you have trouble narrowing down after the ideas start flowing, go back and review the seven-step procedure in Chapter Three.

Step 56 is a great way to end this chapter on team building, and a great way to start your new business.

In a Nutshell

This chapter starts out by helping you understand the basics of management. You will have to do some planning, starting with setting some goals for your business. Leading is a key management function and you'll have to learn how to inspire and empower your team. At the very least, you will have to be able to justify and chart your business structure. We also want you to consider the benefits of a virtual or network organization. Lastly, we want you to think about how you will control and evaluate your business. We suggest, for example, that one of the most effective strategies is to get everyone involved in evaluating their own actions against the business objectives.

Next, we want you to understand that you won't be able do everything yourself. You will need balance and a team with different skills and personalities, depending on your strengths and the needs of the business. Start by taking a look at yourself. The key here is not to clone yourself. You need to be surrounded by people who can complement your skills, strengths and weaknesses and business needs. Use the idea of balance to brainstorm your ideal team and begin scouting potential team members.

Think Points for Success

✓ People tend to "hire themselves." How many more like you can the business take?
✓ A winning team is lurking in your network.
✓ Look to your competitors and vendors for team members.
✓ Your company is *people*.
✓ Balance the people on your team.
✓ Have each team member write objectives for his or her responsibilities within the business.
✓ You can't grow until you have the right people.
✓ How much of your team can be built of part-timers and moonlighters?
✓ How virtual can you make your business structure?

Business Plan Building Block

GENERAL MANAGEMENT

Who's in charge? Investors or vendors are often more interested in the founders than in the business plan itself. Experience in the same type of business and past business successes are powerful positive components of the plan. Focus on responsibility and authority.

A paragraph or two may be sufficient for each key founder. If retail experience is lacking, list consultants or committed strategic partners who can balance the management team. An organizational chart might be included.

MANAGEMENT AND OWNERSHIP

Name the key players and include their résumés, focussing on their contribution to your business and how they will give you a competitive edge. Save the full-blown résumés of the management team members for the appendix in the back of the plan.

The lender, vendor, or venture capital firm weighs the founding team as one of the most important factors. Present balance and diversity with a history of past achievement. It is here where you would explain your business form (incorporation, partnership, limited liability company, sole proprietorship, or co-operative). If you have more than two people on the team, include an organizational chart.

Your turn again: Who are the players in your business and what role will each play?

If this is a one- or two-person venture, list consultants, advisory board members, or strategic partners who can contribute experience or special skills.

HUMAN RESOURCE PLAN

1. Type of workers needed. Include seasonal or part-time workers

2. Compensation, commissions, bonuses, profit sharing

3. Provincial and federal compliance requirements

4. Performance standards, training, and retraining

ACTION STEP REVIEW

53 Understand your personal strengths and weaknesses

54 Consider a virtual team.

55 Find a mentor.

56 Tap your people resources by brainstorming with your team.

5. Workers' compensation and insurance cost

6. Employee handbook (look for professional help)

7. Union contracts

8. Professional certifications

Checklist Questions and Actions to Develop Your Business Plan

BUILDING AND MANAGING A WINNING TEAM

- ❑ What major human resource issues does your business face, and how do you plan to address these issues?
- ❑ Have you included an employment schedule in your appendix and corresponding wage costs for your staff and yourself?
- ❑ Have you allowed for benefits? At a minimum to comply with legal statutory requirements, you need to consider at least 20 percent of your wage and salary costs for benefits.
- ❑ Do you have job descriptions in place and plans to conduct an annual performance appraisal?
- ❑ Do your wage rates fit within the industry norm, and do you pay more than the industry if you are planning to be a "top draw" company?
- ❑ Outline your leadership style, and your strengths and weaknesses as an entrepreneur.
- ❑ How might a "virtual organization" work for you?
- ❑ If you are starting out just with yourself, at what point in sales or other volume indicator will you add a second or a third person?

NOTES

1. Adapted from Rick Spence, *Secrets of Success from Canada's Fastest-Growing Companies* (Toronto: John Wiley & Sons Canada, Ltd., 1997), pp. 98–99. Reprinted by permission of the author.

2. Excerpted from J. Howell and B. Avolio, "The Leverage of Leadership," *The Globe and Mail*, May 15, 1998, p. C1. © 1998 Ivey Management Services. One-time permission to reproduce granted by Ivey Management Services (August 17, 1998).
3. Peter Urs Bender, *Leadership from Within* (Toronto: Stoddart Publishing, 1997), p. 23. Reprinted by permission of Stoddart Publishing Co. Limited, Toronto, Ontario.
4. Adapted from Steven L. Goldman, Roger N. Nagel, and Kenneth Preiss, *Agile Competitors and Virtual Organizations* (New York: Van Nostrand Reinholdt, 1995).
5. Spence, *Secrets of Success from Canada's Fastest-Growing Companies*, pp. 99–100.
6. We encourage you to check out Canadian Business Networks Coalition (CBNC), *How to Network Book: A Practical Guide for Successful Strategic Alliances*. Internet address: <http://strategis.ic.gc.ca/SSG/mi03266e.html>.
7. Spence, *Secrets of Success from Canada's Fastest-Growing Companies*, p. 102.
8. Canadian Youth Business Foundation, Internet address: <http://www.cybf.ca/frames/index.htm>.
9. Cited in Bruce Little, "Statistics Belie Perception of Less Help for the Needy, Part II," *Globe and Mail*, January 20, 1994, pp. A1, A6.

OTHER REFERENCES

Addresso, Patricia J. *Get to Know Your Employees Before You Manage Them*. New York: AMACOM, 1996.

Bendaly, Leslie. *Games Teams Play*. Whitby, ON: McGraw-Hill Ryerson Ltd., 1996.

Bendaly, Leslie. *Organization 2000: The Essential Guide for Companies and Teams in the New Economy*. Toronto: HarperCollins, 1996.

Canadian Business Networks Coalition (CBNC). *How to Network Book: A Practical Guide for Successful Strategic Alliances*. CBNC, 1997.

Kotter, John P. *Leading Change*. Boston, MA: Harvard Business School Press, 1996.

Moss, Kanter Rosabeth, *On the Frontiers of Management*. Boston, MA: Harvard Business School Press, 1997.

Appendix 12.1

The Personality Analysis

Take a few minutes to do the following simple self-assessment. You will learn some fascinating things about yourself in the process. You may also want to compare yourself to others you know — a significant other, your children, or your co-workers.

In the following lists, underline those words (or phrases) that describe you best in a *business* or *work situation*. Total your score for each group of words.

GROUP

A Reserved, uncommunicative, cool, cautious, guarded, seems difficult to get to know, demanding of self, disciplined attitudes, formal speech, rational decision-making, strict, impersonal, businesslike, disciplined about time, uses facts, formal dress, measured actions.

Total score: ________

B Take-charge attitude, directive, tends to use power, fast actions, risk-taker, competitive, aggressive, strong opinions, excitable, takes social initiative, makes statements, loud voice, quick pace, expressive voice, firm handshake, clear idea of needs, initiator.

Total score: ________

C Communicative, open, warm, approachable, friendly, fluid attitudes, informal speech, undisciplined about time, easy-going with self, impulsive, informal dress, dramatic opinions, uses opinions, permissive, emotional decision-making, seems easy to get to know, personal.

Total score: ________

D Slow pace, flat voice, soft-spoken, helper, unclear about what is needed, moderate opinions, calm, asks questions, tends to avoid use of power, indifferent handshake, deliberate actions, lets others take social initiative, risk-avoider, quiet, go-along attitude, supportive, co-operative.

Total score: ________

Write your total scores below:

A = ________ C = ________

B = ________ D = ________

Next, determine which groups are larger and by how much:

A vs. C: Which is larger? ________

By how many points? ________

B vs. D: Which is larger? ________

By how many points? ________

Filling in the Personality Grid

Now mark your results on the grid below:

To determine where you fit on the vertical axis, look at your A vs. C result. For example:

If A was larger than C by 6 points, put a dot (•) at **A-6**.
If C was larger than A by 5 points, put a dot (•) at **C-5**.
If A and C are equal, put a dot (•) at "0," in the centre of the grid.

To find your place on the horizontal axis, use your B vs. D result.

If B was larger than D by 4 points, put a dot (•) at **B-4**.
If D was larger than B by 7 points, put a dot (•) at **D-7**.
If B and D are equal, put a dot (•) at "0," in the centre of the grid.

In the grid below, draw an X where lines extending from your two points meet (as shown in the sample). The quadrant you're in indicates your personality type.*

Sample Grid

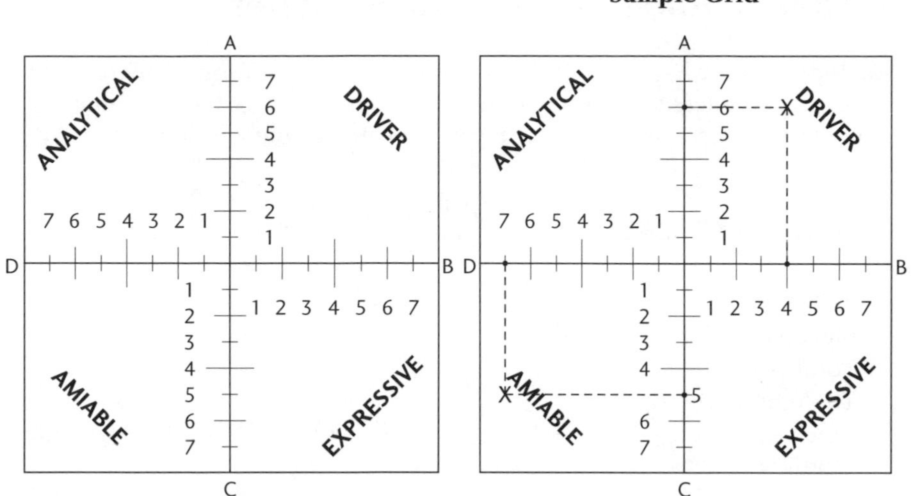

This sample grid shows the results for two different people: one is called a driver; the other is amiable.

Interpreting Your Results

Now that you know where you fit, let's find out what it means!

The following words describe each of the personality types. Read those that apply to you, and see how these words fit your image of your own personality. Then ask others what they think. It helps to get different perspectives.

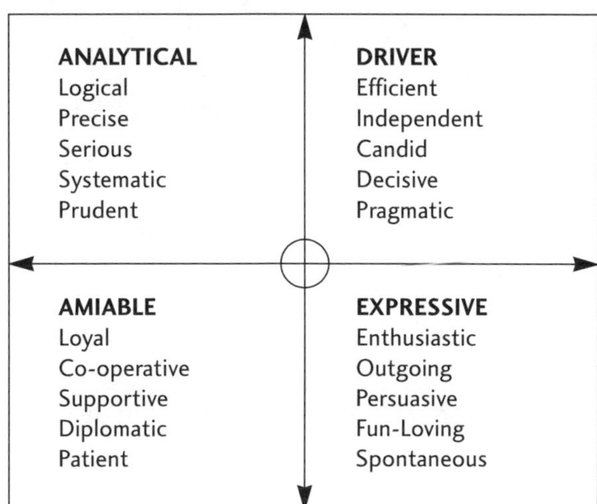

After considering your own personality, look at people around you. What personality types do they exhibit?

*These four personality types are adapted from *Personality Styles and Effective Performance*, by David W. Merrill and Roger H. Reid.

Remember that there is no right or wrong personality type. Different types simply think and act in different ways.

Understanding the Personality Types

Each personality has different needs, values, and motivations. Different levels of assertiveness and responsiveness. Here are some general insights into each type — and some tips to help you get through life a little more easily.

THE ANALYTICAL

Also known as:

Melancholic
Thinker
Thought Man
Processor
Cognitive

The analytical person:

- wants to know "how" things work
- wants to be accurate, and to have accuracy from others
- values numbers, statistics, ideas
- loves details.

Analyticals fear being embarrassed or losing face. They also tend to be introverted and to hide their emotions from others.

THE AMIABLE

Also known as:

Phlegmatic
Feeler
People Man
Helper
Interpersonal

The amiable person:

- wants to know "why?" (e.g., Why am I doing this?)
- wants to build relationships
- loves to give others support and attention
- values suggestions from others.

Amiables fear losing trust or having disagreements with others. While somewhat introverted, they also tend to display their emotions.

THE DRIVER

Also known as:

Choleric
Director
Action Man
Boss
Behavioural

The driver:

- wants to know "what" (What will this do for me/the firm?)
- wants to save time
- values results
- loves being in control, in charge, doing things his or her own way.

Drivers fear giving up control. They tend to be extroverts, but do not like showing their emotions to others.

THE EXPRESSIVE

Also known as:

Sanguine
Intuitive
Front Man
Impulsive
Affective

The expressive person:

- wants to know "who" (Who else is involved; who else have you worked for?)
- values appreciation, applause, a pat on the back
- loves social situations and parties
- likes to inspire others.

Expressives fear being rejected. They are extroverts and usually show their emotions to others.

Source: Peter Urs Bender, *Leadership from Within* (Toronto: Stoddart Publishing, 1997), pp. 60–65. Reprinted by permission of Stoddart Publishing Co. Limited, Toronto, Ontario.

thirteen

Buying a Business

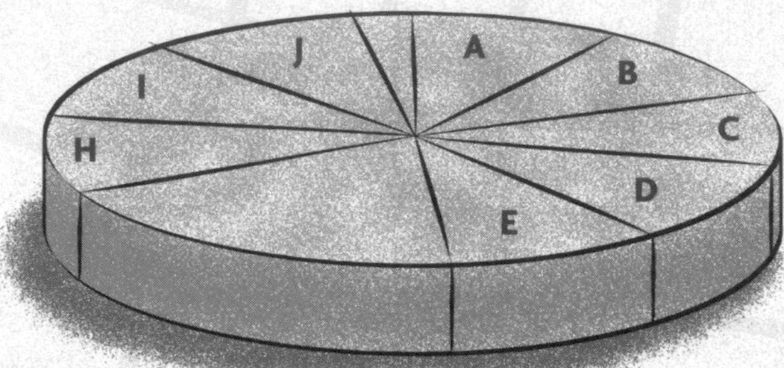

BUSINESS PLAN BUILDING BLOCK

This chapter will help you investigate the advantages and pitfalls of buying a business.

Figure 13.1 Chapter Thirteen investigates the alternative of buying an existing business.

LEARNING OPPORTUNITIES

After reading this chapter, you should be able to:

- Evaluate objectively businesses that are for sale.
- Understand the pros and cons of purchasing an ongoing business.
- Assess the market value of an ongoing business.
- Recognize when you need professional help.
- Decide whether it is better for you to buy an ongoing business or to begin from scratch.

Ben and Sally Raymundo bought a women's sportswear store in a thriving community about two kilometres from a regional shopping mall. They learned too late that the seller had a more profitable store in another part of the county and that she had used that store's records to misrepresent the store they bought. Here are the particulars:

1. The seller moved the cash registers from the higher-volume store to the store she wanted to sell so that the store's sales were greatly inflated.
2. The price was fixed at inventory plus $10 000 for good will. This seemed a bargain for a store whose cash register records showed it was grossing $300 000 per year at a 40 percent average gross margin.
3. Ben and Sally paid full wholesale value ($60 000) for goods that had been shipped there from the other store. The goods were already shopworn and out of date and eventually had to be marked down to less than $20 000.
4. Ben and Sally assumed the remainder of an iron-clad lease at $5 000 per month, and the landlord made them sign a personal guarantee that pledged their home as security on the lease.
5. The location proved to be a dead foot-traffic location in a marginally successful centre.

Fortunately, Ben had kept his regular job. Sally worked at selling off the unwanted inventory and replaced it with more salable stock. They spent another $50 000 for advertising during the twelve months they stayed in business. It was another year before the landlord found a new tenant and Ben and Sally could get out of the lease.

ACTION STEP PREVIEW

57 Prepare a letter of inquiry.
58 Study a business from the outside.
59 Study a business inside out.
60 Probe the depths of ill will.

In this chapter, you'll learn some ways to evaluate businesses that are up for sale. Although we focus on ongoing, independent operations, many of the tactics are the same for evaluating franchise opportunities. We'll discuss franchising more specifically in Chapter Fourteen.

When you buy an ongoing business, you're buying an income stream. You may also be buying inventory, location, good will, and an agreement that the sellers will not compete with you. When you buy a franchise, you're primarily buying the right to use a name. In addition, you may also be buying a training program, a business plan, advertising assistance, lease negotiation assistance, and purchasing advantages.

You should explore businesses for sale whether you're serious about buying or not. By now, you're far enough along on your quest to sense an understanding of the marketplace. Talking to sellers is just one more step in your education in entrepreneurship.

Why Buy an Ongoing Business?

The overwhelming reason for buying an ongoing business is *money*, primarily the income stream, which makes it a good deal. If you do your research and strike a good deal, you can start making money the day you take over an ongoing business. Since most start-ups must plug along for months (even years) before showing a profit, it's smart to consider the business ownership option.

If you find a "hungry seller," you should be able to negotiate good terms. You might get into the business for very little cash up front, and you might also get a good deal on the fixtures and equipment.

HOW TO BUY AND HOW NOT TO BUY

Smart buyers scrutinize everything about a business with microscope, Geiger counter, computer analysis, clipboard, and sage advice from business gurus. They do not plunge into a business for emotional reasons. For example, you may have eaten lunch around the corner at Millie's Cafeteria with your pals for years, and when the place goes up for sale, nostalgia may make you want to write out a cheque for it on the spot. That would be a wrong reason to buy. Don't buy a business that way.

Every business in the country is for sale sometime. Deals are like planes. If you miss one, another will be along soon.

Good buys are always available to the informed and careful buyer, but they may be difficult to discover. Seeking the right business to buy is much like an employment search: the best deals are seldom advertised. In contrast, the worst business opportunities are advertised widely, usually in the classified sections of newspapers. When you see several ads for a particular type of business, you know where the unhappy businesspeople are.

Running your own ad can be a good idea, however. A man ran this ad in the business section (not the classifieds) of a large-circulation Toronto newspaper:

Sold out at 30. Now I'm tired of retirement and ready to start again. Want to buy a business with over $1 million in annual sales. Write me at Box XXXX. H. G.

ACTION STEP 57

Prepare a letter of inquiry.
Write a form letter of inquiry and send it to three to five firms that you may be interested in buying. Keep it open-ended; let them make the disclosures.

It's best to learn about businesses for sale by networking, but you can find some of the most eager sellers by their advertising in the newspaper classified section.

Leave your chequebook right where it is for now. This Action Step will cost you practically nothing. The goal is to learn what's out there and how sellers talk about their businesses.

H. G. received more than 100 replies, and he says that reading the proposals was one of the most educational and entertaining experiences he's ever had. Five of them looked like good deals, but only one fit his talents and interests. After three months of investigation, he decided he would rather start his next venture from scratch. (The firm he almost bought was a beer distributorship whose supplier went out of business the following year. Perhaps the seller knew something.)

GETTING THE WORD OUT

Once you're ready to look for a business to buy, you'll need to learn what's for sale. These tips will help you do that:

1. Spread the word that you are a potential buyer.
2. Contact everyone you can in your chosen industry — manufacturers, resellers, agents, dealers, trade associations, and so on: Let them know you are looking.
3. Ask your network of bankers, lawyers, CAs, CMAs, and community leaders to help you in your search.
4. Advertise your needs in trade journals.
5. Check out the Internet. Strategis would be a good place to start. Here, the "Canadian Company Capabilities" link, for example, will help you connect to buyers and sellers across Canada and around the world.
6. Send letters of inquiry to potential sellers. (See Action Step 57.)
7. Knock on doors.
8. Check with business-opportunities brokers.
9. Talk with firms that deal in mergers and acquisitions.
10. Don't allow yourself to be rushed; time is your ally, and the deals will get better.

Action Step 57 will help you get the word out. It should be quite interesting to read the letters you receive in response to your form letter.

Investigate the Business from the Outside

Once you've found a business that looks promising, check it out in every detail. After analyzing it from the outside, you'll be ready to move inside, to evaluate the financial records and talk to the owner and attempt to learn the real reasons he or she is selling. But the first step is to get your telescope and your telephoto camera and gather as much information as you can from the exterior. In the opening vignette of this chapter, Ben and Sally Raymundo didn't do this, and they learned about fraud the hard way.

LEARN FROM OTHERS' MISTAKES

What could Ben and Sally have done to avoid their mistake? Many things. They could have asked the mall merchants how well the shopping centre was doing. They could have spent some time observing the store and the shopping mall before they committed. They could have insisted that Sally be allowed to work in the store prior to or during the escrow period, with a clause that would have allowed them to bail out.

Ben and Sally were honest, hard-working people who took the seller at face value. This was a huge error. A talk with suppliers might have uncovered the seller's fraud. They are now suing, and the lawyer they have hired could have helped them before they purchased the business. It's only going to get more expensive for them, and their chance of recovery is slim.

Some sellers don't count the value of their own time as a cost of doing business. This makes the firm show an inflated return on investment (ROI). Let's say such a firm earns $60 000 per year and has an inventory of $100 000. This could be a bad buy if the seller, her spouse, and their two children work a total of 200 hours per week and if a $100 000 investment could earn 8 percent or more per year in high-yield bonds.

Look at each deal from the viewpoint of what it would cost to hire a competent manager and staff at market wage rates. In this case, let's suppose you had to pay $40 000 a year for a manager, $30 000 a year for an assistant, and $30 000 a year for two hourly employees. You would have spent $80 000 and lost the opportunity to earn another $8 000 on your investment. Yes, this would be a "no-brainer," but a lot of businesses are bought with even less going for them.

It's time now to go out and investigate a business on your own. Remember what you've learned from Ben and Sally's bad experience, and take along your new eyes and your camera. You'll be surprised how much there is to see. Action Step 58 tells you how to do it.

ACTION STEP 58

Study a business from the outside.

Let's say you've got your eye on a business you think is a real money machine. What can you do to find out more about it without tipping your hand and driving up the asking price?

1. Make sure the business fits into the framework of your industry overview. You want a business that's in the sunrise phase, not the sunset phase, of the life cycle.
2. Diagram the area. What's the location and how does the area fit into the city/regional planning for the future? What is the life-cycle stage of the community? Where is the traffic flow? Is there good access? How far will your TC have to walk? Is parking adequate? Is the parking lot a drop off point for car poolers?
3. Take some photographs of the exterior. Analyze them carefully. Is the building in good repair? What are the customers wearing, driving, and buying? What can you deduce about their lifestyle? Take photographs on different days and at different times of day.
4. Ask around. Interview the neighbours and the customers. What do the neighbours know about the business? Will the neighbours help draw TCs to your business?

   Be up-front with the seller's customers, since they may soon be your customers. What do they like about the store? Is the service good? What changes would they recommend? What services or products would they like to see added? Where else do they go for similar products or services?
5. Check out future competition. Do you want to be close to competitors, or do you want to be kilometres away? Could a competitor move in next door the day after you move in?

Studying the business from the outside will tell you whether you should go inside and probe more deeply.

KNOW WHEN YOU NEED OUTSIDE HELP

We've already discussed the need for a team of small business gurus to help you realize your dream of small business ownership. When you evaluate small business for purchase, however, you may need a special kind of outside help. If you have any lingering doubts about the business you are researching, you may need the perspective of someone who is more objective than one of your team players. If you're not the Sherlock Holmes type yourself, hire someone who is. Your dream may be shattered by this kind of investigation, but you'll save money in the long run.

Here's Georgia's story, worth taking a lesson from.

My husband, Fred, and I wanted to have a business of our own. We both loved sports, so we decided to look around for a sporting goods store.

We found the perfect store, The Sports Factory, by networking with our sports-minded friends. It was located a block from a complex of tennis courts, three blocks from a new racquetball club, and half a kilometre from a park where volleyball tournaments are held every other month.

An accountant friend checked over the books and said they looked perfect. "Great P and L," he said, "and excellent accounting ratios. If you get the right terms, you could clear 30 Gs every quarter, and *that's* only the beginning. This buy doesn't even advertise."

We learned that the owner wanted to sell the store because he was tired of it — the long hours, being tied down, and so on. He'd been doing that for a dozen years.

But I wasn't so sure. I sensed we needed help — some sort of Sam Spade of the business world — but Fred was in a hurry to close the deal. I knew Fred was unhappy in his job, but half the money we were going to invest was mine, and I felt something was not quite right. Frankly, the owner of The Sports Factory didn't look all that tired to me.

So I asked around — networking again — and I located a community college professor who knew a lot about small business and had written a book about going into small business. I called him, and he listened very patiently when I told him our story. He said he'd be glad to check things out for us for a small fee. I told him to go ahead, but I didn't tell Fred about it.

Two days later, Harry, my marketplace detective called and said he had some news.

"Oh?" I said. "So soon?"

"Yes. Do you remember seeing a bulldozer working across the street from The Sports Factory?"

"No, I don't. *What* bulldozer?"

"It started grading last week. Right across the street. I talked to the driver on his lunch break. It seems a developer is putting in a seven-store complex, and one of the stores is going to be a discount sporting goods store." Harry paused.

"Oh, no," I said. "Are you sure?"

He explained that the store going in was part of a monster chain. I could see that we would have a hard time competing with them. I asked him if the owner knew, and if maybe that's why he was so "tired."

"Yes," Harry said, "I double-checked at the city planning office where building permits are issued." And he paused again.

I was having trouble catching my breath. "Could I get this in writing," I asked, "so that I can show my husband? He likes everything documented."

Harry chuckled. "No problem," he said. "I'll e-mail it to you tomorrow. Let me know what you decide, okay?"

"Don't worry," I said. "And thank you very much."

This marketplace detective work cost us $475, but it saved us thousands of dollars and years of heartache. Armed with what we learned through that experience, we examined almost a hundred businesses before we found the right one for us. It pays to investigate.

Georgia and Fred came very close to buying the wrong business. The outsider's perspective helped them avoid making a terrible mistake. Now it's time to get some inside perspectives.

Investigate the Business from the Inside

Once you've learned all you can from the outside, it's time to cross the threshold for a look at the interior. This is an important, time-consuming process, and it's an important milestone in your quest. Action Step 59 will help you.

There are two ways to get inside the business: you can either contact the owner yourself, or you can get assistance from a business-opportunity broker. We recommend that you use a broker because brokers have expertise and detailed knowledge in business opportunities. You can locate them in the Yellow Pages under Real Estate or Business Brokers and in the newspaper classifieds.

Call a broker to learn whether they have any listings in your area of interest. If so, check out the ones that appear interesting. Be prepared for disappointment.

You will probably look at a number of businesses before you find anything close to your requirements. Nevertheless, you will learn a lot from the experience. Make sure you're clear on your business vision before you start. It is all too easy to let your emotions control your decision.

DEALING WITH BROKERS

Business-opportunity brokers are active in most large cities, and they often play an important role in matching up sellers with buyers. Their level of competency ranges from specialists who know as much about fast-food franchises like McDonald's, to part-timers who know so little about business that they will only waste your time. A good broker can save you time and be very helpful in playing a third-party role in negotiations.

A broker has a responsibility to represent the seller and is not paid unless he or she sells something. Typically, the broker's commission is around 10 percent, but it's less on bigger deals, and everything is open to negotiation.

Some sellers list with brokers because they do not want it generally known (to their customers, employees, and competitors) that they want to sell their business. Most sellers who list with brokers, however, do so out of desperation because they've already tried to sell their business to everyone they know. Probably nine out of ten fall into this category.

Spending time with a skilled broker can be a fascinating educational experience. If you want a particular type of business and are able to examine a half dozen that are on the market, you will probably end up with a better grasp of the business than the owners. Network your business contacts to locate a competent broker. Ask brokers for referrals from their former clients. And, as we've said so many times before, leave your chequebook at home. Don't let anyone rush you.

ACTION STEP 59

Study a business inside out.
Looking at a business from the inside enables you to determine its real worth and to see what it would be like to own it. Make an appointment (or have a business-opportunity broker arrange it) to take a serious inside look at the business you think you want to buy. Before you go, review everything we've explained in this section and write down a list of things you hope to learn while you're there. Don't allow anyone to rush you. Leave the chequebook at home; this fun is free.

BUSINESS-OPPORTUNITY BROKER
a real estate broker or consultant who specializes in representing people who want to sell businesses

HOW TO LOOK AT THE INSIDE OF A BUSINESS

Once you have your foot in the door and have established yourself as a potential buyer, you will be able to study the inner workings of the business. Take full advantage of this opportunity.

Study the Financial History What you need to learn from the financial history is where the money comes from and where it goes. Ask to see all financial records (balance sheet, income statement, and bank statement for at least five years back if they're available, and take your time studying them. If you don't understand financial records, hire someone who does. Your aim in buying an ongoing business is to step into an income stream. The financial records give a picture of that stream.

Look at the history of cash flow, profit and loss, and accounts receivable. If the seller has a stack of accounts receivable a foot high, remember that:

- after three months, the value of a current-accounts dollar will have shrunk to 90 cents;
- after six months, it will be worth 50 cents;
- after a year, it will be worth 30 cents.

Like an auditor, review every receipt you can find. If a tavern owner tells you she sells 30–40 kegs of beer per week, ask to see the receipts from the suppliers. If none is offered, ask permission to contact the suppliers for records of shipment. Make her prove to you that she has bought from suppliers. You can then accurately measure sales. If the seller won't co-operate, walk away; she's hiding something.

Evaluate closely any personal expenses that are being charged to the business. (Your accountant could help you determine a course of action that will keep you out of trouble.) This allows you to get a clearer picture of the firm's true profits. Also, compare the financial results to industry standards, such as information prepared by the Robert Morris Annual Financial Statements for your industry.

It's also a good idea to look at cancelled cheques, income tax returns, and the amount of salary the seller has been paying herself. If your seller was stingy with her own salary, decide whether you could live on that amount.

Tip: You can use the seller's accounts receivable as a point for negotiation, but don't take over the job of collecting them.

Compare What Your Money Could Do Elsewhere How much money would you be putting into the business? How long would it take you to make it back? Have you figured in your time?

Let's say you would need to put $50 000 into this business, and that the business will give you a 33.3 percent return, which is full payback in three years. Are there other investments you could make that would yield the same amount on your $50 000?

If you will be working in the business, you need to add in the cost of your time; say that's $25 000 per year (your present salary) over the three-year period, or $75 000 (assuming no raises). In three years, the business would need to return $125 000 after expenses and taxes in order to cover the risks involved with your $50 000 investment and to compensate you for the loss of $25 000 in annual salary.

TANGIBLE ASSETS
things your business owns that you can see and touch, such as real estate, equipment, and inventory

Evaluate the Tangible Assets, the Things You Can See and Touch If the numbers look good, move on to assess the value of everything you can touch, specifically the real estate, the equipment and fixtures, and the inventory.

- *Real estate.* Get an outside, professional appraisal of the building and the land. It may be worth more as vacant land than as a business.
- *Equipment and fixtures.* You can get a good idea of current values by asking equipment dealers and reading the want ads. Scour your area for the best deals, because you don't want to tie up too much capital in equipment that's outmoded or about to come apart. Suppliers have lots of leads on used equipment, so check with them. If you're not an expert in the equipment field, get help from someone who is. Find out the maintenance costs in the last two years.

INVENTORY
items carried in stock and are intended for sale

- *Inventory.* Count the **inventory** yourself, and make sure the boxes are packed with what you think they are. Make certain you specify the exact contents of shelves and cabinets in the purchase agreement. Don't get careless and write in something vague like "All shelves are to be filled." Specify what goes on the shelves. More importantly, find out if the inventory is salable, and if the styles and models of the stock are still valid. Don't accept old stock unless at a very low discount.

  Once you've made your count, contact suppliers to learn the current prices.

  If you find merchandise that is damaged, out of date, out of style, soiled, worn, or not ready to sell as is, don't pay full price for it. Negotiate. This is sacrifice merchandise and it should have a sacrifice price tag.

  Talk to insiders. There's no substitute for inside information. Every detective takes it seriously.
- *Bankers.* It is a must to discuss business with your banker and, ideally, with the current owner's banker. The latter will be limited on what he or she can say, but your banker will be a good help in analyzing the financial statements.

- *Suppliers.* Will suppliers agree to keep supplying you? Are there past difficulties between seller and supplier that you would inherit as the new owner? Remember, you're dependent on your suppliers. How do suppliers evaluate the business?
- *Employees.* Talk to the key employees early. In small business, success can rest on the shoulders of one or two persons, and you don't want them to walk out the day you sign the papers.
- *Competitors.* Identify the major competitors and interview them to learn what goes on from their perspective. You need to understand the industry fully. Expect some bias, but watch for a pattern to develop. (Chapter Five, you'll remember, tells how to identify the competitors.)

Get a Non-competition Covenant Once you buy a business, you don't want the seller to set up the same kind of business across the street. Customers are hard to come by, and you don't want to pay for them and have them spirited away by a cagey seller. So get an agreement, in writing, that the seller will not set up in competition with you — or work for a competitor, or help a friend or relative set up a competitive business — for the next five years. You will need a lawyer to prepare such an agreement. Be sure to specify the exact amount you're paying for the non-competition covenant. That way, Revenue Canada will allow you to deduct it against income over the life of the covenant.

Analyze the Seller's Motives People have all kinds of reasons for selling their business. Some of these reasons favour the buyer, others favour the seller.

Here are some reasons for selling that can favour the buyer:

1. retirement, ill health
2. too busy to manage, seller has other investments
3. divorce, family problems
4. disgruntled partners
5. expanded too fast, out of cash
6. poor management
7. burned out, lost interest

These reasons for selling will favour the seller (Buyer, beware!):

1. local economy in a decline
2. specific industry declining
3. intense competition
4. high insurance costs
5. increasing litigation
6. skyrocketing rents
7. technological obsolescence
8. problems with suppliers
9. high crime location
10. lease not being renewed
11. location in a decline

Examine the Asking Price Many sellers view selling their firms as they would view selling their children; that is, they are emotionally attached to the business and they overvalue its worth. Pride also plays a role; they might want to tell their friends that they started from scratch and sold out for a million. If you run into irrational and emotional obstacles, walk away or counter with unreasonable terms — such as \$100 down and 10 percent of the net profits for the next four years, up to \$1 million.

Some industries have rule-of-thumb benchmarks for pricing. For example, a service firm might be priced at six to twelve months of its total revenue. Such pricing formulas are often unwise. The only formula that makes sense is the return on your investment minus the value of your management time:

Return on Investment (ROI) = (Hours spent × Value of your time per hour)

If you can earn 10 percent without sweating on high-grade bonds, you should earn at least a 30 percent return on a business that will make you sweat.

PRICE/EARNING (P/E) RATIO
a measure of the value of a share of common stock; the ratio of its market price to its earnings per share

It can be useful to consult the newspaper financial pages to learn the **price-to-earning (P/E) ratios** of publicly traded firms. Firms whose P/E ratios are low (the stock price is less than 10 times its earnings) are not regarded as growth opportunities by sophisticated investors. Firms with above-average P/E ratios (price is more than 25 times its earnings) are regarded as having above-average growth potential. Thus, you should be willing to pay a higher price for a firm with above-average growth potential than for one that is declining. In fact, you should not buy a declining business unless you think you can either purchase it very inexpensively and turn it around or dispose of its assets at a profit.

Negotiate the Value of Good Will If the firm has a strong customer base with deeply ingrained purchasing habits, this has value. It takes a while for any start-up to build a client base, and the wait for profitability can be costly.

Some firms have built up a great deal of ill will — customers who have vowed never to trade with them again. A large proportion of the businesses on the market have this problem. If the amount of ill will is great, the business will have little value; it may be that *any* price would be too high.

GOOD WILL
an invisible commodity used by sellers to increase the asking price for a business; technically, good will is the difference between the assets and liabilities of a business

A smart seller will ask you to pay something for **good will**. You'll therefore need to play detective and find out how much good will there is and where it is. For example, consider the seller who has extended credit loosely. Customers are responding, but there's no cash in the bank. If you were to continue that policy and keep granting easy credit, you could be in the red in a couple of months. Or maybe the seller is one of those very special people who is loved by everyone and will take the good will with him — like a halo — when he walks out the door.

So negotiate.

Let's say the asking price for the business you'd like to buy is $145 000 and that its tangible assets (equipment, inventory, and so on) are worth $95 000. In other words, the seller is trying to charge you $50 000 for good will. Before you negotiate, do these things:

1. Compare the good will you're being asked to buy to the good will of a similar business on the market.
2. Figure out how long it would take you to pay that amount. Remember, good will is tangible; you'll be unhappy if it takes you years to pay for it. Even the most cheerful good will comes out of profit.
3. Estimate how much you could make if you invested that $50 000 in a high-yield security.
4. How long would it take you to reach the same level of profitability, starting from scratch?

This gives you a context in which to judge the seller's assessment of the value of good will, and you can use the hard data you have generated to negotiate a realistic — and more favourable — price.

BULK SALES ESCROW
an examination process intended to protect buyers from unknown liabilities

Learn Whether Bulk Sales Escrow Is Needed You need to know whether any inventory you would buy is tied up by creditors. If it is, the instrument you'll use to cut those strings is a bulk sales transfer, a process that will transfer the goods from the seller to you through a qualified third party.

ESCROW COMPANY
a neutral third party that holds deposits and deeds until all agreed-upon conditions are met

If there are no claims by creditors, the transfer of inventory should go smoothly. If there are claims, you'll want to be protected by law. Either consult a lawyer who has experience in making bulk sales transfers, or get an **escrow company** to act as the neutral party in the transfer. Ask your banker or accountant to recommend one. Try to find one that specializes in bulk sales escrow.

An Earn-Out Success Story

Sam Wilson had held several key executive positions in large manufacturing firms after receiving his MBA from Western University in the early 1980s. His last position was as vice-president of a medium-size firm with branch offices throughout North America. Sam got squeezed out when a large conglomerate purchased the firm and moved the headquarters to London.

After doing some freelance management consulting, Sam arranged to purchase an executive search firm that specialized in finding engineering talent in the aerospace industry. Buying the business seemed like a good idea to Sam because the business had been profitable for more than 20 years. The key personnel agreed to stay with the firm. It had loyal customers, a solid reputation, and Sam knew it would take him years to build a similar business from scratch, even though he understood the business.

He purchased the business for no cash down and agreed to pay off the entire purchase price from the earnings over the next five years. (This is called an earn out.) The seller was an older man who had known Sam's reputation as a winner. Sam was one of the few prospective buyers who were willing to pay full price for the business and seemed qualified to continue the growth of the firm.

Buying a business on an earn-out basis is an option only if the seller has great confidence in the buyer's skills and knowledge of the business. Thus, the burden of convincing the seller to agree to such terms is on the buyer. It's necessary to show the seller that the business will continue to show a profit.

The Decision to Buy

Even if you think you're ready to make your decision, don't do it — not yet. Read the checklist in Box 13.1 first. It reminds you of 32 important details you might have overlooked. Even if you know you've found your dream business, complete this checklist before you sign the papers.

PREPARE FOR THE NEGOTIATIONS

Let's say you know you're ready to buy. You've raised the money, and the numbers say you can't lose, so you're ready to start negotiating. (If you're an experienced entrepreneur, you already know how to negotiate. If not, some good books on the fine art of haggling are listed in the references section at the end of this chapter.)

We suggest two things about negotiations. First, when it comes time to talk meaningful numbers, the most important area to concentrate on is *terms*, not asking price. Favourable terms will give you the cash flow you need to survive the first year and then move from survival into success. Unfavourable terms can torpedo your chances for success, even when the total asking price is well below market value.

Second, when the seller brings up the subject of good will, be ready for it. Good will is a "slippery" commodity; it can make the asking price soar. It's

ACTION STEP 60

Probe the depths of ill will.

How many products have you vowed never to use again? How many places of business have you vowed never to patronize again? Why?

Make a list of the products and services you won't buy or use again. Next to each item, write the reason. Does it make you sick? Does it offend your sensibilities? Was the service awful?

After you've completed your list, ask your friends what their negative feelings about particular businesses are. Take notes.

Study the two lists you've made. What are the common components of ill will? How long does ill will last? Is there a remedy for it, or is a business plagued by ill will doomed forever?

Now turn your attention to the business you want to buy. Survey your target customers. How do they feel about the business? You need to learn as much as you can about any ill will that exists toward the business.

Have fun with this step, but take it seriously — and think about the nature of ill will when your seller starts asking you to pay for good will.

Box 13.1 The Before-You-Buy Checklist

- ❑ How long do you plan to own this business?
- ❑ How old is this business? Can you sketch its history?
- ❑ Is this business in the embryonic stage, the growth stage, the mature stage, or the decline stage?
- ❑ Has your accountant reviewed the books and made a sales projection for you?
- ❑ How long will it take for this business to show a complete recovery on your investment?
- ❑ What reasons does the owner give for selling?
- ❑ Will the owner let you see bank deposit records? (If not, why not?)
- ❑ Have you calculated utility costs for the first three to five years?
- ❑ What does a review of tax records tell you?
- ❑ How complete is the insurance coverage?
- ❑ How old are the receivables? (Remember, age decreases their value.)
- ❑ What is the seller paying himself or herself? Is it low or high?
- ❑ Have you interviewed your prospective landlord?
- ❑ What happens when a new tenant takes over the lease?
- ❑ Have you made checks on the currency of the customer lists?
- ❑ Who are your top 20 customers? Your top 50?
- ❑ Is the seller locked into one to three major customers who control the business?
- ❑ How well is the business using technology, computerized systems, and business management?
- ❑ Are you buying inventory? What is the seller asking?
- ❑ Have you checked the value of the equipment against the price of used equipment from another source?
- ❑ To whom does your seller owe money?
- ❑ Has your lawyer checked for liens on the seller's equipment?
- ❑ Do you have maintenance contracts on the equipment you're buying?
- ❑ Has your lawyer or escrow company gone through bulk sales escrow?
- ❑ Have you made certain that:
  - you're getting all brand names, logos, trademarks, and so on that you need?
  - the seller has signed a non-competition covenant?
  - the key lines of supply will stay intact when you take over?
  - the key employees will stay?
  - the seller isn't leaving because of stiff competition?
  - you aren't paying for good will but taking delivery on ill will?
  - you aren't getting the best terms possible?
  - you're buying an income stream?

only natural for the seller to attempt to get as much as possible for good will. Because you know this ahead of time, you can do your homework and go in primed to deal. Action Step 60 will help you do your homework. When the seller starts talking about good will, you can flip the coin over and discuss ill will — which hangs on longer, like a cloud above the business.

PROTECT YOURSELF

Evaluate each business opportunity by the criteria we present in this chapter. When you find one you think is right for you, start negotiating. Your goal is the lowest possible price with the best possible terms. Start low; you can then negotiate up if necessary.

If you are asked to put down a deposit, handle it this way:

1. Deposit the money in an escrow account.
2. Include a stipulation in your offer that says the offer is *subject to your inspection and approval* of all financial records and all aspects of the business.

Doing this gives you an escape hatch so that you can get your deposit returned — and back out of the deal — if things don't look good. Also, consider working in the business for a few weeks with the option to back out if you have a change of heart.

NEGOTIATING THE PRICE

What is a fair price? Obviously, the values of the seller and of the buyer are arrived at from widely separated viewpoints.

The seller has committed considerable time and money to the business, often for less return than could have been earned elsewhere, and sees the sale as the opportunity to make up for the years of "doing without." The buyer, on the other hand, is concerned only with the present state and future potential of the business and cares little for the time and effort invested by the vendor.

The price of a business is related to the ability of that business to generate revenue. This is determined, in large part, by the assets of the business. If you are purchasing assets, the seller will usually have a spec sheet prepared, listing the assets and offering an estimate of their value. The asset value may be calculated using various formulas, including:

- Fair market value: the price of similar assets on the open market;
- Replacement value: what it would cost to replace the asset (i.e., from the original supplier);
- Liquidation value: what the asset would bring if the business were liquidated (as in a bankruptcy); or
- Book value: based on the company's balance sheet.

In that list of assets, however, good will maybe included, representing the value of intangibles, such as location, reputation, and established customer base of the business. Good will is virtually impossible to value objectively. It depends more on instinct and gut feeling than on a strict accounting formula.

The aggregated value of individual assets, however, tells only part of the story. The real value of the business depends on the income that it generates. This may not be directly related to the value of the assets, especially in service businesses. We therefore encourage you to look at the company's income history over a period of years (at least three is usual) to determine what its gross revenues, costs, and profit were. You are really buying that annual profit and one way of looking at the purchase price is in terms of a return on your investment. Start your own investigation by asking for the most recent three years of financial data. Who prepared this data? Is it part of a formal audit? Even if the statements are audited, remember that auditors depend on the paper they are given. There may be a lot hidden under formal statements certified by an accountant.

You can do your own audit by asking the seller for permission to see the actual records of the enterprise. Deposit books, invoices, repair bills, payroll slips, sales slips, and so on will tell you far more about the condition of a business than will an audited statement. You may have to sign a non-disclosure agreement to get access to this type of information, but it gives you a clear picture of the quality of the records and the controls in place to manage the business. If records are scanty and poorly kept, you may not know how much work will be involved in cleaning up the operation if you actually take it over. Adjust your offer accordingly.[1]

As a basis for opening negotiations with a vendor, you might wish to use the following formula, adapted from advice provided by the Business Development Bank of Canada. It is not intended to be an all-inclusive answer to establishing a final price, but it is a valid mathematical approach, based on available hard data, and can serve as a test of the price being asked for the business.

Since we are suggesting that the formula be used to test the asking price, you will need copies of the financial statements for the business. It is only from these figures that a valid analysis can be made.

Pricing Formula

Step 1 Calculate the tangible net worth of the business.

This is, in its simplest form, the total tangible assets (excluding good will, franchise fees, etc.) less total liabilities (both current and long term).

Step 2 Estimate the current earning power of this tangible net worth if this amount was to be invested elsewhere (stocks, bonds, term deposits).

This earning power will vary with economic trends and other factors, but should be based on current interest rates.

Step 3 Determine a reasonable annual salary that could be earned by the owner if similarly employed elsewhere.

Remember to take into consideration benefits paid by the business (automotive, insurance, pensions, etc.) in determining a comparable outside salary.

Step 4 Determine the total earning capacity of the owner that would result from the net worth invested, plus employment sources, by adding the results of steps 2 and 3.

Step 5 Calculate the average annual net profit of the business.

This average will be the total of profit from all financial statements available (before any management salaries or cash withdrawal for partners, proprietors, taxes, etc.), divided by the number of years used in the analysis. We suggest three years minimum, but preferably five years for an accurate result.

Step 6 Calculate the extra earning power of the business, by subtracting the result of step 4 from that of step 5.

This figure represents the additional money you can expect to earn if you buy the business, rather than invest an amount equal to the net worth and obtain or retain outside employment.

Step 7 Calculate the value of intangibles, by multiplying the extra earning power (step 6) by a figure that we will refer to as the development factor.

This development factor is designed to weigh such things as uniqueness of the intangibles, time needed to establish a similar business from scratch, expenses and risk of a comparable start-up, price of good will in similar firms, and so on.

If the business is well established and successful, a suggested factor of 5 or more might be used; a more moderately seasoned firm might rate a factor of 3; and a young but profitable business may rate a factor of only 1.

Step 8 Calculate the final price.

This is arrived at by adding the tangible net worth of the business (step 1) to the value of intangibles (step 7).

Here is one example of how this formula works.

Assume you are interested in purchasing the XYZ Company Limited, and the asking price is $200 000. At your request, the owners of XYZ have given you the following financial statement representing the last complete year of operation. (Note that we are using only one year's statement in this example. When using this formula for real, you should attempt to obtain statements for at least three, but preferably five years.)

XYZ Company Limited
Balance Sheet
As at Dec. 31, 19__

Assets		
Current		
Cash	$ 180	
Accounts Receivable	6 560	
Inventory	13 150	
Total Current	19 890	
Fixed		
Land	5 000	
Buildings	35 000	
Equipment	14 500	
Furniture	1 800	
Vehicles	11 500	
Less: Accumulated Depreciation	8 100	
Total Fixed	59 700	
Total Assets		$79 590

Liabilities		
Current		
Bank	$ 3 000	
Accounts Payable	6 600	
Current Portion—Long-Term	1 100	
Total Current	10 700	
Long-Term Mortgage Loan	21 500	
Equipment Loan	9 600	
Total Long-Term Liabilities	31 100	
Less: Current Portion	1 100	
Total Long-Term	30 000	
Total Liabilities	40 700	
Shareholders' Equity:		
Share Capital	10 000	
Retained Earnings	28 890	
Total Shareholders' Equity	38 890	
Total Liabilities and Shareholders' Equity		$79 590

XYZ Company Limited
Operating Statement
For the 12 months
ended Dec. 31, 19__

Sales (Revenue)		**$250 000**
Cost Of Goods Sold		
Opening Inventory	$ 12 000	
Purchases	151 150	
	163 150	
Closing Inventory	13 150	
Total Cost of Goods Sold		150 000
Gross Profit		100 000
Operating Expenses		
Advertising	1 500	
Automobile	2 400	
Bad Debts	300	
Depreciation	3 700	
Equipment Rental	400	
Insurance	1 200	
Interest and Bank Charges	4 000	
Management Salaries	16 000	
Miscellaneous	400	
Office Supplies	1 100	
Professional Fees	800	
Taxes and Licences (Municipal)	300	
Telephone	800	
Utilities	2 100	
Wages and Benefits	40 000	
Total Operating Expenses		75 000
Operating Profit		25 000
Less: Income Taxes[a]	6 250	
Net Profit		$ 18 750

[a] Arbitrarily set at 25% for demonstration purposes only. Rates can vary not only provincially but within individual businesses.

Formula Calculation (figures have been rounded)

1. Tangible Net Worth	$ 39 000
2. Earning Power (assume 10%)	3 900
3. Reasonable Salary for Owner	15 000
4. Earning Capacity	19 900
5. Average Annual Net Profit (operating profit before taxes, $25 000 + owner's salary, $16 000)	41 000
6. Extra Earning Power	21 100
7. Value of Intangibles (development factor of three)	63 300
8. Final Price (63 300 + 39 000)	102 300

By applying the formula, you come up with a suggested final price of $102 300. This compares with an asking price of $200 000.

Any price negotiated must, of course, be related to the new financing of the business. The combination of personal investment and borrowed money may be very different from the position of the vendor and as such will produce a very different operating result. Your negotiations will be strongly influenced by what you can afford.

Once you are satisfied that you have given full consideration to all factors affecting the proposed acquisition and you are ready to proceed, your offer should be formalized by a purchase agreement. Be sure to seek professional help and advice in the preparation of this agreement.

THE CONTRACT

Ultimately the sale of a business involves a combination of final price, other terms, and overall risk. You may be prepared to pay a higher price as long as other conditions (such as the seller agrees to take a mortgage on easy terms) are suitable. Or you may opt for a lower price in which you assume more of the risks of the transaction. The precise mix will vary in accordance with the nature of the business and the inclinations of the individuals involved.

Once you have arrived at the terms, the details should be spelled out in a contract that itemizes all aspects of the sale. The following is a summary of some standard items that are usually found in such a contract:[2]

- A definition of what is being transferred, from whom to whom, and at what price. This should include an itemized breakdown of costs so that you have a record of the value of each asset, both those you can claim for depreciation and those you cannot.
- Details of any leases or liabilities that you are assuming in making the purchase.
- The method of payment (in cash, by cheque, in shares in another company, in bonds), on what date, and by what means.
- Any adjustments to the price to cover financial transactions occurring between the moment the offer is signed and the closing date (this could include sale of inventory, equipment purchases, tax payments, etc.).
- Guarantees by the seller of the truthfulness of information supplied and provisions for any penalties in the event that information is not accurate.
- A description of the seller's obligations in operating the business up to closing, implementing the transfer of ownership, and performing any post-sale duties or services.
- How to deal with any losses or damages that might occur to the business between the signing of the agreement and the closing date.
- A clause restricting the ability of the seller to compete with the business once the sale is closed, or limiting the seller's freedom to start up similar ventures.
- Any conditions that should be met prior to closing (such as validation of deeds, liabilities, or agreements entered into by the business).
- Details of closing, including the date, time, place, and individuals effecting the transfer.
- Compensation to be paid by the seller to the buyer as damages or compensation if information is to be found to be false.
- The amount of the security deposit the buyer put up and held in escrow for a period of time as a guarantee that all terms and conditions have been satisfied.
- Who would decide the case in the event of a dispute.

EXPECT SOME PLEASANT SURPRISES

Well you've come a long way and you've worked hard on your research. You may be wondering if the digging was worth it. Only you can answer that.

There are bargains to be found out there — businesses like Woolett's Hardware. For hunter-buyers with vision and persistence, beautiful opportunities are waiting behind ugly façades.

I heard about Woolett's being up for sale more than a year ago. I'd just opened up my second store at the time — it's also in the hardware line — and it took me just about a year, April to April, to streamline the paperwork. Thanks to a computer and a good manager, my sanity remained intact.

So, when I finally got over there to check things out, Woolett's had been on the market about a year and a half. One look from the street and I could see why.

The store was a mess. The building was pre-World War II and so was the paint. Out front, the sign was sagging. The parking lot needed lots of work; there were potholes fifteen centimetres deep. The entryway was littered with scraps of paper.

Inside, things weren't much better. The floor needed a good sweeping. The merchandise was covered with dust. And all around there was this feeling of mildew, age, and disuse. It was dark — like a *cave*. It was tough finding a salesperson, and when you did, you couldn't get much help. Yet, there were customers all over the place.

After you've been in business a while, you develop a sort of sixth sense about things. And the minute I stepped into the store, I knew there was something special about it, something hidden, something the eye couldn't see right off. I knew I had to dig deeper.

A visit to the listing real estate broker didn't help much. "Make us an offer," he said. "We just dropped the price yesterday. To $400 000."

"What do the numbers look like?" I asked.

He dug into a slim manila folder. "Last year," he said, "they grossed just under $600 000. The net was around $200 000."

LIEN
a legal obligation filed against a piece of property

"What about inventory?" I asked. "What about loans and **liens** and accounts receivable? When can I interview the manager? And why is the owner selling?"

"Are you just asking that," he said, "or is this for real?"

"This is for my son," I said. "He's new to the business, and we don't want a lot of surprises."

"Like I said, make us an offer."

"Let me check the books," I said. I deposited $500 with an escrow company, making sure I got my usual escape clause — a deposit receipt saying my offer for the business was contingent on my inspection of all assets and my approval of all financial records. Doing this has saved me tons of heartburn medicine over the years.

The minute they got wind of a buyer, the manager and two of the employees up and quit. The back office was a mess, and it took me three days of searching to find something that would tell me I was on the right track. I found a supply of rolled steel. It was on the books at $12 000, but I knew it was worth $150 000. I took that as a buy signal.

The next day, I made an offer: $12 000 down, with the balance to be paid out of profits over the next five years. The owner accepted, and we cleared escrow in 30 days.

The first thing we did was clean the place up. We surfaced the parking lot with asphalt, added a coat of paint, fixed the door, added lighting.

Business picked up right away. My son, newly married, was settling down and learning the business. He seemed to have managerial talents. Buying this business was a pleasant surprise.

ACTION STEP REVIEW

57 Prepare a letter of inquiry.
58 Study a business from the outside.
59 Study a business inside out.
60 Probe the depths of ill will.

In a Nutshell

There are two good reasons to explore businesses for sale: you'll learn a lot by exploring the marketplace, and you might find a gem like Woolett's Hardware — a business that will make money right from the start.

A final note of caution is in order. Buying a business can take time and it certainly involves new risk. In making the purchase, you are assuming new responsibilities to those who helped you finance the deal, to any employees working for the business, to its suppliers, and to its clients. Before you buy, do your homework, complete the checklist provided in Box 13.1, and make sure you have a watertight contract in place.

Think Points for Success

- ✓ Stick to what you know. Don't buy a business you know nothing about.
- ✓ Don't let a seller or a broker rush you. A business is not a used car.
- ✓ If your seller looks absolutely honest, check him or her out anyway.
- ✓ Worry less about price; work harder on terms.
- ✓ Most good businesses are sold behind the scenes, before they reach the open market.
- ✓ Make sure you're there when the physical inventory takes place. Look in those boxes yourself.
- ✓ Get everything in writing. Be specific.
- ✓ Always go through bulk sales escrow.
- ✓ Buying a corporation is tricky. Have an experienced lawyer and accountant help you.

Checklist Questions and Actions to Develop Your Business Plan

BUYING A BUSINESS

- ❑ Why would you buy a business rather than start from scratch?
- ❑ What are the potential "icebergs" (unknowns or major risks) in buying a business?
- ❑ Establish the value of good will. Is the business worth this amount?
- ❑ What would be the cost involved in starting from scratch versus buying a business?

NOTES

1. Industry Canada, Strategis Web site at <http://stratgis.ic.gc.ca/contact>. Reprinted by permission.
2. *Ibid.*

OTHER REFERENCES

Bauman, Robert and Peter Jackson. *From Promise to Performance*. Boston, MA: Harvard Business School Press, 1997. [Merger leads to a brand new company.]

Joseph, Richard A., Anna M. Nekoranec, and Carl H. Steffens. *How to Buy a Business: Entrepreneurship Through Acquisition*. Dearborn Trade, 1993.

Price Waterhouse. *The Buying and Selling a Company Handbook*. Available at local Price Waterhouse offices, 1995.

Snowden, Richard W. *The Complete Guide to Buying a Business*. 1997.

West, Thomas L. *The 1997 Business Reference Guide*. New York: New York Business Brokerage Press, 1997. [Business valuation and contracts.]

Associations:

Institute of Business Appraisers
American Society of Appraisers
International Business Brokers Association

Trade publications (may be available at large business libraries):

The National Review of Corporate Acquisitions
Buyouts
Mergers and Acquisitions

fourteen

Buying a Franchise

LEARNING OPPORTUNITIES

After reading this chapter, you should be able to:

- Appreciate the vast world of franchising.
- Understand key franchising terms and conditions in an agreement.
- Understand the relationship between franchisor and franchisee.
- Learn the benefits and liabilities of owning and operating a franchise.
- Decide whether buying a franchise is the right step for you.

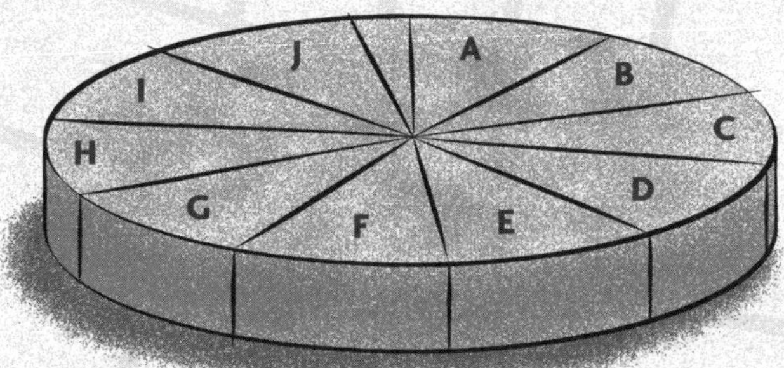

BUSINESS PLAN BUILDING BLOCK

This chapter will introduce you to the world of franchising and help you decide if buying a franchise is right for you.

"You're only here for a cup of coffee," Orv Lahey, our small business professor, told us that first day of class, a few years ago. How ironic. I had a passion — and still do — for coffee and always wanted to own a coffee shop. So it was an omen that Orv came out with this nugget at our first encounter.

I researched the market and came to the conclusion that I needed a partner, a strong partner who could secure me a good location, provide the right training, and be ready to move with the times. I didn't want to be out there alone. I wanted to be part of a strong organization. I felt I couldn't compete in the coffee business as a mom-and-pop operation. After months of investigation, I chose Second Cup.

I've just completed my first year in business, and I can tell you that I made the right decision. Our team has exceeded sales targets and our costs are in line. I know franchising isn't the option for everyone. You hear a lot of horror stories. But it's worked out for me.

My manager, Aaron Cope, and I went through an intensive three-week training program at Second Cup. The company made sure I had a realistic business plan and that my financials were reasonable. I was well prepared and I knew what I wanted. When I was offered a street-front location, I turned it down — it wasn't what I had in mind. Through perseverance and a lot of networking, I finally found a triple-A mall location. I bought the business from a Second Cup franchisee. It impressed me that Second Cup was prepared to do what it could to help her sell the business. Most of all, it was supportive and did what it said it would.

ACTION STEP PREVIEW

61 Investigate the franchise system by interviewing franchisors and franchisees.

62 Visit a franchise exposition and compare various franchise operations.

Figure 14.1 Chapter Fourteen investigates franchising, an important doorway to small business.

On the negative side, I have to follow its system religiously, but I knew going in that that would be the price I would have to pay. However, I still get a chance to vent my entrepreneurial ideas at franchise association meetings.

If you are going to buy a franchise, here's my advice:

- Get a mentor.
- You're more likely to succeed if you stick to what you know best. Make sure you and the franchisor have the same vision.
- Always get advice from a lawyer and an accountant. You don't have to follow it. But at least listen to them.
- Have a business plan.
- Teamwork is everything. If you can't work in a team, you may as well pack it in.
- Find out how the franchisor helps franchisees sell their business. I considered this a litmus test of Second Cup's corporate culture.[1]

Our walk-through of opportunities in small business is almost finished. Decision time approaches. If you've followed the Action Steps, you've spent several months gathering data and talking to people in small business. In Chapter Thirteen, we explored buying a business and talking to sellers. In this chapter, we look at another option: acquiring a franchised business.

The franchising industry is enormous. If you were to buy or rent a car tomorrow morning, put gas in it, buy a coffee and doughnut, purchase some paint, and then go to a fast-food restaurant for lunch, chances are you would support a franchise at every stop. Here are some franchising facts:

- According to Industry Canada, about 40 cents of every retail dollar spent in the retail sector goes to some franchise business.
- There are approximately 1 100 different franchises in Canada.
- Some 13 000 Canadians have chosen franchising as their entrepreneurial gateway and franchises employ over 60 000 people.
- There is one franchise outlet for every 1 200 Canadians.
- Franchise revenues were estimated to be about $90 billion in 1996.
- According to the Canadian Franchise Association, the franchising industry's growth rate in the latter half of the 1990s was 7 percent annually.

Is a franchise for you? When does it make business sense? Are you ready to surrender some of your independence? Is this a good first business, a stepping stone to the future entrepreneurship you seek? We'll try to help you answer these questions in this chapter.

FRANCHISE
authorization granted by a manufacturer or distributor to sell its products or services

FRANCHISOR
the firm that sells the rights to do business under its name and continues to control the business

FRANCHISEE
the individual operator who is licensed to operate under the franchisor's rules and directives

What Is a Franchise?

BUSINESS FORMAT FRANCHISE

A **franchise** is a special kind of partnership in which one company (the **franchisor**) grants the right to sell its products or services to another company or individual (the **franchisee**). It's a distribution system used by businesses to sell or market their products or services.

A variety of franchise business arrangements exists. If you drop by Second Cup for a cup of coffee, buy a dozen doughnuts at Tim Hortons or get your muffler fixed at Speedy, you have just experienced familiar examples of the so-called **business format franchise** system. This type of franchise is one in which the product, method of distribution, and sales and management procedures —the business format — are highly controlled. The franchisor "blueprints" every aspect of the business and then sells this business format to a franchisee. The main job of the franchisee is to staff and run the operation. This is the most popular type of franchise system — one that encompasses most businesses, from used clothing to lawn care and even tax preparation.

BUSINESS FORMAT FRANCHISE
one in which the product, method of distribution, and sales and management procedures are highly controlled

DEALERSHIP RELATIONSHIP FRANCHISE

A second type of popular franchise system is the **dealership relationship franchise** (also termed a licensing or associate relationship). Here the dealer or associate (franchisee) buys the right to distribute a franchisor's product or service. These types of licensing arrangements are less restrictive than the business format arrangement, where the key is standardization. Dealership franchisees distribute and sell the product under the franchisor's conditions, but are left relatively free from any other franchisee obligations. Home Hardware and Century 21 are good examples of this kind of arrangement. Another example would be Coca-Cola and Pepsi, which license or franchise out the right to distribute their products to a local bottler, but don't normally tell the licensees how to run their business operations.

DEALERSHIP RELATIONSHIP FRANCHISE
also called licensing or associate relationship, a type of franchise in which the franchisee buys the right to distribute a franchisor's product or service

This chapter focusses mainly on business format franchising — the most common type of franchising — although much of the discussion also applies to the dealership or licensing format.

Why Buy a Franchise?

In theory, a successful franchise system can benefit the consumer, the franchisee, and the franchisor — a win-win situation.

WHAT THE CUSTOMER GETS

Imagine that you're on a holiday. You have been driving for hours and it's time for lunch. Do you have lunch at Wendy's or Taco Bell, or do you take a chance and pull in at a flashing "Joe's Diner" sign? If you're like the average Canadian, you'll choose a name that is familiar. Why? Because to some degree, you've been branded. You've become comfortable with a product and gained a certain attachment to it. You know what to expect even if it isn't perfect; you keep returning. It's hard to get out of this comfort zone.

"Customer satisfaction" and brand loyalty are the key reasons for buying a franchise. Each franchise outlet is cloned to offer a consistent standard of service and product. If the franchise system runs as planned, customers will know what to expect and how much they will pay every time. Franchises give customers a sense of security. Should a dispute arise, customers know that they can appeal to a larger organization. Franchises give the appearance that they will be around for the long run. Also, there is a good chance the "owner" will be around, and customers like to know that they can speak to the owner should the need arise.

WHAT THE FRANCHISEE RECEIVES

Let's examine what you may receive when you buy a franchise from a franchisor. In principle, a franchise can provide:

1. *Brand-name recognition.* If you pick the right franchise with a high, positive consumer profile, you will have a recognizable brand.
2. *Support from the corporation.* Corporate services can include help with site selection, employee training, inventory control, vendor supplies and connections, a corporate-produced business plan, lease negotiations, layout assistance, and more.
3. *Training.* The franchisor will teach you the business and provide ongoing training.
4. *Financial support.* Lenders often prefer to lend to new franchises over new start-ups.
5. *Template.* You are buying a proven business plan and strategy that work.
6. *Purchasing power.* You may share in economies of scale in purchasing goods, services, and promotion.
7. *Corporate monitoring and assistance.* You are likely to receive psychological hand-holding and field visits from the franchisor.
8. *Less risk of failure.* The failure rate of franchises is less than half of self start-ups.
9. *National/regional promotion.* You will get pretested promotion and marketing programs
10. *Additional units.* You are likely to get opportunities to buy another franchise in your area.

WHAT THE FRANCHISOR ASKS OF YOU

Franchisors earn money in several ways:

FRANCHISE FEE
fee paid by a franchisee for the rights to represent the franchisor in a given geographic area for a specified length of time, commonly five to ten years

ROYALTY FEE
ongoing obligation to pay the franchisor a percentage of the gross sales

1. They collect a **franchise fee** for the rights to use their name and system. This can range anywhere from $3 000 for a small service firm to over $100 000 for a well-established name such as that of a hotel, auto dealership, or major restaurant. The franchise fee is usually paid by the franchisee on the day the franchise agreement is signed.
2. They normally collect a **royalty fee**, which ranges from 2 to 15 percent of the annual gross sales. Some franchisors collect their royalties by charging a percentage on the purchase of supplies rather than on sales.
3. Some may make a profit on the mark-up of items (such as store fixtures) that they sell directly to franchisees.
4. Some may receive volume rebates or other benefits from suppliers, which are not passed on to the franchisees.
5. They may require franchisees to pay advertising and promotion fees. These generally range from 2 to 5 percent of the franchisee's gross sales. Some of these are directed towards local promotions, but most go into the national advertising fund. In some cases, depending on the age of the franchise, it may be possible to ask for some concessions in the payment of these fees.

In addition, growth and market penetration are key benefits. Franchisors can expand their business quickly with limited capital from the original owners. A number of growth options are available. Some franchisors, for example, provide incentives for their successful franchisees to own multiple units. Other aggressive franchisors have been known to sell geographic territories to master or sub-franchisors. The job of master or sub-franchisors is to grow the business (i.e., sell franchises within the designated area). In turn, these quasi-franchisors receive a portion of the franchise fees or royalties.

Investigating Franchise Opportunities

According to Mac Voisin, president of the highly successful M & M Meat Shops Ltd. in Kitchener, Ontario, a franchise chain of over 135 outlets, "True entrepreneurs will die of frustration in a franchise system because they want to do everything their own way."[2] As Voison points out, many of you may not be comfortable operating by the franchisor's strict rules and regulations. Your entrepreneurial spirit may make it difficult for you to follow detailed rules and policies. But that doesn't mean you shouldn't keep your eyes open. You can learn a lot by examining the way good franchises work. It makes sense

Box 14.1 Free Advice

Major banks and financial institutions can help you weigh the pros and cons of franchising. And some advice is free for the asking. Here are three examples.

Royal Bank of Canada: *Doing It Right Franchisor.* This booklet has been developed for the prospective franchisor. It describes the basic elements of a business format franchise, the advantages and disadvantages of franchising, the feasibility of franchising a business, critical success elements, steps to building a franchise plan, and what franchise experts (e.g., consultants, accountants, lawyers and bankers) can do for you. It also includes worksheets and checklists.

Contact:
Royal Bank of Canada
South Tower
24 Floor, 200 Bay Street
Toronto, ON M5J 2J5
Tel: (416) 974-8289 or toll free 1-800-268-3726
Fax: (416) 974-8320
Internet: http://www.franchise-conxions.com

Bank of Nova Scotia: *The Franchise Commitment.* This Bank of Nova Scotia booklet outlines methods for the evaluation of the franchisor, the franchise agreement, and the choice of product or service.

Contact:
Bank of Nova Scotia
Franchising & Independent Business
Canadian Commercial Banking
Scotia Plaza
Suite 1010, 44 King Street West
Toronto, ON M5H 1H1
Tel: (416) 866-4377
Fax: (416) 866-4839

Canadian Imperial Bank of Commerce: *CIBC Guide to Franchising and Its Financing.* This booklet outlines some of the advantages and pitfalls of operating a franchise, and suggests questions that a prospective franchisee should ask before making any commitments. The financial services offered by the Canadian Imperial Bank of Commerce to franchisees are also described.

Contact:
Canadian Imperial Bank of Commerce
National Franchising
Commerce Court Postal Station
Toronto, ON M5L 1A2
Tel: (416) 980-3225
Fax: (416) 980-3229

to evaluate franchise opportunities (especially those in your industry), because, at the very least, it will give you a better picture of the marketplace. To help you get started, do Action Step 61.

ACTION STEP 61

Investigate the franchise system by interviewing franchisors and franchisees.

Franchises are everywhere: Tim Hortons, Boston Pizza, Second Cup, RE MAX, Dale Carnegie, Holiday Inn, Esso, Hertz, and many, many others. To learn more about the system, interview people on both sides of the franchise agreement.

Part A: Franchisors. Leave your chequebook at home and interview at least three franchisors. Here are some questions to start you off:

- What is the business experience of the franchisor's directors and managers?
- How many years has the franchise been operating?
- What are the start-up and ongoing royalty fees and other assessments?
- What level of training and service could I expect before and after I open, and what support is given?
- What is the turnover rate of the franchisees?
- Is the territory well-defined?
- What are the minimum volume requirements?
- Is the franchisor a member of the Canadian Franchise Association?
- Is the franchise registered in Alberta?
- How can the franchise be bought back or cancelled by the franchisor?

Part B: Franchisees. Now interview several franchisees. Ask them the same questions, with emphasis on the type of support they receive from the franchisors.

A handy reference is the *Top Franchises Available: Canadian Business Franchise Handbook*. If you're in a hurry, just log on to Industry Canada's Strategis site, *Franchising in Canada: Information Source*, at <http://strategis.ic.gc.ca/SSG/dm01179e.html#E>, and type the word "franchise" in the search box. Major banks and financial institutions can also help. See, for example, the contacts in Box 14.1

THE FRANCHISE AGREEMENT AND SYSTEM

When you purchase a franchise, you will be required to sign a contract that could be as long as 50 pages and with numerous appendices attached. This contract is the franchise agreement, which lays out the system you will be working within, and the rules and policies that you are bound to operate by. It goes without saying that you need to get legal advice before you sign the agreement. The typical clauses in the contract include:

- Definitions
- Grant and Term
- Franchise Royalty Fee and Sales Taxes
- Reports
- General Services of Franchisor
- Compliance with System
- Manual
- Training
- Advertising and Promotions
- Leasing of the Premises
- Improvements to the Premises
- Engagement in Similar Business: Non-Disclosure of Information
- Trademark
- Insurance
- Indemnification
- Events of Default
- Effect of Termination
- Assignment
- General Provisions
- Renovations
- Schedules: Premises; Trademark; Sublease; Payment Schedule

BUYER BEWARE: SOME PITFALLS OF FRANCHISING

An article in *The Globe and Mail* notes that "Franchising has reached a crossroads. It's in danger of becoming disreputable. Franchise lawyers and desperate franchisees tell the same stories, again and again. Investors are told a location makes $10 000 a week when it actually brings in $2 000; in some cases, refundable deposits are never returned; and some chains ask for deposits as high as $40 000 before giving the franchisee a contract to review."[3]

More notable pitfalls that plague the franchising industry include:

ENCROACHMENT
situation in which franchisors compete with franchisees by putting an outlet nearby or setting up alternative distribution channels such as mail order or the Internet

Encroachment According to some franchise experts, encroachment is the number one issue in the franchise industry. Encroachment is where franchisors compete with franchisees by putting a store nearby or operating through an alternative distribution channel such as mail order or the Internet. For example, H & R Block now offers tax service on the Internet; you can buy a Tim Hortons coffee and doughnut at your local Esso station; and the Body Shop has retail outlets as well as mail-order distribution. What this means is that established franchisees are finding it more and more difficult to protect their territory.

Ground-Floor Opportunities Beware of the so-called "ground-floor" ("grow with us") franchise opportunities. A franchisor offering such "opportunity" is experimenting with your money. If you buy a franchise, you should be buying a recognized brand name, a proven business plan, excellent field support, and experience that demonstrates the particular franchise will work in your location. Otherwise you are better off to do it yourself. A concept is not normally considered established until it has been in business four to five years.

Minimum Franchise Legislation As of 1998, the federal government has no franchise legislation protecting franchisees. As a result, Canada has often been termed the Wild West of the franchise industry. That's because almost any company can become a franchisor. All you need is a franchise agreement and a naïve franchisee ready to sign. There are very few legal requirements or restrictions stopping you from starting your own franchise.

As of 1998, Alberta is the only province that has put in place any franchise legislation. However, franchisors do not have to file any government documents or register with a government agency. They are required to give prospective franchisees a franchise disclosure document. The disclosure document must contain information such as copies of all franchise agreements, financial statements, and all material facts including those relating to the matters set out in Alberta's Franchises Act. From a legal standpoint, what this means is that franchisees are only protected by a "right of recession." Alberta franchisees must settle their disputes with franchisors in the courts (if they have enough money to do so).

The bottom line is that, outside of Alberta, franchisors are not legally required to provide you with the following types of information about the company:

- balance sheet and income statement information
- number of franchises
- bankruptcy history
- background of the owners key officers
- revenues and expenses of the franchisor
- turnover rate of franchisees

Signing Personally If you are going into a partnership with a franchisor, we strongly advise you to keep your legal distance. You don't want to get your personal assets mixed up with a franchisor's business. Form a company, and sign the franchise agreement in the company name. If a franchisor wants personal guarantees, be prepared to say no.

Few Facts Are franchisees more successful? American statistics would support this, but there is no Canadian data. Are franchises more profitable? Again we don't know. Most evidence is anecdotal and relies on information from franchised associations. For example, we told you that franchising grew at about 7 percent per year over the latter half of the 1990s. Here we relied on information from the Canadian Franchise Association. We trusted that its sources were accurate. There are no regular government surveys on franchising in Canada. In fact, no major survey on franchises has been conducted since the early 1990s. Beware of an ambitious franchisor who presents you with an extensive list of franchise benefits and fictitious claims like "only 5 percent of all franchises fail."

The Canadian Franchise Association is one of the few sources of franchise information. The organization has about 300 members who are required to disclose certain types of information to prospective franchisees. As of 1998, you could find this disclosure information on the association Web site at <http://www.cfa.ca/disc.html>. This disclosure requirement, however, is not backed by government legislation. Still, check the Web site for prospective franchisors and see if they are registered. If they are not members, find out why. If they are, you should be able to find some information. Keep in mind, though, that members are not required to file financial information about their operations. In other words, a franchisor could be close to bankruptcy and you may not know it. Beware that some franchises, like Pizza Pizza, have been asked to leave the organization.

Saturated Markets Competition has become intense among competitive franchisors, which has led to a tendency for franchisors, especially fast-food outlets, quick-printing shops, and specialty retailers, to saturate market areas, thus resulting many failures.

Poor Training Some training programs are poor or non-existent.

Supplies Stipulation Some franchise agreements stipulate that you must buy your supplies from the franchisor. Problems emerge when franchisees are required to pay non-competitive prices (i.e., they are overcharged) for products supplied by the franchisor.

Insiders First Typically, current franchisees are offered prime locations before outsiders or first-time franchise buyers are. Rarely is a new player offered a sure thing. Invariably, new players are offered franchisees that have already been passed over.

Non-Refundable Deposits Some franchisors ask for a refundable deposit during the time the buyer is negotiating an agreement. This is supposed to show the buyer's good faith. Be careful if you are presented with this request. Seek legal advice and place the money in trust with your lawyer, not the franchisor's. There have been cases where refundable deposits were never returned.

Evaluating a Franchise

Evaluating a franchise opportunity is much like evaluating any other business that's up for sale, but because of the nature of franchisors, you need to ask some additional questions. For example:

- How long has this franchise been in business?
- Who are the officers?
- Has the franchise gone bankrupt or been convicted of any criminal offenses?
- How many franchise outlets are operating right now?
- How well does this franchise compete with similar franchises?
- Where is this franchise in its life cycle?
- What will this franchise do for me?

In Chapter Thirteen, we presented a checklist to use in evaluating an ongoing business you are considering buying. The majority of that checklist applies to franchises as well. To supplement it, we're giving you a checklist prepared specifically for evaluating franchise opportunities (see Box 14.2). The questions will help you generate a profile of the franchise and make a wise decision.

CHOOSE YOUR PRODUCT OR SERVICE WITH CARE

As a potential franchisee, you should know everything about the product or service the franchise system delivers.

Naturally, an exclusive product or service, or one that is of superior quality and value, is a good business bet. But these aren't the only criteria for judging the competitive strength of the product or service. There are good profits to be made or lost in products that are essentially not different from others in the market — except in how they are marketed. One franchise can

Box 14.2 Franchise Evaluation Checklist

General

	yes	*no*
1. Is the product or service:		
a. considered reputable?	______	______
b. part of a growing market?	______	______
c. needed in your area?	______	______
d. of interest to you?	______	______
e. safe,	______	______
protected,	______	______
covered by guarantee?	______	______
2. Is the franchise:		
a. local?	______	______
regional?	______	______
national?	______	______
international?	______	______
b. full-time?	______	______
part-time?	______	______
possible full-time in the future?	______	______

3. Existing franchises

a. Date the company was founded ______________________

Date the first franchise was awarded ______________________

b. Number of franchises currently in operation or under construction

____

c. References

Franchise 1: owner ______________________
address ______________________
telephone ____________ date started ____________

Franchise 2: owner ______________________
address ______________________
telephone ____________ date started ____________

Franchise 3: owner ______________________
address ______________________
telephone ____________ date started ____________

Franchise 4: owner ______________________
address ______________________
telephone ____________ date started ____________

d. Additional franchises planned for the next twelve months __________

4. Failed franchises

a. How many failed? ______ How many in the last two years? ______

b. Why have they failed?

Franchisor reasons: ______________________

____

Better Business Bureau reasons: ______________________

____

Franchisee reasons: ______________________

____

(Continued)

Box 14.2 Franchise Evaluation Checklist *(Continued)*

5. Franchise in local market area

- **a.** Has a franchise ever been awarded in this area? ________
- **b.** If so, and if it is still in operation:

  owner ________

  address ________

  telephone ________ date started ________
- **c.** If so, and if it is no longer in operation.

  person involved ________

  address ________

  date started ________ date ended ________

  reasons for failure ________

  ____
- **d.** How many inquiries have there been for the franchise from the area in the past six months? _____

6. What product or service will be added to the franchise package:

- **a.** within twelve months? ________

  ____
- **b.** within two years? ________

  ____
- **c.** within two to five years? ________

  ____

7. Competition

- **a.** What is the competition? ________

  ____

  ____

8. Are all franchises independently owned?

- **a.** Of the total outlets, _____ are franchised, and _____ are company owned.
- **b.** If some outlets are company owned, did they start out this way, _____ or were they purchased from a franchisee? _____
- **c.** Date of most recent company acquisition ________

9. Franchise operations

- **a.** What facilities are required, and do I lease or build?

	build	*lease*
office	_____	_____
building	_____	_____
manufacturing facility	_____	_____
warehouse	_____	_____
________	_____	_____
________	_____	_____

- **b.** Getting started — Who is responsible for:

	franchisor	*franchisee*
feasibility study?	_____	_____
design?	_____	_____
construction?	_____	_____
furnishings and equipment?	_____	_____
financing?	_____	_____
employee training?	_____	_____
lease negotiation?	_____	_____

(Continued)

Box 14.2 Franchise Evaluation Checklist *(Continued)*

Franchise Company

1. The company
   a. Name and address of the parent company, if different from the franchise company:
      name ______________________________
      address ______________________________
   b. Is the parent company public ______ or private? ______
   c. If the company is public, where is the stock traded?
      Toronto Stock Exchange ______
      over-the-counter ______
      ______________ ______
2. Forecast of income and expenses
   a. Is a forecast of income and expenses provided? ______
   b. Is it:
      based on actual franchisee operations? ______
      based on a franchisor outlet? ______
      purely estimated? ______
   c. Does it:

	yes	*no*
relate to your market area?	______	______
meet your personal goals?	______	______
provide adequate return on investment?	______	______
provide for adequate promotion and personnel?	______	______

3. What is the best legal structure for my company?
   proprietorship ______
   partnership ______
   corporation ______
4. The franchise contract
   a. Is there a written contract? ______ (Get a copy for lawyer and accountant to review.)
   b. Does it specify:

	yes	*no*
franchise fee?	______	______
termination?	______	______
selling and renewal?	______	______
advertising and promotion?	______	______
patent and liability protection?	______	______
home office services?	______	______
commissions and royalties?	______	______
training?	______	______
financing?	______	______
territory?	______	______
exclusivity?	______	______

Source: Adapted from C.R. Stigleman, *Franchise Index/Profile*, Small Business Management Series, no. 35 (Washington D.C.: Small Business Administration, 1973), 31–41.

be much the same as another, but if its marketing is superior, it can overpower the competition.

So, when you try to assess the competitive strength of the product or service you're interested in, keep your focus wide. Consider everything it takes to deliver that product or service to customers. Then ask yourself how well your prospective franchisor does all of these things.

A good way to learn a lot about franchising and prospective franchisors in a short time is to attend a franchise exposition. You can learn when and where they are to be held in your area by watching for announcements in major newspapers. In Toronto, the Canadian National Franchising Exposition is usually held during the second week of February at the Canadian National Exhibition.

Now complete Action Step 62.

As you look for a good franchise opportunity, bear in mind that the best opportunity may lie with a young franchise that has proven its concept, has 20 to 30 winners, and growth in an area you know. An excellent source of franchise information is *Opportunities Canada*, a franchise and dealership guide by R.A. Sinclair (see references at the end of this chapter).

ACTION STEP 62

Visit a franchise exposition and compare various franchise operations. Most major cities have at least one franchise show a year. An updated source of information is the events calendar of the Canadian Franchise Association, found on its Web site at <http://www.cfa.ca/events.html>.

Attend one and visit with the exhibitors. Learn what you can from the sales presentations.

Collect the exhibitors' literature, compare the data, and select one that seems worth a second look. Write a brief summary of your findings.

Remember, it's usually the small and new franchisors that exhibit at the shows, and their salespeople work on commission. Don't allow yourself to be pursued; you are there to observe and evaluate. You are probably not yet ready to buy.

REASONS FOR NOT BUYING A FRANCHISE

Many entrepreneurs have decided against buying franchises. Here are some of the reasons they have given:

- I know the business as well as they do.
- The franchise name is not all that important.
- Why pay a franchise fee?
- Why pay a royalty and advertising fee?
- My individuality would have been stifled.
- I don't want others to tell me how to run my business.
- I didn't want a ground-floor opportunity where I'd be the guinea pig.
- There were restrictions on selling out.
- If I didn't do as I was told, I would lose my franchise.
- The specified business hours did not suit my location.
- The franchisor's promotions and products did not fit my customers' needs or tastes.
- They offered no territory protection.

A FINAL WORD ABOUT FRANCHISES

After reading about the list of "buyer beware" cautionary notes, you are probably thinking about closing the book on franchising. We're not trying to discourage you, but we want you to be very careful. A franchise is a partnership and you need to make sure you can work under the controls of its system. You need to look at franchising as an option — and an example to learn from. Remember that there is no reason why *you* cannot be the franchisor. If you can develop a winning formula, then with a little entrepreneurial flair you can become a franchisor yourself. Many entrepreneurs have done this and it's another reason for learning all you can about franchising now. In the opening vignette, we discussed a successful franchise, Second Cup. Boston Pizza International Inc. and Yogen Früz World-Wide Inc. are two other notable examples:

Boston Pizza started out as one restaurant in Edmonton called the Boston Pizza and Spaghetti House. By 1997, it had been transformed into a franchise organization and one of the *Financial Post*'s "50 best managed private companies" with over a $140 million in sales.

Aaron and Michael Serruya started Yogen Früz in Toronto's Promenade Mall in the late 1980s. By 1997, it had become a Profit 100 company and had grown into about 3 000 frozen yogurt outlets worldwide, most of which were franchised.

ACTION STEP REVIEW

61 Investigate the franchise system by interviewing franchisors and franchisees.

62 Visit a franchise exposition and compare various franchise operations.

If you are not ready to be on your own yet, franchising may be the start for you. The Second Cup franchisor in our opening vignette made a go of it. But you need to do your homework and get some experienced advice. Before you sign a franchise agreement, read every paragraph in it and find a lawyer with franchise experience. Make sure you understand every clause. Suppose, for example, that your franchise agreement says you must buy supplies from the franchisor at competitive prices. Does competitive mean "competitive relative to what other franchisees in the system are paying"? Or does it mean "competitive in relation to other outside suppliers"? Furthermore, what happens if the franchisor cannot supply the product? As we now know, franchise law in Canada is virtually non-existent, so your lawyer must know how the clauses of a franchise agreement have been interpreted and how the courts have settled franchisee-franchisor disputes. Lastly, we emphasize that you have a right to insist and receive full disclosure of all financial information. Exercise this right.

In a Nutshell

There are many good reasons to consider buying a franchise. Notably, if the brand name is respected, you'll already be positioned in the marketplace; and if the franchisor is sharp, you'll inherit a business plan and a strong corporate partner that can work for you. It's important, however, to examine the franchise's appeal with consumers carefully; you want to get a marketing boost from the name. Depending on the franchise, you may also get other services for your money (e.g., help on site selection, help on interior layout, and vendor connections), but the main thing you're buying is brand-name recognition.

Just as if you were investigating an ongoing independent business, study the opportunity thoroughly. Examine the financial history and compare what you'd make if you bought the business to what you'd make if you invested the same money elsewhere. Most of all, before you sign anything, get good legal and financial advice.

Think Points for Success

- ✓ Avoid ground-floor opportunities. "Grow with us" might really signal *caveat emptor* ("Let the buyer beware").
- ✓ Talk to franchisees.
- ✓ The franchisor gets a percentage of gross sales for advertising and royalty fees whether the franchisee enjoys a profit or not.
- ✓ Do you really need the security blanket of a franchise?
- ✓ Read the proposed agreements carefully.
- ✓ Would you be comfortable relinquishing your independence?

Checklist Questions and Actions to Develop Your Business Plan

BUYING A FRANCHISE

- ❑ Why have you selected a franchise as your method of start-up?
- ❑ What were your lawyer's comments on the franchise agreement?
- ❑ Do your personal vision, goals, and personality match a franchise form of ownership?

NOTES

1. Prepared by Doug Tam, franchise owner, Second Cup, St. Laurent Mall, Ottawa, ON. Reprinted by permission.
2. Mac Voisin is quoted in John Southerst, "If You're 'Entrepreneurial,' Forget Franchising," *The Globe and Mail*, May 8, 1995, p. B5.
3. John Southerst, " Franchising Stumbles Along Perilous Path," *The Globe and Mail*, May 25, 1998, p. B11.

OTHER REFERENCES

Canadian Franchise Association (CFA). *Investigate Before Investing: Guidance for Prospective Franchisees.*

Canadian Franchise Association Web site, *Franchising in Canada: Information Source* at <http://www.cfa.ca/pub.html>.

Industry Canada Strategis Web site, *Franchising in Canada: Information Source* at <http://strategis.ic.gc.ca/SSG/dm01179e.html#E>.

Morton, Neil. "Some Like It Cold." *Canadian Business*, September 1997, pp. 99–103. [Franchising success of Yogen Früz.]

Network Franchising International. Concorde Gate, Ste. 201, Toronto, ON M3C 3N6.

Sinclair, R.A. *Opportunities Canada: Franchise and Dealership Guide*. Mississauga, ON: The Type People Inc., Fall/Winter, 1997–98.

fifteen

Exporting: Another Adventure Beckons

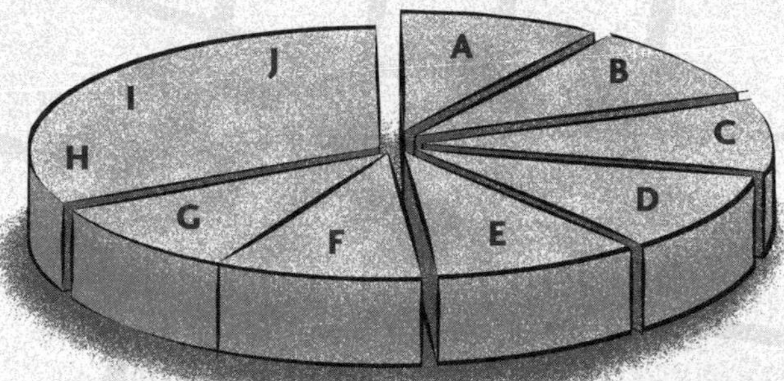

BUSINESS PLAN BUILDING BLOCK

We encourage you to consider exporting your product or service. It's an adventure you will want to investigate before you start your business or once your business is established. If you have chosen exporting to be part of your business, read the chapter carefully and complete the "Export Plan Outline" at the end of the chapter.

Acadian Seaplants Ltd., a small company in Dartmouth, Nova Scotia, harvests seaweed and turns it into products that are used by food, botanical, feed, and agro-chemical industries around the world. Founded in 1991, Acadian is a 1996 Canada Export Award winner, exporting 91 percent of its products to more than 35 countries. Its success has proven that East Coast Canadians can compete and win in the global marketplace.

What has made Acadian Seaplants so successful? According to its president, Louis Deveau, the company's prosperity is due to its high-quality product, advanced technology, and aggressive research. Its competitive strategy is to invest heavily in technology, product, and market research. As much as 15 percent of its revenues are plowed back into sustainable harvesting technology, resource and technology management science, and cultivation.[1]

Figure 15.1 Chapter Fifteen encourages you to consider exporting.

LEARNING OPPORTUNITIES

After reading this chapter, you should be able to:

- Become "export ready."
- Do an export SWOT analysis.
- Become aware of the key exporting issues.
- Understand the basic exporting terminology.
- Understand and use key exporting strategies.
- Become aware of export advisors and sources of help.
- Understand the importance of cultural awareness.
- Draft an export plan.

ACTION STEP PREVIEW

63 Do an export SWOT analysis.
64 Discover export sources.
65 Map out your export strategy.

Mention international business or exporting to a group of entrepreneurs, and some will imagine huge Japanese trading companies, and a few will lapse into bureaucratic comas. International business has been the domain of government and multinational corporations for years. But now you hear about the global economy every day, and that small and medium-sized enterprises account for about 87 000 of Canada's 89 393 exports.

You may already have your plate full with the domestic market. The number of things to do in a day is endless, and you think you simply don't have the time to export. Or do you? If you were convinced that those big international markets were accessible, you'd probably export. Thanks to technology, politics, and the evolving international economy, many markets that were once only accessible to big companies are now within reach of the individual entrepreneur.

We think exporting is an opportunity that should not be overlooked by most entrepreneurs, and for many of Canada's emerging businesses, like Acadian Seaplants, export markets are absolutely essential. Let's take a moment and begin with the global realities facing the Canadian economy.

Global Realities

Whether it's a small company, like Acadian Seaplants, or a corporate giant the size of Nortel, successful Canadian companies consider the world part of their market. The continued prosperity of Canada is linked to the philosophy of looking beyond our borders. Here's what a few of the numbers say to support exporting:[2]

Figure 15. 2

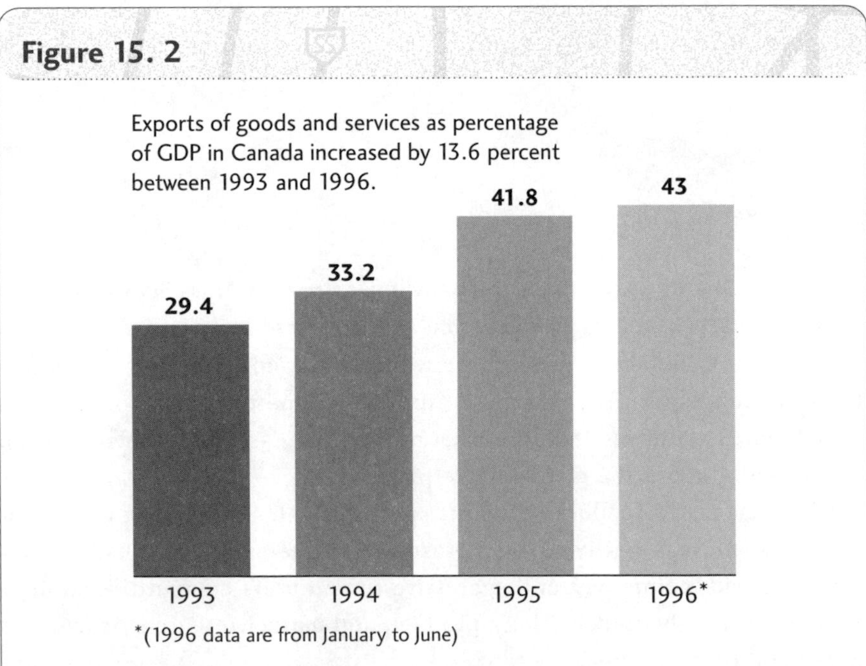
Exports of goods and services as percentage of GDP in Canada increased by 13.6 percent between 1993 and 1996.
29.4
33.2
41.8
43
1993
1994
1995
1996*
*(1996 data are from January to June)

Source: Minister of Supply and Services Canada, *Canada's International Business Strategy, 1997–1998: Overview*, Catalogue No. C2-226/1-1998E, p. 5. Reproduced with the permission of the Minister of Public Works and Government Services Canada, 1998.

- In 1997, exports of goods and services were in the $300 billion range, and accounted for about 43 percent of our economic output (see Figure 15.2).
- Some 3 million working Canadians (one out of every three) owe their jobs to Canada's success in the global marketplace.
- Every $1 billion in exports sustains 11 000 jobs.
- Export firms expand employment 20 percent faster than non-exporting firms, and are 10 percent less likely to fail.
- Our major trading partner is the U.S., which accounts for roughly 80 percent of our exports (see Figure 15.3).

One of the major reasons for Canada's increased reliance on exporting is the North American and global reduction in trade barriers. Signals of this new era for Canadian business in the 1990s included the signing of the Free Trade Agreement with the U.S. (1991) and the North America Free Trade Agreement (1994), the formation of the World Trade Organization (1995), and the free trade agreements with Chile and Israel (1996).

Historically, Canada's small businesses have not taken advantage of the opportunities in the export market. However, while only about 10 percent of our small businesses exported in the 1990s, there were some encouraging indications of change too. For example, almost two-thirds of the Profit 100 companies became heavily involved in exporting over the 1990s. A shining example of this new breed of small business is Oasis Technology Ltd. of North York, Ontario, a software company that develops programs for electronic funds transfer. It was the number one company on the 1997 Profit 100 list. Over a five-year period, Oasis had a mind-boggling growth rate of 10 114 percent. All its revenue came from exporting. "Our strategy has been to attack markets in Latin America, China, and the Middle East, which have no real banking infrastructure," said Ashraf Dimitri who founded the company in 1990. Datalog Technology Inc. in Calgary and Hummingbird Communications Ltd. in North York, Ontario, are two other examples of fast-growing Profit 100 companies that have relied almost exclusively on exporting.[3]

Figure 15.3

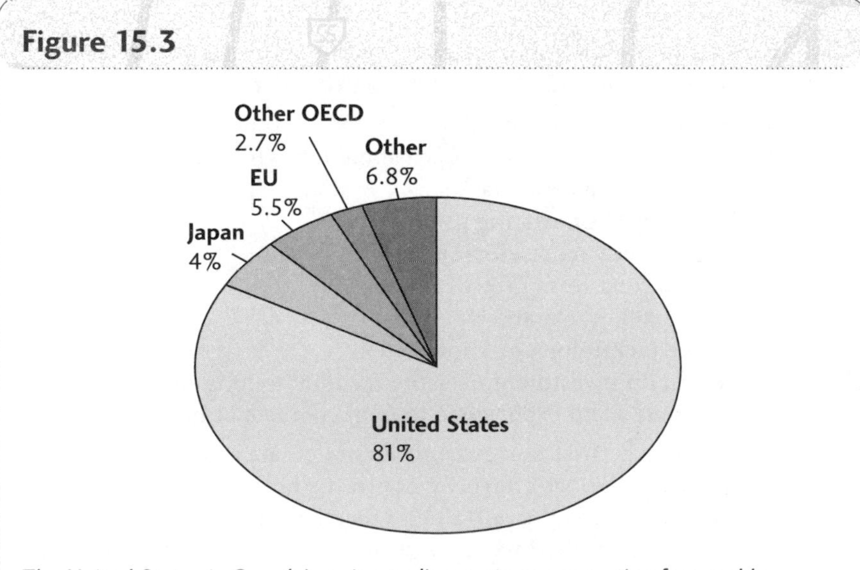

The United States is Canada's major trading partner, accounting for roughly 81 percent of our exports.

Source: Statistics Canada, "The United States Is Canada's Major Trading Partner, Accounting Roughly 81% of Our Exports," adapted from "Canadian International Merchandise Trade," Catalogue No. 65-001. Reprinted with permission.

Today the new knowledge-based economy has levelled the playing field — especially in the service sector. Small companies can serve the world market with a global telecommunications network connected to the Internet. Short production runs in manufacturing industries aided by computer-assisted programs can meet the needs of niche markets more efficiently than long production runs. Small business will continue to prosper in the new world arena that's taking shape. Yes, there are all kinds of entrepreneurial opportunities in the export market. So let's look at the challenges. Chances are, those export markets aren't as far away as you think.

The Start-up Fundamentals[4]

Many first-time exporters often become involved in exporting in an unplanned way. Risk-taking entrepreneurs "fall into" exporting for the following types of reasons:

- A foreign buyer, who sees an opportunity, approaches them.
- They have a surplus of goods that they think they can sell in another market.
- They need a larger market to survive.

Ultimately, many become frustrated, disoriented, and discouraged when they learn that export markets are usually much more difficult to penetrate than expected. We call this situation **export shock**. If you are thinking about exporting, your primary objective right now should be to plan to minimize this export inertia. We suggest you begin by taking a closer look at your export motivations, and follow this up with a **SWOT** — an honest appraisal of your internal Strengths and Weakness and external Opportunities and Threats

EXPORT SHOCK
the difficulty of opening an export market

SWOT ANALYSIS
honest appraisal of your internal Strengths and Weaknesses and external Opportunities and Threats

MOTIVATIONS FOR EXPORTING

What would be your motivation for entering the export market? Review the following list of reasons and choose the ones that apply to you.

- ❑ Dispose of excess domestic product.
- ❑ Supplement domestic sales with occasional foreign orders.
- ❑ Stabilize seasonal domestic markets.
- ❑ Extend the life cycle of existing products.
- ❑ Use existing capacity more efficiently.
- ❑ Build a base for long-term growth.
- ❑ Diversify the company's markets.
- ❑ Exploit unique technology or know-how.
- ❑ Improve return on investment over the medium to long term.
- ❑ Acquire knowledge and experience to help compete at home.

Of these factors, the first four reasons do not create a compelling case for undertaking a major export effort. By contrast, the other factors provide a more solid basis for making a sustained commitment to develop an export business. It takes time and effort to learn the technical aspects of exporting, understand foreign markets, and build relationships with foreign customers and intermediaries. Success in exporting normally stems from following a business strategy that focusses on achieving long-term goals such as market expansion or diversification, acquiring a better understanding of customer needs and market trends, or leveraging a company's specific knowledge or technology.

Entrepreneurs are busy people. Their attitudes and level of commitment towards an exporting goal plays a crucial role in determining whether their company will be successful abroad. Scarcity of managerial time, as well as concern over the risks and barriers that confront the prospective exporter, can deter many small firms from exporting. Now ask yourself the following questions:

- Do you have reservations about entering foreign markets?
- Do you see exporting as a peripheral or sporadic activity for your company?
- Do you believe it is unnecessary to develop a strategic export marketing plan?
- Do you plan to restrict your export effort to selling through Canadian-based "middlemen"?
- Are you willing to devote a significant amount of time to pursuing export business?
- Are you committed to making sufficient funds available to develop foreign markets?
- Are you prepared to trade off profits in the early stages of an export effort for gains in the longer term?
- Do you want to develop long-term international relationships?

A positive answer to the first four questions suggests a relatively weak rationale for developing an export business. A positive answer to the remaining questions indicates a stronger willingness to view exporting as a key strategic goal of your business.

Remember, too, that export success requires both patience and commitment from your team. Everyone involved must understand why the effort is being made, the nature of his or her particular role, and how benefits over time will accrue both to the company and to the individuals who work in it. We therefore suggest you first examine the export motivations of your team members as well as yourself.

SWOT ANALYSIS

You should already have a good perspective on your company because of your planning in the domestic market. What you are trying to do here is to take a strategic look at your business's strengths and weaknesses from an exporting perspective, get some ideas of what you'll need to export successfully, and then use these ideas to focus your market research. Most strategic planning begins with a SWOT analysis — an organizational method of assessing a company's internal Strengths and Weaknesses and external Opportunities and Threats. A SWOT analysis will help you answer a number of key questions. Let's start with your internal strengths and weaknesses.

Internal Strengths and Weaknesses

Here you are trying to define your company's competitive expertise. You'll also want to deal with critical weaknesses and find strategies to improve them. Table 15.1 will help you get started on this process. Before you complete this table, however, be aware of the following:

Product/Service Most successful exporting firms have already established a strong base in their own country. If your sales have been limited to local customers or to just a single Canadian region, you may be better advised to channel your energies into penetrating other Canadian regional markets. Exporting is apt to come easier once you have been successful elsewhere in

Table 15.1 Your Exporting Strengths and Weaknesses

Internal Attributes	Strength	Weakness
Service and Product		
Patented protection	______	______
Production process	______	______
Quality service/product	______	______
Packaging and presentation of service/product	______	______
Timely delivery	______	______
After-sales servicing of products	______	______
Delivery system	______	______
Services strategy	______	______
Responsiveness to customers	______	______
After-sales follow-up	______	______
Financial		
Financial resources	______	______
Cost advantages	______	______
Price advantages	______	______
Knowledge/Skills and Track Record		
Ability to speak foreign languages	______	______
Familiarity with foreign cultures/business practices	______	______
Contacts in a potential foreign target market	______	______
Contacts in the Canadian export community	______	______
Experience in conducting international negotiations	______	______
Experience with the technical aspects of international trade	______	______
Direct experience in exporting	______	______
Knowledge of where to obtain people with required skill sets	______	______
Operating history in domestic market	______	______
Others		
______________________	______	______
______________________	______	______
______________________	______	______

Canada. If you have previously exported on an intermittent basis or have sold your product to a Canadian-based intermediary such as an export trading company, you may have acquired experience that can assist you in making exporting an ongoing part of your business.

Human Resources Exporting is typically more time-consuming than pursuing domestic business. To succeed, you should aim to devote your full-time effort to exporting, at least in the start-up stage. If you have a team, be careful not to add a new set of export-related tasks to the responsibilities of people who already have their plates full. Should that happen, your domestic business will suffer and your export effort will likely not succeed.

Consider hiring (on contract) or assigning someone with prior experience in international business to help you with the mechanics of exporting. Tapping into relevant knowledge and experience from your own team may give your company an edge in evaluating or exploiting possible export opportunities.

Financial Situation A company whose financial position allows it to devote resources to export market development is well placed to make a significant commitment to exploiting international business opportunities.

If immediate profitability, cash, or working capital is a key priority underlying every business decision, export market development may not make sense, since it often requires a willingness to forgo short-term profits for long-term opportunity.

Operating History and Track Record Generally, companies that have been in business for at least a few years will be in a stronger position to try exporting than younger firms. They will have mastered the basics of managing their business, their product or service will have proven itself in the marketplace, and their cash flow will have stabilized.

Now it's your turn to do a SWOT analysis. Try your hand at Action Step 63.

ACTION STEP 63

Do an export SWOT analysis.

If you have a solid business idea, try a SWOT analysis from an exporting perspective. Make a list of your internal strengths and weaknesses, and your external opportunities and threats. Use Tables 15.1 and 15.2 to guide you.

If you still don't have a business in mind, think internationally. Get out a paper and pen and do some international brainstorming. What export opportunities are out there that you can take advantage of? How can you be part of the export revolution?

External Opportunities and Threats

Now that you have taken an inside look at your company's strengths and weaknesses, ask yourself what your company's best external opportunities and possibilities are. Then, identify the most important and emergent threats and how these can affect on your business.

Your external opportunities and threats will depend on the general physical, economic, political, and cultural factors shaping the economic and institutional environment of your potential target markets. Table 15.2 will help you do an external opportunities and threats analysis. First, be aware of some major external issues:

- If your product depends on timely delivery or is expensive to ship, then the foreign markets that are accessible to you will be limited to those within a certain distance or travel time.
- Sophisticated after-sales service or specialized training required to make use of what you have to offer may restrict sales to markets with a population that has relatively high income and literacy levels.
- Luxury products are marketable primarily in wealthier economies where consumers focus on product features rather than price.
- Products that depend on or vary with climatic conditions must be sold in markets where the weather is suitable.
- Products that must be financed in order to be sold will be difficult to sell in countries where such financing is hard to obtain or unavailable.
- Punitive trade barriers or foreign government controls may make some countries difficult export targets.

Key Points You Need to Know for Start-up

So far, we have directed our attention on your export readiness. We've tried to help you be aware of export opportunities, examine your exporting expectations, and analyze your strengths and weaknesses. Many of you may have already decided that exporting, at this time, is not right for you because you still need to focus your business on the local market. If this is the case, you may want to shuffle quickly through this section. Later, when you're ready to move into the export market, you can return to this part of the book.

For those of you who have decided that exporting may be the way to go for your business, this section is designed to help you do your homework. Before you launch into foreign soil, there are some key points about exporting you should be aware of, and several valuable sources of information to tap.

Table 15.2 Opportunities and Threats Checklist, from an Exporting Perspective

Market Characteristics	Opportunity	Threat
Demographic/Physical		
Population/market size	_____	_____
Population density and distribution	_____	_____
Climatic factors	_____	_____
Shipping distances (especially relevant for perishable and expensive-to-transport products)	_____	_____
Physical distribution and communication networks	_____	_____
Communications infrastructure (phones, faxes, modems) and overall technological sophistication (relevant for service providers)	_____	_____
Economic		
Level of economic development	_____	_____
Growth rates and potential	_____	_____
Industrial structure, per capita income	_____	_____
Income distribution	_____	_____
Consumer spending patterns and trends	_____	_____
Openness of the economy to imports	_____	_____
Import penetration and import sources	_____	_____
Currency and exchange rate factors	_____	_____
Balance of payments of the foreign government	_____	_____
Political/Governmental		
Political stability	_____	_____
Government involvement in the economy and in business	_____	_____
Legal framework for doing business	_____	_____
Provisions for the resolution or redress of grievances	_____	_____
Controls over foreign trade	_____	_____
Major trade policy instruments and tariff barriers	_____	_____
Non-tariff barriers such as standards and regulations	_____	_____
General state of relations with Canada	_____	_____
Sociocultural and Environmental		
Literacy rate	_____	_____
Language and customs	_____	_____
Cultural norms and characteristics	_____	_____
Business practices	_____	_____
Others		
______________________	_____	_____
______________________	_____	_____
______________________	_____	_____

FINDING INFORMATION AND ADVICE ABOUT YOUR TARGET MARKET

If you are export-ready, you'll first have to screen out a number of prospective foreign target markets. Then, you'll need to gather more detailed information on those that seem most promising.

For most small Canadian companies just beginning to export, the United States is the most popular initial foreign market. The reasons are easy to understand. Not only is proximity a factor, but also many Canadian compa-

Box 15.1 Planning to Export a Service? Get on The Net

Visit the Web site "Take a World View . . . Export Your Services":
http://strategis.ic.gc.ca/SSG/sc01353e.html

Industry Canada, the Department of Foreign Affairs and International Trade, and service exporters have produced a comprehensive information site for service exporters. The "Service Export Cycle" will take you through the twelve essential steps, from increasing your awareness of service exporting and preparing the tools, to entering your first market and expanding into new world markets. The site also provides answers to the most often asked questions about exporting services, makes it possible to determine export readiness, and helps prepare you for doing business internationally. As well, it offers numerous hot links to other relevant information sources.

nies benefit from close cross-border business ties, common language and culture, and similar consumer tastes and business practices. So the U.S. may be a good place to start.

In your research of foreign markets, many sources of information are available to assist you. Some of the most useful are:

Direct Contact Foreign visits and participation in foreign trade shows and fairs provide many opportunities for direct contact.

Periodicals Various Canadian and U.S. trade and business magazines regularly run features on specific foreign markets.

Department of Foreign Affairs and International Trade (DFAIT) Staff at DFAIT regularly compile market profiles of the countries to which they are posted. Information contained in these profiles and other department publications can be obtained from the Internet at <http://www.infoexport.gc.ca> or <http://exportsource.gc.ca> or by using the International Trade Centre hotline at 1-800-267-8376. You can also order a free newsletter called *CanadExport*. Once you have done your research, contact the Geographic Division at DFAIT for the country or market you are interested in.

Other Federal Government Departments Some of these departments/agencies include: Agriculture Canada, Atlantic Canada Opportunities Agency, Business Development Bank of Canada, Canadian Commercial Corporation, Canadian International Development Agency, Export Development Corporation, Industry Canada, Multiculturalism and Citizenship Canada, Standards Council of Canada, and Statistics Canada.

Trade Commissioners Canada's trade commissioners abroad live and work "on site" in more than 125 cities around the world. They are the eyes, ears, and voice of Canadian exporters and an invaluable link to foreign markets. Trade commissioners abroad can help you enter your target market by assessing your entry strategy, identifying potential partners, and providing you with on-site visit support. Prepare thoroughly before you approach the trade commissioners overseas. Then ask very specific questions to get the detailed and tailor-made answers you need.

Provincial Governments Provincial governments have trade and/or industry departments that deal with export promotion and assemble foreign market intelligence relevant to Canadian businesses.

Business Associations Canadian trade and industry associations also have information about foreign markets. For example, the Canadian Exporters Alliance, the Canadian Chamber of Commerce, and the Canadian Manufacturers Alliance all offer materials and seminars on foreign markets.

Foreign Embassies You should consider contacting the embassies or trade commissions representing countries that interest you and ask for

ACTION STEP 64

Discover export sources.
The Internet has a lot of export information and helpful sources. Check the following sites:

Export Source
http://exportsource.gc.ca/export.html
Export Source is a comprehensive Web site for exporters of both goods and services. It comes with a multi-database search engine and on-line guides. Start with the "Export Preparation" tool to get export-ready.

International Business Information Network
http://strategis.ic.gc.ca/SSG/bi18087e.html
This site will help you search for information on products in demand, market conditions, competitors and business opportunities abroad, business contacts, and the right international business support resources.

Trade Data Online
http://strategis.ic.gc.ca/sc_mrkti/tdst/engdoc/tr_homep.html
Here you will find Canadian and U.S. trade and commodity data. With its search engine, this site will also help you find new export markets and determine competition for your products. It contains information on more than 200 countries and over 5 000 products and 500 industries from which you can create your own reports and graphs.

Forum for International Trade Training FITT
http://www.fitt.ca
FITT Inc.'s mission is to provide businesses and individuals with quality programs and training in international trade so that they are prepared to compete successfully in world markets. This site contains all kinds of information on international training courses, workshops, and seminars.

Multicultural Advisors
http://strategis.ic.gc.ca
The Multicultural Advisors connection on the International Business Opportunities and Investment link in Strategis will help you find a person or organization that could guide you in dealing effectively with culturally different markets, whether at home or abroad. You'll even be able to join in on some on-line multicultural chat.

information on economic conditions, trade patterns, and business conditions and practices in their home countries.

Bilateral Business Councils Numerous bilateral business councils are active in Canada. Examples of country-to-country councils include the Canada–Korea Business Council, the Canada–Poland Chamber of Commerce, and the Canada–India Business Council. Regionally oriented groups include the Pacific Basin Economic Council, the Canada–Arab Business Council, and CUBE, the Council, promote Canadian trade with countries of the former Soviet Union.

Intermediaries Business people in Canada with ties to, or ethnic roots in, a target market can be a valuable source of information and assistance. But it should be remembered that they may not be objective sources of information.

Databases Several major commercial databases (such as Dow Jones, Dow Jones Interactive, and Dun & Bradstreet) carry international economic and business information, country/industry profiles, bibliographic references, and recent newspaper and periodical articles. For information about these databases and how to access them, a good starting point is the nearest public or university library or the Internet.

Export Advisors/Experts Often, the most useful information comes directly from people who possess first-hand knowledge of the market targeted. Such people include:

- Foreign distributors
- Potential foreign customers
- Editors of specialized trade or business magazines
- Diplomatic personnel
- Other federal or provincial government officials
- Canadian companies that currently sell in the market

Internet This should become one of your main sources of export information. There are numerous Web sites dealing with exports. The best place to start is Strategis at <http://strategis.ic.gc.ca>. Box 15.1 contains one primary source "Take a World View . . . Export Your Services." Now Action Step 64 will get you started on other key sites.

MASTER THE TERMINOLOGY OF EXPORTING

As we know by now, exporting is more complex than selling into a domestic market. To succeed, you need to familiarize yourself with key trade expressions and techniques. To get you started on all the terms, we have provided you with a selected list in Table 15.3. You will find many more exporting terms and expressions from the sources we outlined in Action Step 64.

CHOOSING AN ENTRY STRATEGY

Generally, there are three ways to enter a foreign market: through an intermediary, by direct selling, and through a partnership.

Intermediaries

If you're new to the exporting game, your best bet for entering a foreign market may be through an intermediary. This is particularly true if some or all of the following conditions apply:

- You are unfamiliar with the target market.
- You plan to make only small or intermittent export sales.

Table 15.3 General Trade Vocabulary

International trade carries its own particular terminology. The following are only a few general trade expressions that the novice exporter will encounter in published sources or in discussions dealing with trade issues.

Vocabulary	Explanation
Agent	A foreign representative who tries to sell your product in the target market. The agent does not take possession of, and assumes no responsibility for, the goods. Agents are paid on a commission basis.
Certificate of origin	A document that certifies the country where the product was made (i.e., its "origin").
CIF (cost, insurance and freight)	The exporter pays the cost of goods, cargo, and insurance, plus all transportation charges to the named port of destination.
Confirmed letter of credit	A Canadian bank confirms the validity of a letter of credit issued by a foreign bank, on behalf of the foreign importer, guaranteeing payment to the Canadian exporter, provided that the terms outlined in the document have been met. An unconfirmed letter of credit does not guarantee payment so, if the foreign bank or buyer defaults, the Canadian exporter will not be paid. Canadian exporters should accept only confirmed letters of credit as a form of payment.
Confirming house	A company, based in a foreign country, that acts as a foreign buyer's agent and places the "confirm" orders with Canadian exporters. They guarantee payment to the exporter.
Countertrade	A general expression meaning the sale or barter of goods on a reciprocal basis.
Customs invoice	A document used to clear goods through customs in the importing country by providing documentary evidence of the value of the goods.
Export licence	A document required under Canadian law that exporters must obtain before selling certain products abroad (e.g., protected birds, animals, and plants). An export licence may also apply to certain countries.
Factoring house	A company that buys export receivables at a discount.
FOB ("Free on Board")	Goods that are placed on board a shipping vessel by the seller at the port of shipment specified in the sales contract. The risk of loss or damage is transferred to the buyer when the goods pass the ship's rail.
Irrevocable letter of credit	The bank issuing an irrevocable letter of credit agrees to pay the exporter once the terms and conditions of the transaction are met. Because it is irrevocable, none of the terms or conditions may be modified without the consent of all parties, including the exporter. A revocable letter of credit does not provide this assurance and should never be used or accepted by the exporter as an adequate commitment by the foreign buyer to pay.
Landed cost	The cost of the exported product at the port or point of entry into the foreign market, before the addition of foreign tariffs, taxes, local packaging/assembly costs, and local distributors' margins. Product modifications before shipment are included in the landed cost.

- You are selling a low-cost, mass-produced product.
- The target market has a large number of end users and high sales potential.
- Your product requires extensive on-site training and support.
- Your company is not able to provide after-sales service or customer support.
- The product is normally sold through local distributors in the target market.

There are generally three types of intermediaries: agents/representatives, foreign distributors, and trading houses.

AGENT
intermediary, working on commission, who sells an exporter's products to foreign customers

Agents/Representatives An agent obtains and transmits orders from foreign customers and receives a commission from the exporter in return for the effort. The agent sells at prices the exporter sets and does not normally stock the product. If you use an agent, remember that the risk of loss or non-payment and the responsibility for service and warranty remain with you.

MANUFACTURER'S REPRESENTATIVE
specialized agent, working on commission, who sells a manufacturer's products to a specific group of customers within a given geographic area

A **manufacturer's representative** is a specialized agent who generally operates within a given geographic territory and who sells related lines of manufactured goods to a specific group of customers. Using a manufacturer's representative is a common way of distributing industrial and commercial products in the U.S.

Both agents and representatives are authorized to enter into contractual sales agreements with foreign customers on behalf of the Canadian exporter. They usually work on a commission basis and are paid only when they sell your product. Depending on the agreement, they may or may not be paid for their expenses. When searching for foreign agents and representatives, look for those who handle complementary products, which are likely to facilitate sales of your product.

FOREIGN DISTRIBUTOR
intermediary who purchases products from an exporter and resells them

Foreign Distributors The role of a foreign distributor differs from that of an agent or manufacturer's representative. Unlike agents, distributors actually purchase the exporter's product and then resell it to local customers. Because it assumes risks, a foreign distributor typically insists on longer payment terms and on control over your product once it takes possession of it.

A significant potential advantage for the Canadian exporter is that the distributor is often able to provide after-sales service in the foreign market. The main disadvantages of using a foreign distributor are that your margins are reduced, you have less control over the product and price, and you do not benefit from direct contact with foreign customers.

TRADING HOUSES
domestically-based intermediaries that market exporters' goods abroad

Trading Houses Trading houses (about 500 to 600 in Canada) are domestically-based intermediaries that market Canadian goods abroad. A full-service Canadian trading house handles all aspects of exporting, including conducting foreign market research, arranging merchandise transportation, appointing overseas distributors or agents, exhibiting products at trade shows, and advertising and arranging documentation. The trading house can take full responsibility for exporting on behalf of Canadian companies that generally lack direct experience in this area.

In Canada, organizations formed by the Council of Canadian Trading Houses and the Association des maisons de commerce extérieur du Québec may be able to direct you to a trading house that is appropriate for your needs.

Direct Selling

Advances in telecommunications and process technologies, more efficient transportation linkages, the growth of just-in-time delivery systems, improved inventory management techniques, and a host of other developments mean that **direct selling** by exporters in foreign markets became a more viable option for small Canadian companies over the 1990s.

DIRECT SELLING
selling to foreign markets without an intermediary

In the long term, selling directly to foreign retailers or end users may yield higher margins for the exporter than selling through an agent or distributor. It may also mean lower prices for the foreign customer. Moreover, it allows the seller to benefit from closer direct contact with end users. But direct distribution can also have disadvantages. Since the company will not have the services of a foreign representative or distributor, it must take the time to become familiar with the foreign market and with the export process. Building a direct sales force can entail a significant commitment of time, effort, and up-front costs.

Partnerships

Another option open to small business exporters is to develop some form of partnership abroad. One example is given in Box 15.2. Sometimes known also as strategic alliances (covered in Chapter Twelve), partnerships can help overcome the many challenges of doing business internationally. They may be useful to product exporters seeking to overcome various kinds of trade barriers and import restrictions. They are also useful to service exporters seeking a local presence and representation.

A well-structured partnership offers concrete benefits to both sides:

- Each company focusses on what it does and knows best.
- The partners share the risk and therefore minimize the consequences of failure.
- Partnering extends each side's capabilities into new areas or ideas.
- Resources can be pooled to help both sides keep pace with change.
- Small firms can use partnering to take advantage of economies of scale and achieve the critical mass needed for success. Through partners, a company can approach several markets simultaneously.
- Partnering can provide a firm with technology, capital, or market access that it might not be able to afford or achieve on its own. Both sides can translate the synergy gained into a competitive advantage that will help them succeed in the global marketplace.

For all its advantages, partnering also carries a few potential disadvantages:

- You may have to give up some freedom of action.
- You may have to spend considerable energy on just managing the relationship.
- Occasionally, partnerships can lead to dependence on another firm.
- With many forms of partnership, there is always the danger that strategic or proprietary information may be inadvertently shared or leaked outside the alliance.

The different types of international partnering are shown in Table 15.4.

Box 15.2 Dare to Be Different

In Chapter Four, we highlighted Just Kid'n Children's Wear. After several calls from foreign retailers, President Kelly Cahill finally found a global partner he liked: a $4 billion Singapore mail-order company. Cahill created ten mix-and-match items and marketed them under a new name, "Dare to be Different." Almost overnight, he entered the Asian export market. Just Kid'n supplied the product and the Singapore company sold and distributed it.

Alliances, like this, with larger international companies are one of the main reasons Profit 100 companies have been so successful in the export market. "There's no doubt that most Profit 100 companies use bigger international associates to crack the international market," said Cahill.

Source: Adapted from Rick Spence, *Secrets of Success from Canada's Fastest-Growing Companies* (Toronto: John Wiley & Sons Canada, Ltd., 1997), p. 117. Reprinted by permission of the author.

Table 15.4 Types of Export Partnerships

Form of Partnering	Description/Considerations
Joint venture	• An independent business formed through the co-operation of two or more parent firms, normally for a specific purpose. • Traditionally used to avoid restrictions on foreign ownership when the business in question is entering a foreign market. • Useful if the project requires commitments that are more complex and comprehensive than what can be spelled out in a simple contract. • Suitable for longer-term arrangements that require joint product development as well as ongoing manufacturing and marketing. • Can also be used as a way of developing a local presence for the service exporter.
Licensing	• Not usually considered to be a form of partnership, but it can lead to partnerships or be an important element in their formation. • A firm sells the interested party the rights to use its products or services, but it still retains some control over the product or service. • Issues subject to negotiation include royalties, patents, sub-licensing possibilities, rights to sell and manufacture, duration of the arrangement, geographical limitations of the licence, exclusivity, and issues related to the updating of technology.
Cross-licensing	• Increasingly popular form of strategic alliance between two firms, whereby each licenses products or services to the other. • A relatively straightforward way for companies to share products or expertise without the complications of closer collaboration. • Less likely than other partnerships to achieve much synergy because it involves minimal co-operation.
Cross-manufacturing	• A form of cross-licensing in which companies agree to manufacture each other's products. • May be combined with co-marketing or co-promotion agreements through which companies co-operate to advertise and sell each others' products. • A comprehensive co-operative agreement could involve cross-licensing, a shared promotion campaign, or even the formation of a joint venture to market each others' products. • Most agreements do not involve licences or royalties, but some rights to the product may be worked into the agreement.
Co-marketing	• Firms sell and market complementary products. • Sometimes done on the basis of a fee or percentage of sales. • An effective way to take advantage of existing distribution networks and an ally's knowledge of local markets. • Allows firms with complementary products to fill out a product line while avoiding expensive and time-consuming development.

(Continued)

Table 15.4 Types of Export Partnerships (*Continued*)

Form of Partnering	Description/Considerations
Co-production	• Represents co-operation in the production of goods. • Enables firms to optimize the use of their own resources, to share complementary resources, and to take advantage of economies of scale. Co-operation may involve the manufacture of components or even entire products. • Many foreign engineering firms have entered joint production agreements with domestic firms that have manufacturing expertise (in the form of an alliance to make components used by all the competitors).
Franchise	• Represents a more specific form of licensing. • The franchisee is given the right to use a set manufacturing process or service delivery process, along with set business systems or trademarks, and the franchisor controls their use by contractual agreement. • The franchisor is remunerated through an initial franchise agreement fee, from royalties on sales and, in some cases, through control of supplies to the franchisee.

PRICING YOUR PRODUCT OR SERVICE

Even for the experienced exporter, the pricing decision is one of the most challenging aspects of selling in foreign markets. Setting your price is a complex decision, but here are a few basic guidelines

First, you need to understand that pricing is generally a more complicated issue for product exporters than it is for service exporters. In many professional service contracts, price is determined by the exporter's daily rate plus expenses. The crucial pricing decision revolves around the rate that is competitive in the country and what other companies charge for similar types of expertise.

If you are exporting a product, you have to begin by determining what costs will be added to the price of your product as it makes its way to the market. Table 15.5 provides you with a list of the types of costs you may incur, which often makes it more expensive than in Canada. At this stage we strongly advise that you double-check your calculations with customs and insurance brokers and government trade officials. You want to make sure that you have included all the correct costs. Once you know your costs, your next step is to determine what price you have to charge to make it worth your while. Exporters generally rely on a handful of methods to calculate their prices on goods or services sold in foreign markets. Here are three common methods:

Domestic Cost Plus Mark-up This is the simplest pricing approach that allows you to maintain your domestic profit margin. It involves taking your domestic costs and mark-up, and then adding export costs such as packaging, tariffs, freight, and insurance. If you are exporting a service, you would take your basic daily rate and add export-related costs. The main disadvantage of this approach is that it ignores market and demand conditions in the foreign country. For example, you may be able to reduce your domestic cost per unit with a higher volume of sales.

DOMESTIC COST PLUS MARK-UP simplest pricing approach that adds domestic costs and a mark-up to include export costs

FULL-COST PRICING
pricing approach that includes fixed and variable costs and a profit margin

Full-cost Pricing This method considers fixed as well as relevant variable costs, including those specific to exporting, in establishing prices. It allows you to recover your total costs, to which a profit margin is then added to yield the final price. But again, it overlooks the competitive situation in the target market.

MARGINAL-COST PRICING
pricing approach that includes floor price (unit cost) and marginal (export) cost

Marginal-cost Pricing Marginal-cost pricing is a good strategy for some manufacturers and retailers who have surplus capacity on an ongoing basis. This means that the goods or services for export could be produced without a major increase in the company's fixed costs. To calculate your marginal cost price, you would add the following two elements: floor price plus mark-up.

- *The floor price* is the unit cost based on out-of-pocket costs of producing and selling the merchandise for export (including costs specific to exporting, such as product modification, packaging, and labelling). Floor price includes only those extra or incremental costs involved to export your product (i.e., your export or marginal costs).
- A mark-up to the estimated marginal (export) cost to yield export profit margin.

Marginal-cost pricing usually produces a lower export price than domestic cost plus mark-up or full-cost pricing, because it does not include many of the fixed domestic costs such as rent and administration. It is more complicated, though some argue that it provides a more accurate picture of the cost of getting your product to a foreign market, and helps to isolate the profitability of your export business.

Your ultimate decision on the costing method will depend, to a large degree, on your purpose for exporting. For example, if you are exporting to fill export plant capacity (as is the case for many manufacturers) or to keep your employees busy in the off-season, any price that returns more than the marginal cost of exporting may be enough for you.

Once you have determined an export price that will net you a profit, you will then have to deal with the exchange rate. When you sell your product in a foreign country, a critical question is how much you will get in Canadian dollars. That will depend on the exchange rate. Let's assume that the Canadian dollar is trading at $0.70 U.S. You decide that your export price for your product will be $1 Canadian. This would mean you could sell your product in the United States for $0.70 and you would get, in return, $1 Canadian for each product sold. But what if the exchange rate goes to $0.80 U.S.? You would now have to increase your price to $0.80 in the U.S. to maintain your export profit margin. How do you predict these kinds of fluctuations in the exchange rate? To prepare yourself, contact government officials, foreign exchange officials, and international banking officers. Use the experts to guide your guesstimate, and keep in mind that you probably will want a little room for safety in your price policy.

Determining your export price is just one of the many details that goes into selling your product outside of Canada and, with exports, it is sometimes the details that determine success or failure. So, once you have determined your price, you need to do some networking. Review your strategies and plans with those who are familiar with successful export pricing in your target market. Canadian trade commissioners are a good place to start, but we also suggest you revisit our previous list of exporting sources provided above under "Finding Information and Advice About Your Target Market." You will need to know if your price is in line. Will the market respond? Did you forget anything?

Table 15.5 A Typical Export Cost Sheet

1. Unit Cost	$ 650
fixed	300
variable	350
2. Labelling ("Made in Canada" label)	10
3. Tax/Duty Adjustments (subtract)	160
GST rebate	70
duty drawbacks	10
non-applicable fixed costs	80
4. Net Production Cost (1 + 2 – 3)	50
5. Packaging	45
6. Forwarding Agent's Fees	65
7. Promotional Costs	50
8. Other Costs (financing charges, documentation preparation, export credit insurance)	30
9. Export Commissions (10% of selling price to U.S. agent)	140
10. Total (4 + 5 + 6 + 7 + 8 + 9)	830
11. Trucking Costs	130
12. Merchandise Insurance	20
13. Customs and Clearance Fees	45
14. Profit (Export Income)	375
15. Final Price (10 + 11 + 12 + 13 + 14) (truck-delivered selling price, cleared through Customs)	$1 400

PROMOTIONAL STRATEGIES

Well-planned foreign-based promotional strategies often play a key role in the achievement of success in international markets. Here are some important promotional considerations.

Promoting Services A service provider's offerings usually involve some conventional advertising, but personal selling is the most effective. In many service-oriented sectors, a company's reputation spreads by word-of-mouth or personal referrals. Many service contracts are issued by government institutions or international development agencies, and the supplier has to keep an eye on what contracts are being put out for tender. In such cases, the major form of promotion tends to be "lobbying" the support of the Canadian government through the embassy, although the services of an agency such as the Canadian Commercial Corporation or the Canadian International Development Agency can also be important.

Packaging Recognize that it will likely be necessary to redesign your Canadian packaging before trying to sell your product abroad. For example, some colours, signs, pictures, and symbols used on products sold at home may be inappropriate or even offensive in certain foreign markets where consumer tastes and values differ from those at home. Foreign sales agents and distributors will be able to provide useful advice on package design and many other matters related to this facet of promotion.

Promotional Options There are several options for advertising your product or service in foreign markets: trade/business magazines, directories, other publications and media, direct promotional materials such as brochures, and trade fairs and exhibitions.

Promotional Materials The materials for your export promotion campaign must be "internationalized." You cannot simply rely on what you use at home. Here are some important points to remember:

- Where necessary, rewrite your sales letters and literature to adapt the materials for foreign markets.
- Pictures are often an effective way of communicating your message and portraying the application of your product or service.
- Consider whether you should translate your materials into the language of your target market.
- In non-English- and non-French-speaking countries, examine the meaning and acceptability of brand names and logos used in Canada. Make sure that no negative or inappropriate connotations are conveyed.
- Make sure that colour and symbols used in promotional material are sensitive to local tastes and consumer preferences. A special distributor kit can be helpful in responding to inquiries from this source. The contents might include product specifications and a catalogue, background information on the product, product samples, annual reports or other concise summary information on your company, a questionnaire to help you learn more about the foreign agent or distributor, and a proposed understanding or representation agreement.

Trade Fairs and Exhibitions Trade fairs can be an effective way of familiarizing yourself with other markets and promoting your product with prospective foreign buyers. The main goal of trade fairs and shows is to encourage business exchanges between buyers and sellers of a particular category of products. Most trade shows and exhibitions focus on specific industries. As an exporter, your objectives in participating in these events are to display your merchandise, make business contacts, investigate the market, learn more about your competitors and their products, and make some sales.

Promoting in the U.S. Small exporters are advised to approach the United States as a series of distinctive regional markets and to adapt their promotional strategies accordingly. The continental U.S. can be divided into at least five main regions: the northeast, the midwest, the southeast, the southwest, and the Rocky Mountain/western states. Often it makes sense to break these regions into smaller sub-units or even to focus on particular states. American buyers tend to perceive companies based in Canada as being domestic or "North American." They want to make their purchases in the same manner they do when buying from U.S.-based suppliers. As a consequence, many exporters choose to deal directly with any U.S. customs requirements. The priorities of American buyers are generally the same as when they deal with domestic suppliers: a competitive price, good quality, on-time delivery, and superior service.

EXPORT FINANCING

Financing is central to the success of smaller businesses intending to export. In both the product and service areas, exporting brings additional risks in terms of payment delays, disputes, and defaults. The major issues in export financing are: methods of payment, ensuring payment, credit management, and managing exchange rate risk.

Methods of International Payment

There are a variety of ways in which the Canadian exporter can arrange to be paid. Four common short-term financing methods, in order of increasing risk to the exporter, are: cash in advance, letters of credit, documentary collections, and open account transactions.

Cash in Advance This is the most secure option for an exporter, since it eliminates all risk of non-payment and bolsters working capital. Unfortunately, few foreign buyers are willing to pay full cash in advance. On occasion, a buyer will provide a portion of the contract by way of cash in advance as a down payment when Canadian vendors need financing to manufacture the goods ordered by the buyer. In the case of services, a partial payment may be made upon signing a contract, after which progress payments are matched to deliverables.

CASH IN ADVANCE
short-term financing method in which a foreign buyer pays an exporter cash before goods are delivered

Letters of Credit This is frequently used in international commerce. The most common form of payment, a commercial letter of credit or documentary credit is issued by a bank at the request of an importer, in favour of a supplier/exporter, to finance the importation of goods or services. By issuing the documentary credit on behalf of the importer, the bank lends its own name to the transaction. Thus, the bank obligates itself to pay the exporter, provided that the exporter complies strictly with the terms of the credit. In effect, this eliminates the credit risk of the buyer. Both the foreign and the Canadian bank receive fees for providing this service.

LETTER OF CREDIT
document issued by a bank at the request of an importer, in favour of a supplier/exporter, to finance the importation of goods and services; sometimes called documentary credit

There are several varieties of a letter of credit. As we noted in Table 15.3, an irrevocable letter of credit, for example, cannot be amended or cancelled without the consent of all parties, including the exporter. In contrast, a revocable letter of credit can be cancelled without the exporter's consent and, as such, is not a true guarantee of payment. If you are not prepared to accept the credit risk of the issuing bank, you can also insist on a confirmed letter of credit. A letter of credit issued by a foreign bank can be confirmed by a Canadian bank, constituting a guarantee of payment. This is an undertaking by the Canadian bank to pay if the foreign bank does not. The most secure form of letter of credit is one that is both confirmed and irrevocable.

Documentary Collection There are several types of collection methods. A documentary collection is the most common type. It consists of a bill of exchange, which is an unconditional order, signed by the exporter, requiring the importer to pay on demand or at a determined future time, a specified amount of money to a specified person. It is accompanied by commercial documents that confer ownership of the goods shipped. A "clean collection" is a bill of exchange not accompanied by shipping documents, as these are sent directly to the buyer. In both forms of payment, there is evidence of a legal obligation on the part of the importer.

DOCUMENTARY COLLECTION
an unconditional order from the exporter, requiring the buyer to pay on demand or at a determined time a specified amount to a specified person

Collections provide the exporter with a lower level of security than letters of credit, and the bank charges are less. However, in some cases, especially in dealing with countries where the banking system is less developed and letters of credit may not be available, collections may be the only alternative.

Open Account Transactions With this type of collection method, the exporter has sole responsibility for determining the ability and willingness of the purchaser to pay. Banks provide no protection. The exporting party must finance the transaction with its own funds. Selling on open account is arguably the easiest way to make export sales, since this arrangement incurs minimal costs to the exporter and involves little paperwork. However, it may also be risky. Open account transactions are appropriate when you trust your foreign customers and have access to bank credit. The foreign importer should have an established credit record and, preferably, should be located in a country with a stable economy and government.

OPEN ACCOUNT TRANSACTION
a form of collection that involves little or no conditions of payment

Ensuring Payment: Types of Security

When selling into a new and unfamiliar market, one precaution is to demand more secure forms of payment. Apart from the payment terms mentioned earlier, there are other forms of security. The most common is export insurance. Both federal government agencies (such as the Export Development Corporation) and private insurance firms will offer policies to protect your export receivables. Insuring receivables offers exporters another advantage. Because they are essentially guaranteed, most banks will accept insured receivables as security if the exporter wants to borrow additional working capital.

A different type of security is provided by the Canadian Commercial Corporation (CCC). Its role is to facilitate a deal between Canadian suppliers and foreign purchasers by providing assurances to both sides. For foreign buyers, the CCC undertakes to guarantee the performance of the Canadian supplier, ensuring that goods or services will be delivered as specified. For Canadian exporters, the CCC guarantees that payment will be made if the terms of the contract are fulfilled and, in many cases, it can even accelerate payments.

Credit Management

Credit management is a key concern for most businesses when they deal with their domestic customers. The same issue arises when you begin to export. Often, it is necessary to extend credit in order to win and retain foreign customers. But before doing so, always check the buyer's credit worthiness. This is comparatively easy to do in the case of importers located in the United States and many European countries. Also important is to take into account the political/economic stability of the importing country, the availability of credit insurance, and the value of the sale both in absolute terms and in relation to your total sales.

Managing Exchange Rate Risk

International trade can put either the importer or the exporter at a foreign exchange risk. A contract that is to be paid in the exporter's currency (the preferred option for the Canadian exporter), could leave the importer at risk of currency fluctuations. By contrast, the Canadian exporter may be put at risk when the contract specifies payment in the importer's currency.

Such risks can be reduced or avoided by hedging in the foreign exchange market. Hedging involves negotiating the future payment by the importer at the exchange rate prevailing at the time the contract is signed. This eliminates the exporter's exposure to the risk of possible fluctuations in the value of the importer's currency against the Canadian dollar. Banks and other financial institutions can assist you in taking steps to manage your exchange rate risks. Ideally, however, you should try to transfer exchange rate risk to the foreign importer of your product by persuading that company to agree to make payment in Canadian (or perhaps U.S.) dollars. However, as a small business, you will likely lack the expertise or time to become involved in the foreign money market.

GETTING YOUR PRODUCT OR SERVICE TO MARKET

Understanding what is involved in getting your product or service into the foreign target market is an important part of the export process. To a large extent, the challenges you will face in export delivery depend on whether you are exporting a service or a product.

Exporting a Service

The challenges associated with providing services to a foreign market are quite different from those of providing goods. Your ability to deliver services to the customer will depend on factors such as the following:

- The extent and reliability of telecommunications links in the target market.
- The degree to which an infrastructure of computers, Internet, faxes, modems, etc. exists in the target market.
- The frequency and convenience of regularly scheduled transportation links between Canada and the target country.
- The relative technological sophistication, receptivity, and flexibility of customers in the target market.
- The support you may receive from official channels, government departments, and international development agencies.
- Your ability to satisfy legal regulations governing work permits or professional certification.

Exporting a Product

You have four options for getting your goods to your foreign customers: trucking, rail, air, and ocean. No matter what option you choose, the process of international transport is complex. Here are some of the issues you will have to deal with:

Packing of Goods Proper packing and marking is necessary for goods entering international markets. Merchandise shipped internationally, particularly by ocean or regular air freight, is susceptible to damage and loss. In selecting the appropriate packing method, you have to consider such factors as weather conditions, "at port" and handling facilities, risk of damage, and the risk of theft and pilferage.

Marking Marking containers identifies your goods in relation to the consignment or cargoes of other shippers. Marks shown on the shipping containers must conform to those shown on the commercial invoice or bill of lading. Required markings include such items as buyer's name or some other form of agreed identification, point or port of entry into the importing country, and gross and net weights in kilograms and pounds.

Product Labelling Beyond marking the container, you may also have to provide your products with labels suited to the target market. Product labelling is no trivial matter. Your goods may not clear customs or may not be admitted into the country of destination unless your product labels conform to all local requirements. You will have to deal with such issues as use of the local language, name of the country where the product was made or manufactured, name of the producer or shipper, and product details such as weight, ingredients, and so on.

Insurance International carriers assume only limited liability for your goods when they are shipped by air or water. If you are shipping abroad, you will need marine transportation insurance to protect both ocean- and air-bound cargo and to cover connecting land transportation. There are different types of marine insurance, but we strongly suggest you consider "all risk" insurance, which is the most comprehensive type of transportation insurance, protecting against all physical loss or damage from external causes.

Documentation for Overseas Shipping Shipping documents allow your product to pass through customs, be loaded on a carrier, and be transported to the destination. A number of documents are required for overseas shipping. These generally fall into two basic categories: shipping documents and collection documents. Key shipping documents include packing lists, validated export licences (if required by Canadian law), domestic bills of lading, and other export documents. Principal collection documents include commercial invoices (the seller's bill of sale), consular invoices (required by some foreign countries), certificates of origin (attesting to the origin of the exported goods), and import licences.

Freight Forwarders As you can see by now, the transport of goods to a foreign country is complex, and that is why even the most experienced exporters often choose to get expert advice. We strongly recommend that you use the assistance of a freight forwarder for the international transport of goods. Freight forwarders are specialists in handling and shipping goods for sale to foreign countries. Effective use of a forwarder is particularly critical for companies new to exporting. Among the specialized services they offer are:

- Selecting a suitable carrier for your product and target market.
- Negotiating all arrangements with the carrier.
- Co-ordinating the movement of cargo to the port of embarkation.
- Preparing the necessary documents.
- Providing advice on the packing, labelling, and marking of goods.
- Arranging warehouse storage and cargo insurance.

CULTURE AND COMMUNICATION

SLM is a Toronto-based company that sells software systems for electronic banking. In 1996, after just four years in business, it had more than quadrupled its revenues. At least 80 percent of its revenues now come from outside Canada, up from 30 percent in 1992. How did this small Canadian company become so successful in penetrating the world market? According to Govin Misir, SLM's Guyana-born president and chief executive officer, "The company has incorporated cultural awareness into the way it does business." As this example shows, if you want to succeed in the international marketplace, you must ensure that your communications are linguistically and culturally appropriate.[5]

Here are a few interesting illustrations:[6]

- You should always use your right hand when you accept or pass food in India.
- When most Canadians "table" a proposal, they intend to delay a decision. In Britain, "tabling" means that immediate action is to be taken.
- For many Arabs, their signature on a contract is much less meaningful than the fact that they have given their word.
- Pepsico marketers created a promotional campaign, in China, based on the theme "Come Alive with Pepsi." Sales were slow. They later found out that the direct Chinese translation of their slogan was "Bring your ancestors back from the dead."

HIGH-CONTEXT CULTURE
culture in which communication depends not only on the message itself, but also on everything that surrounds it

LOW-CONTEXT CULTURE
culture in which communication tends to rely on explicit written and verbal messages

To help us think about our communication styles, anthropologists tend to divide cultures into two basic types: **high context** and **low context** (see Figure 15.4). Communications in high-context cultures tend to depend not only on the message itself, but on everything that surrounds it. Mexico would be good example of a high-context culture. Communications in low-context cultures tend to rely on explicit verbal and written messages. Examples of countries with low-context cultures include Switzerland, Germany, and Canada. What this means is that if you are the type of Canadian who wants

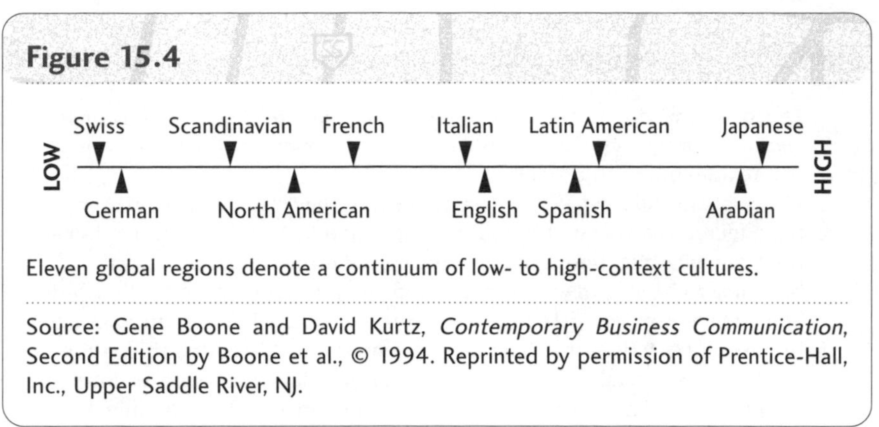

Eleven global regions denote a continuum of low- to high-context cultures.

Source: Gene Boone and David Kurtz, *Contemporary Business Communication*, Second Edition by Boone et al., © 1994. Reprinted by permission of Prentice-Hall, Inc., Upper Saddle River, NJ.

to "shake hands and get down to business," you may hit a cultural roadblock if you are trying to export to Mexico. In Mexico's high-context culture, it's wise to allow lots of time for relaxed meals and relationship building.[7]

Clearly then, before you begin your exporting journey, you are going to have to do your cultural homework. It is not enough to learn how to say a few things in another language or have your mail translated. Communication goes beyond the spoken or written language. It has to do with history, political and social environment, culture, and traditions. This means that you may have to visit your target several times. Or, you may have to get professional advice and training. The point is that the way of conducting business differs in every country and sometimes even within regions of a country. You can't expect to be successful until you have mastered the business and social culture.

A FINAL "EXPORT READY" CHECKLIST

Before you launch your product or service onto foreign soil, we want you to review the following checklist of questions. It might also be a good idea to note some of the most common errors made by novice exporters, shown in Box 15.3.

- ❑ Are you ready to commit the resources and time to attempt exporting?
- ❑ Are you comfortable and knowledgeable with the choice of target market?
- ❑ Are you confident that you have the right product or service for that market?
- ❑ Have you become familiar with the necessary technical information?
- ❑ Are you confident with your choice of entry or distribution strategy, and do you feel you have the right partners or associates?
- ❑ Are you confident your price is competitive?
- ❑ Do you have a promotional plan?
- ❑ Can you finance the transaction?
- ❑ Have you chosen an appropriate way of delivering the shipment?
- ❑ Do you have an adequate understanding of the culture of your target country?

If you're satisfied with these answers, it's time to map out your exporting strategy. Complete Action Step 65. You will then be ready to piece together an export plan. To help you, use the following "Export Plan Outline" as a guideline for the "export plan" section of your business plan or simply on its own as your export plan.

ACTION STEP 65

Map out your export strategy.

By now you should have completed significant export research and a SWOT analysis. You have isolated a target export market. It's necessary to establish your export strategy, which should deal with:

- selection of service offerings or products
- selection of primary and secondary target countries/regions
- market entry strategy (from intermediaries, all the way to on-site manufacturing)
- pricing strategy
- promotion strategy
- payment/collection policies and procedures
- distribution strategy

Once you have completed your strategy, you are ready to draft your export plan.

Box 15.3 Ten Common Exporting Errors

1. The company did not gather all the necessary background information about the target market. It failed to devise a meaningful marketing plan before attempting to export.
2. The company did not have the commitment or the determination to overcome the difficulties associated with exporting, and it lacked the resources to meet the financial obligations incurred during the initial stages of exporting.
3. Not enough attention was paid to choosing a foreign agent or distributor. The one chosen performed poorly and the company became discouraged.
4. In the first flush of enthusiasm, the company spread itself too thin, attempting to enter several different markets, rather than focussing on one and establishing a base of expertise and strength from which further efforts might be undertaken.
5. The company regarded exporting as a safety net, turning to it only when the domestic market experienced a downturn and abandoning it when domestic business recovered. It did not develop a long-term strategy or presence.
6. The company treated its foreign partners, agents, and distributors with less consideration than it treated its partners and associates at home.
7. The company refused to modify its products to respond to regulations or cultural preferences in its target markets.
8. The company attempted to operate exclusively in English and did not bother to provide itself with capabilities in the language of the target market, nor did it seek to produce documents in that language.
9. The firm attempted to do everything by itself instead of engaging specialists such as freight forwarders and customs brokers to handle the technical details of exporting.
10. The company failed to investigate the potential benefits of partnerships, joint ventures, and technology exchanges as a way of enhancing its export efforts

Export Plan Outline[8]

Corporate Overview

- Background
- Description of service or product
- Types of target customers

Export Objectives

- Reasons for pursuing international markets
- Statement of Expectations (e.g., market share, revenues/profits)
- Timeframe for profitability

Export-Related Strengths

- Analysis of strengths and weaknesses
- Strategies for enhancing competitiveness

Export Opportunities/Threats and Target Markets

- Identify market types
- Evaluate markets through market research
- Select target market

Identification of Resource Requirements

- Human resources
- Financial resources
- Facilities requirements
- Marketing requirements

Export Strategy

- Selection of service offerings or products
- Selection of primary and secondary target countries/regions
- Market entry strategy
- Pricing strategy
- Promotion strategy
- Payment/collection policies and procedures
- Distribution strategy
- Detailed marketing and implementation plan

ACTION STEP REVIEW

63 Do an export SWOT analysis.
64 Discover your export sources.
65 Map out your export strategy.

In a Nutshell

The world economy is in a state of change, and change signals opportunity to the entrepreneur. Exporting is a whole new experience for many, and takes commitment, patience, and money. You'll have to learn about new markets, cultures, terms, rules, and behaviours. The purpose of this chapter was to get you started thinking about exporting opportunities. First, we asked you to take a hard look at your export readiness. Then, we suggested that you do an export SWOT analysis — an honest appraisal of the strengths and weaknesses of your business idea, and the market opportunities and threats. Next, we provided you with information on some key export issues. Finally, we encouraged you to draft an export strategy and think about incorporating this into your business plan.

Think Points for Success

✓ Exporting can be a wonderful way to see the world and cultivate an understanding of various cultures.

✓ Use your government officials and agencies, especially at the federal level. Did you know, for example, that the Export Development Corporation (EDC) helped over 3 000 smaller exporters in 1997? Smaller exporters now account for about 90 percent of the EDC's customers.

✓ Make the Internet a primary source of export information. Visit, for example, "InfoExport," the International Trade Web site of the Department of Foreign Affairs and International Trade at <http://www.infoexport.gc.ca>.

✓ If you find yourself balking at exporting because you don't know how to do it, analyze your initial feelings about operating your computer. You didn't know how to work it then, but now you probably couldn't do business without it.

✓ Use your new eyes all the time when your travel. It's amazing what opportunities lie in cultural differences.

✓ If you're going to export, do an export SWOT analysis. Then you'll need an exporting plan and a lot of advice.

NOTES

1. Based on a special supplement by the Department of Foreign Affairs and International Trade, CIBC, Export Development Corporation, and Bell Advantage. The supplement appeared in the "1996 Canada's Export Awards," *The Globe and Mail Report on Business.*
2. Minister of Supply and Services Canada, *Canada's International Business Strategy*, 1997–1998, Catalogue No. C2-226/1-1998E, p. 5; and Colin Campbell with Carol Hood, *Where the Jobs Are: Career Survival in the New Global Economy*, 2nd ed. (Toronto: Macfarlane Walter & Ross, 1997), p. 21.

3. Adapted from Rick Spence, *Secrets of Success from Canada's Fastest-Growing Companies* (Toronto: John Wiley & Sons Canada, Ltd., 1997), pp. 115–16. Reprinted by permission of the author.
4. Information for much of this section came from Industry Canada, Entrepreneurship and Small Business Office, "Exporting for Competitiveness: Ten Steps for Small Business," *Report on Small Business in Canada*, 1992. This source can be accessed on the Internet at <http://strategis.ic.gc.ca/SSG/mi01456e.html>.
5. Patrick Brethour, "Software Company Lands in Tehran," *The Globe and Mail*, October 16, 1996, p. B15.
6. Louis E. Boone, David L. Kurtz, and Ronald A. Knowles, *Business* (Toronto: Dryden, an imprint of Harcourt Brace & Company, Canada, 1998), p. 30.
7. *Ibid.*, p. 236.
8. Adapted from Industry Canada, Strategis Web site, "Take a World View... Export your Service," Module 5: <http://strategis.ic.gc.ca/SSG/sc01353e.html>. Reproduced with the permission of the Minister of Public Works and Government Services Canada, 1998

OTHER REFERENCES

Acuff, Frank L. *How to Negotiate Anything with Anyone Anywhere Around the World*. Whitby, Ontario: McGraw-Hill Ryerson Ltd., 1996.

Campbell, Colin with Carol Hood. *Where the Jobs Are: Career Survival in the New Global Economy*. 2nd ed. Toronto: Macfarlane Walter & Ross, 1997.

Department of Foreign Affairs. *The Exporters' Guide*. ISBN 0-662-24385-4.

International Trade Fairs and Conferences Directory, 1998, Catalogue No. 1800-727-4183.

McInnes, J. David. "Will You Be Paid? International Sales." *Law Now*, October/November, 1995, pp. 15–16.

Osberg, Lars, Fred Wien, and Jon Crude. *Vanishing Jobs: Canada's Changing Workplace*. Toronto: James Lorimer & Company, 1995.

sixteen

Pulling the Plan Together

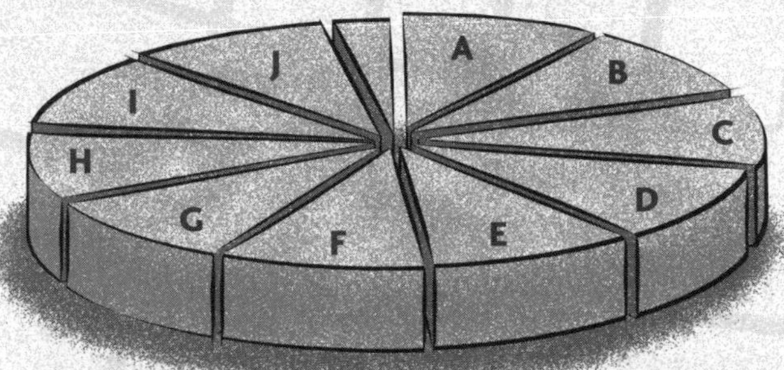

LEARNING OPPORTUNITIES

After reading this chapter, you should be able to:

- Pull all the information you have together into one coherent unit, which becomes a working showcase for your business.
- Study a sample business plan to see how one group of entrepreneurs defined and presented their business.
- Match or surpass the sample business plan in value-added information, research, and effectiveness.
- Put your finished business plan to work.

BUSINESS PLAN BUILDING BLOCK

In this chapter you do the final assembly of your business plan building blocks. Read your plan again and rewrite for maximum clarity and impact. Insert an executive summary, a table of contents, and an appendix, and put the completed plan in an attractive binder.

In 1996, Herb Evans, a business promoter from Florida, presented an idea to Crila Plastics Industries Ltd. in Mississauga, Ontario. Evans claimed he represented someone by the name of Geoff House, who had invented a plastic called Extrudawood that looked and acted like a wood. The staff at Crila studied Herb's proposal and reported to their president, Peter Clark, that the concept looked intriguing. The staff knew that Clark was a man with a willingness to listen to innovative ideas and who had a passion for reading business plans. Fortunately, Herb had drawn up a plan. "Let me take that home," said Peter. He read the document over a weekend. It didn't take long before he signed a joint-venture deal with the inventor, Geoff House, for the North American rights to produce Extrudawood. "One million feet is a nice order in a year. The two companies are both looking at doing that much each month," says Peter. Today, Extrudawood has become the backbone of Crila Industries — largely because of a well-documented business plan.[1]

Figure 16.1 Chapter Sixteen tells you how to draw on all of the materials you have generated in the earlier chapters to create your finished business plan. Each wedge of the pie chart represents a part of your complete business plan — a portable showcase for your business, as well as a personal road map to small business success.

ACTION STEP PREVIEW

66 Write a cover letter for your plan.
67 Write an executive summary.
68 Describe your product or service.
69 Describe the market and the target customer.
70 Describe your major competitors.
71 Describe your marketing strategy.
72 Show off your location.
73 Introduce your management team.
74 Introduce your personnel.
75 Project your cash flow.
76 Project your income statement.
77 Project your balance sheet.
78 Construct a PERT chart and go for it.

Your business plan could be the most important document you've created. It will help keep you focussed while you're out there doing the work on your start-up, researching, finding the gaps, interviewing small business owners, profiling your target customers, and so on.

Staying focussed is important because you're going to get a lot of distracting ideas for more new businesses while you're out there hunting.

A business plan will keep your creativity on track and help you work towards your vision. How? By being a constant reminder of who you are and where you are going.

When you've finished your plan, you've got something in writing to show the people who are important to your business: your banker, lenders, relatives, venture capitalists, vendors, suppliers, key employees, friends, and others. The plan is portable, and you can make as many copies as you need to show to the people who can help you succeed. You can even fax or e-mail it to contacts across the country.

Planning is hard work. You'll stay up nights over this, maybe lose some sleep, but with a plan, implementation is a lot easier. Just as a pilot would not consider a long flight without a flight plan, neither should you consider a business venture without a business plan.

How to Write Your Business Plan

TWO-PART STRUCTURE: WORDS AND NUMBERS

Your business plan tells the world what kind of business you're in. For ease of handling, divide your plan into two sections and provide the needed documentation in appendices at the end. In Section I, use *words* to briefly introduce your strategies for marketing, production, and management. (In this section, you also share your vision, mission, and goals.) Try to "hook" your reader with the excitement of creating a business, assessing the competition, designing a marketing plan, targeting customers, finding the right location, and building a team — all those human things that most people can relate to even if they're not in business.

In Section II present *numbers* such as an income statement, cash flow projection, projected balance sheet, and ratio analysis. This section is aimed primarily at bankers, credit managers, venture capitalists, vendors, and commercial credit lenders. At the same time, you've got to make it accessible to the casual reader who searches for the bottom line.

Support the two sections with *appendices*. This is where you put résumés, maps, diagrams, photographs, tables, reprints from industry journals, letters from customers, letters from vendors, credit reports, personal financial statements, bids from contractors, and other documentation that demonstrates the viability of your plan. Note that in most cases, material in the appendices comes from primary and secondary sources. You're not stating anything new here; you're just supporting what you've already said. (Appendices vary according to each business; for that reason, sample appendices are not included in this book.)

By following the Action Steps in this chapter, you will complete all the components you need to make a successful business plan. If you want to jump ahead for a quick overview of your plan, take a look at our sample table of contents in Box 16.2.

THE RELATIONSHIP OF YOUR PLAN TO THIS BOOK

You may be closer to producing your business plan than you think. If you have completed the Action Steps and Building Blocks in the preceding chapters, you already have the major components of your plan. The earlier chapters gave you the materials; this chapter gives you the structure.

When your entire business plan is assembled, you will notice weaker sections that need more attention. Much of the information that was developed in the Action Steps and Building Blocks will be useful in strengthening the plan and thus building the reader's confidence in it.

HOW TO START WRITING

If you're a creative thinker, chances are your thought processes don't always follow a linear sequence. That's great — it will help you as an entrepreneur! Nonetheless, the Action Steps in this chapter *do* follow a linear sequence, the sequence of the parts of a finished business plan. This is a matter of convenience: you get to see an example of each part as it would appear in the finished product. Bear in mind, however, that we don't expect you to write each part directly in sequence.

The best way to start writing a business plan is to begin with the material with which you feel most comfortable. For example, if you really enjoyed interviewing target customers, you might begin with Part B, "The Market and the Target Customer" referring to Chapters Three and Four for boosts. Once you have a foothold, the other parts will seem easier to reach.

In this chapter, the Action Steps can serve as a checklist for keeping track of which parts of the plan you have written. For example, in practice you would probably write the cover letter last, although that is the first Action Step we present. Think of the writing of this first cover letter as a valuable exercise. The more cover letters you write, the easier it becomes to write them effectively.

The Cover Letter

To aim your plan so that it will achieve the most good, you use a cover letter. Each time you send the plan to someone, you write a special cover letter addressed to that specific reader. The cover letter introduces the excitement of your plan, and it tells the person why you are sending it to him or her.

Read the sample cover letter in Box 16.1.

Let's summarize what's good about our sample cover letter. We can see that:

1. The writer is making use of a previous contact.
2. The writer tells the reader — the manager of a bank — that he is in the market for a loan. He does not put the manager on the spot by asking for money.
3. Instead, he asks for advice on where to find sources of capital.
4. The writer struck the right tone. (To do that, he rewrote the letter several times.)

You can do as well or better — and it's worth the effort! As you draft your cover letter, remember that the reader will pass judgement on your business plan (and on your business ability) on the basis of the letter. Do you want your small business to look bright, attractive, and welcoming? Your cover letter needs to give the same impression. A good cover letter will make its readers want to become involved in your venture.

Action Step 66 will help you write your cover letter.

ACTION STEP 66

Write a cover letter for your plan. Address your letter to a specific person who can help your business. Be brief; aim for about 200 words.

State the reason you are sending the plan. If you are asking for money, tell the person what you want it for and how much you need. One well-written paragraph should be all you need to do this.

Your purpose in writing the cover letter is to open the door gently and prepare the way for further negotiations. The cover letter is bait on your hook.

If you are putting money into the business, or if you have already donated, indicate how much.

The tone you are after in this opening move is confident and slightly formal. You want to appear neat, bright, organized, and in control of your venture.

Be certain to explain briefly how you will repay the money.

Refer to the sample letter in Box 16.1.

Box 16.1

In this sample cover letter, The Software School's CEO introduces his company's business plan to a potential lender.

November 24, 19XX

THE SOFTWARE SCHOOL
47 Turbo Drive
Suites 108-110
Toronto, Ontario

Mrs. Deborah Wallis
Manager, Royal Bank
1400 Market Circle
Anytown, Canada

Dear Mrs. Wallis:

We at The Software School want to extend our appreciation for the advice and guidance you have provided on revising and updating the enclosed business plan. Your input was helpful in the marketing area and invaluable for the financial section. Everyone here at The Software School appreciates the care you took reading over those early drafts.

We're now in the market for a loan of $50 000 (the figure you suggested) to be used for capital expenditures — microcomputers, desks, chairs, and upgrading our curriculum — and we'd appreciate any guidance you could give us concerning sources of capital. (As I'm sure you'll recall, our venture was launched without any debt whatsoever, with each of our five principals putting up $20 000 apiece. And the present Turbo Drive location already has space available for the second classroom.)

We're planning to repay the loan out of new profit over the next three years. (For more information, please refer to the financial section of our plan, beginning on page 14.)

Again, thank you very much for your help and advice. We couldn't have done it without you.

Cordially,

Derek Campbell, CEO

Preliminaries

THE TABLE OF CONTENTS

Box 16.2 provides a sample table of contents to give you a quick overview of a finished business plan. In practice, the table of contents is prepared last.

Box 16.2

The table of contents page of The Software School's business plan.

Table of Contents

*The need for specific appendices varies greatly from business plan to business plan. For that reason, this chapter does not include sample appendices. As you draft your plan, you will need to document and substantiate your business strategies; this kind of documentation is best included as appendices.

THE EXECUTIVE SUMMARY

The executive summary serves as an introduction to the business plan. In function, it is similar to the preface of this book: it is written to acquaint the reader with the nature of the business, to direct the reader's attention to whatever strengths the author (entrepreneur) wants to emphasize, and to make the reader want to turn the page and become involved. Because the executive summary gives perspective to the entire business plan, it needs to be written after the entire plan is completed. All the information should be condensed in one to three pages. Pay special attention to the *business description, current position,* and *future outlook, management, uniqueness,* and — if funds are being sought — *funds sought, how they will be used,* and *when they will be repaid.* This summary will appear right after the table of contents (and the confidentiality statement, if one is used).

As you write your executive summary, remember that lenders prefer "hard" numerical data and facts; they cannot take speculations about things seriously. Therefore, such phrases as "50 percent return on the original investment" and "secured agreements from 17 area businesses" make the example in Box 16.3 a strong executive summary. They help to paint a picture of good management and solid growth potential for The Software School.

ACTION STEP 67

Write an executive summary.
Imagine you had two minutes to explain your business venture to a complete stranger. This gives you an idea of what information you need to put into writing for your executive summary.

Practise explaining your venture to friends and strangers, limiting yourself to two minutes. Ask them to raise questions, and use their questions to guide you as you revise and hone your presentation.

When you are satisfied with your oral summary, write it down and type it up. It should not exceed three typed pages. (The Software School's executive summary that serves as our example was less than one page, single-spaced.)

This may constitute a very small portion of your business plan, but it could be the most important part of it.

Box 16.3

The Software School provides numerical data and hard facts in its executive summary.

Executive Summary
The Software School is a user-friendly, state-of-the-art microcomputer training centre. In our first six months of operation, we demonstrated our unique and profitable way of exploiting a strong and growing market within a fast-growing industry. The Software School's sophisticated electronic classroom provides "hands-on" education that teaches computer users how to use new software programs. By January 2, 19XX, we were operating at 92 percent capacity (50 percent is break-even) and had a waiting list of 168 students.

We plan to add a second classroom in order to double our capacity. This expansion will allow us to attain $400 000 in sales by the end of our eighteenth month. At that time, our pretax profits will have reached almost $50 000, representing a 50 percent return on our original $100 000 investment.

Our target customers seem to have insatiable appetites for software application knowledge, and The Software School anticipates an annual compound growth rate of 50 percent over the next five years. We have secured training agreements from seventeen retail computer stores in the area and firm contracts for more than 700 employees from 84 industrial users.

Our competitors continue to train in the traditional style and currently show no sign of copying our unique instructional approach. Occasional price-cutting by competitors has had no effect on our enrollment.

Management, led by Derek Campbell, has demonstrated how to offer superior training at competitive prices. Our plans for the future include developing additional profit centres by providing on-site counselling and training for firms throughout Southern Ontario. Research and customer surveys indicate that we have just begun to satisfy the ever-increasing need for software education.

You, too, can write an effective executive summary. Action Step 67 will help you to decide which facts and numbers will portray you and your business venture as credible and promising and then to summarize them on paper.

Section I: Description of the Business

You know your business, but you need to prove it with words and numbers. By the time your reader finishes your business plan, you should have a convert to your side. To give you examples to follow, we reprint key sections from the business plan (newly revised and updated) for The Software School, an ongoing business that is seeking financing for acquiring more equipment. Regardless of whether your business is already in existence or just starting up, the goals of Section I are the same: to demonstrate that you know your business and that you're a winner.

PART A: BUSINESS DESCRIPTION

Box 16.4 shows how The Software School tackled this part of Section I.

The Software School will get its funding because the writer of the plan proves that the business is a winning concern. The writer has:

1. let the facts speak for themselves
2. supported all claims with numbers

Box 16.4

The Software School effectively describes its business in Section I.

The Service We Provide
The Software School, a federal corporation, is a microcomputer training facility located in Toronto, between the Pearson International Airport and a high-density executive business complex. The area has a large number of microcomputer users. Now in its seventh month of operation, the school has a waiting list of 168 students (67 percent of whom have paid a deposit).

We train people in computer software systems from the "Top Ten" list of best-selling microcomputer and Internet software packages. Because of their power, these systems are complex. They provide a learning hurdle, especially at first.

Students are drawn to our teaching method because it gives them hands-on experience and because we have a very knowledgeable staff. Our teaching works. Working people are busy, and a student can upgrade a given software skill by 80 percent in eight hours. (Slower learners are guaranteed a second try, and a third, at no additional cost.) Most of our courses can be completed in one day or two evenings. In contrast, the average college course (which emphasizes concepts, rather than hands-on software systems) takes twelve to eighteen weeks. Our price is $100 for most courses, and so far no one has complained about the cost.

The Software School achieves this space-age learning speed with a sophisticated electronic teaching system adapted from flight-simulation techniques used by airlines for training pilots. We are constantly streamlining and upgrading the system, using funds already allocated in our start-up budget.

One especially bright note: We have done far better than we had hoped. Our actual income figures average 24 percent above our original projections. Projected income for the first six months, with an assumed occupancy rate of 50 percent, was just over $10 000 a month. The actual occupancy has not peaked, and for the past two months we have operated at 92 percent capacity.

As a service business, we sell seats as well as skills and information, and as Appendix 1 shows, our promotion has generated a heavy demand for present courses such as Computer Fundamentals, Corel Draw, and Windows 98. At the same time, customers are asking for courses to meet their needs — for example, a course in Lotus Notes.

Until the end of our fifth month, we were open six days a week from 8 AM to 10 PM. To meet demand with our current classroom facilities, we are now open on Sundays from 9 AM to 6 PM, and the Sunday classes are full.

The demand increased dramatically when we contracted with some of Southern Ontario's large computer retailers to develop a training program. (See Appendix 2 for letters from specific sales managers.) These retailers sent us their salespeople for training; the salespeople, in turn, have referred their customers to us. Computer retailers quickly discovered they can sell better systems to buyers who are not afraid of computers, and they are in the business of selling, not training. We combat customers' fears in a logical way, with knowledge.

Our equipment (IBM Pentium PCs) is top-quality. Our staff combines excellent training skills and great practical experience with a focus on people and their needs. We have launched a solid start-up in a heated growth industry, and we plan to continue our growth and success.

ACTION STEP 68

Describe your product or service.
Excite your reader about your business. Excitement is contagious. If you can get your reader going, there's a good chance you'll be offered money. Investors love hot ideas.

If this is a start-up, explain your product or service fully. What makes it unique? What industry is it in? Where does the industry fit in the big picture?

Mention numbers wherever you can. Percentages and dollar amounts are more meaningful than words like *lots* and *many*.

If this is a going business, your records of sales, costs, and profit and loss will substantiate your need for money.

Keep the words going and the keyboard smoking. You need to convince the reader to keep reading.

3. avoided hard-sell tactics
4. refused to puff the product
5. projected a positive future

The writer does a terrific selling job without appearing to be selling at all. Now it's your turn. Do Action Step 68.

ACTION STEP 69

Describe the market and the target customer.
Bring all of your marketing research into this section and *wow* your reader with a picture of your target customer just sitting there waiting for your product or service.

Use data from secondary sources to give credibility to the picture you are painting.

ACTION STEP 70

Describe your major competitors.
Briefly profile the businesses that compete with you directly. Try to be objective as you assess their operations.

What are their strengths? What are their weaknesses? What can you learn from them?

After you've described your competitors, indicate how you're going to out-distance them.

PART B: THE MARKET AND THE TARGET CUSTOMER

Knowledge is power, especially in the Information Age. The Software School — an information business — capitalized on expert knowledge to define the marketplace. In the same way, if your research is sound, that knowledge will show up in your writing.

As you continue to read The Software School's business plan, remember:

1. This is a revised business plan, so the writing flows well. You will need to do several revisions in order to smooth out your writing. (How many revisions are you planning?)
2. The reader of your business plan is a special kind of target customer. (How can you use your marketing abilities to look at this reader with new eyes? Have you developed a profile of this very special target customer?) Action Step 69 gives you a chance to show what you know about your market and target customer. If you need help getting started, review your work in Chapters Three and Four. You can also review what the business plan for The Software School says about its market and TCs (see Box 16.5). Be sure to use secondary sources (like documents, tables, and quotes) to lend credibility to this portion of your plan.

PART C: THE COMPETITION

Obviously, if you know who your competitors are and how they fail to meet market needs, you are well on your way to strategic competition. You need to persuade your reader how great your competitive tactics are. (If you need a reminder, reread Chapters Four and Five. Competition changes according to the life-cycle stage of the industry, so a good way to begin your section on competition is to place your industry in the proper life-cycle phase.)

How tough do your competitors look? As you read The Software School's assessment of its competition, note that the writer takes a cool, objective look at the competition. He does not belittle them, and he certainly doesn't underestimate them. (See Box 16.6.)

How will you handle the competition in your business plan? Your readers will expect you to be cool and objective. Now you should be ready to complete Action Step 70.

PART D: MARKETING STRATEGY

Now it's time to describe your marketing strategy. Need a reminder? Look back at your work in Chapter Six.

The marketing strategy excerpt from The Software School's business plan (Box 16.7) demonstrates a carefully reasoned approach. The excerpt describes conscious marketing policies that will help this small business be competitive. If you read a business plan in which the writer did not demonstrate this care and deliberation, how much faith would you have in the writer's business abilities?

Note that The Software School uses a three-pronged approach to reaching the public. This business understands the importance of finding a good promotional mix.

The entrepreneurs who run The Software School stay on top of the changing market picture. They have demonstrated this by:

1. dropping discount inducements from their ongoing print campaign,
2. looking ahead to radio and TV exposure,

Box 16.5

The Software School clearly describes its market and target customer.

The Market and Our Target Customer

Industry Overview

Fifteen years ago, the personal computer (PC) did not exist in the marketplace. There were mainframes, of course, and terminals linked to invisible data banks — but nothing you could carry home in a suitcase.

Things are different today. Approximately 200 firms are making PCs. The lions's share of the market goes to IBM, Dell Computers, Compaq, and so forth, and yet someone brings out a new PC almost every day of the year. The microcomputer industry and the Internet are moving so fast that statistics can hardly keep pace.

The growth in computer purchases tripled over the 1990s. By 1997, almost one in three Canadian households owned a computer. At least 50 percent of employed Canadians now use a computer at work. About 25 percent of Canada's 2+ million self-employed workers are hooked up to a modem and the Internet. In the next few years, up to three-quarters of the self-employed people in Canada will use the Internet as an indispensable business tool, according to a report by the Canadian Federation of Independent Business.

With all this sales flurry and emphasis on space-age speed and the Internet, some people are being left behind because they don't know how to use computers. A computer can be your best friend, but only if you learn how to use it. This makes training people to use computers a booming industry, and The Software School is on the leading edge of a major growth segment.

Target Market

Our potential total market is Southern Ontario, with a logical concentration in Metropolitan Toronto, whose population is expected to reach some 3.5 million by the year 2000.

Geographically, our target market or industry segment includes Mississauga, Brampton, the area north to Barrie, and those areas east to Oshawa.

For now, our focus is Metropolitan Toronto. Within this highly concentrated population area, our target customer is the small business person.

Given the success we have projected, we plan by the third year to better service our clients in Brampton and Oshawa by opening offices in these locations.

Our Target Customer

Our primary target is the small business, profiled here:

Size: 1–30 employees
Annual sales: $250 000 to $5 000 000
Type of business: service industry
Major output: paper (reports, letters, documents, etc.)

Our secondary target is the home user:

Sex: 50% male, 50% female
Age: 18–45
Education: some college
Owns PC: 30%
Access to computer at work: 52%
Lives near computer store: 73%
Household income: $55 000+
Occupation: professional, managerial, executive, entrepreneurial

ACTION STEP 71

Describe your marketing strategy.
Now that you've profiled your target customer and assessed your competition, take some time to develop the thrust of your market strategy. Which techniques will get the best and most cost-effective response?

Because pricing is such an important consideration, you might start with what your TC sees as a good value, and then develop your marketing mix.

Box 16.6

The Software School assesses its competition objectively.

The Competition
The Software School has four main competitors:

Traherne Schools. Our oldest, most entrenched competitor. Three locations in Metro: Etobicoke, North York, and Scarborough. Traherne conducts a six-hour course Introduction to Microprocessors for $95. They currently run a course on desktop publishing for the Mac, and they have been planning to introduce an Internet course, but to-date have not done so.

Traherne operates within our geographic market. Their Scarborough operation is closed on Saturdays.

Big Micro Computer Instruction. Excellent classroom facilities, located in East York near the Don Valley Parkway. All instruction is tied to Macintosh machines, and is free if you buy your hardware from Big Micro. Otherwise, courses usually cost around $95 and take six to eight hours.

The instructors try hard, but Big Micro is really in the business of pushing hardware.

Micro Hut Computer Center. Friendly salespeople with teaching skills double as teachers. Courses at Micro Hut are Microsoft-related. Prices range between $100 and $200 per student/day: VisiCalc, $89; Word Processing, $149.

Your Micro and You. Local facility developed by professional educators. The atmosphere of YMAY is excellent. They offer a normal range of programs and a course in using the computer in a small business, each course costing about $125. Their market seems to be divided between adults with casual interest in computers and children aged 10 to 15.

These people have done it right.

Other Competitors. Secondary competitors are colleges, which offer a range of six- to twelve-week courses. As well, more companies today are supplying in-house training for their employees.

Meeting the Competition
The Software School is in the computer education business. We do not sell hardware or software.

Our program of instruction is relevant. We teach software, and we are constantly on the lookout for trends that will lead us to new markets. For example, we have just added a course on how to create your own home page. Furthermore, our prices are competitive, and we teach classes seven days a week.

Our price per hour may be higher than the college courses, but time and results are important to our students. Therefore, we are seen as price competitive.

3. logging calls and gathering information on the callers to maintain a base of up-to-date information on their target market, and
4. determining how they have gained their largest accounts, and planning to intensify their efforts in that area.

Action Step 71 will help you to refine your marketing strategy. Note that you must continue to focus on the target customer.

PART E: LOCATION

The next part of your business plan is the one on location. You may want to review your work in Chapter Seven now.

Box 16.7

The Software School takes a carefully reasoned approach in its description of its marketing strategy.

Marketing Strategy

An analysis of our competitors indicates that our prices — $99 for a one-day course, $198 for a two-day course — are between two extremes. These prices are competitive but still maintain our image of quality.

We use a wide range of strategies to let our customers know where we are: mass-media advertising (newspapers, television, and radio), special promotions (press releases, brochures, newsletter, etc.), and personal selling (commissioned salespeople, networking, corporate contracts, trade shows, etc.).

Mass-Media Advertising

The Software School places ads in the *Toronto Star* and smaller area newspapers to keep a continuous presence in front of our target customers. In the beginning, we used inducement (two-for-one offers, 15 percent reductions, etc.), but that is no longer necessary as our waiting lists grow. As we continue to expand, we will develop advertising on radio and TV.

Creative Promotions/Ink/Free Ink

In our first month of operation, we sponsored a scholarship contest in the local high schools, which resulted in some very positive press. In addition, the school has been featured in several local newspapers.

We are in the information business, and toward that end we are developing three different publications: a computer handbook, a newsletter, and a brief history of the founding of The Software School. In time, we hope that this history (a how-to for computer educators) will become a guide for the industry. We have also developed our own Web site (www.software.com).

Our mailing list grows daily. We log all in-coming phone calls and e-mail with information on the callers and how they found out about us. This information helps us define our target market.

Personal Selling

Personal contact has gained us our largest accounts so far. (Please refer to letters from computer retailers in Appendix 2.) We intend to intensify our efforts along these lines. Fortunately, our directors have experience and talent in the area of personal selling.

We maintain a booth at the major computer trade shows in the area. Approximately 17 percent of our hobbyist/home-user business has been generated this way.

ACTION STEP 72

Show off your location.

The great thing about a location is that it's so *tangible*. A potential lender can visit your site and get a feel for what's going on.

A banker will often visit your business site. That's good news for you because now the banker is on your turf.

Clean up the place before your banker arrives.

In this section, you want to persuade potential lenders to visit your site. Describe what goes on here. Use photographs, diagrams, and illustrations to make it feel almost like home.

Read how The Software School shows off its location to advantage (Box 16.8).

You need to paint an attractive picture of your business site and, at the same time, keep your reader interested by inspiring confidence in your choice. Location takes a tremendous amount of analysis. The Software School writer gives himself a subtle pat on the back by describing the lease arrangements and by identifying the need for a second classroom. The reader who needs more is referred to the appendix. This is smart writing.

Your plan will become very real when you showcase your physical facility. Complete Action Step 72.

ACTION STEP 73

Introduce your management team.
Almost every study you read on small business failure puts the blame on management. Use this section to highlight the positive qualities of your management team.

Focus on quality first: their experience, accomplishments, education, training, flexibility, imagination, tenacity. Be sure you weave in experience that relates to your particular business.

Remember — dreamers make terrific master builders, but they make lousy managers. Your banker knows this, and potential investors will sense it. A great team can help you raise money.

The key to a great team is balance.

Box 16.8

The Software School paints an attractive picture of its location.

Our Location
The Software School is currently in the first year of a three-year lease at 47 Turbo Drive, Toronto, Ontario. The facility is all on the ground floor and occupies 210 square metres.

The area, which is zoned for business use, is a hotbed of high-technology activity. Within the immediate area, there are two computer stores, one computer furniture store, one software dealer, an electronics store, and two printers, one of which does typesetting directly from software diskettes. Within a seven-kilometre radius are 27 computer dealers.

During our lease negotiations, we persuaded the landlord to make extensive improvements in the interior, and to spread the cost out over the three-year term of the lease. The decor — blue carpet, white walls, orange furniture — gives the effect of a solid, logical, somewhat plush business environment in which our target customer will be comfortable and learn fast.

The building is divided into four areas: a reception area (30 square metres), a director's office (10 square metres), a classroom (75 square metres), and a storage area (90 square metres).

The principals envision the storage area as a second classroom. See diagram in Appendix 9.

The area is easily accessible by public transportation, and we offer free parking.

PART F: MANAGEMENT

Management will make or break your small business. You are a member of the management team, and you want this business plan to inspire confidence in your team. Writing this section will help you focus more closely on your management team members. (If you need a refresher, review your work in Chapters Eleven and Twelve.)

Now let's see how The Software School introduces *its* management (Box 16.9).

Nothing is more important than the people who will make your business work. Present their pedigree and focus on their track records and accomplishments as you complete Action Step 73. It is also helpful to include résumés in the appendix.

PART G: HUMAN RESOURCES

Part G of your plan shows off your human resources. For a start-up business, you're peering into the future with confidence, conducting informal job analyses for key employees who will help you to succeed. For an ongoing business, you need to list your present employees and anticipate your future personnel needs. If you have five employees now and you want to indicate growth, try to project how many jobs you'll be creating in the next five years.

When you start thinking about tasks and people to do them, review your work in Chapters Eleven and Twelve. Preparing a human resource plan is important because it gives you one more chance to analyze job functions and

Box 16.9

The Software School shows off its winning management team.

Management

Derek Campbell. Mr. Campbell was born in Stratford, Ontario, in 19--. He took a B.Sc. degree in Industrial Engineering from McGill University and then spent five years in the Armed Forces, where he was a flight instructor, a check pilot, and a maintenance officer. While in the service, Mr. Campbell completed an M.A. degree in Marketing Management and Human Relations.

Following military service, Mr. Campbell was employed as a pilot for Air Canada. He is currently the CEO of EuroSource, a software importing company. He is the author of several articles on computers and the Information Age.

Roberta Jericho. Ms. Jericho was born in Lethbridge, Alberta, in 19--. She has a B.Sc. degree in Geology and Physical Sciences from the University of Calgary.

She has completed the Microsoft training program and has been the IT manager for EuroSource for the past five years.

Directors

C. Hughes Smith. Mr. Smith was born in Halifax, Nova Scotia, in 19--. He has a B.A. degree in Political Science and Philosophy from Dalhousie University, an M.B.A. from Stanford, and a law degree from the University of Toronto.

Mr. Smith is a senior vice-president of Lowes and Lockwood, a residential homebuilding firm, and a partner in Graebner and Ashe, a Toronto law firm. He is the author of numerous articles in the field of corporate planning and taxes.

Philu Carpenter. Ms. Carpenter was born in Winnipeg, Manitoba, in 19--. Her B.A. degree is from the University of Manitoba and her M.B.A., with a marketing specialty, is from the University of Western Ontario.

Ms. Carpenter spent 20 years in the corporate world (IBM, DEC, InterComp, etc.), where she worked in marketing and industrial sales. Currently a professor of Business at York University, Ms. Carpenter is the general partner in two businesses and a small business consultant. She has written and lectured widely in the area of small business.

Dan Masters. Mr. Masters was born in Mississauga, Ontario, in 19--. His degrees (B.A., M.B.A.) are from the University of Western Ontario, where he specialized in marketing and finance. Mr. Masters has worked for Kodak and Northern Telecom (as senior account sales executive and sales manager, respectively) for a total of 25 years.

Mr. Masters is currently a professor of Business at Seneca College. He is active in several small businesses, lectures widely, and has published numerous articles in the field of small business.

Personal résumés of all personnel are provided in Appendix 4.

Other Available Resources

The Software School has retained the legal firm of Farney and Shields and the accounting firm of Hancock and Craig. Our insurance broker is Sharon Mandel of Fireman's Fund. Our advertising agency is George Friend and Associates.

develop job descriptions before you start interviewing, hiring, and paying benefits — all of which are expensive.

You'll notice that The Software School gives a very brief overview of its human resource situation (Box 16.10).

In describing their lean operation, the entrepreneurs who run The Software School keep their description brief as well. They show good sense

ACTION STEP 74

Introduce your personnel.
Describe the kinds of people you will need as employees and how they fit into your plan.

What skills will they need? How much will you have to pay them? Will there be a training period? How long? What benefits will you offer? How will you handle overtime?

If you haven't yet written job descriptions, do that now. Job descriptions will help you hire people who best match the skills required.

Box 16.10

The Software School provides a brief overview of its human resources.

Human Resources
At the end of six months of operation, The Software School has three full-time employees and fourteen part-time employees. The full-time employees include:

1. Manager, salaried at $3 000 per month
2. Receptionist, salaried at $8 per hour
3. Training Director, salaried at $1 500 per month

The part-time employees include three directors, who assist in the marketing function, three outside commissioned salespeople, and eight part-time instructors. According to our plan, one salesperson will become full-time at the end of the seventh month.

We will continue to hold down overhead with qualified part-time employees as long as it is feasible. We believe that running a lean operation is important to our success.

when they express a commitment to control operating costs. Their decision reflects business discipline and foresight. If you were a potential investor in this business, wouldn't you appreciate some purse strings?

Every person on your team is important. Action Step 74 will help you describe the kinds of people you will need and how you will help them be productive.

Section II: Financial Section

GOOD NUMBERS

The financial section is the heart of your business plan. It is aimed at lenders — bankers, credit managers, venture capitalists, vendors, commercial credit lenders — people who think in numbers. Lenders are professional skeptics by trade; they will not be swayed by the enthusiasm of your writing in Section I. Your job, therefore, is to make your numbers do the talking.

You started collecting financial information in Chapter Eight, when you began thinking about money. You projected cash flow and income in Chapter Nine. In Chapter Ten, you tested your numbers on real lenders in the real world. Now you're ready to organize your numbers into four standard instruments:

1. the opening and projected balance sheets
2. the cash flow projection (also called a pro forma)
3. the projected income statement
4. other important financial information

Examples from The Software School will serve as models for you. You can adapt them to fit your business.

The idea is to know where every dollar is going. You need to show when you'll make a profit and you need to show you are efficient, conservative, and in control. You'll know you've succeeded when a skeptical lender looks up from your business plan and says, "You know, these numbers look good."

GOOD NOTES

One way to spot a professional lender is to hand over your business plan and watch to see which section is read first. Most lenders study the notes that accompany income and cash flow projections first. Knowing this allows you to be forewarned. Use these notes to list all assumptions and to tell potential lenders how you generated your numbers (for example, "Advertising is projected at 5 percent of sales") and to explain specific entries (for example, "Leased Equipment — monthly lease costs on IBM microcomputers").

Make these notes easy to read, with headings that start your readers off in the upper left-hand corner and march them down the page, step-by-step, to the bottom line. (Some sample projection charts use tiny footnotes, on the same page. We prefer *large* notes on a separate page. Notes are important, no less important than the rest of the plan.)

Creating your business plan takes a lot of time. It's only natural for you to hope that lenders will read it, get excited, and ask questions. These notes can help you accomplish that, even if you haven't started up and the numbers and assumptions are projections into the future.

PART H: PROJECTED CASH FLOW

Next, focus your attention on the projected cash flow, the lifeblood of your business. By projecting cash flow month-by-month, you get a picture of how healthy your business will be.

The Software School's cash flow projection is set out in Table 16.1. The notes for these numbers are reprinted in Box 16.11. If you compare the projected income statement (Table 16.2) with the cash flow projection, you will see that some items are treated differently in the tables. For example, expenses in the projected income statement are divided into monthly installments, whereas the same expenses in the cash flow projection are shown as bulk payment when due. Now look at insurance expense. In the projected income statement, we find a total expense of $960 shown as twelve monthly debits of $80 each. The same expense in the cash flow projection is shown as two payments of $480 each, falling due in the seventh and thirteenth months. If the entrepreneurs running the business had only $80 available to pay for insurance in the seventh month — that is what is shown in the income statement — they would be in trouble.

Profits don't pay the bills and the payroll; cash flow does. Potential lenders look at cash flow projections first, so Action Step 75 can make or break you.

ACTION STEP 75

Project your cash flow.
Get used to doing cash flow. Once a month is not too often to do it. If you prepared a cash flow for your business back in Chapter Nine, bring those numbers forward. If you skipped that step, do it now. Here's how it's done:

1. Write down all the cash you will have for one year.
2. Add net profit.
3. Add any loans.
4. Figure your total cash needs for the year.
5. Spread these numbers out across the year. You may have a lot of cash at the start of the year; you want to make sure you have enough to get all the way through.
6. Now list all disbursements. Spread these out too.
7. Now examine the figures. Is there any time during the year when you will run short of cash? It's better to know the truth now, when you're still working on paper.
8. If your cash picture looks good, drop in a couple of what-ifs. (Let's say you've budgeted $300 for utilities, and the air conditioner goes out. It will cost $200 to repair it, and the lease says it is your expense. Or let's say you see an opportunity for a sale, but you would have to hire someone to handle it for you. Can your cash flow handle such surprises?)

PART I: PROJECTED INCOME STATEMENT

Your next task is to put together your projected income statement (sometimes called a profit and loss statement). With the information you've gathered so far, it shouldn't be too hard. In fact, it will be enjoyable — if the numbers look good.

The Software School's projected income statement is shown in Table 16.2, and the careful documentation of each item is reprinted here. For instance, if a lender wanted to know how the figures for commissions were generated, Note 6 explains that they are estimated as 10 percent of sales (Box 16.12).

Table 16.1 The Software School's Cash Flow Projection

	Cash Flow: Software School												
	7th Month	8th Month	9th Month	10th Month	11th Month	12th Month	13th Month	14th Month	15th Month	16th Month	17th Month	18th Month	Total
Cash-Receipts													
Beginning of Month	$3 970	$7 365	$6 015	$51 575	$47 060	$35 275	$31 840	$28 645	$27 900	$33 115	$43 895	$47 800	$364 455
Sales	23 500	25 200	26 900	28 500	30 200	31 900	33 600	35 300	38 350	40 100	43 300	43 300	400 150
Less: Credit Card Expense	(295)	(315)	(335)	(355)	(380)	(400)	(420)	(440)	(480)	(500)	(540)	(540)	(5 000)
Loan			60 000										60 000
Total Sales	$27 175	$32 250	$92 580	$79 720	$76 880	$66 775	$65 020	$63 505	$65 770	$72 715	$86 655	$90 560	$819 605
Disbursements													
Books	$175	$190	$200	$210	$225	$235	$250	$305	$350	$370	$370	$385	$3 265
Inst./Materials		6 000			7 500			9 000			9 000		31 500
Salaries													
Instruction	2 000	2 000	2 040	2 080	2 120	2 160	2 200	2 240	2 280	2 320	2 360	2 360	26 160
Administration	2 640	2 640	2 640	3 120	3 600	3 600	3 600	3 600	3 600	3 600	3 600	3 600	39 840
Commissions	1 730	1 865	1 995	2 130	2 255	2 390	2 530	2 660	2 795	3 030	3 170	3 420	29 970
Payroll Taxes	2 045	2 195	2 250	2 435	2 690	2 755	2 805	2 870	2 925	3 025	3 075	3 170	32 240
Advertising	1 080	1 175	1 250	1 335	1 410	1 495	1 580	1 660	1 750	1 895	1 980	2 135	18 475
Leased Equip.	1 270	1 270	1 270	1 270	1 270	1 270	1 270	1 270	1 270	1 270	1 270	1 270	15 240
Licences/fees	2 160	2 330	2 495	2 665	2 820	2 990	3 160	3 325	3 495	3 790	3 960	4 275	35 305
Accounting	500	500	500	500	500	500	500	500	500	500	500	500	6 000
Rent	3 890	3 890	3 890	3 890	3 890	3 890	3 890	3 890	3 890	3 890	3 890	3 890	46 680
Office Supplies	60	65	65	70	75	80	85	90	95	100	110	110	1 005
Dues/Subscript.	20	20	20	20	20	20	200	20	20	20	20	20	420
Repair/Maint.	235	250	265	285	300	320	335	355	385	395	435	435	3 995
Insurance	480						480						960
Telephone	325	355	380	405	430	455	480	505	530	575	600	650	5 690
Utilities	430	470	505	540	570	605	640	670	705	765	800	865	7 565
Interest				650	650	650	650	650	650	595	595	595	5 685
Loan Payback									5 000				
Miscellaneous	705	755	805	855	905	955	1 010	1 060	1 150	1 205	1 300	1 300	12 005
Inc. Tax Reserve	65	265	435	200	375	565	710	935	1 265	1 475	1 820	1 820	9 930
Total Disbursements	$19 810	$26 235	$21 005	$22 660	$31 605	$24 935	$26 375	$35 605	$32 655	$28 820	$38 855	$30 800	$339 360
Net Cash Before Capital Invest.	$7 365	$6 015	$71 575	$57 060	$45 275	$41 840	$38 645	$27 900	$33 115	$43 895	$47 800	$59 760	$480 245
Capital Equipment			10 000										10 000
Contracted Course Development			10 000	10 000	10 000	10 000	10 000						50 000
	$7 365	$6 015	$51 575	$47 060	$35 275	$31 840	$28 645	$27 900	$33 115	$43 895	$47 800	$59 760	$420 245

Box 16.11

The Software School's notes for its cash flow projection.

1. **Beginning of the Month.** Cash available as the month begins.
2. **Sales.** Includes all sales by cash, cheque, or credit card at the time the class is taken. Does not include accounts receivable.
3. **Credit Card Expense.** Fees of 2.5 percent paid to credit card companies. Approximately 50 percent of customers use charge cards.
4. **Loans.** Loan for new course development and audiovisual equipment.
5. **Total Cash Available.** Sum of all money available during the month.
6. **Books.** Books for sale are ordered and paid for one month in advance of projected sale.
7. **Instructional Materials.** Covers course materials purchased from licenser.
8. **Salaries.** Net salaries paid employees approximate 80 percent of gross salaries paid.
9. **Payroll Taxes.** Total of amount withheld from employees, plus Income Statement payroll tax item.
10. **Advertising.** Established as 30-day accounts with all media companies.
11. **Leased Equipment.** Lease payments are due the first of each month.
12. **Licences and Fees.** Licence fees are due the fifteenth of the following month.
13. **Legal and Accounting.** Due 30 days after bill is received.
14. **Rent.** Due the first of each month.
15. **Office Supplies.** Paid at time of purchase or with subscription. No credit.
16. **Insurance.** Paid every six months in advance.
17. **Telephone and Utilities.** Paid within 30 days of receipt of bill.
18. **Interest.** Interest only, paid each month.
19. **Loan Payback.** $5 000 loan payment due every six months.
20. **Miscellaneous.** Paid in month when expense occurs.
21. **Income Tax Reserve.** Paid into a special tax account at the bank.
22. **Total Disbursements.** Total cash expended during the month.
23. **Net Cash Before Capital Investment.** Cash balance before capital investment payments.
24. **Capital Equipment.** Purchase of additional audiovisual equipment.
25. **Contracted Course Development.** Contract payment due for new course development.
26. **Monthly Cash Flow.** Cash balance after all payments at the end of the month.

ACTION STEP 76

Project your income statement.
What you're driving at here is *net profit* — what's left in the kitty after expenses — for each month and for the year.

First, you figure your *sales*. The first big bite out of the figure is the cost of *goods sold*. (In a service business, the big cost is labour.) Subtracting that gives you a figure called *gross margin*.

Now add up all your *expenses* (rent, utilities, insurance, etc.) and subtract them from the gross margin. This gives you your net *profit before taxes*. (Businesses pay quarterly installments.)

Subtract taxes. There's your net profit.

Action Step 76 will help you project your own monthly profits and losses for twelve months. Refer to Table 16.2 as you predict your income.

PART J: PROJECTED BALANCE SHEET

The professionals will look at your balance sheet (sometimes called a statement of financial position) to analyze the state of your finances at a given point in time. They are looking at things like liquidity (how easily your assets can be converted into cash) and capital structure (what sources of financing have been used, how much was borrowed, and so on). Professional lenders will use such factors to evaluate your ability to manage your business.

Table 16.3 shows two balance sheets for The Software School. Note that the first one shows its actual position at the end of its first six months and the second is a projection of where it will be at the end of its first eighteen months. If you're just starting up, *all* figures will be projections.

Table 16.2 The Software School's Projected Income Statement

Income Statement: Software School	7th Month	8th Month	9th Month	10th Month	11th Month	12th Month	13th Month	14th Month	15th Month	16th Month	17th Month	18th Month	Total
Sales													
Instruction	$23 285	$24 950	$26 630	$28 215	$29 900	$31 580	$33 265	$34 945	$37 915	$39 600	$42 770	$42 770	$395 825
Books	215	250	270	285	300	320	335	355	435	500	530	530	4 325
Total Sales	$23 500	$25 200	$26 900	$28 500	$30 200	$31 900	$33 600	$35 300	$38 550	$40 100	$43 300	$43 300	$400 150
Cost of Instruction													
Clssrm. Matrls.	$1 765	$1 890	$2 020	$2 140	$2 265	$2 395	$2 520	$2 650	$2 875	$3 000	$3 240	$3 240	$30 000
Inst./Personnel	2 500	2 500	2 600	2 600	2 700	2 700	2 800	2 800	2 900	2 900	3 000	3 000	33 000
Books	150	175	190	200	210	225	235	250	305	350	370	370	3 030
Total Cost/Instr/Books	4 415	4 565	4 810	4 940	5 175	5 320	5 555	5 700	6 080	6 250	6 610	6 610	66 030
Gross Profit	$19 085	$20 635	$22 090	$23 560	$25 025	$26 580	$28 045	$29 600	$32 270	$33 850	$36 690	$36 690	$334 120
Expenses													
Sales													
Commissions	$2 330	$2 495	$2 665	$2 820	$2 990	$3 160	$3 325	$3 495	$3 790	$3 960	$4 275	$4 275	$39 580
Advertising	1 175	1 250	1 335	1 410	1 495	1 580	1 660	1 750	1 895	1 980	2 135	2 135	19 800
Credit Cards	295	315	335	355	380	400	420	440	480	500	540	540	5 000
Administrative													
Salaries	3 300	3 300	3 300	4 500	4 500	4 500	4 500	4 500	4 500	4 500	4 500	4 500	50 400
Payroll Taxes	570	580	600	695	715	725	745	755	785	795	825	825	8 615
Leased Equip.	1 270	1 270	1 270	1 270	1 270	1 270	1 270	1 270	1 270	1 270	1 270	1 270	15 240
Licences/fees	2 300	2 495	2 665	2 820	2 990	3 160	3 325	3 495	3 790	3 960	4 275	4 275	39 580
Accounting	500	500	500	500	500	500	500	500	500	500	500	500	6 000
Rent	3 890	3 890	3 890	3 890	3 890	3 890	3 890	3 890	3 890	3 890	3 890	3 890	46 680
Office Supplies	60	65	65	70	75	80	85	90	95	100	110	110	1 005
Dues/Subscript.	20	20	20	20	20	20	200	20	20	20	20	20	420
Repair/Maint.	235	250	265	285	300	320	335	355	385	395	435	435	3 995
Insurance	80	80	80	80	80	80	80	80	80	80	80	80	960
Telephone	355	380	405	430	455	480	505	530	575	600	650	650	6 015
Utilities	470	505	540	570	605	640	670	705	765	800	865	865	8 000
Depreciation	1 170	1 170	1 170	1 335	1 335	1 335	1 335	1 335	1 335	1 335	1 335	1 335	15 525
Interest				650	650	650	650	650	650	595	595	595	5 685
Miscelleaneous	705	755	805	855	905	955	1 010	1 060	1 150	1 205	1 300	1 300	12 005
Total Expenses	$18 755	$19 320	$19 910	$22 555	$23 155	$23 745	$24 505	$24 920	$25 955	$26 485	$27 600	$27 600	$284 505
Net Profit	$330	$1 315	$2 180	$1 005	$1 870	$2 835	$3 540	$4 680	$6 315	$7 365	$9 090	$9 090	$49 615
Reserve for taxes	65	265	435	200	375	565	710	935	1 265	1 475	1 820	1 820	9 930
Net Profit After Taxes	$265	$1 050	$1 745	$805	$1 495	$2 270	$2 830	$3 745	$5 050	$5 890	$7 270	$7 270	$39 685

Box 16.12

The Software School's notes for its projected income statement.

1. **Instruction.** Based on 2.5 percent occupancy growth per month, starting at 35 percent (235 students) and growing to 69 percent. Students pay $99 per course.
2. **Books.** Revenue from books sold averages approximately 1 percent of instructional sales, rounded to bring total sales to an even $100 figure.
3. **Classroom Materials.** $7.50 per student.
4. **Instruction Personnel.** Instructor cost is $100 per eight-hour class, starting with 25 classes and growing to 30 classes by the end of the year.
5. **Books.** Cost of books is 70 percent of selling price.
6. **Commissions.** Average 10 percent of instructional sales.
7. **Advertising.** Projected at 5 percent of sales.
8. **Credit Cards.** Approximately 50 percent of sales are paid with credit cards. The cost is 2.5 percent of the sale.
9. **Salaries.** Start with three full-time employees. Bring on one additional person beginning the tenth month.
10. **Payroll Taxes.** The company's share of employee taxes averages 7 percent of commissions and salaries.
11. **Leased Equipment.** Monthly lease costs on IBM microcomputers.
12. **Licences and Fees.** Licence (right to use copyrighted material) costs 10 percent of instruction sales.
13. **Accounting.** Average accounting and bookkeeping costs for the area and size of the business.
14. **Rent.** Based on three-year lease.
15. **Office Supplies.** Estimated at 0.25 percent of sales.
16. **Dues and Subscriptions.** Estimated costs for magazines, newspapers, and membership in organizations.
17. **Repair and Maintenance.** Projected to be 1 percent of sales.
18. **Insurance.** Based on current insurance contract for next twelve months, payable every six months.
19. **Telephone and Fax.** Figured at 1.5 percent of sales.
20. **Utilities.** Figured at 2 percent of sales.
21. **Depreciation.** Schedule established by accounting firm.
22. **Interest.** Loan at 13 percent, with $5 000 payments due every six months until paid off.
23. **Miscellaneous.** Figured at 3 percent of sales.
24. **Reserve for Taxes.** Local, provincial, and federal taxes estimated at 20 percent of net profit.

OTHER IMPORTANT FINANCIAL INFORMATION

The ratios tell you a lot about the health of your business. They allow you to compare it with industry benchmarks and also to compare your results to your objectives.

Let's talk for a minute about **ROI (or return on investment).** It is a bottom-line figure that shows how much is earned on the total dollars invested in the business. You have this kind of information up front if you invest money in bonds. The interest tells you your ROI. Imagine that you had two funds, Bond A and Bond B, and Bond A paid you a 4 percent return and Bond B paid you 25 percent. Which bond would have the better ROI?

ROI (RETURN ON INVESTMENT) net profit to owner's investment

Table 16.3 The Software School's Balance Sheet

	Actual Balance Sheet of Software School as of September 30, 19xx (after first 6 months)			Projected Balance Sheet of Software School as of September 30, 19xx (after first 18 months)		
Assets						
Cash	$3 970			$59 670		
Inst. Materials & Books	2 500			4 495		
Total Current Assets			$6 470			$64 165
Leasehold Improvements	$41 000			$41 000		
Furniture	15 100			15 100		
Audio/Visual	10 600			20 600		
Office Equipment	3 600	$70 300		3 600	$80 300	
Less Depreciation		7 020	63 280		22 545	57 755
License Agreement			25 000	$25 000		
New Courses			–0–	50 000		75 000
Total Assets			$94 750			$196 920
Liabilities						
Instructors' Salaries	$1 250			$1 500		
Administrative Salaries	1 650			2 250		
Commissions	2 165			4 275		
Accounts Payable	4 495			9 020		
Current Liabilities		$9 560			$17 045	
Long-Term Debt		–0–			55 000	
Total Liabilities			$9 560			$72 045
Net Worth (Owner's Equity)						
Capital Stock	$100 000			$100 000		
Retained Earnings	(14 810)		85 190	24 875		124 875
Total Liabilities & Net Worth			$94 750			$196 920

You compute ROI for a business by dividing the net profit by investing dollars. For The Software School, the profit after taxes is $39 685 (from Table 16.2). Divide that by the owner's investment of $100 000 (from Table 16.3):

$39 685 / $100 000 = 39.7%

Could you get 39.7 percent from a savings account or a bond fund? It's not a bad ROI. It would dazzle lenders and probably draw the attention of a venture capitalist.

It is also helpful to include a comparison of your ratios to industry standards. Don't forget to include your break-even analysis as well.

The Software School did not provide notes to its balance sheets because, in this case, no notes are needed. In conjunction with the income statement and the cash flow projection, all the entries in the balance sheet will make sense to your professional readers. Under some circumstances, you would want to note unusual features of a balance sheet for an actual fiscal year, but in most cases — and in most projections — this won't be necessary.

Now project a balance sheet for your business. Action Step 77 will help you.

Epilogue: Act on What You Know

Well, do you feel like you're ready? You are. You have thoroughly researched your product or service, your market and target customer, your competition, your marketing strategy, and your location. You've discovered how to prepare for surprises you can't afford, how to handle numbers, how to pursue financing, when and why you should incorporate, how to build a winning team, and whether you should buy, franchise, or start on your own. You've surveyed the vistas that a small business computer training school can open up for you. And you've written it all up in a workable business plan that can be implemented.

Before you take off running, we want to give you one more tool that we think every entrepreneur should have — a tool to help you put your business plan to work. It's called **PERT,** an acronym for Program Evaluation and Review Technique, and it's often used to establish schedules for large projects.

A PERT chart is just the thing if you feel overwhelmed by the tasks of starting up and don't know where to begin. If you're a person who sometimes tries to do everything at once, PERT is also recommended. It will help you focus your energy on the right job at the right time. A sample PERT chart is provided in Table 16.4. Yours will need to be bigger and more detailed. You can use days, weeks, or months to plot the tasks ahead. (If you think you should use years, reassess your industry.)

Action Step 78 is the last one we give you in this book, and it symbolizes the first one taken on your own as an entrepreneur. It's the end, yes, but also the beginning. All our best wishes go with you as you embark on your great adventure. We hope that this book and its Action Steps have convinced you that you can achieve success — whatever it means to *you* — and have fun at the same time. Good luck! Work smart, and enjoy your adventure!

Table 16.4 A Sample PERT Chart

	Week					
Task	**1**	**2**	**3**	**4**	**5**	**6**
Befriend banker	X	X	X	X	X	X
Order letterhead		X				
Select site	X					
Get business name statement	X					
Register company			X			
Select ad agency	X					
Lunch, lawyer			X			
Appointment, accountant				X		
Prepare vendor statement					X	
Make utilities deposit					X	
Review promotional material					X	
Survey phone system			X	X	X	
Order phone system						X
Hold open house						X

ACTION STEP 77

Project your balance sheet.
A projected balance sheet is simply a prediction, on paper, of what your business will be worth at the end of a certain period of time. This prediction allows you to figure your actual and projected ROI, which is the real bottom line.

1. Add up your assets. For convenience, divide these into *current* (cash, notes, receivables, etc.), *fixed* (land, equipment, buildings, etc.), and *other* (intangibles like patents, royalty deals, copyrights, goodwill, contracts for exclusive use, and so on). You'll need to depreciate fixed assets that wear out. For value, you show the net of cost minus the accumulated depreciation.
2. Add up your liabilities. For convenience, divide these into *current* (accounts payable, notes payable, accrued expenses, interest on loans, etc.), and *long-term* (trust deeds, bank loans, equipment loans, balloon payments, etc.).
3. Subtract the smaller figure from the larger one.

You now have a prediction of your net worth. Will you be in the red or in the black?

PERT
abbreviation for Program Evaluation and Review Technique

ACTION STEP 78

Construct a PERT chart and go for it.
Rehearsal is over. Now it's time to step onto the stage and get the drama under way. One way to shift from planning into action is to develop your own personal PERT chart. A PERT chart will serve as a script for you. It also will tell you and the other members of your team how long certain jobs should take.

List the tasks you need to accomplish — befriending a banker, filing a fictional name statement, taking a lawyer to lunch, ordering business letterhead, selecting a site, contacting vendors, and so on — and set your deadlines.

As you already know, a successful package is made up of many details. If you take the details one at a time, you'll get there without being overwhelmed. The sample PERT chart in Table 16.4 can guide you.

Box 16.13 Bookmark This

Writing a Business Plan — The Long Version
http://www.dtonline.com/writing/wrcover.htm

What Venture Capital Firms Want in the Business Plan
http://www.benlore.com/files/emexpert1_5.html

Creating an Effective Business Plan
http://www.americanexpress.com/smallbusiness/resources/starting/biz_plan/

A Sample Business Plan
http://www.morebusiness.com/bplan

I Don't Need a Business Plan
http://www.morebusiness.com/management/v1n5.html

Business Plan Template
http://www.moneyhunter.com/htm/btemp_dload.htm

In a Nutshell

It's been a long haul, and you're now ready to create your business plan. The business plan is a portable showcase for your business. When you visit vendors, bankers, and potential lenders, you can take along a copy of your business plan to speak for you, to show them you've got a blueprint for success.

Begin writing by starting with the material you feel most comfortable with. Once you have finished one part of the plan, the other parts will fall into place more easily. Fortunately, your work in earlier chapters has prepared you for each section. The executive summary will be written last.

You'll need to write a cover letter for each copy of the plan you send out. The cover letter will personalize the plan and target the prime interests of each reader.

Think Points for Success

✓ Section I should generate excitement for your business. Section II should substantiate the excitement with numbers.
✓ Be sure to use sufficient footnotes to explain the numbers in your financial statements — Parts H, I, and J.
✓ The executive summary should read like ad copy. Hone it till it's tight and convincing.
✓ Now that you have Plan A, have you thought about Plan B?

Checklist Questions and Actions to Develop Your Business Plan

PULLING THE PLAN TOGETHER

❑ How will your business idea contribute to society in general?
❑ In what way does your product or service differ from that of your competitors?
❑ What are the critical success factors for your business?

- ❑ How would your customers define your quality and level of customer service?
- ❑ In completing your business plan, ask yourself: Have I been consistent in my thinking that the quality of sales staff fits the image I wish to convey, and that money is set aside for appropriate training?
- ❑ What social responsibility practices do you intend to follow?
- ❑ What business-related ethical issue might surface about your business venture?
- ❑ If your business is successful, what is your long-term growth plan?
- ❑ Are you going to achieve your personal vision?

ACTION STEP REVIEW

66 Write a cover letter for your plan.
67 Write an executive summary.
68 Describe your product or service.
69 Describe the market and the target customer.
70 Describe your major competitors.
71 Describe your marketing strategy.
72 Show off your location.
73 Introduce your management team.
74 Introduce your personnel.
75 Project your cash flow.
76 Project your income statement.
77 Project your balance sheet.
78 Construct a PERT chart and go for it.

NOTES

1. Adapted from Rod McQueen, "Canada's 50 Best Managed Private Companies: Crila Plastics Industries Ltd.," *Financial Post*, December 13, 1997, p. 19. Reprinted by permission of The Financial Post.

OTHER REFERENCES

BDC Business Plan, Business Development Bank of Canada.

Brodsky, Norm. "Why You Need a Personal Business Plan." *Inc.* January 1997, pp. 27–28.

Burstiner, Irving. *The Small Business Handbook,* 3rd edition. New York: Simon & Schuster, 1997. [A comprehensive guide to starting and running your own business.]

Deloitte & Touche. *The Business Plan.* 1998.

Dupree, James V. *A Business Plan for the Small Business with Software.* Saddle River, NJ: Prentice Hall, 1996.

Good, Walter S. *Building a Dream: A Comprehensive Guide to Starting a Business of Your Own.* Whitby: McGraw-Hill Ryerson Limited, 1997.

King, Jan B. *Business Plans to Game Plans: A Practical System for Turning Strategies into Actions.* New York: Merritt Publishing, 1994.

Royal Bank of Canada. *Starting a Business: A Guide for Independent Business.* 1998.

Sherman, Andrew J. *Running and Growing Your Business.* New York: Times Business, 1997. [Making your small business bigger.]

seventeen

Fast-Start Business Plan

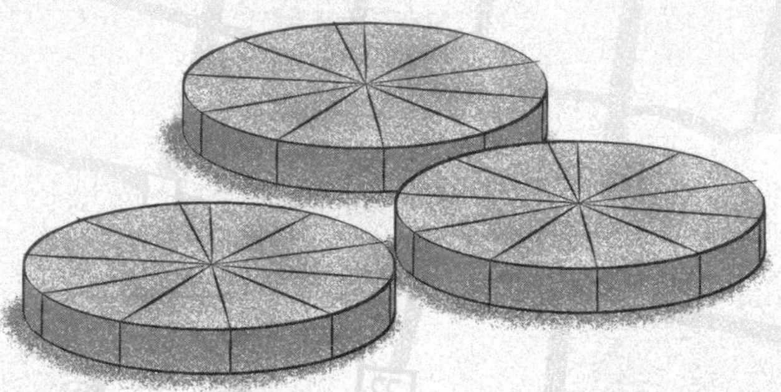

BUSINESS PLAN BUILDING BLOCK

If your business concept is very simple or short-term, perhaps you don't need a fully developed business plan. This chapter was developed to allow you to respond quickly to a narrow window of opportunity, and to demonstrate to yourself that the venture is viable.

LEARNING OPPORTUNITIES

After reading this chapter, you should be able to:

- Admit that you're in a hurry.
- Launch a start-up without getting financial help from bankers.
- Capitalize on a hot opportunity in the marketplace.
- Start small while you explore the possibilities of growing larger.
- Work with numbers so that you can keep going when the going gets tough.
- Make some money now.
- Plan as you work in your new business.

George Finklestein had a lot of experience in window cleaning over the three summers he was attending university. As a matter of fact, it paid for his education. After graduating, and after a fruitless job search that involved sending out over 100 résumés, Finklestein decided that he could have a career in business. He knew that there was money to be made in window cleaning, and so he decided that this is where he would start. He wasn't looking for financing and wanted to get going right away. When he registered his business name, "Yes, We Do Windows," he knew he had to have some kind of plan. He created a fast-start plan. It took him only about a month to fill in the details since he already knew the business quite well.

Did the plan work? Here is George's response. "In February of my first year, I took three weeks off and did some deep sea fishing. Turned out window cleaning was quite profitable. While on vacation, I made a decision: when I got home I would spend my spare hours developing a detailed plan and a franchise package for my student employees." The next summer, he had twelve student franchisees, and was making plans to go biking in Europe during his off-season.

Figure 17.1 Chapter Seventeen hands you a "Fast-Start Business Plan" that is almost ready to fly.

ACTION STEP PREVIEW

79 Describe your new business.
80 Describe the business you are really in.
81 Describe what your competitors look like.
82 Describe your pricing strategy.
83 Describe your target customer and your main market area.
84 Describe your advertising and sales program.
85 Calculate what it will cost you to open your doors.
86 Determine how much you will sell in your first month and how much you will spend.
87 Make a "things to do" list.

Many of you, like George Finklestein, may not need an exhaustive business plan. You are in a hurry. You probably won't need to go to the bank. You just want to get started. If the business doesn't work, fine, you'll dream up something else. If this is your situation, Chapter Seventeen will help. But first, you need to make sure the fast start is the right start for you. In this chapter, we help you give thought to your big decision. We also provide a model "Yes, We Do Windows" business plan based on George Finklestein's experience.

The Big Decision

If you're going it alone with money you can afford to lose ($500, $1 000, even $5 000), and if the loss of that money won't jeopardize your loved ones and make wolves howl at your door, use the fast-start business plan.

If other people are involved — investors, bankers, advisers, company officers — then return to Chapter Sixteen and write a comprehensive plan.

The comprehensive plan gives you a blueprint to follow month by month through the first year. It gives you the framework to go for a four-year projection following that first year. It tracks your business through seasonal ups and downs. It allows for contingencies.

The fast-start business plan lets you get going now. It's great if you've been in business before and know the footwork of entrepreneurship. With the fast-start business plan, you're using the business as a probe into the marketplace. You can start quickly because you have an instinct for what to expect and where you are going. You have a market sense. You also have a good sense of the business you are starting.

The fast-start business plan is quicker to write than the more detailed plan. Marketing, pricing, and advertising employ a low-key approach. As you gain experience, you fold that experience into a rolling projection. You can write the fast-start plan in one to three months. The full business plan, because of the extensive data gathering and need to pass through many hands, can take six months to a year.

QUICK CHECKLIST

Here's a quick checklist for implementing the fast-start business plan:

- ❑ Can you afford to lose your dollar investment? How much money can you afford to lose at the slots in Reno or Las Vegas or Windsor, Ontario? Can you lose $100? $1 000? $5 000? More? What's your deductible on your car insurance? Your boat? Your major medical? Write down the amount you can afford to lose. If you have excess money to speculate with, then the fast-start business plan is for you.
- ❑ How easy is it to enter this business? Are the barriers to entry low? Is it easy to talk to owners? Are role models in great abundance? Do the prospective customers have a clear understanding of the goods and services provided? Examples of business with wide doors: window washing, auto detailing, landscape maintenance, pet-sitting, house-sitting, consulting.
- ❑ Can you start this business on a part-time basis? Starting part time lessens your risk. You have a chance to prove the business. You see how much you really like it. You keep a running tally of customer responses. You keep your other job.
- ❑ How tough is it to gather the data needed to formulate a fast-start business plan? In breaking new ground, be careful. In a venture like this, the

market is not clearly defined. There are very few competitors. Pricing is not clear. Remaining part-time is essential. You must make certain you've got a market out there.

❑ Can you start using only your own funds? Bill Gates, the founder of Microsoft, could use the fast-start business plan for a business start-up costing $50 000 to $1 000 000. A single parent of two with rent and a car loan to pay might afford much less. Be honest with yourself. Be honest with your family.

STRUCTURING YOUR PLAN

Use these questions to structure your fast-start business plan:

1. How do you describe your business?
2. What business are you really in?
3. Who is your main and secondary competition? How are they doing?
4. What is your entry strategy?
5. What is your pricing strategy?
6. Who is your target customer? Why should they buy from you?
7. How will you advertise?
8. What are your start-up costs?
9. What are your sales goals for the first three months?
10. What are your operating expenses for the first three months?
11. If you crash and burn, what can you salvage for cash?

Business Description

It's night. The family's gone to bed. The house is quiet. The pets are snoozing.

It's time to sit back in your favourite chair, time to relax, time to dream about your new business. Think about your vision, and then write down your dream:

You step out of your van. It's a handsome vehicle, spotless, white, and gleaming. On the side, in red letters, is your sign: My Carpet Cleaners — Quality and Service Is Our Number One Job. Your company phone number is underneath. You are all in white, white jumpsuit, white shoes. The starched look gives you the image of being the best carpet cleaner in town. You catch your reflection in the mirror. The jumpsuit makes you look taller. The company logo stitched on your breast pocket makes you proud.

The house of your prospective customer is large. Three stories, well-kept lawn, a three-car garage, a curved driveway. The walkway leading to the front door is paved. The doorway is large enough to drive a truck through. Out back, you can hear the happy shrieks of children as they splash in the pool.

Cut to the job. You're in a big room with wall-to-wall carpet. Your machine sucks up the dirt. The customer enters, walking on a drop cloth you laid down for your equipment. Pointing to a transparent tube attached to your super-steam vacuum, you show the customer the dirt coming out of her carpet. The carpet sparkles in the sunlight as you go after those drapes. The customer, overwhelmed with such service, hands you the biggest cheque you've ever seen.

This cheque is two metres long and one metre high. The customer smiles. You read the amount — fantastic money for a fantastic job — and dance your way out of the house and down the walkway to your van.

GREAT DREAM EQUALS GREAT BUSINESS

A business dream separates your business from everyone else who's out there trying to clean carpets.

You're clean and you're in the cleaning business. You're proud of being in business. You care. The customer, owner of expensive things, cares that you care. We like to do business with people who care about what they're doing. Such people take pride in a job well done.

By being spotless when you enter this home, you show the customer respect. Your equipment is spotless. You're not dragging someone else's dirt into the place. The drop cloth is a nice touch.

You look like a carpet cleaner. You act like a carpet cleaner and are very knowledgeable about carpet cleaning. Your dream gives you a jump start. Now you add in details.

What products and services will you offer? Will you limit yourself to carpets? Or will you clean chairs and drapes? Will you specialize in homes? Or will you do offices? Will you provide a simple service? Or will you also sell spot remover, touch-up cleaners, other extras?

Complete Action Step 79.

ACTION STEP 79

Describe your new business.

What will your business look like?

To your customers?
To your competitors?
To yourself.

Write quick descriptions of your products and/or services. What do they look like? How do they feel? How much time do they take? How much do they cost? Next, describe them in terms of benefits to your customers. How will Target Customer A benefit from buying your product or service?

Keep going.

What is unique about your product or service? What separates you from your competitors?

Research the marketplace. Is your type of business growing? If so, how fast? Where are you on the life-cycle chart? Is your market area growing?

Try to describe your business in 50 words or less. When you tell people about your business, you want to have a clear, crisp picture. You want to use the right words.

This is your business. You want to know exactly what it is.

WHAT BUSINESS ARE YOU REALLY IN?

Are you selling clean carpets? Are you selling a better-looking home or office? Are you selling better health? Are you helping the customer preserve an investment? Remember, in the eyes of the customer you are selling benefits.

To help you get an appreciation of this, let's profile two different businesses in the same industry.

Business A is a family restaurant. It's open 24 hours a day. There's nothing on the menu over $9.95. The menu for children is extensive. On each table is a digital clock and a sign that says you eat free if your meal is not on the table within ten minutes of being ordered. The clock invites the customer to set it, invites the waiter to beat the clock.

Business B is a restaurant with limited hours. Weekdays it's open from 11 A.M. to 2 P.M. and from 5 P.M. to 10 P.M. Weekends it's open from 5 P.M. until midnight. Each table features large, comfortable chairs. The lighting is soft. The china is fine, the silverware first class. The waiters wear tuxes, and their manners are impeccable. The wine list contains fine vintages from Europe and California. If you can stump the bartender by requesting a drink she cannot mix, your drink is served free by the maître d'hotel. The cheapest entrée on the menu is $25 (this restaurant rounds prices off).

Both A and B are in the food service business. You can find both in the restaurant section in the Yellow Pages. But are they both in the same business?

For your answer, look at the customers.

Customers go to Business A for fast service. Their desire is to feed the whole family without going broke. They don't want a long travel time, so Business A is close to home. The food is good. Not wonderful, not divine, but good.

Customers go to Business B for excellent food and superior service. They go to relax, to enjoy a perfect moment over a rare vintage. They may be driven by fantasy or romance or escape. They may go just to watch the staff perform. That's entertainment.

What business is A in? What business is B in?

Business A is in the family-feeding business. But B is in the entertainment business. While A provides nourishment at affordable prices, B provides more than food — it provides a dining experience. If you were the manager of Business A, you would do these things:

- purchase good food in quantity
- get it at the lowest price
- control waste in the kitchen
- develop a fast and efficient delivery system
- turn those tables

If you were the manager of Business B, you would do these things:

- hire and train employees to fit the up-scale image
- provide ambience
- select top-quality food, rare food, specialty food, and top-quality wines
- find a bartender who knows the latest mixes and has excellent human relations skills

To figure out what business you're in, take a couple of steps back. Look at your business from the viewpoint of the customer. Complete Action Step 80. Then plan your course of action.

ACTION STEP 80

Describe the business you are really in. This is a tough task.

Start by interviewing customers of your competitors. Why do they buy what they buy? Why do they shop here instead of somewhere else? What are they after? What are they trying to satisfy? What itch does this business scratch?

Stimulate your thinking by analogy. What, for example, do you get when you have your car washed? It costs you anywhere from $2 to $25, and for what? A clean car? A savings in time? Pride of ownership? A car your customer will ride in? Does washing the car make you feel clean? Or maybe it's maintenance. Do you live near the beach, where the salt air eats your chrome?

Where do you buy clothes? Why? Where do you buy gas? Why? Who cleans your carpet? Why?

Probe your own buying habits. Probe the buying habits of your friends. Keep an open mind. Gather data. All this will lead you to discover what business you're really in.

WHO ARE YOUR COMPETITORS?

This is a good time to try out your new eyes. How much can you learn from your competitors?

How do you find them? If you're hunting for retailers or restaurant owners, you hop in your car and drive around. But how do you find a home-based word-processing business? How do you find a home-based cleaning service? How do you find a mobile auto detailer?

You know this: in order to stay in business, a business must communicate with potential customers. So you tune in your entrepreneurial radar. Check your Yellow Pages. Check area newspapers. Look for business cards in copy services. Check the Internet and visit your competitors' Web sites. Look in trade magazines.

Once you find your competitors, take a closer look. Were they easy to find? How visible was their advertising? As you study their advertising strategy, what kind of a customer profile can you draw? Are they spending a lot on their advertising? Are they working on a shoestring?

What can you tell from their pricing? Are prices firm? Are they negotiable? Are they high, low, or competitive? What kind of customer will go for these prices? Who will get shut out? Do your competitors understand the marketplace? Is their pricing structure positioned properly? Where is their pricing in the product life cycle?

Are your competitors zeroed in on a specific target customer, or are they using the shotgun approach? Just for practice, profile the target customer of your competitors.

Which of your competitors are successful? Can you tell why? Which are just hanging in there? Why? If a business has been operating for some time, there's a good chance the owner's doing something right. What is your competitors' market niche? What is their marketing strategy? What customer benefits do they offer? Fast service? Quality work? Free delivery and pick-up? Low prices? Better use of technology?

Even the most successful business overlooks something. Find out what they missed. Did they overlook a market segment? Did they get sloppy with their advertising? Is their range of services actually limited? Is their inventory sparse? Thousands of businesses have been built on the weaknesses of competition.

Take the time to chat with the customers of your competitors. Are they satisfied? If not, why not? How do they see the competition? What image does the competition project? How do customers feel about price, quality, timeliness, and so on?

Take the time to chat with competitors outside your area. Is there a gap no one has thought to close? Complete Action Step 81.

HOW MUCH SHOULD YOU CHARGE?

Pricing is key. Don't be misled by thinking you can whisk customers away from established competitors by charging less for the same thing. It didn't work for now bankrupt department stores. It won't work for you. Price should never be your only strategy.

Find out what is important to the customers. Is it time? Dependability? Quality? Convenience? Once you find out what it is, learn to see the value of your product or service through your customers' eyes.

For example, when you eat lunch at a fast-food restaurant, you buy french fries, coffee, tea, a soft drink. You pay a dollar or more for each of these items. The cost to the seller is a quarter or two per item. Within limits, these items are not price-sensitive. The question is, what is the customer's perception of value?

When you shop, train yourself to make price comparisons. You might notice, for example:

Newspapers at the newsstand	
Profit magazine	$3.50
The Globe and Mail	$0.65
local paper	$0.60
Coffee	
at local doughnut shop	$0.90
at a luxury hotel	$2.00
Car wash	
high school students' Saturday special	$1.00
do-it-yourself	$2.00
done for you	$8.00
Transportation	
Ford	$20 000
Mercedes	$60 000
Bentley	$275 000
Education	
a year at university	$7 000
a year at college	$2 000

Almost everyone has a price limit for every product or service. What is the maximum that people will pay for your product? Take a look at Action Step 82.

PROFILE YOUR TARGET CUSTOMER

Who will receive the biggest benefit from your business? Who can afford your product? Who are your main, secondary, and invisible target customers?

ACTION STEP 81

Describe what your competitors look like.

Are they winners? Losers? Why? What things are they doing right? What are they doing wrong?

How many competitors do you have? What customer groups are they serving? Whom are they overlooking? Where do they advertise? Where do they promote? What do you think of their location? What market area do they cover?

If you owned a competitor's business, what would you change?

What can you learn from studying your competitors? After you have opened your business, do some more marketplace detecting as you study your competitors. You'll learn more because you know more. A veteran entrepreneur knows what to look for.

ACTION STEP 82

Describe your pricing strategy.

What does your target customer see as good value?

What is most important to your target customer? Convenience? Quality? On-time delivery? Image? Price?

What stage of the product or service life cycle are you in? How many competitors do you have? How close are they?

If price is the main decision factor, try to add a little extra something. What's unique about your product? Is it sufficient to let you charge a little extra?

ACTION STEP 83

Describe your target customer and your main market area.

Who is your primary target customer? Do a profile: sex, age, income, occupation, residence, vehicle driven — anything that gives you a picture of needs and wants. What do they read? What do they watch? What do they listen to?

When you have profiled your primary customer, do the same thing for secondary customers.

How large is your main market area? Will you sell in one section of town? The whole town? The province? The region? The country? If you're driving around to service accounts, how far will you have to drive?

ACTION STEP 84

Describe your advertising and sales program.

How will you let potential customers know that you are open for business? How will you let them discover the benefits of buying from you?

Start with the budget. How much money can you spend on promotion? Once you know what you can afford, select the advertising to match your budget.

As part of your plan, set up an evaluation procedure. You want to know how well each promotion works.

Where do they live? What's their income range? What do they need? What benefits do they want? What work do they do? Are they married? Single? Divorced? Retired?

To profile your customers, become a marketplace detective. To practise, study the customers that buy from your competitors.

Do the women outnumber the men? What's the average age? What cars do they drive? What make? Price range? How are the customers dressed? How expensive are their shoes? Can you tell what methods of payment they use? Cash? Cheques? Credit? Debit? How expensive are the items they're buying?

Practice trains your eyes to consider the person as a prospect. Now complete Action Step 83. The bottom line: what are the three or four critical success factors that characterize your target customer?

HOW DO YOU MAKE THAT CUSTOMER CONNECTION?

Before you spend a bundle on a TV ad, or three months knocking on doors of houses along Golf Course Drive, take some time to put together a message.

What image do you want to project? How do you want the marketplace to perceive your product or service? What position do you want to assume among your competitors? What are the key benefits your business will offer customers? How soon do you want to start? How many autos can you detail — or homes can you clean — in one day?

Once you answer these questions, develop your overall marketing strategy. Start by designing your business card. Use a logo that offers an insight into your business. If you're starting a computer training business, use something along the lines of "Computer Training That Works for You Tomorrow." If you're thinking of house cleaning: "Only Sparkle — Not a Speck of Dust." Always carry lots of business cards. They're inexpensive memory seeds, handy reminders, and often your most cost-effective advertising.

Once your business cards are done, research ways of reaching customers. Do they gather at church? At school? At football games? At little league baseball? What do they read? Watch? Listen to? Could you reach them best through the Yellow Pages? Through radio? On a billboard? The Internet? What can you afford? Match that up with the most effective communication channel.

Stay visible. If your target customers gather in groups, try to reach them there. Attend their meetings. Get on their list of speakers. Give a demonstration. Hand out business cards. Offer a freebie.

If you must find your customers one at a time, spend a few hours each day knocking on doors. Telephone prospects. Work your mailing list. If you use mail or e-mail contacts, be sure you do phone follow-ups.

Join the local chamber of commerce. If you're lucky, your chamber will run a short piece about you, the newcomer, in its newsletter. Stay visible at chamber meetings. Don't get pushy with your business cards, but have them handy.

While you're connecting with customers, don't overlook organizations that might act as your sales force. For example, let's say you've found a school where the parents' group is trying to raise funds to support an athletic endeavour. Put together a flyer for students to take home. In return for each sale from the flyer, your business will donate 10 to 25 percent to the fundraising group. Consider the donation a part of your promotional budget.

Try your hand at Action Step 84.

What Are Your Start-up Costs?

At your local office supply store, make these purchases: a travel log, an expense journal, and a folder to hold receipts. You can deduct travel and expenses related to your business start-up.

List everything that you need to get started. Don't worry whether the list would cost a bundle. You're brainstorming at this point. The key here is not to overlook anything. A visit to your competitors will add ideas to your list. An interview with an owner will trigger new items. When you're chatting with business people, ask questions: What kind of cash register or computer system and software do you use? What kind of bookkeeping system do you have? What's the cost of a start-up inventory? When your list is fat, add price tags.

When you start purchasing, check the large discount stores. Also investigate mail-order houses. If one company in your area can supply most of your needs, try to make a package deal and develop a long-term relationship.

On equipment items, save by buying used. Used equipment might be scratched or dented, but you stand to save 50 to 90 percent. Check the newspaper classifieds under "Equipment for Sale" or "Office Furniture." Talk with potential suppliers — they usually know someone who's going out of business. You can find good deals from an owner who's folding.

You should also consider leasing your equipment. Leasing costs more in the long run, less when you're getting started. As your business grows, and your leases expire, you can decide whether to replace by buying new or used. Leasing provides you a lot of flexibility up front.

Divide your start-up list into two columns. Column 1 should contain items that are absolutely necessary. Column 2 should contain "nice-to-haves."

Check Column 1. Is there anything you can borrow from home, parents, friends? Scrape to the bottom of the barrel here. Your goal is to cut costs so that you'll have cash to run the business. Whatever the case, allow for a cash contingency of at least 10 percent of your first three months' expenses, as you will likely forget something.

ACTION STEP 85

Calculate what it will cost you to open your doors.

List your expenses, equipment, rentals, inventory — everything you'll need to start your business. Start your list with business cards. End with the key for the front door. What comes in between?

When you have listed all the items, give each one an estimated cost. On equipment, buy used. If you can't buy used, try leasing. On inventory, negotiate with each supplier to see whether you can get credit terms right from the start. If you can't get credit, find out how you can get quality.

When the list is complete — items and costs — go through it with a black marker, deleting items you can do without for a month or so. You are trying to keep your up-front cash outlay to a minimum.

CHARTING YOUR SALES GOALS FOR THE FIRST THREE MONTHS

How much would you like to sell the first month? The second? The third? How much can you afford to sell? What is a realistic target for your business?

Sales goals provide the information you need to forecast your variable expenses — those expenses forced to change in relation to sales volume. If you are selling a product, sales goals will allow you to estimate the cost of goods sold.

Sales goals provide the driving force for your team. They help you focus on your target for the month. When the month is finished, compare how you did with your initial sales goals. Did you make it? If not, why not? Did you exceed your goal by 25 percent? Why? What worked well? What didn't? As you evaluate, decide how to improve next month, and how to keep improving.

To chart a reasonable sales goal, focus on three factors:

1. *The weight of your advertising program.* Do you plan a wide-area campaign? Or will you start by calling on friends and neighbours, counting on them to spread the word slowly? How much energy are you putting into this? Will you start full-time? Will you keep your job? If you're in school, will you stay enrolled?

2. *The experience of entrepreneurs in business like yours who operate in a non-competing area.* How much effort does entrepreneur A have to put out to make a $100 sale in his or her area?
3. *The capacity you have to deliver the product or service.* What do you need to make this venture go? If it costs you $500 for materials to build one computer cabinet and you only have $500 worth of capital, then you will be limited to building one cabinet at a time. You have to get paid before you can build a second cabinet.

Or let's say you're starting a part-time business detailing, or cleaning, autos. Detailing one auto takes three hours. Driving time takes almost a half hour per auto. Your maximum sales activity per week will be based on the number of hours you can devote to your business after you put in your hours at your full-time job. If you can devote 20 hours a week, then your sales would be 20 hours, divided by time, multiplied by your charge. Let's try that:

20 divided by 3.5 = 6 autos per week.
Your charge per auto is $60.
6 times $60 = $360 per week.

Make a list of your friends and relatives. Find out how many of them have their autos detailed. Add the repeat factor: how often do they want detailing? Once a month? Once every quarter? Once a year? When your list is finished, suppose you have 24 prospects. Let's say you have a realistic shot at eighteen of those prospects. You are then going to have to determine if that's enough for a start-up.

As a wise entrepreneur, you know that your first few jobs will take longer than later ones. You're new. You're learning the business. You want to make sure you do a super job. You have four prospects who want monthly detailing. You have six who want it quarterly. Start with these ten prospects and lay out a chart. (See Figure 17.2.)

Figure 17.2 First Sales Forecast

	1	2	3	4	5	6	7	8	9
1									
2	First Sales Forecast								
3									
4		1st Month		2nd Month		3rd Month		4th Month	
5	Monthly Detailing (2)	$240	(4)	$240	(4)	$300	(5)	$360	(6)
6	Quarterly Detailing (3)	180	(3)	180	(3)	0		180	(3)
7	Rest of 18 Prospects (4)	180	(3)	300	(5)	0			
8	Need to Find (5)			360	(6)	1500	(25)		
9	Sales	600		1080		1800			
10									
11									
12									

Make these assumptions:

1. Assume that the first and second months contain four weeks and the third month has five weeks.
2. Assume sign-ups of four monthly detailing prospects from your list of 24. Add one new monthly prospect out of every six new customers from the "need-to-find" group.
3. Assume a sign-up of six quarterly customers from your list of 24 prospects. Add one new quarterly customer out of every six new customers from the "need-to-find" group.
4. Assume a sign-up of eight one-time prospects from your list of 24 prospects.
5. Action: Must find new customers from the remaining six prospects on the list of 24 names. Other sources are referrals, sales calls, and advertising.
6. We only plan for the first three months, but continue to update the plan every month. The fourth month is easy to start building from monthly and quarterly customers.

EXPENSE FORECAST

List everything you'll need to pay for on a regular basis to operate your business — for example, phone, cell phone, fax, supplies, truck, and advertising/promotion. Next, list everything you can think of under each heading. Here's a partial example:

Supplies	Truck
rags	gas
soap	oil/maintenance
wax	insurance
cleaner	
Q-Tips	

Now consider each specific item. Which ones can you tie to the detailing job? For example, for each auto detailing job, you use two packages of rental rags, one-half can of wax, one-quarter can of cleaner, ten Q-Tips, $1 for gas, and so on.

Add these expenses to your first sales forecast. Also add expense items that don't change. (See Figure 17.3.)

Assumptions:

1. Monthly basic rate, plus pager.
2. $20 per month plus $1 per job.
3. $10 per month toward oil change, tires, and maintenance, plus 50 cents per job.
4. $1 200 a year, $100/month expense paid quarterly for insurance.
5. Estimated at $10 per job.
6. Yellow Pages ad at $35 a month, plus $15 a month for four-line ad in weekly paper for the first month and $125 for flyers and business cards in the second and third months.
7. Depreciation should be factored in for truck and buffer.
8. Set aside: contingency (surprise) expenses.
9. Profit before depreciation (a non-cash expense). In time, you should get an estimate from your accountant for depreciation.

Now we want you to get started on your sales and expense forecast. Complete Action Step 86.

ACTION STEP 86

Determine how much you will sell in your first month and how much you will spend.

Your aim in this Action Step is to set realistic goals. To do that, you need to know your maximum capacity. For example, how many houses with an area of 1 500 to 2 000 square feet can you clean in one day? One week? One month? This will give you the top sales figure you could reach. That's your ideal.

Fixed expenses don't change with sales volume. List those first. Then list the variable expenses.

For fixed expenses, check with people who can give you answers: public utility companies (water, gas, electricity, natural gas); a leasing agent for rental rates; an insurance agent for estimated insurance costs.

For variable expenses, those that change with sales volume, figure out how far they go up relative to some fixed unit of change — for example, $100 of sales per house cleaned. If you can establish a percentage relationship between sales and each individual variable expense, then it will be easy to fill in your projections each month.

Figure 17.3 First Income Statement Forecast

	1	2	3	4	5	6	7
1	First Income Statement Forecast						
2							
3		1st Month	2nd Month	3rd Month			
4	Sales						
5	Monthly	$240	$240	$300			
6	Quarterly	180	180				
7	Original Prospects	180	300				
8	Need to Find		360	1500			
9							
10	Sales Total	600	1080	1800			
11							
12	Expenses:						
13	Phone (1)	20	20	20			
14	Gasoline (2)	30	38	50			
15	Oil/Maint. (3)	15	19	25			
16	Insurance (4)	100	100	100			
17	Supplies (5)	100	180	300			
18	Ad./Promotion (6)	50	75	75			
19	Depreciation (7)						
20	Miscellaneous (8)	50	50	50			
21							
22	Expense Total	365	482	620			
23	Profit (9)	235	598	1180			
24							
25							

Final Pass

Out of the 24 prospects, you manage to sign up fifteen for auto detailing. That's good. Six of those who want monthly detailing bargained you down to $50. Two of those six agreed to a weekly hand wash at $12. Five prospects agreed to a quarterly detailing, and one of those five agreed to a weekly hand wash. Five prospects decided on a one-time trial. You'd like to snag 25 new customers by the third month. A more reasonable estimate, however, is fifteen new customers.

New expenses include $5 a week for a Leads Club breakfast; $75 to join the chamber of commerce; $2 for the car washes; $1 for gas. The new numbers go into your forecast. (See Figure 17.4.)

Figure 17.4 Start-up Income Statement Forecast

	1	2	3	4	5	6	7
1	Start-Up Income Statement Forecast						
2							
3		1st Month	2nd Month	3rd Month			
4							
5	Sales						
6	Monthly	250	250	300			
7	Car Washes	108	120	156			
8	Quarterly	180	120				
9	Rest of 15	120	180				
10	Need to Find		360	900			
11							
12	Sales Total	658	1030	1356			
13							
14							
15	Expenses:						
16	Phone	20	20	20			
17	Gas	39	41	54			
18	Oil/Maint.	19.5	23	27			
19	Insurance	100	100	100			
20	Supplies	100	180	236			
21	Ad./Promotion	145	95	95			
22	Depreciation						
23	Miscellaneous	50	50	50			
24							
25	Expense Total	491.5	510	582			
26	Profit	166.5	520	774			
27							

"THINGS TO DO" LIST

Now that your plan is complete; act on it. Your first step is to write up a list of things that need doing. You need this list for at least three reasons:

1. It gives you easy steps to follow.
2. It keeps you on target.
3. It gives you a sense of getting there at last.

Following is a sample "things to do" list from a catering service started by Doris and Mike.

ACTION STEP 87

Make a "things to do" list.
Use lists — they work for you. When you write down things to do, do them and cross them off. You'll feel good. As you move from item to item, you'll feel even better.

Set up a pre-start list and continue right on into your business. You'll find that you are more in control of your time and business by keeping lists.

List of Necessities Before Opening Day

1. Talk with experienced caterers.
2. Prepare fast-start business plan.
3. Stay focussed on the business.
4. Choose a business name.
5. Make arrangements with food service kitchen.
6. Determine what market area to service.
7. Have business phone installed with voice mail. Purchase office supplies.
8. Set up business bank accounts and establish relationship with banker.
9. Locate suppliers: refrigeration, cooking, baking, utensils, cash register, tables, chairs, other.
10. Check business licence regulations.
11. Get PST and GST numbers.
12. Select an insurance agent and appropriate insurance policy.
13. Develop job descriptions and application forms.
14. Hire employees. Full-time or part-time? How many? Make sure to get all information.
15. Complete marketing plan and advertising for the opening.
16. Join a discount-price warehouse.
17. Choose food suppliers.
18. Establish support business contracts:
    a. Rental tents, equipment
    b. Florists
    c. Entertainment
    d. Service staff
    e. Other bakeries, specialty suppliers, ice carvers, props, lighting, etc.
19. Order business cards and get ready to hand them out.
20. Order preprinted billing statements for customers who do not pay on receipt (but preferably get money up front).
21. Record all income and expenses daily in a ledger.
22. Find a bookkeeper to prepare financial statements. Check out computerized accounting systems.
23. Contact a lawyer for all lease and legal agreements.
24. Network with friends, relatives, other caterers.
25. Join chamber of commerce. Good place to meet potential customers.
26. Do projected profit and loss statement for three months.

It's your turn. Complete Action Step 87. Make up your "to do" list. Now it's time to take a look at the model business plan for "Yes, We Do Windows," created by George Finklestein.

In a Nutshell

The fast-start business plan is not a substitute for preparing a full-fledged plan. Use the fast-start for a specific venture that is easy to start, carrying minimal risk. Also use it for a business that's breaking new ground, where there is little information available.

The key to any business, and to any business plan, is how well you understand the needs of your target customer. Find an itch that isn't being scratched and you can ace your competitors.

Write your own fast-start business plan. Keep it handy. Refer to it often. Use it to keep your business on track in those early months of operation. When you've been in business for three months, use your fast-start business plan as a launching pad for your next nine months of operation. For your second year, write a full-fledged business plan.

ACTION STEP REVIEW

79 Describe your new business.
80 Describe the business you are really in.
81 Describe what your competitors look like.
82 Describe your pricing strategy.
83 Describe your target customer and your main market area.
84 Describe your advertising and sales program.
85 Calculate what it will cost you to open your doors.
86 Determine how much you will sell in your first month and how much you will spend.
87 Make a "things to do" list.

Think Points for Success

- ✓ Your business plan, fast-start or full-fledged, is your pathway to success.
- ✓ Looking at your competition helps you see your target customer. Seeing your target customer clearly helps you position your business strategically in the marketplace.
- ✓ Building a plan builds confidence. Confidence breeds excitement. If you don't feel excited and confident about your business, bail out now.
- ✓ Once you get started heading around the track, don't forget to keep your new eyes on the marketplace.

Model Business Plan: Yes, We Do Windows

1. Definition of your business
2. What business am I really in?
3. Competition
4. Pricing
5. Target customer
6. Ad/sales program
7. Start-up costs
8. Sales goals and expenses — first three months
9. "Things to do" list

1. DEFINITION OF YOUR BUSINESS

I have been a window washer for three years. For two years I worked for Windowlite Ltd., a large organization with over 250 satellites across three provinces. For the next year, I worked for a local operator who owned a truck and three squeegees. I feel that I know the business from both ends.

My idea — and the subject of this plan — is to do window washing and house cleaning.

Window washing. I will clean windows, screens, and window casings.

House cleaning: I will vacuum, dust, polish/wash, and mop. I will do bathrooms, mirrors, kitchens, range tops, and ovens.

A customer may contract for one or more services. House cleaning will be offered on a once-a-week or once-every-two-weeks basis. Window washing will be offered monthly, quarterly, twice a year, or as needed.

2. WHAT BUSINESS AM I REALLY IN?

I have determined the answer by identifying the following customer benefits:

1. Pride of ownership — a home is a person's most expensive investment. Keeping it clean makes the customer proud.

2. Time-saving — homeowners work hard to pay for their investment; many homes today are supported by double incomes; few homeowners have the time to do their own cleaning.
3. Preserving the value of the investment — dirt and grime damage the home. Cleaning on a regular basis enhances and preserves the value of the home.
4. Comfortable, healthy living area — a clean home is a healthier home. Who wants to live with dirt?

The business I am really in: "Providing a clean and healthy environment, while at the same time preserving the value of an investment and deepening pride of ownership."

3. COMPETITION

At this writing, there are 77 window cleaning services and 102 house cleaning services listed in my metropolitan area's Yellow Pages.

Taking the time to make phone calls to these competitors made me feel even better about my idea for a business. Their phone skills need retooling. The clerks who answered were impolite. They didn't seem interested in the prospect of making money. Out of 59 businesses polled, a hefty 68 percent charged for an on-site estimate.

The phone bids were vague. When pressed, the people who answered the phone said they would have to call me back. Very few did call back.

I can see two "musts" for the business. (1) My bids must be firm. (2) My phone skills must be customer-oriented. If I can't answer the phone, I must find a phone person who can fulfil these two musts. The image we're presenting here is "We aim to please. We're interested in servicing your home."

One question I asked was: "Will the same person be in my home every time?" A mere 6 percent said yes. The other respondents were vague. That indicated a problem in scheduling.

Measuring the competition has given my start-up a real advantage. Since I'll be doing all the work myself, I can gather customer data as I work. As I expand, I shall match employees to homeowners. A home is a private place. It's a place where you go to escape from the day. You don't want it invaded by different strangers every week. My plan is to expand only when I find the three right employees.

4. PRICING

My strategy is to price my services just slightly higher than the current competitors' rates. Every three months, to stay current, I will survey the competition.

Basic Rates for Cleaning:

First Cleaning

Square Feet	*Price*
1 000	$ 50
1 000–1 500	75
1 500–2 000	100
2 000+	100 + $25 per 1 000 sq. ft.
Weekly Cleaning	
1 000	$ 35
1 000–1 500	55
1 500–2 000	75
2 000+	75 + $15 per 1 000 sq. ft.
Bi-monthly	
1 000	$ 45
1 000–1 500	70
1 500–2 000	90
2 000+	90 + $20 per 1 000 sq. ft.

Window Washing

One-story house	
up to 15 windows	$ 25
each additional 5 windows	10
Two-story house	
up to 25 windows	$ 60
each additional 5 windows	10

5. TARGET CUSTOMER

I can classify three types of target customers for my business.

Customer A — Family Dwelling

A married couple with one or more children. The household income is $75 000 or more. Two vehicles. Both parents work. Reason for the service: spare time is at a premium for child care, recreation, and entertainment. Parents cannot spare the time to do windows or other cleaning.

Customer B — Single Person Condo

Customer B is a single or divorced person living alone, usually in an apartment or waterside condo. Age range from 28 to 40. The income here runs from $32 000 to $50 000. Time is at a premium. Customers are seldom at home on nights or weekends.

Customer C — High Roller

Customer C is distinguished by income in the six-figure range. Home values start at $400 000 and move up the scale to $1 million. Customer C has high standards, zero desire to perform menial tasks, wants a spotless home. If work is excellent and customer feels there is no rip-off, price is mainly no object.

6. ADVERTISING AND SALES PROGRAM

1. I will maintain an image of high visibility. My truck is washed daily. The colour is white. If there is mud on the tires after a job, the mud is washed off before the next job. I wear a white jumpsuit that bears the company logo. My employees wear similar jumpsuits. Our footgear is white sneakers. They're easy on the feet and look professional, almost a sporty image.
2. My business cards are white with blue lettering. On the reverse side is a list of my services. I make it a habit to get a business card whenever I hand one out. Data from these cards are entered into a computer. Names are added to a master list.
3. Flyers will be placed door to door in target neighbourhoods. I plan to do one neighbourhood of 100 to 200 homes, and then evaluate the response. I ask questions of each person who calls about the flyer: What did they like? What was missing? From this marketing survey, I'll redesign the flyer before approaching a second neighbourhood.

I make a habit of leaving flyers and business cards at all day-care centres in the area. In exchange for each customer I gain, I donate to a fund for school books or toys.

7. START-UP COSTS

Truck	$10 000*
Paint truck white	1 000
Ladder rack (custom-made)	350
Ladders	412
Supplies — window washing	400

Supplies — house cleaning	500
Signs for new truck	195
Advertising	250
Answering machine	75
Phone and pager installation	200
Post office box per month (first and last month)	40
Chamber of commerce	200
Business name	65
Business licence	55
Used desk and chair	275
Desk calendar	6
Date book, home	65
Date book, truck	15
Rolodex, supplies, file system	50
Bank account and accounting system	125
Total Estimate for Start-up Expenses	$14 278*

*I should be able to buy a used truck for $1 000 down and $175 to $200 per month for 36 months. Thus, start-up cash may be as low as $5 078.

8. SALES GOALS AND EXPENSES — FIRST THREE MONTHS

My plan is to work six days per week. Until I gain experience, I can work a maximum of three jobs per day. As an incentive for customers, I will do windows at half price with the first house cleaning. I will devote two full weeks to marketing my new business. On the schedule at present, I have four weekly customers and two bimonthly scheduled for the third week. When not on the job, I plan a strong marketing effort so that I can add one customer per week until I'm up to eighteen customers, my maximum for the week. At that time, I will evaluate my ability to add additional customers and/or hire a part-time employee. (See Figure 17.5.)

9. "THINGS TO DO" LIST

- File for business name.
- Design business logo, cards, and flyer.
- Order phone installation.
- Purchase phone.
- Lease pager.
- Set up bank account.
- Order one-write cheque system.
- Order business cards.
- Set up post office box.
- Locate source of supplies.
- Purchase supplies.
- Purchase truck.
- Obtain quotes and arrange for truck painting.
- Order signs for truck.
- Purchase answering machine.
- Buy ladder rack for truck.
- Buy ladders.
- Join chamber of commerce.
- Purchase desk, chair, and office supplies.

Figure 17.5 Sales Goals and Expenses

	1	2	3	4	5	6	7
1	Sales Goals and Expenses						
2							
3		1st Month	2nd Month	3rd Month			
4							
5	Sales (1)	$1 087.50	$2 580	$4 580.50			
6							
7	Expenses:						
8	Gas (2)	73	91	115			
9	Maintenance (3)	25	25	25			
10	Insurance (4)	125	125	125			
11	Phone (5)	45	45	45			
12	Advertising (6)	80	80	80			
13	Supplies (7)	65	155	275			
14	Truck Loan Interest	60	60	60			
15	Expense Total	473	581	725			
16	Profit	$614.50	$1999	$3855.50			
17							

NOTES FOR FIGURE 17.5

1. Average customer will own a one-storey house of $2 000 square feet with fifteen windows. Month 1 = four weeks. Month 2 = four weeks. Month 3 = five weeks. Every other new customer bi-monthly. All window washing contracts on a quarterly basis.
2. Gas, $15 per week plus $1 per job.
3. Maintenance — mainly a reserve for tires, repairs, oil changes, $25 per month.
4. Auto insurance and bonding, $1 500 per year.
5. Basic phone, pager, post office box.
6. Approximately 400 flyers per month comes to $55, plus $25 for distribution.
7. Approximately $5 per job.

index

Reader Reply Card

We are interested in your reaction to *Small Business: An Entrepreneur's Plan,* Third Canadian Edition, by Ronald A. Knowles and Cliff G. Bilyea. You can help us to improve this book in future editions by completing this questionnaire.

1. What was your reason for buying this book?

   ❑ university course ❑ professional development
   ❑ college course ❑ personal interest
   ❑ continuing education course ❑ other ______________

2. If you are a student, please identify the university, college or school you attend and the course in which you used this book.

3. Which chapters or parts of this book did you use? Which did you not?

4. What did you like best about this book?

5. What did you like least about this book?

6. Please identify any topics you think should be added to future editions.

7. Please add any further comments or suggestions.

8. May we contact you for further information? ______ Yes ______ No

   Name: ________________________________

   Address ________________________________

   ____

   Phone: ________________________________

(fold here and tape shut)

Canada Post Corporation / Société canadienne des postes

Postage paid If mailed in Canada | **Port payé** si posté au Canada

Business Reply | **Réponse d'affaires**

0116870399 01

0116870399-M8Z4X6-BR01

Larry Gillevet
Director of Product Development
HARCOURT CANADA
55 HORNER AVENUE
TORONTO, ONTARIO
M8Z 9Z9